In Conflict and Order

Understanding Society

Second Edition

D. Stanley Eitzen
Colorado State University

ALLYN AND BACON, INC. — Boston, London, Sydney, Toronto

To my parents,
David and Amanda

Chapter opening credits:
Chapter 1: © Charles Gatewood/Magnum Photo, Inc.   *Chapter 2:* Joseph P. Schuyler/Stock, Boston.   *Chapter 3:* Nicholas Sapieha/Stock, Boston.   *Chapter 4:* Daniel S. Brody/Stock, Boston.   *Chapter 5:* Larry C. Morris/*The New York Times.*   *Chapter 6:* David S. Strickler/The Picture Cube.   *Chapter 7:* Eric A. Roth/The Picture Cube.   *Chapter 8:* Owen Franken/Stock, Boston.   *Chapter 9:* Bernard Pierre Wolff/Photo Researchers, Inc.   *Chapter 10:* © Roger Lubin/Jeroboam 1972.   *Chapter 11:* Bill Strode/Black Star.   *Chapter 12:* Ellis Herwig/Stock, Boston.   *Chapter 13:* © Frank Siteman MCMLXXXI.   *Chapter 14:* © Jean-Claude Lejeune/Stock, Boston.   *Chapter 15:* © William Thompson/Jeroboam.   *Chapter 16:* Andrew Sacks/Black Star.   *Chapter 17:* © George Gardner.

Library of Congress Cataloging in Publication Data
Eitzen, D. Stanley.
    In conflict and order.

    Bibliography
    Includes index.
    1. Sociology.   2. Social structure.   3. Social psychology.   4. United States—Social conditions—1960–   .   I. Title.
HM51.E336   1981   973.92   81–10978
ISBN 0-205-07644-0   AACR2

Contents

17
The Structure of Power in American Society/465
Models of the National Power Structures/465

Preface

This is *not* a *traditional* textbook for the introductory course in sociology. Several foci separate it from most mainstream books. Foremost, the book examines social organizations from a critical perspective. Far from a dispassionate description of the way things are, this book enumerates the positive *and* negative consequences of social structure. The book will introduce sociology, then, by showing how structure is important and necessary while simultaneously leading to social problems. This view of social life provides an integrated framework that will aid the reader in developing a sociological perspective. The book is designed to provide a coherent, consistent, and critical view of society.

Many introductory students will only be exposed to sociology once. They should leave that course with a new and meaningful way of understanding themselves, others, and society. The most fundamental goal of this book is to assist the student in developing a sociological perspective—all else is secondary.

I have made a number of major changes in this second edition.

1. The materials have been updated.

2. Some chapters have been reworked completely, especially the chapters on social change, culture, race/ethnicity, sexual stratification, the family, and power.

3. New topics have been added, including: evangelical politics, the rise of evangelicals and the decline of mainline churches, family violence, primary and secondary groups, sunbelt migration, undocumented workers, social movements, the social contruction of reality, cultural relativity, brainwashing, social mobility, Hispanics, residential segregation, abortion, dual career marriages, capitalism, socialism, Political Action Committees, the bias of the political/economic system, and the Trilateral Commission.

4. New boxed materials have been added, such as cross-cultural and methods panels.

5. Pedagogical devices, such as new chapter opening material, methods panels, and itemized chapter reviews have been added.

Although the final responsibility for this book is mine, it reflects the influence, work, and support of many persons. I am indebted to a number of scholars whose ideas I have incorporated, especially Marvin Olsen, Peter Berger, R. P. Cuzzort, William Ryan, Jerome Skolnick, and Michael Parenti. My editor, Al Levitt, has had an active part in developing this new edition. With his guidance, a number of sociologists reviewed the first edition and drafts of the second edition. I am especially indebted to one of these reviewers, Maxine Baca Zinn, whose scholarship, thorough attention to detail, and insistence on consistency were invaluable in developing the final product.

D. S. E.

Fort Collins, Colorado
September, 1981

Prologue:
From Author to Reader

When I took my first course in sociology in 1953, the approach, typical of that day, emphasized the formal theoretical concepts of the discipline in a manner equivalent to premed courses. The result was that most students were left with the impression that sociology was composed of unrelated concepts, that it made simple events into abstract "principles," and that it had no meaning for their lives. By the time I had taught my first college course in sociology in 1967, a new approach was in ascendancy. In contrast to the tedious, concept-memorizing approach, the new mode was to make sociology relevant at all costs. The topics considered centered on such issues as racism, imperialism, gay rights, pornography, victimless crimes, welfare mothers, and alternative life-styles. While classes using this approach were interesting, the students were frequently left with little else than unrelated facts and titillating anecdotes. These students, as did the students of my day, had a serious failing—the inability to understand the importance of social factors in explaining the behavior of individuals and groups and to apply sociological explanations to new issues as they arise.[1]

This book will attempt to provide the student with the best of these two approaches while eliminating their weaknesses. The concepts of sociology are important to understand—but not as representing unrelated social phenomena. Social life coheres, and so should the concepts that identify its structure and processes. Sociology is inherently interesting, fascinating, relevant, and exciting, and any text that does not convey these qualities is misrepresenting and betraying the discipline.

The ultimate objectives of this book are to provide the reader with (1) an intuitive grasp of the sociological perspective; and (2) a consistent framework from which to view, understand, and interpret social life. The first goal, the adoption of the sociological perspective, will be emphasized explicitly in the first chapter and implicitly throughout the book. The sociological perspective focuses on the social sources of behavior. It requires the shedding of existing myths and ideologies by questioning all social arrangements. One of the most persistent questions of the sociologist is: Who benefits from the existing customs and social order and who does not? Since social groups are created by people, they are not sacred. Is there a better way? One editorial writer has posed a number of questions that illustrate the critical approach typical of the sociological perspective:

Must we [Americans] try to perpetuate our global empire, maintaining far-flung military outposts, spending billions on the machinery of death, meddling in the affairs of other nations—or is there a better way? Must we continue to concentrate power and wealth in the hands of a few, preserving the income gaps that have remained virtually undisturbed through New Deal, Fair Deal, New Frontier, and Great Society—or is there a better way? Must millions of our people be subjected to the cruel displacements of an irrational economy—or is there a better way? Must we stand by while our liberties are undermined, our resources squandered, our environment polluted—or is there a better way? Must private profit be the nation's driving force—or is there a better way?[2]

Although there will be disagreement on the answers to these questions, the answers are less important, sociologically, than the willingness to call into question existing societal arrangements that many people consider sacred. This is the beginning of the sociological perspective. But being critical is not enough. The sociologist must have a coherent way to make sense of the social world, and this leads us to the second goal of this book—the elaboration of a consistent framework from which to understand and interpret social life.

This book is guided by the assumption that there is an inherent duality in all societies. The realistic analysis of any one society must include both the integrating and stabilizing forces, on the one hand, and the forces that are conducive to malintegration and change, on the other. American society is characterized by harmony *and* conflict; integration *and* division; stability *and* change. This synthesis is crucial if the intricacies of social structure, the mechanisms of social change, and the sources of social problems are to be understood fully.

This objective of achieving a balance between the order and conflict perspectives is not fully realized in this book, however. Although both perspectives are incorporated into each chapter, the scales tend to be tipped in favor of the conflict perspective. This slight imbalance is the conscious product of the way I, as author and teacher, view the structure and mechanisms of society. In addition to presenting what I think is a realistic analysis of society, it counters the prevailing view presented in contemporary sociology textbooks—the order perspective with its implicit sanctification of the status quo. Such a stance is untenable to me, given the spate of social problems that persist in American society. The emphasis of the conflict approach, on the other hand, questions the existing social arrangements, viewing them as sources of social problems, a position with which I agree. Implicit in such a position is the goal of restructuring society along more humane lines.

The fact that I stress the conflict approach over the order model does not suggest that this book is a polemic. To the contrary, the social structure is also examined from a sympathetic view. The existing arrangements do provide for the stability and maintenance of the system. But the point is that by including a relatively large dose of the conflict perspective the discussion *is* a realistic appraisal of the system rather than a look through rose-colored glasses.

This duality theme will be shown primarily at the societal level in this book. But while the societal level is the focus of our inquiry, the small group and individual levels will not be ignored. The principles that apply to societies are also appropriate for the small social organizations to which we belong, such as families, work groups, athletic teams, churches, and clubs. Just as important, the sociological perspective shows how the individual is affected by groups of all sizes. Moreover, it shows how the identity of the individual is shaped by social forces and how in many important ways the individual's thoughts and actions are determined by group memberships.

The linkage of the individual to social groups will be shown throughout the book. The relationship of the individual to the larger society will be illustrated by special panels. These will examine how societal changes and forces impinge on individuals and the choices available to us as we attempt to cope with these societal trends.

The book is divided into four parts. The first introduces the reader to the sociological perspective, the fundamental concepts of the discipline, and the duality of social life. These chapters will set the stage for an analysis of the structure (organization) and process (change) of American society. The emphasis will be on the characteristics of societies in general and the United States in particular.

Part II describes the way human beings are shaped by society. The topics include the values that direct our choices, the social bases of social identity and personality, the cultural tyranny of sex roles, the mechanisms that control individual and group behavior, and the violation of social expectations—deviance. Throughout this section we will examine the forces that, on the one hand, work to make all Americans similar and those that, on the other hand, make us different.

Part III examines in detail the various forms of social inequality present in American society. The opening chapter deals with how societies rank people in hierarchies. Also examined are the mechanisms that ensure that some people will have a greater share of wealth, power, and prestige than others and the positive and negative consequences of such an arrangement. Other chapters focus on the specific aspects of stratification—poverty, majority—minority relations, and sexism.

Part IV discusses another characteristic of all societies—the presence of social institutions. Every society has developed historically a fairly consistent way of meeting its survival needs and those of its members. The family, for example, ensures the regular input of new members, provides for the stable care and protection of the young, and regulates sexual activity. In addition to the family, a separate chapter is devoted to religion, the economy, and the polity. The understanding of institutions is vital to the understanding of society because these social arrangements are part of its structure, resist change, and have such a profound impact on the public and private lives of people.

The sociological analysis of American society is especially important and interesting now because of a unique combination of historical and structural factors. No American generation but the present has faced possible extinction from the effects of nuclear weapons and ecological disasters. No American generation but the present has faced the possibility of a future with severe energy and resource shortages that threaten the American values of progress, growth, and materialism. No generation but the present has grown up with the instant history and the constant violence of television. No generation has undergone such a rapid rate of change. The trend toward greater bureaucratization continues in business, religion, labor, school, sport, and government. All Americans are caught in its impersonal clutches.

While these and other changes have occurred with fantastic speed, American institutions have become afflicted with old age, unwilling to change. The intransigence of American institutions in the face of rapid social and technological change has caused a gap which, if not breached, will lead to increasing despair, discontent, alienation, and hostility by dislocated individuals and perhaps the ultimate demise of society.

The problems of American society are of great magnitude, and solutions must be found. But understanding must precede action—and that is one goal of this book.

The analysis of American society is a challenging task. It is frustrating because of the heterogeneity of the population and the complexity of the forces impinging upon American social life. It is frustrating because the diversity within the United States leads to many inconsistencies and paradoxes. Furthermore, it is difficult if not impossible for an American to be objective and consistently rational about his or her society. Nevertheless, the sociological study of American society is fascinating and rewarding. It becomes absorbing as one gains insights about his or her own actions and the behavior of others. Understanding the intricate complex of forces leading to a particular type of social structure or social problem can be liberating and lead toward collective efforts to bring about social change. This book will attempt to give the reader just such a sociological perspective.

Finally, I am unabashedly proud of being a sociologist. My hope is that you will capture some of my enthusiasm for exploring and understanding the intricacies and mysteries of social life.

NOTES AND REFERENCES

1. For a critique of past approaches and a plea for one similar to that used in this volume, see Amitai Etzioni, "The Importance of Humanistic Sociology," *The Chronical of Higher Education,* January 19, 1976, p. 32.

2. "Voting for What We Want," *The Progressive,* November, 1976, p. 5.

In Conflict and Order

Understanding Society

Part I

The Sociological Approach

1

The Sociological Perspective

Life appears to be a series of choices for each of us. We decide how much schooling is important and what to major in. We choose a job, a mate, and a lifestyle. But how free are we? Have you ever felt trapped by events and conditions beyond your control? Your religious beliefs may make you feel guilty for some behaviors. Your patriotism may cost you your life—even willingly. These ideological traps are powerful, so powerful that we usually do not even see them as traps.

Have you ever felt trapped in a social relationship? Have you ever continued a relationship with a friend, group of friends, lover, or spouse when you were convinced that it was wrong for you? Have you ever participated in an act because others wanted you to that later seemed absolutely ridiculous, even immoral? Most likely your answers to these questions are in the affirmative because those closest to us effectively command our conformity.

At another level, have you ever felt that because of your race, gender, age, ethnicity, or social class certain opportunities were closed to you? For example, if you are a black football player certain positions on the team (usually quarterback, center, offensive guard, and kicker) will very likely be closed to you regardless of your abilities. If you are a white male recent affirmative action legislation makes it especially difficult for you in the job market. As a female you may want to try certain sports or jobs but to do so is to call your "femininity" into question.

Even more remotely, each of us is controlled by decisions made in corporate boardrooms, in government bureaus, and in foreign capitals. Our tastes in style are decided on and manipulated by corporate giants through the media. High interest rates affect individual workers and their families in the housing and automobile industries by increasing unemployment. A war in the Middle East reduces the supply of oil and the price rises dramatically, restricting personal use here in the United States. That same war may mean that you will be called to action because you are the right age and sex. The weather in China and Russia affects grain prices in the United States, meaning bankruptcy or prosperity for individual farmers and high or low prices for individual consumers.

Finally, we are also trapped by our culture. We do not decide what is right or wrong, moral or immoral. These are decided for us and incorporated inside us. We do not decide what is beautiful and what is not. Even the decision on what is important and what is not is a cultural bias embedded deep inside each of us.

Sociology is the science dealing with social forces—the forces outside us that shape our very lives, interests, and personalities. As the science of society and social behavior, sociology is interesting, insightful, and important. This is because sociology explores and analyzes the ultimate issues of our personal lives, of society, and of the world. At the personal level sociology investigates the causes and consequences of such phenomena as romantic love, violence, identity, conformity, deviance, personality, and interpersonal power. At the societal level sociology examines and explains poverty, crime rates, racism, sexism, pollution, and political power. At the global level sociology researches such phenomena as war, conflict resolution, and population growth. While other disciplines are also helpful in the understanding of these social phenomena, sociology makes a unique contribution.

The insights of sociology are important for the individual because they help us understand why we behave as we do. This understanding is not only liberating but is a necessary precondition for meaningful social action to bring social change. As a scholarly discipline, sociology is important because it complements and in some cases supersedes other disciplines concerned with understanding and explaining social behavior.

ASSUMPTIONS OF THE SOCIOLOGICAL PERSPECTIVE

To discover the underlying order of social life and the principles that explain human behavior, scientists have focused on different levels of phenomena. The result of this division of labor has been the creation of scholarly disciplines, each concentrating on a relatively narrow sphere of phenomena. Biologists interested in social phenomena have focused on the organic bases for behavior. Psychological explanations assume the source of human behavior in the psyches of individuals.

The understanding of human behavior benefits from the emphases of the various disciplines. Each makes important contributions to knowledge. Of the three major disciplines focusing on human behavior, sociology is commonly the least understood. The explicit goal of this book is to remedy this fault by introducing the reader to the sociological ways of perceiving and interpreting the social world. Let us begin by enumerating the assumptions of the sociological approach that provide the foundation for this unique, exciting, and insightful way of viewing the world.

1. *Individuals are, by their nature, social beings.* There are two fundamental reasons for this assumption. First, children enter the world totally dependent on others for their survival. This initial period of dependence means, in effect, that each of us has been immersed in social groups from birth. A second basis for the social nature of human beings is that throughout history people have found it to their advantage to cooperate with others (for defense, for material comforts, to overcome the perils of nature, and to improve technology).

2. *Individuals are socially determined.* This essential assumption stems from the first, that people are social beings. Individuals are products of their social environments for several reasons. During infancy, the child is at the mercy of adults, especially parents. These persons can shape the infant in an infinite variety of ways, depending on their proclivities and those of their society. The parents will have a profound impact on that child's ways of thinking about himself/herself and about others. The parents will transmit religious views, political attitudes, and attitudes toward how other groups are to be rated. The child will be punished for certain behaviors and rewarded for others. Whether that

child becomes a bigot or integrationist, traditionalist or innovator, saint or sinner, depends in large measure on the parents, peers, and others who interact with him or her.

The parents may transmit to their offspring some idiosyncratic beliefs and behaviors, but most significantly they act as cultural agents, transferring the ways of the society to their children. Thus, the child is born into a family but also into a society. This society into which the individuals are born shapes their personality and perceptions. Berger has summarized the impact of this in the following:

Society not only controls our movements, but shapes our identity, our thoughts and our emotions. The structures of society become the structures of our own conscious-ness. Society does not stop at the surface of our skins. Society penetrates us as much as it envelops us.[1]

The individual's identity is socially bestowed. Who we are, how we feel about ourselves, and how others treat us are typically consequences of our location in society. Individuals' personalities are also shaped by the way we are accepted, rejected, and/or defined by others. Whether an individual is attractive or plain, witty or dull, worthy or unworthy, depends on the values of society and the groups in which the individual is immersed. Although genes determine one's physiology and potential, the social environment deter-mines how those characteristics will be evaluated.

Suggesting that human beings are socially determined is another way of saying that they are similar to puppets. They are dependent on and manipulated by social forces. A major function of sociology is to identify the social forces that affect us so greatly. Freedom, as McGee has pointed out, can only come from a recognition of these unseen forces:

Freedom consists in knowing what these forces are and how they work so that we have the option of saying no to the impact of their operation. For example, if we grow up in a racist society, we will be racists unless we learn what racism is and how it works and then choose to refuse its impact. In order to do so, however, we must rec-ognize that it is there in the first place. People often are puppets, blindly danced by strings of which they are unaware and over which they are not free to exercise control. A major function of sociology is that it permits us to recognize the forces operative on us and to untie the puppet strings which bind us, thereby giving us the option to be free.[2]

So, one task of sociology is to learn, among other things, what racism is and to determine how it works. This is often difficult because we typically do not recognize its existence—because we have been puppets, socialized to believe and behave in particular ways.

To say that we are puppets is too strong. This assumption is not meant to imply a total **social determinism**.* The metaphor is used to convey the idea that much of who we are and what we do is a product of our social environment. But there are nonconformists, deviants, and innovators. Society is not a rigid, static entity composed of robots. While the members

---

*Advocates of social determinism are guilty of oversimplifying complex phenomena, just as are genetic de-terminists, psychological determinists, geographical determinists, and economic determinists.

of society are shaped by their social environment, they also change that environment. Human beings are the *shapers* of society as well as the *shapees*. This is the third assumption of the sociological approach.

3. *Individuals create, sustain, and change the social forms within which they conduct their lives.* While individuals are largely puppets of society, they are also puppeteers. Chapter 2 will describe this process of how people in interaction are the architects of society. In brief, the argument is that social groups of all sizes and types (families, peer groups, work groups, corporations, communities, and societies) are made by people. What interacting persons create becomes a source of control over those individuals (that is, they become puppets of their own creation). But the continuous interaction of the group's members also changes the group.

There are three important implications of this assumption that groups are human-made. First, these social forms that are created have a certain momentum of their own that defies change. The ways of doing and thinking common to the group are "natural" and "right." Although human-made, the group's expectations and structures take on a sacred quality—the sanctity of tradition—that constrains behavior in the socially prescribed ways.

A second implication is that social organizations, because they are created and sustained by people, are imperfect. Slavery benefited some segments of society by taking advantage of others. A competitive free enterprise system creates "winners" and "losers." The wonders of technology make worldwide transportation and communication easy and relatively inexpensive but create pollution and waste of natural resources. These examples show that there are positive and negative consequences of the way people have organized.

A final implication is that individuals through collective action are capable of changing the structure of society and even the course of history.[3]

PROBLEMS WITH THE SOCIOLOGICAL PERSPECTIVE

Sociology is not a comfortable discipline and therefore will not appeal to everyone. To look behind the "closed doors" of social life is fraught with danger. The astute observer of society must ask such questions as: How does it really work? Who really has the power? Who benefits under the existing social arrangements and who does not? To ask such questions means that the inquirer is interested in looking beyond the commonly accepted "official" definitions. As Berger has put it, "[the] sociological perspective involves a process of 'seeing through' the facades of social structures."[4] The underlying assumption of the sociologist is that things are *not* as they seem. Is the mayor of your town the most powerful person in the community? Is the system of justice truly just? Is professional sport free of racism? Is the United States a meritocratic society where talent and effort combine to stratify the people fairly? To make such queries is to call into question existing myths, stereotypes, and official dogma. The critical examination of society will demystify and demythologize. It sensitizes the individual to the inconsistencies present in society. Clearly that will result if you ask: Why does the United States, in the name of freedom, protect dictatorships around the world? Why do we encourage subsidies to the affluent but resent those directed to the poor? Why was Richard Nixon pardoned while his lackeys who followed orders in the Watergate situation were penalized? How powerful would Ted Kennedy be if his surname were Garcia? Why have over 50 percent of those killed by capital punishment in the United States been black? Why are many women opposed to the Equal Rights Amendment? Why in a democracy such as the United States are there so few truly democratic organizations?

The sociological assumption that provides the basis for this critical stance is that the social world is human-made—and therefore not sacred. The beliefs, the economic system, the law, the way power is distributed are created and sustained by people. They can, therefore, be changed by people. But if the change is to correct imperfections, then we must truly understand how social phenomena work. The central task of this book is to aid in such an understanding of American society.

The sociological perspective is also discomforting to many because the understanding of the constraints of society is liberating. Traditional sex roles, for example, are no longer "sacred" for many persons. But while this is liberating from the constraints of tradition, it is also freedom from the protection that custom provides. The robotlike acceptance of tradition is comfortable because it frees us from choice (and therefore blame) and from ambiguity. So the understanding of society is a two-edged sword, freeing us, but also increasing the probability of frustration, anger, and alienation.

Sociology is also uncomfortable because the behavior of the subjects is not always certain. Prediction is not always accurate, because people can choose between options or be persuaded by irrational factors. The result is that if sociologists know the social conditions, they can predict, but in terms of probabilities. In chemistry, on the other hand, scientists know exactly what will occur if a certain measure of sodium is mixed with a precise amount of chlorine in a test tube. Civil engineers armed with the knowledge of rock formations, type of soils, wind currents, and temperature extremes know exactly what specifications are needed in building a dam in a certain place. They could not, however, if the foundation and building materials kept shifting. That is the problem—and the source of excitement—for the sociologist. The political proclivities of Americans over the past few decades offer a good example of shifting attitudes. In 1964 the Republican candidate for President, Barry Goldwater, was soundly defeated and many observers predicted the demise of the Republican Party. But in 1968, Richard Nixon, the Republican, won. He won again in 1972 by a record-setting margin, leading to the prognostication that the Democratic Party would no longer be viable. Two years later, however, Nixon resigned in disgrace and in 1976 the Democratic candidate, Jimmy Carter, was the victor. In 1980 President Carter was defeated by Ronald Reagan and a number of liberal Senators were defeated by conservatives, leading many observers to predict the demise of liberalism. These dramatic political shifts illustrate that social life is highly complex and its study is beset by change and uncertainties. Although the goal is to reduce the margin of error, its complete elimination is impossible as long as human beings are not robots.

SOCIOLOGICAL METHODS: THE CRAFT OF SOCIOLOGY

Sociology is dependent on reliable data and logical reasoning. These necessities are possible, but there are problems that must be acknowledged. Before we describe the ways that sociologists use to gather reliable data and make valid conclusions, let's examine, in some detail, two major obstacles.

A fundamental problem with the sociological perspective is that bane of the social sciences—objectivity. We are *all* guilty of harboring stereotyped conceptions of social categories such as blacks, hard hats, professors, homosexuals, fundamentalists, business tycoons, communists, jet-setters, and jocks. Moreover, we interpret people's behavior, events, and material objects through the perceptual filter of our religious and political beliefs. When fundamentalists oppose the use of certain books in schools, when abortion is approved by a legislature, when Ronald Reagan advocates cutting billions from the Federal budget by eliminating social services, or when the Supreme Court denies private schools the right to exclude certain racial groups, then most of us rather easily take a position in the ensuing debate.

Sociologists are caught in a dilemma. On the one hand, they are members of society with beliefs, feelings, and biases. At the same time, though, their professional task is to study society in a disciplined (scientific) way. This latter requirement is that scientist-scholars be dispassionate, objective observers. In short, if they take sides, they lose their status as scientists.

This ideal of **value neutrality** can be attacked from three positions. The first is that scientists should not be morally indifferent to the implications of their research. Gouldner has argued this in the following statement:

It would seem that social science's affinity for modeling itself after physical science might lead to instruction in matters other than research alone. Before Hiroshima, physicists also talked of a value-free science; they, too, vowed to make no value judgments. Today many of them are not so sure. If we today concern ourselves exclusively with the technical proficiency of our students and reject all responsibility for their moral sense, or lack of it, then we may someday be compelled to accept responsibility for having trained a generation willing to serve in a future Auschwitz. Granted that science always has inherent in it both constructive and destructive potentialities. It does not follow from this that we should encourage our students to be oblivious to the difference.[5]

The second argument against the purely neutral position is that such a stance is impossible. Becker, among others, has argued that there is no dilemma—because it is impossible to do research that is uncontaminated by personal and political sympathies.[6] This argument is based on several related assumptions. One is that the values of the scholar–researcher enter into the choice of what questions will be asked and how they will be answered. For example, in the study of poverty a critical decision involves the object of the study—the poor or the system that tends to perpetuate poverty among a certain segment of society. Or, in the study of the problems of youth, we can ask either: Why are some youth troublesome for adults, or, alternatively, why do adults make so much trouble for youth? In both illustrations there are quite different questions that will yield very different results.

Similarly, our values lead us to decide from which vantage point we will gain access to information about a particular social organization. If researchers want to understand how a prison operates, they must determine whether they want a description from the inmates, from the guards, from the prison administrators, or from the state board of corrections. Each view provides useful insights about a prison, but obviously a biased one. If the researchers obtain data from more than one of these levels, they are faced with making assessments as to which is the more accurate view, clearly another place in the research process where the values of the observers will have an impact.

Perhaps the most important reason why the study of social phenomena cannot be value-free is that the type of problems researched and the strategies employed tend either to support the existing societal arrangements or to undermine them. Seen in this way, social research of both types is political. Ironically, however, there is a strong tendency to label only the research aimed at changing the system as political. By the same token, whenever the research sides with the underdog, the implication is that the hierarchical system is being questioned—thus, the charge that this type of research is biased. Becker has provided us with the logic of this in the following:

When do we accuse ourselves and our fellow sociologists of bias? I think an inspection of representative instances would show that the accusation arises, in one important class of cases, when the research gives credence, in any serious way, to the perspective of the subordinate group in some hierarchical relationship. In the case of deviance, the hierarchical relationship is a moral one. The superordinate parties in the relationships are those who represent the forces of approved and official morality; the subordinate parties are those who, it is alleged, have violated that morality.[7]

It is odd that, when we perceive bias, we usually see it in these circumstances. It is odd because it is easily ascertained that a great many more studies are biased in the direction of the interests of responsible officials than the other way around.[8]

In summary, bias is inevitable in the study and analysis of social problems. The choice of a research problem, the perspective from which one analyzes the problems, and the solutions proposed all reflect a bias that is either supportive of the existing social arrangements or not. Moreover, unlike biologists, who can dispassionately observe the behavior of an amoeba under a microscope, sociologists are participants in the social life they seek to study and understand. As they study the busing riots in South Boston, children living in poverty, or urban blight, sociologists cannot escape from their own feelings and values. They must, however, not let their feelings and values render their analysis invalid. In other words, research and reports of research must "tell it like it is," not as the researcher might want it to be. Sociologists must display scientific integrity, which requires recognizing biases in such a way that they do not invalidate the findings.[9] Properly done in this spirit, an atheist can study a religious sect, a pacifist can study the military–industrial complex, a divorcee can study marriage, and a person who abhors the political stance of the Moral Majority can study that phenomenon in American politics.

In addition to bias, people gather data and make generalizations about social phenomena in a number of faulty ways. In a sense everyone is a "scientist" seeking to find valid generalizations to guide their behavior and make sense of their world. But most people are, in fact, very unscientific about the social world. The first problem, as we have noted, is the problem of bias. The second is that people tend to generalize from their experience. Not

METHODS PANEL

Panel 1–1
Minimizing Bias

The essential problem for social scientists involves the credibility of their research. How is objectivity possible, though, when they cannot escape their personal values, biases, and opinions? The answer lies in the norms of science.

Sociologists share with other scientists norms for conducting research that minimize personal bias. Their research must reflect the standards of science before it is accepted in scholarly journals. These journals function as gate-keepers for a discipline. What they accept for publication is assumed by their readers to be scientific. The editors of scholarly journals send manuscripts to referees who are unaware of the identity of the authors. This system of anonymity allows the referees to make objective judgments about the credibility of the studies. They review, among other things, the methods used to assess validity and reliability. **Validity** is the degree to which a study actually measures what it purports to measure. **Reliability** is the degree to which another study repeating the same methods would yield the same results.

To guide sociologists, their professional association—the American Sociological Association—has a code of ethics, which includes a number of standards for objectivity and integrity in sociological research.*

*Excerpted from the "Revised ASA Code of Ethics," *ASA Footnotes* (August 1980), p. 12.

only is one's interpretation of things that happen to him or her subjective, but there is a basic problem of sampling. The chances are that one's experience will be too idiosyncratic to allow for an accurate generalization. For example, if you and your friends agree that abortion is appropriate, that does not mean that others in the society, even those of your age, will agree with you. Very likely, your friends are quite similar to you on such dimensions as socioeconomic status, race, religion, and geographic location. Another instance of faulty sampling leading to faulty generalizations is when we make assumptions from a single case. An individual may argue that blacks can make it economically in this country as easily as whites because he or she knows a wealthy black person. Similarly, one might argue that all Chicanos are dumb because the one you know is in the slowest track in high school. This type of reasoning is especially fallacious because it blames the victim.[10] The cause of poverty or crime or dropping out of school or scoring low on an IQ test is seen as a result of the flaw in the individual, ignoring the substantial impact of the economy or school.

Another typical way that we explain social behavior is to use some authority other than our senses. The Bible, for example, has been used by many persons to support or condemn certain activities, such as slavery, capital punishment, war, or monogamy. The Bible, however, is ambiguous on many subjects, offering contradictory statements. The media provide other sources of authority for individuals. The media, however, are not always

1. Sociologists should be sensitive to the potential for damage to individuals or groups from public disclosure of research based on ungeneralizable samples or unsubstantiated interpretation. Especially where there is the potential to harm groups or individuals, sociological research should adhere to the highest methodological standards.

2. Sociologists must not misrepresent their own abilities, or the competence of their staff, to conduct a particular research project.

3. Sociologists—regardless of their work setting—must present their findings honestly and without distortion. There must be no omission of data from a research report which would significantly modify the interpretation of findings. And sociologists should indicate where and how their own theory, method and research design may bear upon or influence the interpretation.

4. Sociologists must report fully all sources of financial support in their research publications and must note any special relations to the sponsor that might affect the interpretation of findings.

5. Sociologists must not accept such grants, contracts or research assignments as appear likely to require violation of the principles above, and should dissociate themselves from the research if they discover a violation and are unable to achieve its correction.

6. The American Sociological Association may ask an investigator for clarification of any distortion by a sponsor or consumer of the findings of a research project in which he or she has participated.

reliable sources of facts either. Stories are often selected because they are unusually dramatic, giving the faulty impression of, for example, a crime wave or questionable air safety.

Finally, we use aphorisms to explain many social occurrences. The problem with this common tactic is that society supplies us with ready explanations that fit contradictory situations and are therefore useless. For instance, if we know a couple who are alike in religion, race, socioeconomic status, and political attitudes, that makes sense to us because "birds of a feather flock together." But the opposite situation also makes sense. If a couple are very different on a number of dimensions, we can explain this by the obvious explanation—"opposites attract." There are a number of other proverbs that we use to explain behavior. The only problem is that there is often a proverb or aphorism to explain either of two extremes:

Absence makes the heart grow fonder.
Out of sight, out of mind.

Look before you leap.
He who hesitates is lost.

Familiarity breeds contempt.
To know her is to love her.

Women are unpredictable.
Isn't that just like a woman.

You can't teach an old dog new tricks.
It's never too late to learn.

Above all, to thine own self be true.
When in Rome, do as the Romans do.

Variety is the spice of life.
Never change horses in the middle of the stream.

Two heads are better than one.
If you want something done right, do it yourself.

You can't tell a book by its cover.
Clothes make the man.

Many hands make light work.
Too many cooks spoil the broth.

Better safe than sorry.
Nothing ventured, nothing gained.

Haste makes waste.
Strike while the iron is hot.

Work for the night is coming.
Eat, drink and be merry for tomorrow you may die.

There's no place like home.
The grass is always greener on the other side of the fence.

These contradictory explanations are commonly used and, of course, explain nothing. The job of the sociologist is to specify under what conditions certain rates of social behaviors occur.

Sociologists do not use aphorisms to explain behavior nor do they speculate based on faulty samples or authorities. Because we are part of the world that is to be explained, sociologists must get evidence that is beyond reproach. In addition to observing scrupulously the canons of science, there are four basic sources of data that yield valid results for sociologists: survey research, experiments, observation, and the use of existing documents. We shall describe these techniques only briefly here.*

1. *Survey research.* Sociologists are interested in obtaining information about certain kinds of persons. They may want to know how political beliefs and behaviors are influenced by differences in sex, race, ethnicity, religion, and social class. Or sociologists may wish to know whether religious attitudes are related to racial antipathy. They may want to determine whether poor people have different values from others in society, the answer to which will have a tremendous impact on the ultimate solution to poverty (see Chapter 11). To answer these and similar questions, the sociologist may use personal interviews or written questionnaires to gather the data. The researcher may obtain information from all the possible subjects or from a selected sample. Since the former is often impractical, a random sample of subjects is selected from the larger population. If the sample is selected scientifically, a relatively small proportion can yield satisfactory results—that is, the inferences made from the sample will be reliable about the entire population. For example, a probability sample of only 2000 from a total population of 1 million will provide data very close to what would be discovered if a survey were taken of the entire 1 million.[11]

Typically with survey research, sociologists use sophisticated statistical techniques to control the contaminating effects of confounding variables, to determine whether the findings could have occurred by chance or not, to determine whether variables are related, and whether such a relationship is a causal one.

2. *Experiments.* To understand the cause-and effect relationship among a few variables, sociologists use controlled experiments. Let's assume, for example, that we want to test whether white students in interracial classrooms have more positive attitudes toward blacks than whites in segregated classrooms. Using the experimental method, the researcher would take a number of white students previously unexposed to blacks in school and randomly assign a subset to an integrated classroom situation. Before actual contact with the blacks, however, all the white students would be given a test of their racial attitudes. This pretest establishes a bench mark from which to measure any changes in attitudes. One group, the **control group**, continues school in segregated classrooms while the other group, the **experimental group**, now has blacks as classmates. Otherwise the two groups are the same. Following a suitable period of time, the whites in both groups are tested again (posttest) for their racial attitudes. If the experimental group is found to differ from the control group in racial attitudes (the **dependent variable**), then it is assumed that interracial contact (the **independent variable**) is the source of the change.

As an example of a less contrived experiment, a researcher could test the results of two different treatments on the subsequent behavior of juvenile delinquents. Delinquent boys

*See the bibliography at the end of the chapter for references on the methods of sociology. Methodological footnotes and methods panels appear occasionally throughout this book to give insight into how sociologists obtain and analyze data.

who had been adjudicated by the courts could be randomly assigned to a boys' industrial school or a group home facility in the community. After release from incarceration, records would be kept on the boys' subsequent behavior in school (grades, truancy, formal reprimands) and in the community (police contacts, work behavior). If the boys from the two groups differ appreciably, then we can say with assurance, since the boys were randomly assigned to each group, that the difference in treatment (the independent variable) was the source of the difference in behavior (the dependent variable).[12]

3. *Observation.* The researcher, without intervention, can observe as accurately as possible what occurs in a community, group, or social event. This type of procedure is especially helpful in understanding such social phenomena as the decision-making process, the stages of a riot, the attraction of cults for their members, and the depersonalization of patients in a mental hospital. Case studies of entire communities have been very instrumental in the understanding of power structures[13] and the intricacies of social stratification.[14] Long-time participant observation studies of slum neighborhoods and gangs have been very insightful in showing the social organization present in what the casual observer might think of as very disorganized activity.[15]

4. *Existing sources.* The sociologist can also make use of existing data to test theories. The most common sources of information are the various agencies of the government. Data are provided for the nation, regions, states, communities, and census tracts on births, deaths, income, education, unemployment, business activity, health delivery systems, prison populations, military spending, poverty, migration, and the like. Important information can also be obtained from such sources as business firms, athletic teams and leagues, unions, and professional associations. Statistical techniques can be used with these data to describe populations and the effects of social variables on various dependent variables.

SUMMARY

The sociological perspective allows us to understand ourselves, others, and social organizations. It requires of us the ability to stand back from social life to see the patterns, regularities, and constraints. This means not only a certain amount of detachment but also, and most fundamentally, the realization that the customs and existing forms of social organization are not sacred. This critical examination of social life will allow us to see the positive *and* negative consequences and, we hope, will lead us to work for more humane social arrangements. This critical analysis of social life is a two-edged sword, however. On the one hand, to know the forces constraining us is to be freed from their power. But while this is liberating, it also frees us from the protection that custom and tradition provide.

Sociology, because its subject matter is social life, has problems of separating fact from myth. There are the problems of bias and of generalizing from faulty samples. Sociologists, although they are part of the social reality under investigation, employ vigorous scientific methods to overcome these obstacles. Most important, they employ methods designed to get valid information that allows for accurate probability statements about social reality.

CHAPTER REVIEW

1. Sociology is the science dealing with social forces—the forces outside us that shape our very lives, interests, and personalities. Sociologists, then, work to discover the underlying order of social life and the principles regarding it that explain human behavior.

2. The assumptions of the sociological perspective are that: (a) individuals are, by their nature, social beings; (b) individuals are socially determined; and (c) individuals create, sustain, and change the social forms within which they conduct their lives.

3. Sociology is uncomfortable for many because it looks behind the facades of social life. This requires a critical examination of society that questions the existing myths, stereotypes, and official dogma.

4. The basis for the critical stance of sociologists is that the social world is not sacred because it is made by humans.

5. Sociology is dependent on reliable data and logical reasoning. Although value neutrality is impossible in the social sciences, bias is minimized by the norms of science.

6. Survey research is a systematic means of gathering data to obtain information about people's behaviors, attitudes, and opinions.

7. Sociologists may use experiments to assess the effects of social factors on human behavior. One of two similar groups—the experimental group—is exposed to an independent variable. If this group later differs from the control group, then the independent variable is known to have produced the effect.

8. Observation is another technique for obtaining reliable information. Various social organizations such as prisons, hospitals, schools, churches, cults, families, communities, and corporations can be studied and understood through systematic observation.

9. Sociologists also employ existing sources of data to test their theories.

10. Sociology is a science and the rules of scientific research guide the efforts of sociologists to discover the principles of social organization and the sources of social constraints on human behavior.

FOR FURTHER STUDY

The Sociological Perspective

Peter L. Berger, *Invitation to Sociology: A Humanistic Perspective* (Garden City, N.Y.: Doubleday (Anchor Books), 1963).

Stephen Cole, *The Sociological Orientation: An Introduction to Sociology* (Chicago: Rand McNally, 1975).

Lewis A. Coser (ed.), *The Pleasures of Sociology* (New York: New American Library, 1980).

C. Wright Mills, *The Sociological Imagination* (New York: Oxford University Press, 1959).

The Craft of Sociology

Earl R. Babbie, *The Practice of Social Research*, Second Edition (Belmont, Calif.: Wadsworth, 1979).

Robert Sommer and Barbara B. Sommer, *A Practical Guide to Behavioral Research* (New York: Oxford University Press, 1980).

Gideon Sjoberg (ed.), *Ethics, Politics, and Social Research* (Cambridge, Mass.: Schenkman, 1967).

NOTES AND REFERENCES

1. Peter L. Berger, *Invitation to Sociology: A Humanistic Perspective* (Garden City, N.Y.: Doubleday (Anchor Books), 1963), p. 121.

2. Reece McGee, *Points of Departure: Basic Concepts in Sociology*, 2nd ed. (Hinsdale, Ill.: Dryden Press, 1975), pp. x–xi.

3. See Charles H. Anderson, *Toward a New*

Sociology, rev. ed. (Homewood, Ill.: Dorsey Press, 1974), p. 3.

4. Berger, *Invitation to Sociology*, p. 31.

5. Alvin W. Gouldner, "Anti-Minotaur: The Myth of Value-Free Sociology," *Social Problems* 9 (Winter, 1962), p. 212.

6. Howard S. Becker, "Whose Side Are We On?" *Social Problems* 14 (Winter, 1967), pp. 239–247.

7. Becker, "Whose Side Are We On?" p. 240.

8. Becker, "Whose Side Are We On?" p. 242.

9. Berger, *Invitation to Sociology*, p. 5.

10. See William Ryan, *Blaming the Victim*, rev. ed. (New York: Pantheon Books, 1976).

11. Bernard S. Phillips, *Social Research: Strategy and Tactics*, 2nd ed. (New York: Macmillan, 1971), pp. 307–313.

12. E. L. Philips, E. A. Phillips, D. L. Fixsen, and M. M. Wolf, "Behavior Shaping Works for Delinquents," *Psychology Today* 7 (June, 1973), pp. 75–79.

13. See Floyd Hunter, *Community Power Structure* (Chapel Hill, N.C.: University of North Carolina Press, 1953); and Robert Dahl, *Who Governs?* (New Haven, Conn.: Yale University Press, 1961).

14. See W. Lloyd Warner and Paul S. Lunt, *The Social Life of a Modern Community* (New Haven, Conn.: Yale University Press, 1941); and Robert S. Lynd and Helen Merrill Lynd, *Middletown in Transition* (New York: Harcourt Brace Jovanovich, 1937).

15. See William Foote Whyte, *Street Corner Society: The Social Structure of an Italian Slum*, rev. ed. (Chicago: University of Chicago Press, 1955); Herbert J. Gans, *The Urban Villagers* (New York: Free Press, 1962); and Elliot Liebow, *Tally's Corner* (Boston: Little, Brown, 1967).

2

The Structure of Social Groups

An experiment was conducted some years ago when 24 previously unacquainted boys, aged 12, were brought together at a summer camp.[1] For three days the boys, who were unaware that they were part of an experiment, participated in camp-wide activities. During this period the camp "counselors" observed the friendship patterns that emerged naturally. The boys were then divided into two groups of 12. The boys were deliberately separated in order to break up the previous friendship patterns. The groups were then totally separated for a period of five days. During this period the boys were left alone by the "counselors" so that what occurred was the spontaneous result of the boys' behavior. The experimenters found that in both groups, there developed (1) a division of labor; (2) a hierarchical structure of ranks—that is, differences among the boys in power, prestige, and rewards; (3) the creation of rules; (4) punishments for violations of the rules; (5) argot—that is, specialized language such as nicknames and group symbols that served as positive in-group identifications; and (6) member cooperation to achieve group goals.

This experiment illustrates the process of social organization. The "counselors" did not insist that these phenomena occur in each group. They seemed to occur "naturally." In fact, they happen universally.[2] The goals of this chapter are to understand this process, to understand the components of social structure that emerge, and how they operate to constrain behavior. Although the process is generally the same regardless of group size, we will examine it at two levels—the micro level and the societal level.

THE MICRO LEVEL

The Process of Social Organization[3]

"**Social organization** refers to the ways in which human conduct becomes socially organized, that is, the observed regularities in the behavior of people that are due to the social conditions in which they find themselves rather than to their physiological or psychological characteristics as individuals."[4] The social conditions that constrain behavior can be divided into two types: (1) **social structure**—the structure of behavior in groups and society; and (2) **culture**—the shared beliefs of group members that unite them and guide their behavior.

Social structure. Sociology is the study of the patterns that emerge when people interact over time. The emphasis is on the linkages and network that emerges, which transforms an **aggregate** of individuals into a **group**. We start, then, with **social interaction**. When the actions of one person (or persons) affect another person, social interaction occurs. The most common method is communication through speech, the written word, or symbolic acts (for example, a wink, a wave of the hand, or the raising of a finger). Behavior can also be altered by the mere presence of others. The way we behave (from the way we eat to what we think) is affected by whether we are alone or with others. Even physical reactions such as crying, laughing, or passing gas are controlled by the individual because of the fear of embarrassment. It could even be argued that, except in the most extreme cases, people's actions are always oriented toward other human beings whether they are physically present or not. We, as individuals, are constantly concerned about the expected or actual reactions of others. Even when alone, an individual may not act in certain ways because of having been taught that such actions are wrong.

Social interaction may be either transitory or enduring. Sociologists are interested in the latter type because only then does patterned behavior occur. A case of enduring social interaction is a **social relationship**. Relationships occur for a number of reasons. It may be sexual attraction, familial ties, because the members have a common interest (for example, collecting coins or growing African violets), because they share a common political or religious ideology, because they cooperate to produce or distribute a product, or because of propinquity (neighbors). Regardless of the specific reasons, the members of a social relationship are united at least in some minimal way with the others. Most important, the members of a social relationship behave quite differently than they would as participants in a fleeting interaction. Once the interaction is perpetuated, the behavior of the participants is profoundly altered. An autonomous individual is similar to an element in chemistry. As soon as there is a chemical reaction between two elements, however, they become parts of a new entity, as Olsen has noted:

The concepts of "elements" and "parts" are analogous to terms in chemistry. By themselves, chemical elements—sodium and chlorine, for instance—exhibit characteristics peculiarly their own, by which each can be separately identified. This condition holds true even if elements are mixed together, as long as there is no chemical reaction between them. Through a process of chemical interaction, however, the elements can join to form an entirely new substance—in this case, salt. The elements of sodium and chlorine have now both lost their individual identities and characteristics, and have instead become parts of a more inclusive chemical compound, which has properties not belonging to either of its component parts by themselves. In an emergent process such as this, the original elements are transformed into parts of a new entity.[5]

Olsen's description of a chemical reaction is also appropriate for what arises in a social relationship. Most sociologists assume that the whole is not identical to the sum of its parts—that is, through the process of enduring interaction something is created with properties different from the component parts.* The two groups artificially formed at the summer camp, for example, developed similar structural properties regardless of the unique personalities of the boys in each group.

*This assumption—the **realist position**—is one side of a fundamental philosophical debate. The **nominalists**, on the other hand, argue that to know the parts is to know the whole. In sociology the realist position is dominant and found especially in the works of Emile Durkheim[6] and the contemporary classic by Charles Warriner.[7] The minority position in sociology is represented most prominently by George Homans.[8]

Although groups may differ in size or purpose, they are similar in structure and the processes that create the structure. In other words, one group may exist to knit quilts for charity while another may do terrorist bombings, but they will be alike in many important ways. Their social structure involves the patterns of interaction that emerge, the division of labor, and the linking and hierarchy of positions. The social structure is an emergent phenomenon bringing order and predictability to social life within the group.

Culture. The other component of social organization is culture—the shared beliefs of a group's members that serve to guide conduct. Through enduring social interaction common expectations emerge about how people should act. These are called **norms**. Criteria for judging what is appropriate, correct, moral, and important also emerge. These criteria are the **values** of the group. Also part of the shared beliefs are the expectations group members have of individuals occupying the various positions within the group. These are **social roles**. The elements of culture will be described briefly below for the micro and macro levels and in detail in Chapter 5.

To summarize, social organization refers to both culture and social structure. Blau and Scott describe how they operate to constrain human behavior:

The prevailing cultural standards and the structure of social relations serve to organize human conduct in the collectivity. As people conform more or less closely to the expectations of their fellows, and as the degree of their conformity in turn influences their relations with others and their social status, and as their status in further turn affects their inclinations to adhere to social norms and their chances to achieve valued objectives, their patterns of behavior become socially organized.[9]

Norms

All social organizations have rules (norms) that specify appropriate and inappropriate behaviors. In essence, norms are the behavioral expectations that members of a particular group collectively share. They ensure that action within social organizations is generally predictable.

Some norms are not considered as important as others and consequently are not severely punished if violated. These minor rules are called **folkways**. Folkways vary, of course, from group to group. A particular sorority may expect its members to wear formal dress on certain occasions and to never wear curlers to the library. In a church, wine may be consumed by the parishioners at the appropriate time—communion. To bring one's own bottle of wine to communion, however, would be a violation of the folkways of that church. Could you imagine an announcement in your church bulletin that communion will be next Sunday—B.Y.O.B.? These examples show that folkways involve etiquette, customs, and regulations which, if violated, do not threaten the fabric of the social organization.

The violation of the group's **mores**, on the other hand, is considered important enough so that it must be punished severely. This type of norm involves morality—in fact, mores can be thought of as moral imperatives. In a sorority, for instance, examples of the mores might be: disloyalty, stealing from a "sister," and conduct that brings shame to the organization, such as blatant sexual promiscuity.

Status and Role

One important aspect of social structure is comprised of the positions of a social organization. If one determines what positions are present in an organization and how they are interrelated (hierarchy, reciprocal pairs, etc.), then the analyst has a structural map of that social group. The existence of positions in organizations has an important consequence for individuals—the bestowing of a social identity. Each of us belongs to a number of organizations and in each we occupy a position (**status**). If you were asked—who are you?—chances are you would respond by listing your various statuses. An individual may at the same time be a student, sophomore, daughter, sister, friend, female, Baptist, Sunday School teacher, Democrat, waitress, American citizen, and Secretary-Treasurer of the local chapter of Weight Watchers.

The individual's social identity, then, is a product of the particular matrix of statuses that she or he occupies. Another characteristic of positions in organizations that has an important influence on social identity is that they tend to be differentially rewarded and esteemed. This hierarchical element of status reinforces the positive or negative image individuals have of themselves depending on placement in various organizations. Some individuals consistently hold prestigious positions (bank president, deacon, caucasian, male, chairman of United Fund), while others may hold only those statuses negatively esteemed (welfare recipient, aged, Chicano, janitor) and some occupy mixed statuses (bus driver, 32nd-degree Mason, union member, church trustee).

So group memberships are vital sources of our notion of our own identity. Similarly, when others know of our status in various organizations, they assign a social identity to us. When we determine a person's age, race, religion, and occupation, we tend to stereotype that person—that is, we assume that the individual is a certain "type." This has the effect of conferring a social identity on that person, raising expectations for certain behaviors which, very often, result in a self-fulfilling prophecy.

While the mapping of statuses provides important clues about the social structure of an organization, the most important aspect of status is the behavior expected of the occupant of a status. To determine that an individual occupies the status of father does not tell us much about what the group expects of a father. In some societies, for example, the biological father has no legal, monetary, or social responsibility for his children. His children are cared for by the mother and her brother. In American society, there are norms (legal and informal) that demand of the father that he be responsible for his children. Not only must he provide for them, but he must also, depending on the customs of the family, be a disciplinarian, buddy, teacher, Santa Claus, and tooth fairy.

The behavior expected of a person occupying a status in a group is the **role.*** The norms of the social organization constrain the incumbents in a status to behave in prescribed and therefore predictable ways, regardless of their particular personalities. Society insists that we play our roles correctly. To do otherwise is to risk being judged by others as abnormal, crazy, incompetent, and/or immature. These pressures to conform to role demands ensure that there is stability in social groups even though member turnover occurs. For example, ministers to a particular congregation come and go, but certain actions are predictable in particular incumbents because of the demands on their behavior. These demands come

---

*This section will introduce the concept of role as it is appropriate to the context of social organization. We shall elaborate on it in Chapter 7.

from the hierarchy of the denomination, from other ministers, and most assuredly from the members of the parish. The stability imposed by role is also seen with other statuses, such as professor, janitor, policemen, students, and even President of the United States.

The organizational demands on members in the various statuses do *not* make behavior totally predictable, however. Occupants of the statuses can vary within limits. There are at least three reasons for this. First, personality variables can account for variations in the behavior of persons holding identical status. People can be conformist or unconventional, manipulated or manipulators, passive or aggressive, followers or inspirational leaders, cautious or impetuous, ambitious or lackadaisical. The particular configuration of personality traits can make obvious differences in the behavior of individuals, even though they may face identical group pressures.

A second reason why role does not make social actors robots is that the occupants of a status may not receive a clear, consistent message as to what behavior is expected. A minister, for example, may find within his or her congregation individuals and cliques that make conflicting demands. One group may insist that the minister be a social activist. Another may demand that the pastor be apolitical and spend his or her time exclusively meeting the spiritual needs of the members.

Another circumstance leading to conflicting expectations—and unpredictability of action—results from multiple-group memberships. The statuses we occupy may have conflicting demands on our behavior. As one example of this, the black Lieutenant Governor of Colorado, George Brown, when inaugurated was faced with the demands of his office, on the one hand, and the demands of his black constituency, on the other, who demanded that he do more for blacks. He opted to go slow on the latter, which resulted in a black walkout during his swearing-in ceremony. Other illustrations of conflicting demands because of occupying two quite different statuses are: daughter and lover, son and peer-group member, and businessman and church deacon. Being the recipient of incompatible demands results in hypocrisy, secrecy, guilt, and most important for our consideration—unpredictable behavior.

Although role performance may vary, stability within organizations remains. The stability is a consequence of the strong tendency of persons occupying statuses in the organization to conform. Let us look briefly at just how powerfully roles shape behavior. First, the power of role over personal behavior is seen very dramatically as one moves from one status to another. If you could observe your father's behavior, for example, at work, at parties, at church, and at a convention in a faraway city, chances are that the behavioral patterns would be inconsistent. Or, even closer to home, what about your own behavior at home, at church, at school, in the dorm, or in a parked car? In each of these instances the same individual occupies multiple statuses and faces conflicting role expectations, resulting in overall inconsistent behavior but very likely behavior that is expected for each separate role.

The power of role to shape behavior is also demonstrated as one changes status within an organization. The Amish, for instance, select their minister by lot from among the male adults of the group. The eligible members each select a Bible. The one choosing the Bible with the special mark in it is the new pastor. His selection is assumed to be ordained by God. Now this individual has a new status in the group—the leader with God's approval. Such an elevation in status will, doubtless, have a dramatic effect on that person's behavior. Without special training (the Amish rarely attend school beyond the eighth grade), the new minister will in all likelihood exhibit leadership, self-confidence, and wisdom. Less dramatically, but with similar results nonetheless, each of us undergoes shifts in status within the organizations to which we belong—from freshman to senior, bench warmer to first team, assembly-line worker to foreman, and from adolescent to adult. These changes in status mean, of course, a concomitant shift in the expectations for behavior (role). Not only does our behavior change but so too our attitudes, perceptions, and perhaps even our personality.

A dramatic example of the power of role over behavior is provided by an experiment conducted by Philip Zimbardo. He wanted to study the impact of prison life on guards and prisoners. Using student volunteers, he randomly assigned some to be guards and others to be inmates. By utilizing subjects who were unassociated with a prison, the researcher could actually study the effects of social roles on behavior without the confounding variables of personality traits, character disorders, and the like.

Zimbardo constructed a mock prison in the basement of the psychology building at Stanford University. The students chosen as prisoners were "arrested" one night without warning, dressed in prison uniforms, and locked in the cells. The "guards" were instructed to maintain order. Zimbardo found that the college students assigned the roles of guard or inmate actually *became* guards and inmates in just a few days. The guards showed brutality and the prisoners became submissive, demonstrating that roles effectively shape behavior because they have the power to shape consciousness (thinking, feeling, and perceiving). Interestingly, Zimbardo, who is a psychologist, concluded that *social factors superseded individual ones*: "Individual behavior is largely under the control of social forces and environmental contingencies rather than personality traits, character, will power or other empirically unvalidated constructs."[10]

Finally, roles have the power to protect individuals. The constraints on behavior, implied in the role, provide a blueprint that relieves the individual from the responsibility for action. Thus, the certainty provided by role makes us comfortable. Gay liberation and women's liberation, to name two contemporary movements, are aimed at liberation from the constraints of narrowly prescribed sex roles. But to be free of these constraints brings not only freedom but also problems. So, too, when one is freed from the constraints of a particular community, job, or marriage, the newfound liberty, independence, and excitement are countered by the frustrations involving ambiguity, choice, loneliness, and responsibility.

Social Control

Although social groups vary in the degree of tolerance for alternative behaviors, they universally demand conformity to some norms. In the absence of such demands, groups would not exist because of the resulting anarchy. The mechanisms of social control are varied. They can occur subtly in the socialization process (see Chapter 6), so that persons feel guilty or proud, depending upon their actions. They can occur in the form of rewards (medals, prizes, merit badges, gold stars, trophies, praise) by family members, peers, neighbors, fellow workers, employers, and the community to reinforce certain behaviors. Also common are negative sanctions such as fines, demerits, imprisonment, and excommunication that are used to ensure conformity. More subtle techniques, such as gossip or ridicule, are also quite successful in securing conformity because of the common fear of humiliation before one's friends, classmates, coworkers, or neighbors.

An example of a particularly devastating and effective technique is the practice of "shunning" the sinner, used by some of the Amish and Mennonite religious sects. No one in the religious community, not even the guilty party's spouse and children, is to recognize his or her existence. In one celebrated case, Robert Bear was the victim of shunning. He took the case to court on the grounds that this practice was unconstitutional because it was too severe. Since the shun was invoked, Bear's wife had not slept with him, his six children were alienated from him, and his farm operation was in ruin because no one would work for him or buy his produce.[11] The courts ruled, however, that it was within the province of the church to punish its members for transgressions. The severity of the "shun" is an extremely effective social control device for the Amish community, guaranteeing, except in rare cases, conformity to the dictates of the group.

Whatever the mechanism used, social control efforts tend to be very effective, whether they be within a family, peer group, organization, community, or a society. Most of the people, most of the time, conform to the norms of their groups and society. Otherwise, the majority of the poor would riot, most of the starving would steal, and more young men would refuse to fight in wars. The pressure to conform comes from within us (internalization of the group's norms and values from the socialization process) and from outside us (sanctions or the threat of sanctions) and we obey. In fact, what we consider self-control is really the consequence of social control. These constraints are usually not oppressive to the individual. Indeed, we want to obey the rules.

Primary and Secondary Groups

A social **group** is a social organization created through enduring and patterned interaction. It consists of people who have a common identity, share a common culture, and define themselves as a distinct social unit. Groups may be classified in a number of ways, the most significant of which involves the kind and quality of relationships that members have with each other. Sociologists have delineated two types of groups according to the degree of intimacy and involvement among the members—primary and secondary.

Primary groups are those whose members are the most intimately involved with each other.[12] These groups are small and display face-to-face interaction. They are informal in organization and long lasting. The members have a strong identification, loyalty, and emotional attachment to the group and its members. Examples are the nuclear family, a child's play group, a teenage gang, and close friends. Primary groups are crucial to the individual because they provide members with a sense of belonging, identity, purpose, and security. Thus, they have the strongest influence on the attitudes and values of members.

Secondary groups, in contrast to primary groups, are much larger and more impersonal. They are formally organized, task oriented, and relatively nonpermanent. The individual member is relatively unimportant. The members may vary considerably in beliefs, attitudes, and values. Americans are greatly affected by this type of group. The government at all levels deals with us impersonally. So, too, does our school, where we are a number in a computer. We live in large dormitories or in neighborhoods where we are barely acquainted with those near us. We work in large organizations and belong to large churches.

One significant impact of the impersonal nature of secondary groups is that they spawn the formation of primary groups. Primary groups emerge at school, at work, in an apartment building, in a neighborhood, in a church, or in an army. In other words, intensely personal groups develop and are sustained by their members in largely impersonal settings.

The existence of primary groups within secondary groups is an important phenomenon that has ramifications for the goals of the secondary group. Two examples from military experience make this point. In World War II the German army was organized to promote the formation of primary groups. The men were assigned to a unit for the duration of the war. They trained together, fought together, went on furloughs together, and were praised or punished as a group. This was a calculated organizational ploy to increase social solidarity in the small fighting units. This worked to increase morale, loyalty, and a willingness to die for the group. In fact, they often became more loyal to their fighting unit than to the nation.[13]

In contrast, the American army in Vietnam was organized in such a way as to minimize the possibility for forming primary groups. Instead of being assigned to a single combat unit until the war was over, soldiers were given a twelve-month tour of duty in Vietnam. This rotation system meant that in any fighting unit soldiers were continually entering and leaving. This prevented the development of a close relationship and a feeling of "all for one and one for all." Since each soldier had his own departure date his goal was not to win the war but to survive until he was eligible to go home. This individualism made morale difficult to maintain and loyalty to one's unit difficult if not impossible to achieve. It also made the goal of winning the war less attainable than would a system that fostered primary groups.[14]

The Power of the Social Group

We have seen that primary and secondary groups structure the behavior of their members by providing rules, roles, and mechanisms of social control. The result is that most of us, most of the time, conform to the expectations of social groups. Let us examine some illustrations of the profound influence of social groups on individuals, beginning with the classic study of suicide by Emile Durkheim.

1. *One's attachment to social groups affects the probability of suicide.* Suicide would appear on the surface to be one area that could strictly be left to psychological explanations. An individual is commiting the ultimate individual act—ending one's own life— presumably because of excessive guilt, anxiety, and/or stress. Sociologists, however, are interested in this seemingly individual phenomenon because of the social factors that may produce the feelings of guilt or the undue psychological stress. Sociologists are not interested, however, in the individual suicide case as psychologists would be, but in a number of people in the same social situation. Let us look at how sociologists would study suicide by examining in some detail the classic study by the nineteenth-century French sociologist Emile Durkheim.[15]

Durkheim was the consummate sociologist. He reacted to what he considered the excessive psychologism of his day by examining suicide rates (the number of suicides per 100,000 people in a particular category) sociologically. Some of the interesting results of his study were that single people had higher rates than married people, childless married people had a higher rate than those with children, the rate of city dwellers exceeded that of rural people, and Protestants were more likely to be self-destructive than Catholics or Jews. Societal conditions were also correlated with suicide rates. As expected, rates were higher during economic depressions than in periods of economic stability, although surprisingly high rates were found during economic booms.

Durkheim went an important step beyond just noting that social factors were related to suicide rates. He developed a theory to explain these facts—a theory based on the individual's relationship to a social organization. Three types of suicide—the egoistic, altruistic, and anomic—were posited by Durkheim to illustrate the effect of one's attachment to a group (society, religion, family) on self-preservation. **Egoistic suicide** occurs when an individual has minimal ties to a social group. The person is alone, lacking group goals and group supports. This explains why married people are less likely to commit suicide than single people and why married people with children are not as likely to kill themselves as those who are childless. Being an important part of a group gives meaning and purpose to life. This lack of group supports also explains why Protestants during Durkheim's day had a higher suicide rate than Catholics. The Catholic religion provided believers with many group supports, including the belief in the authority of religious leaders to interpret the scriptures. Catholics also believed that through the confessional, sinners could be redeemed. Protestants, on the other hand, were expected to be their own priests, reading and interpreting God's word. When guilty of sin, Protestants again were alone. There was no confessional where a priest would assure one of forgiveness. The differences in theology left individual Protestants without religious authority and with a greater sense of uncertainty. This relatively greater isolation left Protestants without the group of believers and the authority of priests in times of stress.

Altruistic suicide occurs in a completely different type of group setting. When groups are highly cohesive, the individual member of such a collectivity tends to be group oriented. Such a group might expect its members to kill themselves for the good of the group under certain conditions. Soldiers may be expected to leave the relative safety of their foxholes and attack a strategic hill even though the odds are very much against them. The strong allegiance to one's group may force such an act, which would otherwise seem quite irrational. The kamikaze attacks by Japanese pilots during World War II were suicide missions where the pilot guided the ammunition-laden plane into a target. These pilots gave their lives because of their ultimate allegiance to a social group—clearly an example of altruistic suicide. Another example of obligatory suicide for the good of the group is found among Eskimos. Because life is so tenuous in their harsh environment, Eskimos are expected to carry their full burden in providing for the survival of the group. When individuals become too old and feeble to provide their share, they provide for the survival of the group by taking their own lives.

The third type of suicide—the **anomic**—is also related to the individual's attachment to a group. It differs from the other two types in that it refers especially to the condition where the expectations of a group are ambiguous or they conflict with other sets of expectations. Typically, behavior is regulated by a clear set of rules (norms). But there are times when these rules lose their clarity and certainty for individuals. This is a condition of anomie (normlessness). Anomie usually occurs in a situation of rapid change. Examples of anomic situations are: emigration from one society to another, movement from a rural area to an urban one, rapid loss of status, overnight wealth, widowhood, divorce, and drastic inflation or deflation. In all these cases, people are often not sure how to behave. They are not certain of their goals. Life may appear aimless. Whenever the constraints on behavior are suddenly lifted, the probability of suicide increases. The irony is that we tend to be comfortable under the tyranny of the group and that freedom from such constraints is often intolerable. The sexual freedom of married persons in American society, for example, is highly regulated. There is only one legitimate sex partner. The unmarried person is not limited. But while married persons might fantasize that such a life is "nirvana," the replacement of regulated sexual behavior with such freedom is a condition of normlessness conducive to higher suicide rates.[16]

2. *The group may affect our perceptions.* Apparently, our wish to conform is so great that we often give in to group pressure. Solomon Asch, a social psychologist, has tested this proposition by asking the subjects in an experiment to compare the length of lines on cards.[17] The subjects were asked one at a time to identify verbally the longest line. All the subjects but one were confederates of the experimenter, coached to give the same wrong answer, placing the lone subject in the awkward position of having the evidence of his senses unanimously contradicted. Each experiment consisted of 18 trials, with the confederates giving wrong responses on 12 and correct ones on six. For the 50 subjects going through this ordeal, the average number of times they went along with the majority with incorrect judgments was 3.84. While 13 of the 50 were independent and gave responses in accord with their perceptions, 37 (74 percent) gave in to the group pressure at least once (12 did eight or more times). In other experiments where the confederates were not unanimous in their responses, the subjects were freed from the overwhelming group pressure and generally had confidence enough in their perceptions to give the correct answer.

Muzafer Sherif also conducted a series of experiments to determine the extent of conformity among individuals.[18] An individual subject was placed in a dark room to observe a pinpoint of light. The subject was asked to describe how many inches the light moved (the light appears to move, even though it is stationary, because of what is called the "autokinetic effect"). In repeated experiments each of the subjects tended to be consistent as to how far they felt the light had moved. When placed in a group, however, individuals modified their observations to make them more consistent with those of the others in the room. After repeated exposures, the group arrived at a collective judgment. The important point about this experiment is that the group, unlike the one in the Asch experiment, was composed entirely of naive subjects. Therefore, the conclusion about group pressure on individual members is more valid, reflecting natural group processes.

3. *Sectarians with group support maintain their conviction despite contrary evidence.* Leon Festinger and his associates at the University of Minnesota carefully studied a group which believed that a great flood would submerge the West Coast from Seattle to Chile on December 21 of that year.[19] On the eve of the predicted cataclysm the leader received a message that her group should be ready to leave at midnight in a flying saucer that had been dispatched to save them. The group of ten waited expectantly at midnight for the arrival of the saucer. It did not appear and finally at 4:45 A.M. the leader announced that she had received another communication. The message was that the world had been spared the disaster because of the force of good found among this small band of believers. Festinger was especially interested in how the group would handle this disconfirmation of prophecy. But this group, like other millennial groups of history, reacted to the disconfirmation by reaffirming their beliefs and doubling their efforts to win converts.

4. *Membership in a group may have an effect on one's health and even life itself.* Pakistan has a caste system. This means that children are destined to occupy the stratum of

society that they are born into. Their occupation will be that of their parents with no questions asked. One of the lowest castes is that of beggar. Since the child of a beggar will be a beggar and the most successful beggars are deformed, the child will be deformed by his family (usually by an uncle). Often the method is to break the child's back because the resulting deformity is so wretched. All parents wish success for their children, and the beggar family wishing the same is forced by the constraints of the rigid social system to physically disable their child for life.

There is a religious sect in Cortez, Colorado, the "Church of the First Born," which does not believe in traditional medical care. Recently a three-year-old boy, whose mother belonged to this sect, died of diphtheria. The boy had never been immunized for this disease. Moreover, the mother refused medical treatment for her son after the illness had been diagnosed. The mother knew the consequences of her refusal of medical treatment because her nephew had died of diphtheria, but her faith and the faith of the other members kept her from saving her son's life. This is dramatic evidence for the power of the group to curb what we erroneously call "maternal instinct."

Another example of a group demanding hazardous behavior of its members is found among some religious sects of Appalachia that encourage the handling of poisonous snakes (rattlesnakes, water moccasins, and copperheads) as part of worship. Members pick up handfuls of poisonous snakes, throw them on the ground, pick them up again, thrust them under their shirts and blouses, and even cover their heads with clusters of snakes. The ideology of the group, thus, encourages members to literally put their faith to the ultimate test—death. The ideology is especially interesting because it justifies death by snakebite as well as being spared the bite or recovering if bitten.

The serpent-handlers say the Lord causes a snake to strike in order to refute scoffers' claims that the snakes' fangs have been pulled. They see each recovery from snakebite as a miracle wrought by the Lord—and each death as a sign that the Lord "really had to show the scoffers how dangerous it is to obey His commandments." Since adherents believe that death brings one to the throne of God, some express an eagerness to die when He decides they are ready. Those who have been bitten and who have recovered seem to receive special deference from other members of the church.[20]

5. *The group can alter the behavior of members, even behaviors that involve basic human drives.* Human beings are biologically motivated to eat, drink, sleep, and engage in sexual activity. But human groups significantly shape how these biological drives are met. How we eat, when we eat, and what we eat are all greatly influenced by social groups. Some groups have rigid rules that require periods of fasting. Others have festivals where huge quantities of food and drink are consumed. Sexual behavior is also controlled. Although there is a universal sex drive, mating is not a universal activity among adults. Some persons, because of their group membership, take vows of chastity. Some persons, because they have certain physical or mental traits, are often labeled by groups as undesirable and are therefore involuntarily chaste. Some societies are obsessed with sex while others are not. An example of the latter is the Dani tribe of New Guinea. Sexual intercourse is delayed between marriage partners until exactly two years after the ceremony. After the birth of a child there is a five-year period of abstinence.

These dramatic examples of the power of groups over individuals should not keep us from recognizing the everyday and continual constraints on behavior. Our everyday activities, our perceptions and interpretations, and our attitudes are the product of our group memberships. The constraints, however, are for the most part subtle and go unrecognized as such. In short, what we think of as autonomous behavior is generally not.

Summary

Social groups undergo a universal process—the process of social organization. Through enduring social interaction a matrix of social expectations emerges which guides behavior in prescribed channels, making social life patterned and therefore predictable. Thus, social organizations tend to be stable. But this is also a process, as Figure 2–1 indicates.

Interaction among the social actors in a social organization is constant and continuous, reinforcing stability but also bringing about change. Social organizations are never static. New ideas and new expectations emerge over time. Social change, however, is generally gradual. This is because, as shown in Figure 2–1, while social organizations are human-made, the creation, like Frankenstein's monster, to an important degree controls the creator. The culture that emerges takes on a sacred quality (the sanctity of tradition) that is difficult to question. This profoundly affects the attitudes and behaviors of the social actors in the social organization and the organization itself. As Wilbert Moore, the distinguished sociologist, has put it:

Man is an inevitably social animal, and one whose social behavior is scarcely guided by instinct. He learns social behavior, well or poorly of one sort or another. [As a member of social groups] he invents values for himself and his collectivities, rules for his conduct, knowledge to aid him in predicting and controlling his environment, gods to reward and punish him, and other ingenious elements of the human condition. . . . Once [the products of this activity] are established in the human consciousness, they become, in turn, guides to behavior.[21]

FIGURE 2–1   Process of Social Organization

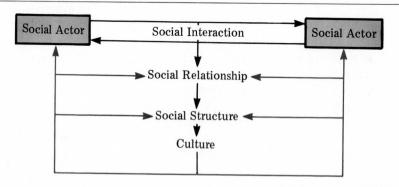

Source: This scheme is adapted from that developed by Marvin E. Olsen, *The Process of Social Organization*, 2nd ed. (New York: Holt, Rinehart and Winston, 1976).

THE SOCIAL STRUCTURE OF SOCIETY

We have focused on primary and secondary groups. These illustrate nicely the process and the components of social organization. But each of these groups exists in a larger social setting—a context that is also structured with norms, statuses, roles, and mechanisms of social control. These are the components of social structure through which society affects our attitudes and behaviors regardless of our other group memberships.

A **society** is the largest social organization to which persons owe their allegiance. It is an aggregate of people, united by a common culture, who are relatively autonomous and self-sufficient, and who live in a definite geographical location. It is difficult to imagine a society undergoing the same processes as other, smaller, social organizations because societies are typically composed of so many different persons and groups, none of whom

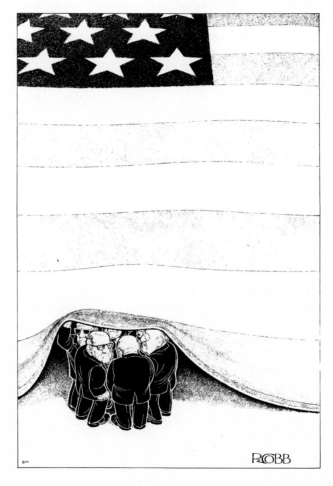

were present at the beginning of the society. But the conceptual scheme for the process of social organization shown in Figure 2–1 is also applicable at the societal level. Continuing interaction among the members reinforces stability but also is a source of change. At any given time, the actors in the society are constrained by the norms, values, and roles that are the result of hundreds of years of evolution.

Society as a Social System

A society is a **social system**, composed of interdependent parts that are linked together into a boundary-maintaining whole. This concept of system implies that there is order and predictability within. Moreover, there are clear boundaries to a system in terms of membership and territory. Finally, the parts are interdependent. The economy illustrates this interdependence nicely. There is a division of labor in society that provides a wide range of products and services meeting the needs of society's members. The presence of economic booms and depressions illustrates further the interdependence in society. For example, a depression comes about (in overly simplistic terms) when the flow of money is restricted by high taxes, high interest rates, high unemployment, and restricted buying practices by individuals. When large numbers of persons delay buying items such as a new car or refrigerator because they are uncertain of the future, the sales of these decline dramatically. This decrease itself is a source of further pessimism, thereby further dampening sales. The price of stocks in these companies will, of course, plummet under these conditions, causing further alarm. Moreover, many workers in these industries will be laid off. These newly unemployed persons, in turn, will purchase only the necessities, thereby throwing other industries into panic as their sales decline. A depression, then, is the result of actions by individual consumers, boards of directors of corporations, banks, savings and loan associations, individual and institutional investors, and the government. Additionally, the actions of this nation and the actions of other nations greatly affect the economic conditions of each other because they, too, form an interdependent network.

The Culture of Society

Culture explains much individual and group behavior, as well as the persistence of most aspects of social life. Social scientists studying a society foreign to them must spend months, perhaps years, learning the culture of that group. They must learn the meanings for the symbols (written and spoken language, gestures, and rituals) which are employed by the individuals in that society. They must know the feelings people share as to what is appropriate or inappropriate behavior. Additionally, they need to know the rules of the society: which activities are considered important, the skills members have in making and using tools, as well as the knowledge members need to exist in that society. In short, analysts must discover all the knowledge that people share—that is, they must know the culture. A full discussion of culture and its transmission is found in Chapters 5–7.

Social Classes

A structural component of societies is the hierarchical arrangement of people in terms of power, prestige, and resources. This universal phenomenon of social inequality is so important for the understanding of individual behavior and the structure of society that Chapters 10 through 13 are devoted to it. At the individual level, one's placement in the hierarchy directly affects self-perception, motivation, political attitudes, and the degree of advantage or disadvantage in school, in the economy, in the courts, and even for life itself. At the societal level, the extent of inequality affects the types and magnitude of social problems, societal stability, and economic growth.

Social Institutions

One distinguishing characteristic of societies is the existence of a set of institutions. The popular usages of this term are imprecise and omit some important sociological considerations. An institution is not anyone or anything that is established and traditional (for example, a janitor who has worked at the same school for forty-five years). An institution is not limited to specific organizations such as a school or a prison or a hospital. An institution is much broader in scope and importance than a person, a custom, or a social organization. **Institutions** are social arrangements that channel behavior in prescribed ways in the important areas of social life. They are interrelated sets of normative elements—norms, values, and role expectations—that the persons making up the society have devised and passed on to succeeding generations in order to provide "permanent" solutions to society's perpetually unfinished business.

Institutions are cultural imperatives. They serve as regulatory agencies, channeling behavior in culturally prescribed ways.

Institutions provide procedures through which human conduct is patterned, compelled to go, in grooves deemed desirable by society. And this trick is performed by making the grooves appear to the individual as the only possible ones.[22]

For example, a society instills in its members predetermined channels for marriage. Instead of allowing the sexual partners a whole host of options, it is expected in American society that they will marry and set up a conjugal household. Although the actual options are many, the partners choose what society demands. In fact, they do not consider the other options as valid (for example, polygyny, polyandry, group marriage). The result is a patterned arrangement that regulates sexual behavior and attempts to ensure a stable environment for the care of dependent children.

Institutions arise from the uncoordinated actions of multitudes of individuals over time. These actions, procedures, and rules evolve into a set of expectations that appear to have a design, because the consequences of these expectations provide solutions that help maintain social stability. The design is accidental, however; it is a product of cultural evolution.

All societies face problems in common. Although the variety of solutions is almost infinite, there is a functional similarity in their consequence, which is stability and maintenance of the system. Table 2–1 on page 34 gives a number of common societal problems and the resulting institutions. This partial list of institutions shows the type of societal problems for which solutions are continually sought. All societies, for instance, have some form of the family, education, polity, economy, and religion. The variations on each of these themes that are found in societies are almost beyond imagination. These

TABLE 2-1   Common Societal Problems and Their Institutions

Societal problems	Institution
Sexual regulation; maintenance of stable units that ensure continued births and care of dependent children	Family
Socialization of the newcomers to the society	Education
Maintenance of order; the distribution of power	Polity
Production and distribution of goods and services; ownership of property	Economy
Understanding the transcendental; the search for meaning of life and death and the place of humankind in the world	Religion
Understanding the physical and social realms of nature	Science
Providing for physical and emotional health care	Medicine

variations, while most interesting, are beyond the scope of this book. By looking at the interrelated norms, values, and role expectations that provide "pat" solutions to fundamental societal problems, we shall begin to understand American society.

Institutions are, by definition, conservative. They are the answer of custom and tradition to questions of survival. While absolutely necessary for unity and stability, institutions in contemporary American society are often outmoded, inefficient, and unresponsive to the incredibly swift changes brought about by technological advances, population shifts, and increasing worldwide interdependence. Let us look briefly at problems within two institutions—the polity and the economy.

The polity is based on a set of norms that were for the most part appropriate for another age. Current laws, for example, penalize the cities, which have experienced an eroding tax base, and benefit the wealthier suburbs. The government bureaucracy is so large and unwieldy that it is unresponsive to all but the large and powerful interest groups. A final example is of ultimate importance. This is the inability to control the expansion and use of nuclear weapons throughout the world.

The American economic system, based on a philosophy of free enterprise, is also outmoded in many respects. Capitalism has always thrived in an environment when there were people to exploit (slaves, unskilled and semiskilled labor, colonies); but these exploited groups worldwide are no longer passive. The free enterprise mentality, while appropriate in an expansionist setting with seemingly inexhaustible resources, is inappropriate in a world of shortages. Consumption for its own (and profit's) sake is no longer a legitimate goal, for it hastens the end of resources and eventual chaos. The profit orientation has also meant pollution and ecological catastrophes. The resistance to government planning increases the probability of booms and busts, surpluses and shortages, and high unemployment.

As we look at the institutions of American society we must not forget that institutions are made by people and can therefore be changed. We should be guided by the insight that while institutions appear to have the quality of being "sacred," they are not. They can be changed. But critical examination is imperative. Social scientists must look behind the facades. They must not accept the patterned ways as the only "correct" ways. This is in the

American heritage—as found in the Declaration of Independence. As Skolnick and Currie have put it:

Democratic conceptions of society have always held that institutions exist to serve man, and that, therefore, they must be accountable to men. Where they fail to meet the tests imposed on them, democratic theory holds that they ought to be changed. Authoritarian governments, religious regimes, and reformatories, among other social systems, hold the opposite: in case of misalignment between individuals or groups and the "system," the individuals and groups are to be changed or otherwise made unproblematic.[23]

SUMMARY

Sociologists are interested in two levels of social organization—relatively small groups (the micro level) and the societal (macro) level. The micro level is characterized by the same structural components and social processes as occur at the societal level except for social classes and institutions, which are strictly macro phenomena. Social organizations of all types are created and sustained by the social interaction of the members. Enduring social interaction is the basis for a social relationship. A social relationship requires the patterning and therefore the predictability of behavior. The shared knowledge that emerges from this continuous interaction guides the behavior, giving it a sacred quality. While social organizations are constantly changing, the rate of change is relatively slow because of the sanctity of the cultural components (norms, values, roles, and ideologies).

Although we shall refer occasionally to the micro level, the thrust of this book is on the societal level. The goal is to understand the structure of American society—its norms, values, roles, and institutions. This endeavor will provide the reader with a grasp of the sociological perspective and the tools to understand not only the machinery of society but also the bias of that machinery.

The focus of our inquiry throughout the remainder of this book, then, is on the positive and negative consequences of the way American society is structured. This is spelled out in Chapter 3. To anticipate the argument, the positive consequences of the traditional features of society are unity and stability—both necessary ingredients for social survival.

On the negative side, we shall focus on the structure of society as a source of social problems. Such social problems as poverty, racism, pollution, and unemployment are the result of the unequal distribution of wealth and power in society; the values of Americans; the tendency of Americans to blame individuals rather than the social environment ("blaming the victim"), which is translated into person-change solutions rather than system-change answers; and the inability of institutions to cope with the massive changes occurring in society and throughout the world.

CHAPTER REVIEW

1. Social organization refers to the observed regularities in the behavior of people that are due to social conditions rather than the physiology or psychology of individuals.

2. Social organization includes both social structure and culture. These emerge through enduring social interaction.

3. Social structure involves the linkages and network that transform individuals into a group. It includes the patterns of interaction that emerge, the division of labor, and the links and hierarchy of positions.

4. Culture, the shared beliefs of a group's members, guides conduct. The elements of culture include the norms (rules), roles (behavioral expectations for the occupants of the various positions), and values (the criteria for judging of people, things, and actions).

5. Norms are the rules specifying appropriate and inappropriate behaviors. The important norms are called mores and the less important ones are called folkways.

6. Each of us belongs to a number of social organizations and in each we occupy a position (status). These statuses are a major source of identity for individuals.

7. The behavior expected of a person occupying a status in a social organization is the role. The pressures to conform to role demands ensure that there is stability and predictability in social groups even though member turnover occurs.

8. There are three reasons, however, why role expectations do not make behavior totally predictable: (a) personality differences; (b) inconsistent messages as to what behavior is expected; and (c) multiple group memberships resulting in conflicting demands.

9. Social organizations employ positive sanctions (rewards) and negative sanctions (punishments) to enforce conformity to the norms, values, and roles of the group.

10. One way to classify social groups is on the basis of size and the quality of interaction. Primary groups are those whose members are involved in intimate, face-to-face interaction, with strong emotional attachments. The organization is informal and long lasting. The members identify strongly with each other and the group. In contrast, secondary groups are large, impersonal, and formally organized. The individual member is relatively unimportant.

11. Primary groups often emerge within secondary groups.

12. Social groups have enormous power over their members and affect their beliefs, behaviors, perceptions, and even health.

13. A society is the largest social organization to which persons owe their allegiance. The society provides the social context for primary and secondary groups. Society places constraints on these groups and their members through its own norms, values, roles, and mechanisms for social control.

14. A society is a social system composed of interdependent parts that are linked together in a boundary-maintaining whole. There is order and predictability within. There is a division of labor providing for self-sufficiency.

15. A society, like other social organizations, has a culture involving norms, roles, values, symbols, and technical knowledge.

16. Unlike other social organizations, a society has a set of institutions. These are social arrangements that channel behavior in prescribed ways in the important areas of social life.

17. Institutions are conservative, providing the answers of custom and tradition to questions of social survival. While absolutely necessary for unity and stability, institutions can be outmoded, inefficient, and unresponsive to the swift changes of contemporary life.

FOR FURTHER STUDY

The Process of Social Organization

S. F. Nadel, *The Theory of Social Structure* (New York: Free Press, 1957).

Marvin E. Olsen, *The Process of Social Organization*, Second Edition (New York: Holt, Rinehart and Winston, 1976).

Max Weber, *The Theory of Social and Economic Organization*, A. M. Henderson and Talcott Parsons, trans. (New York: Free Press, 1947).

Micro Structure

Elliot Aronson, *The Social Animal*, Third Edition (San Francisco: W. H. Freeman, 1980).

Harold Garfinkel, *Studies in Ethnomethodology* (Englewood Cliffs, N.J.: Prentice-Hall, 1967).

Erving Goffman, *Presentation of Self in Everyday Life* (Garden City, N.Y.: Doubleday (Anchor Books), 1957).

A. Paul Hare, Robert F. Bales, and Edward Borgatta, eds., *Small Groups* (New York: Alfred A. Knopf, 1965).

Macro Structure

Gerhard Lenski, *Human Societies: A Macrolevel Introduction to Sociology* (New York: McGraw-Hill, 1970).

Robert Marsh, *Comparative Sociology* (New York: Harcourt Brace Jovanovich, 1967).

Robin Williams, Jr., *American Society: A Sociological Interpretation*, Third Edition (New York: Alfred A. Knopf, 1970).

NOTES AND REFERENCES

1. Muzafer Sherif and Carolyn W. Sherif, *Groups in Harmony and Tension* (New York: Farrar, Straus & Giroux (Octagon Books), 1966).
2. Two classic sociological studies of this phenomenon are: William F. Whyte, *Street Corner Society* (Chicago: University of Chicago Press, 1943); and Elliot Liebow, *Tally's Corner: A Study of Negro Street Corner Men* (Boston: Little, Brown, 1967). Other illustrations can be found in literature; see William Golding, *The Lord of the Flies* (London: Faber & Faber, 1954); and George Orwell, *Animal Farm* (New York: Harcourt, Brace, 1946).
3. The view of social organization presented here is fundamentally indebted to Marvin E. Olsen, *The Process of Social Organization*, 2nd ed. (New York: Holt, Rinehart and Winston, 1976).
4. Peter M. Blau and W. Richard Scott, *Formal Organizations: A Comparative Approach* (San Francisco: Chandler, 1962), p. 2. Blau and Scott's distinction between social structure and culture is incorporated in the following analysis.
5. Olsen, *The Process of Social Organization*, p. 37.
6. See Emile Durkheim, *The Rules of Sociological Method*, 8th ed., Sarah A. Solovay and Hohn H. Mueller, trans. (Glencoe, Ill.: Free Press, 1938).
7. Charles K. Warriner, "Groups Are Real: A Reaffirmation," *American Sociological Review* 21 (October, 1956), pp. 549–554.
8. George Homans, "Bringing Men Back In," *American Sociological Review* 29 (December, 1964), pp. 809–818.
9. Blau and Scott, *Formal Organizations*, pp. 4–5.
10. Philip G. Zimbardo, "Pathology of Imprisonment," *Society* 9 (April, 1972), p. 6.
11. "Shun Thy Neighbor," *Newsweek* (December 8, 1975), p. 68.
12. The term "primary group" was coined by Charles H. Cooley, *Social Organization* (New York: Scribner's, 1909).
13. Edward A. Shils and Morris Janowitz, "Cohesion and Disintegration in the Wehrmacht in World War II," *Public Opinion Quarterly* 12 (Summer, 1948), pp. 280–315.
14. Charles C. Moskos, Jr., "The American Combat Soldier in Vietnam," *The Journal of Social Issues* 31 (Fall, 1975), pp. 25–37.

15. Emile Durkheim, *Suicide*, reprinted ed. (Glencoe, Ill.: Free Press, 1951). For an update and a confirmation of Durkheim, see Jack P. Gibbs, "Suicide," in *Contemporary Social Problems*, 2nd ed., Robert K. Merton and Robert A. Nisbet, eds. (New York: Harcourt, Brace and World, 1966), pp. 281–321.

16. See Stephen Cole, *The Sociological Orientation: An Introduction to Sociology* (Chicago: Rand McNally, 1975), p. 9.

17. Solomon E. Asch, "Effects of Group Pressure upon the Modification and Distortion of Judgments," in *Readings in Social Psychology*, 3rd ed., Eleanor E. Maccoby, Theodore M. Newcomb, and Eugene L. Hartley, eds. (New York: Holt, Rinehart and Winston, 1958), pp. 174–183.

18. Muzafer Sherif, "Group Influences upon the Formation of Norms and Attitudes," in *Readings in Social Psychology*, pp. 219–232.

19. Leon Festinger, Henry W. Riecken, Jr., and Stanley Schacter, *When Prophecy Fails* (Minneapolis, Minn.: University of Minnesota Press, 1956).

20. Nathan L. Gerrard, "The Serpent Handling Religions of West Virginia," *Trans-action* 5 (May, 1968), p. 23.

21. Wilbert E. Moore, "Social Structure and Behavior," in *The Handbook of Social Psychology*, 2nd ed., Vol. IV, Gardner Lindzey and Elliot Aronson, eds. (Reading, Mass.: Addison-Wesley, 1969), p. 283.

22. Peter L. Berger, *Invitation to Sociology: A Humanistic Perspective* (Garden City, N.Y.: Doubleday, Anchor Books, 1963), p. 87.

23. Jerome H. Skolnick and Elliott Currie, "Approaches to Social Problems," in *Crisis in American Institutions*, Jerome H. Skolnick and Elliott Currie, eds. (Boston: Little, Brown, 1970), p. 15.

3

The Duality of Social Life: Order and Conflict

Jerome Skolnick, an analyst of American society who is highly sensitive to the role of the powerful, has observed (in his report to the National Commission on the Causes and Prevention of Violence) that what is considered violence and what is not will actually be determined by those in power.

First, "violence" is the term used for any act that threatens the power structure. In this way the lynching of a black is less shocking (and therefore less violent) than the behavior of the black that provoked it. In other words, violence is perceived as a quality of those individuals and groups who challenge existing arrangements rather than those who uphold them. Thus, what the victimized group may see as "police brutality" is viewed by those in power as legitimate and not as violence.

Violence always refers to a disruption of some condition of order. But Skolnick has pointed out that order, like violence, is also politically defined. "Order" itself can be very destructive to some categories of persons. Carmichael and Hamilton illustrated this in their book *Black Power*. They noted that when white terrorists bombed a black church as they did in Birmingham, Alabama, and killed five children, the act was deplored by most elements of American society. But when hundreds of black babies die each year in Birmingham because of the effects of racism, no one in the power structure gets upset and calls this violence.[1] Although high infant mortality and rates of preventable disease, which are perpetuated through discrimination, take many times more lives than civil disorder, the term "violence" is not applied. Skolnick has suggested that we should indeed identify such outcomes as "institutional violence," implying that the system itself injures and destroys.

Violence is also defined politically through the selection process. Some acts of force (to injure persons or to destroy property) are not always forbidden or condemned in American society. Property damaged during football games, Halloween, or the Mardi Gras is often overlooked. Even 10,000 beer-drinking, noisy, and sometimes destructive college students on the beaches of Florida are allowed to go on such a binge because "boys will be boys." But if the same 10,000 college students were to destroy the same amount of property in a demonstration where the goal was to change the system, then the acts would be defined as "violent" and the police called to restore order by force if necessary (which, of course, would not be defined as violence by the authorities). Thus, violence is condemned or condoned through political pressures and decisions. The basic criterion is whether the act is in approved channels or is supportive of existing social and political arrangements. If not supportive, then the acts are by definition to be condemned and punished.

The decision of whether or not to use violence to control protest is also a political one. Although the use of force by those in power ("official violence") is violent, it is not usually perceived as such. When the mayor of a large city tells his police to shoot looters, or when police

41

officers injure persons for alleged violations of the law, we have instances of
official violence.

Skolnick's analysis of the relationship
between the power structure and violence
is important and useful to the analyst of
any society. It highlights the benefits accruing to those persons and groups
highly situated because of existing social

arrangements. It also aids in understanding the behavior of those not well situated who work to change the existing
system.

Source: Summarized from Jerome Skolnick,
The Politics of Protest (New York: Ballatine
Books, 1969), pp. 3–8.

The analyst of society begins with a mental picture of its structure. For scientists, this
image (or **model**) influences what they look for, what they see, and how they explain the
phenomena that occur within the society.

SOCIAL SYSTEMS: ORDER AND CONFLICT

Among the characteristics of societies is one—the existence of segmentation—that is the
basis for the two prevailing models of society. Every society is composed of parts. This
differentiation may result from differences in age, race, sex, physical prowess, wisdom,
family background, wealth, organizational membership, type of work, or any other
characteristic considered to be salient by the members. The fundamental question concerning differentiation is this: What is the basic relationship among the parts of society?
The two contradictory answers to this question provide the rationale for the two models of
society—order and conflict.

One answer is that the parts of society are in harmony. They cooperate because of
similar or complementary interests and because they need each other to accomplish those
things beneficial to all (for example, production and distribution of goods and services,
protection). Another answer is that the subunits of society are basically in competition
with each other. This view is based on the assumption that the things people desire most
(wealth, power, autonomy, resources, high status) are always in short supply; hence,
competition and conflict are ubiquitous social phenomena.

The Order Model

The **order model*** attributes to societies the characteristics of cohesion, consensus, cooperation, reciprocity, stability, and persistence. Societies are viewed as social systems,
composed of interdependent parts that are linked together into a boundary-maintaining
whole. The parts of the system are basically in harmony with each other. The high degree

---

*This model is most often referred to in sociology as the functional or structural-functional model. It is the basis
for the analysis of American society by Robin M. Williams, Jr.[2]

of cooperation (and societal integration) is accomplished because there is a high degree of consensus on societal goals and on cultural values. Moreover, the different parts of the system are assumed to need each other because of complementary interests. Because the primary social process is cooperation and the system is highly integrated, all social change is gradual, adjustive, and reforming. Societies are therefore basically stable units.

For order theorists, the central issue is: What is the nature of the social bond? What holds the group together in a boundary-maintaining whole? This was the focus of one of the most important figures in sociology, Emile Durkheim, the French social theorist of the early 1900s. The various forms of integration were used by Durkheim to explain differences in suicide rates, social change, and the universality of religion.[3]

One way to focus on integration is to determine the manifest and latent consequences of social structures, norms, and social activities. Do these consequences contribute to the integration (cohesion) of the social system? Durkheim, for example, noted that the punishment of crime has the **manifest** (intended) **consequences** of punishing and deterring the criminal. The **latent consequence** of punishment, however, is the societal reaffirmation of what is to be considered moral. The society is thereby integrated through belief in the same rules.[4]

Taking Durkheim's lead, sociologists of the order persuasion have made many penetrating and insightful analyses of various aspects of society. By focusing on *all* the consequences of social structures and activities—intended and unintended, as well as negative (malintegrative)—we can see behind the facades and thereby understand more fully such disparate social arrangements and activities as ceremonials (from rain dances to sporting events), social stratification, fashion, propaganda, and even political machines.*

The Conflict Model

The assumptions of the **conflict model** are opposite from those of the order model. The basic form of interaction is not cooperation but competition, which often leads to conflict. Because the individuals and groups of society compete for advantage, the degree of social integration is minimal and tenuous. Social change results from the conflict among competing groups and therefore tends to be drastic and revolutionary. The ubiquitousness of conflict results from the dissimilar goals and interests of social groups. It is, moreover, a result of social organization itself.

The most famous conflict theorist was Karl Marx, who, after examining history, theorized that there exists in every society (except, Marx believed, in the last historical stage of communism) a dynamic tension between two groups—those who own the means of production and those who work for the owners. The powerful will use and abuse the powerless, thereby "sowing the seeds" of their own destruction. The destruction of the elite is accomplished when the dominated unite and overthrow the dominants.

Ralf Dahrendorf, a contemporary conflict theorist, has also viewed conflict as a ubiquitous phenomenon, not because of economic factors as Marx believed, but because of other aspects of social organization. Organization means, among other things, that power will be distributed unequally. The population will therefore be divided into the

---

*See Robert K. Merton's *Social Theory and Social Structure* for an excellent discussion of sociological research from the order (functionalist) perspective.[5]

"haves" and the "have-nots" with respect to power. Because organization also means constraint, there will be a situation in all societies where the constraints are determined by the powerful, thereby further ensuring that the "have-nots" will be in conflict with the "haves"—thus, the important insight that conflict is endemic to social organization.*

One other emphasis of conflict theorists is that the unity present in society is superficial because it results not from consensus but from coercion. The powerful, it is asserted, use force and fraud to keep society running smoothly, with benefits mostly accruing to those in power.

The basic duality of social life can be seen by summarizing the opposite ways in which order and conflict theorists view the nature of society. If asked, "What is the fundamental relationship among the parts of society?" the answers of order and conflict theorists would disagree. This disagreement leads to and is based upon a number of related assumptions about society. These are summarized in Table 3–1.

One interesting but puzzling aspect of Table 3–1 is that these two models are held by different scientific observers *of the same phenomenon.* How can such different assumptions be derived by experts on society? The answer is that both models are correct. Each focuses on reality—but only part of that reality. Scientists have tended to accept one or the other of these models, thereby focusing on only part of social reality, for at least two reasons: (1) one model or the other was in vogue at the time of the scientist's intellectual development[†]; or (2) one model or the other made the most sense for the analysis of the particular problems of interest—for example, the interest of Emile Durkheim, who devoted his intellectual energies to determining what holds society together, or the fundamental concern of Karl Marx, who explored the causes of revolutionary social change. The analysis of social problems is one important area where sociologists have been influenced by the order and conflict models. Let us turn to these contrary ways to view social problems before examining a synthesis of the two models.

SOCIAL PROBLEMS FROM THE ORDER AND CONFLICT PERSPECTIVES

There is a general agreement among sociologists that a **social problem** reflects a violation of normative expectations.[8] It is a situation that is incompatible with the values of a significant number of people, who agree that the situation should be altered. Under this rubric fall such different phenomena as unemployment, poverty, crime, prejudice, drug addiction, political extremism, and mental illness.

The order and conflict perspectives constrain their adherents to view the causes, consequences, and remedies of social problems in opposing ways. The order perspective focuses on deviants themselves. This approach (which has been the conventional way of studying social problems) asks: Who are the deviants? What are their social and psycho-

---

*This description is a very superficial account of a complex process that has been fully described by Ralf Dahrendorf.[6]

†Order theorists have dominated American sociology since the 1930s. This has led to the charge by "radical" sociologists that the contemporary sociology establishment has served as the official legitimator of the system—not the catalyst for changing the system.[7] This radical challenge to order theory gained momentum in the 1960s and has generated a great deal of subsequent conflict theorizing.

TABLE 3–1   Duality of Social Life: Assumptions of the Order and Conflict Models of Society

	Order model	Conflict model
Question:	What is the fundamental relationship among the parts of society?	
Answer:	Harmony and cooperation.	Competition, conflict, domination, and subordination.
Why:	The parts have complementary interests. Basic consensus on societal norms and values.	The things people want are always in short supply. Basic dissensus on societal norms and values.
Degree of integration:	Highly integrated.	Loosely integrated. Whatever integration is achieved is the result of force and fraud.
Type of social change:	Gradual, adjustive, and reforming.	Abrupt and revolutionary.
Degree of stability:	Stable.	Unstable.

logical backgrounds? With whom do they associate? Deviants somehow do not conform to the standards of the dominant group; they are assumed to be out of phase with conventional behavior. This is believed to occur most often as a result of inadequate socialization. In other words, deviants have not internalized the norms and values of society because they either are brought up in an environment of conflicting value systems (as are children of immigrants or the poor in a middle-class school) or are under the influence of a deviant subculture such as a gang. Because the order theorist uses the prevailing standards to define and label deviants, the existing practices and structures of society are accepted implicitly. The remedy is to rehabilitate the deviants so that they conform to the societal norms.

The conflict theorist takes quite a different approach to social problems. The adherents of this perspective criticize order theorists for **"blaming the victim."**[9] To focus on the individual deviant is to locate the symptom, not the disease. Individual deviants are a manifestation of a failure of society to meet the needs of individuals. The sources of crime, poverty, drug addiction, and racism are found in the laws, the customs, the quality of life, the distribution of wealth and power, and in the accepted practices of schools, governmental units, and corporations. In this view, then, the schools are the problem, not the dropouts; the quality of life, not mental illness; the maldistribution of wealth, not poverty; the roadblocks to success for minority-group members, not apathy on their part. The established system, in this view, is not "sacred." Because it is the primary source of social problems, it, not the individual deviant, must be restructured.

Although most of this book attempts to strike a balance between the order and conflict perspectives, the conflict model is clearly favored when social problems are brought into focus. This is done explicitly for three reasons: (1) the focus on the deviant has dominated sociology and there is a need for balance; (2) the subject matter of sociology is not individuals, who are the special province of psychology, but society. If sociologists do not make a critical analysis of the social structure, who will? Also (3) I am convinced that the source of social problems is found within the institutional framework of society. Thus, a recurrent theme of this book is that social problems are societal in origin and not the exclusive function of individual pathologies.

SYNTHESIS OF THE ORDER AND CONFLICT MODELS

The assumptions of both models are contradictory for each comparison shown in Table 3–1, and their contradictions highlight the duality of social life. Social interaction can be harmonious or acrimonious. Societies are integrated or divided, stable or unstable. Social change can be fast or slow, revolutionary or evolutionary.

Taken alone, each of these perspectives fosters a faulty perception and interpretation of society, but taken together, they complement each other and present a complete and realistic model. A synthesis that combines the best of each model would appear, therefore, to be the best perspective for understanding the structure and process of society.[10]

The initial assumption of a synthesis approach is that *the processes of stability and change are properties of all societies*. There is an essential paradox to human societies: they are always ordered; they are always changing. These two elemental properties of social life must be recognized by the observer of society. Within any society there are forces providing impetus for change *and* there are forces insisting on rooted permanence. Allen Wheelis has labeled these two contrary tendencies as the instrumental process and the institutional process, respectively.[11]

The instrumental process is based upon the desire for technological change—to find new and more efficient techniques to achieve goals. The institutional process, on the other hand, designates all those activities that are dominated by the quest for certainty. We are bound in our activities, often by customs, traditions, myths, and religious beliefs. So there are rites, taboos, and mores that persons obey without thinking. So, too, are there modern institutions such as monotheism, monogamy, private property, and the sovereign state, all of which are coercive in that they limit freedom of choice, but they are assumed proper by almost all individuals in American society.

These two processes constitute the dialectic of society. As contrary tendencies, they generate tension because the instrumental forces are constantly prodding the institutions to change when it is not their nature to do so.

The second assumption is that *societies are organized but the very process of organization generates conflict*. Organization implies, among other things, differential allocation of power. Inequalities in power are manifested in at least two conflict-generating ways: differentials in decision making, and inequalities in the system of social stratification (social classes and minority groups). Scarce resources can never be distributed equally to all persons and groups in society. The powerful are always differentially rewarded and make the key decisions as to the allocation of scarce resources.

A third basic assumption for a synthesis model is that *society is a social system*. The term **"social system"** has several important implications: (1) that there is not chaos but some semblance of order—that action within the unit is, in a general way, predictable; (2) that boundaries exist which may be in terms of geographical space or membership; and (3) that there are parts which are interdependent—thus conveying the reality of differentiation and unity. A society is a system made up of many subsystems (for example, groups, organizations, communities). Although these are all related in some way, some are strongly linked to others, while others have only a remote linkage. The interdependence of the parts implies further that events and decisions in one sector may have a profound influence on the entire system. A strike in the transportation industry, for example, eventually impinges upon all individuals and groups. But some events have little or no effect upon all of American society. Most important for the synthesis approach is the recognition that the parts of the system may have complementary interests with other parts but may also have exclusive, incompatible interests and goals. There is generally some degree of cooperation and harmony found in society because of consensus over common goals and because of similar interests (for example, defense against external threats). Some degree of competition and dissensus is also present because of incompatible interests, scarcity of resources, and unequal rewards. Societies, then, are imperfect social systems.

A fourth assumption is that *societies are held together by complementary interests, by consensus on cultural values, but also by coercion*. Societies do cohere. There are forces that bind diverse groups together into a single entity. The emphasis of both order and conflict models provides twin bases for such integration—consensus and coercion.

Finally, *social change is a ubiquitous phenomenon in all societies. It may be gradual or abrupt, reforming or revolutionary*. All social systems change. Order theorists have tended to view change as a gradual phenomenon occurring either because of innovation or because of differentiation (for example, dividing units into subunits to separate activities and make the total operation more efficient within the society). This view of change is partially correct. Change can also be abrupt; it can come about because of internal violence, or it may result from forces outside the society (that is, reaction to events outside the system, or accepting the innovations of others).

To summarize, a synthesis of the order and conflict models views society as having ". . . two faces of equal reality—one of stability, harmony, and consensus and one of change, conflict, and constraint."[12]

The remainder of this chapter illustrates the duality of social life by examining American society from the perspectives of the conflict and order theorists. We will consider the sources of disunity in the United States and the major instances of violence that have occurred throughout American history. Despite the existence of division and violence, the United States is unified at least minimally. We will, therefore, also consider the factors that work to unify.

Division and Violence in American Society

Societies are integrated but disunity and disharmony also exist to some degree in all societies. It is especially important to examine the segmenting influences in American society, for they aid in explaining contemporary conflict and social change.

The divisive forces in American society. Social scientists have found that in small groups, the more heterogeneous the group, the more likely cliques will form. A group composed of members of one religion, for example, cannot form cliques on the basis of religion, but one with three religions represented has the potential of subdividing into three parts.[13] This principle applies to larger organizations as well, including societies. The United States, then, has the potential of many, many subgroups since it is so diverse. The United States is, in effect, a mosaic of different groups—different on a number of dimensions, such as occupation, racial background, education, and economic circumstances. Let us briefly examine these and other dimensions and the manner in which they bring about segmentation in American society.

1. *Size.* The United States is large in size, in both number of people and expanse of land. Both of these facts have a segmenting influence in American society. With respect to population size, there is an accepted sociological proposition that states: "As the population of a social organization increases, the number of its parts and the degree of their specialization also increase."[14] If, as in the United States, there is not only a large population (over 230 million) but also a high level of technology, then the division of labor becomes very refined. This division is so refined that there are over 30,000 different occupations recognized and catalogued by the Bureau of the Census.

If people have specialized occupations, they will probably interact most often with persons like themselves. Because of similar interests, they will tend to cooperate with each other and perhaps compete with other groups for advantage. An important social theorist of the early 1900s, Robert Michels, wrote about this tendency for exclusion and conflict as a universal tendency in all social organizations.

By a universally applicable social law, every organ of the collectivity, brought into existence through the need for the division of labor, creates for itself, as soon as it becomes consolidated, interests peculiar to itself. The existence of these special interests involves a necessary conflict with the interests of the collectivity.[15]

A second segmenting factor related to size has to do with land rather than population. The United States, excluding Alaska and Hawaii, has an area of 3,615,123 square miles. Found within this large territory is a wide range in topography and climate. Some areas are sparsely settled, others not. Some regions are attracting new residents at a much faster rate than others.

Traditionally there have been pronounced regional differences (and sometimes rivalries) because each region had its own economic specialization (that is, its own industry and agriculture) and each was relatively isolated from the influences of the others. The revolutions in manufacturing, transportation, and communication have helped to break down this regionalism.

Although regionalism has been declining, it remains a force that sometimes divides Americans. As evidence of this, many votes in Congress show that regional considerations often outweigh national ones. Many nonsouthern Americans have stereotyped ideas of southerners. Southerners often hold stereotypes of the "Yankee" that may cause the rejection of ideas and innovations from such a source. Consequently, communication within American society is often blocked and interaction stifled because persons from one region feel not only physically separate from but also superior to persons from other regions.

2. *Social class.* Economic differences provide important sources of division in American society. There is the natural resentment of persons without the necessities of life

toward those with a bountiful supply of not only the necessities but luxuries as well. There is also hostility toward a system that provides excessive benefits (or excessive hurdles) to persons not on the basis of demonstrated skills but on family background.

Status (prestige) differentials also divide Americans. Organizations, residential areas, and social clubs sometimes exclude certain persons and groups because of their social "inferiority."

3. *Race.* Throughout human history race has been used as a criterion for differentiation. If any factor makes a difference in American society, it is race. Blacks, American Indians, Mexican Americans, and other minority racial groups have often been systematically excluded from residential areas, occupations, and organizations, and even sometimes denied equal rights under the law. Although the overt system of racial discrimination has changed, racist acts continue in American society, with the result that these disadvantaged groups continue to be second-class citizens.

Racial strife has occurred throughout American history. Slave revolts, Indian battles, race riots, and lynchings have occurred with regularity. Racial conflict continues today not only in the ghettos of large cities but in most neighborhoods where the minority group is large enough to be perceived by the majority as a threat, in universities and secondary schools, in factories and other places of work, and in the armed forces. The rhetoric of violence has been escalated recently by minority-group leaders. The appeal of militant groups is ever greater, particularly among the young. Minority-group members are no longer willing to wait for slow racial reform. They are bent upon seeing justice done now. It is equally clear that many majority-group members will do virtually anything to keep the status quo (that is, to retain an advantageous position for themselves). Many minority persons seeking to shake the status quo may participate in various acts of violence. This violence brings repression by the powerful which further angers and frustrates the minority—thus a treadmill of violence and division.

The racial composition of the United States is changing and this will likely lead to increased tension and conflict. The two largest racial minorities are increasing in number faster than the rest of the population. By 1990, blacks will number nearly 30 million (12.2 percent of the population) and Hispanics, the fastest growing minority, will likely number 17 million (7 percent of the population—up from 4 percent in 1970).[16] Also in recent years refugees in great numbers have fled to the United States. In 1980 there were a total of 375,000 Indochinese; 900,000 Cubans; and 100,000 Haitian refugees in the United States. Not classified as refugees are the millions of undocumented immigrants mostly from Mexico and South America, estimated to number between 3.5 and 12 million in 1980.[17] These refugees have brought problems that have led to growing hostility. Jobs are in short supply. Taxes are already high and these groups require large amounts of aid. The poor fear that these new refugees will take jobs, increase demands on cheap housing, and decrease welfare currently allocated to them. Schools and other public agencies cannot meet the demands of these new groups.

4. *Ethnic groups.* The United States is inhabited by a multitude of **ethnic groups** that migrated to this country in different waves and continue to do so. These groups have distinctive lifestyles and customs. One reason for this is that they have retained a cultural heritage brought to this country from another society. Another, and very important for their continued distinctiveness, is the structure of American society. The persistence of

Panel 3–1
Los Angeles and the New Immigrants

More immigrants (legal and undocumented) are coming to Los Angeles than to any other American city. This is because of the warm climate and the easy access from Asia and Mexico. In 1960 the principal minority groups—blacks, Hispanics, and Asiatics—accounted for 28 percent of the city's population. The estimates in 1980 were: 20 percent black, 30 percent Hispanic, 10 percent Asiatic, and 40 percent Anglo out of a population of 2.9 million. Most of the change occurred from 1975 to 1980 with heavy migrations of Mexicans, Vietnamese, and Koreans.

The immigrants have strained city services and schools. There are 83 languages spoken in Los Angeles County and every government agency lacks employees who can communicate with the refugees. The schools, however, are especially affected. Hollywood High School, for example, has students who speak 60 different languages and dialects. In Grant Elementary School, 95 percent of the new pupils enrolling in 1980 could speak no English.

The potential for social unrest in this situation is heightened in a number of ways, as noted in the following account from the *Wall Street Journal*:

"We're very concerned about the hostility here and the potential for a riot," says Carl Martin, executive director of the Los Angeles County Commission on Human Relations; he and everyone else here remember the carnage of the Watts riots in 1965. "We haven't had any overt, major incidents in recent years, and we're hoping the lid can be kept on," he adds.

But the pot is bubbling. There were 783 murders in the city last year, 50% more than in 1975. Many were due to gang warfare involving minorities battling for turf. For many immigrants, joining a gang gives them an identity and a measure of protection; in the sprawling barrio of East Los Angeles, three generations in the same house may belong to the same gang.

Blacks and Hispanics here have been fighting between and among themselves for many years, and so have rival Hong Kong and Taiwanese gangs, including the Wah Chings and Jo Fongs. Vietnamese of Chinese extraction now are joining them, and Korean gangs such as the American Burgers, Korean Killers, and Black Ji are slugging it out with black and Hispanic gangs from adjoining neighborhoods.

* * * *

Ironically, immigrants also have trouble adjusting to the other immigrants and minorities they find here. Many Asians have ingrained prejudices against, and fear of, blacks. They don't necessarily get along with other Asians, either; though An-

subordination, discriminatory housing and work patterns, and other forms of structured inequality encourages solidarity among the disadvantaged.[18] The uniqueness and strong ethnic identification of immigrant groups is a source of internal strength for them but causes resentment, negative stereotypes, competition, hatred, and conflict as other ethnic groups or members of the dominant majority question their loyalty, resent their success, fear being displaced by them in the job market, and worry about maintaining the integrity of their schools and neighborhoods.

glos lump them together as one minority, the Asians include dozens of nationalities and regional groups with a history of animosity in their home countries. "We've been fighting each other for centuries," one Japanese-American says.

Unskilled immigrants from traditional rural societies have the hardest adjustment of all. Jo Marcel, head of the county's Indochina social-service project, says wife-beating, divorce, and alcoholism are all rising as the Indochinese struggle with a foreign urban culture, ideas such as women's liberation, and even indoor plumbing. . . .

Most newcomers must settle for rock-bottom jobs. Some become the pawns of employers who play off one minority against another to keep wages low. Recently more than a dozen Vietnamese hired by an assembly plant in the San Fernando Valley complained of harassment from Hispanic co-workers; the community agency that got them the positions discovered that the Vietnamese had replaced Hispanics fired because they had wanted to start a union.

The influx of foreigners also is creating restlessness in Watts and other predominantly black areas of south-central Los Angeles, where youth unemployment hovers at around 50 per cent. "We are opening our arms to immigrants, but we aren't opening our arms to our own black citizens who've been here much longer," says John Mack, president of the Los Angeles Urban League. Adds an AFL-CIO official here: "Charity should begin at home."

Blacks, however, have political influence the others lack. Mayor Tom Bradley is black, and so are three of the 15 city councilmen—while Hispanics, by far the biggest minority and possibly a majority within 10 or 20 years, haven't any elected representatives in city government. That may change. One political analyst says: "As the Anglos fade, you may see the blacks running the political establishment and the Chicanos fighting them for power."

Meanwhile, more people keep coming. Some 200 miles south, they penetrate the border, move north by night and melt into "East Los," uncounted and uncountable. They come from Russia, Samoa, Manila. Some 1,500 Indochinese are arriving every month, mostly after stays in other American cities; they like the climate in Los Angeles and are drawn by the presence of so many countrymen. Smiling in the sunlight, one recent arrival says cheerfully: "After a year or two, we all move here."

Source: Laurel Leff, "The Immigrants: A Flood of Newcomers Is Turning Los Angeles Into Tense Melting Pot." Reprinted by permission of *The Wall Street Journal* (September 25, 1980), © Dow Jones & Company, Inc. (1980). All Rights Reserved.

5. *Religion.* Religion, like race and ethnicity, evokes an emotional response in individuals. It is difficult to be neutral about religion. It is almost impossible to accept the idea that religious beliefs other than one's own are equilegitimate. Religion also has a polarizing effect because it is often the basis for selecting (or rejecting) mates, friends, neighbors, schools, and employees. Therefore, religious differences in the United States not only differentiate persons but also may provide the basis for conflict.[19]

Religious intolerance is not unknown in American history. Although the nation was founded on the principle of religious freedom, at various times and places Jews, Catholics, Quakers, Mennonites, and atheists have been targets of religious bigotry.

There have been political parties (Know-Nothing Party), organizations (Ku Klux Klan and the American Nazi Party), and demagogues (Gerald L. K. Smith and George Lincoln Rockwell) that have been anti-Catholic and anti-Semitic. Their moderate success in attracting followers demonstrates that some Americans are susceptible to such appeals. The effect has been to lessen the probability of interfaith cooperation and enhance the likelihood of conflict.

These segmenting factors create some groups in society that are advantaged and others that are disadvantaged. The former work to perpetuate their advantages while the latter sometimes organize to protest and change the system they consider unfair.[20] But how can these persons change the system if they are self-defined as powerless? A first step is legitimate, polite protest, which usually takes the form of voting, petitions, or writing public officials. A second option is to use impolite, yet legitimate forms of protest (for example, peaceful demonstrations, picket lines, boycotts, and marches). The third alternative, used when others fail, is to employ illegitimate forms of protest (for example, civil disobedience, riots, bombings, and guerilla warfare).[21]

Illegitimate protest is selected by dissident groups because of the intransigence of those in power toward change. The dissident groups consider their actions legitimate because they are for a just cause ("the ends justify the means"), but these protests are perceived as illegitimate by those in power. Those in authority resort to force, often intensifying the zeal and purpose of the protester, and frequently rallying previously uncommitted persons to the cause of the dissidents.

Implicit in this section is the notion that highly differentiated social systems, like that in the United States, must cope with the realities of disharmony, conflict of interest, and even violence. There is no alternative to conflict because of the diverse conditions of the American social structure. This is not to say that conflict is altogether bad. There can be positive consequences of conflict for both parties to the conflict and for society as well.[22]

All societies have the potential for cleavage and conflict because of the differential allocation of power. Concomitant with having power is the holding of other advantages (prestige, privilege, and economic benefits). Persons with advantage almost invariably wish to keep it, and those without often want to change the reward system.

Coupled with the stratification system in the United States are other aspects of social structure that increase the probability of conflict. The United States, perhaps more than any other society, is populated by a multitude of ethnic groups, racial groups, and religious groups. The diversity is further increased by the existence of regional differences and a generation gap. Although assimilation has occurred to some degree, the different groups and categories have not blended into a homogeneous mass, but continue to remain separate—often with a pride that makes assimilation unlikely and conflict possible.

Violence in the United States and the Myth of Peaceful Progress

There are two beliefs held typically by Americans that combine to make the "**myth of peaceful progress**."[23] First, there is a widely held notion that the United States is made up of diverse groups that have learned to compromise differences in a peaceful manner.

Second, there is the belief that any group in the United States can gain its share of power, prosperity, and respectability merely by playing the game according to the rules. Hence, there is no need for political violence in America, since the system works for the advantage of all.

It is precisely because these beliefs are widely shared that most Americans do not understand dissent by minority groups. These are believed to be aberrations, and are explained away by saying that they are communist-inspired, or that some groups (for example, blacks) are exceptions to the rule because they are basically immoral and irrational. Perhaps the most prevalent explanation locates the source of all violence in the individual psyches of the persons involved.

These explanations are incomplete because they locate the blame outside the system itself. American history shows that, with but few exceptions, powerless and downtrodden groups seeking power have not achieved it without a struggle. American institutions, Rubenstein has noted, are better designed to facilitate the upward mobility of talented individuals than of oppressed groups. "Most groups which have engaged in mass violence have done so only after a long period of fruitless, relatively nonviolent struggle in which established procedures have been tried and found wanting."[24] The problem is that the United States, like all other societies, has not and does not allow for the nonviolent transfer of power.

Throughout American history groups that were oppressed resorted to various legitimate and illegitimate means to secure rights and privileges which they believed to be rightfully theirs. Those in power typically reacted either by doing nothing or by repression—the choice depending upon the degree to which the minority groups' actions were perceived as a real threat. The following is a partial list of groups which at various times in American history have resorted to violence to achieve social, economic, or political objectives.[25]

Revolutionary colonists. The most notable case of violence by a minority in early American history was the Revolutionary War. The United States was literally born through violence. The American colonists first petitioned the King of England to redress grievances, and when this failed they turned to acts of civil disobedience and finally to eight years or war. "The Declaration of Independence," clearly a revolutionary document, provided the rationale for mass violence:

We hold these truths to be self-evident, that all men are created equal, that they are endowed by their Creator with certain unalienable Rights, that among these are Life, Liberty, and the pursuit of Happiness. That to secure these rights, Governments are instituted among Men, deriving their just powers from the consent of the governed. That whenever any Form of Government becomes destructive of these ends, it is the Right of the People to alter or to abolish it, and to institute new Government, laying its foundation on such principals and organizing its powers in such form as to them shall seem most likely to effect their Safety and Happiness. Prudence, indeed, will dictate that Governments long established should not be changed for light and transient causes; and accordingly all experiences hath shewn that mankind are more disposed to suffer, while evils are sufferable, than to right themselves by abolishing the forms to which they are accustomed. But when a long train of abuses and usurpations, pursuing invariably the same Object evinces a design to reduce them under absolute Despotism, it is their right, it is their duty, to throw off such Government, and to provide new Guards for their future security . . .

This document, a cornerstone of American heritage, legitimates the use of violence by oppressed peoples. It could have been written by a modern-day militant. While still revered, its content is no longer taken literally by those in power or by the bulk of the American citizenry.

American Indians.   Long before the Revolutionary War, and continuing to the present day, Indians attempted to change the order established by whites. When white settlers took their land, ruined their hunting, and imprisoned them on reservations, the Indians fought these occurrences and were systematically suppressed by the United States government.[26] In recent years Indians have occasionally boycotted, used violence (for example, trashing of the Bureau of Indian Affairs headquarters in 1972), tried to take land by violence (for example, Alcatraz in 1969 and Wounded Knee, South Dakota, in 1973), or used legal offensives to regain former Indian lands. The last tactic has become especially

© 1975 Ron Cobb. All rights reserved. From *The Cobb Book*, Wild & Woolley, Sydney, Australia.

popular. More than half of the 266 federally recognized tribes have claims in various federal courts. These are not trivial claims, as evidenced by the case brought by the Passamaquoddy and Penobscot tribes to regain 8 million sparsely settled acres in Maine.[27]

Exploited farmers. Farmers have used violence on occasion to fight economic exploitation. Between the Revolutionary War and 1800, for example, three such revolts took place—Shays's Rebellion, the Whiskey Rebellion, and Fries's Rebellion. The protesting farmer has used various forms of violence (destruction of property, looting, and killing) throughout American history. Some modern farmers have resorted to acts of violence to publicize their demands and to terrorize other farmers in order to present a united front against their opponents.

Slaveholders. Feeling the threat of the abolitionist movement, white southerners beginning in about 1820 used violent means to preserve slavery. In the early stages this amounted to civil disobedience, and later it burst out into fighting in places like "bleeding Kansas." Eventually the South seceded and the Civil War was waged—a classic example of a minority group using violence to force a change and being suppressed by the power of the majority.

WASP supremacists. Following the Civil War and continuing to the present day, some whites have engaged in guerilla warfare, terrorism, and lynching in order to maintain the subjugation of blacks. From 1882 to 1903, for example, 1,985 blacks were killed by southern lynch mobs.[28]

Riots, lynchings, and mob actions are not solely southern phenomena. Many Americans from other sections of the country have used these techniques against various "alien" groups (usually Catholics and immigrants from non-Teutonic Europe) in order to maintain their superiority. American history is rife with examples of this phenomenon: "Native Americans" tore apart the Irish section of Philadelphia in 1844; a Catholic church and homes of Irish Catholics were destroyed in Boston in 1854; Chinese and Japanese immigrants were victims of both riots and discrimination, particularly on the West Coast; Japanese, even those who were American citizens, were put in "concentration camps" during World War II because their patriotism was suspect; and Jews have been the objects of physical attack, boycotts, intimidation, and discrimination throughout American history. Perhaps the best contemporary example of mob violence against intruders can be seen in some communities where an all-white neighborhood is faced with one or more black families moving in. Threats, burning crosses, ostracism, and occasional physical violence have occurred with alarming regularity where black "invasion" of previously all-white areas has taken place. This is not a southern phenomenon but an American one.*

Ethnic minorities. Immigrant groups (that is, those groups most recently immigrant) as well as racial groups, because they have been the target of discrimination, threats, and physical violence, have themselves participated in violence. Sometimes gangs have at-

---

*Ironically, this type of violence usually occurs in blue-collar areas (black "invasion" is not a threat in the more expensive neighborhoods) where individuals are more prone toward "law-and-order" political candidates. Apparently when individuals feel personally threatened, "law and order" becomes vigilantism.

tacked the groups responsible for their deprived condition. Most often, however, hostility by immigrants has been aimed at groups with less power, either toward blacks or toward more newly arrived immigrants.

Violence by blacks has occurred throughout American history. Always the victims, they have sometimes responded to violence in kind. During the years of slavery more than 250 insurrections took place. Mass black violence has occurred in many major cities (for example, Chicago and Washington, D.C., in 1919, Detroit in 1943, and again in 1967, Los Angeles in 1965, and Newark in 1967).

The rage that blacks must feel against whites has surfaced sporadically in small and diffuse ways as well. Most commonly it has been manifested in individual crimes (murder, theft, and rape) or gang assaults on whites or in destruction of property owned by whites.

Labor disputants. Another relatively powerless group resorting to violence to achieve their aims was American labor. The workingmen of the 1870s attempted to organize for collective action against unfair policies of the industrialists. Unions, such as the Knights of Labor, American Federation of Labor, and the Industrial Workers of the World, formed. Their primary tactic was the strike, which in itself is nonviolent. But strikers often used force to keep persons from crossing the picket lines. Nor were the owners blameless. Their refusal to change existing wages, hours, and working conditions was the source of grievance. They sometimes turned to violence themselves to suppress the unions (for example, threats and hiring persons to physically break up picket lines).

The intransigent refusal of the owners to change the truly awful conditions of nineteenth-century workers resulted in considerable violence in many industries, particularly in the coal mining, steel, timber, and railroad industries. Labor violence, as in other cases mentioned previously, was ultimately effective. Working conditions, wages, and security of the workingman improved. Legislation was passed providing for arbitration of differences, recognition of unions, and so on. Clearly, the use of force was necessary to gain advances for the laboring man.

Given the evidence just cited, it is remarkable that people still hold to the "Myth of Peaceful Progress." Violence was necessary to give birth to the United States. Violence was used both to keep the blacks in servitude and to free them. Violence was used to defeat rebellious Indians and to keep them on reservations. Additionally, violence has been a necessary means for many groups in American society to achieve equality or something approaching parity in power and in the rights that all Americans are supposed to enjoy.

The powerful have not been munificent in giving a break to the powerless. To the contrary, much effort has been expended by the powerful to keep the powerless in that condition. Many times in American history, violence has been the only catalyst for change. Minority groups in the United States (for example, blacks, women, farmers) have repeatedly gone outside of existing law. To these groups, the use of force was justified because of the need to right insufferable wrongs—the very reason the colonists gave for breaking from England. We should note, however, that violence does not always work. The Indian revolts were not beneficial in any way to the Indians. Moreover, some groups, such as the Jews, have advanced with comparatively little violence.[29] Historically, however, "violence is as American as cherry pie." The Presidential Commissions on Civil Disorders and Violence have laid bare the inaccuracies of the "peaceful progress" idea held by so many Americans. The uniform remedy suggested by these commissions for minimizing violence is to solve the cause of social unrest and perceived injustice. It cannot be a surprise that minority groups occasionally use violence because they are reacting against a system that systematically disadvantages them with little hope for change through peaceful means.

The Integrative Forces in American Society

Most order theorists recognize that conflict, disharmony, and division occur within societies, particularly in complex, heterogeneous societies. They stress, however, the opposite societal characteristics of cooperation, harmony, and unity. They see American society as "We the people of the United States . . ." rather than a conglomerate of sometimes hostile groups.

In particular, order theorists focus on what holds society together. What are the forces that somehow keep anarchy from becoming a reality—or as the philosopher Hobbes asked long ago, "Why is there not a war of all against all?" The answer to this fundamental question is found in the combined effects of a number of factors.

Functional integration. Probably the most important unifying factor is the phenomenon of **functional integration**. In a highly differentiated society such as the United States with its very specialized division of labor, interaction among different segments occurs with some regularity. Interdependence often results because no group is entirely self-sufficient. The farmer needs the miller, the processor, and retail agents, as well as the fertilizer manufacturer and the agricultural experimenters. Manufacturers need raw materials, on the one hand, and customers, on the other. Management needs workers and the workers need management.

These groups, because they need each other, because each gains from the interaction, work to perpetuate a social framework that maximizes benefits to both parties and minimizes conflict or the breaking of the relationship. Written and unwritten rules emerge to govern these relationships, usually leading to cooperation rather than either isolation or conflict, and to linkages between different (and potentially conflicting) groups.

Consensus on societal values. A second basis for the unification of diverse groups in American society is that almost all Americans hold certain fundamental values in common. Order theorists assume that commonly held values are like social glue binding otherwise diverse people in a cohesive societal unit. Unlike functional integration, unity is achieved here through similarity rather than through difference.

Most Americans believe that democracy is the best possible government. Americans accept the wishes of the majority on election day. Defeated candidates, for example, do not go off into the hills with their followers to blow up bridges and otherwise harass the government. Most Americans are patriotic. They revere American heritage and believe strongly in individualism, free enterprise, and the Judeo-Christian ethic.

There are many symbols that epitomize the consensus of Americans with respect to basic values. One such unifying symbol is the American flag. Although a mere piece of cloth, the flag clearly symbolizes something approaching the sacred. Reverence for the flag is evidenced by the shock shown when it is defiled and by the punishment given to defilers. The choice of the flag as an object to spit on, or burn, is a calculated one by dissident groups. They choose to defile it precisely because of what it represents and because most Americans revere it so strongly.

Similarly, such documents as the Declaration of Independence and the Constitution are held in high esteem and serve to unify Americans.

The American heritage is also revered through holidays such as Thanksgiving and Independence Day. Consensus is also achieved through the collective "worship" of such American heroes as George Washington, Abraham Lincoln, and Dwight Eisenhower.

The social order. A third factor that unifies all Americans, at least minimally, is that they are all subject to similar influences and "rules of the game." Americans are answerable to the same body of law (at the national level) and they are under the same government. Additionally, Americans use the same language, the same system of monetary exchange, the same standards for measurement, and so on. The order in society is evidenced by the fact that Americans take for granted such assorted practices as obeying traffic lights, the use of credit, and the acceptance of checks in lieu of money.

Group membership. A source of unity (as well as cleavage) is group memberships. Some groups are exclusive, since they limit membership to a particular race, ethnic group, income category, religion, or other characteristic. The existence of exclusive organizations creates tension if persons are excluded who want to be included, because exclusiveness generally implies feelings of superiority. Country clubs, fraternities, some churches, and some neighborhoods are based on the twin foundations of exclusiveness and superiority. In American society, however, there are groups whose membership consists of persons from varying backgrounds (that is, the membership includes rich and poor or black and white). Consequently, heterogeneous organizations such as political parties, religious denominations or churches, and veterans' organizations allow members the chance not only to interact with persons unlike themselves but also to join together in a common cause.

Many, if not most, Americans who belong to several organizations belong to organizations with different compositions by race, religion, or other salient characteristics. To the extent that these cross-cutting memberships and allegiances exist, they tend to "cancel out" potential cleavages along social class, race, or other lines. Individuals belonging to several different organizations will probably feel some "cross-pressures" (that is, pulls in opposite directions), thereby preventing polarization.

Additionally, most Americans belong to at least one organization such as a school, church, or civic group with norms that support those of the total society. These organizations support the government and what it stands for and they expect their members to do the same.

International competition and conflict. External threats to the society's existence unify. the advice Machiavelli gave his "prince" is a regrettable truth: "if the Prince is in trouble he should promote a war." This was the advice that Secretary of State Seward gave to President Lincoln prior to the Civil War. Although expedient advice from the standpoint of preserving unity, it was, Lincoln noted, only a short-term solution.

A real threat to security unifies those groups, no matter how diverse, who feel threatened. Thus, a reasonable explanation for lack of unity in America's involvement in an Indochina war was that the Viet Cong were not perceived by most Americans as a real threat to their security. The Soviet buildup in armaments in the late 1970s and early 1980s, on the other hand, was perceived as a real threat, unifying most Americans in a willingness to sacrifice in order to catch up with and surpass the Russians.

The mass media.   The world is in the midst of a communications revolution. Only in very recent times has television, for example, expanded to encompass virtually every home in the United States. This phenomenon—universal exposure to television—has been blamed, among other things, for rising juvenile delinquency, lowering cultural tastes, contributing to general moral deterioration, and suppressing creativity.[30] These damning criticisms are countered by order theorists, who see television and the other forms of mass media as performing several integrative functions. Government officials, for example, can use the media to shape public opinion (for example, to unite against an "enemy" or to sacrifice by paying higher taxes). The media also reinforce the values and norms of society. Newspaper editorials extol certain persons and events while decrying others. Soap operas are stories involving moral dilemmas, with virtue winning out. Newspaper and magazine stories under the caption, "It Could Only Have Happened in America," abound. The media do not, except for a few exceptions, "rock the boat." American heroes are praised and her enemies vilified. The American way is the right way; the ways of others are considered incorrect, or downright immoral.

Planned integration.   Charismatic figures or other persons of influence may work to unite segmented parts of the system (conversely, they can promote division). Thus, a union leader or the archbishop of a Catholic diocese can, through personal exhortation or by example, convince his members to cooperate rather than compete, or to open membership requirements rather than maintain exclusiveness.

   Public officials on the local, state, and national levels can use their power to integrate the parts of the society in three major ways: (1) by passing laws to eliminate barriers among groups; (2) by working to solve the problems that segment the society; (3) by providing mediators to help negotiate settlements between such feuding groups as management and labor.[31] High officials such as the President utilize various means of integration. First, there is the technique of co-optation (that is, appointing a member of a dissident group to a policy-making body to appease the dissenting group). Second, he can use his executive powers to enforce and interpret the laws in such a way as to unite groups within the society. Finally, the President may use the media to persuade the people. The President can request television time on all networks during prime time, thereby reaching most of the adult population in order to use whatever powers of persuasion he has to unite diverse groups.

False consciousness.   Most Americans do not feel oppressed. Even many persons who do not have many material blessings tend to believe in the American creed that anyone can be upwardly mobile—if not themselves, then at least their children.

   Thus, contrary to Karl Marx's prediction over a century ago that capitalism would be overthrown by an oppressed majority, most Americans today consider themselves as "haves" rather than as "have-nots." There has been little polarization along purely economic lines because blue-collar workers are often relatively well-off financially (many make more money than persons with more prestigious jobs).

SUMMARY

There are two contradictory models of society—the order and conflict models. The order model views society as basically cooperative, consensual, and stable. The system works. Any problems are the faults of people, not society. At the other extreme, the adherents of the conflict model assume that society is fundamentally competitive, conflictual, coercive, and radically changing. Social problems are the faults of society, not individuals, in this view.

The order and conflict models of society are both significant, and they will be utilized in the remainder of this book. While each, by itself, is important, a realistic analysis must include both. The order model must be included because there is integration, order, and stability; because the parts are more or less interdependent; and because most social change is gradual and adjustive. The conflict model is equally important because society is not always a harmonious unit. To the contrary, much of social life is based on competition. Societal integration is fragile; it is often based on subtle or blatant coercion.

A crucial difference between the two models is the implicit assumption of each as to the nature of the social structure (rules, customs, institutions, social stratification, and the distribution of power). The order perspective assumes that the social structure is basically right and proper because it serves the fundamental function of maintaining society. There is, therefore, an implicit acceptance of the status quo, assuming that the system works. As we examine the major institutions of society in this book, one of the tasks will be to determine how each of these institutions aids in societal integration.

Although order theorists also look for the **dysfunctions** of institutions, rules, organizations, and customs (dysfunctions refer to those consequences that are malintegrative), the critical examination of society is the primary thrust of conflict theorists. While this book will describe the way American society is structured and how this arrangement works for societal integration, a major consideration will center around the question, "who benefits under these arrangements and who does not?" Thus, the legitimacy of the system will always be doubted.

CHAPTER REVIEW

1. Sociologists have a mental image (model) of how society is structured, how it changes, and what holds it together. There are two prevailing models—order and conflict—that provide contradictory images of society.

2. Order model theorists view society as ordered, stable, and harmonious, with a high degree of cooperation and consensus. Change is gradual, adjustive, and reforming. Social problems are seen as the result of problem individuals.

3. Conflict model theorists view society as competitive, fragmented, and unstable. Social integration is minimal and tenuous. Social change, which can be revolutionary, results from clashes among conflicting groups. Social problems are viewed as resulting from society's failure to meet the needs of individuals. Indeed, the structure of society is seen as the problem.

4. The order and conflict models present extreme views of society. Taken alone, each fosters a faulty perception and interpretation of society. A realistic model of society combines the strengths of both models. The assumptions of such a synthesis are: (a) the processes of stability and change are properties of all societies; (b) societies are organized but the very process of organization generates conflict; (c) society is a social system, with the parts linked through

common goals and similar interests, *and* competitive because of scarce resources and inequities; (d) societies are held together by consensus on values *and* by coercion; and (e) social change may be gradual or abrupt, reforming or revolutionary.

5. The divisive forces bringing about segmentation in American society are size, social class, race, ethnic groups, and religion. Thus, society has the potential for cleavage and conflict.

6. Americans tend to believe in the "myth of peaceful progress"—that disadvantaged groups throughout history have gained prosperity and equality without violence. The evidence, however, is that oppressed groups have had to use force or the threat of force to achieve gains.

7. There are a number of integrative forces in American society. These are functional integration, consensus on values, the social order, group memberships, threats from other societies, the mass media, planned integration, and false consciousness.

FOR FURTHER STUDY

Sociological Theories: General

Graham C. Kinloch, *Sociological Theory: Its Development and Major Paradigms* (New York: McGraw-Hill, 1977).

John C. McKinney and Edward A. Tiryakian, eds., *Theoretical Sociology: Perspectives and Developments* (New York: Appleton-Century-Crofts, 1970).

George Ritzer, *Sociology: The Multiple-Paradigm Science*, Revised Edition (Boston: Allyn and Bacon, 1980).

Jonathan H. Turner, *The Structure of Sociological Theory* (Homewood, Ill.: Dorsey Press, 1974).

The Order Model

Kingsley Davis, *Human Society* (New York: Macmillan, 1937).

Robert K. Merton, *Social Theory and Social Structure*, Revised Edition (New York: Free Press, 1968).

Robin Williams, Jr., *American Society: A Sociological Interpretation*, Third Edition (New York: Alfred A. Knopf, 1970).

The Conflict Model

Charles H. Anderson and Jeffry R. Gibson, *Toward a New Sociology*, Third Edition (Homewood, Ill.: Dorsey Press, 1978).

William J. Chambliss, ed., *Sociological Readings in the Conflict Perspective* (Reading, Mass.: Addison-Wesley, 1973).

Karl Marx and Friedrich Engels, *The Communist Manifesto*, Eden Paul and Cedar Paul, trans. (New York: Russell and Russell, 1963).

C. Wright Mills, *The Power Elite* (New York: Oxford University Press, 1956).

Michael Parenti, *Power and the Powerless* (New York: St. Martin's Press, 1978).

Richard E. Rubenstein, *Rebels in Eden: Mass Political Violence in the United States* (Boston: Little, Brown, 1970).

Albert J. Szymanski and Ted George Goertzel, *Sociology: Class, Consciousness, and Contradictions* (New York: D. Van Nostrand, 1979).

NOTES AND REFERENCES

1. Stokely Carmichael and Charles V. Hamilton, *Black Power: The Politics of Liberation in America* (New York: Random House (Vintage Books), 1967), p. 4.

2. Robin M. Williams, Jr., *American Society: A Sociological Interpretation*, 3rd ed. (New York: Alfred A. Knopf, 1970).

3. Emile Durkheim, *Suicide*, John A. Spaulding and George Simpson, trans. (New York: Free Press, 1951), originally published in 1897; Emile Durkheim, *The Division of Labor in Society*, George Simpson, trans. (New York: Free Press, 1933), first published in 1893; and Emile Durkheim, *The Elementary Forms of*

Religious Life, Joseph Ward Swain, trans. (New York: Macmillan (Collier Books), 1961), first published in 1912.

4. Emile Durkheim, *The Rules of the Sociological Method,* 8th ed. (Glencoe, Ill.: Free Press, 1938), pp. 64–75.

5. Robert K. Merton, *Social Theory and Social Structure*, 2nd ed. (Glencoe, Ill.: Free Press, 1957), pp. 19–84.

6. Ralf Dahrendorf, *Class and Class Conflict in Industrial Society* (Stanford, Calif.: Stanford University Press, 1959).

7. *Sociological Inquiry* 40 (Winter, 1970).

8. This section depends largely on the insights from three sources: John Horton, "Order and Conflict Theories of Social Problems as Competing Ideologies," *American Journal of Sociology* 71 (May, 1966), pp. 701–713; Jerome H. Skolnick and Elliott Currie, "Approaches to Social Problems," in *Crisis in American Institutions*, Jerome H. Skolnick and Elliott Currie, eds. (Boston: Little, Brown, 1970), pp. 1–16; and Earl Rubington and Martin S. Weinberg, eds., *The Study of Social Problems: Five Perspectives* (New York: Oxford University Press, 1971).

9. William Ryan, *Blaming the Victim* (New York: Pantheon Books, 1971).

10. A number of analysts in recent years have attempted such a synthesis: Pierre van den Berghe, "Dialectics and Functionalism: Toward a Theoretical Synthesis," *American Sociological Review* 28 (October, 1963), pp. 697–705; Gerhard E. Lenski, *Power and Privilege: A Theory of Social Stratification* (New York: McGraw-Hill, 1966); and Chalmers Johnson, *Revolutionary Change* (Boston: Little, Brown, 1966).

11. Allen Wheelis, *The Quest for Identity* (New York: W. W. Norton, 1958).

12. Ralf Dahrendorf, "Out of Utopia: Toward a Reorientation of Sociological Analysis," *American Journal of Sociology* 64 (September, 1968), p. 127.

13. James A. Davies, "Structural Balance, Mechanical Solidarity, and Interpersonal Relations," *Sociological Theories in Progress I,* Joseph Berger, Morris Zelditch, Jr., and Bo Anderson, eds. (Boston: Houghton Mifflin, 1966), pp. 74–101.

14. Paul E. Mott, *The Organization of Society* (Englewood Cliffs, N.J.: Prentice-Hall, 1965), p. 50.

15. Robert Michels, *Political Parties*, Eden Paul and Cedar Paul, trans. (New York: Free Press, 1966), p. 389.

16. "U. S. Population Headed for Change in the '80s," *Intercom* 8 (January, 1980), p. 12.

17. "Refugees: Stung by a Backlash," *U. S. News & World Report* (October 13, 1980), pp. 60–63.

18. See Ronald L. Taylor, "Black Ethnicity and the Persistence of Ethnogenesis," *American Journal of Sociology* 84 (May, 1979), pp. 1401–1423; and William L. Yancey, Eugene P. Ericksen, and Richard N. Juliani, "Emergent Ethnicity: A Review and Reformulation," *American Sociological Review* 41 (June, 1976), pp. 391–402.

19. Earl Raab (ed.), *Religious Conflict in America* (Garden City, N.Y.: Doubleday (Anchor Books), 1964); and Robert Lee and Martin E. Marty, eds., *Religion and Social Conflict* (New York: Oxford University Press, 1964).

20. See Lynne B. Iglitzin, *Violent Conflict in American Society* (San Francisco: Chandler, 1972).

21. David O. Arnold, "The American Way of Death: The Roots of Violence in American Society," *The Age of Protest*, Walt Anderson, ed. (Pacific Palisades, Calif.: Goodyear, 1969), pp. 262–268.

22. Lewis Coser, *The Functions of Social Conflict* (New York: Free Press, 1956); and Joseph S. Himes, "The Functions of Racial Conflict," *Social Forces* 45 (September, 1966), pp. 1–10.

23. The following discussion is drawn largely from three staff reports to the National Commission on the Causes and Prevention of Violence: Jerome H. Skolnick, *The Politics of Protest* (New York: Ballantine Books, 1969); Hugh Davis Graham and Ted Robert Gurr, *The History of Violence in America* (New York: Bantam Books, 1969); and James F. Kirkham, Sheldon G. Levy, and William J. Crotty, *Assassination and Political Violence* (New York: Bantam Books, 1970). Also helpful were: Richard E. Rubenstein, *Rebels in Eden: Mass Political Violence in the United States* (Boston: Little, Brown, 1970), and a series of analyses by a number of eminent

social scientists appearing in *The New York Times Magazine* (April 28, 1968) under the title, "Is America by Nature a Violent Society?"

24. Rubenstein, *Rebels in Eden*, p. 8.
25. Graham and Gurr, *The History of Violence in America*; Skolnick, *The Politics of Protest*, pp. 10–15; Kirkham, Levy, and Crotty, *Assassination and Political Violence*, pp. 212–237; John Higham, *Strangers in the Land* (New Brunswick, N.J.: Rutgers University Press, 1955); David W. Chalmers, *Hooded Americanism* (Chicago: Quadrangle Books, 1968); Graham Adams, Jr., *Age of Industrial Violence* (New York: Columbia University Press, 1966); and Arthur I. Waskow, *From Race Riot to Sit-In* (Garden City, N.Y.: Doubleday, 1966).
26. Dee Brown, *Bury My Heart at Wounded Knee* (New York: Holt, Rinehart and Winston, 1971).
27. See "Should We Give the U.S. Back to the Indians?" *Time* (April 11, 1977), p. 51; and "If Indian Tribes Win Legal War to Regain Half of Maine—," *U.S. News & World Report*, April 4, 1977, pp. 53–54.
28. James E. Cutler, *Lynch-Law: An Investigation into the History of Lynching in the United States* (New York: Longmans, Green, 1905), p. 177.
29. Rubenstein, *Rebels in Eden*, p. 18.
30. Melvin L. De Fleur, *Theories of Mass Communication*, 2nd ed. (New York: David McKay, 1970), p. 5.
31. Paul E. Mott, *The Organization of Society* (Englewood Cliffs, N.J.: Prentice-Hall, 1965), pp. 283–284.

4

The Duality of Social Life: Stability and Change

Technological breakthroughs are a major source of social change. In modern society these occur with ever greater rapidity and often with dramatic impact on individuals. Consider, for example, the possible implications of the following technology-related incidents for individuals and society:

—Cancer kills some 400,000 Americans every year, and the Department of Health, Education and Welfare estimated that at least one-fourth of this total can be attributed to conditions of the workplace. Other estimates are that up to 90 percent of all cancers are environmentally related.[1]

—In March 1979 the risk of nuclear plant failure became clear when the people of Pennsylvania faced the real possibility of a fuel core meltdown at Three Mile Island.

—In 1980 the Supreme Court ruled that the new gene splicing technology could be patented. This ruling opened the door for patenting new life forms with genetic information never before in existence.[2]

—In 1981 it was reported that: "About once every four days, on the average, the Pentagon discovers that the United States is being attacked by Soviet missiles. In the last eighteen months there have been 151 nuclear alerts, each requiring a 'missile display conference' by radio or telephone among U.S. technicians in various parts of the world. Fortunately, all 151 alerts turned out to be equipment failures or false alarms that were identified in time—sometimes barely in time."[3]

There are some major economic and social problems that appear inevitable for the decade of the 1980s. Some of these are: (1) inflation and high unemployment will continue; (2) the standard of living will decline; (3) the cost of energy will continue to surge; (4) competing business and political interest groups will make central planning difficult, if not impossible, to achieve; (5) huge government expenditures for the military will reduce the monies spent for social projects; (6) the gap between the "haves" and the "have nots" will widen; (7) the large cities will be increasingly unable to meet their needs; (8) resources will grow short; and (9) business will continue to refuse to halt pollution.

Given the strong probability of these and other problems escalating in proportion and severity, will the system adapt and stabilize or change, even dramatically?[4] There are adaptive mechanisms and trends that may neutralize or at least minimize the potential for social unrest and tumultuous change. These are: (1) the state's ability to adapt by increasing benefits such as unemployment compensation in times of crisis;[5] (2) the tendency of unrest by minorities and other groups to be localized and segmented; (3) the increasing frequency with which both spouses are in the labor force to offset declining family incomes; (4) patriotism's ability to unify people in times of international tensions; and (5) patriotism's ability to foster a spirit of sacrifice in times of scarcity.

There is an alternative scenario. The problems could reach unprecedented proportions. The government could become more and more ineffective in solving problems. The masses or a significant number of people could focus on a major national problem whose source was clearly identified. Leaders could emerge. The people could become committed to activism with the goal of major structural changes.

The question, then, is just how resilient is our social system? Will the 1980s be a time of turmoil and major change or will this decade be characterized by adaptation and relative stability? The answer is not easy because there are structural forces that work to achieve change and there are others that operate to promote stability. The dialectic between these opposing forces is the subject of this chapter.

CHANGE IN SOCIAL SYSTEMS

Social systems, if they are to survive, require two opposite tendencies—stability and change. They require stability so that interaction and behaviors will be relatively predictable. These must be predictable for goods and services to be produced and distributed, for work to be coordinated, and for chaos in everything from traffic to politics to be averted.

But while societies and their members need stability and predictability, social change is both inevitable *and* necessary. To say that change is inevitable is another way of saying that it is normal. Inevitable changes in the environment or within a social system require changes in the social system. Changes occur in response to external forces that impinge on the system such as war, flood, famine, and economic conditions. Changes occur also because of conditions within the social system such as shortages or surpluses, technological innovations, population growth or decline, conflict between factions, and economic booms or declines. Because societies are never completely stable and tranquil, adjustments (minor or major) are necessary to meet members' needs. These changes may be gradual or abrupt, reforming or revolutionary, deliberate or accidental.

Thus, the duality of social systems introduced in the last chapter includes not only order and conflict but also the related conditions of stability and change. This chapter is organized to describe how society is buffeted by these two seemingly contrary tendencies. We will begin by examining the structural sources for stability, and follow by examining the sources of change.

FORCES FOR STABILITY

Societies strain toward persistence. We are bound in our activities, for example, by the constraints of customs, traditions, myths, and ideologies that we have been taught to accept without thinking. Some of these are so important that we will sacrifice—even our lives, if necessary—to perpetuate them. Religious beliefs and nationalism evoke this kind of response in most of us. Clearly, perceived threats to religious dogma and to the foundations of our political heritage will be resisted by most. We will consider three especially important impediments to social change—institutions, bureaucracy, and organizations bent on preserving the status quo—in addition to the values and ideologies held by the members of society.

Barriers to Social Change

All **institutions** are by definition reactionary. They provide answers from tradition and thus preserve stability. Each institution, whether it be the family, education, religion, the economy, or the polity, channels behavior in prescribed ways. Any deviation from these demands is punished, either formally or informally. For example, we do not have the option in American society to marry more than one spouse at a time. Similarly, school districts do not hire those who are known atheists, Communists, or homosexuals. Let's look briefly at two institutions and some other elements of society and see how they operate to resist change in American society.

The polity. The government is structured to inhibit change. For example, the choices of decision-makers are often limited by various **systemic imperatives**. In other words, there is a bias that pressures the government to do certain things and not to do other things. Inevitably, this bias favors the status quo, allowing those with power to continue as they are, because no change is always easier than change. The current political and economic systems have worked and generally are not subject to question, let alone change. In this way the laws, customs, and institutions of society resist change. Thus the propertied and the wealthy benefit while the propertyless and the poor continue to be disadvantaged. As Parenti has argued the law has such a bias:

The law does not exist as an abstraction. It gathers shape and substance from a context of power, within a real-life social structure. Like other institutions, the legal system is class-bound. The question is not whether the law should or should not be neutral, for as a product of its society, it *cannot* be neutral in purpose or effect.[6]

In addition to the inertia of institutions, there are other systemic imperatives. One such imperative is for the government to strive to provide an adequate defense system against our enemies, which stifles any external threat to the status quo. Domestically, government policy is also shaped by the systemic imperative for stability. The government promotes domestic tranquility by squelching dissidents. This last point is significant. The job of the government is to keep order. By definition, this function works against change. The "enemies" of society therefore are harassed by the FBI, the CIA, and other government agencies.

The very way that the government is organized promotes stability. For example, the requirement that three fourths of the state legislatures, each by a two-thirds vote, must ratify proposed amendments, makes it extremely difficult to amend the Constitution. Thus, though a majority of the Congress, the people, and the state legislators favor the Equal Rights Amendment, it has failed to be ratified. Similarly the law resists change because the Courts use the principle of precedent to determine current cases. The way Congress is organized is another example. Committee chairs are selected on the basis of seniority not expertise. Longevity in public office is rarely achieved by taking radical stances. Thus the very powerful positions of committee chairs are occupied by people oriented toward the status quo.

As a final example, the two party system is organized to preserve the status quo. A multi-party system, as is common in Western Europe, means that each party has a narrow appeal because of its principles. Our system of two parties, in contrast, requires that both parties have wide appeal. A radical position is not acceptable in this system. Although there is no mention of political parties in the Constitution, our two party system has evolved in such a way as to make third parties inconsequential. Attempts to add parties are thwarted by the election laws, which make it difficult for candidates other than Republicans and Democrats to get on the ballots in each state.[7] At the presidential level, it is difficult for third party candidates to qualify for public campaign funds. They also have difficulty being allowed to participate in televised debates and receiving equal time on television, as John Anderson found out in 1980. Finally, the way Congress is organized, one must be a Republican or a Democrat to be effective.

The educational system. The formal system of education in American society (and in all societies, for that matter) is conservative. This must be the case, since the avowed function of the schools is to teach to newcomers the attitudes, values, roles, specialties, and training necessary to the maintenance of society. In other words, the special task of the schools is to preserve the culture, not to transform it. Thus, the schools indoctrinate their pupils in the culturally prescribed ways. Children are taught to be patriotic. They learn the myths, the superiority of their nation's heritage, who are the heroes and who are the villains. Jules Henry has put it this way:

Since education is always against some things and for others, it bears the burden of the cultural obsessions. While the Old Testament extols without cease the glory of the One God, it speaks with equal emphasis against the gods of the Philistines; while the children of the Dakota Indians learned loyalty to their own tribe, they learned to hate the Crow; and while our children are taught to love American democracy, they are taught contempt for totalitarian regimes.[8]

There is always the explicit or implicit assumption in American schools that the American way is the only really right way. When this assumption is violated on the primary and secondary school level by the rare teacher who asks students to consider the viability of world government, or who proposes a class on the life and teachings of Karl Marx or about world religions, then strong enough pressures usually occur from within the school (administrators, school board) or from without (parents, the American Legion, and the Daughters of the American Revolution) to quell the disturbance. The consequence is that creativity and a questioning attitude are curtailed in school. But the school really has no choice.

Schools also promote the status quo by certifying which individuals are able to hold the most prestigious and financially rewarding jobs in society. The schools enhance stability through this "sifting and sorting" function in two ways. First, schools reinforce the existing system of stratification by disproportionately rewarding those from upper-class backgrounds. Secondly, schools inhibit change by demanding conformity to the norms of society and by punishing deviants. Since deviants do not succeed in school, they will not be certified to take the best jobs in society.

The preoccupation of the schools with conformity is manifested in a number of ways. The school day is regimented by the dictates of the clock. Activities begin and cease on a timetable, not by the degree of interest shown or whether the students have mastered the subject. Silberman characterizes this as the "tyranny of the lesson plan," where teachers too often see the lesson plan as the end rather than as a means to an end.[9] Another indicator of order is the preoccupation with discipline (that is, absence of unwarranted noise and movement as well as the following of orders).

Schools in their quest for order also demand conformity in clothing and hair styles. Dress codes are infamous for their constraints upon the freedom to dress as one pleases. School athletic teams also restrict freedom, and these restrictions are condoned by the school authorities. Conformity is also demanded in what to read, where to set the margins on the typewriter, and how to give the answers the teacher wants. The brilliant poet E. E. Cummings, because he did not follow the rules on capitalization, would doubtless fail English composition in a vast majority of American schools.

A major consequence of this excessive concern with conformity is that students learn to follow orders from authority figures. This emphasis is highlighted in the following excerpt from a famous (or infamous) work entitled *The Student as Nigger*.

[Students] haven't gone through twelve years of public school for nothing. They've learned one thing and perhaps only one thing during those twelve years. They've forgotten their algebra. They've grown to fear and resent literature. They write like they've been lobotomized. But Jesus, can they follow orders! . . . Students don't ask that orders make sense. They give up expecting things to make sense long before they leave elementary school. Things are true because the teacher says they're true. At a very early age we all learn to accept "two truths," as did certain medieval churchmen. Outside of class, things are true to your tongue, your fingers, your stomach, your heart. Inside class things are true by reason of authority. And that's just fine because you don't care anyway. Miss Wiedemeyer tells you a noun is a person, place or thing. So let it be. You don't give a rat's ass; she doesn't give a rat's ass. The important thing is to please her. Back in kindergarten, you found out that teachers only love children who stand in nice straight lines. And that's where it's been at ever since.[10]

Bureaucracy. The process of **bureaucratization** refers to the changes within organizations toward greater rationality—that is, improved operating efficiency and more effective attainment of common goals. As the size and complexity of an organization grow, there is a greater need for coordination if efficiency is to be maintained or improved. Organizational efficiency would be maximized (ideally) under these conditions:

1. when the work is divided into small tasks performed by specialists;
2. when there is a hierarchy of authority (chain of command) with each position in the chain having clearly defined duties and responsibilities;
3. when all decisions are made on the basis of technical knowledge, not personal considerations;
4. when the members are judged solely on the basis of proficiency, and discipline is impartially enforced.[11]

In short, a bureaucracy is an organization designed to perform like a machine.

Panel 4–1
The Bureaucracy as a Rational Tool:
The Organization of Power

Bureacucracy is a remarkable product of gradual, halting, and often unwitting social engineering. Most elements were in place before the spurt of industrialization in the nineteenth century; it was this spurt and the associated control over employees that destroyed most other forms of large-scale organized activity. Without this form of social technology, the industrialized countries of the West could not have reached the heights of extravagance, wealth, and pollution that they currently enjoy. . . .

First . . . I would like to state my own biases. After twenty years of studying complex organizations, I have come to two conclusions that run counter to much of the organizational literature. The first is that the sins generally attributed to bureaucracy are either not sins at all or are consequences of the failure to bureaucratize sufficiently. In this respect, I will defend bureaucracy as the dominant principle of organization in our large, complex organizations. My second conclusion is that the extensive preoccupation with reforming, "humanizing," and decentralizing bureaucracies, while salutary, has served to obscure from organizational theorists the true nature of bureaucracy and has diverted us from assessing its impact upon society. The impact upon society in general is incalculably more important than the impact upon the members of a particular organization, that most critics concern themselves with. . . .

The push toward increased bureaucratization pervades nearly all aspects of American life including the government (at all levels), the church (the Catholic Church, the Methodist Church), education (all school systems), sports (NCAA, A.A.U., athletic departments at "big time" schools, professional teams), corporations (General Motors, IBM), and even crime ("mafia").

The majority of social scientists have viewed with alarm what they conceive to be the trend toward greater and greater bureaucratization. Individuals will, it is typically predicted, increasingly become small cogs in very big machines. Narrowly defined tasks, a rigid chain of command, and total impersonality in dealing with others will be our organizational lot in the future. Human beings will be rigid conformists—the prototype of the organization man or woman.

Several aspects of bureaucracies as they operate in reality work to promote the status quo.* First, the blind obedience to rules and the unquestioned following of orders means that new and unusual situations cannot be handled efficiently because the rules do not apply. Rigid adherence to the rules creates automatons. Secondly, bureaucracies tend to be stagnant in selecting people for leadership roles. Leaders in bureaucracies typically follow two principles when choosing new leaders. The first is to select from the pool of

---

*These forces promoting the status quo may actually foster change when bureaucracies are unable to adapt. Thus, individuals may subvert the bureaucracy or form new organizations to meet new conditions. Bureaucracies, then, provide the interesting paradox that in their quest for rationality, they may actually accomplish irrationality.[12]

these services cost approximately $18,000 for each new person added to the population[29]—or a saving of $900 billion if the population were 50 million fewer.

It is interesting to speculate as to the impact of having 50 million fewer persons on social problems in the society. With 250 million people instead of 300 million, several predictions seem appropriate. Because wealth will be spread over fewer people, a smaller proportion of the population will likely be poor. The number of crimes will be less. Because there will be less overcrowding, intergroup tensions and violence will likely be less. Moreover, a smaller population would free governmental monies, if the officials were so inclined, to help alleviate material suffering and increase the probability of equality of opportunity.

The boom generation. Birth rates in this century, while showing a definite downward trend, had one period that reversed the trend, resulting in a baby boom. This aberration has had and will continue to have a profound effect on American society.[30]

The depression period was a time of low fertility as families postponed having children or restricted their family size because of economic difficulties and uncertainties. These uncertainties were compounded further by World War II. Again fertility was kept low by the conscious acts of families or now because many husbands and wives were physically separated. So following 15 years of depression and war persons who had delayed child bearing began to make up for lost time. The result was a period of rising fertility from 1947 through 1960. Between 1947 and 1957, for example, 43 million babies were born—10 million more than in the previous decade—and one fifth of the present population. This created a 10-million-person bulge in the age structure. Like a pig that has been swallowed by a python, this bulge has been slowly moving through the age structure, creating problems and dislocations at every stage. It will continue to create problems of adjustment for the duration of the 70-year life span of the baby boom—until 2020 or so.

The immediate effect of the baby boom was to reduce the number of women in the labor force. By 1950 there were 858,000 fewer women working than in 1945 and the proportion of working women was below that of 1940. Increased family size also increased the need for room, hence the trend to move to the suburbs. In the 1950s the suburbs grew by nearly 20 million, and homeownership increased from 44 percent of total housing in 1940 to 62 percent in 1960.[31]

In the mid-fifties this bulge in the age structure created a crisis for elementary schools— a tremendous shortage in classrooms and teachers. By 1960 the nation had 1.4 million classrooms, about half of which had been built since 1950 to accommodate the boom generation. In the early 1960s these shortages hit the secondary schools and by the end of that decade the colleges faced up to these problems. During this time, for example, one new institution of higher learning was opening *every week*. The baby boom had caused a rapid expansion of facilities and teachers at every level but when the population bulge moved on the schools faced another problem—empty classrooms and a surplus of teachers. The colleges that had geared up to the teacher shortage continued to graduate teachers with the jobs rapidly drying up. The colleges themselves face a difficult adjustment period as the number of students declines sharply.

As the new wave of humanity entered adolescence, the society faced new problems. Traffic accidents increased because of the tremendous number of young drivers. The volume of crime increased dramatically. The Commission on Population Growth reported that "about 28 percent of the reported increase between 1960 and 1970 in the number of arrests for serious crimes can be attributed to an increase in the percentage of the population under 25."[32]

FIGURE 4–1   Progress of Depression Cohort, Baby Boom Cohort, and Baby Bust Cohort Through U.S. Population Age-Sex Pyramid: 1960–2050

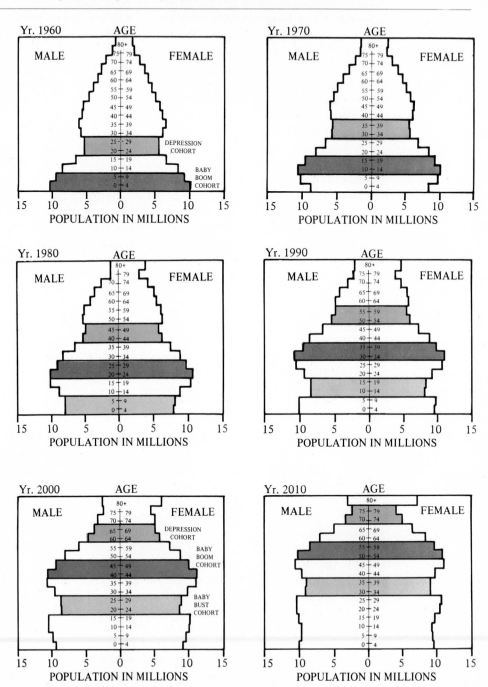

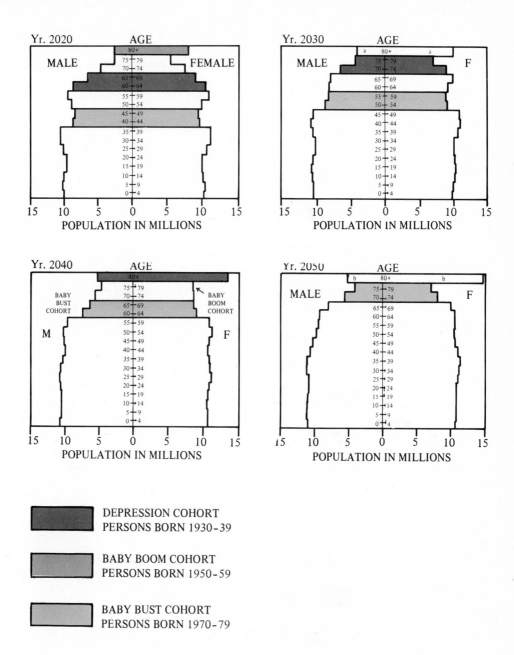

DEPRESSION COHORT
PERSONS BORN 1930–39

BABY BOOM COHORT
PERSONS BORN 1950–59

BABY BUST COHORT
PERSONS BORN 1970–79

Source: Leon F. Bouvier, "America's Baby Boom Generation: The Fateful Bulge," *Population Bulletin* Vol. 35, No. 1 (Population Reference Bureau, Inc., Washington, D.C., 1980), Figure 4.

Of special concern for society and the boom generation will be employment. During the 1970s "3.5 million persons entered the labor force for the first time each year—700,000 more per year than in the sixties."[33] In other words, each year 700,000 jobs had to be created *just to stay even* with the employment level of the 1960s. The problem is exacerbated further by: (1) the increasing number of women who will seek employment; (2) the largest single source of available jobs in the sixties, teaching, will offer very few openings; (3) openings for professional and technical jobs are created more slowly than the number of persons trained for such jobs; and (4) increased demands by minorities for better jobs. One consequence of these factors is that many college graduates will have to accept jobs *below* their level of competence and training. As these college-trained persons acquire jobs below their level (a condition known as **underemployment**) they will in turn "bump" many non-college-trained individuals also to a level below their training and competence. This will create a condition of **status inconsistency** for those individuals affected—that is, having an occupational status that does not measure up to one's educational attainment. This condition causes resentment for the individual who is underrewarded for his efforts (investment in education) and the potential increases for social unrest.[34]

The members of boom generation will, as they move through the age structure, also affect the economy in a number of ways. For example, their large numbers will ensure a growing market for housing, furniture, and other items. There will be a continual problem of economic dislocations. Companies supplying goods for the boom generation will face expansion followed by a rapid decline as the "boomers" age and move on to another stage, just as the schools built rapidly and then found themselves overbuilt. These dislocations added to the problems of unemployment could be a continual source of economic booms and recessions.

A concern to demographers is what will happen to population growth as the population bulge reaches marriage. Although these couples will doubtless have small families, the overall effect will be a surge in population growth. We may experience a second baby boom (even with a low birth rate) as an "echo effect" of the postwar baby explosion.

In the decade from 2010 to 2020 the boom generation will reach retirement. The number of persons over 65 in 2030 will be 52 million (compared to 23 million in 1977). "That age group then would equal more than half of what the entire U.S. population was in 1900."[35] The problem, of course, is that these people on pensions and Social Security will have to be supported by the younger working population. Mayer has informed us of the magnitude of this burden in the following quote:

In what may turn out to be the most dramatically unfair action against the outsize cohorts of the twenty-year bulge, their parents in 1971 rewrote the social-security laws to assure themselves a highly comfortable retirement at four to five times the monthly income that social security yields today—an income based not on the social-security taxes they were paying themselves but on the taxes that will be paid by the larger work force now coming on. But when the current demographic bulge reaches retirement age, its successors will be too few to support so many old people in so fine a style: the unfunded liabilities of the social-security system will then total well over 2 *trillion* of today's dollars. Assuming only minor growth in longevity from all the medical research now in progress, a social-security tax rate approaching 30 percent of the national payroll will then be necessary in order to meet the payouts prescribed by law, and nobody believes that social-security taxes of those dimensions will actually be assessed.[36]

Finally, 70 years after it had begun, the population bulge created by the baby boom will have passed through the age structure. By then, presuming a steady birth rate at or below the replacement rate, the U.S. population will have stabilized at about 270 million with a balanced age structure.

The Government

Although the government can resist change, it can also be a powerful force for change.[37] For example, in the United States the government has fought wars and made peace, been imperialistic, opened the West, subsidized the transcontinental railroad, seized land from the Indians, built dams and canals, harnessed the atom, and initiated space travel. Through laws the government has stimulated farming (the Homestead Act of 1862 gave farmers tracts of land), encouraged education (the Morrill Act of 1862 instituted land grant colleges in each state), desegregated schools (Brown v. Board of Education), and attempted to eliminate sexism in the schools (Title IX).

The government has been active in all major changes in American history. It has not been a disinterested bystander but rather an impetus for change in a particular direction. Most important, the government has tended to promote changes that benefitted those already affluent segments of society. Those actions providing equity for the lower strata of society generally have occurred when there was a threat of social unrest.[38]

Social Movements Oriented to Changing Society

There are three types of social movements that are political in nature. There are those that are organized to prevent changes, the "resistance" movements discussed earlier. There are **reform movements,** which seek to alter a specific part of society. These movements commonly focus on a single issue such as women's rights, gay liberation, or ecology. Typically there is an aggrieved group such as blacks, Indians, homosexuals, farmers, or workers which focuses its strategy on changing the laws and customs to improve their situation. As noted in the previous chapter, at various times in American history oppressed groups have organized successful drives to change the system to provide more equity. The Civil Rights Movement of the 1950s and 1960s provides an example. Blacks had long been exploited in American society. A series of events in this period such as the jailing of Rosa Parks, a black woman, for not giving her seat on a bus to a white man as was the custom, raised the consciousness of blacks and whites. A leader emerged, Martin Luther King, Jr., who inspired blacks to stand up against oppression. He and others organized marches, sit-ins, boycotts, and court cases, which eventually succeeded in destroying the racist laws and customs of the South. King's reform movement was bent on tearing down existing norms and values and substituting new ones. Many individuals and groups resisted these efforts.

The third type of social movement—**revolutionary movements**—seeks radical changes. These movements go beyond reform by seeking to replace the existing social structure with a new one. For example, a shift from a capitalist to a socialist economy would dramatically change all areas of social life. Castro's 1959 socialist revolution in Cuba illustrates this type of movement as do the French Revolution in 1789 and the Russian Revolution in 1918.

Several categories of persons are particularly susceptible to the appeal of social movements. Obvious candidates for recruits are the disadvantaged. The American economic system, because it encourages private property, profit, and accumulation, divides

Panel 4–3
The American Future Is Being Bumbled Away

Some people plan, others are planned upon. Some governments plan, others are planned upon.

The American future is being stolen, dribbled, and bumbled away by a government that does not plan for the long range, does not know how to plan, is afraid to talk about the need for long-range planning, and is therefore out-planned at every step by major corporations who are staking out pieces of the future for themselves, as well as by foreign nations who are doing the same on a global scale.

Failure to look at America's current economic and political crisis in terms of the next 25–50 years is costing us unmeasurable billions of dollars in lost economic and social opportunities, and is leading us toward technological and military policies that threaten the survival of the entire planet.

The U.S., in order to avoid bloodshed over the next few decades, must begin now to develop very long-range strategies—and must invent wholly new forms of planning that involve not merely a handful of technocratic experts, but millions of ordinary citizens. We must become an "anticipatory democracy."

The Super-Industrial Revolution

A dramatically new approach to the future is now required because the U.S.—along with other technological nations—has reached the end of its industrial stage and is about to move into its super-industrial stage of development. Economic strategies, business plans, social policies designed for an industrial society are no longer effective. Old economic theories like Keynesianism or traditional "laissez-faire-ism" or "socialism" are all obsolete in this new situation. We are entering into the super-industrial revolution—a transition that may bring changes even deeper than those brought by the industrial revolution itself. And it is likely that these high-powered changes will be compressed into decades instead of centuries.

Industrialism was a world-system based on

—Cheap raw materials
—Non-renewable fossil fuel energy
—Electro-mechanical technologies
—Nuclear family system
—Mass education
—Mass communication
—High urban concentrations
—A predominance of employment in the manufacturing sector
—Materialist values and growth ethic

Today massive changes are occurring at very high speeds in resource prices, the world energy system, and the very nature of technology. We are beginning a shift from the old electro-mechanical technologies typical of industrialism, such as rail, auto, steel, or rubber production, to new industries such as aerospace, petrochemicals, electronics, and, eventually, to ocean mining, new forms of agriculture, and industries based on molecular biology. In the family system, we are witnessing a radical shift away from the nuclear family as the standard model in society. (Even now, one out of seven American children is raised in a single-parent household; one out of four in the urban areas.) More and more "aggregate families" are cropping up composed of intertwined members from several divorces. Homosexuality is gradually assuming a more open role in the society. Our cities are becoming worn out and losing their economic base. The proportions of the work force engaged in service and other non-manufacturing functions has risen. We are moving away from simpleminded, uni-dimensional growth policies toward a broader acceptance of the idea of "balanced growth"—ecologically and socially responsible growth.

All these taken together are parts of a world-wide transformation, and similar changes are being felt in most of the industrial nations, not merely the U.S. What is happening is the emergence of a new stage of technological civilization, a super-industrial stage. This transition could take from 20 to 50 years, at a guess, and it could, unless understood and planned for, result in extreme turbulence—wars, insurrections, secessionist movements, riots, revolutions, technological disasters, ecological catastrophes, military outbreaks, nuclear accidents, and the like.

The industrial revolution, which occurred on a much smaller scale and at much slower and more easily absorbed rates of change, was accompanied by massive shifts in population, starvation, civil wars in many countries (including our own), the break-up of the old family structures, and tremendous geo-political changes on the face of the earth. It was also accompanied by a period of "Grand Imperialism" that underwrote economic development in the West by exploiting the people and raw materials of the rest of the world, at the cost of many wars.

If we want to make the transition to super-industrialism a peaceful one, we must begin now to plan for it—to lay out long-term democratic strategies that will help us completely overhaul our industry, reconstruct our cities, reshape our family system, create a new, more rational energy base, deescalate our military expenditures and the dangers of global nuclear confrontation, and to re-think our community structures.

Faced by changes of such overpowering magnitude, the failure to engage in futurism, the failure to plan ahead, the attempt to deal with legislative and other policy issues on a purely ad hoc basis, the lack of any administration to put forward a positive image of America 2000, all result in decisions that are self-cancelling, wasteful, and ineffective. The result is a radical loss of public confidence in government, mounting disillusionment, cyncicism, and anger. The potentials are in place for the current passivity—even paralysis—to explode into violence.

Source: Excerpted from Alvin Toffler, "The American Future Is Being Bumbled Away," *The Futurist* 10 (April 1976), pp. 97–99. Reprinted with permission.

people into rich and poor, powerful and powerless.[39] The result, as suggested by the theory of Karl Marx, is a class which bears all the burdens of society without sharing its advantages.[40] At the other end of the scale there is a class that lives in affluence at the expense of the oppressed. The antagonism between these two groups will ultimately result in the attempt by the oppressed to change the system. Clearly, individuals who define themselves as oppressed are ripe for appeals to change a system they consider unjust.

There are other categories of persons who, because of their status in the social system, are also candidates for involvement in social movements.[41] These types share a condition called **status anguish**—a fundamental concern with the contradictions in the individual's status set. One type of status anguish results from **marginality**.[42] Some examples of categories experiencing marginality are second-generation immigrants, recent migrants from rural areas to urban centers, and interracial couples. These people are in two different worlds but not fully part of either. The result, commonly, is psychic stress which may manifest itself in attempts by the marginal group to seek change that would allow them to be accepted.

Another form of status anguish that occurs is the condition of **status inconsistency**. A black physician, for example, has high occupational status in American society but ranks low on the racial dimension of status. Such an individual is accepted and treated according to his or her high status by some while others ignore the occupational dimension and consider only his or her race. Faced with this kind of contradiction, individuals may react by withdrawal from painful situations, accommodation, or aggression.

The third form of status anguish—**status withdrawal**—occurs as a result of losing status. Those individuals whose occupations have lost out to new technology are included in this category. Another example would be small entrepreneurs who cannot compete with huge corporations. These downwardly mobile persons are typically going to blame outside conditions for their problems and seek reforming or revolutionary means to restore their lost status.

SUMMARY

This chapter has focused on an apparent contradiction—the co-existence of stability and change. Social systems are, on the one hand, ordered, stable, and predictable while on the other they are always changing. There are, as we have seen, elements of the social structure that impede change while others impel change. This tension leads to the inevitability of change, most often in gradual adjustments and reforms but occasionally in swift and revolutionary ways.

The changes in American history have generally been in the general direction of increased freedom. Although the freedom we now have is far from absolute, it is important to note that modern American women and men, while still greatly affected by traditional sex roles, are freer than ever before. This shift toward freedom is a mixed blessing, however, as Silberman has noted in the following passage:

In the past men inherited their occupations, their status, their religion, and their life style; their wives were selected for them, and their struggle to survive gave them little time to question anything. Today, by contrast, they are presented with a bewildering range of options; they are forced to choose their occupations, jobs, places to live, marital partners, number of children, religion, political allegiance and affiliation, friendships, allocation of income, and life style. This widening of the range of choice and enhancement of individuality have had the effect of reducing the authority of tradition, which in turn requires still more choices to be exercised.

The burden is heavy. The choices are frightening, for they require the individual, perhaps for the first time in history, to choose, and in a sense to create, his own identity.[43]

CHAPTER REVIEW

1. Within societies there are structural forces that work to achieve change while there are others that operate to promote stability. Both change and stability are inevitable and necessary for the survival of societies. These contradictory forces present another inherent duality in social systems.

2. The forces for stability are the constraints of customs, traditions, myths, and ideologies.

3. Institutions are barriers to social change because they provide answers from tradition. The institution of the government inhibits change because of systemic imperatives (the necessity of order, the stifling of dissent, enforcing the law, and promoting the political and economic systems). Also the organization of the government preserves the status quo.

4. The institution of education inhibits change. The schools impart to the young the attitudes, roles, specialties, and training necessary to fit into society. The schools' special task is to preserve the culture by transmitting it, not transforming it.

5. Bureaucracies are complex organizations designed to increase efficiency by dividing work into small tasks performed by specialists; by having a chain of command in which each position has clearly defined responsibilities; by making decisions based on technical knowledge; and by judging performance by proficiency.

6. Bureaucracies promote the status quo in several ways. Unquestioned following of rules and orders means that new and unusual situations cannot be handled because the rules do not apply. Promotions within the hierarchy are made on the basis of conformity, loyalty, and productivity.

7. Ideological beliefs can stifle change. Religious beliefs, for example, have rejected new ideas and technologies throughout history.

8. A social movement is a collective attempt to promote or resist change. A resistance movement is explicitly organized to resist change.

9. Technology is a major force for change, altering roles, rules, ideas, and behaviors. A few examples are the automobile, television, contraceptives, and computers, which have affected the family, created and destroyed occupations, and changed perceptions.

10. Urbanization, the concentration of people in limited geographical areas, is another force for social change. The growth of cities and suburbs, and the racial transformation of the central cities in this century have greatly affected changes in American society.

11. Migration is having a profound effect on contemporary life. Migration patterns away from central cities to suburbs and from the industrial Northeast to the sunbelt are bringing economic problems to the abandoned areas and increased economic and political power to the growing regions.

12. Immigration, legal and illegal, is adding as it always has to the ethnic diversity of the United States. It is also bringing problems, such as increased hostilities among competing groups and increased costs for social services.

13. Population growth is another source of societal change. The baby boom generation provides an excellent example. This bulge of an extra 10 million people has had dramatic effects on society as they move through the age structure.

14. The government, although it can resist

change, can also be a prime mover by financing new technologies, opening or closing trade with other nations, stimulating the economy, and the like.

15. There are two types of social movements organized to promote change. A reform movement seeks to alter a specific part of society such as discrimination against a certain category. The goal of a revolutionary movement is more ambitious, seeking the transformation of the entire society.

16. Social movements to enhance or inhibit change appeal to certain categories of persons. These are the disadvantaged and oppressed and those who share a condition called "status anguish." These persons are marginal in status (such as children of immigrants, recent migrants from rural to urban areas, and interracial couples), have inconsistent status, or have lost status.

FOR FURTHER STUDY

Social Change: General

Daniel Bell, *The Coming of Postindustrial Society* (New York: Basic Books, 1973).
William Kornhauser, *The Politics of Mass Society* (New York: Free Press, 1959).
Robert Lauer, *Perspectives on Social Change*, Second Edition (Boston: Allyn and Bacon, 1977).
Steven Vago, *Social Change* (New York: Holt, Rinehart and Winston, 1980).

Forces for Social Change

Daniel Bell, *The Cultural Contradictions of Capitalism* (New York: Basic Books, 1976).
Jacques Ellul, *The Technological Society* (New York: Alfred A. Knopf, 1964).

Hugh Davis Graham and Ted Robert Gurr (eds.), *Violence in America: Historical and Comparative Perspectives*, Revised Edition (Beverly Hills, Calif.: Sage, 1979).
Michael Harrington, *Decade of Decision* (New York: Simon and Schuster, 1980).
John Oosterbaan, *Population Dispersal* (Lexington, Mass.: Lexington, 1980).
Michael Parenti, *Power and the Powerless* (New York: St. Martin's, 1978).
Max Weber, *The Theory of Social and Economic Organization*, A. M. Henderson and Talcott Parsons (trans.), (New York: Free Press, 1947).
John R. Weeks, *Population* (Belmont, Calif.: Wadsworth, 1978).

NOTES AND REFERENCES

1. "The Politics of Cancer," *The Progressive* 43 (May, 1979), pp. 1–10.
2. "Out of the Bottle," *The Progressive* 44 (August, 1980), p. 8.
3. Sidney Lens, "The Doomsday Prerogative," *The Progessive* 45 (January, 1981), p. 10.
4. This debate is considered in a series of articles appearing in *Social Policy* 11 (May/June, 1980): S. M. Miller, "Turmoil and/or Acquiescence for the 1980s? (pp. 22–25); Heather Booth and Steve Max, "Citizen vs. Corporation," (pp. 26–28); Robert Lekachman, "Acquiescence for Now," (p. 35); Peter Marcuse, "The Establishment in Crisis," (pp. 36–38); and Alan Wolfe, "Left: Out of Step," (pp. 39–40).
5. See Frances Fox Piven and Richard A. Cloward, *Regulating the Poor* (New York: Random House, 1971).
6. Michael Parenti, *Power and the Powerless* (New York: St. Martin's Press, 1978), p. 188.
7. Jim McClellan, "Two-Party Monopoly," *The Progressive* 45 (January, 1981), pp. 28–31.
8. Jules Henry, *Culture Against Man* (New York: Random House (Vintage Books), 1963), pp. 285–286.
9. Charles E. Silberman, *Crisis in the Classroom* (New York: Random House, 1970).

10. Jerry Farber, *The Student as Nigger* (New York: Simon and Schuster (Pocket Books), 1970), p. 92.

11. See the classic statement on bureaucracy by Max Weber, *The Theory of Social and Economic Organization*, A. M. Henderson and Talcott Parsons (trans.), (New York: The Free Press, 1947), pp. 329–341. Originally published in 1922.

12. See Robert K. Merton, *Social Theory and Social Structure* (Glencoe, Ill.: The Free Press, 1968).

13. Laurence F. Peter and Raymond Hull, *The Peter Principle* (New York: Morrow, 1969).

14. Peter M. Blau and Marshall W. Meyer, *Bureaucracy in Modern Society*, Second Edition (New York: Random House, 1971), p. 104.

15. Gerald R. Leslie, Richard F. Larson, and Benjamin L. Gorman, *Introductory Sociology*, 3rd ed. (New York: Oxford University Press, 1980), p. 283.

16. The examples in this section are taken from Robert H. Lauer, *Perspectives on Social Change* (Boston: Allyn and Bacon, 1973), pp. 120–122.

17. For the classic treatment on social movements and other forms of collective behavior see Herbert Blumer, "Collective Behavior," in Alfred McClung Lee (ed.), *New Outline of the Principles of Sociology* (New York: Barnes and Noble, 1951). See also Neil Smelser, *Theory of Collective Behavior* (New York: The Free Press, 1962).

18. Gresham M. Sykes, *Social Problems in America* (Glenview, Ill.: Scott, Foresman, 1971), p. 30; see also Michael Harrington, *The Accidental Century* (Baltimore, Md.: Penguin, 1965).

19. Silberman, *Crisis in the Classroom*, p. 22.

20. Philip Slater, *The Pursuit of Loneliness: American Culture at the Breaking Point* (Boston: Beacon, 1970), pp. 44–45.

21. Alvin Toffler, *Future Shock* (New York: Bantam, 1970), p. 24.

22. The data in this section on urban population are taken from several sources: Bureau of the Census, *Current Population Reports*, "Population Profile of the United States: 1977," Series P–20, No. 324 (Washington, D.C.: U.S. Government Printing Office, 1978); Bureau of the Census, *Current Population Reports*, "Household and Family Character: March 1979," Series P–20, No. 352 (Washington, D.C.: U.S. Government Printing Office, 1980); and *The World Almanac & Book of Facts 1980* (New York: Newspaper Enterprise Association, 1980).

23. The data presented in this section are taken from *Population and the American Future: The Report of the Commission on Population Growth and the American Future* (New York: New American Library, 1972), pp. 37–43.

24. David L. Kaplan and Cheryl Russell, "What the 1980 Census Will Show," *American Demographics* (October, 1979), pp. 11–17.

25. *Population and the American Future*, p. 2.

26. *Population and the American Future*, p. 15; "Looking to the ZPG Generation," *Time* (February 28, 1977), pp. 71–72.

27. *Population and the American Future*, p. 46. See also "Next 25 Years—How Your Life Will Change," *U.S. News & World Report* (March 22, 1976), pp. 39–42.

28. Shirley Foster Hartley, "Our Growing Problem: Population," *Social Problems* 21 (Fall 1973), p. 195.

29. Daniel Bell, quoted in the *Kansas City Star* (September 30, 1973).

30. The following is taken primarily from two sources: Leon F. Bouvier, "America's Baby Boom Generation," *Population Bulletin* 35 (Washington, D.C.: Population Reference Bureau, April, 1980); and Richard A. Easterlin, "What Will 1984 Be Like? Socioeconomic Implications of Recent Twists in Age Structure," *Demography* 15 (November, 1978), pp. 397–419.

31. James W. Kuhn, "The Immense Generation," *Intellectual Digest* 4 (February, 1974), p. 68.

32. *Population and the American Future*, p. 17. See also "Yesterday's 'Baby Boom' Is Overcrowding Today's Prisons," *U.S. News & World Report* (March 1, 1976), pp. 65–67.

33. Kuhn, "The Immense Generation," p. 68.

34. See James O'Toole, "The Reserve Army of the Under-Employed," *Change* 7 (May, 1975), pp. 28–30; and Linda Baer, D. Stanley Eitzen, Charles Duprey, Norman Thompson, and Curtis Cole, "The Consequences of Objective and Subjective Status Inconsistency,"

The Sociological Quarterly 17 (Summer, 1976), pp. 389–400.

35. See David Stolberg, "American Population Aging; Over-75 Group Grows Fastest," *Rocky Mountain News* (February 5, 1975), p. 92; "The Graying of America," *Newsweek* (February 28, 1977), pp. 48–65; and "Age Distribution Shifts in U.S.," *The Futurist* 10 (April, 1976), p. 109.

36. Martin Mayer, "Growing Up Crowded," *Commentary* 60 (September, 1975), p. 45.

37. Lauer, *Perspectives on Social Change*, pp. 153–159.

38. Ibid., pp. 156–157; and Piven and Cloward, *Regulating the Poor.*

39. See Alan Wolfe, *The Limits of Legitimacy: Political Contradictions of Contemporary Capitalism* (New York: The Free Press, 1977).

40. See Karl Marx, *Capital: A Critique of Political Economy*, vol. 1 (New York: International Publishers, 1967). Originally published in 1866.

41. Lauer, *Perspectives on Social Change*, pp 159–165.

42. The classic statement on marginality is by Everett C. Hughes, "Dilemmas and Contradictions of Status," *American Journal of Sociology* 50 (July 1944–May 1945), pp. 353–359.

43. Silberman, *Crisis in the Classroom*, pp. 22–23.

Part II

The Individual in Society; Society in the Individual

5

Culture

Let's begin with a bold assertion—American values taken to the extreme, kill. Although such a statement is too strong, there is some truth to it. The American values of individualism, according to which we are judged by our personal accomplishments, our success in competitive situations, and our accumulation of material goods as evidence of our success, drives many persons toward premature death from heart disease. The medical profession, following the pioneering work of Drs. Meyer Friedman and Ray H. Rosenman, has accepted the thesis that persons exhibiting "Type A" behavior (resulting from the intense drive to be No. 1) are likely candidates for early heart trouble.

The Type A Behavior Pattern: You possess this pattern:

1. If you always move, walk, and eat rapidly.
2. If you feel an impatience with the rate at which most events take place. The signs of such impatience are: (a) hurrying the speech of others; (b) attempting to finish the sentences of persons speaking to you before they can; (c) becoming unduly irritated when a car ahead of you in your lane runs at a pace you consider too slow; (d) becoming irritated at having to perform necessary but repetitious duties (writing out the monthly checks); and (e) hurrying your own reading or always attempting to obtain condensations or summaries of truly interesting and worthwhile literature.
3. If you think of or do two or more things at once. Examples of this would be to eat breakfast, read the paper, and watch the Today Show simultaneously or to shave with an electric razor while driving to work.
4. If you find it always difficult to refrain from talking about or bringing the theme of any conversation around to those subjects which especially interest and intrigue you.
5. If you almost always feel vaguely guilty when you relax and do absolutely nothing.
6. If you fail to notice or be interested in your environment or things of beauty.
7. If you do not have any time to spare to become the things worth being because you are so preoccupied with getting the things worth having.
8. If you attempt to schedule more and more activities into less and less time. A concomitant of this is a chronic sense of time urgency.
9. If you resort to certain characteristic gestures or nervous tics. For example, if you frequently clench your fist or bang your hand on a table in conversations you are exhibiting Type A gestures. Similarly, if you habitually clench your jaw or grind your teeth, this suggests the presence of a continuous struggle.
10. If you measure your own or others' successes in terms of numbers (number of books read, articles written, sales made).
11. If you play every game to win, even when playing with children.

The Type B Behavior Pattern: You possess this pattern:

1. If you are completely free of all the habits and exhibit none of the traits that harass the Type A person.
2. If you never suffer from a sense of urgency with its accompanying impatience.
3. If you feel no need to display or discuss either your achievements or accomplishments unless such exposure is demanded by the situation.
4. If, when you play, you do so to find fun and relaxation, not to exhibit your superiority at any cost.
5. If you can relax without guilt, just as you can work without agitation.

Source: Meyer Friedman and Ray H. Rosenman, *Type A Behavior and Your Heart* (Greenwich, Conn.: Fawcett Publications, 1975), pp. 100–103.

An important focus of sociology is on the social influences on human behavior. As people interact over time two fundamental sources of constraints on individuals emerge—social structure and culture. As noted in Chapter 2, **social structure** refers to the linkages and network among the members of a social organization. **Culture**, the subject of this chapter, is the knowledge that these members share. Because this shared knowledge includes ideas about what is right, how one is to behave in various situations, religious beliefs, and communication, culture constrains not only behavior but how people think about and interpret their world.

This chapter is divided into two parts. The first describes the nature of culture and its importance for understanding human behavior. The second part focuses on one aspect of culture—values. This discussion is especially vital for understanding the organization and problems of society, in this case, American society.

CULTURE: THE KNOWLEDGE THAT PEOPLE SHARE

Social scientists studying a society foreign to them must spend months, perhaps years, learning the culture of that group. They must learn the meanings for the symbols (written and spoken language, gestures, and rituals) the individuals in that society employ. They must know the feelings people share as to what is appropriate or inappropriate behavior. Additionally, they need to know the rules of the society: which activities are considered important, the skills members have in making and using tools, as well as the knowledge members need to exist in that society. In short, the analyst must discover all the knowledge that people share—that is, he or she must know the culture. Let us examine each of the characteristics of this important social concept.

Characteristics of Culture

1. *Culture is an emergent process.* As individuals interact on any kind of sustained basis, they exchange ideas about all sorts of things. In time they develop common ideas,

common ways of doing things, and common interpretations for certain actions. In so doing, the participants have created a culture. The emergent quality of culture is an ongoing process; it is built up slowly rather than being present at the beginnings of social organization. The culture of any group is constantly undergoing change because the members are in continuous interaction. Culture, then, is never completely static.

2. *Culture is learned behavior*. Culture is not instinctive or innate in the human species; it is not part of the biological equipment of human beings. The biological equipment of man, however, makes culture possible. That is, we are symbol-making creatures capable of attaching meaning to particular objects and actions and communicating these meanings to others. When a person joins a new social organization, she or he must learn the culture of that group. This is true for the infant born into a society as well as for a college girl joining a sorority or a young man inducted into the armed forces, or for immigrants to a new society. This process of learning the culture is called **socialization**.

3. *Culture channels human behavior*. Culture, since it emerges from social interaction, is an inevitable development of human society. More important, it is essential in the maintenance of any social system because it provides two crucial functions—predictability of action and stability. To accomplish these functions, however, culture must restrict human freedom (although as we shall see, cultural constraints are not normally perceived as such); through cultural patterns the individual is expected to conform to the expectations of the group.

How does culture work to constrain individuals? Or put another way, how does culture become internalized in people so that their actions are controlled? Somehow culture operates not only outside individuals but also inside them. Sigmund Freud recognized this process when he conceptualized the "superego" as that part of the personality structure that inhibits people from committing acts considered wrong by their parents, a group, or the society.

The process of **internalization** (and therefore control) is accomplished mainly in three ways. First, culture becomes part of the human makeup through the belief system into which a child is born. This belief system, provided by parents and those persons immediately in contact with youngsters, shapes their ideas about the surrounding world as well as giving them certain ideas about themselves. The typical American child, for example, is taught to accept Christian beliefs without reservation. These beliefs are literally "force fed," since alternative belief systems are considered unacceptable by the "feeders." It is interesting to note that after Christian beliefs are internalized by the child, they are often used by the "feeders" as levers to keep the child in line.

Second, culture is internalized through psychological identification with the groups to which individuals belong (membership groups), or to which they want to belong (**reference groups**). Individuals want to belong; they want to be accepted by others. Therefore, they tend to conform to the behavior of their immediate group as well as to the wishes of society at large.

Finally, culture is internalized by providing the individual with an identity. People's age, sex, race, religion, and social class have an effect upon the way others perceive them and the way they perceive themselves. To be a male, for example, requires in American society that one be aggressive, ambitious, and competitive. Berger has said, "in a sociological perspective, identity is socially bestowed, socially sustained, and socially transformed."[1]

Culture, then, is not freedom but rather constraint. Of the entire range of possible behaviors (which probably are considered appropriate by some society somewhere), the person of a particular society can only choose from a narrow range of alternatives. The paradox, as Peter Berger has pointed out, is that while society is like a prison to the persons trapped in its cultural demands and expectations, it is not perceived as limiting to individual freedom. Berger has stated it well in the following passage:

For most of us the yoke of society seems easy to bear. Why? . . . because most of the time we ourselves desire just what society expects of us. We *want* to obey the rules. We *want* the parts that society has assigned to us.[2]

Individuals do not see the prisonlike qualities of culture because they have internalized the culture of their society. From birth children are shaped by the culture of the society into which they are born. They retain some individuality because of the configuration of forces unique to their experience (gene structure, peers, parents' social class, religion, and race), but the behavioral alternatives deemed appropriate for them are narrow.

Culture even shapes thought and perception. What we see and how we interpret what we see is determined by culture. CBS News staged an experiment several years ago that illustrates this point. A black man with something in his hand ran down a crowded city street. White bystanders were asked what they saw. The typical response was that they had perceived the black as carrying a gun, knife, or stolen property, and running from the authorities. In fact, the man was running to catch a bus with a rolled-up newspaper in his hand. Would the respondents have interpreted the actions differently if the person were white? Many white Americans believe that blacks tend toward criminal activity. This stereotype can, therefore, affect negatively the interpretation of a socially acceptable act.

For a dramatic illustrative case of the kind of mental closure that may be determined by culture, consider the following riddle about a father and son driving down a highway:

There is a terrible accident in which the father is killed, and the son, critically injured, is rushed to a hospital. There the surgeon approaches the patient and suddenly cries, "My God, that's my son!"

How it is possible that the critically injured boy is the son of the man in the accident as well as the son of the surgeon? Answers might involve the surgeon being a priest, or a stepfather, or even artifical insemination. The correct answer to this riddle is that the surgeon is the boy's mother. Americans, male and female alike, have been socialized to think of women as occupying roles less important than physician/surgeon. If Russians were given this riddle, they would almost uniformly give the correct answer since approximately three-fourths of Rissian physicians are women. So culture may be confining—not liberating. It constrains not only actions but also thinking.

4. *Culture is boundary maintaining.* Culture not only limits the range of acceptable behavior and attitudes but it instills in its adherents a sense of "naturalness" about the alternatives peculiar to a given society (or other social organization). Thus there is a universal tendency to deprecate the ways of persons from other societies as wrong,

old-fashioned, inefficient, or immoral, and to think of the ways of one's own group as superior (as the only right way). The concept for this phenomenon is **ethnocentrism**. The word combines the Greek word *ethnikos*, which means nation or people, and the English word for center. So one's own race, religion, or society is the center of all and therefore superior to all.

Ethnocentrism is demonstrated in statements such as "My fraternity is the best," "Reincarnation is a weird belief," "We are God's chosen people," or "Polygamy is immoral." To name the playoff between the American and National Leagues the "World Series" implies that baseball outside the United States (and Canada) is inferior. Religious missionaries provide a classic example of one among several typical groups convinced that their own faith is the only correct one.

A resolution passed at a town meeting in Milford, Connecticut, in 1640 is a blatant example of ethnocentrism. It stated:

Voted, the earth is the Lord's and the fulness thereof
Voted, the earth belongs to the saints
Voted, we are the saints.

Further examples of ethnocentrism taken from American history are: "manifest destiny," "white man's burden," exclusionary immigration laws such as the Oriental Exclusion Act, and "Jim Crow" laws. A current illustration of ethnocentrism can be seen in the activities of the United States as it engages in exporting the "American way of life," because it is believed that democracy and capitalism are necessities for the good life and therefore best for all peoples.

Ethnocentrism, because it implies feelings of superiority, leads to division and conflict between subgroups within a society and between societies, each of which feels "superior."

Ethnocentric ideas are real because they are believed and they influence perception and behavior. Analysts of American society (whether they are Americans or not) must recognize their own ethnocentric attitudes and the way these affect their own objectivity.

To summarize, culture emerges from social interaction. The paradox is that although culture is human-made, it exerts a tremendous complex of forces that *constrain* the actions and thoughts of human beings. The analyst of any society must be cognizant of these two qualities of culture, for they combine to give a society its unique character; culture explains social change as well as stability; culture explains existing social arrangements (including many social problems); culture explains a good deal of individual behavior because it is internalized by the individual members of society and therefore has an impact (substantial but not total) on their actions and personalities.

Types of Shared Knowledge

The concept of culture refers to knowledge that is shared by the members of a social organization. In analyzing any social organization and, in this case, any society, it is helpful to conceive of culture as combining six types of shared knowledge—symbols, technology, roles, ideologies, norms, and values.

1. *Symbols.* By definition, language refers to symbols that evoke similar meanings in different people. Communication is possible only if persons attribute the same meaning to

stimuli such as sounds, gestures, or objects. Language, then, may be written, spoken, or unspoken. A shrug of the shoulders, a pat on the back, the gesturing with a finger (which one may be significant), a wink, or a nod are examples of unspoken language and vary in meaning from society to society.

2. *Technology*. Technology refers to the information, techniques, and tools used by people to satisfy their varied needs and desires. For analytic purposes two types of technology can be distinguished—material and social. *Material technology* refers to knowledge of how to make and use things. It is important to note that the things produced are not part of the culture but represent rather the knowledge that people share and that makes it possible to build and use the object. The knowledge is culture, not the object.

Social technology is the knowledge about how to establish, maintain, and operate the technical aspects of social organization. Examples of this are procedures for operating a university, a municipality, or a corporation through such operations as Robert's Rules of Order, bookkeeping, or the kind of specialized knowledge citizens must acquire to function in society (knowing the laws, how to complete income tax forms, how to vote in elections, how to use credit cards and banks).[3]

3. *Ideologies*. These are shared beliefs about the physical, social, and metaphysical worlds. They may, for example, be statements about the existence of supernatural beings, the best form of government, or racial pride.

Ideologies help individuals interpret events. They also provide the rationale for particular forms of action. They can justify the status quo or demand revolution. A number of competing ideologies exist within American society—for example, fundamentalism and atheism, capitalism and socialism, and white supremacy and black supremacy. Clearly, ideology unites as well as divides and is therefore a powerful human-made (cultural) force within societies.

4. *Societal norms*. There are societal prescriptions for how one is to act in given situations—for example, at a football game, concert, restaurant, church, park, or classroom. We also learn how to act with members of the opposite sex, with our elders, with social inferiors, and with equals. Thus, behavior is patterned. We know how to behave and we can anticipate how others will behave. This allows interaction to occur smoothly.

There is a subdiscipline in sociology called **ethnomethodology**, which is the scientific study of the commonplace activities of daily life. The goal is to discover and understand the underpinnings of relationships (the shared meanings that implicitly guide social behavior). The assumption is that much of social life is "scripted"; that is, the players act according to society's rules (the script). The conduct in the family, in the department store between customer and salesperson, between doctor and patient, between boss and secretary, between coach and player are, in very real sense, determined by societal scripts.

But what happens when persons do not play according to the common understandings (the script)? Harold Garfinkel, an ethnomethodologist, has used this technique to discover the implicit bases of social interaction.[4] Examples of possible rule breaking include: (1) when answering the phone, you remain silent; (2) when selecting a seat in the audience, you ignore the empty seats and choose rather to sit next to a stranger (violating that person's privacy and space); (3) you act as a stranger in your family; (4) in talking with a friend, you insist that that person clarify the sense of his or her commonplace remarks; and (5) you bargain with clerks over the price of every item of food you wish to purchase. Now these behaviors violate the rules of interaction in American society. When they are violated, the other persons in the situation do not know how to respond. Typically, they become confused, anxious, and angry. This buttresses the notion that most of the time social life is very ordered and orderly. We behave in prescribed ways and we anticipate that others will do the same. The norms are strong and we tend to follow them automatically.

In addition to societal norms being necessary for the conduct of behavior in society, they vary in importance, as we saw in our discussion of norms at the micro level. There are those norms that are less important—the **folkways**—that are not severely punished if violated. Examples of folkways in American society are: it is expected that men should rise when a woman enters the room (unless she is the maid); women should not wear curlers to the opera; and one does not wear a business suit but go barefoot.

Violation of the **mores** of society is considered important enough by society that it must be punished severely. This type of norm involves morality. Some examples of mores are: one must have only one spouse at a time; "thou shalt not kill" (unless defending one's country or one's own property); and one must be loyal to the United States.

There is a problem, however, for many Americans in deciding the degree of importance for some norms. Figure 5–1 shows the criteria for deciding whether a norm should be classified as a folkway or a mos (the singular of the Latin term mores).

Figure 5–1 shows that on the basis of the two defining criteria there are four possibilities, not just two. It is difficult to imagine cases that would be located in cell (b). The only possibilities are activities that have only recently been designated as very harmful but against which laws have not yet been passed for strict punishment (either because of the natural lag in the courts and legislatures or because powerful groups have been influential in blocking the necessary legislation). The best current example of cases that would fall in cell (b) would be the pollution of lakes, streams, and air by large commercial enterprises. These acts are recognized a having serious consequences for present and future generations, but either go unpunished or receive only minor fines.

Cell (c), on the other hand, is interesting because there are acts not important to the survival of society or the maintenance of its institutions that receive severe punishments (at least relative to the crime). Some examples would be a male student being suspended from school until he gets his hair cut; persons caught smoking marijuana being sentenced to a jail term; young men burning their draft cards being jailed or drafted; and a woman being fired from her job for not wearing a bra.

FIGURE 5–1 Classification of Norms

| | | Severity of Punishment | |
		High	Low
Degree of Importance	High	Mores (a)	(b)
	Low	(c)	Folkways (d)

CROSS-CULTURAL PANEL

Panel 5-1
The Kiss as a Cultural Creation

Nothing seems more natural than a kiss. Consider the French kiss, also known as the soul kiss, deep kiss, or tongue kiss (to the French, it was the Italian kiss, but only during the Renaissance). Western societies regard this passionate exploration of mouths and tongues as an instinctive way to express love and to arouse desire. To a European who associates deep kisses with erotic response, the idea of one without the other feels like summer without sun.

Yet soul kissing is completely absent in many cultures of the world, where sexual arousal may be evoked by affectionate bites or stinging slaps. Anthropology and history amply demonstrate that, depending on time and place, the kiss may or may not be regarded as a sexual act, a sign of friendship, a gesture of respect, a health threat, a ceremonial celebration, or disgusting behavior that deserves condemnation. . . .

One of the first modern studies to dispel the belief that sexual behavior is universally the same (and therefore instinctive) was *Patterns of Sexual Behavior*, written in 1951 by Clellan Ford and Frank Beach. Ford and Beach compared many of the sexual customs of 190 tribal societies that were recorded in the Human Relations Area Files at Yale University.

Unfortunately, few of the field studies mentioned kissing customs at all. Of the 21 that did, some sort of kissing accompanied intercourse in 13 tribes—the Chiricahua, Cree, Crow, Gros Ventre, Hopi, Huichol, Kwakiutl, and Tarahumara of North America; the Alorese, Keraki, Trobrianders, and Trukese of Oceania; and in Eurasia, among the Lapps. Ford and Beach noted some variations: The Kwakiutl, Trobrianders, Alorese, and Trukese kiss by sucking the lips and tongue of their partners; the Lapps like to kiss the mouth and nose at the same time. (I would add Margaret Mead's observation of the Arapesh. They "possess the true kiss," she wrote; they touch lips, but instead of pressing, they mutually draw the breath in.)

But sexual kissing is unknown in many societies, including the Balinese, Chamorro, Manus, and Tinguian of Oceania; the Chewa and Thonga of Africa; the

Both criteria used to delineate types of norms—degree of importance and severity of the punishments—are determined by those in power. Consequently, activities that are perceived by the powerful as being disruptive of the power structure or institutional arrangements that benefit some and not others are viewed as illegitimate and punished severely. For example, if 10,000 young persons protest against the political system with marches, speeches, and acts of civil disobedience, they are typically perceived as a threat and jailed, beaten, gassed, and harassed by the police and the National Guard. Compare the treatment of these young people with another group of 10,000 on the beaches of Florida during their annual spring break. These people often drink to excess, are sexually promiscuous, and are destructive of property. Generally, the police consider these behaviors as non-threatening to the system and therefore treat them relatively lightly.

Norms are also situational. Behavior expected in one societal setting may be inappro-

Siriono of South America; and the Lepcha of Eurasia. In such cultures the mouth-to-mouth kiss is considered dangerous, unhealthy, or disgusting, the way most Westerners would regard a custom of sticking one's tongue into a lover's nose. Ford and Beach report that when the Thonga first saw Europeans kissing they laughed, remarking, "Look at them—they eat each other's saliva and dirt."

Deep kissing apparently has nothing to do with the degree of sexual inhibition or repression in a culture. Donald S. Marshall, an anthropologist who studied a small Polynesian island he called Mangaia, found that all Mangaian women are taught to be orgasmic and sexually active; yet kissing, sexual and otherwise, was unknown until Westerners (and their popular films) arrived on the island. In contrast, John C. Messenger found that on a sexually repressed Irish island where sex is considered dirty, sinful, and, for women, a duty to be endured, tongue kissing was unknown as late as 1966. . . .

Small tribes and obscure Irish islanders are not the only groups to eschew tongue kissing. The advanced civilizations of China and Japan, which regarded sexual proficiency as high art, apparently cared little about it. In their voluminous production of erotica—graphic displays of every possible sexual position, angle of intercourse, variation of partner and setting—mouth-to-mouth kissing is conspicuous by its absence. Japanese poets have rhapsodized for centuries about the allure of the nape of the neck, but they have been silent on the mouth; indeed, kissing is acceptable only between mother and child. (The Japanese have no word for kissing—though they recently borrowed from English to create "kissu.") Intercourse is "natural"; a kiss, pornographic. When Rodin's famous sculpture, *The Kiss*, came to Tokyo in the 1920s as part of a show of European art, it was concealed from public view behind a bamboo curtain.

Among cultures of the West, the number of nonsexual uses of the kiss is staggering. The simple kiss has served any or all of several purposes: greeting and farewell, affection, religious or ceremonial symbolism, deference to a person of higher status. (People also kiss icons, dice, and other objects, of course, in prayer, for luck, or as part of a ritual.) Kisses make the hurt go away, bless sacred vestments, seal a bargain. In story and legend a kiss has started wars and ended them, and awakened Sleeping Beauty and put Brunnhilde to sleep.

Source: Excerpts from "The Kiss" by Leonore Tiefer from *Human Nature*, July 1978, pp. 28, 30. Copyright © 1978 by Human Nature, Inc. Reprinted by permission of the publisher.

priate for another. Several examples should make this point clear. One may ask for change from a clerk, but one would not put money in a church collection plate and remove change. Clearly, behavior considered acceptable by fans at a football game (yelling, booing authority figures, even destroying property) would be inexcusable behavior at a poetry reading. Behavior allowable in a bar probably would be frowned upon in a bank. Or doctors may ask patients to disrobe in the examining room but not in the subway.

Finally, because norms are properties of groups, they vary from society to society and from group to group within societies. Thus, behavior appropriate in one group of society may be absolutely inappropriate in another. Some examples of this are:

item: The "couvade" is a practice surprisingly common throughout the world, but in sharp contrast to the expectations in the United States. This refers to the time when

Panel 5-2
Cultural Time

To find social time it is necessary to look beyond the individual perceptions and attitudes, to the temporal construct of the society or culture. Temporal constructs are not to be found in human experience, but rather in the cultural symbols and institutions through which human experience is construed. Our own Indo-European language imposes the concept of time on us at a very early age, so it is difficult to identify with the concept of timelessness. Societies do exist without a consciousness of time. But most societies possess a concept of time. Conceptualizations of time are as varied as the cultures, but most can be categorized by one of three images. Time in the broad sense is viewed as a line (linear), a wheel (cyclical), or as a pendulum (alternating phenomenon). But within these central images, numerous other distinctions must be made. One is tense. Is there a past or present or future, or all three? If more than one, to which is the society oriented and in what way? Another is continuity. Is time continuous or discontinuous? Does the continuity or hiatus have regularity? Another is progressiveness. Is evolutionary transformation expected with the passage of time? Still another is use. Is time used for measuring duration or is it for punctuality? The metaphysical distinctions are numerous. Is there a mode for measuring time? Is it reversible or irreversible? Subjective or objective, or both? Unidirectional? Rectilinear?

These distinctions come into focus when one studies various cultures. The Pawnee Indians, for example, have no past in a temporal sense; they instead have

a woman is in childbirth. Instead of the wife suffering, the husband moans and groans and is waited on as though he were in greater pain. After his wife has had the baby she will get up and bring her husband food and comfort. The husband is so incapacitated by the experience that in some societies he stays in bed for as many as 40 days.

item: Among the Murgin of Australia, a woman giving birth to twins kills one of the babies because it makes her feel like a dog to have a litter instead of one baby. A tribe along the Niger Delta puts both the mother and the twins to death. With the Bankundo of the Congo valley, on the other hand, the mother of twins is the object of honor and veneration.

item: In some Latin American countries high-status males are expected to have a mistress. This practice is even encouraged by their wives because it implies high status (given the cost of maintaining two households). In the United States, such a practice is grounds for divorce. American wives would never find such a circumstance something to brag about.

item: In Pakistan one never reaches for food with his or her left hand. To do so would make the observers physically sick. The reason is that the left hand is used to clean oneself after a bowel movement. Hence, the right hand is symbolically the only hand worthy of accepting food.

5. *Values.* Another aspect of a society's structure are the **values**, which are the bases

a timeless storehouse of tradition, not a historical record. To them, life has a rhythm but not a progression. To the Hopi, time is a dynamic process without past, present, or future. Instead, time is divided vertically between subjective and objective time. Although Indo-European languages are laden with tensed verbs and temporal adjectives indicating past, present, and future, the Hopi have no such verbs, adjectives, or any other similar linguistic device. The Trobriander is forever in the present. For the Trobriander and the Tiv, time is not continuous throughout the day. Advanced methods of calculating sun positions exist for morning and evening, but time does not exist for the remainder of the day. For the Balinese, time is conceived in a punctual rather than a durational sense. The Balinese calendar is marked off, not by even duration intervals, but rather by self-sufficient periods which indicate coincidence with a period of life. Their descriptive calendar indicates the *kind* of time, rather than what time it is. The Maya had probably the most complicated system of time yet discovered. Their time divisions were regarded as burdens carried by relays of divine carriers—some benevolent, some malevolent. They would succeed each other, and it was very important to determine who was currently carrying in order to know whether it was a good time or a bad time.

Source: Excerpted from F. Gregory Hayden, "A Critical Analysis of Time Stream Discounting for Social Program Evaluation," *The Social Science Journal* 17 (January 1980), pp. 26–27.

for the norms. These are the criteria used in evaluating objects, acts, feelings, or events as to their relative desirability, merit, or correctness. Values are extremely important, for they determine the direction of individual and group behavior, encouraging some activities and impeding others. For example, efforts to get Americans to conserve energy and other resources run counter to the long-held American values of growth, progress, and individual freedom. Consequently, the prevailing values have thwarted the efforts of various presidents and others to plan carefully about future needs and restrict usage and the rate of growth now.

6. *Role.* Societies, like other social organizations, have social positions (**statuses**) and behavioral expectations for those who occupy these positions (**roles**). There are family statuses (son or daughter, sibling, parent, husband, wife); age statuses (child, adolescent, adult, aged); sex statuses (male, female); racial statuses (black, chicano, Indian, white); and socioeconomic statuses (poor, middle class, wealthy). For each of these statuses there are societal constraints on behavior. To become 65 years old in American society is an especially traumatic experience for many. The expectations of society dramatically shift when one reaches this age. A sixty-five-year-old person is no longer considered an employable adult. The aged are forced into a situation of dependence rather than independence. To be a male or female in American society is to be constrained in a relatively rigid set of expectations. Similarly, blacks and other minorities, because of their minority status, have been expected to "know their place." The power of the social role is

best illustrated, perhaps, by the person who occupies two relevant statuses—for example, the black physician or the woman airline pilot. Although each of these persons is a qualified professional, they will doubtless encounter many situations where persons will expect them to behave according to the dictates of the traditional role expectations of their **ascribed status** (race or sex, statuses over which the individual has no control) rather than their **achieved status** (that is, their occupation).

The Social Construction of Reality

A society's culture determines how the members of that society will interpret their environment.[5] Language, in particular, influences the ways in which the members of a society perceive reality. Two linguists, Edward Sapir and Benjamin Whorf, have shown this by the way the Hopi Indians and Anglos differ in the way each speak about time.[6] The Hopi language has no verb tenses and no nouns for times, days, or years. Consequently the Hopi think of time as continuous—without breaks. The English language, in sharp contrast, divides time into seconds, minutes, hours, days, weeks, months, years, decades, centuries, and the like. The use of verb tenses in English clearly informs everyone whether an event occurred in the past, present, or future (see Panel 5–2 for other examples of how time is conceived of in various societies). Clearly precision regarding time is important to English speaking peoples while unimportant to the Hopi.

There is an African tribe that has no word for the color gray. This implies that they do not see gray even though we "know" that there is such a color and readily see it in the sky and in hair. The Navajo do not distinguish between *blue* and *green* yet they have two words for different kinds of *black*.

The Aimore tribe in eastern Brazil has no word for *two*. The Yancos, an Amazon tribe, cannot count beyond *poettarrarorincoaroac*, their word for *three*. The Temiar people of West Malaysia also stop at three.[7] Can you imagine how this lack of numbers beyond two or three affects the way these people perceive reality?

Our language helps us to make order out of what we experience. Our particular language allows us to perceive differences among things or to recognize a set of things to be alike even when they are not identical. Language permits us to order these by what we think they have in common. As Bronowski has put it:

Habit makes us think the likeness obvious; it seems to us obvious that all apples are somehow alike, or all trees, or all matter. Yet there are languages in the Pacific Islands in which every tree on the island has a name, but which have no word for tree. To these islanders, trees are not at all alike; on the contrary, what is important to them is that the trees are different.[8]

The social interpretation of reality is not limited to language. For example, some people believe that there is such a thing as "holy water." Now there is no chemical difference between water and holy water but some people believe that the differences in properties and potential are enormous. To understand holy water we must examine priests and parishioners, not water.[9] Similarly, consider the difference between spit and saliva.[10] There is no chemical difference between them, the only difference being that in one case the substance is inside the mouth and in the other it is outside. We swallow saliva continuously and think nothing about it yet one would not gather his or her spit in a container and then drink it. Clearly saliva is defined positively and spit negatively, yet the only difference is a social definition.

There is a debate in philosophy and sociology on this issue of reality. One position—**ontology**—accepts the reality of things because their nature cannot be denied (a chair, a tree, the wind, a society). The opposite side—**epistemology**—argues that all reality is socially constructed. In this view all meaning is created out of a world that generates no meanings of its own.[11] The world is absurd and humans make sense out of it to fit their situation. This extreme position is expressed by two sociologists in the following quotation:

> Fundamental to our view is the assumption that the universe has no intrinsic meaning—it is, at bottom, absurd—and that the task of the sociologist is to discover the various imputed or fabricated meanings constructed by [people] in society. Or, to put it another way, the sociologist's job is to find out *by what illusions people live*. Without these artifacts, these delicately poised fantasies, most of us would not survive. Society, as we know it, could not exist. Meaninglessness produces terror. And terror must be dissipated by participating in, and believing in, collective fictions. They constitute society's "noble lie," the lie that there is some sort of inherent significance in the universe. It is the job of sociology to understand [how people] impute meaning to the various aspects of life.[12]

Cultural Relativity

A number of customs from around the world have been described in this chapter. These typically seem to us weird, cruel, or stupid. Anthropologists, though, have helped us to understand that in the cultural context of a given society, the practice may make considerable sense. For example, anthropologist Marvin Harris has explained why sacred cattle are allowed to roam the countryside in India while the people may be starving.[13] Outsiders see cow worship as the primary cause of India's hunger and poverty, because cattle do not contribute meat while eating crops that would otherwise go to humans. Harris, however, argues that cattle must not be killed for food because they are the most efficient producer of fuel and food. To kill them would cause the economy to collapse. Cattle contribute to the Indian economy in a number of significant ways. They are the source of oxen, which are the principal traction animals for farming. Their milk helps to meet the nutritional needs of many poor families. India's cattle annually excrete 700 million tons of recoverable manure, half of which is used for fertilizer and the rest for fuel. Cow dung is also used as a household flooring material. If cows were slaughtered during times of famine, the economy would not recover in good times. To Western experts it looks as if the Indian would rather starve to death than to eat his cow. But as Harris has argued, "They don't realize that the farmer would rather eat his cow than starve, but that he will starve if he does eat it."[14] The practice of cow worship also allows for a crude redistribution of wealth. The cattle owned by the poor are allowed to roam freely. In this way the poor are able to let their cows graze the crops of the rich and come home at night to be milked. As Harris has concluded:

> The sacredness of the cow is not just an ignorant belief that stands in the way of progress. Like all concepts of the sacred and the profane, this one affects the physical

world; it defines the relationships that are important for the maintenance of Indian society.

Indians have the sacred cow; we have the "sacred" car and the "sacred" dog. It would not occur to us to propose the elimination of automobiles and dogs from our society without carefully considering the consequences, and we should not propose the elimination of zebu cattle without first understanding their place in the social order of India.

Human society is neither random nor capricious. The regularities of thought and behavior called culture are the principal mechanisms by which we human beings adapt to the world around us. Practices and beliefs can be rational or irrational, but a society that fails to adapt to its environment is doomed to extinction. Only those societies that draw the necessities of life from their surroundings, inherit the earth. The West has much to learn from the great antiquity of Indian civilization, and the sacred cow is an important part of that lesson.[15]

This extended example is used to convey the idea that the customs of a society should be evaluated in the light of the culture and their functions for that society. These customs should *not* be evaluated by our standards, but by theirs. This is called **cultural relativity**. The problem with cultural relativity, of course, is ethnocentrism—the tendency for the members of each society to assume the rightness of their own customs and practices and the inferiority, immorality, or irrationality of those found in other societies.

AMERICAN VALUES

While all of the components of culture are essential for an understanding of the constraints on human behavior, perhaps the quickest way to reach this understanding is to focus on its values. These are the criteria used by the members of society to evaluate objects, ideas, acts, feelings, or events as to their relative desirability, merit, or correctness.

Humans are valuing beings. They continually evaluate themselves and others. What objects are worth owning? What makes people successful? What activities are rewarding? What is beauty? Of course, different societies have distinctive criteria (values) for evaluating. People are considered successful in the United States, for example, if they accumulate many material things as a result of hard work. In other societies people are considered to be successful if they attain total mastery of their emotions or if they totally reject materialism.

One objective common to any social science course is the hope that students will become aware of the various aspects of social life in an analytical way. For Americans studying their own society this means that while immersed in the subject matter, they also become participant observers. This implies an objective detachment (as much as possible) so that one may understand better the forces which in large measure affect human behavior, individually and in groups.

The primary task for the participant observer interested in societal values is to determine what the values are. There are a number of clues that are helpful for such as task.* The first clue is to determine what most preoccupies people in their conversations and actions. So one might ask: Toward what do people most often direct their action? Is it, for

*A good but partial list of methods to determine empirically the values of American society has been developed in a text by Robin M. Williams.[16]

example, contemplation and meditation or physical fitness or the acquiring of material objects? In other words, what gives individuals high status in the eyes of their fellows?

A second technique that might help delineate the values is to determine the choices that people make consistently. The participant observer should ascertain what choices tend to be made in similar situations. For example, how do individuals dispose of surplus wealth? Do they spend it for self-aggrandizement or for altruistic reasons? Is there a tendency to spend it for the pleasure of the present, save it for security in the future, or spend it on others?

A third procedure is used typically by social scientists—that is, to find out through interviews or written questionnaires what people say is good, bad, moral, immoral, desirable, or undesirable. There is often a difference between what people say and what people do. This is always a problem in the study of values because there will sometimes be a discrepancy between values and actual behavior. Even if there is difference between what people write on a questionnaire or say in an interview and their actual behavior, they will probably say or write those responses they feel are appropriate, and this by itself is a valid indicator of what the values of the society are.

One may also observe the reward–punishment system of the society. What behavior is rewarded with a medal, or a bonus, or public praise? Alternatively, what behavior brings condemnation, ridicule, public censure, or imprisonment? The greater the reward or the punishment, the greater the likelihood that important societal values are involved. Consider, for example, the extraordinary punishment given to Americans who willfully destroy the private property of others (for example, a cattle rustler, a thief, a looter, or a pyromaniac).

Closely related to the reward–punishment system are the actions that cause individuals to feel guilt or shame (losing a job, living on welfare, declaring bankruptcy) or those actions which bring about ego enhancement (a better-paying job, getting an educational degree, owning a business). Individuals feel guilt or shame precisely because they have internalized the norms and values of society. When values and behavior are not congruent, feelings of guilt will be a typical response.

Another technique is to examine the principles that are held as part of "the American way of life." These principles are enunciated in historical documents such as the Constitution, the Declaration of Independence, and the Bible. We are continually reminded of these principles in speeches by elected officials, by editorials in the mass media, and from pulpits. The United States has gone to war to defend such principles as democracy, equality, freedom, and the free enterprise system. One question the analyst of values should ask, therefore, is, "For what principles will the people fight?"

The remainder of this chapter is devoted to the description of the American system of values. Understanding American values is essential to the analysis of American society, for they provide the basis for America's uniqueness as well as the source of many of its social problems.

American Values as Sources of
Societal Integration and Social Problems

American society, while similar in some respects to other advanced industrial societies, is also fundamentally different. Given the combination of geographical, historical, and

religious factors found in the United States, it is not surprising that its cultural values are unique.

Geographically, the United States has remained relatively isolated from other societies for most of its history. Americans have also been blessed with an abundance of rich and varied resources (land, minerals, and water). Until only recently, Americans were unconcerned with conservation and the careful use of resources (as many societies must be to survive) because there was no need. The country provided a vast storehouse of resources so rich they were often used wastefully.

Historically, the United States was founded by a revolution that grew out of opposition to tyranny and aristocracy. Hence, Americans have verbally supported such principles as freedom, democracy, equality, and impersonal justice.

Another historical factor that has led to American culture having its particular nature is that it has been peopled largely by immigrants. This fact has led, on the one hand, to a blending of many cultural traits, such as language, dress, and customs, and alternatively, to the existence of ethnic enclaves that resist assimilation.

A final set of forces that has affected American culture stems from its religious heritage. First is the Judeo-Christian ethic that has prevailed throughout American history. The strong emphases on humanitarianism, the inherent worth of all individuals, a morality based on the Ten Commandments, and even the Biblical injunction to "have dominion over all living things" have had a profound effect upon how Americans evaluate each other.

Another aspect of America's religious heritage, the Protestant (Puritan) work ethic, has been an important determinant of the values that are believed to typify most Americans.[17] The majority of early European settlers in America tended to believe in a particular set of religious beliefs that can be traced back to two individuals, Martin Luther and John Calvin. Luther's contribution was essentially twofold: each person was considered to be his or her own priest (stressing the person's individuality and worth), and each person was to accept his or her work as a "calling." To be "called" by God to do a job, no matter how humble, was to give the job and the individual dignity. It also encouraged everyone to work very hard to be successful in that job.

The contribution of John Calvin was based upon his belief in "Predestination." God, because He is all-knowing, knows who will be "saved." Unfortunately, individuals do not know whether they are "saved" or not, and this is very anxiety-producing. Calvinists came to believe that God would look with more favor upon those preordained to be "saved" than those who were not. Consequently, success in one's business became a sign that one was "saved," and this was therefore anxiety-reducing. Calvinists worked very hard to be successful. As they prospered, the capital they accumulated could only be spent on necessities, for to spend on luxuries was another sign that one was not "saved." The surplus capital was therefore invested in the enterprise (purchasing more property or better machinery, hiring a larger work force, or whatever).

Luther and Calvin produced an ethic that flourished in America. This ethic stressed the traits of self-sacrifice, diligence, and hard work. It stressed achievement, and most importantly, it stressed a self-orientation rather than a collectivity orientation. Indirectly, this ethic emphasized private property, capitalism, rationality, and growth.

Thus geography, religious heritage, and history have combined to provide a distinctive set of values for Americans. However, before we describe these dominant American values, several caveats should be mentioned. First, the tremendous diversity of the United States precludes any universal holding of values. There are persons and groups that reject the dominant values. Moreover, there are differences in emphasis for the dominant values by region, social class, age, and religion. Second, the system of American values is not always consistent with behavior. Third, the values themselves are not always consistent. How does one reconcile the coexistence of individualism with conformity? or competition and cooperation? Robin Williams, an eminent analyst of American society, has concluded that:

We do not find a neatly unified "ethos" or an irresistible "strain toward consistency." Rather, the total society is characterized by diversity and change in values. Complex division of labor, regional variations, ethnic heterogeneity, and the proliferation of specialized institutions and organizations all tend to insulate differing values from one another.[18]

To minimize the problem with inconsistencies, we will present only the most dominant of American values in this section.[19] Let's examine these in turn.

Success (individual achievement). The highly valued individual in American society is the self-made person—i.e., one who has achieved money and status through his or her own efforts in a highly competitive system. Our culture heroes are persons like Abe Lincoln and John D. Rockefeller, each of whom rose from humble origins to the top of his profession.

Success can be achieved, obviously, by outdoing all others, but it is often difficult to know exactly the extent of one's success. Hence, economic success (one's income, personal wealth, and type of possessions) is the most commonly used measurement. Economic success, moreover, is often used to measure personal worth. As Robin Williams has put it, "The comparatively striking feature of American culture is its tendency to identify standards of personal excellence with competitive occupational achievement."[20]

Competition. Competition is highly valued in American society. Most Americans believe it to be the one quality that has made America great because it motivates individuals and groups to be discontented with the status quo and with being second best. Motivated by the hope of being victorious in competition, or put another way, by fear of failure, Americans must not lose a war or the Olympics or be the second nation to land men on the moon.

Competition pervades almost all aspects of American society. The work world, sports, courtship, organizations like the Cub Scouts, and schools all thrive on competition. The pervasiveness of competition in schools is seen in how athletic teams, cheerleading squads, debate teams, choruses, bands, and casts are composed. In each case, competition among classmates is used as the criterion for selection. Of course, the grading system is also often based on the comparison of individuals with each other.

The Cub Scouts, because of its reliance on competition, is an all-American organization. In the first place, individual status in the den or pack is determined by the level one has achieved through the attainment of merit badges. Although all boys can theoretically attain all merit badges, there is competition as the boys are pitted against each other to see who can obtain the most. Another example of how the Cub Scouts use competition is their annual event—the Pinewood Derby. Each boy in a Cub pack is given a small block of wood and four wheels that he is then to shape into a racing car. The race is held at a pack meeting with one boy eventually being the winner. The event is rarely questioned even though nearly all of the boys go home disappointed losers. Why is such a practice accepted—indeed publicized? The answer, simply, is that it is symbolic of the ways things are done in virtually all aspects of American life.

An important consequence of this emphasis on the "survival of the fittest" is that some persons take advantage of their fellows to compete "successfully." Perhaps the best recent example is the abuses by high administration officials during the 1972 election campaign (the Watergate break-in, bugging, "laundering of money," taking of illegal contributions from individuals and corporations, use of the Internal Revenue Service to punish enemies, and the "dirty tricks" against political opponents) were done in the cause of a "higher good"—i.e., insuring the reelection of Richard Nixon. Sociologist Amitai Etzioni has captured the essence of this relationship between "success" and illegal means in the following statement:

Truth to be told, the Watergate gang is but an extreme manifestation of a much deeper and more encompassing American malaise, the emphasis on success and frequent disregard for the nature of the means it takes to achieve it. Not only high level administration officials, but many Americans as well, seem to have accepted the late football coach Vince Lombardi's motto, "Winning is not the most important thing, it's the only thing." Thus, the executives of ITT who sought to overthrow the government of Chile to protect their goodies, the Mafia chieftans who push heroin, the recording company executives who bribe their records onto the top-40 list, and the citizens who shrug off corruption in the local town hall as "that's the way the cookie crumbles," all share the same unwholesome attitude. True, the Watergate boys have broken all known American precedents in their violation of fair play, but they are unique chiefly in the magnitude of their crime—not in the basic orientation that underlies it. John Mitchell captured the perverted spirit of Watergate best when he stated that "in view of what the opposition had to offer" (i.e., McGovern), he felt justified in doing anything necessary to secure Nixon's reelection.[21]

In the business world we find theft, fraud, interlocking directorates, and price-fixing are techniques used by some individuals to "get ahead" dishonestly. A related problem, abuse of nature for profit, while not a form of cheating, nevertheless takes advantage of others, while one pursues economic success. The current ecology crisis is caused by individuals, corporations, and communities, which find pollution solutions too expensive. Thus, in looking out for themselves, they ignore the short- and long-range effects on social and biological life. In other words, competition, while a constant spur for individuals and groups to succeed, is also the source of some illegal activities and hence social problems in American society.

Similar scandals are also found in the sports world. The most visible type of illegal activity in sports is illegal recruiting of athletes by colleges and universities. In the quest to succeed (i.e., win), some coaches have felt it necessary to violate NCAA regulations by altering transcripts to insure an athlete's eligibility, allowing substitutes to take admissions tests for athletes of marginal educational ability, paying athletes for nonexistent jobs, illegally using government work-study monies for athletes, and offering money, cars, and clothing to entice athletes to their school.[22]

The valued means to achieve. There are three related highly valued ways to succeed in American society. The first is through hard work. Americans, from the early Puritans to the present day, have elevated persons who were industrious and denigrated those who were not. Most Americans, therefore, assume that poor people deserve to be poor because they are allegedly unwilling to work as hard as persons in the middle and upper classes. This type of explanation places the blame on the victim rather than on the social system that systematically thwarts efforts by the poor. Their hopelessness, brought on by their lack of education, or by their being black, or by their lack of experience, is interpreted as their fault and not as a function of the economic system.

The two remaining valued means to success are continual striving and deferred gratification. Continual striving has meaning for both the successful and the not-so-successful. For the former, one should never be content with what he or she has; there is always more land to own, more money to make, or more books to write. For the poor, continual striving means a never-give-up attitude, a belief that economic success is always possible through hard work, if not for yourself, at least for your children.

Deferred gratification refers to the willingness to deny immediate pleasure for later rewards. The hallmark of the successful person in American society is just such a willingness—to stay in school, to moonlight, or to go to night school. One observer has asserted that the difference between the poor and the nonpoor in this society is whether they are future or present-time oriented.[23] Superficially, this assessment appears accurate, but we would argue that this lack of a future-time orientation among the poor is not a subcultural trait but basically a consequence of their hopeless situation.

Progress. Societies differ in their emphasis on the past, the present, and the future. American society, while giving some attention to each time dimension, stresses the future. Americans neither make the past sacred nor are they content with the present. They place a central value on progress—on a brighter tomorrow, a better job, a bigger home, a move to the suburbs, college education for their children, and on self-improvement.

Americans are not satisfied with the status quo; they want growth (bigger buildings, faster planes, bigger airports, more business moving into the community, bigger profits, and new world's records). They want to change and conquer nature (dam rivers, clear forests, rechannel rivers, seed clouds, and spray insecticides).

Although the implicit belief in progress is that change is good, some things are not to be changed, for they have a sacred quality (the political system, the economic system, American values, and the nation-state). Thus, Americans while valuing technological change, do not favor changing the system (revolution).

The commonly held value of progress has also had a negative effect on contemporary American life. Progress is typically defined to mean either growth or new technology. Every city wants to grow. Chambers of Commerce want more industry and more people (and incidentally more consumers). No industry can afford to keep sales at last year's figures. Everyone agrees that the gross national product (GNP) must increase each year. If all these things are to grow as Americans wish, then concomitant with such growth must be increased population, more products turned out (using natural resources), more electricity, more highways, and more waste. Continued growth will inevitably throw the tight ecological system out of balance since there are but limited supplies of air, water, and places to dump waste materials. Not only are these limited but they diminish as the population increases.

Progress also means a faith in technology. It is commonly believed by Americans that scientific knowledge will solve problems. Scientific breakthroughs and new technology have solved some problems and do aid in saving labor. But often new technology creates problems that were unanticipated.* Although the automobile is of fantastic help to humankind, it has polluted the air, and it kills about 60,000 Americans each year in accidents. It is difficult to imagine life without electricity, but the creation of electricity pollutes the air and causes the thermal pollution of rivers. Insecticides and chemical fertilizers have performed miracles in agriculture but have polluted food and streams (and even "killed" some lakes). Obviously, the slogan of the Du Pont Corporation—"better living through chemistry"—is not entirely correct.

Material progress. An American belief holds that "work pays off." The payoff is not only success in one's profession but also in economic terms—income and the acquisition and consumption of goods and services that go beyond adequate nutrition, medical care,

---

*Sociologists have a term for this phenomenon—**latent functions**—which means, in effect, unintended consequences. The intended consequences of an activity or social arrangement are called **manifest functions**.

shelter, and transportation. The superfluous things that we accumulate or strive to accumulate, such as country club memberships, jewelry, lavish homes, boats, second homes, pool tables, electric toothbrushes, and season tickets to the games of our favorite teams are symbols of success in the competitive struggle. But these have more than symbolic value because they are elements of what Americans consider the "good life" and, therefore, a right.

This emphasis on *having* things has long been a facet of American life. This country, the energy crisis notwithstanding, has always been a land of opportunity and abundance. Although many persons are blocked from full participation in this abundance, the goal for most is to accumulate those things that bring status and that provide for a better way of life by saving labor or enhancing pleasure in our leisure.

Individual freedom. Americans value individualism. They believe that people should generally be free from government interference in their lives and businesses and free to make their own choices. Implied in this value is the responsibility of each individual for his or her own development. The focus on individualism places responsibility on the individual for his or her acts—not on society or its institutions. The individual is blamed for being poor, not the maldistribution of wealth and other socially perpetuated disadvantages that blight many families generation after generation. Blacks are blamed for aggressive behavior, not the limits placed on social mobility for blacks by the social system. Individual students are blamed for dropping out of high school before graduation, not the educational system that fails to meet their needs. This attitude helps to explain the reluctance by persons in authority to provide adequate welfare, health care, and compensatory programs to help the disadvantaged. This common tendency of individuals to focus on the deviant rather than the system that produces deviants has also been true of American social scientists analyzing social problems.

Individual freedom, is, of course, related to capitalism and private property. The economy is supposed to be competitive. Individuals, through their own efforts, business acumen, and luck can (if successful) own property and pyramid profits.

The belief that private property and capitalism are not to be restricted has led to several social problems: (1) unfair competition (monopolies, interlocking directorates, price fixing); (2) a philosophy by many entrepreneurs of *caveat emptor* ("Let the buyer beware"), whereby the aim is profit with total disregard for the welfare of the consumer; and (3) the current ecology crisis, which is due in great measure to the standard policy of many Americans and most corporations to do whatever is profitable—thus a total neglect for conservation of natural resources.

All these practices have forced the federal and state governments to enact and enforce regulatory controls. Clearly, Americans have alway tended to abuse nature and their fellows in the name of profit. Freedom if so abused must by curtailed, and the government (albeit somewhat reluctantly, given the pressures from various interest groups) has done this.

The related values of capitalism, private property, and self-aggrandizement (individualism) have also led to an ecology crisis. Industries fouling the air and water with refuse, farmers spraying pesticides that kill weeds and harm animal and human life, are but two examples of how individual persons and corporations look out for themselves with an almost total disregard for the short- and long-range effects of their actions on life. As long as Americans hold a narrow self-orientation rather than a collectivity orientation this crisis will not only continue but steadily worsen. The use people make of the land (and the water on it or running through it, and the air above it) has traditionally been theirs to decide because of the American belief in private property. This belief in private property has meant, in effect, that individuals have had the right to pave a pasture for a parking lot, tear up a lemon grove for a housing development, put down artificial turf for a football field, dump waste products into the air and water, and so on. Consequently, individual decisions have had the collective effect of taking millions of acres of arable land out of production permanently, polluting the air and water, covering land where vegetation once grew with asphalt, concrete buildings, and astroturf even though green plants are the only source of oxygen.

Values and Behavior

The discrepancy between values and behavior has probably always existed in American society. Inconsistencies have always existed, for example, between the Christian ethic of love, brotherhood, and humanitarianism, on the one hand, and the realities of religious bigotry, the maximization of self-interest, and property rights over human rights on the other. The gap may be widening because of the tremendous rate of social change taking place (the rush toward urbanization, the increased bureaucratization in all spheres of social life). Values do not change as rapidly as do other elements of the culture. Although values often differ from behavior, they remain the criteria for evaluating objects, persons, and events. It is important, however, to mention behaviors that often contradict the values because they demonstrate the hypocrisy prevalent in American society that so often upsets young people (and others) who, in turn, develop countercultures (a topic that we shall cover shortly).

Perhaps most illustrative of the inconsistency between values and behavior is the belief in the American Creed held by most Americans—generally assumed to encompass equality of all persons, freedom of speech and religion, and the guarantees of life, liberty, and prosperity—as against the injustices perpetuated by the system and individuals in the system on members of minority groups.

Americans glorify individualism and self-reliance. These related traits, however, are not found in bureaucracies, where the watchword is, "don't rock the boat." Whyte in his classic *The Organization Man* has noted that bureaucracies are not tolerant of individualists (except at the highest levels). They desire persons who adjust to the wishes of the group. They generally prefer that committees reach decisions, not individuals.[24]

The value placed on "hard work" is still found in many Americans. But for many it has been replaced by a philosophy of "getting by." Unions sometimes enforce a policy of restricted output so as not to embarrass slower (or lazier) workers. Some observers have noted that the current generation, unlike its predecessor, is overrepresented by either: (1) "corner cutters" and "angle players"—persons interested in "easy money"; or (2) persons who value a subsistence existence.

Successful persons in America have always been self-made. They have been the ones who achieved wealth, fame, and power through their own achievements. The value placed on achievement rather than ascription (inherited advantages) began in American history as an antiaristocracy bias. This has changed over time, and now the wealthy are considered successful whether they made the money or not. Americans now tend to give great weight to the opinions expressed by the wealthy, as evidenced by the electorate's tendency to elect them to public office.

Americans have always placed high value on the equality of all persons (in the courts or in getting a job). This value is impossible to reconcile with the racist and superiority theories held by some individuals and groups. It is also impossible to reconcile with many of the formal and informal practices on jobs, in the schools, and in the courts.

Related to the stated belief in equality are the other fundamental beliefs enunciated by the Founding Fathers: the freedoms guaranteed in the Bill of Rights and the Declaration of Independence. Ironically, although the United States was founded by a revolution, the same behavior (called for by the Declaration of Independence) by dissident groups is now squelched (in much the same way as by King George III).

Americans value "law and order." This reverence for the law has been overlooked throughout American history whenever "law-abiding" groups, such as vigilante groups, took the law in their own hands (by threatening that anyone who disobeys vigilante law will be lynched). Currently, the very groups to make the loudest demands for "law and order" are ones who disobey certain laws—for example, southern politicians blocking federal court orders to integrate schools, American Legion posts that notoriously ignore local, state, and federal laws about gambling and liquor, and school administrators allowing prayer in public schools despite the ruling of the Supreme Court.

A final example of disparity between American values and behavior involves the pride Americans have in solving difficult problems. Americans are inclined to be realists. They are pragmatic, down-to-earth problem solvers ready to apply scientific knowledge and expertise to handle such technical problems as getting human beings to and from the moon safely. This realism tends to be replaced by mere gestures, however, when it comes to social problems. Americans have a compulsive tendency to avoid confrontation with chronic social problems. They tend to think that social problems will be solved if one has "nice" thoughts, such as "ban the bomb," "the population problem is everybody's baby," or "black is beautiful." Somehow the verbal level is mistaken for action. If we hear our favorite television personality end the program with a statement against pollution, the problem will somehow be solved.

This is evidenced at another level by proclaiming a "war on poverty," or setting up a commission to study violence, pornography, or civil disorders. Philip Slater has said that the typical American approach to social problems is to decrease their visibility—out of sight, out of mind.

When these discarded problems rise to the surface again—a riot, a protest, an expose in the mass media—we react as if a sewer had backed up. We are shocked, disgusted, and angered. We immediately call for the emergency plumber (the special commission, the crash program) to ensure that the problem is once again removed from consciousness.[25]

The examples just presented make clear that while Americans express some values, they often behave differently. The values do, however, still provide the standards by which individuals are evaluated. These inconsistencies are sometimes important in explaining individual behavior (guilt, shame, aggression), and the emergence of insulating personal and social mechanisms such as compartmentalization and racial segregation.

Not only is there an inconsistency between values and behavior, but there is also a lack of unity among some of the values themselves. Some examples of this phenomenon, which has been called "ethical schizophrenia," are individualism vs. humanitarianism, materialism vs. idealism, and pragmatism vs. utopianism.[26]

Cultural Diversity

Americans are far from unanimous on a number of public issues. Table 5–1 shows this diversity on issues that reflect the American values of capitalism, technological growth, women's rights, equality of opportunity, and individual freedom.

Despite the inconsistencies and ambiguities just noted, Americans do tend to believe in certain things—for example, that democracy is the best form of government; that capitalism is the best economic system; that success can be defined in terms of hard work, initiative, and the amassing of wealth and property; that Christianity should be the country's dominant religion; and that there should be equality of opportunity and equal justice before the law. It is important to note that while these values are held generally by the American populace, there is never total agreement on any of them. The primary reason for this is the tremendous diversity found within the United States.

It is composed of too many people who differ on important social dimensions: age, sex, race, region, social class, ethnicity, religion, rural/urban, and so on. These variables suggest that groups and categories will differ in values and behavior because certain salient social characteristics imply differential experiences and expectations. These will be noted often in the remainder of this book.

Let us examine a few differences held by various groups and categories to illustrate the lack of consistency among Americans. Values are the criteria used to determine, among other things, morality. A Gallup survey asked a national sample in 1980 their opinions on abortion. Table 5–2 breaks down the data by sex, race, age, income, and education. Clearly on this issue Americans differ. The differences are systematic rather than random. The older the person and the lower his or her income or education, the more likely to be anti-abortion.

TABLE 5–1   Diversity of Public Opinion
(percentages)

Issue	Yes	No	No opinion
Favor Equal Rights Amendment	58%	31%	11%
We should have a draft	58	34	8
Women should be drafted	49	47	4
Nuclear plants are safe	30	55	15
There should be a gun control law	31	65	4
Favor wage-price controls	57	34	9
U. S. should permit Cubans to immigrate here	34	57	9
Favor Constitutional amendment permitting prayer in public schools	76	15	9

Source: Gallup Opinion Index, various issues from 1980.

TABLE 5–2   The Legality of Abortion
(percentages)

Question: "Do you think abortions should be legal under any circumstances, legal under only certain circumstances, or illegal in all circumstances?"

	Legal, any circumstances	*Legal, certain circumstances*	*Illegal, all circumstances*	*No opinion*
National	25%	53%	18%	4%
Sex				
Men	24	51	20	5
Women	26	54	16	4
Race				
White	25	55	17	3
Nonwhite	23	42	25	10
Education				
College	35	53	9	3
High school	23	56	17	4
Grade school	13	42	37	8
Age				
Under 30	30	50	16	4
30–49 years	27	54	15	4
50 and older	19	54	22	5
Income				
$25,000 and over	30	57	11	2
$10,000–14,999	24	47	23	6
Under $5,000	22	38	26	14

Source: Gallup Opinion Index, Report No. 178 (June 1980), p. 7.

There are rural–urban differences in American society that are well known. An interesting example is the probability that rural people are more humanitarian, yet more intolerant of deviance among their neighbors than are urban dwellers. But there are variations among rural communities as there are among urban places on these and other differences.

Region of the country accounts for some variation in values held. But the generalizations made about southerners, easterners, and midwesterners, while having some validity, gloss over many real differences. Within any one region there are differences among rural and urban people, among different religious groups, among different ethnic groups, and so on. Perhaps the best study of cultural variation within the United States (and even within one geographical region) was done by Kluckholn and Strodtbeck.[27] These researchers studied five small communities in the same general area in the American southwest—a Mormon settlement, a Texan settlement, a village of Spanish-Americans, a Zuñi reservation, and a Navajo reservation. They found that these groups were quite different with respect to individual versus collective orientation, time dimension, the relationship of human beings to nature, and so on. Because each of these communities differed in their answers to various human dilemmas, their values also differed significantly.

Kluckhohn and Strodtbeck, of course, did not choose American communities at random. They were very selective, hoping to demonstrate the existence of real cultural

METHODS PANEL

Panel 5-3
Participant Observation

A common method of data collection is the direct observation of social phenomena in natural settings. One way to accomplish this is for the researcher to become part of what he or she is studying. There are several roles that observers may
take in this regard. One is to hide the fact that one is a researcher and participate
as a member of the group being studied. Another is to let the subjects know that
you are a scientist but remain separate and detached from the group. A third option is to identify oneself as a researcher and become friends with those being studied. Each of these alternatives has its problems, such as the ethics of deceiving subjects and the fundamental problem of subjects altering their behavior if they know
they are being investigated.

Elliot Liebow—a white, Jewish, and middle-class researcher—investigated the
subculture of poor black males in one section of the Washington, D.C. ghetto.*

differences within the United States. What they found were four subcultures (all but the
Texas community) within one geographical region within the border of the United States.

The concept, **subculture**, has been defined typically as a relatively cohesive cultural
system that varies in form and substance from the dominant culture. Under the rubric
"subculture," then, there are ethnic groups, delinquent gangs, and religious sects. Milton
Yinger has proposed that the concept "subculture" be defined more precisely. He has
suggested that it be used for one type of group and "contraculture" for another type that
had been previously called a subculture.[28] For Yinger the concept "subculture" should be
limited to relatively cohesive cultural systems that differ from the dominant culture in such
things as language, values, religion, and style of life. Typically, a group that is a subculture
differs from the larger group because it has immigrated from another society and because
of physical or social isolation has not been fully assimilated. The cultural differences, then,
are usually based on ethnicity. Tradition keeps the culture of this group somewhat unique
from the dominant culture. There are a number of examples of such subcultures in the
United States—the Amish, the Hutterites, some Orthodox Jewish sects, many Indian
tribes, Appalachian snake handlers, and Poles, Croatians, Hungarians, Italians, Greeks,
and Irish groups at one time or another in American history. The existence of numerous
subcultures within the United States explains much of the lack of consistency with respect
to American values.

A **contraculture**, as defined by Yinger, is a culturally homogeneous group that has
developed values and norms that differ from the larger society because the group opposes
the larger society. This type of group is in conflict with the dominant culture. The
particular values and norms can only be understood by reference to the dominant group.

The values held by delinquent gangs are commonly believed to be a reaction against the
values held by the larger society (and hence would represent a contraculture). Albert K.

From the beginning Liebow identified himelf as a researcher. He became deeply involved with his subjects. He partied with them, visited in their homes, gave them legal advice, and just generally "hung around" with them in their leisure hours. As the research progressed he became more and more a part of the streetcorner life he was investigating. As a white, though, he never escaped completely being an outsider.

At first Liebow's field notes concentrated on individuals: what they said, what they did, and the contexts in which they said or did them. Through this beginning he ultimately saw the patterns of behavior and how the subjects perceived and understood themselves. He was able to understand the social structure of streetcorner life. More important, his research enabled him to see the complexity of the social network of society's "losers" and how they continuously slip back and forth between the values and beliefs of the larger society and those of their own social system.

Tally's Corner (Boston: Little, Brown, 1967).

Cohen has noted, for example, that lower-class juvenile gangs not only reject the dominant value system but they exalt the exact opposite values.[19] These boys, Cohen argues, are ill-equipped because of their lower-class origins and other related drawbacks to be successful in the game as it is defined by the dominant society. They, therefore, repudiate the commonly held values for a new set that have meaning for them and under which they can perform satisfactorily. These values differ from the values of the larger culture because the delinquents actually want the larger values but cannot attain them. If Cohen's thesis is correct, then delinquent gangs indeed form a contraculture (although Cohen specifically names them subcultures).

SUMMARY

Culture, the knowledge that the members of a collectivity share, is the product of sustained interaction. At the societal level people create language and other symbols, norms, values, technical knowledge, and belief systems and pass them from generation to generation through socialization. (The process of socialization is the topic of the following chapter.) This human creation is a powerful determinant of people's subsequent behavior. It shapes their thoughts and perceptions. It guides their choices by providing the criteria for evaluation. It includes societal rules. In many ways culture provides the script for social life. Violating this script invites social ostracism, the label of mental illness, or even prison (see Chapters 8 and 9).

The second part of this chapter focused on American values. Values are the culturally prescribed criteria by which individuals evaluate persons, behavior, objects, and ideas as to their relative morality, desirability, merit, or correctness. Although there is not complete agreement on American values because of the diversity present in American society, there are some dominant value orientations that make Americans unique. These are success through individual achievement, competition, hard work, continual striving, and deferred gratification. Other American values are progress, materialism, and individual freedom.

These values are sources of both societal integration and social problems. Order theorists assume that sharing values solves the most fundamental problem of societal integration. The values are symbolic representations of the existing society and therefore promote unity and consensus among Americans. They must, therefore, be preserved.

Conflict theorists, on the other hand, view the mass acceptance of values as a form of cultural tyranny that promotes political conservatism, inhibits creativity, and gets people to accept their lot because they believe in the system rather than joining with others to try and change it. Thus, conflict theorists believe that slavish devotion to society's values inhibits necessary social change. Moreover, American values are assumed by conflict theorists to be the actual source of social problems such as crime, conspicuous consumption, planned obsolescence, the energy crises, pollution, and the artificial creation of winners and losers.

Regardless of which side one may take on the consequences of American values, most would agree that the traditional values of individual freedom, capitalism, competition, and progress have made America relatively affluent. The future, however, will very likely be very different from the past, requiring a fundamental change in these values. The future of slow growth or no growth, lower levels of affluence, and resource shortages will require that Americans adapt by adopting values that support cooperation rather than competition, that support group goals over individual goals, and a mode of "making do" rather than the purchasing of unnecessary products and the relentless search for technological solutions.

CHAPTER REVIEW

1. Culture, the knowledge the members of society or other social organizations share, constrains behavior and how people think about and interpret their world.

2. Culture emerges as a result of continued social interaction.

3. Culture is learned behavior. The process of learning the culture is called socialization.

4. Through the socialization process, individuals internalize the culture. Thus the control that culture has over individuals is seen as natural.

5. Culture channels behavior by providing the rules for behavior and the criteria for judging.

6. Culture is boundary maintaining. One's own culture seems right and natural. Other cultures are considered inferior, wrong, or immoral. This tendency to consider the ways of one's own group superior is called ethnocentrism.

7. Six types of shared knowledge constitute the culture—symbols, technology, ideologies, norms, values, and roles.

8. Norms are divided into two types by degree of importance and severity of punishment for their violation. Folkways are less important while the mores are considered more vital and thereby more severely punished if violated.

9. Roles are the behavioral expectations of those who occupy the statuses in a social organization.

10. Through language and other symbols culture determines how the members of a society will interpret their environment. The important

point is that through this "construction of reality" the members of a society make sense out of a world that has no inherent meaning.

11. The variety of customs found throughout the world is staggering. The members of one society typically view the customs found elsewhere as weird, cruel, and immoral. If we understand the cultural context of a given society, however, their practices generally make sense. This is called cultural relativity.

12. Knowing the values (the criteria for evaluating) of a society is an excellent way of understanding that society.

13. American values are the result of three major factors: (a) geographical isolation and being blessed with abundant resources; (b) founding of the nation in opposition to tyranny and aristocracy and supporting freedom, democracy, equality, and impersonal justice; and (c) a religious heritage based on the Judeo-Christian ethic and the Protestant work ethic.

14. The dominant American values are: success through individual achievement, competition, hard work, progress through growth and new technology, material progress, and individual freedom.

15. These American values are the sources of societal integration as well as social problems.

16. Despite the power of culture and American values over individual conduct, the diversity present in American society means that for many there are inconsistencies between values and actual behavior. There are clear variations in how Americans feel on public issues based on their different social situations.

17. A major source of cultural variation in the United States is the existence of subcultures. Because of different religions and ethnicity some groups retain a culture different from the dominant one. Other groups form a culture because they oppose the larger society. The latter are called contracultures.

FOR FURTHER STUDY

Culture: General

Ruth Benedict, *Patterns of Culture* (Baltimore, Md.: Penguin, 1946).

Peter L. Berger and Thomas Luckman, *The Social Construction of Reality* (Garden City, N.Y.: Doubleday (Anchor Books), 1967).

Marvin Harris, *Cows, Pigs, Wars, and Witches: The Riddles of Culture* (New York: Random House (Vintage Books), 1974).

American Values

Florence Kluckhohn and Fred L. Strodtbeck, *Variations in Value Orientations* (New York: Harper & Row, 1961).

Philip Slater, *Wealth Addiction* (New York: E. P. Dutton, 1980).

Robin Williams, *American Society: A Sociological Interpretation*, Third Edition (New York: Alfred A. Knopf, 1970).

Subcultures

Elliot Liebow, *Tally's Corner* (Boston: Little, Brown, 1967).

Rosabeth M. Kanter, *Commitment and Community: Communes and Utopias in Sociological Perspective* (Cambridge, Mass.: Harvard University Press, 1972).

William M. Kephart, *Extraordinary Groups: The Sociology of Unconventional Life-Styles* (New York: St. Martin's Press, 1976).

NOTES AND REFERENCES

1. Peter L. Berger, *Invitation to Sociology* (Garden City, N.Y.: Doubleday (Anchor Books), 1963), p. 98. See also R. P. Cuzzort, *Humanity and Modern Sociological Thought* (New York: Holt, Rinehart and Winston, 1969), pp. 203–204.

2. Berger, *Invitation to Sociology*, p. 93.

3. Marvin E. Olsen, *The Process of Social Organization* (New York: Holt, Rinehart and Winston, 1968), p. 60; and Gerhard Lenski, *Human Societies: A Macrolevel Introduction to Sociology* (New York: McGraw-Hill, 1970), pp. 37–38.

4. See Harold Garfinkel, *Studies in Ethnomethodology* (Englewood Cliffs, N.J.: Prentice-Hall, 1967).

5. See Peter L. Berger and Thomas Luckman, *The Social Construction of Reality* (Garden City, New York: Doubleday (Anchor Books), 1967).

6. John B. Carroll (ed.), *Language, Thought, and Reality: Selected Writings of Benjamin Lee Whorf* (Cambridge, Mass.: MIT Press, 1956).

7. Norris and Ross McWhirter, *Guinness Book of World Records*, 11th ed. (New York: Sterling, 1972), p. 167.

8. J. Bronowski, *The Common Sense of Science* (Cambridge, Mass.: Harvard University Press, 1978), p. 21.

9. Thomas Szasz, *Ceremonial Chemistry* (Garden City, N.Y.: Doubleday (Anchor Books), 1974), p. 17.

10. This insight comes from my colleague Ronny Turner, Colorado State University.

11. Charles Edgley and Ronny E. Turner, "Masks and Social Relations," *Humboldt Journal of Social Relations* 3 (Fall/Winter 1975), p. 6.

12. Harvey Farberman and Eric Goode, *Social Reality* (Englewood Cliffs, N.J.: Prentice-Hall, 1973), p. 2.

13. Marvin Harris, *Cows, Pigs, Wars, and Witches: The Riddles of Culture* (New York: Random House (Vintage Books), 1975), pp. 11–32.

14. Ibid., p. 21.

15. Marvin Harris, "India's Sacred Cow," *Human Nature* 1 (February, 1978), p. 36.

16. Robin M. Williams, *American Society: A Sociological Interpretation*, 3rd ed. (New York: Alfred A. Knopf, 1970), pp. 444–446.

17. See especially the insights of Max Weber, *The Protestant Ethic and the Spirit of Capitalism*, Talcott Parsons (trans.), (New York: Scribner's, 1958). This work was first published in 1904.

18. Williams, *American Society*, p. 451.

19. Much of the following material is taken from D. Stanley Eitzen and George H. Sage, *Sociology of American Sport*, 2nd ed. (Dubuque, Iowa: Wm. C. Brown, 1982), chapter 3.

20. Williams, *American Society*, pp. 454–455.

21. Amitai Etzioni, "After Watergate—What?: A Social Science Perspective," *Human Behavior* 2 (November 1973), p. 7.

22. See George H. Hanford, "Controversies in College Sports," *The Annals* 445 (September 1979), pp. 66–79; and John Underwood, "The Writing is on the Wall," *Sports Illustrated* (May 19, 1980), pp. 36–72.

23. Edward C. Banfield, *The Unheavenly City Revisited* (Boston: Little, Brown, 1974).

24. William H. Whyte, Jr., *The Organization Man* (Garden City, N.Y.: Doubleday (Anchor Books), 1956), p. 150.

25. Philip Slater, *The Pursuit of Loneliness: American Culture at the Breaking Point* (Boston: Beacon, 1970), p. 15.

26. Jane C. Record and Wilson Record, "Ideological Forces and the Negro Protest," *The Annals* 357 (January, 1965), pp. 89–96.

27. Florence Kluckhohn and Fred L. Strodtbeck, *Variations in Value Orientation* (New York: Harper & Row, 1961).

28. J. Milton Yinger, "Contraculture and Subculture," *American Sociological Review* 25 (October, 1962), pp. 625–635. The following discussion relies principally upon this article.

29. Albert K. Cohen, *Delinquent Boys: The Culture of the Gang* (Glencoe, Ill.: Free Press, 1955).

6

Socialization

Oscar Stohr and Jack Yufe are identical twins separated as babies by their parents' divorce. Oscar was raised by his maternal grandmother in the Sudetenland of Czechoslovakia. He was a strict Catholic. As a loyal Nazi, he hated Jews. His brother, Jack, was raised by his Jewish father in Trinidad. During World War II he was loyal to the British and hated the Germans.

The twins were united briefly in 1954, but Jack was warned by the translator to not tell his brother that he was Jewish. In 1979, at age 47, the brothers were reunited by scientists who wished to establish the degree to which environment shapes human behavior. Because they had the same genes, any differences between the brothers must result from how they were raised.

The scientists found not only that they were physically alike but that the twins were strikingly similar in temperament, tastes, tempo, and the way that they did things. Both had been excellent athletes. Both had had trouble in school with mathematics. But the twins also differed in many important respects. Jack is a workaholic, while Oscar enjoys his leisure time. Jack is a political liberal while Oscar is a traditionalist. This difference is seen in Jack's tolerance of feminism and Oscar's resistance to that movement. Jack is proud of being Jewish while Oscar never mentions his Jewish heritage.

In this chapter we will examine this process of socialization that is so powerful in shaping human thought and behavior as to make identical twins different.

Every day a horde of savages appears on the scene in American society. How do these savages become members of society? How do they lose their "savageness"? How do they become "human"? The answer to these questions is that they learn to be human by acquiring the meanings, ideas, and actions appropriate for that society. This process of learning the culture is called **socialization**.*

Children are born with the limits and potential established by their unique genetic compositions. Their physical features, size and shape, rate of physical development, and even temperament will unfold within predetermined boundaries. The limits of their intellectual capabilities are also influenced by biological heritage. But, while children are biologically human, they do not have the instincts or the innate drives that will make them human. They acquire their "humanness" through social interaction. Their concepts of

---

*That this chapter focuses on how children learn the culture should *not* be interpreted to mean that the socialization process stops at the end of adolescence. To the contrary, socialization is a lifelong process and occurs in all social groups, not just the society.

themselves, personality, conception of love, freedom, justice, right and wrong, and interpretation of reality are all products of social interaction. In other words, human beings are essentially the social creations of society.

Evidence for this assertion is found by examining the traits and behaviors of children raised without much human contact. There have been occasional accounts of **feral** children throughout history. These are children believed to have been raised by animals. When found, they look human but act like the animals with whom they have had contact. A recent case involved a Tarzan-like child reported to have been raised by monkeys in the jungles of central Africa. The boy was discovered in 1974 at about the age of six with a troop of gray monkeys. Two years later after painstaking efforts to "rehabilitate" him, he remained more monkey than human. "He is unable to talk and communicates by 'monkey' grunts and chattering. He will eat only fruit and vegetables, and when excited or scared jumps up and down uttering threatening monkey cries."[1] If a child's personality were largely determined by biological heritage, this child would have been much more human than simian. But, there is a consistent finding in all cases of feral children—they are not normal. They cannot talk and have great difficulty in learning human speech patterns. They do not walk or eat like human beings. They express anger differently. In essence, the behavior that arises in the absence of human contact is not what we associate with human beings.

The most famous case of a child who was raised with only minimal human contact was a girl named Anna.[2] Anna was an illegitimate child. Her grandfather refused to acknowledge her existence, and to escape his ire, the mother put her in an attic room and, except for minimal feeding, ignored her. Anna was discovered by a social worker at about age six and she was placed in a special school. When found, Anna could not sit up or walk. She could not talk and was believed to be deaf. She was immobile and completely indifferent to those around her. Staff members worked with Anna (during one year a single staff member had to receive medical attention more than a dozen times for bites she received from Anna[3]), and eventually Anna learned to take care of herself, walk, talk, and play with other children.

By the time Anna died of hemorrhagic jaundice approximately four and a half years [after she was found], she had made considerable progress as compared with her condition when found. She could follow directions, string beads, identify a few colors, build with blocks, and differentiate between attractive and unattractive pictures. She had a good sense of rhythm and loved a doll. She talked mainly in phrases but would repeat words and try to carry on a conversation. She was clean about clothing. She habitually washed her hands and brushed her teeth. She would try to help other children. She walked well and could run fairly well, though clumsily. Although easily excited, she had a pleasant disposition. Her involvement showed that socialization, even when started at the late age of six, could still do a great deal toward making her a person. Even though her development was no more than that of a normal child of two or three years, she had made noteworthy progress.[4]

The conclusion from those who had observed Anna and other cases of isolated children is that being deprived of social interaction during one's formative years deprives individuals of their humanness.

The second essential to socialization is language. Language is the vehicle through which socialization occurs. In Anna's case, what little human contact she had during her first six years was physical and not communicative interaction. As Kingsley Davis has noted, Anna's case illustrates "that communicative contact is the core of socialization."[5] This principle is also illustrated by Helen Keller. This remarkable person became deaf and blind as a result of illness during infancy. She was locked into her own world until her teacher, Anne Sullivan, was able to communicate to her that the symbol she traced on Helen's hand represented water. That was the beginning of language for Helen Keller and the beginning of her understanding of who she was and the meaning of the world and society in which she was immersed.[6]

Learning language has profound effects on how individuals think and perceive. Through their languages societies differ in the way they conceive of time, space, distance, velocity, action, and specificity. To illustrate this last dimension—specificity—let's consider the Navajo language. With respect to rain, the Navajo make much finer distinctions than the English who generally leave it to: "It has started to rain;" "It is raining;" and "It has stopped raining." When the Navajo reports his or her experiences

he uses one verb form if he himself is aware of the actual inception of the rain storm, another if he has reason to believe that the rain has been falling for some time in his locality before the occurrence struck his attention. One form must be employed if rain is general round about within the range of vision; another if, though it is raining about, the storm is plainly on the move. Similarly, the Navaho must invariably distinguish between the ceasing of rainfall (generally) and the stopping of rain in a particular vicinity because the rain clouds have been driven off by the wind. The [Navaho] people take the consistent noticing and reporting of such differences . . . as much for granted as the rising of the sun.[7]

In short, the languages of different societies are not parallel methods for expressing the same reality. Our perception of reality depends on our language. In this way experience itself is a function of language. As the distinguished linguist B. L. Whorf has put it: ". . . no individual is free to describe nature with absolute impartiality but is constrained to certain modes of interpretation even while he thinks himself most free."[8]

In learning language we discover the meaning of symbols not only for words but also for objects, such as the cross, the flag, and traffic lights. Through language we can think about the past and the future. Language symbolizes the values and norms of the society, thus enabling the user to label and evaluate objects, acts, individuals, and groups. The words we use in such instances can be positive, such as beautiful, wise, moral, friend, and appropriate, or negative, such as ugly, dumb, immoral, enemy, or inappropriate. Moreover, the description of the same act can portray a positive or a pejorative image. This can be seen in the sports world, as reported by syndicated columnist Jim Murray:

"On our side, a guy is 'colorful.' On their side, a 'hotdog'."

"Our team is 'resourceful.' Theirs is 'lucky'."

"Our guys are 'trusted associates.' Theirs are 'henchmen'."

"Our team gives rewards. Theirs, bribes."

"Our team plays 'spirited' football. Theirs plays dirty."

"Our team is 'opportunistic.' Theirs gets all the breaks."

"Our guy is 'confident.' Theirs is an egotist."[9]

Thus, language is a powerful labeling tool, clearly delineating who is "in" and who is "out." Finally, children learn who they are by using words to describe themselves. The words they use are those that others, in turn, have used in talking about them and their actions.

THE PERSONALITY AS A SOCIAL PRODUCT

In Chapter 2, we noted the dialectic character of society. Society is at once a product of social interaction, yet that product continuously acts back on its producers. As Berger has put it, "Society is a product of man. . . . Yet it may also be stated that man is a product of society."[10] In this section, the emphasis will be on this second process—human beings as a product of society. In particular, we shall examine the emergence of the human personality as a social product.

We develop a sense of self (our personality) in interaction with others. Newly born infants have no sense of self-awareness. They are unable to distinguish between themselves and their surroundings. They cry spontaneously when uncomfortable. They eventually become aware that crying can be controlled and that its use can bring a response from others. In time, and especially with the employment of language, the child begins to distinguish between "I" and "you" and "mine" and "yours"—signs of self-awareness. But this is just the beginning of the personality-formation process. Let us look now at several classical theories of how children develop personalities and how they learn what is expected of them in the community and society.

Charles H. Cooley: The Looking-Glass Self

Cooley (1864–1929) believed that children's conceptions of themselves arise through interaction with others.[11] He used the metaphor of a looking glass to convey the idea that all persons understand themselves through the way in which others act toward them. They judge themselves on how they think others judge them. Cooley believed that each of us imagines how we look to others and what their judgment of us is. Bierstedt has summarized this process: "I am not what I think I am and I am not what you think I am. I am what I think you think I am."[12]

The critical process in Cooley's theory of personality development, then, is the feedback the individual receives from others. Others behave in particular ways with regard to an individual. The individual interprets these behaviors positively or negatively. When the behaviors of others are perceived as consistent the individual accepts this definition of self, which in turn has consequences for his or her behavior. In sum, there is a self-fulfilling prophecy—the individual is as defined by others. Suppose, for example, that whenever you entered a room and approached a small knot of people conversing with each other, they promptly melted away with lame excuses. Clearly, this experience, repeated many times, would affect your feelings about yourself. Or, if wherever you appeared, a conversational group quickly formed around you, would not such attention tend to give you self-confidence and ego strength?

Cooley's insight that our self-concepts are a product of how others react to us is important in understanding behavior. Why are some categories of persons more likely to be school dropouts or criminals or malcontents or depressed while others fit in? As we will see in Chapter 9, deviance is the result of the successful application of a social label, a process akin to the "looking-glass self." So, too, does this concept help us to understand the tendency of minority-group members to have low self-esteem. If black children, for example, receive a consistent message from whites that they are inferior, that they are incapable of success in intellectually demanding tasks, and that they are not trustworthy, the probability is that they will have these traits. Many black children and adults fulfill this prophecy, thereby reinforcing the stereotypes of the majority and the low self-esteem of the blacks.

George Herbert Mead:
Taking the Role of the Other

Mead (1863–1931) theorized about the relationship of self and society.[13] In essence, he believed that children find out who they are as they learn about society and society's expectations. This occurs in several important stages. Infants learn to distinguish between themselves and others from the actions of their parents. By the age of two or so, children have become self-conscious. By this Mead meant that the children are able to react to themselves as others will react to them. For example, they will tell themselves "No-No," as they have been told many times by their parents, and not touch the hot stove. The importance of this stage is that the children have internalized the feelings of others. What others expect has become a part of them. They have become conscious of themselves by incorporating the way others are conscious of them.

The next stage is the play stage. Children from age four to seven spend many hours a day in a world of play. Much of this time is spent in pretending to be mothers, teachers, doctors, policemen, ministers, grocers, and other roles. Mead called this form of play "taking the role of the other." As children play at a variety of social roles, they act out the behavior associated with these social positions and thus develop a rudimentary understanding of adult roles and why people in those positions act the way they do. They also see how persons in these roles interact with children. Thus, children learn to look at themselves as others see them. As McGee has put it, "he learns who he is by 'being' who he is not."[14] The play stage, then, accomplishes two things. It provides further clues for children as to who they are and it prepares them for later life.

The game stage occurs at about age eight and is the final stage of personality development in Mead's scheme. In the play stage the children's activities were fluid and spontaneous. The game stage, in contrast, involves activities that are structured. There are rules that define, limit, and constrain the participants. Mead used the game of baseball to illustrate what occurs in the game stage. In baseball children must understand and abide by the rules. They must also understand the entire game—that is, when playing second base what they and the other players must do if there is a player on first, one out, and the batter bunts down the first base line. In other words, the various individuals in a game must know the role of all the players and adjust their behavior to that of the others. The assessment of the entire situation is what Mead called the discovery of the "generalized other." In the play stage, children learned what was expected of them by "significant others" (parents, relatives, teachers). The game stage provides children with constraints from many others, including people they do not know. In this way children incorporate and understand the pressures of society. By passing through these stages children have finally developed a social life from the expectations of parents, friends, and society.

Sigmund Freud: The Psychoanalytic View

Freud (1856–1939) emphasized the biological dimension along with social factors in personality development.[15] For Freud, the infant's first years are totally egocentric, with all energies directed toward pleasure. This is an expression of a primitive biological force—the **id**—that dominates the infant. The id, although a force throughout life, is gradually stifled by society. Parents, as the agents of society, hamper children's pleasure seeking by imposing schedules for eating, punishing them for messy behavior and masturbation, forcing them to control their bowels, and the like.

The process of socialization is, in Freud's view, the process of society controlling the id. Through this process children develop egos. The **ego** is the rational part of the personality that controls the id's basic urges, finding realistic ways of satisfying these biological cravings. The individual also develops a superego (conscience) which regulates both the id and ego. The **superego** is the consequence of the child's internalizing the parents' morals. A strong superego represses the id and channels behavior in socially acceptable ways.

Freud presents a view of socialization that differs significantly from the theories of Mead and Cooley. Whereas Mead and Cooley saw the socialization process as a complete and nonconflictual one, Freud believed the process to be incomplete and accomplished by force. Freud saw the person pulled by two contradictory forces—the natural impulses of biology and the constraints of society—resulting in the imperfection and discontent of human beings. Mead and Cooley, in contrast, did not view the child as one who is repressed, led kicking and screaming into adulthood. For Mead the child passed through natural stages as a willing apprentice to become a conforming member of society. Thus, Mead's conception of the socialization process is deterministic—the individual is a creature of society. Freud's view is quite different.

To Freud man is a *social* animal without being entirely a *socialized* animal. His very social nature is the source of conflicts and antagonisms that create resistance to socialization by the norms of any of the societies which have existed in the course of human history.[16]

Society's Socialization Agents

Two themes stand out in this section. First, the personality of the child is, to a large degree, socially created and sustained. Second, through the process of socialization, the child internalizes the norms and values of society. In a sense, the child learns a script for acting, feeling, and thinking that is in tune with the wishes of society. Before we leave this topic, let us look briefly at the special transmitters of the cultural patterns—the family, the schools, and the media.

The family. Aside from the obvious function of providing the child with the physical needs of food, clothing, and shelter, the family is the primary agent of socialization. The family will indoctrinate the child in the ways of society. The parents equip the child with the information, etiquette, norms, and values necessary for the functioning member of society. Parents in blatant and subtle ways emit messages of what is important, appropriate, moral, beautiful, correct, and what is not. There is no option for young children. They must accept the messages of their parents of what is and what ought to be. As Everett Wilson has put it:

But when he [the child] enters the human group, he is quite at the mercy of parents and siblings. They determine both what and when he shall eat and wear, when he shall sleep and wake, what he shall think and feel, how he shall express his thoughts and feelings (what language he shall speak and how he shall do it), what his political and religious commitments shall be, what sort of vocation he shall aspire to. Not that parents are ogres. They give what they have to give: their own limited knowledge, their prejudices and passions. There is no alternative to this giving of themselves; nor for the receiver is there any option. Neither can withhold the messages conveyed to the other.[17]

Thus, children learn from their parents. They learn from them the meaning of physical objects such as the Bible, poison, and the police officer's badge. They also learn the relative worth of social groups such as Jews or blacks. Panel 6–1 provides an example of how one southern white girl was raised to hate blacks.

The schools. The schools perform several vital functions for the maintenance of the prevailing social, political, and economic order. Education, along with the institutions of the family and religion, has a primary responsibility for the socialization of newcomers to the society. A second function of education is the shaping of personalities so that they are

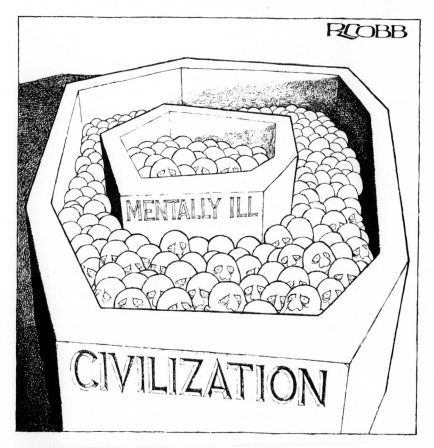

© 1975 Ron Cobb. All rights reserved. From *The Cobb Book*, Wild & Woolley, Sydney, Australia.

in basic congruence with the demands of the culture. In other words, one goal of the educational system of any society is to produce people with desired personality traits (for example, competitiveness, altruism, bravery, conformity, or industriousness, depending upon the culture of the society). A third function is to prepare individuals for their adult roles. In American society this means the preparation of individuals for the specialized roles of a highly complex division of labor. It also means the preparation of youngsters for life in a rapidly changing world. In early American history the primary aims of schooling

Panel 6-1
The Teaching of Prejudice

A southern child's basic lessons were woven of such dissonant strands as these; sometimes the threads tangled into a terrifying mess; sometimes archaic, startling designs would appear in the weaving; sometimes, a design was left broken while another was completed with minute care. Bewildered teachers, bewildered pupils in home and on the street, driven by an invisible Authority, learned their lessons:

The mother who taught me what I know of tenderness and love and compassion taught me also the bleak rituals of keeping Negroes in their "place." The father who rebuked me for an air of superiority toward schoolmates from the mill and rounded out his rebuke by gravely reminding me that "all men are brothers," trained me in the steel-rigid decorums I must demand of every colored male. They who so gravely taught me to split my body from my mind and both from my "soul," taught me also to split my conscience from my acts and Christianity from southern tradition.

Neither the Negro nor sex was often discussed at length in our home. We were given no formal instruction in these difficult matters but we learned our lessons well. We learned the intricate system of taboos, of renunciations and compensations, of manners, voice modulations, words, feelings, along with our prayers, our toilet habits, and our games. I do not remember how or when, but by the time I had learned that God is love, that Jesus is His Son and came to give us more abundant life, that all men are brothers with a common Father, I also knew that I was better than a Negro, that all black folks have their place and must be kept in it, that sex has its place and must be kept in it, that a terrifying disaster would befall the South if ever I treated a Negro as my social equal and as terrifying a disaster would befall my family if ever I were to have a baby outside of marriage. I had learned that God so loved the world that He gave His only begotten Son so that we might have segregated churches in which it was my duty to worship each Sunday and on Wednesday at evening prayers. I had learned that white southerners are a hospitable, courteous, tactful people who treat those of their own group with consideration and who carefully segregate from all the richness of life "for their own good and welfare" thirteen million people whose skin is colored a little differently from my own.

I knew by the time I was twelve that a member of my family would always shake hands with old Negro friends, would speak graciously to members of the Negro race unless they forgot their place, in which event icy peremptory tones would draw lines beyond which only the desperate would dare take one step. I knew that to use the word "nigger" was unpardonable and no well-bred southerner

were teaching the basics of reading, writing, spelling, and arithmetic. These were needed to read the Bible, write correspondence, and do simple accounting—the required skills for adults in an agrarian society. Modern society, on the other hand, demands people with specialized occupational skills, with expertise in narrow areas. The educational system is saddled with providing these skills in addition to the basics. Moreover, the schools have taken over the teaching of citizenship skills, cooking, sewing, and even sex education, skills and knowledge that were once the explicit duty of each family to transmit to its offspring.

was quite so crude as to do so; nor would a well-bred southerner call a Negro "mister" or invite him into the living room or eat with him or sit by him in public places.

I knew that my old nurse who had cared for me through long months of illness, who had given me refuge when a little sister took my place as the baby of the family, who soothed, fed me, delighted me with her stories and games, let me fall asleep on her deep warm breast, was not worthy of the passionate love I felt for her but must be given instead a half-smiled-at affection similar to that which one feels for one's dog. I knew but I never believed it, that the deep respect I felt for her, the tenderness, the love, was a childish thing which every normal child outgrows, that such love begins with one's toys and is discarded with them, and that somehow—though it seemed impossible to my agonized heart—I too, must outgrow these feelings. I learned to use a soft voice to oil my words of superiority. I learned to cheapen with tears and sentimental talk of "my old mammy" one of the profound relationships of my life. I learned the bitterest thing a child can learn: that the human relations I valued most were held cheap by the world I lived in.

From the day I was born, I began to learn my lessons. I was put in a rigid frame too intricate, too twisting to describe here so briefly, but I learned to conform to its slide-rule measurements. I learned it is possible to be a Christian and a white southerner simultaneously; to be a gentlewoman and an arrogant callous creature in the same moment; to pray at night and ride a Jim Crow car the next morning and to feel comfortable in doing both. I learned to believe in freedom, to glow when the word *democracy* was used, and to practice slavery from morning to night. I learned it the way all of my southern people learn it; by closing door after door until one's mind and heart and conscience are blocked off from each other and from reality.

I closed the doors. Or perhaps they were closed for me. One day they began to open again. Why I had the desire or the strength to open them, or what strange accident or circumstance opened them for me would require in the answering an account too long, too particular, too stark to make here. And perhaps I should not have the wisdom that such an analysis would demand of me, nor the will to make it. I know only that the doors opened, a little; that somewhere along that iron corridor we travel from babyhood to maturity, doors swinging inward began to swing outward, showing glimpses of the world beyond, of that bright thing we call "reality."

Source: Excerpted from Lillian Smith, *Killers of the Dream* (New York: Norton, 1949), pp. 17-19. By permission of W. W. Norton & Company, Inc. Copyright © 1949, 1961 by Lillian Smith.

Contemporary schools go beyond these functions, however. They exist to meet the needs of the economy by providing employers with a disciplined and skilled labor force and a means to control individuals in order to maintain political stability. To understand these points, let's review the changing role of the school in American history.[18]

When most Americans were farmers and artisans, the schools had a relatively simple task because the skills society required were essentially unchanged from generation to generation and were learned generally at home. As the economy changed to a factory system in urban settings, the family became less important as an agent of economic socialization, and the school grew in importance. Work became specialized, technology changed rapidly, and work was done in large organizations with rigid authority structures. The workers were no longer in control of their own labor but were controlled by the owners of the factories. Thus, workers were placed in potentially oppressive and alienating work situations. This was a concern to capitalists because the workers might unite to

SOCIAL DILEMMAS AND CRITICAL CHOICES

Panel 6–2
What is the Purpose of Education?

What is the purpose of education? The typical answer to this question is that the task of formal education is to preserve the culture by passing it on to the new-comers of society. This is traditionally done by teaching the accumulated wisdom of the past. This has often meant, in effect, that the schools have taught dogma, insisting that certain ideas and practices are considered correct, perhaps even sacred (nationalism, capitalism, Christianity, monogamy), while other ideas and practices are believed to be wrong and even immoral.

In the late 1960s a social science curriculum for grade-school children was devel-oped by the National Science Foundation that had a different purpose. This cur-riculum, known by the acronym MACOS (Man: A Course of Study), was de-signed to acquaint children with what makes us human (by contrasting us with other animals) and with the alternative ways human beings have adapted to their environment. About one half of the course is devoted to an in-depth study of the Netsilik Eskimos. This society is composed of people living in the harshest of phys-ical environments. They have adapted by being unusually inventive and coopera-tive. Most important, they have customs very different from those found in the United States. Some of these are senilicide, infanticide (especially of first-born daughters), trial marriage, wife swapping, and occasional cannibalism.

By 1976, some 1700 schools throughout the United States had adopted the MACOS curriculum. There has been a considerable amount of controversy in many of these schools generated by the concerns of many parents and conservative political and religious organizations. The fundamental issues raised by these critics are that: (1) children are exposed to alternatives rather than indoctrinated with our ways; (2) this may lead children to question America's cherished values; (3) child-ren will be tolerant of practices that we consider deviant; (4) children would implic-itly receive the message that there are no moral absolutes, leading to the adoption

challenge the existing system. Stability was also threatened by the rising numbers of immigrants who entered the United States to live in urban centers and work in factories.

According to radical educational historians, mass public education was perceived by those in power as the answer to these problems in a changing society since the church and family were no longer effective in teaching the skills and uniformity in belief necessary for an effective and tractable work force.

An ideal preparation for factory work was found in the social relations of the school: specifically, in its emphasis on discipline, punctuality, acceptance of authority outside the family, and individual accountability for one's work. The social relations of the school would replicate the social relations of the workplace, and thus help young people adapt to the social division of labor. Schools would further lead people to accept the authority of the state and its agents—the teachers—at a young age, in part by fos-

---

of situational ethics; and (5) the long-range consequences will be a breakdown of nationalism and the consensus that unites Americans.

If you were a parent of a child in a MACOS program, how would you feel? Would you want some modifications in a program that presents alternative cultures and lifestyles to small children? How far would you agree with the critics of MACOS?

One group of concerned parents in Fort Collins, Colorado, was so upset by the MACOS program in the local schools and its presumed effects on the values of chidren that they drafted a document, which each individual parent would address to his or her child's principal. This letter said, in part:

This letter is to inform you that certain rights and privileges with regard to the instruction of our child are permanently specifically reserved by us, the parents. The familial relationship involving personal relationships, attitudes, responsibilities, religious and social training are the sole prerogative of the parents. We demand that you not enroll, prepare or instruct our child in any course or class, workshop, study group, etc., known as, or including 'sensitivity training,' 'MACOS,' Human Development programs, social awareness, self-awareness, situation ethics, value judgment, values clarification, Ethnic Studies, 'Humanities,' the philosophies of the Humanist religion, the Occult or any other additional specific courses attempting to modify moral values without our prior informed written consent, which shall also be required for any sex education program, course or study whatever.

Other parents hailed MACOS as a necessary program to prepare children for a shrinking world undergoing ever-faster-paced change.

The School Board in Fort Collins resolved the issue by providing a traditional program in any school where a parent objected to MACOS. Thus, parents were given a very important choice because exposure to one or the other curriculum will make a difference in their children. Children will be more tolerant of deviance, more receptive to alternatives, and less bound by tradition than those children denied access to MACOS. How would you feel about this issue if your children were in a MACOS school?

Panel 6–3
"Brainwashing"

The socialization process does not affect everyone alike in a complex society. There are persons who as adults reject society's institutions and "sacred" values. Some may refuse to go to war. Others disdain work. In recent years thousands of young people have converted to religious cults like Hare Krishna, Sun Myung Moon's Unification Church, and the Children of God. These groups require that members reject their families, cut off all ties with former friends, give up traditional career patterns, and renounce American values.

These religious groups are labeled as deviant by the larger society because they threaten the foundation of society—in particular the family, traditional religion, and American values. The conversion of young people to groups antithetical to tradition is viewed, therefore, as sinister. The assumption is that the young converts have been tricked and manipulated in some way—i.e., brainwashed. In this view, conversion to an alien value system is considered an illness in the convert. The cure is to recapture the convert's mind through "deprogramming" by a psychiatrist or other agent of the societal status quo. In the following passage, sociologist Barbara Hargrove discusses the attraction of these alien cults from a different perspective, a perspective that looks at society rather than at the individual.

Harvey Cox has suggested that in all societies where new religious movements have attracted young people, their parents and others in the "establishment" will develop some "evil eye" theory, insisting that their children have been bewitched. Brainwashing, in this case, may be seen as the evil eye theory appropriate to a modern scientific culture. . . .

An evil eye definition of conversion has both its source and its consequences in the willingness by members of the dominant society to avoid dealing with those weaknesses of the society that create needs which are met by new religious groups. Bewitchment or brainwashing must be the fault of the deceiver, not of those whose children are deceived nor of the society from which they come. No critical examination of other possible causes is thought necessary. And so no remedial action is required other than the exorcism of the evil influence. That way of dealing with the situation is always open to the kind of criticism carried in the parable of the man who, freed from an evil spirit, swept out the house of his soul so thoroughly that the spirit returned with seven even more evil companions. To assume that the

tering the illusion of the benevolence of the government in its relations with citizens. Moreover, because schooling would ostensibly be open to all, one's position in the social division of labor could be portrayed as the result not of birth, but of one's own efforts and talents.[19]

The media. The mass media—consisting of newspapers, magazines, movies, radio, and television—play a vital role in promoting the existing values and practices of society. For example, they *select* most of the information that helps us to define socio-political reality. As Parenti has suggested:

Almost all the political life we experience is through the media. How we view issues—indeed, what we even define as an issue or event—what we see and hear and what we

sole source of religious conversion is the evil influence of the converter is to refuse to deal with sources of the conversion which should be faced by those most concerned. Why are young people so impressed by a group of people who show genuine love and concern? Have they never met such responses elsewhere? Why is it so attractive to be recruited to save the world? In what ways have recruits come to understand that it is so in need of saving? What are the interstices of our culture through which important human needs are falling unmet; and how may these be filled? These are the kinds of questions which conversions elicit, and which definitions like brainwashing allow us to ignore.

Solutions like deprogramming reinforce a view of humankind as incapable of decision making or any exercise of the will. They reflect a kind of scientific determinism that is frequently identified as a source of youthful discontent, and in fact as a source of conversions to new lifestyles and meaning systems. If one assumes that individual lives are entirely the product of impersonal social forces, and that all human responses are the result of some kind of conditioning, then it becomes very difficult for a person to see any particular meaning in his or her life. Yet there are expectations in our society that the particular task of youth is to choose a career pattern and life plan that will be meaningful. It seems logical that, placed in this position, young people should be attracted to groups which offer such meaning, and that they might consider it a sinister act if they are pursued by people bent on conditioning them to a different response.

Much of the *ideology* behind the deprogramming movement has involved a critique of the religious groups for substituting a communal will for the autonomy of the individual. But the basic view of humanity which underlies the *method* of deprogramming is less one of autonomy and more that of a stimulus-response psychology which is indeed "beyond freedom and dignity." The young involved appear to be given the choice between being directed by an authoritarian community or used as subjects of an abstract technology. While some of the religious movements appear to be authoritarian and potentially if not actually repressive, so also do the methods by which they are opposed. It is not much of a choice to pick domination by psychological manipulators over that by religious demagogues. In fact, the latter at least seem usually to offer more of the warmth of human community than do the deprogrammers.

Source: Excerpts from Barbara Hargrove, "Evil Eyes and Religious Choices." Published by permission of Transaction, Inc. from *Society*, Vol. 17, No. 3, pp. 20–24. Copyright © 1980 by Transaction, Inc.

do *not* see and hear are greatly determined by those who control the mass media. By enlarging our vision through technology, we have actually surrendered control over much of our own sensory experience.[20]

The media promote traditional American values. In his study of *CBS Evening News, NBC Nightly News, Newsweek*, and *Time*, sociologist Herbert Gans found that these news sources portrayed eight clusters of enduring values: ethnocentrism, altruistic democracy, responsible capitalism, small-town pastoralism, individualism, moderatism, social order, and national leadership.[21] The promotion of these values is especially effective because it appears to the consumers as independent and objective.

Television, through its entertainment shows, also functions to promote the status quo.

Stereotypes of the aged, women, and minorities are promoted on these programs.[22] Crime shows, for example, provide a series of morality plays in which:

Wrongs are righted, victims avenged, and victimizers awarded for just deserts. The timing is the same, the rhythm, the choreography, the cast, the denouement—everyone has learned just what to expect. On the top of the heap are television's Good Guys, for years mainly mature white males. On the bottom of the heap lie the Victims—piled up bodies of children, old people, poor people, nonwhites, young people, lone women— all done in by Bad Guys recruited principally from the lower social strata many of the so-called victims come from. . . . Our modern morality plays . . . point the finger at the social strata from which evil emanates and signal the conditions that make it quite proper to shoot, kill, maim, hurt, rip, smash, slash, crush, tear, burn, bury, excise. What starts out as shocking becomes routine then is converted into ritual.[23]

The impact of television is of special importance because children are so exposed to it. Children age two through five, for example, watch television an average of 27 hours a week.[24] The messages they receive are consistent: they are bombarded with materialism and consumerism, what it takes to be a success, and the value of law and order. In short, the media have tremendous power to influence us all, but particularly our youth. This influence can be in the direction of acceptance or criticism of the system. Overwhelmingly, the media are supportive of that system.

SIMILARITIES AND DIFFERENCES AMONG MEMBERS OF SOCIETY

Modal Personality Type

In Chapter 2, we described the condition that Durkheim called "anomie." This refers to a situation where an individual is unsure of his or her social world—the norms are ambiguous or conflicting. In other words, an anomic situation lacks consistency, predictability, and order. Since this condition is upsetting, individuals and groups seek order. Every society provides a common **nomos** (meaningful order) for its members.[25] "Every society has its specific way of defining and perceiving reality—its world, the universe, its overarching organization of symbols."[26] Through the socialization process, the newcomer to society is provided a reality that makes sense. By learning the language and the ready-made definitions of society, the individual is given a consistent way to perceive the world. The order that is created for each of us is taken for granted by us; it is the only world that we can conceive of; it is the only system in which we feel comfortable.

This order, by which the individual comes to perceive and define his world, is thus not chosen by him, except perhaps for very small modifications. Rather it is discovered by him as an external datum, a ready-made world that simply is *there* for him to go ahead and live in, though he modifies it continually in the process of living in it.[27]

Each society has its unique way of perceiving, interpreting, and evaluating reality. This common culture, and nomos, is internalized by the members of society through the process of socialization—thus, people are a product of their culture. It follows, then, that the members of a society will be similar in many fundamental respects. Although there are individual exceptions and subcultural variations, we can say that Americans differ fundamentally from Mexicans, Germans, the French, and others. Let us illustrate how people in a society will develop similarly by briefly characterizing two categories of Indians of North America.[28]

1. *The Pueblo Indians of the southwest.* The Zuñi and Hopi Indians are submissive and gentle peoples. Children are treated with warmth and affection. They live in highly cooperative social structures where individualism is discouraged. One who thirsts for power is ridiculed.

Life in these societies is highly structured. The rules are extremely important and order is highly valued. They never brew intoxicants and reject the use of drugs. In these orderly and cooperative settings, people are trusted. Life is pleasant and relatively free from hatred. The kind of person that develops in these societies tends to be confident, trusting, generous, polite, cooperative, and emotionally controlled.

2. *The Indians of the northern plains.* The Plains Indians are aggressive peoples. They are fierce warriors exhibiting almost suicidal bravado in battle. They stress individuality with fierce competition for prestige. They boast of their exploits. They stress individual ecstasy in their religious experiences, brought about by fasting, self-torture, and the use of drugs (peyote and alcohol).

The Plains Indians, in contrast to the Pueblo Indians, are more individualistic, competitive, and aggressive. They are more expressive as individuals and less orderly in group life.

These examples show that each society tends to produce a certain type of individual—a **modal personality type**. The individual growing up in American society, with its set of values, will tend to be individualistic, competitive, materialistic, and oriented toward work, progress, and the future. While this characterization of Americans is generally correct, there are some problems with the assumption that socialization into a culture is so all-powerful. First, the power of socialization can vary by the type of society. Small, homogeneous societies like those of American Indian tribes provide the individual member of society with a consistent message, while in a heterogeneous society like the United States, individuals are confronted with a number of themes, variations, and counterthemes. More fundamental, though, is the second problem—is the socialization process completely deterministic? The views of Cooley and Mead noted earlier would seem to suggest this. Dennis Wrong has criticized this position. He has argued that, from a Freudian position, the individual and society are never completely in harmony. While individuals are socialized and generally comply with the demands of society, the process is never complete.[29] The distance from complete socialization is maximized in modern, heterogeneous societies.

Why Aren't We All the Same?

Every society has its deviants. Clearly, people are not robots. Given the power of society, through the socialization process, what are the forces that allow for differences in people in the United States? We begin with a discussion of the major agencies of socialization.

1. *The family.* We have said that the family is the ultimate societal agency for socialization. Families teach their children the language, etiquette, skills; and the like that will enable the child to find his or her niche in society. But families differ in a variety of important ways (for example, in religion, political views, optimism, and affluence). Socioeconomic status is an especially important variable. In Chapter 14 we shall provide the details as to how the different social classes tend to rear children and the consequences. Two examples will suffice for the present discussion. Working-class parents tend to be authoritarian, demanding control of their youngsters, and providing punishment for failure to comply. Authority figures are to be obeyed without question. In contrast, upper-middle-class parents have tended to allow their children to explore, experiment, and question. The family is democratic. Rules are not necessarily absolute. Clearly, children growing up in authoritarian and permissive families will differ in their acceptance of authority, political proclivities, and view of the world.

The family may have little influence on the child if the parents disagree on politics, religion, values, and the like. Or, if the parents' values are consistent, they may be neutralized by contrary values held by their friends. This is facilitated by the decreasing amount of time that parents spend with the children compared to the time spent in previous generations.[30] As parents spend less and less time raising and influencing their

SOCIAL DILEMMAS AND CRITICAL CHOICES

Panel 6-4
Socialization of Children for the Future

American youth have been socialized to be individualistic and highly competitive. Through institutions such as the family, school, and sport, Americans have been socialized to be restless, ambitious, self-reliant strivers who are intolerant of losers, and who place the individual above the group. These traits may have had positive consequences when the United States was isolated, underpopulated, and blessed with abundant resources. But Americans are now part of an interdependent worldwide economic system. The planet's resources are rapidly being depleted and its environment is being fouled with pollutants and waste.

Are the typical American traits that we pass on to our children proper for a world that will be overcrowded and characterized by shortages? A strong case can be made that if we continue to raise individualistic, competitive, grasping children, then we will produce a society whose inhabitants will be increasingly irrational— that is, unable to cope with the demands of a future that will likely include rationing and other forms of sacrifice for the good of the society and the world.

Do you think that your children will be better prepared for the future if they learn less competitiveness and more cooperation? If so, how much should you do to help them learn more cooperation in a competitive society? There are societies

children, their youngsters are influenced more and more by not only peers but also baby sitters, schools, and television.

Some families may have little or negative influence on their children because they are hopelessly disorganized. One or both parents may be alcoholics, unstable, or uncommunicative.

In sum, although children raised in American society are affected by a common culture, family experiences and emphases can vary enough to result in behavioral and attitudinal differences. That children and families can be fundamentally different is seen in the occasional value conflicts between parents and school authorities on sex education, the use of certain literature, rules, and the proper way to enforce rules. But the schools themselves also vary, resulting in different products by type of school.

2. *The schools.* American schools, as are schools in all societies, are conservative. But, there are differences that have a substantial impact on students. There are schools, for example, where the curriculum, schedule, and philosophy are very rigid. Children sit in straight rows, may talk only with permission, wear the prescribed clothing, and accept without question the authority of the teacher. There are other schools, however, where the curriculum, schedules, teachers, and rules are flexible. The products of these two types of schools are likely to differ in much the same way as do the children of autocratic or permissive homes.

3. *Religion.* In general, organized religion in the United States reinforces American values and the policies of the government (see Chapter 16). But there are significant

that appear to inculcate a predominantly cooperative ethic.* How far should these form partial models for rewarding cooperation while discouraging aggressiveness? For example, what if we established a general principle that parents, teachers, and other authorities should reward cooperative behavior by children and either ignore or punish competitive, individualistic behavior. Parents might then also reward their children whether they achieved or not. Games can be used that encourage teamwork. Honors could be equally distributed for participation in sports and other activities that presently glorify the achievements of stars. Schools could abolish tournaments and playoffs. Grades, if used at all, could be based on meeting universal standards, and never on outdoing one's classmates. Absolutely forbidden should be contests such as those sponsored by various corporations and civic groups that reward a small elite at the expense of the masses (for example, the Punt, Pass, and Kick competition).

Do you think that you should encourage a modification of our competitive society by raising your children along these lines? If so, or if not, what modifications would you suggest for the upbringing of your children to cope with life in the future?

*See Ruth Benedict, *Patterns of Culture* (Baltimore, Md.: Penguin Books, 1946); Urie Bronfenbrenner, *Two Worlds of Childhood: U.S. and U.S.S.R.* (New York: Pocket Books, 1973); and Linden L. Nelson and Spencer Kagan, "Competition: The Star-Spangled Scramble," *Psychology Today* 6 (September, 1972), pp. 53–56, 90–91.

differences among and within the various religious bodies. There are religious disagreements on morality, birth control, abortion, capital punishment, evolution, and other volatile issues. Moreover, religious ideas can conflict with those of one's peers, and with what is taught in school. The more salient one's religion, then, the more likely one will differ from those who do not share one's religious views.

4. *Social location*. Each of us is located in society, not only geographically, but also socially. Depending on our wealth, occupation, education, ethnic or racial heritage, and family background, we see ourselves and others see us as being superior to some persons and inferior to others (see Chapters 10 through 13). Our varying positions in this hierarchy will have an effect on our attitudes and perceptions. In particular, those who are highly placed will tend to be supportive of the status quo, while those who are less advantaged will likely be more antagonistic to the way things are and desirous of changes beneficial to them.

5. *Contradictory influences*. We have seen that youngsters may experience pulls in opposite directions from their family, church, and school. Other sources of contradictory attractions are peer groups and the media. Parents may insist, for instance, that their children not fight. Yet, their peers might demand such behavior. Moreover, children are bombarded by violence (much of which is considered appropriate) in the movies and on television. How are these children to behave, faced with such opposing and powerful stimuli? Some will follow their parents' dictates, while others will succumb to other pressures.

6. *Conflicts in role definition*. Some societies are clear and consistent in their expectations for members' behavior. There is no such consensus in American society. An examination of a few fundamental social roles illustrates the disagreement on the expectations of the occupants. Adolescents are often unsure of what is expected of them. The law sometimes defines them as children and at other times as adults. Parents and other adults often lack consistency in what they expect of teenagers. The aged are another category that experiences ill-defined expectations. At times they are treated as adults and at other times they are not taken seriously. Some must retire from work at age 65 while others may continue.

Sex roles, the topic of Chapter 7, provide another example of varying expectations depending on the individual, audience, and community. Traditional masculine and feminine roles are in flux. What precisely is expected of a man and woman as they enter a building? Does the man open the door for the woman? This was appropriate behavior in the past and it may be now, but one is never sure, for some women find such behavior offensive. What are the expectations of a newly married husband and wife? How will they divide the household chores? Who is to be the breadwinner? And later, if there is a divorce, who will take the children? Twenty years ago, or even five years ago, the answers to these questions were certain, but no longer.

SUMMARY

The theme of this chapter is that people are the products of society. Society shapes our identity, our thoughts, our emotions, our perceptions, and our behavior. Through the various agencies of the society—the family, school, church, voluntary associations, and the media—children internalize the norms and values of society. In short, they learn the societal script for living successfully in society.

The socialization process tends to create a relatively uniform product (modal personality type). But, while there is some uniformity in language, understanding, perception, world view, values, and personality, there are differences. A heterogeneous society like the United States will have a good deal of variance among its members because families, churches, and schools may differ in their emphases and because there is often no solid agreement about societal expectations.

Both order and conflict theorists acknowledge the power of the socialization process. They differ, however, in their interpretation of this universal process. The order theorists view this as necessary to promote unity and law-abiding citizens. Conflict theorists, on the other hand, view the process as one in which persons are led to accept the customs, laws, and values of society uncritically and therefore become willing participants in a society that may be in need of change. The ultimate irony is that most of the powerless in American society do not rebel because they actually believe in the system that systematically disadvantages them.

CHAPTER REVIEW

1. Socialization is the process of learning the culture. Children must learn the culture of the society in which they are born. Socialization, however, is a lifelong process and occurs in all social groups, not just society.

2. Infants become human only through learning the culture.

3. The socialization of youth requires social interaction.

4. Another essential to socialization is language, which has profound effects on how individuals think and perceive.

5. The personality emerges as a social product. We develop a sense of self only through interaction with others.

6. One theory of how personality develops is Cooley's "looking-glass self." Through interaction children define themselves according to how they interpret how others think of them.

7. Mead's theory of self development involves

several stages. Through interaction with their parents, infants are able to distinguish between themselves and others. By age two they are able to react to themselves as others react to them. In the play stage (from age four to seven) children pretend to be in a variety of adult roles (taking the role of the other). In the game stage (about age eight) children play at games with rigid rules. They begin to understand the structure of the entire game with the expectations for everyone involved. This understanding of the entire situation is called the "generalized other."

8. According to Freud's theory, socialization is the process by which society controls the id (the biological needs for pleasure). Through this process children develop egos (the control of the id by finding appropriate ways to satisfy biological urges). A superego also emerges which is the internalization of the morals of the parents, further channeling behavior in socially acceptable ways.

9. Through interaction children internalize the

norms and values of society. There are three special transmitters of the cultural patterns—the family, the schools, and the media.

10. Because the socialization agents of society present a relatively consistent picture, the members of a society tend to be alike in fundamental ways (modal personality type). The smaller and more homogeneous the society, the more alike the members of that society will be.

11. Despite the tendency for the members to be alike, people, especially in large, heterogeneous societies, are not all the same. The sources of deviation are the differences found in families (e.g., in social class, religion, ethnic background); schools with differing philosophies (rigid or flexible, public or sectarian); religions, social locations, contradictory influences, and conflicts in role definitions.

FOR FURTHER STUDY

The Socialization Process

Charles Horton Cooley, *Human Nature and the Social Order* (New York: Schocken, 1964).

Erik Erikson, *Childhood and Society* (New York: W. W. Norton, 1950).

Frances FitzGerald, *America Revised* (Boston: Atlantic-Little, Brown, 1979).

Sigmund Freud, *Civilization and Its Discontents*, Joan Riviere, trans., (London: Hogarth, 1946).

Herbert J. Gans, *Deciding What's News* (New York: Pantheon, 1979).

Rose K. Goldsen, *The Show and Tell Machine: How Television Works and Works You Over* (New York: Delta, 1977).

George Herbert Mead, *Mind, Self and Society* (Chicago: University of Chicago Press, 1934).

Jean Piaget and Barbara Inhelder, *The Psychology of the Child* (New York: Basic Books, 1969).

Modal Personality

Victor Barnouw, *Culture and Personality*, 3rd ed. (Homewood, Ill.: Dorsey, 1979).

Ruth Benedict, *Patterns of Culture* (Baltimore, Md.: Penguin Books, 1946).

Urie Bronfenbrenner, *Two Worlds of Childhood: U.S. and U.S.S.R.* (New York: Simon and Schuster (Pocket Books), 1973).

Stanley Elkins, *Slavery: A Problem of American Institutional and Intellectual Life* (New York: Universal Library, 1963).

Margaret Mead, *Sex and Temperament in Three Primitive Societies* (New York: William Morrow, 1935).

David Reisman, *The Lonely Crowd* (New York: Doubleday, 1953).

NOTES AND REFERENCES

1. "Jungle Boy Remains More Like Monkey," Associated Press release, May 15, 1976. See also J. A. L. Singh and Robert M. Zingg, *Wolf-Children and Feral Man* (New York: Harper, 1942).

2. Kingsley Davis, *Human Society* (New York: Macmillan, 1948), pp. 204–205; Kingsley Davis, "Extreme Social Isolation of a Child," *American Journal of Sociology* 45 (January, 1940), pp. 554–564.

3. Bruno Bettelheim, "Feral Children and Autistic Children," *American Journal of Sociology* 54 (March, 1959), p. 458.

4. Davis, *Human Society*, p. 205.

5. Ibid.

6. Helen Keller, *The Story of My Life* (Garden City, N.Y.: Doubleday, 1954).

7. Clyde Kluckhohn and D. Leighton, *The Navaho* (Cambridge, Mass.: Harvard University Press, 1946), p. 194.

8. B. L. Whorf, "Science and Linguistics," in E. E. Maccoby, T. M. Newcomb, and E. L. Hartley (eds.), *Readings in Social Psychology* (New York: Holt, 1956), p. 1. See also Alfred

R. Lindesmith, Anselm L. Strauss, and Norman K. Denzin, *Social Psychology*, 4th ed. (Hinsdale, Ill.: Dryden, 1975), pp. 161–166.

9. Jim Murray, "Vocabulary Takes on a Ruddy-Faced Look," *Rocky Mountain News* (December 9, 1976), p. 150.

10. Peter Berger, "Religion and World Construction," *Life as Theatre*, Dennis Brissett and Charles Edgley, eds. (Chicago: Aldine, 1975), p. 234.

11. Charles Horton Cooley, *Human Nature and the Social Order* (New York: Schocken, 1964).

12. Robert Bierstedt, *The Social Order*, 4th ed. (New York: McGraw-Hill, 1974), p. 197.

13. George Herbert Mead, *Mind, Self and Society* (Chicago: University of Chicago Press, 1934). For a summary, see Reece McGee, *Points of Departure: Basic Concepts in Sociology*, 2nd ed. (New York: Dryden Press, 1975), pp. 63–77.

14. McGee, *Points of Departure*, pp. 74–75.

15. Sigmund Freud, *Civilization and Its Discontents*, Joan Riviere, trans. (London: Hogarth Press, 1946).

16. Dennis Wrong, "The Oversocialized Conception of Man in Modern Sociology," *Sociological Theory*, 3rd ed., Lewis A. Coser and Bernard Rosenberg, eds. (New York: Macmillan, 1969), p. 130.

17. Everitt K. Wilson, *Sociology: Rules, Roles and Relationships* (Homewood, Ill.: Dorsey Press, 1966), p. 92.

18. See Samuel Bowles, "Unequal Education and the Reproduction of the Social Division of Labor," in *Power and Ideology in Education*, Jerome Karabel and A. H. Halsey, eds., (New York: Oxford, 1977), pp. 137–153; Joel H. Spring, *Education and the Rise of the Corporate State* (Boston: Beacon, 1972); and Michael B. Katz, *The Irony of Early School Reform: Educational Innovation in Mid-Nineteenth Century Massachusetts* (Cambridge, Mass.: Harvard University Press, 1968).

19. Bowles, "Unequal Education," p. 139.

20. Michael Parenti, *Democracy for the Few*, 3rd ed. (New York: St. Martin's, 1980), p. 168. See also Robert Cirino, *Don't Blame the People* (New York: Vintage, 1972), pp. 30–31.

21. Herbert J. Gans, *Deciding What's News* (New York: Pantheon, 1979), pp. 39–69, 196–203.

22. *Window Dressing On the Set: An Update*, A Report of the U.S. Commission on Civil Rights (Washington, D.C., 1979).

23. Rose K. Goldsen, *The Show and Tell Machine: How Television Works and Works You Over* (New York: Delta, 1977), pp. 223–224, 234.

24. Kate Moody, "The Research on TV: A Disturbing Picture," *The New York Times* (April 20, 1980), EDUC 17.

25. This discussion is dependent on the insights of Peter Berger on the "social construction of reality," especially Peter L. Berger and Thomas Luckman, *The Social Construction of Reality: A Treatise in the Sociology of Knowledge* (Garden City, N.Y.: Doubleday (Anchor Books), 1967); and Peter Berger and Hansfred Kellner, "Marriage and the Construction of Reality," in Brissett and Edgley, *Life as Theatre*," pp. 219–233.

26. Berger and Kellner, "Marriage and the Construction of Reality," p. 219.

27. Ibid., p. 220.

28. These accounts are taken from Victor Barnouw, *Culture and Personality*, 3rd ed. (Homewood, Ill.: Dorsey, 1979), pp. 59–75.

29. Wrong, "The Oversocialized Conception of Man," p. 130.

30. The evidence is summarized in Sarane S. Boocock, "Is U.S. Becoming Less Child Oriented?" *National Observer* (February 22, 1975), p. 12.

7

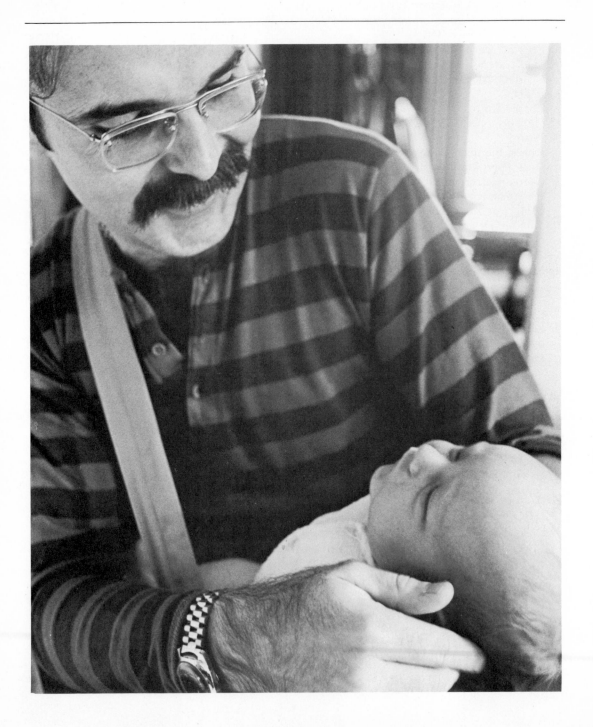

Socialization and Sex Roles

When you are on a date: Who initiates the action? Who pays for the food and entertainment? Who drives the car? Who opens the door for the other? Whose parents set the time when you should be home?

In the home where you grew up: Who made the decisions and over what domains? How was the housework divided? Which parent was responsible for the nurturing of the children? Which parent was the breadwinner? What childhood activities did your parents encourage and discourage?

What are your beliefs about: the double standard concerning sexual behavior? dual career marriages? women in traditional "male" occupations? men in traditional "female" occupations? married women who retain their maiden names?

Because of the women's movement we have become aware in the last fifteen years or so of the profound significance and power relations symbolized in the verbal gestures, forms of address, rituals, and expectations common in society regarding the relations between the sexes. In this chapter we will consider the social forces behind traditional sex role behavior in American society. In particular we will see how individuals acquire traditional sex roles in the course of socialization and how these roles are reinforced by society's institutions.

All societies have clear expectations for their members on the basis of sex. The division of tasks in the family, occupations, the expression of emotion, and even personality traits are assigned by gender. The socialization process in this regard is so powerful that these arrangements seem natural. This chapter will analyze this phenomenon in American society by examining stereotyped sex roles and the societal mechanisms that bombard Americans from infancy with blatant and subtle demands to conform to these expectations.

THE ROLES OF MEN AND WOMEN

The concept **role** is borrowed directly from the theater and is a metaphor intended to convey the idea that conduct adheres to positions (**statuses**) in a social system. This is to say that because of one's position in an organization (for example, family, corporation, community, society) one has certain rights and privileges as well as duties and obligations to persons occupying other positions in the social structure. In occupying a specific position, a person experiences a number of normative expectations, and these expectations are the role. They specify what one should, ought, and must do, and usually how to do it. In this chapter we shall concentrate on the specific roles (that is, behavior expectations) of males and females in American society.

What are the traditional expectations for males and females in American society? For one thing a man is expected to pursue a career while a woman is to raise children and provide emotional support for her husband. In the occupational world men are expected to have the positions of leadership, responsibility, and initiative while women hold the service and subservient positions. In terms of personality characteristics, American men are expected to be aggressive, courageous, tough, independent, ambitious, competitive, unemotional, pragmatic, and rational. American women, on the other hand, are expected to have the opposite personality traits: passive, submissive, gentle, dependent, family oriented, emotional, sentimental, idealistic, and intuitive.

Are Sex Roles Based on Physiological Differences

There is a controversy among scientists concerning the basis for sex roles. One school argues that there is a biogenetic foundation for the observed differences in male and female behavior while their counterparts are convinced that the differences are explained largely by differential learning.[2] We know that there are biological differences between the two sexes. The key question is whether these unlearned differences in the sexes contribute to the sex role differences found in societies. To answer this question, let's first review the evidence for both positions.

The biological bases for sex roles. Males and females are different from the moment of conception. Chromosomal and hormonal differences make males and females physically different. These differences, for example, give the female health superiority. At every age, from conception until old age, more males than females get sick and die. Approximately 120 males are conceived for every 100 females, yet there are only 105 live male births for

CROSS-CULTURAL PANEL

Panel 7-1
Sexism Among the Yanomamo

Along the Brazil/Venezuela border is a tribe of about ten thousand Yanomamo. This group is one of the most aggressive, war-like, and male-oriented societies in the world. For our purposes we will concentrate on the extreme sexism found in that society.

All Yanomamo men physically abuse their wives. Men expect their wives to serve them promptly and without protest. If a woman does not respond quickly enough the husband will likely beat her, burn her with a burning stick, or yank on the sticks of cane that the women wear through their pierced ear lobes. A man's image is enhanced if he publicly beats his wife with a club. The women expect to be beaten by their husbands and perceive the beatings as acts of caring. In fact, they measure their status as wives by the frequency of beatings they receive from their husbands.

Yanomamo females are victimized from infancy. Most dramatically, women

each 100 female births, meaning that fetuses spontaneously aborted (miscarried) or stillborn are typically males. Various studies have shown that males are more susceptible than females to respiratory, bacterial, and viral infections, hepatitis, and childhood leukemia. The explanation for females being the healthier sex is that they have twice as many of a group of genes that program the production of immunological agents.[3] This means that females, compared to males, produce larger amounts of antibodies to combat a number of infectious agents.

Hormonal differences in the sexes are significant. The male hormones (androgens) and female hormones (estrogens) direct the process of sex differentiation from about six weeks after conception throughout life. They make males taller, heavier, and more muscular. At puberty they trigger the production of secondary sexual characteristics. In males, these include body and facial hair, a deeper voice, broader shoulders, and a muscular body. In females, puberty brings pubic hair, menstruation, the ability to lactate, prominent breasts, and relatively broad hips. Actually, males and females have both sets of hormones. It is the relative proportion of androgens and estrogens that gives one masculine or feminine physical traits.

These hormonal differences may explain in part why males tend to be more active, aggressive, and dominant than females.[4] Studies in animals provide some evidence for this assertion. Castrated rats and monkeys, deprived of the sex hormones created by the testes, have decreased levels of aggression. When testosterone is injected into these castrated males, their aggression levels increase.[5]

Critics of the biological determinist approach have argued that research on animals is irrelevant for humans because of the importance of socialization and culture. But the force of this argument has been negated somewhat by a recent study of a unique group of children from the Dominican Republic.[6] Because of a rare genetic disease, eighteen

kill their babies until they have a male child because the father will not accept a female first born. Little girls are beaten by their brothers. The brothers are *never* punished for this but the sisters are if they hit back. The father decides who his daughter will marry and when. The marriage may occur as early as age 8 or 9 for the girl.

The Yanomamo consider menstrual blood evil and dangerous. Consequently when a girl has her first menses she is locked in a cage without food. Subsequently she must isolate herself from the tribe at every menstrual period.

A husband gladly shares his wife sexually with his brothers and comrades without her consent. He will not, however, condone his wife's extramarital affairs. If caught in such a relationship, the wife is severely beaten or killed by her husband.

Because there is a shortage of women in the society due to female infanticide and polygyny (one husband and several wives), a prime objective of warfare is the capture of women from enemy villages. After capture the females are gang-raped by the warriors. On return to the home village the female captives are turned over to the men who stayed home and gang-raped again. Later, after much arguing, the women are assigned as wives to individual warriors.

children were raised as girls because their parents believed them to be female. However, at puberty a surge of testosterone caused their voices to deepen, their muscles to develop, and their genitals to turn masculine. The "girls" had become men. Although two of the eighteen chose to remain in the female role as they had been socialized, the remainder changed to the male role, leading some researchers to conclude that sexual identity is more a function of the predominant sex hormone than a function of the environment.

The social bases for sex roles. Probably the best, although still imperfect, way to determine an answer to this dilemma is to examine the male and female roles in a variety of cultures. If the expectations for males and females are uniform throughout the world, then the basis for the difference between the sexes is physiological. If, however, the male and female roles are found to vary from society to society, we can assume that the basis for masculine and feminine role differences is very likely sociocultural.

The cross-cultural evidence shows a wide variation of behaviors for the sexes. Table 7-1

TABLE 7-1   Sex Allocation in Selected Technological Activities in 224 Societies

| Activity | Number of societies in which the activity is performed by: | | | | | % Male |
	Males exclusively	Males usually	Both sexes equally	Females usually	Females exclusively	
Smelting of ores	37	0	0	0	0	100.0
Hunting	139	5	0	0	0	99.3
Boat building	84	3	3	0	1	96.6
Mining and quarrying	31	1	2	0	1	93.7
Land clearance	95	34	6	3	1	90.5
Fishing	83	45	8	5	2	86.7
Herding	54	24	14	3	3	82.4
House building	105	30	14	9	20	77.4
Generation of fire	40	6	16	4	20	62.3
Preparation of skins	39	4	2	5	31	54.6
Crop planting	27	35	33	26	20	54.4
Manufacture of leather products	35	3	2	5	29	53.2
Crop tending	22	23	24	30	32	44.6
Milking	15	2	8	2	21	43.8
Carrying	18	12	46	34	36	39.3
Loom weaving	24	0	6	8	50	32.5
Fuel gathering	25	12	12	23	94	27.2
Manufacture of clothing	16	4	11	13	78	22.4
Pottery making	14	5	6	6	74	21.1
Dairy production	4	0	0	0	24	14.3
Cooking	0	2	2	63	117	8.3
Preparation of vegetables	3	1	4	21	145	5.7

Source: Adapted from George P. Murdock and Caterina Provost, "Factors in the Division of Labor by Sex: A Cross-Cultural Analysis," *Ethnology* 12 (April, 1973), p. 207

provides some interesting cross-cultural data from 224 societies on the division of labor by sex. This table shows that for the majority of activities, societies are not uniform in their sexual division of labor. Even activities requiring strength, presumably a male trait, are not strictly apportioned to males. In fact, activities such as burden bearing and water carrying are done by females more than by males. Even an activity like house building is not exclusively male.

Although these data show variation, they also indicate a pattern. Almost universally, females do the tasks related to nurturance of the family (home care, preparation of food, and making of clothes). Males, on the other hand, typically do the hunting and mining. These differences are due at least indirectly to biology. Males are physically larger and stronger. Females give birth to children and are equipped to feed the newborn children. Since women in preindustrial societies tend to have a large number of children, they are bound by biology to domestic duties. Males, however, can leave their offspring for extended periods, and therefore are logically more likely to become engaged in activities such as hunting and fighting.

But there are now rapid changes that make this traditional sexual division of labor unnecessary, especially in modern technological societies. First, women are no longer fated to incessant pregnancy, child rearing, and early death. In American society, most women want few children and to have them within a short period of time before age thirty. This is easily accomplished with modern contraceptive methods. Thus, when the last child enters school, women have the majority of their adult lives before them. Women, therefore, are no longer bound into their activities by the biology of reproduction. A second major change in modern societies is that work is no longer the result of muscle power but now depends on machines and brains. Thus, there is no longer any objective basis for a sexual division of labor. But the division of labor on that basis remains. Stark has suggested why in the following statement:

The problem is that we are still following cultural patterns that built up over thousands of years—ways of life that made the relative subordination of women seem necessary. It is difficult to change our whole system of sex roles and the arrangements that sustain them, and it is especially difficult to change them without considerable trauma. That the problem is fundamentally in our heads—in how we think about sex roles rather than in social necessities—only makes change possible, not inevitable. Change must be won against the inertia of past traditions, and this, of course, is precisely what necessitates and motivates the contemporary women's movement.[7]

To summarize, the anthropological evidence is that masculine and feminine roles are basically cultural, not physiological phenomena. Slater has summarized it as follows:

We know by now . . . that there is virtually nothing in the way of personal characteristics or behavior that is defined in every culture as masculine or feminine. In some societies women are assumed to be stronger, and carry all the heavy burdens. In some societies women are supposed to be impractical and intuitive, in others men are. In most societies women are seen as earthy, men as spiritual, but Victorian England reversed this order. Even within our own society, there are odd contradictions: activity is seen as a masculine characteristic, passivity as feminine. Yet men are supposed to move and talk slowly, while women are expected to be birdlike in body movement—constantly moving their hands, using many more facial muscles, talking rapidly. Paradoxically, a man who is too active in the most physical sense of using many muscles from moment to moment is considered "effeminate." It should be emphasized, then, that when we talk of "masculine" and "feminine" we are referring only to the ways in which these are customarily defined in our culture, and since sex role definitions change from time to time there is ample room for confusion.[8]

The question of whether biology predetermines one's destiny or not is exceedingly important. To accept the biological argument is to justify and accept traditional sex roles. A woman's place is in the home; if she takes a place in the work force, then her appropriate job is an extension of the domestic role—as a support for men or to provide care for young children. If, however, the social environment is the key determinant in the sexual division of labor, then changes in the social order can bring equality of opportunity regardless of gender.

Both sides in this debate of whether nature or nurture is the predominant force behind traditional sex roles have valid arguments. Clearly, biological factors are important as are social ones. The weight of the evidence, however, is that most sex role behaviors are learned. Society, not biology, is responsible for assigning to one sex or the other such traits as: decision-making, tenderness, breadwinning, and dependence. If the customs, laws, and institutions of society did not demand these preferences, then behavior would be unrelated to gender. Instead of a sex-polarized society, there would be an androgynous one. Individuals would, in such a society, be "tender and dominant, dependent and decisive, ambitious and nurturing according to their human temperament, not their gender."[9]

But societies have not opted for androgny. In American society, for example, the consistent theme throughout all institutions has been a subtle and active promotion of traditional sex roles. The next section provides ample proof for this assertion.

THE INSTITUTIONAL REINFORCEMENT OF TRADITIONAL SEX ROLES

Traditional sex roles are the result of the consistent messages from a number of societal sectors—the family, peers, the language, religion, the media, and the schools.

The family. Children learn very quickly in their families what is expected of them as boys and girls. Boys are dressed in blue and given trucks, guns, and balls, while girls are dressed in pink, frilly clothes, have teddy bears, dolls, and playhouses. Boys are expected to be rough and tumble, while girls are expected to be gentle and look pretty. Parents expect their sons to strive for a good occupation; they expect their daughters to become housewives and raise a family. As Frazier and Sadker have put it:

The way parents treat their children may be the most important factor of all in the creation of sex stereotypes. When one compares the life of the young girl to that of the young boy, a critical difference emerges: She is treated more protectively and she is subjected to more restrictions and controls; he receives greater achievement demands and higher expectations.[10]

This process of sex differentiation begins very early. For example, research has shown that parents from birth treat boys differently from girls. Girl infants are talked to more. Girls are the objects of more physical contact such as holding, rocking, caressing, and kissing.[11] We also know that fathers, especially working-class fathers, are more concerned than mothers about their young children engaging in behaviors considered inappropriate for their sex.[12] Mothers have a more covert role in the sex role socialization process, with the same result. They provide role models for their daughters. The mother's work status (at home, blue collar, professional) has a pronounced effect on the aspirations of daughters.[13]

In addition to the parents' active role in reinforcing conformity to society's sex role demands, a subtler message is emitted from picture books for preschool children that parents purchase for their children. One study of eighteen award-winning children's books from 1967 to 1971 found the following to be true:

1. Females were virtually invisible. The ratio of male pictures to female pictures was 11:1. The ratio of male to female animals was 95:1.
2. The activities of boys and girls varied greatly. Boys were active in outdoor activities, while girls were passive and most often found indoors. The activity of the girls typically was that of some service for boys.
3. Adult men and women (role models) were very different. Men led, women followed. Females were passive and males active. Not one woman in these books had a job or profession; they were always mothers and wives.[14]

Two books by the same author best illustrate how children's books are biased toward traditional occupational roles apportioned by sex. The first, *What Boys Can Be*, lists fourteen occupations: fireman, baseball player, bus driver, policeman, cowboy, doctor, sailor, pilot, clown, zoo manager, farmer, actor, astronaut, and President.[15] The book, *What Girls Can Be*, also lists fourteen occupations: nurse, stewardess, ballerina, candy-shop owner, model, actress, secretary, artist, nursery school teacher, singer, dress designer, bride, housewife, and mother.[16] In analyzing these two books, Weitzman et al., make several interesting observations. First, the ultimate goal presented for boys is to become president and for girls to be mothers. Second, while three of the male occupations are performed inside, eleven of the female jobs are. Third, the jobs for women are either glamorous or service-oriented. Males, in contrast, have a much greater range of choice. Finally, the male jobs tend to be more prestigious, better paid, and require more education than those for females.[17]

Another book designed for preschool children lists the difference between boys and girls in another way that implies the limited abilities of females. Two examples will suffice:

Boys fix things. Girls need things fixed.
Boys invent things. Girls use what boys invent.[18]

Before formal schooling, parents often send their child to day-care centers and nursery schools. The teachers there serve as surrogate parents, also reinforcing traditional sex roles. A study of 15 preschools found that teachers act and react in quite different ways to boys and girls. The teachers, for example, responded over three times as often to males as to females who hit or broke things. Boys were typically punished by a loud public reprimand while girls were taken aside for a soft rebuke. In task-learning situations, boys were twice as likely as girls to receive individual instructions on how to do things. Summarizing their study, the researchers noted:

As nursery-school children busily mold clay, their teachers are molding behavior. Unwittingly, teachers foster an environment where children learn that boys are aggressive and able to solve problems, while girls are submissive and passive. The clay impressions are transient, but the behavioral ones last into adulthood and present us with people of both sexes who have developed only parts of their psychological and intellectual capabilities.[19]

Peers. The friends and playmates of young children constitute an important source of socialization to sex role stereotypes. Through their peers youth find out what those outside the family consider appropriate behavior. Sex role differences can easily be observed in the play of children. Janet Lever studied this among fifth graders.[20] She found that boys, more than girls: (1) played outdoors; (2) played in larger groups; (3) played in age-heterogeneous groups; (4) were less likely to play in games dominated by the opposite gender; (5) played more competitive games; and (6) played in games that lasted longer.

These differences in play by sex reinforce the traditional sex roles. Boys play at competitive games that require aggressiveness and toughness, while girls tend to play indoors with dolls and play-acting scenarios of the home. Thus, boys and girls in their play are practicing and perfecting the adult roles expected for their sex.

The English language and sex role stereotypes. The English language is sexist. The following words and phrases, although including women in the categories, treat women as outsiders, inferior, and/or invisible:[21] mankind, prehistoric man, men of science, forefathers, frontiersmen, Frenchmen, chairman, salesman, mailmen, spacemen, horsemen, manpower, statesmen, foreman, history, "Men helping Man" (General Electric advertising slogan), one-man show, man-hour, man and wife, man overboard, manslaughter, workmen's compensation, and man's achievements. The problem common to these examples is the generic use of man to include all of humankind. This usage may be grammatically correct but it is demeaning to females and confusing as to its referent. It is demeaning because the use of man forces us to think male and not female. Further, it implies power and dominance for males and the lack of these traits for females.

The generic use of man is ambiguous because man has several clearly different meanings. *Webster's New World Dictionary of the American Language*, for example, provides ten meanings for "man," three of which are pertinent for our discussion:

1. a human being, whether male or female.
2. the human race.
3. an adult male human being.

The obvious question is how can the same word include women in two meanings and exclude them in the other.[22]

Many traditionalists consider these criticisms of English trivial. But what are the subtle effects on females of the constant bombardment of sexism through one's language? Lynn T. White, when president of Mills College, argued that the impact is clearly negative.

The grammar of English dictates that when a referent is either of indeterminate sex or both sexes, it shall be considered masculine. The penetration of this habit of language into the minds of little girls as they grow up to be women is more profound than most people, including most women, have recognized: for it implies that personality is really a male attribute, and that women are a human subspecies. . . . It would be a miracle if a girl baby, learning to use the symbols of our tongue, could escape some wound to her self-respect: whereas a boy baby's ego is bolstered by the pattern of our language.[23]

Religion and traditional sex roles. The customs, beliefs, and laws that discriminate against women are clearly reinforced and perpetuated by religion. Limiting discussion to the Judeo-Christian heritage, let's examine some of the teachings from the Old and New Testaments regarding the place of women. The Old Testament clearly established male supremacy in a number of ways.[24] To begin, God is believed to be a male. Women were obviously meant to be second to males because Eve was created from Adam's rib. According to the scriptures, only a male could divorce a spouse. A woman who was not a virgin at marriage could be stoned to death. Girls could be purchased for marriage. Even employers were enjoined to pay women only three-fifths the wages of men: "If a male from 20 to 60 years of age, the equivalent is 50 shekels of silver by the sanctuary weight; if it is a female, the equivalent is 30 shekels."[25]

The Old Testament devotes inordinate space to the listing of long lines of male descent to the point where it would seem that for centuries women "begat" nothing but male offspring. Although there are heroines in the Old Testament—Judith, Esther and the like—it's clear that they functioned like the heroines of Greek drama and later of French: as counterweights in the imaginations of certain sensitive men to the degraded position of women in actual life. The true spirit of the tradition was unabashedly revealed in the prayer men recited every day in the synagogue: "Blessed art Thou, O Lord . . . for not making me a woman."[26]

The New Testament generally continued the tradition of male dominance. Jesus was a male. He was the son of a male God, not Mary, who remained a virgin. All the disciples were male. The great leader of the early church, the Apostle Paul, was especially adamant in arguing for the primacy of the male over the female. According to Paul: "the husband is supreme over his wife," "woman was created for man's sake," and "women should not teach, nor usurp authority over the man, but be silent."

Important Christian theologians of the Middle Ages were also consistent in their view of women as secondary to male. Two quotations make this point:

Nor is there a parallel between wife and husband: because, since the husband has to rule the wife and not vice versa, the wife is bound to follow her husband rather than the husband the wife.

Thomas Aquinas (1225–1274)

No gown worse becomes a woman than the desire to be wise.

Martin Luther (1483–1546)

Contemporary religious thought reflects this heritage. Some conservative denominations severely limit or even forbid women from any decision-making. Others allow women to vote but limit their participation in leadership roles. The best evidence of the reluctance of established churches to allow women equal participation is the paucity of women ministers.[27]

Mass-communications media and sex-role stereotypes. The mass media (television, radio, newspapers, magazines, movies, and popular music) reflect the culture of society and nowhere more than in their sex-role assumptions. To document this, let's begin by analyzing contemporary American magazines. For many years, the picture of women that has emerged from various stories and articles has been that of the happy housewife meeting the demanding but fulfilling needs of her husband and children. The wife tends to be younger than her spouse and dependent upon him in almost a childlike way.[28]

Janet Saltzman Chafetz and a number of her students analyzed sex-role stereotypes in newspapers and newsmagazines and found that these media were actively promoting the traditional sex roles.[29] Of special interest were departments of the publications devoted to women. They found here a consistent emphasis on parties, weddings, beauty hints, recipes, and child care and the virtual exclusion of legal, political, intellectual, and economic matters.

Chafetz and her students also found that popular songs reflect very traditional sex-role stereotypes. Their data show that the majority of songs are male oriented and support commonly accepted sex-role definitions. This is significant because:

Today's young adults are considered by many to be more willing to experiment with new ideas, role structures, and so on than their parents and grandparents. Surely, if any medium could be expected not to reflect traditional sex-role definitions, it would be the one that is most specifically and explicitly created and consumed by youth; popular songs. However, the same medium that protested war, pollution, racism, and middle-class materialism, and extolled peace, love, drugs, and a generally more free and humane life style, continued to reflect very traditional sex role stereotypes.[30]

Depictions of males and females in films have consistently upheld the popular images. Males have been typically portrayed as aggressive, decisive, action oriented, independent, and emotionally strong while women were seen has having the opposite traits. They especially were used as blatant sex objects.[31]

Television continues to reinforce traditional sex-role stereotypes. This can be seen best perhaps by the type of programming on daytime television whose audience is composed almost entirely of women. Here the fare is dominated by "soap operas" and game shows. One study of the female characters in daytime soap operas found 53 percent of them "dependent," 80 percent "emotional," and 80 percent "expressive."[32] In prime time, television has been primarily an all-male world. This has been changing as women are being included on news teams and as leads in dramas and variety shows. Even with these changes, however, the overall pattern that emerges continues to uphold the commonly accepted sex roles.[33]

Advertising plays a very significant part in the reinforcement of traditional sex roles. Komisar has said it well in the following passage:

There once was some concern over the danger of subliminal advertising that would force people to make subconscious decisions about products or politics. Advertising today is not subliminal, but its subtle psychological effect is as devastating as any secret message flashed at high speeds to unsuspecting viewers. Advertising exploits and reinforces the myths of woman's place with messages of such infinite variety and number that one might as easily deny that the earth revolves around the sun as entirely reject their influence. Advertising is an insidious propaganda machine for a male supremacist society. It spews out images of women as sex mates, housekeepers, mothers and menial workers—images that perhaps reflect the true status of most women in society, but which also make it increasingly difficult for women to break out of the sexist stereotypes that imprison them.[34]

A review of the research on television advertising has shown, for example, that: (1) almost all commercials with voice-overs are spoken or sung by men; (2) men are found in a wider variety of roles than women; (3) the roles depicted for females are typically family roles; (4) women tend to be doing activities in the home that benefit men; (5) women tend to be inside the home with men outside; (6) women are younger than men; and (7) in commercials during children's programming, women and girls are seen less often than men and boys.[35]

The sexism prevalent in advertising can be very subtle as noted by Erving Goffman:

1) overwhelmingly a woman is taller than a man only when the man is her social inferior; 2) a woman's hands are seen just barely touching, holding or caressing—never grasping, manipulating, or shaping; 3) when a photograph of men and women illustrates an instruction of some sort the man is always instructing the woman—even if the men and women are actually children (that is, a male child will be instructing a female child!); 4) when an advertisement requires someone to sit or lie on a bed or a floor that

METHODS PANEL

Panel 7–2
Sampling

In 1980 the Roper Organization selected a sample of 3,000 women age eighteen and over to determine the attitudes of women on various issues. The results from that survey (and one taken in 1970) for one question are found in the following table.

Efforts To Strengthen Women's Status

Question: There has been much talk recently about changing women's status in society today. On the whole, do you favor or oppose most of the efforts to strengthen and change women's status in society today?

	1980			1970		
	Favor	Oppose	Not sure	Favor	Oppose	Not sure
	%	%	%	%	%	%
Total Women	**64**	**24**	**11**	**40**	**42**	**18**
Single	75	15	10	53	33	14
Married	64	25	11	38	45	17
Divorced/separated	75	18	8	61	27	12
Widowed	48	35	17	36	41	23
White	62	26	12	37	46	17
Black	77	14	9	60	20	20
18 to 29	74	16	10	46	39	15
30 to 39	70	19	11	40	44	16
40 to 49	60	31	9	39	43	18
50 and over	55	31	14	35	45	20
Non-high school graduate	54	30	16	36	38	26
High school graduate	63	26	11	38	45	17
College	73	18	8	44	40	16
Northeast	68	21	11	41	40	19
Midwest	61	26	12	38	46	16
South	60	27	13	39	41	20
West	70	21	9	42	43	15
Cities	72	19	9	47	36	17
Suburbs	68	20	12	41	44	15
Towns	60	28	12	37	46	17
Rural	58	29	12	34	45	21

Source: Roper Organization, Inc.: *The 1980 Virginia Slims American Women's Opinion Poll*, p. 17. [machine-readable data file]. New York: Roper Organization producer, 1980; Storrs, CT: Roper Public Opinion Research Center, University of Connecticut distributor.

someone is almost always a child or a woman, hardly ever a man; 5) when the head or eye of a man is averted it is only in relation to a social, political, or intellectual superior, but when the eye or head of a woman is averted it is always in relation to *whatever* man is pictured with her; 6) women are repeatedly shown mentally drifting from

The data in this table lead to several generalizations: (1) American women in 1980 when compared to American women in 1970, regardless of their social characteristics, were more favorable to the strengthening of women's status in society; (2) single and divorced women are more liberal on this question than married and widowed women; (3) blacks are more liberal than whites; (4) the younger the woman, the more liberal; (5) the higher the education, the more favorable to changing women's status; (6) women in the Northeast and West are more sympathetic to change than women in the Midwest and South; and (7) the larger the community in which a woman lives, the more liberal she will be on this issue.

How confident can we be about these generalizations? Do they represent the attitudes of American women? After all, Roper asked 3,000 women out of a potential pool of almost 100 million. How similar are these 3,000 to the 100 million they are supposed to represent. Our confidence depends on the sampling procedures used. Since it is too costly and even impossible to contact all women in America age 18 and over, a subset of that population—a sample—is drawn to represent the category investigated. A sample will probably never perfectly represent the actual population, but the error can be estimated statistically. This amount of error can be very small, if the sample is carefully drawn.

There are two fundamental types of sampling designs. In a *random sample* each member of the population to be studied has an equal chance of being selected. For example, every woman's Social Security number could be stored in a computer and a sample of 3,000 selected at random by the computer.

A *stratified sample* (the method used by Roper) is based on choosing persons whose characteristics are representative of the total population. If the investigator knows, for instance, the percentage of American women by age category, size of community, race, amount of education, and marital status, then she or he would select individuals for inclusion in the sample so that the total sample would have the characteristics of the population under investigation *in the correct proportion*. For example, if 12 percent of the nation's women are black, then 12 percent of the sample must be black. The key, though, is that the individuals selected because of their social characteristics be selected randomly.

Properly done, sampling can provide very accurate information about those groups too large to investigate in their entirety. Thus, it is appropriate to generalize from the findings of a survey when we have confidence about the representativeness of the sample.

For further information on sampling see: Earl R. Babbie, *The Practice of Social Research*, Second Edition (Belmont, Ca.: Wadsworth, 1979), Chapter 7; and Robert Sommer and Barbara B. Sommer, *A Practical Guide to Behavioral Research* (New York: Oxford University Press, 1980), Chapter 16.

the scene while in close physical touch with a male, their faces lost and dreamy, "as though his aliveness to the surroundings and his readiness to cope were enough for both of them" 7) concomitantly, women, much more than men, are pictured at the kind of psychological loss or remove from a social situation that leaves one unoriented for action (e.g., something terrible has happened and a woman is shown with her hands over her mouth and her eyes helpless with horror).[36]

Formal education and sex role stereotypes.   By the time youngsters graduate from high school, they have each spent approximately thirteen thousand hours in the classroom. Obviously, school has a profound influence on a child's world. The question to be answered in this section is: To what degree do the schools contribute to channeling people into narrow roles according to sex? To answer this question, we shall examine several areas: course offerings, textbooks, teacher-student interactions, sports, female role models, counseling, and teacher education.

1. *Curriculum.*   Home economics, business education, shop classes, and vocational agriculture have traditionally been rigidly sex-segregated. Reflecting society's expectations, schools taught girls child rearing, cooking, sewing, and secretarial skills. Boys, on the other hand, were taught mechanics, woodworking, and other vocationally oriented skills. These courses were usually segregated by custom and sometimes by official school policy.

2. *Sex bias in textbooks.*   The content of textbooks transmits messages to readers about society, about children, and about what adults are supposed to do. For this reason, individuals and groups concerned about the potential for sexist bias in schools have looked carefully at how males and females are portrayed in textbooks assigned to students. Their findings provide a consistent message: textbooks commonly used in American schools have been overtly and covertly sexist. Let us look at this evidence.

A study of 134 elementary textbooks from 12 different publishers found that the ratio of boy-centered stories to girl-centered stories was 5:2; the ratio of male biographies to female biographies was 6:1. Moreover, clever girls occurred only 33 times, compared to 131 clever boys.[37] A study of elementary texts used in Kalamazoo, Michigan, reported similar results. The books showed only 40 occupations for women compared to 215 for men. The female adult is always a mother and always at home.[38]

An extensive survey of the words used in elementary texts revealed that "he" occurred three times as often as "she." "Boy" occurred twice as often as "girl." In an interesting switch, however, "wife" was found three times more than the word "husband." This is not necessarily inconsistent, though, because the emphasis on wife suggests that society heavily stresses that role, but for the boy, husband is not necessarily such an important role.[39]

Textbooks, then, have given official sanction to the subordinate roles that society imposes on women in real life. In assessing what textbooks should be, Marjorie U'Ren has said:

No one asks that stories be artificially measured out part by part to assure an absolute equality of material. What is needed is a distribution of stories that inspire all peoples and both sexes to aim high and achieve their best, and an end to a textbook world where male figures outnumber and dominate, and female characters lack spirit, curiosity, and originality.[40]

3. *Teacher-student interactions.*   The purpose of schools at every level is to educate everyone based on the assumption of equal opportunity for all. This idealistic goal is not

met in a number of areas which include a bias against females. Here we will examine how this works in only one area—teacher expectations for pupils by sex.

Typically, teachers expect boys to be aggressive, active, and independent achievers while girls should be submissive, quiet, and conforming.[41] These expectations result in a self-fulfilling prophecy that is beneficial to boys, for the "masculine" traits encouraged are exactly the ones that promote achievement, motivation, and success. Conversely, the "feminine" traits encouraged by teachers suppress creativity and inhibit achievement.

The differing attitudes teachers hold for boys and girls have other subtle effects that result in advantages for boys. One representative study of twenty-one fourth and sixth grade classes found that male and female teachers interacted *more* with boys than with girls in four major categories of teaching behavior: approval, instruction, listening to the child, and disapproval.[42] The boys got more attention than girls which likely encourages them to participate in classroom discussions, to be inquisitive, to be tougher in their thinking processes, and to be more confident in their ability to solve problems.

4. *The reinforcement of sex roles in school sports.* Sport in American schools has historically been almost exclusively a male preserve. This is clearly evident as one compares by sex the number of participants, facilities, support of school administrators, and financial support.

Such disparities are based on the assumption that competitive sport is basically a masculine activity and that the proper role of girls is that of spectator and cheerleader. What is the impact on a society that encourages its boys and young men to participate in sports while expecting its girls and young women to be spectators and cheerleaders? The answer is that sport thereby serves to reinforce societal expectations for males and females. Males are to be dominant, aggressive—the doers—while females are expected to be passive supporters of men, attaining status through the efforts of their menfolk. Kathryn Clarenback of the University of Wisconsin has made this point well in the following passage:

The overemphasis on protecting girls from strain or injury, and underemphasis on developing skills and experiencing teamwork, fits neatly into the pattern of the second sex. Girls are the spectators and the cheerleaders. They organize the pep clubs, sell pompons, make cute, abbreviated costumes, strut a bit between halves and idolize the current football hero. This is perfect preparation for the adult role of women—to stand decoratively on the sidelines of history and cheer on the men, who make the decisions. [43]

A very important consequence of minimizing sport participation for women is that approximately one-half of the population is denied access to all that sport has to offer (enjoyment, teamwork, goal achievement, ego enhancement, social status, competitiveness, and character building). School administrators, school boards, and citizens of local communities have long assumed that sports participation has general educational value. If so, then clearly girls should also be allowed to receive the benefits.

In June, 1975, the federal government set forth guidelines to equalize opportunities for females in education. Every school that receives federal aid is affected: 2700 colleges and universities and 16,000 public school districts. With respect to sport, these guidelines insist that schools: integrate their physical education classes; provide athletic supplies, equipment, facilities, and travel allowances for women equal to those of men; sponsor separate women's teams for contact sports if requested; and allow women and men to participate together on teams in noncontact sports.

This act by the government will have far-reaching consequences. The most important for our consideration is that increased numbers of women will participate, and this will have a dramatic impact in time on the breaking down of sex-role stereotypes. As David Auxter has put it:

In America we use athletics extensively to teach, not fact so much as attitudes. Above all, we value athletics because they are competitive. That is, they teach that achievement and success are desirable, that they are worth disciplining oneself for. By keeping girls out of sports, we have denied them this educational experience. Our male-dominated society prefers females to be physically and psychologically dependent. Denying them athletic opportunities has been a good way of molding girls into the kind of human we want them to be. Better athletic programs will develop more aggressive females, women with confidence who value personal achievement and have a strong sense of identity.[44]

5. *Female role models in education.* A subtle form of sex-role reinforcement in education is found in the types of jobs held by men and women. The pattern is the familiar one found in hospitals, business offices, and throughout the occupational world—women occupying the bottom rungs while men are in the prestigious and decision-making positions. In 1971 less than 1 percent of superintendents, 3 percent of high school principals, 4 percent of middle school and junior high principals, and 21 percent of elementary school principals were women. A study of women administrators in New England done in 1977–1978 indicates little change in the situation from 1971.[45] This pattern is a hidden bias that presents a subtle message to youngsters, reinforcing the prevailing sex-role stereotype.

Whenever an issue is too big or troublesome for the teacher (usually female) to handle, the principal (usually male) is called upon to offer the final decision, to administer the ultimate punishment or reward. And children, so alert to body cues, so sensitive to messages transmitted through the silent language, must detect the teacher's change in demeanor, the slight shift in posture that transforms confidence into deference and respect. It would be hard to misinterpret the relationship. The teacher is the boss of the class; the principal is boss of the teacher. And the principal is a man.[46]

If women elementary teachers portray a negative image to youngsters, then the problem is compounded many times as the level of education increases. For whereas 88 percent of elementary school teachers are women, only 47 percent are at the junior and senior high school level, and the proportion decreases to 26 percent at the junior college level, 23 percent at the college level, and 15 percent at the university level.[47]

This declining proportion of women instructors as the level of education increases demonstrates the relative absence of women as positive role models. Moreover, the message is clear—the higher the intellectual level, the more men predominate because they are more capable. But apparently being capable is not as relevant as gender. There are several indications that discrimination is the source of the paucity of women at these higher levels. Women at these levels tend to be lower in academic rank than men, make less money (even when statistically controlling for academic level), are less likely to have tenure, and are virtually excluded from administrative positions.

The bias against women is clearly evident in higher education. In 1979 the pay for women faculty averaged 20 percent less than for men. Although the women's share of teaching jobs was 24.2 percent, it was only 10 percent at the top level—full professor. Between 1975 and 1979 about 10 times more men than women became tenured full professors and twice as many men became associate professors.[48]

6. *Counseling.* A fundamental task of school guidance personnel is to aid students in their choice of a career. This involves testing students for their occupational preference and aptitude, advising them on course selection and what kind of post-high-school training they should get. The guidance that students receive on career choice tends to be biased in at least two ways. Foremost are the attitudes of the counselors themselves. As products of society, they typically hold traditional assumptions about what is a "normal" career for a boy and what is "normal" for a girl. Several research studies provide some proof that counselors do retain traditional sex-role stereotypes. One study found that there is a counselor bias against women entering a "masculine" profession. Another found that male school counselors tended to think of women in feminine roles characterized by feminine personality traits, and that male counselors associated college-bound girls with tradition-ally feminine occupations at the semiskilled level, while female counselors associated college-bound girls with occupations requiring a college education.[49]

7. *Teacher education.* Each year about 200,000 prospective teachers graduate from colleges and universities in the United States. A recent study indicates that the major textbooks used in teacher education courses are sexist.[50] The researchers found that the 24 most widely adopted texts used in teacher training were sexist in: (1) the lack of experi-ences and contributions by females; (2) the treatment of sex differences; (3) the percentage of total content concerning males; (4) the percentage of total content concerning females; and (5) the use of sexist language. Although the textbooks were sexist in these areas, the researchers felt that the major finding from their analysis was that teacher education texts are characterized by an overwhelming lack of information on sex equity in education. Of these twenty-four widely used texts, twenty-three allocated less than one percent of narrative space to the issue of sexism, and one third of the books failed to mention the topic. Most of the texts characterized by these omissions were in methods of teaching mathematics and science—the very areas in which girls are most likely to experience difficulties.[51]

THE CONSEQUENCES OF TRADITIONAL SEX-ROLE STEREOTYPES

Chapter 13 will be devoted to an extensive discussion of the consequences of sexism. Here we shall limit the discussion to the consequences of the consistent sex-role demands in American society.

Society suppresses the choices of males and females through cultural tyranny. The socialization process forces males and females into behavioral modes, personality charac-teristics, and occupational roles deemed appropriate by society. Most important, these

Panel 7–3
Barriers in Education: Sexism in Academe

The following essay considers the sexism present in one university—Colorado State. It is representative of what might be found at almost any college or university in the United States.

At Colorado State University, there are 332 male full professors and only 10 female full professors. The difference their average salaries is $3,200. At the associate professor level, there are 316 men and only 20 women. In the assistant position we find 163 men and 52 women. Not until we reach the lowest rank, that of instructor, do women outnumber men, 21 to 18. Even there, the trend of paying men higher salaries is followed. . . . We find this paucity of women at the administrative level also. There are no female vice-presidents, and only one female dean out of nine.

At the graduate level, we find that in 1977 there were 213 male [Graduate Teaching Assistants] and only 101 female. Male [Graduate Research Assistants] outnumber women almost 5 to 1 (588 to 140). . . .

In a university that boasts a freshmen (for lack of a better word) class of 52% women, the above figures seem to point to one fact—women are not encouraged and, indeed, may be discouraged, from pursuing a higher education.

Discrimination is also found in classrooms. How often do students encounter a textbook that utilizes the pronoun "she" instead of "he" when talking about a person in general? We are all familiar with the so-called "generic man." At the beginning of this school year, 13 departments were sent letters, asking that course titles that included the term "man" be changed, and suggestions were given for each.* Four responses were received. Only two of

*Course titles which were requested to be changed:
Zoology & Entomology: *Man and the Animal World*
Chemistry: *Man and Society*
Botany and Plant Pathology: *Fungi and Man*
Anthropology: *Beginnings of Mankind*
Philosophy: *Philosophy of Man*

constraints bring about a system that is biased in favor of males. Men possess power and status while women have inferior and supportive roles. Men have the opportunity to develop their talents fully while women may only develop within a severely limited range. In this section we will enumerate the consequences of this pernicious system for individuals in American society.

Cultural tyranny and the stifling of individuality for women. Society expects females to be dependent and passive, and to serve in positions secondary to men. There are three basic responses to this condition. A common response is for women to accept the role that society has imposed and that they have been taught. They are devoted mothers and attentive wives; if they enter the occupational world, they accept servile positions as their rightful place. It must be made clear that to want to be a parent, a housewife or househusband, a nurse, or a secretary is perfectly appropriate. To be passive, emotional, and caring are positive traits. The point, however, is that the socialization process has forced these roles and these traits on half the population regardless of their wishes. The

Social Control in Society

At 9:34 p.m. on July 13, 1977 the electricity went out in New York City and in some areas did not work again for twenty-five hours. Under the cover of darkness many areas of the city were pillaged. More than two thousand stores were broken into with property losses estimated at $1 billion. The plunderers were of all ages. They stole appliances, jewelry, shoes, groceries, clothes, furniture, liquor, and automobiles (fifty new Pontiacs from one dealer). The atmosphere was a mixture of revenge, greed, and festival. Observers characterized the looting binge as a carnival atmosphere in which the actors had no concept of morality. It was as if they were immune from the law and from guilt. All of society's constraints were removed resulting in anarchy. When the lights went out, the social controls on behavior left as well for many citizens.

All social groups have mechanisms to ensure conformity—mechanisms of **social control**. The socialization process is one of these ways by which individuals internalize the norms and values of the group. Persons are taught what is proper, moral, and appropriate. This process is generally so powerful that individuals conform, not out of fear of punishment, but because they *want* to. In other words, group demands *out there* become demands *inside* us. But socialization is never perfect—we are not all robots. As we will see in Chapter 9, people deviate. To cope with this, social groups exert external control—that is, rewards and punishments. These controls are the subject of this chapter.

The focus of this chapter is on social control at the societal level. The dominant modes of socialization vary by type of society. Small, homogeneous societies, for example, are dominated by tradition, while large, modern societies are very much less affected by the force of tradition. Traditional societies tend to have an overriding consensus on societal values; therefore, the family, religion, and the community convey to each individual member a consistent message of which behaviors are appropriate and which ones are not. Although the formal punishment of norm violators does occur in traditional societies, informal controls are usually quite effective and more typical.

In a complex society such as the United States, social control is more difficult to attain because of the existence of different groups with values that are often competing. Therefore, social control tends to be more formal and appears more repressive (because it is more overt) than that which is found in traditional societies. It occurs in many forms and disguises. Social control is accomplished in the home and school and through various other institutions. It is attained through the overt and covert activities of political agencies, psychotherapists, and even genetic engineers. Efforts to manipulate the masses through various techniques of persuasion also keep deviance in check.

The remainder of this chapter is devoted to an extensive examination of the various agents of social control in American society. These are divided into two types by the means used to achieve social control: ideological and direct intervention. The former aims at control through manipulation of ideas and perceptions, while the latter controls the actual behavior of citizens.[1]

AGENTS OF IDEOLOGICAL SOCIAL CONTROL

Ideological social control is the attempt to manipulate the consciousness of citizens so that they accept the ruling ideology and refuse to be moved by competing ideologies. Other goals are to persuade the members of society to comply willingly with the law and to accept without question the existing distribution of societal power and rewards. These goals are accomplished in at least three ways. First, ideological social control is accomplished through the socialization of youth. Young people, for example, are taught the values of individualism, competition, patriotism, and respect for authority at home, in school, in scouting organizations, in sports, and through the media. The socialization process could be referred to as cultural control, since the individual is given authoritative definitions of what should and should not be done, which make it appear as if there were no choice.[2] Second, ideological conformity occurs by frontal attacks on competing ideologies by politicians, ministers, teachers, and other persons in authority. Finally, there are propaganda efforts by political authorities to persuade the public what actions are moral, who the enemies are, and why certain courses of governmental action are required. Let us examine these in detail by describing the agents of social control that are especially important in accomplishing the goal of ideological conformity.

The Family

The primary responsibility of parents is to teach their children the attitudes, values, and behaviors considered appropriate by the parents (and society). Parents universally want their children to succeed. Success is not only measured in terms of monetary achievement but also in whether the child fits in society. This requires that the child learn to behave and think in the ways that are deemed "proper." Although, as noted in Chapter 6, there is a wide latitude in the actual mode of socialization in the family,[3] most children do behave in acceptable ways.

The School

The formal system of education is an important societal agent for conformity. The school insists that the behavioral standards of the community be maintained in speech, dress, and demeanor. More than this, the schools indoctrinate their pupils in the "correct" attitudes about work, respect for authority, and patriotism. The textbooks used in schools have typically not provided an accurate account of history, for example, but rather an account that is biased in the direction the authorities wish to perpetuate. The treatment given minorities in these texts is one indicator of the bias. Another is the contrast between descriptions of the behavior of the United States and the behavior of its enemies in wars.[4]

The schools promote respect for American institutions and the "American Way of

Life." State legislatures, for instance, have passed laws similar to the one in Arizona requiring every student to take a one-semester course in "the essentials and benefits of the free enterprise system."[5] Florida requires a course for high school graduation called *Americanism versus Communism*. The legislation requiring this course noted that the best method for meeting the challenge of communism is "to have the youth of the state and nation thoroughly and completely informed as to the evils, dangers and fallacies of Communism. . . ."[6] Clearly, the goal of such a course is not education but indoctrination.

One critic of the schools is concerned with the problem of conformity, which taken to the extreme results in blind obedience to such malevolent authority figures as Adolph Hitler, Charles Manson, and the Rev. Jim Jones. Rather than turning out conformists the schools should be turning out individuals with the courage to disobey false prophets.

The power of socialization can conceivably be harnessed so as to develop individuals who are rational and skeptical, capable of independent thought, and who can disobey or disagree at the critical moment. Our society, however, continues systematically to instill exactly the opposite. The educational system pays considerable lip service to the development of self-reliance, and places huge emphasis on lofty concepts of individual differences. Little notice is taken of the legions of overly obedient children in the schools; yet, for every overly disobedient child, there are probably twenty who are obeying too much. There is little motivation to encourage the unsqueaky wheels to develop as noisy, creative, independent thinkers who may become bold enough to disagree.[7]

Religion

Established religion in America tends to reinforce the status quo. Few clergy and their parishioners work actively to change the political and economic system. Instead they preach sermons extolling the virtues of "the American Way of Life," and "giving unto Caesar the things which are Caesar's." Directly or indirectly there has been a strong tendency for religious groups throughout American history to accept existing governmental policies, whether they are slavery, war, or the conquest of the Indians.

Religious groups also preserve the status quo by teaching that people should accept an imperfect society (poverty, racism, and war) because they are born sinners. In this way, religion, as Marx suggested, *is* an opiate of the masses because it convinces them to accept an unjust system rather than work to change it. The downtrodden are advised to accept their lot because they will be rewarded in the next life. Thus, they have no need to change the system from below. As Szymanski has argued:

The doctrine of the omnipotence of God and total submission to His will pervades the general world views of religious people, and hence is sublimated as submission to political rulers and the upper class. Religion provides a consolation for the suffering of people on earth and a deflection of one's hopes into the future. Combined with its advocacy of the earthly status quo, religion thus typically serves as a powerful legitimatizing force for upper-class rule. Further, most religions, especially the religions of the working class and the poor—Baptism, Methodism, the Messianic sects, and Catholicism—in their sermons typically condemn radical political movements and preach instead either political abstention or submission to governmental authority.[8]

CROSS-CULTURAL PANEL

Panel 8–1
The Amish

The Amish are a religious sect found mainly in Pennsylvania, Indiana, and Kansas. They are farmers who resist modern technology. They forbid the use of motorcycles, automobiles, and electricity. They wear simple clothes of the nineteenth century. They believe that they are only temporary visitors on earth, and hence remain aloof from it. This explains why they insist on being different. Most important, the Amish insist on conformity within their community.

The Amish descend from Jacob Amman, a Mennonite preacher in Switzerland. The Mennonites and other Anabaptists of that day differed from mainstream Protestants because they believed in the separation of church and state, adult baptism, refusal to bear arms and take oaths. Amman and his followers split away from the Mennonites in 1700 over an issue of church discipline—the *Meidung*. Amman felt that the Mennonites were too lax in their discipline of deviants and that the *Meidung* must be enforced in severe cases. The *Meidung* is one of the most potent of all social control mechanisms. The following is a description by William Kephart of this device used by the Amish to ensure conformity within the community.

The ultimate sanction is imposition of the *Meidung*, or ban, but because of its severity, this form of punishment is used only as a last resort. The Amish community relies heavily on the individual's conscience to tell him what is right and wrong. And since the typical Amishman has a finely developed conscience, actions like gossip or reprimand are usually sufficient to bring about conformity. The *Meidung* would be imposed only if a member

Sport

School and professional sports work to reinforce conforming attitudes and behaviors in the populace in several ways.[9] First, there is the strong relationship between sport and nationalism. Success in international sports competition tends to trigger pride among that nation's citizens. The Olympics and other international games tend to promote an "us vs. them" feeling among athletes, coaches, politicians, the press, and fans. It can be argued, then, that the Olympic Games is a political contest, a symbolic world war in which nations win or lose. Because this interpretation is commonly held, citizens of the nations involved unite behind their flag and their athletes.[10]

The integral interrelationship of sport and nationalism is easily seen in the blatantly militaristic pageantry that surrounds sports contests. The playing of the national anthem, the presentation of the colors, the jet-aircraft fly-overs, the band forming a flag or a liberty bell, are all political acts supportive of the existing political system.

For whatever reason, sport competition and nationalism are closely intertwined. When American athletes compete against those of another country, national unity is the result (for both sides, unless one's athletes do poorly). Citizens take pride in their representatives' accomplishments, viewing them as collective achievements. This identification with ath-

were to leave the church, or marry an outsider, or break a major rule (such as buying an auto) without being repentant.

Although the *Meidung* is imposed by the bishop, he will not act without the near-unanimous vote of the congregation. The ban, however, is total. No one in the district is permitted to talk or associate with the errant party, including members of his own family. Even normal marital relations are forbidden. Should any member of the community ignore the *Meidung*, that person would also be placed under the ban. As a matter of fact, the *Meidung* is honored by *all Amish districts*, including those which are not in full fellowship with the district in question. There is no doubt that the ban is a mighty weapon. Jacob Amman intended it to be.

On the other hand, the ban is not irrevocable. If the member admits the error of his ways—and asks forgiveness of the congregation, in person—the *Meidung* will be lifted and the transgressor readmitted to the fold. No matter how serious the offense, the Amish never look upon someone under the ban as an enemy, but only as one who has erred. And while they are firm in their enforcement of the *Meidung*, the congregation will pray for the errant member to rectify his mistake.

Although imposition of the ban is infrequent, it is far from rare. Males are involved much more often than females, the young more frequently than the old. The *Meidung* would probably be imposed on young males more often were it not for the fact that baptism does not take place before age sixteen, and sometimes not until eighteen. Prior to this time, young males are expected to be—and often are—a little on the wild side, and allowances are made for this fact. The prebaptismal period thus serves as a kind of safety valve.

Baptism changes things, however, for this is the rite whereby the young person officially joins the church and makes the pledge of obedience. Once the pledge is made, the limits of tolerance are substantially reduced. More than one Amish youth has been subjected to the *Meidung* for behavior which, prior to his baptism, had been tolerated.

Source: William M. Kephart, *Extraordinary Groups: The Sociology of Unconventional Life-Styles* (New York: St. Martin's Press, 1976), pp. 26–28. Reprinted by permission of St. Martin's Press, Inc. and Macmillan & Co., Ltd.

letes and their cause of winning for the nation's glory tends to unite a nation's citizens regardless of social class, race, and regional differences. Thus, sport can be used by political leaders whose nations have problems with divisiveness.

We have seen that sport success can unite a nation through pride. After Brazil won the world cup in soccer (*futebol*) for the third time in succession, one observer noted:

The current *futebol* success has promoted a pride in being Brazilian and a unifying symbol without precedent. Even the lower classes of the cities, thanks to television, felt a sense of participation in something representing national life. They know that Brazil is now internationally significant, not necessarily for reasons of interest to the scholar or public figure, but of importance to the common man. It is estimated that over 700 million soccer fans throughout the world watched Brazil defeat England and Italy. The Englishman in his pub, the French worker, the German with a Volkswagen all know that Brazil is not just another large "tropical country," but the homeland of the world's best *futebol* and a legend named Pelé.[11]

This pride in a nation's success, because it transcends the social classes, serves as an opiate of the masses. Sanders has asserted that *futebol* in Brazil enables the poor to forget partially the harshness of their life. It serves also as a safety valve for releasing tensions that might otherwise be directed toward disrupting the existing social order.[12]

The same situation appears to be true of the United States. Virtually all homes have television sets, making it possible for almost everyone to participate vicariously in and identify with local and national sports teams. Because of this, their minds and energies are deflected away from the hunger and misery that are disproportionately the lot of the lower classes in American society.

Sport also acts as an opiate by perpetuating the belief that persons from the lowest classes can be upwardly mobile by success in sports. Clearly this is a myth since for every major leaguer who has come up from poverty, tens of thousands have not. The point, however, is that most Americans *believe* that sport is a mobility escalator and that it is merely a reflection of the opportunity structure of the society in general. Again, poor youth who might otherwise invest their energies to changing the system, work instead on a jump shot. The potential for revolution is thus impeded by sport.

Another way that sport serves to control persons ideologically is by reinforcing American values among the participants.[13] Sport is a vehicle by which the American values of success in competition, hard work, perseverance, discipline, and order are transmitted. This is the explicit reason given for the existence of little league programs for youngsters and the tremendous emphasis on sports in American schools. While vice president, Spiro Agnew voiced the prevailing view well in a speech delivered to the Touchdown Club of Birmingham, Alabama. The following are some excerpts:

Not the least of these values is the American competitive ethic which motivates young Americans . . . to strive toward excellence in everything they undertake. For such young Americans—whether on the athletic field, in the classroom, or on the job—the importance of our competitive ethic lies in the fact that it is only by trial of their abilities—by testing and challenging—can they discover their strengths and, yes, their weaknesses. Out of this process of self-discovery, painful though it may be at times, those young Americans who compete to excel learn to cope with whatever challenges lie ahead in life. And having given their best, they also emerge from the competitive test with greater ability to determine for themselves where their individual talents lie. Life is a great competition. In my judgment it will remain so despite the efforts of the social architects to make it a bland experience, controlled by their providing what they think is best for us. Success is sweet but it entails always the risk of failure. It is very, very important to learn how to lose a contest without being destroyed by the experience. For a man who has not known failure cannot fully appreciate success. . . .

And so, to me, that is the message of competitive sports: not simply trying to win, and to achieve, but learning how to cope with a failure—and to come back. In this regard, let me say something about my personal philosophy concerning the meaning of success and failure in sports for young Americans.

First, I believe that sports—all sports—is one of the few bits of glue that holds society together, one of the few activities in which young people can proceed along avenues where objectives are clear and the desire to win is not only permissible but encouraged.

Opponents of the free-enterprise system tell our young people that to try for material success and personal status is bad; that the only thing worthwhile is to find something to wring your hands about; that the ultimate accomplishment is to make everybody feel better.

I, for one, would not want to live in a society that did not include winning in its philosophy; that would have us live our lives as identical lemmings, never trying to best anybody at anything, all headed in the same direction, departing not from the appointed route, striving not for individual excellence. In short, I would rather be a failure in a competitive society which is our inheritance than to live in a waveless sea of nonachievers.[14]

One explicit goal of sports is to build character. The assumption is that participation in sports from the Little Leagues through the Big Leagues (professional ranks) provides the athletes with those values that are American: achievement in competitive situations through hard work, materialism, progress, and respect for authority. As David Matza has put it: "The substance of athletics contains within itself—in its rules, procedures, training, and sentiments—a paradigm of adult expectations regarding youth."[15] Schools want individuals to follow rules, be disciplined, to work hard, to fit in, and sports accomplish these goals.

Not only do schools insist that athletes behave a certain way during practice and games, but they also strictly monitor the behavior of the athletes in other situations as well. The athletes must conform to the school's norms in dress, speech, demeanor, and grades if they want to continue to participate. In this way, school administrators use athletes as models of decorum. If others in the school and community admire athletes, then athletes serve to preserve the community and school norms.

The Media

The movies, television, newspapers, and magazines also serve basically to reinforce the system. There is clearly a conservative bias among the various corporations involved because their financial success depends on whether the public will buy their product and whether advertisers will use their vehicles. As Wolfe has put it:

Because the media are part of the capitalist system, and because a change in the system would significantly alter the power of a small group of men, it is not surprising that the media engage much of their time in preserving the existing state of affairs. They do this by being conscious propagandists for the system, by reinforcing indirect consciousness manipulation, and by *not* serving as an information vehicle.[16]

That the media reinforce the values and norms of society is seen in newspaper editorials that extol certain persons and events while decrying others and in stories under the caption, "It Could Only Have Happened in America." Soap operas also accomplish this since they are stories involving moral dilemmas with virtue winning out. Television, in particular, has had a significant impact on the values of Americans. The average American child will watch 4000 hours of television before he or she enters elementary school. What are the consistent messages that television emits? One study has concluded that:

Television influences the way children think about jobs, job values, success and social surroundings. It stresses the prestige of upper-middle-class occupations: the professions and big business. It makes essentially middle-class value judgments about jobs and success in life.[17]

In short, the media shape how we evaluate ourselves and others. Just as important, they affect directly the way viewers or readers perceive and interpret events. The media, therefore, have tremendous power to influence us to accept or question the system. Although the media do investigative reporting and occasionally question the system (for example, Watergate, the CIA scandal), the overall impact of the media is supportive of the system.

The Government

Governmental leaders devote a great deal of energy toward ideological social control. One governmental effort is to convince the public that capitalism is good and communism is bad. This is done in political speeches and books. Blatant examples were noted earlier in this chapter of how state legislatures have tried to control the ideological content (patriotism, procapitalism, anticommunism) in schools. Another example of ideological control is seen in government agencies such as the Defense Department and the departments of Agriculture, Commerce, and Education. Each maintains active public relations programs which spend millions of dollars to persuade the public of their views.

The public can also be manipulated by being convinced that their security is threatened by an enemy. This could be done to unify a nation troubled by internal strife. The advice Machiavelli gave his "prince" is a regrettable truth: "if the Prince is in trouble, he should promote a war." This was the advice that Secretary of State Seward gave to President Lincoln prior to the Civil War. Although expedient advice from the standpoint of preserving unity, it was, Lincoln noted, only a short-term solution. Similar efforts to unite by suggesting an external threat, although short of declaring war, have been tried by various American political leaders or candidates for office.

Perhaps the most obvious way that government officials attempt to shape public opinion is through speeches, especially on television. The President can request free prime-time television to speak to the public. These efforts are typically intended to unite the American people against an enemy (inflation, deflation, the energy crisis, communism).

Conclusion

We have described how the various agents of ideological social control operate. Perhaps the best evidence that they are successful is that few of the downtrodden in American society question the legitimacy of the political and economic system. Karl Marx theorized that the "have-nots" in a capitalist society (the poor, the minority group members, the workers) would eventually feel their common oppression and unite to overthrow the owners of capital. That this has not happened in America is due, in large part, to the success of the various agents of ideological social control.[18]

AGENTS OF DIRECT SOCIAL CONTROL

Direct social control refers to attempts to punish or neutralize organizations or individuals who deviate from society's norms. The deviant targets here are essentially four: the poor, the mentally ill, criminals, and political dissidents. This section will be devoted to three agents of social control whose efforts are directed at these targets—social welfare, sciences/ medicine, and the government.

Welfare

Piven and Cloward, in their classic study of public welfare, have argued that public assistance programs serve a social control function in times of mass unemployment by defusing social unrest.[19] When large numbers of people are suddenly barred from their traditional occupations, the legitimacy of the system itself may be questioned. Crime, riots, looting, and social movements bent on changing the existing social and economic arrangements become more widespread. Under this threat, relief programs are initiated or expanded by the government. Piven and Cloward show how during the Great Depression, for example, the government remained aloof from the needs of the unemployed until there was a great surge of political disorder. The function of social welfare, then, is to defuse social unrest through direct intervention of the government. Added proof for Piven and Cloward's thesis is the contraction or even abolishment of public assistance programs when political stability is restored.*

Science and Medicine

The practitioners and theoreticians in science and medicine (physicians, psychotherapists, geneticists, electrical engineers, and public health officials) have devised a number of techniques for shaping and controlling the behavior of nonconformists.

Drugs are often used to control the behavior of deviants. Powerful drugs have revolutionized the practice of psychiatry.[21] These drugs, called neuroleptics, are used to quell the disordered thoughts of schizophrenics, shorten psychotic episodes, and control violent behavior. They do not cure the problems, however, only mask them. Moreover, critics have charged, the use of drug therapy for mental problems too often replaces talking to people and making them feel wanted.

Drugs are often used in nursing homes to control disruptive behaviors in the elderly. A 1980 study, for example, found that in 173 nursing homes in Tennessee, 43 percent of the nearly 6,000 residents received antipsychotic drugs.[22]

Drugs are prescribed by school psychologists to tranquilize hyperactive students in American schools.[23] They are also commonly used in mental hospitals and prisons to calm aggressive inmates. Rebellious prison inmates have been given such drugs as Anectine, which induces sensations of extreme terror, suffocation, and imminent death. After such an episode the individual is told to reform or face another dose of the drug. In one Iowa prison the drug Apomorphine, which causes uncontrolled vomiting, has been used on inmates who used abusive language or smoked illegally. The drug Prolixin, which

---

*The second function of welfare mentioned by Piven and Cloward is more subtle (and fits more logically as an agent of ideological social control). Even in good times some people must live on welfare (the disabled, the husbandless who must care for dependent children). By having a category of persons on welfare who live in wretched conditions and who are continuously degraded, work is legitimized. Thus, the poor on welfare serve as an object lesson—keeping even those who work for low wages relatively satisfied with their lot. As Piven and Cloward have concluded:

> In sum, market values and market incentives are weakest at the bottom of the social order. To buttress weak market controls and ensure the availability of marginal labor, an outcast class—the dependent poor—is created by the relief system. This class, whose members are of no productive use, is not treated with indifference, but with contempt. Its degradation at the hands of relief officials serves to celebrate the virtue of all work and deters actual or potential workers from seeking aid.[20]

CROSS-CULTURAL PANEL

Panel 8-2
The Control of Illicit Sex Among the Arabs

In the kinship culture of the Arab world . . . family bonds are so strong that all members suffer "blackening of the face" after the dishonorable act of any one. However, within this general context, there is for the Arab mind a sharp distinction between those shameful events that do involve women and those that do not. In the Arab world, the greatest dishonor that can befall a man results from the sexual misconduct of his daughter or sister, or *bint 'amm* (one's father's brother's daughter). The marital infidelity of a wife, on the other hand, brings to the Arab husband only emotional effects and not dishonor.

The roots of this particular view of male honor go deep into the structure and dynamics of the Arab kin group. The ties of blood, of patrilineal descent, can never be severed, and they never weaken throughout a person's life. This means that a woman, even though she marry into a different kin group, never ceases to be a member of her own paternal family. Her paternal family, in turn, continues to be responsible for her. This has beneficial effects for the married woman, especially during that difficult period in her life which precedes the time when her sons reach maturity and become her supporters and defenders. Prior to that time, the young wife, who is considered something of an outsider by her husband's family, can always count on the aid and sympathy of her own father and brothers. The very knowledge that these men are lined up solidly behind her, and are ready, if need be, even to fight for her, puts a restraint on her husband's family in their treatment of a young daughter-in-law.

Whatever credit or discredit a woman earns reflects back on her own paternal family. This continuing responsibility comes powerfully into play if a woman becomes guilty of a sexual indiscretion, or if her behavior arouses as much as a suspicion that she may be tempted to do something forbidden by the traditional code. The most powerful deterrent devised by Arab culture against illicit sex (which means any sexual relations between a man and a woman who are not married to each other) is the equation of family honor with the sexual conduct of its daughters, single or married. If a daughter becomes guilty of the slightest sexual indiscretion (which is defined in various terms in various places), her father and brothers become dishonored also. Family honor can be restored only by punishing the guilty woman; in conservative circles, this used to mean putting her to death.

That the sexual conduct of women is an area sharply differentiated from other areas of the honor-shame syndrome is reflected in the language. While honor in its non-sexual, general connotation is termed *"sharaf,"* the specific kind of honor that

produces a catatonic state, has also been used on prison inmates who are judged by their captors to need additional control.

Another social control use of drugs is through methadone maintenance.[24] In these programs heroin addicts are provided by an official agency with an addictive drug that is cheap and easy to administer—methadone. The purpose of such programs is to reduce the

is connected with women and depends on their proper conduct is called " *'ird*." *Sharaf* is something flexible: depending on a man's behavior, way of talking and acting, his *sharaf* can be acquired, augmented, diminished, lost, regained, and so on. In contrast, *'ird* is a rigid concept: every woman has her ascribed *'ird*; she is born with it and grows up with it; she cannot augment it because it is something absolute, but it is her duty to preserve it. A sexual offense on her part, however slight, causes her *'ird* to be lost, and once lost, it cannot be regained. It is almost as if the physical attribute of virginity were transposed in the *'ird* to the emotional-conceptual level. Both virginity and *'ird* are intrinsically parts of the female person; they cannot be augmented, they can only be lost, and their loss is irreparable. The two are similar in one more respect: even if a woman is attacked and raped, she loses her *'ird* just as she loses her virginity. Where the two differ, of course, is in the circumstance that the legal, approved, and expected loss of virginity during the wedding night has no counterpart in the *'ird*: a good woman preserves it, guards it jealously until her dying day.

What is even more remarkable is that the *sharaf* of the men depends almost entirely on the *'ird* of the women of their family. True, a man can diminish or lose his *sharaf* by showing lack of bravery or courage, or by lack of hospitality and generosity. However, such occurrences are rare because the men learn in the course of their early enculturation to maintain at all cost the appearances of bravery, hospitality, and generosity. Should a man nevertheless become guilty of an open transgression of any of these, he will, of course, lose his honor, but this is not accompanied by any institutionalized and traditionally imposed physical punishment. Over crimes which are outside the focus of the code of ethics, such as killing, stealing, breaking promises, accepting bribes, and other such misdeeds, Arab opinion is divided: some say such acts would affect a man's *sharaf*, others feel they would not. But as to the results of a woman's transgression of the *'ird* there is complete and emphatic unanimity: it would destroy the *sharaf* of her menfolk. This led one student of Arab ethics to the conclusion that the core of the *sharaf* "is clearly the protection of one's female relatives' *'ird*." To which we can add that this attitude is characteristic of the Arab world as a whole, and that, moreover, a transgression of the *'ird* by a woman and by her paramour is the only crime (apart from homicide) which requires capital punishment according to the Arabic ethical code. Since any indiscretion on her part hurts her paternal family and not her husband's, it is her paternal family—her father himself, or her brothers, or her father's brother's son—who will punish her, by putting her to death, which is considered the only way of repairing the damage done to the family honor.

Source: Excerpt from *The Arab Mind* by Raphael Patai, pp. 119–122. Copyright © 1973 by Raphael Patai. Reprinted by permission of Charles Scribner's Sons.

crime rate among heroin addicts by eliminating their dependence on that drug, the costs of which are so prohibitive that criminal activity is almost mandatory. In some of the more responsible programs addicts are eventually weaned from the methadone over a period of months. While such programs do serve this social control function, most do not attempt to treat the source of the addiction.

Psychologists and psychotherapists are clearly agents of social control. Their goal is to aid persons who, in the patient's eyes and the eyes of others, do not follow the expectations of the society. In other words, they attempt to treat persons considered "abnormal" in order to make them "normal." By focusing on the individual and his adjustment, the mental health practitioners validate, enforce, and reinforce the established ways of society. The implicit assumption is that the individual is at fault and needs to change, not that society is the root cause of mental suffering.

A special category of psychiatrists—forensic psychiatrists—are explicitly involved as agents of social control. These persons are employed as consultants by the courts to advise whether a particular defendant: (1) is competent to stand trial or not; (2) should be involuntarily committed to a mental hospital or not; and (3) can, if already confined to a mental hospital, be released. Obviously, these duties give forensic psychiatrists unusual powers. They, because of their expertise, can determine the defendant's fate. Especially powerful is their ability to even take away the defendant's right to a trial by recommending that he or she is incompetent. Studies have shown that forensic psychiatrists are quite conservative in their judgments—that is, they are prone to err in the direction of confinement rather than freedom. The reasons for this tendency are two. First, the community pressures are usually for confinement of persons thought to act abnormally. Second, there is always the fear that a person released on their recommendation might be charged later with a serious crime. If this were to happen, the credibility of the psychiatrist would be challenged and he or she probably would not be asked to consult for the court again. One observer, Henry Steadman, has summed up the role of the forensic psychiatrist this way: "Forensic psychiatry is intimately connected with the political forces of social control. Its legitimation appears to be greatly tied up in its ability to apply social control in a manner favorable to existing power structures."[25]

Psychosurgery is yet another method with important implications for social control. As with drug therapy or psychotherapy, individuals who are considered abnormal are treated to correct the problem, but this time through brain surgery.[26] With modern techniques, surgeons can operate on localized portions of the brain that govern particular behaviors (for example, sex, aggression, appetite, or fear). The technology has advanced to the point where surgeons can now implant small electrodes that not only make it possible to record the brain's electrical activity but also, by stimulating a particular area of the brain, to control the behavior of the subject.

Clearly, such a telemetric system, with its ability to monitor and control behavior by remote control, approaches the ultimate technique of social control. All deviants or potential deviants could be outfitted with the electronic device and they would remain "normal." The procedure could replace jails. Instead of jail, or as a condition of parole, individuals could be equipped with a telemetric control system. This would presumably benefit the offender because it is an alternative to jail. Society would benefit in three ways: (1) telemetry is less costly than maintaining jails; (2) the offender would continue to support his or her dependents; and (3) the offender is conditioned to nondeviant behavior, thus reducing to zero the probability of recidivism.[27]

Although some of the preceding techniques have the potential for absolute social control in a "Brave New World," another scientific endeavor, **genetic engineering**, if successfully applied, would herald its ultimate achievement. The rationale of **eugenics**, the improvement of the human race through control of hereditary factors, has operated for some time in American society. Through sterilization, categories of persons labeled defective have not been allowed to reproduce. From 1907 to 1964, for instance, over 64,000 persons in 30 states were legally sterilized for abnormalities such as drunkenness, criminality, sexual perversion, and feeblemindedness.[28] By 1971, 21 states still had laws authorizing eugenic sterilization of "mental defectives."

The sterilization of the poor is accomplished also by more subtle techniques.[29] In 1975, for example, the Department of Health, Education and Welfare proposed that the government pay 90 percent of the costs of sterilization of the poor but only 50 percent for abortions. By such a tactic, of course, HEW encourages the long-term eugenics solution of sterilization over abortions.

Experts inform us that the potential for eugenics will progress dramatically in the next few decades. **Cloning,** the creating of large numbers of genetically identical individuals (with the traits deemed desirable by society) may be possible in the future.[30] An important question, if cloning were feasible, is which human traits will be included and which ones will be excluded? Should aggression be omitted from the behavioral traits of future people? If so, passive subjects could be totally controlled without fear of revolution. The social–political–economic system, whatever its composition, would go unchallenged and society would be tranquil. The logic of genetic engineering, while positive in the sense of ridding future generations of hereditary diseases, is frightening in its basic assumption that problems arise, not from the faults of society, but from the genes of individuals in society.

Should the poor be forbidden to reproduce? They should if one accepts the argument of psychologist Richard Herrnstein that the poor are poor (see Chapter 11) for genetic reasons.[31] Or should those males with an extra Y chromosome be sterilized since some research findings have noted that these persons tend to have a greater probability than those with a normal XY arrangement to be criminals or mentally ill? Or should blacks be sterilized because they score noticeably lower than whites on IQ tests and they are more likely to be adjudicated as criminals?

Similar questions can be raised about the other techniques in this section. The creativity of the scientific community has presented the powerful in society with unusually effective means to enforce conformity. The aggressive in schools, prisons, mental hospitals, and in society can be anesthetized. But what is aggressive behavior? What is violence? In 1973, for example, the then-Governor of California, Ronald Reagan, endorsed a proposal, which came from his Director of Corrections, that would allow psychosurgery as a "cure" for violence. But who is violent? Should psychosurgery have been used on the protestors in the political demonstrations of the late 1960s? Was Martin Luther King, Jr., violent? Although he advocated nonviolent techniques, his goal was to change a system oppressive to blacks and this brought violence in its wake. Society would have been much more tranquil without a Martin Luther King, Jr., aggressively seeking changes the majority did not want. Thus, it could be argued, he would have been a likely candidate for psychosurgery to cure him of his "violent" inclinations.

Obviously, the identification of deviants to be controlled is a crucial one. The Law Enforcement Assistance Administration (LEAA) of the Department of Justice provided a grant to develop a technique to identify individuals who are violence prone. But can an instrument be developed to measure such a tendency accurately? Moreover, what if it could? The labeling of persons as violence-prone will doubtless have a self-fulfilling prophecy effect as others interact with them on the basis of that label. As an extreme example of how far this could go, Dr. Arnold Hutchnecker, former physician to President Nixon, has suggested a plan whereby all six- to eight-year-olds in the nation would be

Panel 8–3
The Sterilization Solution

Throughout recent American history various public officials have supported the involuntary sterilization of persons considered undesirable. Three examples make this point.

In 1924 Virginia passed a law permitting the involuntary sterilization of mental patients, the mentally retarded, habitual criminals, and others considered misfits by society. Three years later the U.S. Supreme Court upheld this law by a vote of 8 to 1. Justice Oliver Wendell Holmes declared in the majority opinion:

In order to protect us from being swamped by incompetents it is better for all the world instead of waiting to execute degenerate offspring for crimes or let them starve for their imbe-

given a predictive psychological test for their criminal potential. Those who were thus labeled as potential criminals would then be sent to rehabilitation centers. This plan was not implemented by the government, but the implications of such a proposal are staggering.

Although the Hutchnecker plan was not put into effect, a potential forerunner of it was planned by the Department of Health, Education and Welfare in 1975. Under this plan, a massive psychological screening would occur for all those children eligible for Medicaid (approximately 13 million of the nation's poorest children). The danger of the mental screening of these youngsters is that the tests, themselves subject to errors of measurement and interpretation, would result in stigmatizing labels such as "mentally retarded," "brain damaged," "hyperkinetic," and "learning disabled." These designations tend to control the individuals so labeled by excluding them in "special" classes or institutions.[32]

The Government

The government, as the legitimate holder of power in society, is directly involved in the control of its citizens. A primary objective of the government is to provide for the welfare of its citizens. This includes protection of their lives and property. It requires, further, that order be maintained within the society. There is a clear mandate, then, for the government to apprehend and punish criminals. Not so clear, however, is the legitimacy of a government in a democracy to stifle dissent, which is done in the interests of preserving order. The American heritage, best summed up in the Declaration of Independence, provides a clear rationale for dissent:

Governments are instituted among men, deriving their just powers from the consent of the governed. That whenever any form of government becomes destructive of these ends [the rights of life, liberty, and the pursuit of happiness], it is the right of the people to alter or to abolish it, and to institute a new government, laying its foundation on such principals and organizing its powers in such form as to them shall seem most likely to effect their safety and happiness.

cility, if society can prevent those who are manifestly unfit from continuing their kind. . . . The principle that sustains compulsory vaccination is broad enough to cover cutting Fallopian tubes. . . .

A representative in the Oklahoma House sponsored a bill in 1979 that would provide for the castration of rapists whose victims were under the age of 18, whose crime was especially cruel, or who seem to demonstrate a high probability of recidivism. Requiring 51 votes for passage, the bill received 49 votes for and 47 against.

In 1980 the chairperson of the Texas Welfare Board and mayor of Richmond, Texas for thirty-two years said that he supported sterilization of welfare recipients. "I've always felt that when you cannot support yourself or your family, you give up certain rights. One of these is bringing in more children, and if you don't want to give that up, then get a job and get off welfare."

The American government, then, is faced with a dilemma. American tradition and values affirm that dissent is appropriate. Two facts of political life work against this principle, however. First, for social order to prevail, a society needs to ensure that existing power relationships are maintained over time (otherwise anarchy will result). Second, the well-off in society benefit from the existing power arrangements so they use their influence (which is considerable, as noted in the previous chapter) to encourage the repression of challenges to the government. The evidence is strong that the American government has opted for repression of dissent. Let us examine this evidence.

To begin with, we must peruse the processes of law enactment and law enforcement. These two processes are both directly related to political authority. Some level of government determines what the law will be (that is, which behaviors are to be allowed and which ones are to be forbidden) and the agents of political authorities then apprehend and punish violators. Clearly, the law is employed to control behaviors that might otherwise endanger the general welfare (for example, the crimes of murder, rape, and theft). But laws also promote certain points of view at the expense of others (for example, the majority instead of the minority, or the status quo rather than change). With this in mind, let us turn to the two schools of thought on the function of the law—the prevailing liberal view and the Marxist interpretation.[33]

The dominant view in American society is based on liberal democratic theory and is congruent with the order model. The state exists to maintain order and stability. Law is a body of rules enacted by representatives of the people in the interests of the people. The state and law, therefore, are essentially neutral, dispensing rewards and punishments without bias. A basic assumption of this view is that the political system is pluralistic—that is, the existence of a number of interest groups of more-or-less equal power. The laws, then, reflect compromise and consensus among these various interest groups. In this way the interests of all are protected.

Contrary to the prevailing view of law based on consensus for the common good is the view of the radical criminologists, which is based on conflict theory. The assumptions of this model are: (1) the state exists to serve the ruling class (the owners of large corporations and financial institutions); (2) the law and the legal system reflect and serve the needs of the ruling class; and (3) the interests of the ruling class are served by the law when domestic order prevails and challenges to changing the economic and political system are successfully thwarted. In other words, the law does not serve society as a whole, but the interests of the ruling class prevail.

Closely related to the Marxian view of the role of law in capitalist societies is the interest-group theory of Richard Quinney.[34] The essence of this theory is that a crime is behavior that conflicts with the interests of those segments of society that have the power to shape criminal policy.

Law is made by men, representing special interests, who have the power to translate their interests into public policy. Unlike the pluralist conception of politics, law does not represent a compromise of the diverse interests of society, but supports some interests at the expense of others.[35]

Quinney's view is in the conflict model tradition. Society is held together by some segments coercing other segments. Interest groups are unequal in power. The conflict among interest groups results in the powerful getting their way in determining public policy. Evidence for this position is seen in the successful efforts of certain interest groups to get favorable laws: the segregation laws imposed by whites on blacks, the repression of political dissidents whose goal is to transform society, and the passage of income tax laws that benefit the rich at the expense of wage earners.

Quinney's model makes a good deal of sense. The model is not universally applicable, however, because certain crimes—burglary, murder, and rape—would be regarded as crimes no matter which interest group was in power.[36] A very important part of his theory that does fit almost universally is his proposition that: "*The probability that criminal definitions will be applied varies according to the extent to which the behaviors of the powerless conflict with the interests of the power segments* (italics in the original)."[37]

The law, of course, provides the basis for establishing what is criminal behavior. Enforcement of the law is accomplished by the police and the courts. The evidence is overwhelming that the law is unequally enforced in American society. Let us direct our attention here, rather, to the efforts of other agencies in the political system to control deviance, especially political deviance.[38]

Government agencies have a long history of surveillance of citizens.[39] The pace quickened in the 1930s and increased further with the Communist threat in the 1950s. Surveillance reached its peak during the height of antiwar and civil rights protests of the late 1960s and early 1970s. The FBI's concern with internal security, for example, dates back to 1936 when President Roosevelt directed J. Edgar Hoover to investigate domestic Communist and Fascist organizations in the United States.[40] In 1939, as World War II began in Europe, President Roosevelt issued a proclamation that the FBI would be in charge of investigating subversive activities, espionage, and sabotage, and directed that all law enforcement offices should give the FBI any relevant information on suspected activities. These directives began a pattern followed by the FBI under the administrations of Presidents Truman, Eisenhower, Kennedy, Johnson, Nixon, Ford, Carter, and Reagan.

The scope of these abuses by the FBI and other government agencies such as the CIA,

the National Security Agency, and the Internal Revenue Service, is incredible. In the name of "national security" the following actions have been taken against American citizens:

item: The Internal Revenue Service monitored the activities of 99 political organizations and 11,359 individuals during the period of 1969 to 1973. During and since that period the IRS has used a variety of methods to invade the private lives of individuals, including the use of seizure-liens, assessments, penalties, wiretaps, and even hiring prostitutes to occupy suspects while agents photocopied the contents of briefcases.[41]

item: From 1967 to 1973 the NSA (National Security Agency) monitored the overseas telephone calls and cables of approximately 1,650 Americans and U.S. organizations, as well as almost 6,000 foreign nationals and groups.[42]

item: The CIA opened and photographed nearly 250,000 first class letters in the United States between 1953 and 1973.[43]

item: As Director of the CIA, William Colby acknowledged to Congress that his organization had opened the mail of private citizens and accumulated secret files on more than 10,000 Americans.[44]

item: The FBI over the years conducted about 1,500 break-ins of foreign embassies and missions, mob hangouts, and the headquarters of such organizations as the Ku Klux Klan and the American Communist Party.[45]

item: The FBI confessed to the Senate Intelligence Committee that it had committed 238 burglaries against 14 domestic organizations during a 26-year period ending in 1968.[46]

item: The FBI collected over 500,000 dossiers between 1959 and 1971 on Communists, black leaders, student radicals, and feminists.[47]

item: The husband of an officer in ACTION, a St. Louis civil rights organization, received a handwritten note that said: "Look man, I guess your old lady doesn't get enough at home or she wouldn't be shucking and jiving with our black men in ACTION, you dig? Like, all she wants to integrate is the bedroom and we black sisters ain't gonna take no second best from our men. So lay it on her man or get her the hell off Newstead (Street)." The couple soon separated and the local FBI officer wrote to headquarters: "This matrimonial stress and strain should cause her to function much less effectively in ACTION."[48]

item: In 1972 the FBI paid 7,402 "ghetto informants" to provide information about racial extremists.[49]

item: In 1970 actress Jean Seberg helped raise money for a militant organization, the Black Panthers. According to documents released by the FBI after the suicide of Ms. Seberg in 1979, the FBI tried to discredit the actress by planting the rumor that the father of her baby was a prominent Black Panther leader. This false story led to a miscarriage and psychotic behavior, and possibly to her suicide.[50]

These are but a few examples of government abuses against its citizens. To make the point clearer, we will describe in greater detail two nefarious (but representative) campaigns of the government: (1) the FBI's vendetta against Martin Luther King, Jr.; and (2) the FBI's campaign to nullify the effectiveness of the Socialist Workers party.

The FBI had a campaign to destroy civil rights groups. The most infamous of these was the attempt to negate the power of Martin Luther King, Jr. King had been openly critical of the Bureau's ineffectual enforcement of civil rights laws, which apparently led the Director, J. Edgar Hoover, to label King "the most notorious liar in the U.S." and to launch a vendetta against him.[51] From 1957, when King became prominent in the Montgomery Bus Boycott, the FBI monitored King's activities under its vague authority to investigate "subversives." The more powerful King became the greater the FBI's surveillance of him. King was indexed in the files as a Communist and someone to be imprisoned in the event of a "national emergency." This charge against King was based on the allegation that two of his associates in the Southern Christian Leadership Conference were Communists.

Because Hoover had convinced the Attorney General, Robert Kennedy, of the possible link between King and the Communists, Kennedy authorized wiretaps of King's phones, which continued for the next two years. Unknown to Kennedy was that the FBI planned to use the wiretaps to discredit King.

The FBI's efforts to neutralize or even destroy King were intensified with King's increasing popularity as exemplified by his *I had a Dream* speech before 250,000 in Washington, D.C. in August of 1963. King was thus characterized in an FBI memo:

He stands head and shoulders over all other Negro leaders put together when it comes to influencing great masses of Negroes. *We must mark him now . . . as the most* dangerous Negro of the future of this Nation from the standpoint of Communism, the Negro and national security.[52]

The efforts now escalated to include physical and photographic surveillance and the placement of illegal bugs in his living quarters. The tapes of conversations in a Washington hotel were used by the FBI to imply that King engaged in extramarital sexual activities. They used these tapes, which may or may not have been altered, to dishonor King. At the very time King was receiving great honors such as the Nobel Peace Prize, *Time* magazine's "Man of the Year" award, and numerous honorary degrees, the FBI countered with briefings, distribution of the "tapes" to newspeople and columnists, and congressional testimony about King's "Communist" activities and "private" behavior. The FBI even briefed officials of the National Council of Churches and other church bodies about King's alleged deviance.

The smear campaign against King reached its zenith when the FBI mailed the "tapes" to the Southern Christian Leadership Conference offices in Atlanta with a covering letter suggesting that he commit suicide or face humiliation when the tapes were made public on the eve of the Nobel award ceremonies in Sweden.

Summing up the sordid affair, Halperin and his associates have editorialized:

The FBI had turned its arsenal of surveillance and disruption techniques on Martin Luther King and the civil rights movement. It was concerned not with Soviet agents nor with criminal activity, but with the political and personal activities of a man and a movement committed to nonviolence and democracy. King was not the first such target, not the last. In the end we are all victims, as our political life is distorted and constricted by the FBI, a law enforcement agency now policing politics.[53]

This comment is justifiably critical of the FBI. I believe that the FBI's tactics were illegal whether King was a communist or not. But that is a moot point because King was not a communist. In testimony before a Senate committee, the FBI's assistant deputy director James Adams was asked by Senator Frank Church if the FBI ever found that King was a communist. Replied Adams, "No, we did not."[54]

Another example of an FBI vendetta against a non-existent threat involved the Socialist Workers party, a small, peaceful, and legal political party.[55] This party became the target of FBI abuses because it supported such causes as Castro's Cuba and worked for racial integration in the South. For these transgressions, the FBI kept the SWP under surveillance for 34 years. FBI documents have revealed that in one 6½-year period in the early 1960s the agency burglarized the offices of the party in 94 raids, often with the complicity of the New York City police department. Over this period FBI agents photographed 8,700 pages of party files and compiled dossiers totaling 8 million pages.

The FBI tried to destroy the party by sending anonymous letters to members' employers, working to keep the party's candidates off the ballot, and by otherwise sabotaging political campaigns. They also used informants to collect information about the political views of the organization.*

---

*The SWP has sued the FBI (and won) for its violations of the SWP's civil rights.

Several points need to be made about these FBI activities. Obviously, these were a thorough waste of time and money. As one observer put it: "If they had devoted tens of thousands of man-hours to pursuing true criminals—say, those involved in organized crime—they might have served the public interest as they were meant to."[56] Most important, the FBI's tactics were not only illegal but they were directed at an organization that was working legally *within* the system.

Just as the FBI's illegal assumption of the authority to investigate subversive activities led to illegal methods, the failure of those methods to produce evidence that could be used to take legal action against radical and liberal political movements led to further lawlessness: active efforts to destroy them. In October, 1961, for example, the FBI put into operation its "S.W.P. Disruption Program." The grounds for this program, as a confidential Bureau memorandum described them, were that the Socialist Workers Party had been "openly espousing its line on a local and national basis through running candidates for public office. . . ." The memorandum is astonishingly revealing about the political sophistication of the FBI. If these Socialists were openly espousing their line by running candidates for public office, including the Presidency, these activities obviously weren't illegal. And if their support for the civil-rights movement was subversive, then so was that of many millions of Americans.[57]

One should remember that the government *must* exert some control over its citizens. There must be a minimum of control if the fabric of society is to remain intact. But in exerting control, there are serious problems that came to the forefront during the Nixon

SOCIAL DILEMMAS AND CRITICAL CHOICES

Panel 8-4
Genetic Control of Future Generations

A long-time dream of science, genetic engineering, is at hand. Scientists have been able to combine segments of the DNA from the bacterium known as *Escherichia coli* (*E. coli*) with the DNA of plants, animals, and other bacteria. The *E. coli* combined with a DNA molecule from another source can reproduce billions of exact duplicates of the hybrid in a single day. This technology for genetic manipulation will eventually be applied to higher organisms, and this has fantastic potential for good and ill. Positively, it may lead to a cure for cancer, eliminate hereditary diseases, and create plants that take their nitrogen from the air rather than fertilizers. There are great dangers, however, many that are unforeseeable, such as new diseases for which humans have no immunity, or the creation of new human forms.

Despite these dangers, varied experimentation with genetic manipulation will continue on a number of fronts. In the near future, we will very likely be able to test unborn fetuses and abort them if they possess undesirable traits (mongoloidism and other genetic defects, which can be detected now, but also "aggressive" fetuses). Cloning (the genetic recreation of an individual from a single cell) has been

years. First, there is the problem of the violation of individual rights as guaranteed in the Constitution. Under what conditions can these be violated by the government—if ever? A closely related problem can be framed in the form of a question: Who monitors the monitors? The problem inherent in this question is not only the tactics of the monitors but also the criteria used to assess who should be controlled or who should not.

A most serious charge is that the government squelches protest, which Thomas Jefferson said is the hallmark of a democracy. The implication is that the government is beyond questioning—the dissidents are the problem. But as Donner has put it:

> To equate dissent with subversion, as intelligence officials do (the FBI, CIA, IRS, Justice Department, and the Department of Defense), is to deny that the demand for change is based on real social, economic, or political conditions."[58]

SUMMARY

In 1949 George Orwell wrote a novel about life as he envisioned it to be in 1984. The essence of his prediction was that every word, every thought, and every facial expression of citizens would be monitored by government using sophisticated electronic devices. The evidence, as presented in this chapter, is that as we approach the year 1984, we are indeed moving toward fulfilling Orwell's prophecy. The government has exhibited a strong tendency to watch closely the activities of persons who threaten it. But it is not only the political dissident whose freedoms are being threatened. As Howard Zinn has put it:

accomplished in a submammalian species and soon may be possible for humans. Eventually, too, we may be able to "order" a child with just the right characteristics (sex, height, hair color, disposition, mental ability). These possibilities lead to the question: will this genetic technology lead to a higher level of evolution, or will it threaten humankind with a new source of bondage? Other ethical and political questions we must answer are: Who has the power over the unborn fetus? Should society remove certain undesirable genetic traits from the population (hemophilia, Tay-Sachs disease, cystic fibrosis, diabetes, sickle cell anemia) by insisting on a prenatal test and automatic abortion if the tests determine that the fetus has the undesirable trait? Or should eugenics be voluntary, even if this runs the risk of the undesirable traits being passed on to unborn generations that might have been saved this grief?

What kind of political/social interference would you agree to or vote for? What kind of restraints would you advocate to limit government power in this area? Would you advocate any restraints to limit the power of individuals over their offspring? The answers to these questions have important implications for individuals and society. For example, if you favor governmental intervention to control physical defects, there is the important question of limits. How can you be sure the government will promote the genes you favor? Most important, a totalitarian political regime could use genetic manipulation as the ultimate means of social control, ensuring that all offspring will be docile, compliant, and willing workers—shades of Orwell's *1984*.

Our actual freedom is determined . . . by the power the policeman has over us on the street, or that of the local judge behind him; by the authority of our employers; by the power of teachers, principals, university presidents, and boards of trustees if we are students; by parents if we are children; by children if we are old; by the welfare bureaucracy if we are poor; by prison guards if we are in jail; by landlords if we are tenants; by the medical profession or hospital administration if we are physically or mentally ill.[59]

The technology for "1984" exists in drugs, psychosurgery, and telemetry. Currently, various arms of the government have used some of these techniques in their battle to fight crime, recidivism, political dissidence, and other forms of nonconformity. But at what point does the government go too far in its control of nonconformity? The critical question, as stated earlier, is who monitors the monitors? One can easily envision a future when the government, faced with anarchy or political revolution, might justify ultimate control of its citizens—in the name of national security. If this were to take place, then obviously, the freedoms rooted in 200 years of history will have been washed away.

The future may resemble Orwell's vision, however, not because of a tyrannical government, but rather because it is in the interests of society that people be controlled. The time may come when people, because human survival depends on it, will not have the freedom to have as many children as they want or the freedom to squander energy on eight-cylinder cars or air-conditioned homes, or to own a gun. B. F. Skinner, the famous behavioral psychologist, has argued that we must give up our outmoded notions of freedom and dignity and build a society in which the behavior of people will be controlled for their own good—for the sake of their survival, happiness, and satisfaction.[60] In other words, if not enough people exercise self-control, the government, for the common good, may be forced to impose controls from the outside. And with the technology available to the government, absolute control is a real threat.

CHAPTER REVIEW

1. All societies have mechanisms to ensure conformity—mechanisms of social control.

2. The socialization process through which the demands of the group become internalized is a fundamental mechanism of social control. This process is never complete, however, otherwise we would be robots.

3. Ideological social control is the attempt to manipulate the consciousness of citizens so they accept the status quo and ruling ideology.

4. The agents of ideological social control are the family, education, religion, sport, and the media.

5. Direct social control refers to attempts to punish or neutralize organizations or individuals who deviate from society's norms, especially the poor, the mentally ill, criminals, and political dissidents.

6. According to Piven and Cloward, public assistance programs serve a direct social control function in times of mass unemployment by defusing social unrest.

7. Science and medicine provide the techniques for shaping and controlling the behavior of nonconformists. Drugs, psychosurgery, and genetic engineering are three such techniques.

8. The government is directly involved in the control of its citizens. It apprehends and punishes criminals. It is also involved in the suppression of dissent, which, while important for pre-

serving order, runs counter to the American democratic heritage. Order theorists argue that the state exists to maintain order. The state and the law in this view are neutral, dispensing re-

wards and punishments without bias. Conflict theorists, however, believe that the state and the law exist to serve the ruling class. Squelching political dissent, therefore, benefits the powerful.

FOR FURTHER STUDY

Ideological Social Control

Martin Carnoy, *Education as Cultural Imperialism* (New York: Longman, 1974).

Jules Henry, *Culture Against Man* (New York: Random House (Vintage Books), 1963).

Donald B. Kraybill, *Our Star-Spangled Faith* (Scottsdale, Pa.: Herald Press, 1976).

Elliot S. Valenstein (ed.), *The Psychosurgery Debate: Scientific, Legal, and Ethical Perspectives* (San Francisco: W. H. Freeman, 1980).

Alan Wolfe, *The Seamy Side of Democracy: Repression in America*, second edition. (New York: Longman, 1978).

Direct Social Control

Philip Agee, *Inside the Company: CIA Diary* (New York: Bantam, 1975).

Michael Dorman, *Witch Hunt: The Underside of American Democracy* (New York: Dell, 1976).

Jack D. Douglas and John M. Johnson (eds.), *Official Deviance: Readings in Malfeasance, Misfeasance, and Other Forms of Corruption* (Philadelphia: J. B. Lippincott, 1977).

Vance Packard, *The People Shapers* (Boston: Little, Brown, 1977).

Frances Fox Piven and Richard A. Cloward, *Regulating the Poor: The Functions of Public Welfare* (New York: Random House, 1971).

Richard Quinney, *Critique of Legal Order: Crime Control in Capitalist Society* (Boston: Little, Brown, 1973).

David R. Simon and D. Stanley Eitzen, *Elite Deviance* (Boston: Allyn and Bacon, 1982).

B. F. Skinner, *Beyond Freedom and Dignity* (New York: Alfred A. Knopf, 1972).

Thomas Szasz, *The Manufacture of Madness* (New York: Harper & Row, 1970).

Roy Wilkins and Ramsey Clark, in *Search and Destroy: A Report of the Commission of Inquiry into the Chicago Police Raid on the Black Panther Headquarters* (New York: Harper & Row, 1973).

David Wise, *The American Police State: The Government against the People* (New York: Random House, 1976).

NOTES AND REFERENCES

1. This distinction and much of the material that follows is taken from Alan Wolfe, *The Seamy Side of Democracy: Repression in America* (New York: David McKay, 1973).

2. Richard Stivers, "Introduction to the Social and Cultural Control of Deviant Behavior," in *The Collective Definition of Violence*, F. James Davis and Richard Stivers, eds. (New York: Free Press, 1975), p. 372.

3. There are a number of sources that document the differences in mode of socialization by social class. Especially important is the article that summarizes twenty-five years of studies of parent–child relationships by Urie Bron-

fenbrenner, "Socialization and Social Class through Time and Space," in *Readings in Social Psychology*, E. E. Maccoby, T. M. Newcomb, and E. L. Hartley, eds. (New York: Holt, Rinehart and Winston, 1958), pp. 400–425. See also Melvin L. Kohn, "Social Class and Parental Values," *American Journal of Sociology* 64 (January, 1959), pp. 337–351.

4. See Francis FitzGerald, *America Revised: History Schoolbooks in the Twentieth Century* (Boston: Atlantic-Little, Brown, 1979).

5. James J. Kilpatrick, "Education, Not Indoctrination," *Washington Star* (Jan. 20, 1974).

6. Quoted in Wolfe, *The Seamy Side of Democracy*, p. 162.

7. Sarah J. McCarthy, "Why Johnny Can't Disobey," *The Humanist* (September/October 1979), p. 34.

8. Albert Szymanski, *The Capitalist State and the Politics of Class* (Cambridge, Mass: Winthrop, 1978), p. 253.

9. Most of the material in this section is taken from D. Stanley Eitzen and George H. Sage, *The Sociology of American Sport*, 2nd ed. (Dubuque, Iowa: Wm. C. Brown, 1982), Chap. 7.

10. See Donald W. Ball, "Olympic Games Competition: Structural Correlation of National Success," *International Journal of Comparative Sociology* 13 (September/December, 1972), pp. 186–199; and Phillip Goodhart and Christopher Chataway, *War without Weapons* (London: W. H. Allen, 1968).

11. Thomas G. Sanders, "The Social Functions of *Futebol*," *American Universities Field Staff Reports*, East Coast South America Series 14 (July, 1970), p. 7.

12. Sanders, "The Social Functions," pp. 8–9. See also Janet Lever, "Soccer: Opium of the Brazilian People," *Trans-action* 7 (December, 1969), pp. 36–43.

13. See Eitzen and Sage, *The Sociology of American Sport*, Chap. 4; and Harry Edwards, *Sociology of Sport* (Homewood, Ill.: Dorsey Press, 1973), Chap. 5.

14. Excerpts from the press release of the address by the Vice President of the United States, Spiro Agnew, Birmingham, Alabama (January 18, 1972), pp. 5–6. For a critique of the Agnew position see Nicholas von Hoffman, "The Sport of Politicians," *The Washington Post* (January 24, 1972), p. B1.

15. David Matza, "Position and Behavior Patterns of Youth," *Handbook of Modern Sociology*, Robert E. L. Faris, ed. (Chicago: Rand McNally, 1964), p. 207.

16. Wolfe, *The Seamy Side of Democracy*, p. 145.

17. Hilde Himmelweit, A. N. Oppenheim, and Pamela Vance, *Television and the Child* (London: Oxford University Press, 1958).

18. Michael Parenti, *Power and the Powerless* (New York: St. Martin's Press, 1978).

19. The following section is taken from Frances Fox Piven and Richard A. Cloward, *Regulating the Poor: The Functions of Public Welfare* (New York: Random House, 1971).

20. Frances Fox Piven and Richard A. Cloward, "The Relief of Welfare," *Trans-action* 8 (May, 1971), p. 52.

21. See "Drugs and Psychiatry: A New Era," *Newsweek* (November 12, 1979), pp. 98–104.

22. Cited in Dava Sobel, "Psychiatric Drugs Widely Misused, Critics Charge," *The New York Times* (June 3, 1980), pp. C1–C2.

23. Charles Witter, "Drugging and Schooling," *Trans-action* 8 (July/August, 1971), pp. 31–34. See also "About Drugs for 'Unruly' Schoolchildren," *U.S. News & World Report* (April 5, 1976).

24. Florence Heyman, "Methadone Maintenance as Law and Order," *Society* 9 (June, 1972), pp. 15–25.

25. Henry J. Steadman, "The Psychiatrist as a Conservative Agent of Social Control," *Social Problems* 20 (Fall, 1972), p. 270.

26. For an elaboration on the psychosurgery debate, see Elliot S. Valenstein (ed.), *The Psychosurgery Debate: Scientific, Legal, and Ethical Perspectives* (San Francisco, W. H. Freeman, 1980); Lani Silver, et. al., "Surgery to the Rescue," *The Progressive* (December, 1977), p. 23; and Vernon H. Mark, "A Psychosurgeon's Case for Psychosurgery," *Psychology Today* 8 (July, 1974), pp. 28–33, 84–86.

27. Barton L. Ingraham and Gerald W. Smith, "The Use of Electronics in the Observation and Control of Human Behavior and Its Possible Use in Rehabilitation and Parole," *Issues in Criminology* 7 (Fall, 1972), pp. 35–53.

28. Associated Press release (March 23, 1980).

29. See Sheila M. Rothman, "Sterilizing the Poor," *Society* 14 (January/February 1977), pp. 36–40.

30. See Martin Ebon, *The Cloning of Man: A Brave New Hope—or Horror?* (New York: New American Library, 1978).

31. Richard Herrnstein, "I.Q." *The Atlantic* 228 (September, 1971), pp. 43–64.

32. Sharland Trotter, *APA Monitor* 6 (September/October, 1975), pp. 1, 5, 23. See also "'Screening' Children of the Poor," *The Progressive* 39 (September, 1975), pp. 6–7.

33. The following is taken from Richard Quinney, *Criminal Justice in America: A Critical*

Understanding (Boston: Little, Brown, 1974), pp. 18–25. See also Richard Quinney, *Critique of Legal Order: Crime Control in Capitalist Society* (Boston: Little, Brown, 1973).

34. Richard Quinney, *The Social Reality of Crime* (Boston: Little, Brown, 1970), especially pp. 29–42.

35. Quinney, *The Social Reality of Crime*, p. 35.

36. Marshall B. Clinard, *Sociology of Deviant Behavior*, 4th ed. (New York: Holt, Rinehart and Winston, 1974), p. 258.

37. Quinney, *The Social Reality of Crime*, p. 18.

38. Of special importance to this section is Frank Donner's "The Theory and Practice of American Political Intelligence," *The New York Review of Books* 16 (April 22, 1971), pp. 27–39; and David Wise, *The American Police State: The Government against the People* (New York: Random House, 1976).

39. The remainder of this chapter is taken from David R. Simon and D. Stanley Eitzen, *Elite Deviance* (Boston: Allyn and Bacon, 1982), Chapter 7. For a history of the government's monitoring of its citizens, see Alan Wolfe, "Political Repression and the Liberal Democratic State," *Monthly Review* 23 (December, 1971), pp. 18–38; Donald B. Davis, "Internal Security in Historical Perspective: From the Revolution to World War II," *Surveillance and Espionage in a Free Society*, Richard H. Blum, ed. (New York: Praeger, 1972), pp. 3–19; "It's Official, Government Snooping Has Been Going On for 50 Years," *U.S. News & World Report* (May 24, 1976), p. 65; and Select Committee to Study Governmental Operations with Respect to Intelligence Activities, U.S. Senate, *Intelligence Activities and the Rights of Americans: Book II*, Report 94–755 (April 26, 1976), pp. 1–20, found in *Corporate and Governmental Deviance*, M. David Ermann and Richard J. Lundman, eds. (New York: Oxford University Press, 1978), pp. 151–173.

40. This brief history of the FBI is taken from Richard Harris, "Crime in the FBI," *The New Yorker* (August 8, 1977), pp. 30–42.

41. See Blake Fleetwood, "The Tax Police: Trampling Citizens' Rights," *Saturday Review* (May, 1980), pp. 33–36.

42. "Project Minaret," *Newsweek* (November 10, 1975), pp. 31–32.

43. U.S. Senate, *Intelligence Activities*, in Er-

mann and Lundman, p. 156. See also, "Who's Chipping Away at Your Privacy," *U.S. News & World Report* (March 31, 1975), p. 18.

44. Ibid.

45. "The FBI's 'Black-Bag Boys,'" *Newsweek* (July 28, 1975), pp. 18, 21.

46. Associated Press release (March 29, 1979).

47. United Press International release (November 19, 1975).

48. "Tales of the FBI," *Newsweek* (December 1, 1975), p. 36.

49. "Curbing the Spooks," *The Progressive* 42 (November 1978), pp. 10–11.

50. "The FBI vs. Jean Seberg," *Time* (September 24, 1979), p. 25.

51. The following account is taken from several sources: Morton H. Halperin, et al., *The Lawless State: The Crimes of the U.S. Intelligence Agencies* (New York: Penguin, 1976), pp. 61–89; "The Truth about Hoover," *Time* (December 22, 1975), pp. 14–21; "Tales of the FBI," and "The Crusade to Topple King," *Time* (December 1, 1975), pp. 11–12.

52. Final Report of the Select Committee to Study Governmental Relations with Respect to Intelligence Activities, U.S. Senate, *Supplementary Detailed Staff Reports on Intelligence Activities and the Rights of Americans: Book III*, "Dr. Martin Luther King, Jr., Case Study" (Washington, D.C.: U.S. Government Printing Office, 1976), pp. 107–198, cited in Halperin, et al., *The Lawless State*, p. 78.

53. Halperin, et al., *The Lawless State*, p. 89.

54. Quoted in "The Crusade to Topple King," p. 11.

55. The evidence presented on the FBI's campaign against the SWP is taken from Harris, "Crime in the FBI;" Associated Press release (March 29, 1976); and "Monitoring Repression," *The Progressive* 41 (January, 1977), p. 7.

56. Harris, "Crime in the FBI," p. 40.

57. Ibid.

58. Donner, "The Theory and Practice of American Political Intelligence," p. 35.

59. Quoted in Tom Wicker, "The Long Arm of the Military," *The New York Times*, December 31, 1973.

60. B. F. Skinner, *Beyond Freedom and Dignity* (New York: Alfred A. Knopf, 1972).

9

Deviance

Who are the deviants in American society? There is considerable evidence that most of us at one time or another break the laws. For example:

—In 1980 it was estimated that about 80 million Americans shoplifted about $8 billion worth of goods (more than the combined 1979 net incomes of Exxon and IBM). During the 1979 Christmas buying season alone approximately $2 billion in goods were stolen by shoppers and dishonest employees.[1]

—In 1979 between $250 and $400 billion earned in business transactions (10 percent of the entire United States economy) went unreported to the Internal Revenue Service (a loss in revenues to the federal government of as much as $100 billion). Most of these monies come from the selling of goods or services for cash, tips received, and second incomes. It is estimated that between 15 and 20 million Americans are involved in these illegal practices.[2]

—A study by the IRS revealed that 27 to 32 percent of the sample interviewed were dishonest in completing their 1978 tax returns, and another 9 to 13 percent admitted that they "stretched the truth just a little."[3]

—In 1980 at Princeton University 34 percent of those polled admitted cheating on an exam at least once during their undergraduate years. Another study, at the University of Nebraska, found 60 percent who said that they would cheat if under severe pressure to do well.[4]

—Company executives were asked by the *Harvard Business Review* if they would abide by a code of business ethics and 4 out of 7 said that they would violate such a code whenever they thought they could avoid detection.[5]

These illustrations indicate that many of us are guilty of cheating and stealing —behaviors clearly considered wrong. But are those of us who commit these illegal or immoral acts deviant? The complexities of the designation of "deviant" are the topics of this chapter.

The previous four chapters have analyzed the ways in which human beings, as members of society, are constrained to conform. We have seen how society is not only outside of us coercing us to conform but also inside of us making us *want* to behave in the culturally prescribed ways. But despite these powerful forces, people deviate from the norms. These acts and actors are the subjects of this chapter.

WHAT IS DEVIANCE?

Deviance is that behavior which does not conform to social expectations. It violates the rules of a group (custom, law, role, or moral code). *Deviance, then, is socially created.*[6]

Social organizations create right and wrong by originating norms, the infraction of which constitutes deviance. This means that nothing inherent in a particular act makes it deviant. Whether an act is deviant or not depends on how others react to it. As Kai Erikson has put it: "Deviance is not a property *inherent* in any particular kind of behavior; it is a property *conferred upon* that behavior by the people who come into direct or indirect contact with it."[7] This means that *deviance is a relative, not an absolute notion*. Evidence for this is found in two sources: inconsistencies among societies as to what is deviance and inconsistencies in the labeling of behavior as deviant within a single society.

There is abundant anthropological evidence that what is right or wrong varies from society to society. The following are a few examples:

item: The Ila of Africa encourge sexual promiscuity among their adolescents. After age ten girls are given houses of their own during harvest time, where they can play at being husband and wife with boys of their choice. The Tepoztlan Indians Mexico, in contrast, do not allow girls to speak or encourage any boy after the time of the girl's first menstruation.
item: Egyptian royalty were required to marry their siblings, whereas this was prohibited as incestuous and sinful for European royalty.
item: Young men of certain Indian tribes are expected, after fasting, to have a vision. This vision will be interpreted by the tribal elders to decide that young man's future occupation and status in the tribe. If an American youth were to tell his elders that he had had such a vision, he would likely be considered mentally ill.

Differential treatment for the same behavior by different categories of persons within a single society provides further proof that deviance is *not* a property of the act but depends upon the reaction of the particular audience. Several examples illustrate these inconsistencies in American society:

item: Unmarried fathers escape the severe censure that unmarried mothers typically receive.
item: Sexual intercourse between consenting adults is not deviant except if one partner pays another for his or her services and then the deviant is the recipient of the money, not the donor.
item: Murder is a deviant act but the killing of an enemy during wartime is rewarded with praise and medals.
item: A father would be considered a deviant if he removed his bathing suit at a public beach but his two-year-old son could do this with impunity. The father can smoke a cigar and drink a martini every night, but if his young son did, the boy (and his parents, if they permitted this) would be considered deviant.[8]
item: Women smokers were once considered deviants but are no longer considered so.

In a heterogeneous society there will often be widespread disagreement on what the rules are and therefore what constitutes deviance. There are differences over, for example, sexual activities between consenting adults (regardless of sex, marital status), smoking marijuana, public nudism, pornography, drinking alcohol, remaining seated during the national anthem, and refusal to fight a war. Concerning this last instance, who was the deviant in the Vietnam war, for example, the person who killed Viet Cong or the person who refused to kill them? There is a difference of opinion among Americans on this with the majority likely to define the draft evaders and protesters as the deviants even though they were officially pardoned by President Carter.

This leads to a further insight about deviance: *the majority determines who is a deviant*. If most people believe that the Viet Cong are the enemy, then napalming them and their villages is appropriate and refusal to do so is deviant. If most people believe there is a God you can talk to, then such a belief is not deviance (in fact, the refusal to believe in God may then be deviant). But if the majority are atheists, then those few who believe in God would be deviant and subject to ridicule, job discrimination, and mental treatment.

Another example of this "safety in numbers" principle is the effort by some parents to deprogram their children if they have adopted a different religion—for example, pentecostal Christian, Children of God, or Hare Krishna. These parents had their children kidnapped. The children were confined for days with little food or sleep and badgered by hired experts into recanting their beliefs. As Mewshaw has described it:

Euphemistically called "deprogramming," the process amounts to little more than a methodical and sometimes violent attempt to exorcise not Satan, but unpopular, misunderstood, or inarticulate notions about God.[9]

Erikson has summarized how deviance is a relative rather than an absolute notion in the following:

Definitions of deviance vary widely as we range over the various classes found in a single society or across the various cultures into which mankind is divided, and it soon becomes apparent that there are no objective properties which all deviant acts can be said to share in common—even within the confines of a given group. *Behavior which qualifies one man for prison may qualify another for sainthood, since the quality of the act itself depends so much on the circumstances under which it was performed and the temper of the audience which witnessed it.*[10] (italics added)

An insight of the order theorists is important to note. Deviance is an integral part of all healthy societies.[11] Deviant behavior, according to Durkheim, actually has positive consequences for society because it gives the nondeviants a sense of solidarity. By punishing the deviant, the group expresses its collective indignation and reaffirms its commitments to the rules.

Crime brings together upright consciences and concentrates them. We have only to notice what happens, particularly in a small town, when some moral scandal has just been committed. They stop each other on the street, they visit each other, they seek to come together to talk of the event and to wax indignant in common. From all the similar expressions which are exchanged, for all the temper that gets itself expressed, there emerges a unique temper . . . which is everybody's without being anybody's in particular. That is the public temper.[12]

Durkheim believed that the true function of punishment was not the prevention of future crimes. He asserted, rather, that the basic function of punishment is to reassert the importance of the rule being violated. It is not that a murderer is caught and put in the electric chair to keep potential murderers in line. That argument assumes people to be more rational than they really are. Instead, the extreme punishment of a murderer reminds each of us that murder is wrong. In other words, the punishment of crimes serves to strengthen our belief as individuals and as members of a collectivity in the legitimacy of society's norms. This enhances the solidarity of society as we unite in opposition to the deviant.

Crime, seen from this view, has positive functions for society. In addition to reaffirming the legitimacy of the society, defining certain acts as crimes creates the boundaries for what is acceptable behavior in the society.

Deviance, from the order perspective, is not only a consequence of social order (a violation of society's rules) but also is necessary for social order. As Rubington and Weinberg have said: "Each [social order and deviance] presupposes the other. And from studying one, sociologists frequently learn more about the other."[13]

The conflict theorists have pointed out that all views of rule violations have *political* implications.[14] When persons mistreat rule breakers they are saying, in effect, that the norms are legitimate. Thus, the bias is conservative, serving to preserve the status quo, which includes the current distribution of power. The opposite view, that the norms of society are wrong and should be rejected, is also political. When people and groups flaunt the laws and customs (for example, the draft, segregation, and marijuana smoking) they are not only rejecting the status quo but also questioning the legitimacy of those in power. As Edwin Schur has argued:

Deviance issues are inherently political. They revolve around some people's assessments of other people's behavior. And power is a crucial factor in determining which and whose assessments gain an ascendancy. Deviance policies, likewise, affect the distribution of power and always have some broad political significance.[15]

TRADITIONAL THEORIES FOR THE CAUSES OF DEVIANCE[16]

The Individual as the Source of Deviance

Biological, psychological, and even some sociological theories have assumed that the fundamental reason for deviance is a fatal flaw in certain people.[17] The criminal, the dropout, the addict, the schizophrenic, have something wrong with them. These theories are deterministic, arguing that the individual ultimately has no choice but to be different.

1. *Biological theories.* Biological explanations for deviance have focused on physiognomy (the determination of character by facial features), phrenology (the determination of mental abilities and character traits from the configuration of the skull), somatology (the determination of character by physique), genetic anomalies (for example, XYY chromosome in males), and brain malfunctions.

Some of these theories have been discredited (for example, Lombroso's theory that some distinct body types are more likely to be criminal because they are throwbacks to an earlier stage of human development—closer to the ape stage than nondeviants). Other biological theories have shown a statistical link between certain physical characteristics and deviant behavior. Chances are, though, that when such a relationship is found, it is likely a result of social factors. The learning disability known as dyslexia, for example, is related to school failure, emotional disturbance, and juvenile delinquency. A survey of all youngsters admitted to reform schools in Colorado found that 90 percent had clinically provable learning disabilities. Another study in Cleveland found that 74 percent were afflicted in that way.[18] This disability is a brain malfunction where visual signs are scrambled. Average skills in reading, spelling, and arithmetic are impossible to attain if the malady remains undiagnosed. Teachers and parents often are unaware that the child is dyslexic and assume, rather, that she or he is retarded, lazy, or belligerent. The child (who actually may be very bright—Thomas Edison and Woodrow Wilson were dyslexic) finds school frustrating. Such a child is therefore much more likely than those not affected to be a troublemaker, to be alienated, to be either pushed out of school or a dropout, and to never reach full intellectual potential.

2. *Psychological theories.* These theories also consider the source of deviance to reside within the individual, but they differ from the biological theories in that they assume conditions of the mind or personality to be the fault. Deviant individuals, depending on the particular psychological theory, are psychopaths (asocial, aggressive, impulsive) as a result of a lack of affection during childhood, Oedipal conflict, psychosexual trauma, or other early life experience.[19] Using Freudian assumptions, the deviant is one who has not developed an adequate ego to control deviant impulses (the id). Or, alternatively, deviance can result from a dominating superego. Persons with this condition are so repulsed by their own feelings (such as sexual fantasies, or ambivalence toward parents and siblings) that they may commit deviant acts in order to receive the punishment they deserve. Freudians, therefore, place great stress on the relationship between children and their parents. The parents, in this view, can be too harsh or too lenient, or too inconsistent in their treatment of the child. Each situation leads to inadequately socialized children and immature, infantile behavior by adolescents and adults.

Since the fundamental assumption of the biological and psychological theories of deviance is that the fault lies within the individual, the solutions are aimed at changing the individual. Screening of the population for those individuals with the presumed flaws is considered the best preventive. Doctors could routinely determine which boys had the XXY or XYY chromosome pattern. Psychological testing in the schools could find out which persons were unusually aggressive, guilt ridden, or fantasy oriented. Although the screening for potential problem people may make some sense (to detect dyslexics, for example), there are some fundamental problems with this type of solution. First, the screening devices likely will not be perfect, thereby mislabeling some persons. Second, screening is based on the assumption that there is a direct linkage between certain characteristics and deviance. If identified as a predeviant by these methods, the subsequent treatment of that individual and his own new definition of self would likely lead to a self-fulfilling prophecy and a false validation of the screening procedures, increasing their usage and acceptability.

A related problem with these screening procedures is the tendency to overpredict. In one attempt to identify predelinquents, a panel of experts examined a sample of youths already in the early stages of troublemaking and made predictions regarding future delinquency. Approximately 60 percent of the cases were judged to be predelinquents. A follow-up twenty years later revealed, however, that less than one third actually became involved with the law.[20]

For those identified as potential deviants or those who are actually deviants, the "kinds-of-people" theorists advocate solutions aimed at changing the individuals. The person is treated by drug therapy, electrical stimulation of the brain, electronic monitoring, surgery, operant conditioning, counseling, psychotherapy, probation with guidance of a psychiatric social worker, or incarceration. The assumption is clearly that deviants are troubled and sick persons who must be changed to conform to the norms of society.

3. *The socialization approach.* There are a number of sociological theories that are also "kinds-of-people" explanations for deviance. Instead of individual characteristics distinguishing the deviant from the nondeviant, these focus on differing objective social and economic conditions. These are based on the empirical observations that crime and mental illness rates, to name two forms of deviance, vary by social class, ethnicity, race, place of residence, and sex.

From these gross differences, the sociologist infers that something beyond the intimacy of family surroundings is operative in the emergence of delinquent patterns; something in the cultural and social atmosphere apparent in certain sectors of society.[21]

Let us look at some of these theories, which emphasize that certain social conditions are conducive to the internalization of values that encourage deviance.

a. *Urbanism.* One theory that purports to explain the high crime rates in cities rests its argument on the characteristics of the city and city living.[22] The assumption is that people living in cities are crowded together, and that urban relations tend to be impersonal and anonymous. A fundamental difference between rural and city living is that the former is characterized by face-to-face relations as a form of social control while the latter is basically free of these constraints. Interaction is often with strangers. Thus, "city life does not provide the restraints on social behavior formerly built into the rural social structure."[23] Free of the constraints of rural life, individuals in the city may engage in activities that they would have foregone in rural settings.

A variant of this theory is that some places in the city are especially conducive to criminal activity because of their characteristics. The highest crime rates, for example, occur precisely in those geographical areas of the city where poverty, substandard housing, overcrowding, disease, and population instability are also the highest. As Hartjen has summarized it, "crime and human wretchedness seem to go hand in hand."[24]

b. *Cultural transmission.* Sutherland's theory of differential association sought to explain why some persons are criminals while others are not, even though both may share certain social characteristics such as social class position.[25] Sutherland believed that through interaction, one learns to be a criminal. If our close associates are deviants, there is a strong probability that we will learn the techniques and the deviant values that make criminal acts possible. In sum,

the significant feature of Sutherland's theory is his claim that procriminal sentiments are acquired, as are all others, by association with other individuals in a process of social interaction. Criminal orientations do not, thus, stem from faulty metabolism, inadequate superego development, or even poverty.[26]

   c. *Societal goals and differential opportunities.* Robert Merton has presented an explanation for why the lower classes (who coincidentally live in the cities) disproportionately commit criminal acts.[27] In Merton's view, societal values determine both what are the appropriate goals (success through the acquisition of wealth) as well as the approved means for achieving these goals. The problem, however, is that some people are denied access to the legitimate means of achieving these goals. The poor, especially those from certain racial and ethnic groups, in addition to the roadblocks presented by negative stereotypes, often receive a second-class education or they have to drop out of school prematurely because of financial exigencies, all of which effectively exclude them from high-paying and prestigious occupations. Because legitimate means to success are inaccessible to them, they often resort to certain forms of deviant behavior to attain success. Viewed from this perspective, deviance is a result of social structure and not the consequence of individual pathology. McGee makes this point in his analysis of Merton's scheme.

[In each of the deviant adaptations] the individuals are behaving as they have been taught by their societies. They are not sinful or weak individuals who choose to deviate. They are, in fact, doing what they have learned they are supposed to do in order to earn the rewards which their society purports to offer its members. But either because their positions in the social structure do not permit them access to the means through which to seek the rewards they have learned to want, or because the means do not in fact guarantee goal attainment, they become frustrated and experience loss of self-esteem. In a final attempt to do and be what they have been taught they must, they engage in what is called deviant behavior. Such behavior is simply an attempt to gain the same self-esteem which others are presumed to have and which the society has made it intolerable to be without.[28]

   Although Merton's analysis provides many important insights, the emphasis is on the adjustments people make to the circumstances of society. Deviance is a property of people because they cannot adapt to the discrepancy between the goals and the means of society. The problem is that Merton accepts the American success ethic. In the words of Doyle and Schindler:

What is missing is the perspective that the winner, firster, money mentality could be a pathology rather than a value in America, a pathology that so powerfully corrupts our economy, polity, and way of life that it precludes any possibility of a cohesive, healthy, community. Certainly it is valid and worthwhile to explore the situation of the deprived in a success oriented society, but it is also valid to question the viability of a social system with such a "value" at its core. The sociology of deviance has turned too quickly and too exclusively to hypotheses about "bad" people. The analysis of "bad" societies has been neglected.[29]

   d. *Subcultural differences by social class.* We shall explore the "culture of poverty" hypothesis in Chapter 11. Since it has special relevance for explaining differential crime rates, we will briefly characterize it here with that emphasis. The argument is that people because of their social class position differ in resources, power, and prestige and hence have different experiences, lifestyles, and ways of life. The lower-class culture has its own values, many of which run counter to the values of the middle and upper classes. There is a unique morality (a "right" action is one that works and can be gotten away with) and a unique set of criteria that make one successful in the lower-class community (being tough, willingness to take risks).[30] Panel 9–1 provides what Banfield considers the elements of propensity to crime by the lower class. Banfield may be correct in his assertions about the "lower-class culture," but there is strong evidence that it is incorrect (see Chapter 11).[31] Assuming that Banfield's characterization of the lower-class propensity to crime is correct, the critical question is whether these differences are durable or not. Will a change in monetary status or peer groups make a difference because the individual has a dual value system—one that is a reaction to his deprived situation and one that is middle class? This is a key research question because the answer determines where to attack the problem—at the individual or societal level.

Panel 9–1
The Lower-Class Propensity to Criminal Activity

The elements of propensity [toward criminal activity] seem to be mainly these:

Type of morality. This refers to the way in which an individual conceptualizes right and wrong and, therefore, to the weight he gives to legal and moral rules in making choices. One whose morality is "preconventional" understands a "right" action to be one that will serve his purpose and that can be gotten away with; a "wrong" action is one that will bring ill success or punishment. An individual whose morality is preconventional cannot be influenced by authority (as opposed to power). One whose morality is "conventional" defines "right" action as doing one's "duty" or doing what those in authority require; for him, laws and moral rules have a constraining effect even in the absence of an enforcement apparatus. One whose morality is "postconventional" defines "right" action as that which is in accord with some universal (or very general) principle that he considers worthy of choice. Such an individual is constrained by law as such only if the principle that he has chosen requires him to be; if it requires him to obey the law only when he thinks that the law in question is just, he is, of course, not under the constraint of law at all.

Ego strength. This refers to the individual's ability to control himself— especially to his ability to adhere to and act on his intentions (and therefore to manage his impulses) and to his ability to make efforts at self-reform. One who is radically deficient in ego strength cannot conceive or implement a plan of action; he has a succession of fleeting resolves, the last of which eventuates in action under the pressure of circumstances.

Time horizon. This refers to the time perspective an individual takes in estimating costs and benefits of alternative courses of action. The more present-oriented an individual, the less likely he is to take account of consequences that lie in the future. Since the benefits of crime tend to be immediate and its costs (such as im-

The "Blaming-the-Victim" Critique of the
Individual-Oriented Explanations for Deviance

Although the socialization theories focus on forces external to individuals that push them toward deviant behavior, they, like the biological and psychological theories, are "kinds-of-people" theories that find the fault within the individual. The deviant has an acquired trait—the internalization of values and beliefs favorable to deviance—that is social in origin. The problem is that this results in **"blaming the victims,"** as William Ryan has forcefully argued:

The new ideology attributes defect and inadequacy to the malignant nature of poverty, injustice, slum life, and racial difficulties. The stigma that marks the victim and accounts for his victimization is acquired stigma, a stigma of social, rather than genetic origin. But the stigma, the defect, the fatal difference—though derived in the past from environmental forces—is still located *within* the victim, inside his skin. With such an

---

prisonment or loss of reputation) in the future, the present-oriented individual is *ipso facto* more disposed toward crime than others.

Taste for risk. Commission of most crimes involves a certain amount of risk. An individual who places a very low (perhaps even a negative) value on the avoidance of risk is thereby biased in the direction of crime.

Willingness to inflict injury. Most crimes involve at least the possibility of injury to others and therefore a certain willingness on the part of the actor to inflict injury. It may be useful to distinguish among (a) individuals with a distaste for inflicting any injury ("crimes without victims" would still be open to them, of course); (b) those with a distaste for injuring specifiable individuals (they might steal from a large enterprise, but they would not cheat the corner grocer); (c) those with a distaste for doing bodily (but not necessarily other) injury to people; and (d) those with no distaste for inflicting injuries, along with those who positively enjoy inflicting them.

These several elements of propensity tend to exist in typical combinations. In general, an individual whose morality is preconventional also has little ego strength, a short time horizon, a fondness for risk, and little distaste for doing bodily harm to specifiable individuals. The opposites of these traits also tend to be found together.

It also happens that individuals whose propensity toward crime is relatively high—especially those with high propensity for violent crime—tend to be those whose situation provides the strongest incentive to crimes of common sorts. The low-income individual obviously has much more incentive to steal than does the high-income one. Similarly, a boy has much more incentive to "prove he is not chicken" than does a girl. In general, then, high propensity and high inducement go together.

Source: Excerpted from Edward C. Banfield, *The Unheavenly City Revisited* (Boston: Little, Brown, 1974), pp. 182–183. Copyright © 1968, 1970, 1974 by Edward C. Banfield. By permission of Little, Brown and Co.

elegant formulation, the humanitarian can have it both ways. He can, all at the same time, concentrate his charitable interest on the defects of the victim, condemn the vague social and environmental stresses that produced the defect (some time ago), and ignore the continuing effect of victimizing social forces (right now). It is a brilliant ideology for justifying a perverse form of social action designed to change, not society, as one might expect, but rather society's victim.[32]

Let us contrast, then, two ways to look at deviance—blaming the victim or blaming society. The fundamental difference between these two approaches to deviance is whether the problems emanate from the pathologies of individuals or because of the situation in which deviants are immersed. The answer is doubtless somewhere between these two extremes, but since the individual blamers have held sway, let us look carefully at the critique of this approach.[33]

Let us begin by considering some victims. One group of victims is composed of children in slum schools who are failures. Why do they fail? Victim blamers point to the children's "cultural deprivation."* They do not do well in school because their families speak a different dialect, because their parents are uneducated, because they have not been exposed to all the educational experiences of middle-class children (for example, visits to the zoo, extensive travel, attendance at cultural events, exposure to books). In other words, the defect is in the children and their families. System blamers, however, look elsewhere for the sources of failure. They ask: What is there about the schools that makes slum children more likely to fail? The answer for them is found in the irrelevant curriculum, the class-biased IQ tests, the tracking system, the overcrowded classrooms, the differential allocation of resources within the school district, and insensitive teachers whose low expectations for poor children comprise a prophecy that is continually fulfilled.

Another victim is the criminal. Why is the recidivism rate (reinvolvement in crime) of criminals so high? The individual blamer would point to the faults of the individual criminals: their greed, feelings of aggression, weak impulse control, and lack of a conscience (superego). The system blamers' attention is directed to very different sources for this problem. They would look, rather, at the penal system, the employment situation for ex-criminals, and the schools. For example, studies have shown that 20 to 30 percent of inmates are functionally illiterate.[34] This means they cannot meet minimum reading and writing demands in American society such as filling out job applications. Yet these persons are expected to leave prison, find a job, and stay out of trouble. Because they are illiterate and ex-criminals, they face unemployment or at best the most menial jobs (where there are low wages, no job security, and no fringe benefits). The system blamer would argue that these persons are not to blame for their illiteracy but rather that the schools at first and later the penal institutions have failed to provide these people with the minimum requirements for citizenship. Moreover, the lack of employment and the unwillingness of potential employers to train functional illiterates forces many to return to crime in order to survive.

*The term "cultural deprivation" is a loaded ethnocentric term. It implies that the culture of the group in question is not only deficient but that it is inferior. This label is applied by members of the majority to the culture of the minority group. It is not only a malicious "putting down" of the minority, but the concept itself is patently false because no culture can be inferior to another; it can only be different. The concept does remind, us, however, that people can and do make invidious distinctions about cultures and subcultures. Furthermore, they act on these definitions as if they were true.

While still President, Richard Nixon made the following statement:

Americans in the last decade were often told that the criminal was not responsible for his crimes against society, but that society was responsible. I totally disagree with this permissive philosophy. Society is guilty of crime only when we fail to bring the criminal to justice. When we fail to make the criminal pay for his crime, we encourage him to think that crime will pay. Such an attitude will never be reflected in the laws supported by this Administration, nor in the manner in which we enforce those laws.[35]

Aside from the obvious irony of this statement by the now-disgraced former president, it does present a classic statement that blames the victim. In support of Nixon's position, an editorial writer for *The National Observer* said that the system is not to blame for crime because of the opportunity for upward mobility that exists. The poor do not have to stay poor. There is not, in his opinion, a cycle of poverty that dooms the individual.[36] The system blamer, on the other hand, would argue that for every individual who breaks out of a cycle of poverty, many are trapped by their inferior education, their lack of salable skills, their greater likelihood to be ill because of poor nutrition and inadequate medical care, and their lack of self-esteem because of the negative labels the system gives them. As Tom Wicker, in response to the Nixon speech, argued:

Conditions of poverty and unemployment, social and economic disadvantage tend to breed criminal behavior. . . . Poverty and inequity lead more and more young people into the only career that seems to offer them any hope—crime. And an ineffective and counterproductive prison system tends to keep them in that career.[37]

Blacks (and other racial minorities) constitute another set of victims in American society. What accounts for the greater probability for blacks than whites to be failures in school, to be unemployed, to be criminals, and to be heroin addicts? The individualistic approach places the blame on the blacks themselves. They are "culturally deprived," they have high rates of illegitimacy, a high proportion of transient males, and a relatively high proportion of black families have a matriarchal structure. But this approach neglects the pervasive effects of racism in American society, which limits the opportunities for blacks, provides them with a second-class education, and renders them powerless to change the system through approved channels.

Why is there a strong tendency to place the blame for deviance on individuals rather than on the social system? The answer lies in the way that persons tend to define deviance. Most people define deviance as behavior that deviates from the norms and standards of society. Because people do not ordinarily question the norms or the way things are done in society, they tend to question the exceptions. The system is not only taken for granted, but it has, for most people, an aura of sacredness because of the traditions and customs behind it. Logically, then, those who deviate are the source of trouble. The obvious question, then, is why do these people deviate from the norms? Because most persons abide by society's norms, the deviation of the exceptions must be the result of some kind of unusual circumstance—accident, illness, personal defect, character flaw, or maladjustment.[38] The key to this approach, then, is that the flaw is within the deviant and not a function of societal arrangements.

The position taken in this debate his serious consequences. Let us briefly examine the effects of interpreting social problems solely within a person-blame framework.[39] First, this interpretation of social problems frees the government, the economy, the system of stratification, the system of justice, and the educational system from any blame. The established order is protected against criticism, thereby increasing the difficulty encountered in trying to change the dominant economic, social, and political institutions. A good example is found in the strategy of social scientists studying the origins of poverty. Since the person blamer studies the poor rather than the nonpoor, the system of inequality (buttressed by the tax laws, welfare rules, and employment practices) goes unchallenged. A related consequence of the person-blame approach, then, is that the relatively advantaged segments of society retain their advantages.

Not only is the established order protected from criticism by the person-blame approach, but the authorities can control dissidents under the guise of being helpful. Caplan and Nelson have provided an excellent illustration of this in the following quote:

Normally, one would not expect the Government to cooperate with "problem groups" who oppose the system. But if a person-blame rather than system-blame action program can be negotiated, cooperation becomes possible. In this way, the problem-defining process remains in the control of the would-be benefactors, who provide "help" so long as their diagnosis goes unchallenged.

In 1970, for example, while a group of American Indians still occupied Alcatraz Island in San Francisco Bay, a group of blacks took over Ellis Island in New York Harbor. Both groups attempted to take back lands no longer used by the Federal Government. The Government solved the Ellis Island problem by getting the blacks to help establish a drug-rehabilitation center on it. They solved the Alcatraz problem by forcibly removing the Indians. Had the Indians been willing to settle for an alcoholism-treatment center on Alcatraz, thereby acknowledging that what they need are remedies for their personal problems, we suspect the Government would have "cooperated" again.[40]

Another social control function of the person-blame approach is that troublesome individuals and groups are controlled in a publicly acceptable manner. Deviants, whether they be criminals, homosexuals, or social protestors are controlled by incarceration in prison or mental hospital, drugs, or other forms of therapy. In this manner, not only is blame directed at individuals and away from the system, but the problems (individuals) are in a sense eliminated.

A related consequence is the manner in which the problem is to be treated. A person-blame approach demands a person-change treatment program. If the cause of delinquency, for example, is defined as the result of personal pathology, then the solution lies clearly in counseling, behavior modification, psychotherapy, drugs, or some other technique aimed at changing the individual deviant. Such an interpretation of social problems provides and legitimates the right to initiate person-change rather than system-change treatment programs. Under such a scheme, norms that are racist or sexist, for example, will go unchallenged.

The person-blame ideology not only invites person-change treatment programs but also programs for person control. If local governments spent less than 2 percent for social services while 75 percent were for public safety, chiefly to police departments, as was the case in the 1970s, then the system blamer would argue that such an emphasis treats the symptom rather than the disease.[41]

A final consequence of person-blame interpretations is that they reinforce social myths about the degree of control we have over our fate. It provides justification for a form of Social Darwinism—that is, a person's placement in the stratification system is a function of ability and effort. By this logic, the poor are poor because they *are* the dregs of society. In short, they deserve their fate, as do the successful in society. Thus, there is little sympathy for governmental programs to increase welfare to the poor.

We should recognize, however, that the contrasting position—the system-blame orientation—also has its dangers. First, it is only part of the truth. Social problems and deviance are highly complex phenomena that have both individual and systemic origins. Individuals, obviously, can be malicious and aggressive for purely psychological reasons. Perhaps only a psychologist can explain why a parent is a child abuser, or why a sniper shoots at cars passing on the freeway. Clearly, society needs to be protected from some individuals. Moreover, some persons require particular forms of therapy, remedial help, or special programs on an individual basis if they are to function normally. But much that is labeled deviant is the end product of social conditions.

A second danger in a dogmatic system-blame orientation is that it presents a rigidly deterministic explanation for social problems. Taken too far, this position views individuals as robots controlled totally by their social environment. A balanced view of people is needed, since human beings have autonomy most of the time to choose between alternative courses of action. This raises the related question as to the degree to which people are responsible for their behavior. An excessive system-blame approach absolves individuals from the responsibility of their actions. To take such a stance would be to argue that society should never restrict deviants. This extreme view invites anarchy.[42]

Despite the problems with the system-blame approach just noted, it will be emphasized in this chapter. The rationale for this is, first, that the contrasting view (individual-blame) is the prevailing view in American society. Since average citizens, police personnel, legislators, judges, and social scientists tend to interpret social problems from an individualistic perspective, a balance is needed. Moreover, as was noted earlier, to hold a strict person-blame perspective has many negative consequences, and citizens must realize the effects of their ideology.

A second basis for the use of the society-blaming perspective is that the subject matter of sociology is not the individual, who is the special province of psychology, but society. If sociologists do not emphasize the social determinants of behavior and if they do not make a critical analysis of the social structure, then who will? As noted in Chapter 1, an important ingredient of the sociological perspective is the development of a critical stance toward societal arrangements. The job of the sociologist is to look behind the facade to determine the positive and negative consequences of societal arrangements. The persistent question is: Who benefits under these arrangements and who does not? This is why there should be such a close fit between the sociological approach and the societal-blaming perspective. Unfortunately, this has not always been the case.

SOCIETY AS THE SOURCE OF DEVIANCE

We have seen that the traditional explanations for deviance, whether they be biological, psychological, or sociological, have found the source of deviance in individual deviants, their families, or their immediate social settings. The basic assumption of these theories is

that because deviants do not fit in society, something is wrong with them.[43] In this section we shall provide an antidote to the medical analogy implicit in those theories by focusing instead on two theories that place the blame for deviance on the role of society—labeling theory and conflict theory.

Labeling Theory

All the explanations for deviance described so far assume that deviants differ from nondeviants in behavior, attitude, and motivation. This is buttressed by the commonly held belief that deviance is the actions of a few weird people who are either criminals, insane, or both. In reality, however, most persons break the rules of society at one time or another. The evidence from this comes from a number of studies. For example, two researchers asked 700 middle-class citizens if they had ever committed (after age 15) any one or more of 49 crimes that were punishable in New York State by at least one year in prison. The results were that 99 percent of the respondents admitted committing at least one such offense. The average number of offenses by men was 18 and by women, 11. Moreover, about two thirds of the men admitted at least one serious crime—a felony—as did about one third of the women.[44] There is also a considerable amount of evidence that indicates little or no difference in magnitude between lower-class delinquent behavior and middle-class delinquent behavior.[45] Hirschi has summarized these studies by saying:

While the prisons bulge with the socioeconomic dregs of society, careful quantitative research shows again and again that the relation between socioeconomic status and the commission of delinquent acts is small, or nonexistent.[46]

These studies do not mesh with our perceptions and the apparent facts. Crime statistics do show that the lower classes are more likely to be criminals. Even data on mental illness demonstrate that the lower classes are more prone than the middle classes to have serious mental problems.[47] The difference is that most persons break the rules at one time or another, even serious rules for which they could be placed in jail (for example, theft, statutory rape, vandalism, violation of drug or alcohol laws, fraud, violations of the Internal Revenue Service), but only some get the *label* of deviant.[48] As one adult analyzed his ornery but normal youth:

I recall my high school and college days, participating in vandalism, entering locked buildings at night, drinking while under age—even while I made top grades and won athletic letters. I was normal and did these things with guys who now are preachers, professors, and businessmen. A few school friends of poorer families somehow tended to get caught and we didn't. They were failing in class, and we all believed they were too dumb not to know when to have fun and when to run. Some of them did time in jail and reformatories. *They* were "delinquents" and *we* weren't.[49]

This chapter began with the statement that society creates deviance by creating rules, the violation of which constitutes deviance. But rule breaking itself does "not a deviant make." The successful application of the label "deviant" is crucial.[50]

Who gets labeled as a deviant (criminal, psychotic, queer, or junkie) is not just a matter of luck or random selection but the result of a systematic societal bias against the powerless. Chambliss has summarized the empirical evidence for criminals:

The lower class person is (1) more likely to be scrutinized and therefore be observed in any violation of the law, (2) more likely to be arrested if discovered under suspicious circumstances, (3) more likely to spend the time between arrest and trial in jail, (4) more likely to come to trial, (5) more likely to be found guilty, (6) if found guilty, more likely to receive harsh punishment than his middle- or upper-class counterpart.[51]

We can see how the well-to-do tend to avoid the criminal label by examining the disposition of those persons actually found guilty of a felony (major crime) by their socioeconomic characteristics. The judicial procedures in Florida provide a revealing glimpse of this bias. For persons accused of a felony but placed on probation, Florida law allows a judge the option of withholding adjudication of guilt. The importance of avoiding this label is that such persons lose none of their civil rights and may truthfully assert that they have never been convicted of a felony. To be a "convicted felon," on the other hand, means that one loses the rights to vote, hold public office, serve on juries, and possess certain firearms. The stigma of "felon" also makes employment more difficult as well as acceptance in other situations. A study of the legal and social characteristics of 2419 consecutive felony probation cases found that defendants who were older, black, poorly educated, had a prior record, and were defended by a court-appointed attorney were the most likely to be so labeled.[52] Clearly, the judges reflected the bias present in society by formally imposing criminal labels on those persons *expected* to be the most criminal (the poor, the uneducated, racial minorities), who coincidentally are the least powerful segments in society.

Not only are the more well-to-do less likely to receive a punishment of imprisonment, but those who are imprisoned receive advantages over the lower-class and minority inmates. The most blatant example of this is found by examining what type of person actually receives the death penalty. A former Attorney General has summarized the findings in the following quote:

The poor and the black have been the chief victims of the death penalty. Clarence Darrow observed that "from the beginning, a procession of the poor, the weak, the unfit, have gone through our jails and prisons to their deaths. They have been the victims." It is the poor, the sick, the ignorant, the powerless and the hated who are executed.
Racial discrimination is manifest from the bare statistics of capital punishment. Since we began keeping records in 1930, there have been 2,066 Negroes and only 1,751 white persons put to death. Hundreds of thousands of rapes have occurred in America since 1930, yet only 455 men have been executed for rape—and 405 of them were Negroes. There can be no rationalization or justification of such clear discrimination. It is outrageous public murder, illuminating our darkest racism.[53]

The social class of the prisoner on death row is also related to whether an individual receives the ultimate punishment or not. In a study of death row in Pennsylvania from 1914 to 1958, those offenders with court-appointed counsel were much more likely to be executed than offenders with private counsel. Likewise, there is a greater probability of the death penalty being imposed on persons of low-prestige occupations than for those of higher prestige.[54]

Who gets paroled is another indicator of a bias in the system. Parole is a conditional release from prison that allows prisoners to return to their communities under the supervision of a parole officer before the completion of their maximum sentence. Typically, parole is granted by a parole board set up for the correctional institution or for the state. Often the parole board members are political appointees without training.[55] The parole board reviews a prisoner's social history, past offenses, and behavior in prison and makes its judgment. The decision is rarely subject to review and can be made arbitrarily or discriminatorily.

The bias that disadvantages minorities and the poor throughout the system of justice continues as parole board members, corrections officers, and others make judgments that often reflect stereotypes. What type of prisoner represents the safest risk, a black or a white? An uneducated or an educated person? A white-collar worker or a chronically unemployed unskilled worker? One study shows vividly how the parole system tends to continue the bias against blacks and those of low socioeconomic status. Petersen and Friday compared prisoners in Ohio who were granted "shock probation" (release after a short period of incarceration) with those who were eligible for early release but were not.[56] They found that while 44 percent of whites received "shock probation," only 20 percent of blacks did. Educational attainment was also a significant variable affecting early release from prison. Only 25 percent of those inmates with less than nine years of education were released early, while 53 percent of those with some college were. Especially interesting to note is the effect of race and education combined (see Table 9-1). These data show that blacks have about one half of the choice of early release that whites have *at each educational level*. The researchers also examined the effects of race, holding constant a number of other variables (for example, type of offense, number of previous adult arrests, and father's education) and found invariably that whites are much more likely than blacks to receive the preferential treatment of "shock probation" by the authorities. The conclusion that the procedure favors whites over blacks, then, is inescapable.

Currently in the United States there are about 5000 city and county jails, 400 state and federal prisons, plus a variety of other forms of detention centers. On an average day about 1.3 million persons are confined in these places. We have shown that the underdogs in society (the poor and the minorities) are disproportionately represented in the prison population. An important consequence of this is that it reinforces the negative stereotypes already present in the majority of the population. The large number of blacks and the poor in prison "prove" that they have criminal tendencies. This belief is reinforced further by the high **recidivism** rate of 70 percent of ex-prisoners.

At least four factors relative to the prison experiences operate to fulfill the prophecy that the poor and the black are prone toward criminal behavior. The first is that the entire criminal justice system is viewed by the underdogs as unjust. There is a growing belief among prisoners that because the system is biased against them, all prisoners are, in fact, political. This "consciousness raising" increases the bitterness and anger among them.[57]

A second reason for the high rate of crime among those processed through the system of criminal justice is the accepted fact that prison is a brutal, degrading, and altogether dehumanizing experience. Mistreatment by guards, sexual assaults by fellow prisoners, overcrowding, unsanitary conditions, are commonplace in American prisons.[58] Prisoners cannot escape the humiliation, anger, and frustration. These feelings, coupled with the knowledge that the entire system of justice is unjustly directed at certain categories of persons, creates within many ex-cons the desire for revenge.

A third factor is that prisons provide learning experiences for prisoners in the art of crime. Through the interaction of the inmates, individuals learn the techniques of crime from the masters and develop the contacts that can be used later.

TABLE 9-1   Early Release from Prison According to the Race of the Offender, with Education Held Constant (percentages)

Education	Shock probation		Incarceration	
	White	Black	White	Black
Less than 9 years	31.9	11.9	68.1	88.1
Some high school	51.4	25.4	48.6	74.6
High school graduate	64.4	30.8	35.6	69.2
Some college	56.3	33.3	43.8	66.7

Source: Adapted from David M. Petersen and Paul C. Friday, "Early Release from Incarceration: Race as a Factor in the Use of 'Shock Probation,' " *The Journal of Criminal Law and Criminology* 66 (March, 1975), p. 82. Reprinted by special permission of the Journal of Criminal Law and Criminology. Copyright © 1975 by Northwestern University School of Law.

Finally, the ex-con faces the problems of finding a job and being accepted again in society. Long-termers face problems of adjusting to life without regimentation. More important, since good-paying jobs, particularly in times of economic recession, are difficult for anyone to find, the ex-con who is automatically assumed to be untrustworthy is faced with either unemployment or those jobs nobody else will take. Even the law works to his disadvantage by prohibiting certain jobs to ex-cons.

In 46 states and the District of Columbia, for example, they cannot become barbers. In New York, he or she is prohibited from being an auctioneer, junk dealer, pharmacist, undertaker, embalmer or poolroom operator, among other things. In Kentucky, ex-cons are not even allowed to perform the foul job of cleaning septic tanks.[59]

The result of nonacceptance by society is often to return to crime. Previous offenders, on the average, are arrested for crime within six weeks after leaving prison. This, of course, justifies the beliefs by policemen, judges, parole boards, and other authorities that certain categories of persons should receive punishment while others should not.

The consequences of labeling. We have just seen that the labeling process is a crucial factor in the formation of a deviant career. In other words, the stigma of the label leads to subsequent deviance. This is what Lemert meant by the concept of secondary deviance.[60] **Primary deviance** is the rule breaking that occurs prior to labeling. **Secondary deviance** is that behavior resulting from the labeling process. Being labeled a criminal means being rejected by society, by employers,[61] by friends, and even relatives. There is a high probability that such a person will turn to behavior that fulfills the prophecies of others. Put another way, persons labeled as deviants tend to become locked into a deviant behavior pattern. Looking at deviance this way turns the tables on conventional thought.

Instead of assuming that it is the deviant's difference which needs explanation, [the labeling perspective] asks why the majority responds to *this* difference as it does. This shift of the question reverses the normal conception of causation; the labeling school suggests that the other person's peculiarity has not caused us to regard him as different so much as our labeling hypothesis has caused his peculiarity.[62]

Ex-mental patients, like ex-convicts, usually have difficulty in finding employment and establishing close relationships because of the stigma of the label. This, of course, leads to frustration, anger, low self-esteem, and other symptoms of "mental illness." Moreover, the consistent messages from others (remember Cooley's looking-glass self) that one is sick will likely lead the individual to behavior in accord with these expectations. Even while a patient is in the mental hospital, the actions of the staff may actually foster in the person a self concept of "deviant" and behavior consistent with that definition. Patients who show insight about their "illness" confirm the medical and societal diagnosis and are positively rewarded by psychiatrists and other personnel.[63] The opposite also occurs, as illustrated so vividly by the character R. P. McMurphy in *One Flew Over the Cuckoo's Nest*.[64] Although the mythical McMurphy fought this tendency to confirm the expectations of powerful others, the pressures to conform were great. Cole has summarized this process of how the deviant role is sustained in the following:

After someone is labeled as deviant, he often finds it rewarding to accept the label and act deviant. Consider, for example, a patient in a mental hospital who has been diagnosed as a schizophrenic. If the patient refuses to accept the diagnosis, claims that he is not mentally ill, and demands to be immediately released, the staff will consider him to be hostile and uncooperative. He may be denied privileges and treated as hopelessly insane. After all, the person who cannot even recognize that he is ill must be in a mental state in which he has no perception of reality! On the other hand, if the patient accepts the validity of the diagnosis, admits his illness, and tries to cooperate with the staff in effecting a cure, he will be rewarded. He will be defined as a good cooperative patient who is sincerely trying to get better. Any weird or unusual behavior he engages in will be ignored; after all, he is mentally ill, and such types of behavior should be expected from a person in his mental state. He may even be rewarded for engaging in behavior which is considered to be characteristic of schizophrenia. Such behavior serves to reassure the staff that the patient is indeed mentally ill and that the social organization of the mental hospital makes sense.[65]

The labeling perspective is especially helpful in understanding the bias of the criminal justice system. It shows, in summary, that when society's underdogs are disproportionately singled out for the criminal label, the subsequent problems of stigmatization and segregation they face result in a tendency toward further deviance, thereby justifying the society's original negative response to them. This tendency for secondary deviance is especially strong when the imposition of the label is accompanied by a sense of injustice. Lemert argued that a stronger commitment to a deviant identity is greatest when the label (stigma) is believed by the individual to be inconsistently applied by society.[66] The evidence of such inconsistency is overwhelming.

From this perspective, then, the situations which show that society's underdogs engage in more deviance than persons from the middle and upper classes are invalid, since they reflect the differential response of society to the deviance by them at every phase in the process of criminal justice. Hartjen has provided an excellent statement that summarizes this process.

Criminal sanctions are supposedly directed toward a person's behavior—what he does, not what kind of person he is. Yet, the research on the administration of criminal justice . . . reveals that just the opposite occurs. A person is likely to acquire a social identity as a criminal precisely because of what he is—because of the kind of personal or social characteristics he has the misfortune to possess. Being black, poor, migrant, uneducated, and the like increases a person's chances of being defined as a criminal. . . . What I am suggesting here is that the very structure and operation of the judicial system, which was created to deal with the problem called crime, are not only grounded in an unstated image of the criminal but also—merely because the system exists—serve to produce and perpetuate the "thing" it was created to handle. That is to say, the criminal court (and especially the juvenile court) does not exist in its present form because the people it deals with are what they are. Rather, the criminals and delinquents become the way they are characterized by others as being because the court (and the world view it embodies) exists in the form that it does. *The criminal, thus, is a "product" of the structural and procedural characteristics of the judicial system.*[67]

"Solutions" for deviance from the labeling perspective. The labeling theorist's approach to deviance leads to unconventional solutions.[68] The assumption is that deviants are not basically different—except that they have been processed (and labeled) by official sources (judges and courts; psychiatrists and mental hospitals). The primary target for policy, then, should be neither the individual nor the local community setting, but the process by which some persons are singled out for the negative label. From this approach, organizations produce deviants. Speaking specifically about juvenile delinquency, Schur has argued that the solution should be what he has called **"radical nonintervention."**

We can now begin to see some of the meanings of the term "radical nonintervention." For one thing, it breaks radically with conventional thinking about delinquency and its causes. Basically, radical nonintervention implies policies that accommodate society to the widest possible diversity of behaviors and attitudes, rather than focusing as many individuals as possible to "adjust" to supposedly common societal standards. This does not mean that anything goes, that all behavior is socially acceptable. But traditional delinquency policy has proscribed youthful behavior well beyond what is required to maintain a smooth-running society or to protect others from youthful depredations.

Thus, the basic injunction for public policy becomes: *leave kids alone wherever possible*. This effort partly involves mechanisms to divert children away from the courts but it goes further to include opposing various kinds of intervention by diverse social control and socializing agencies. . . . Subsidiary policies would favor collective action programs instead of those that single out specific individuals; and voluntary programs instead of compulsive ones. Finally, this approach is radical in asserting that major and intentional sociocultural change will help reduce our delinquency problems. Piecemeal socioeconomic reform will not greatly affect delinquency; there must be throughgoing changes in the structure and the values of our society. If the choice is between changing youth and changing society (including some of its laws), the radical noninterventionist opts for changing the society.[69]

One way to accomplish this "leave the deviants alone whenever possible" philosophy would be to treat fewer acts as criminal or deviant. For adults this could be accomplished by decriminalizing victimless crimes, such as gambling, drug possession, prostitution, and homosexuality. Youth should not be treated as criminals for behavior that is legal if one is old enough. Truancy, running away from home, curfew violations, and purchasing alcohol are acts for which persons below the legal age can receive the label "delinquent," yet they are not crimes for adults. Is there any wonder, then, why so many youthful rule breakers outgrow their "delinquency," becoming law-abiding citizens as adults?

Acts dangerous to society do occur, and these must be handled through legal mechanisms. But when a legal approach is required, justice must be applied evenly. Currently, the criminal label is disproportionately applied to individuals from the "other side of the tracks." This increases the probability of further deviance by these persons because of "secondary deviance" and justifies further stern punishment for this category. This unfair cycle must be broken.

A critique of labeling theory. The strengths of labeling theory are: (1) that it concentrates on the role of societal reactions in the creation of deviance, (2) the realization that the label is applied disproportionately to the powerless, and (3) that it explains how deviant careers are established and perpetuated. There are problems with the theory, however.[70] First, it avoids the question of causation (primary deviance). Labeling, by definition, occurs after the fact. It disregards undetected deviance. As McCaghy has put it,

By minimizing the importance of explaining initial (primary) deviance, whatever meaning the behavior originally had for the deviant is ignored as a contributor to subsequent behavior. Although societal reaction may become a crucial factor in behavior, it is questionable that whatever purpose of reward the behavior first held is invariably replaced. For example, if a person first steals for thrills, do thrills fail to be a factor once societal reaction has taken its toll?[71]

Another problem with labeling involves the assumption that deviants are really normal—because we are all rule breakers. Thus, it overlooks the possibility that some persons are unable to cope with the pressures of their situation. Some people are dangerous. Individuals who are disadvantaged tend to be more angry, frustrated, and alienated than their more fortunate fellows. The result may be differences in quantity and quality of primary deviance.

This perspective also relieves the individual deviant from blame. The underdog is seen as victimized by the powerful labelers. Further, individuals enmeshed in the labeling process are so constrained by the forces of society that they are incapable of choice. Once again, McCaghy has put it well: "Although it is true that deviants may be pawns of the powerful, this does not mean that deviants are powerless to resist, to alter their behavior, or to acquire power themselves."[72]

Perhaps the most serious deficiency of labeling theory, though, is that it focuses on certain types of deviance but ignores others. The attention is directed at society's underdogs, which is good. But those forms of deviance emanating from the social structure or from the powerful are not considered a very serious omission. As Liazos has put it, the themes of labeling theory focus attention on those who have been successfully labeled as deviants ("nuts, sluts, and perverts"), the deviant subculture, and the self-fulfilling prophecy that perpetuates their deviant patterns.[73] While this is appropriate and necessary, it concentrates on the powerless. The impression is that deviance is an exclusive property of the poor in the slum, the minorities, and street gangs.

But what of the deviance of the powerful members of society and even society itself? Liazos has chronicled these for us.[74]

1. The unethical, illegal, and destructive actions found in the corporate world, such as robbery through price fixing, low wages, pollution, inferior and dangerous products, deception, and outright lies in advertising.
2. The covert institutional violence committed against the poor by the institutions of society: schools, hospitals, corporations, and the government.
3. The political manipulators who pass laws that protect the interests of the powerful and disadvantage the powerless.
4. The power of the powerful is used to deflect criticism, labeling, and punishment even when deserved.

In short, labeling overlooks the deviant qualities of the society and its powerful members. Although social structure should be central to sociologists, the labeling theorists have minimized its impact on deviance. Liazos has summarized the problem this way:

We should banish the concept of "deviance" and speak of oppression, conflict, persecution, and suffering. By focusing on the dramatic forms, as we do now, we perpetuate most people's beliefs and impressions that such "deviance" is the basic cause of many of our troubles, that these people (criminals, drug addicts, political dissenters, and others) are the real "troublemakers"; and, necessarily, we neglect conditions of inequality, powerlessness, institutional violence, and so on, which lie at the bases of our tortured society.[75]

Another way deviance is explained—conflict theory—extends labeling theory by focusing on social structure, thereby overcoming the fundamental criticisms of Liazos and others.

Conflict Theory

Why is certain behavior defined as deviant? The answer, according to conflict theorists, is that powerful economic interest groups are able to get laws passed and enforced that protect their interests.[76] We must begin, then, with the law.

Of all the requirements for a just system, the most fundamental is the foundation of nondiscriminatory laws. Many criminal laws are the result of a consensus among the public as to what kinds of behaviors are a menace and should be punished (for example, murder, rape, theft). The laws devised to make these acts illegal and the extent of punishment for violators are nondiscriminatory (although, as we have seen, the administration of these laws is discriminatory) since they do not single out a particular social category as the target.

There are laws, however, that discriminate because they result from special interests using their power to translate their interests into public policy.[77] These laws may be discriminatory because some segments of society (for example, the poor, minorities, youth, renters, debtors) rarely have access to the lawmaking process and therefore often find the laws unfairly aimed at them. Vagrancy, for example, is really a crime that only the poor can commit.[78] Perhaps a better example of this interest group approach to the law is to examine certain crimes of the Jim Crow days in the South. The majority created laws to keep the races separate and unequal. Burns has summarized the situation this way:

In classical theories of democracy, the laws are supposed to reflect "the will of the people"—or at least of the majority. From the point of view of black people in this country, American law has been all too successful in this regard; for, in a country permeated by white racism, the legal system has been and continues to be racist in character.[79]

Let's examine a few specific examples of the historical bias of the law against blacks:[80]

item: the law played a critical role in defining and sanctioning slavery. For instance, the law made slavery hereditary and a lifetime condition.

item: the slave codes denied blacks the rights to bring law suits or testify against a white person.

item: Jim Crow laws codified the customs and usages of segregation.

item: after reconstruction, the grandfather clause, the literary test, and the poll tax were all legal devices designed to block blacks from the polls.

item: in the nineteenth century, the law reserved exclusively for white men the right to sit on juries.

Not only is the formation of the law political, but so, too, is the administration of the law.[81] This is because at every stage in the processing of criminals, choices are made by authorities based on personal bias, pressures from the powerful, and the constraints of the status quo. Some examples of the political character of law administration are: (1) the attempt by the powerful to coerce others to their view of morality, hence laws against homosexuality, pornography, drug usage, and gambling; (2) the powerful may exert pressure on the authorities to crack down on certain kinds of violators, especially those individuals and groups who are disruptive (protesters); (3) there may be political pressure exerted to keep certain crimes from public view (embezzlement, stock fraud, the Watergate coverup); (4) there may be pressure to protect the party in power, the elected officials, the police, CIA, and FBI; and (5) any effort to protect and preserve the status quo is a political act. Hartjen has summarized why the administration of justice is inherently political in the following quote:

Unless one is willing to assume that law-enforcement agents can apply some magic formula to gauge the opinions of the public they serve, unless one is willing to assume that citizens unanimously agree on what laws are to be enforced and how enforcement is to be carried out, unless one is willing to assume that blacks, the poor, urbanites, and the young are actually more criminalistic than everyone else, it must be concluded, at least, that discriminatory law enforcement is a result of differences in power and that actual decisions as to which and whose behavior is criminal are expressions of this power. One need only ask himself why some laws, such as those protecting the consumer from fraud, go largely unenforced while the drug addict, for example, is pursued with a paranoiac passion.[82]

The fundamental assumption of the conflict approach to deviance is that the state is a political organization that is controlled by the ruling class for its advantage. This assumption has been summarized by Sykes:

At the heart of this orientation lies the perspective of a stratified society in which the operation of the criminal law is a means of controlling the poor (and members of minority groups) by those in power who use the legal apparatus to (1) impose their particular morality and standards of good behavior on the entire society; (2) protect their property and physical safety from the depredations of the have-nots, even though the cost may be high in terms of the legal rights of those it perceives as a threat; and (3) extend the definition of illegal or criminal behavior to encompass those who might threaten the status quo. . . . The coercive aspects of this arrangement are hidden—at least in part—by labeling those who challenge the system as "deviants" or "criminals" when such labels carry connotations of social pathology, psychiatric illness and so on. If these interpretative schemes are insufficient to arouse widespread distaste for the rule-breaker as "bad" or "tainted," official statistics can serve to create a sense of a more direct and personal danger in the form of a crime wave that will convince many people (including many of the people in the lower classes) that draconian measures are justified.[83]

Thus, the focus of the conflict perspective is on the political and economic setting in society. The power of certain interests determines what gets defined as deviance (and who, then, is a deviant), and how this "problem" is to be solved. Since the powerful benefit from

SOCIAL DILEMMAS AND
CRITICAL CHOICES

Panel 9–2
The Politics of Pot

Until about 1965 public consensus supported strict enforcement of the marijuana laws. Marijuana was believed to be a dangerous drug associated with other forms of deviance, such as sexual promiscuity and crime. Even college students were virtually unanimous in their condemnation of marijuana smokers as deviants of the worst sort. But the social upheavals of the 1960s included experimentation with drugs and the questioning of society's mores. Rapid changes in attitudes and behavior, especially among the young and college educated, took place. Most significantly, the use of marijuana skyrocketed. In 1965 some 18,815 persons were arrested for violations of state and local marijuana laws, but this number rose to 420,700 in 1973. A survey of high school seniors in 1976 revealed that 53 percent had tried marijuana (up 5 percent from the previous year) and 30 percent were regular users. By 1978 some 43 million Americans had tried marijuana and 16 million used the drug on a regular basis.

While behavior patterns have changed since the mid-1960s, the laws have essentially remained punitive to marijuana users. This gap between the law and behavior has had some interesting consequences: (1) many white, affluent, and middle-class parents saw their children treated as criminals; (2) many persons spent time in jail and were stigmatized as drug users, making reintegration into society hard and thereby creating a deviant drug culture (that is, repressive societal controls created secondary deviance); (3) there was a growing disrespect for the law, because the law was perceived by many of the users and their families as governmental interference in a private matter; and (4) insolence for the law was also encour-

the status quo, efforts to reform society are vigorously thwarted by them. The solution, from the conflict theorists, however, requires not only reform of society but its radical transformation. It is the structure of society that is the problem. The radical therapists, for example, assume that society is the root cause of all mental suffering.[84] Mental illness in this view is really a process that an individual is going through in a relationship to his environment. The depressed person, the chronic alcoholic, and the schizophrenic are each trying to survive in a mad world. Rather than focusing on the individual and his adjustment (although this may be necessary in the short term), which validates and reinforces the established system, the radical therapist argues that the only real and lasting form of therapy is a radical transformation of society.

Critique of the conflict approach to deviance. The strengths of the conflict perspective on deviance are[85]: (1) its emphasis on the relationship between political order and nonconformity; (2) the understanding that the most powerful groups use the political order to protect their interests; (3) that it emphasizes how the system of justice is unjust, and that the distribution of rewards in society is skewed; and (4) the realization that the institutional

aged by those who saw the crackdown on marijuana as discrimination, not based on pharmacological grounds but on political laws—laws that made marijuana use a crime but not the use of other drugs, such as alcohol and tobacco. Informed persons also realized that some drugs were illegal and others were not because of the particular distribution of power. Powerful interests promoted the use of tobacco and alcohol (corporations and the Department of Agriculture), whereas marijuana had only the support of isolated individuals (and underworld suppliers who benefited by its illegality).

Essentially, there are four options to solve this "problem." The first option would be to make the penalties harsh for the use and sale of marijuana. In this way, society could continue to impose its will to protect the health, safety, and morals of its citizens. A second possibility would be to decriminalize the smoking of pot. The penalty for usage would be reduced from a crime to a civil infraction akin to a traffic violation. This solution would recognize that persons likely will continue to use marijuana for recreational purposes but that society mildly disapproves. Another alternative would be to legalize the sale and use of marijuana. Similar to the present sale and use of tobacco and alcohol, the state and local governments would permit over-the-counter purchases with some regulations, such as restricting the age of the buyer. Finally, there is the suggestion by libertarians that it is none of the government's business what drug people put into their bodies. Therefore, there should be no governmental interference in this private act.

Obviously, the decision to use drugs is your personal choice to make. But there are also the larger questions of society's role in the control of their usage. The political apparatus is slowly moving in the direction of greater liberalization of the drug laws. So, too, the people, especially middle-class young people, are becoming more tolerant of marijuana use. What can you do to clarify the discrepancy between law and society? Where are the boundaries to society's control of its citizens? Once these boundaries are established, should society be consistent for all types of drugs?

framework of society is the source of so many social problems (for example, racism, sexism, pollution, unequal distribution of health care, poverty, and economic cycles). There are some problems with this perspective, however. First, there is the tendency to assume a conspiracy by the well-to-do. Because the empirical evidence is overwhelming that the poor, the uneducated, and the members of minority groups are singled out for the deviant label, some persons make the too facile imputation of motive.

Second, the answer of the conflict theorists is too utopian. The following quotation by Quinney is representative of this naivete:

The alternative to the contradictions of capitalism is a truly democratic society, a socialist society in which human beings no longer suffer the alienation inherent in capitalism. When there is no longer the need for one class to dominate another, when there is no longer the need for a legal system to secure the interests of a capitalist ruling class, then there will no longer be the need for crime.[86]

But, would crime and other forms of deviance disappear under such a socialist system?

This, like Marx's final stage of history, is a statement of faith rather than one based on proof.

SUMMARY

The preceding descriptions of the theories on the causes of deviance indicate clearly their social nature. To recapitulate, they are social because they involve: (1) the violation of societal norms, values, and expectations; (2) the perceptions of the citizenry which are shaped, of course, by the way they have been socialized; (3) the labeling process, whereby society designates certain persons as deviants; (4) the role of the powerful in all these processes; and (5) the structure of society itself as a source of human suffering.

Despite the social nature of deviance, however, there is a very strong tendency for individuals (laypeople, police personnel, judges, lawmakers, and social scientists alike) to perceive social problems and prescribe remedies from a psychological perspective. The individual is blamed for being poor, not the maldistribution of wealth and other socially perpetuated disadvantages which blight many families generation after generation. The black is blamed for his or her aggressive behavior, not the limits placed on social mobility for blacks by the social system. Dropouts are blamed for leaving school prematurely, not the educational system that fails to meet their needs. This type of explanation helps to explain the reluctance by persons in authority to provide adequate welfare, health care, and compensatory programs to help the disadvantaged. This common tendency of individuals to focus on the deviant rather than the system that produces deviants has also been true of American social scientists analyzing social problems. Although one might logically expect psychologists to have such a bias, sociologists, because their unit of analysis is society, should logically focus on institutions rather than the deviant. Since this has not been the case, let us examine more closely the theoretical perspectives within sociology to determine why sociology has tended to view social problems as a result of individual pathologies rather than the structure of society.

The two contrasting theoretical perspectives in sociology—the order model (functionalism) and the conflict model—constrain their adherents to view the causes, consequences, and remedies of social problems in opposing ways (see Table 9–2).

The order perspective focuses on deviants themselves. This approach (which has been the conventional way of studying social problems) asks: Who are the deviants? What are their social and psychological backgrounds? With whom do they associate? Deviants somehow do not conform to the standards of the dominant group; they are assumed to be out of phase with conventional behavior. This is believed to occur most often as a result of inadequate socialization. In other words, deviants have not internalized the norms and values of society because they are either brought up in an environment of conflicting value systems (as are children of immigrants or the poor in a middle-class school) or are under the influence of a deviant subculture such as a gang. Since the order theorist uses the prevailing standards to define and label deviants, the existing practices and structures of society are accepted implicitly. The remedy is to rehabilitate the deviants so that they conform to the societal norms.

The conflict theorist takes a quite different approach to social problems. The adherents of this perspective criticize order theorists for "blaming the victim." To focus on the individual deviant is to locate the symptom, not the disease. Individual deviants are a manifestation of a failure of society to meet the needs of individuals. The sources of crime,

TABLE 9–2   Assumptions of the Order and Conflict Models about Deviance[87]

Order model	Conflict model
Who is deviant?	
Those who break the rules of society.	Those who break the rules but also those who make the rules. Deviance is created by the powerful, who make the rules. Enactment and enforcement of these rules are used by the powerful to control potentially dissident groups and to maintain their own interests at the expense of those being ruled.
The legitimacy of deviance:	
Deviance is illegitimate, by definition.	Deviance of rule breakers can be legitimate because the rules are arbitrarily made and reflect a class bias. Deviance is also necessary to change an unjust society.
The causes of deviance:	
People are deviant because they have not been socialized to accept and obey the customs of society.	Deviance is caused by society, which makes the rules, the violation of which constitutes deviance. The inequities of society generate the behavior that the powerful label as deviant.
The solutions for deviance:	
Control by punishment and rehabilitation of deviant individuals (therapy, behavior modification, incarceration).	Restructure society (eliminate inequities, provide adequately for the needs of all members, a fair system of justice, laws that reflect the interest of all groups).

poverty, drug addiction, and racism are found in the laws, the customs, the quality of life, the distribution of wealth and power, and in the accepted practices of schools, governmental units, and corporations. The established system, in this view, is not "sacred." Since it is the primary source of social problems, it, not the individual deviant, must be restructured.

Since this is a text on society, we have emphasized and will continue to emphasize the conflict approach. The insights of this approach will be clarified further in the remainder of this book as we examine the structure and consequences of social inequality in the next five chapters, followed by four chapters describing the positive and negative effects of institutions.

CHAPTER REVIEW

1. Deviance is behavior that violates the laws and expectations of a group. This means that deviance is not a property inherent in a behavior but a property conferred upon that behavior by others. In short, deviance is socially created.

2. What is deviant varies from society to society and within a society the same behavior may be interpreted differently as it is done by different categories of persons.

3. The norms of the majority determine what behaviors will be considered deviant.

4. Order theorists point out that deviant behavior has positive consequences for society because

it gives the nondeviants a sense of solidarity and it reaffirms the importance of society's rules.

5. Conflict theorists argue that all views of rule violations have political implications. Punishment of deviants reflects a conservative bias by legitimating the norms and the current distribution of power. Support of the deviant behavior is also political because it rejects the legitimacy of those in power and their rules.

6. There are several traditional theories for the causes of deviance that assume the source as a fatal flaw in certain people. These are theories that focus on physical or psychological reasons for deviant behavior.

7. "Kinds-of-people" explanations for deviance also apply to some theories by sociologists. One theory argues that crime results from the conditions of city life. Another places the blame on the influences of peers. A third focuses on the propensity of the poor to be deviants because of the gap between the goal of success and the lack of the means for these people to attain it. Finally, some have argued that lower-class culture is responsible.

8. These "kinds-of-people" theories have been criticized for blaming the victim. Because they blame the victim, the society (government, system of justice, education) is freed from blame. Because the established order is protected from criticism, necessary social change is thwarted.

9. An alternative to person-blame theories is labeling theory. This approach argues that while most people break the rules on occasion, the crucial factor in establishing a deviant career is the successful application of the label "deviant."

10. Who gets labeled as a deviant is not a matter of luck but the result of a systematic societal bias against the powerless.

11. Primary deviance is the rule breaking that occurs prior to labeling. Secondary deviance is that behavior resulting from the labeling process.

12. Labeling theorists argue that because deviants are not much different from nondeviants, the problem lies in organizations that label. Thus, these organizations should: (a) leave the deviants alone whenever possible; and (b) apply justice fairly when the legal approach is required.

13. Labeling theory has been criticized because it: (a) disregards undetected deviance; (b) assumes that deviants are really normal because we are all rule-breakers; (c) relieves the individual from blame; and (d) focuses on certain types of deviance but ignores deviance by the powerful.

14. Conflict theory focuses on social structure as the source of deviance. There is an historical bias in the law that favors the powerful. The administration of justice is also biased. In short, the state is a political organization controlled by the ruling class for its own advantage. The power of powerful interests in society determines what and who is deviant.

15. From the conflict perspective the only real and lasting solution to deviance is the radical transformation of society.

FOR FURTHER STUDY

Social Deviance

Howard S. Becker, *The Outsiders: Studies in the Sociology of Deviance*, 2nd ed. (New York: Free Press, 1973).

Kai Erikson, *Wayward Puritans: A Study in the Sociology of Deviance* (New York: John Wiley, 1966).

Erving Goffman, *Stigma: Notes on the Management of Spoiled Identity* (Englewood Cliffs, N.J.: Prentice-Hall, 1963).

David Matza, *Becoming Deviant* (Englewood Cliffs, N.J.: Prentice-Hall, 1969).

Richard Quinney, *Class, State and Crime: On the Theory and Practice of Criminal Justice* (New York: David McKay, 1977).

Theories of Deviance

Clayton Hartjen, *Crime and Criminalization*, 2nd ed., (New York: Praeger, 1978).

Edwin M. Lemert, *Human Deviance, Social Problems, and Social Control*, 2nd ed. (Englewood Cliffs, N.J.: Prentice-Hall, 1972).

Charles H. McCaghy, *Deviant Behavior: Crime, Conflict, and Interest Groups* (New York: Macmillan, 1976).

Gwynn Nettler, *Explaining Crime* (New York: McGraw-Hill, 1974).

Richard Quinney, *The Social Reality of Crime* (Boston: Little, Brown, 1970).

Jeffrey H. Reiman, *The Rich Get Richer and the Poor Get Prison: Ideology, Class, and Criminal Justice* (New York: John Wiley & Sons, 1979).

Earl Rubington and Martin S. Weinberg, *The Study of Social Problems: Five Perspectives*, rev. ed. (New York: Oxford University Press, 1977).

William Ryan, *Blaming the Victim*, rev. ed. (New York: Random House (Vintage Books), 1976).

Leonard D. Savitz and Norman Johnston (eds.), *Crime in Society* (New York: John Wiley & Sons, 1978).

Edwin M. Schur, *The Politics of Deviance* (Englewood Cliffs, N.J.: Prentice-Hall, 1980).

Edwin M. Schur, *Interpreting Deviance: A Sociological Introduction* (New York: Harper & Row, 1979).

David R. Simon and D. Stanley Eitzen, *Elite Deviance* (Boston: Allyn and Bacon, 1982).

NOTES AND REFERENCES

1. "Shoplifting Soars—and Merchants Strike Back," *U.S. News & World Report* (December 3, 1979), pp. 71–72; Associated Press release (August 25, 1980); and Pat Cloud, "Shoplifting Deterrents Cut Deeply into Profit Margins," Colorado State University *Collegian* (October 9, 1980), p. 4.

2. "The Underground Economy," *U.S. News & World Report* (October 22, 1979), pp. 49–56; and Terri Schultz, "How Millions Cheat (and Beat) the IRS," *Dallas Times Herald* (March 30, 1980), pp. 1M, 6M.

3. Deborah Rankin, "Cheating Found on the Rise," *The New York Times* (April 22, 1980), p. D2.

4. "Cheating in College Becomes an Epidemic," *U.S. News & World Report* (October 20, 1980), pp. 39–42.

5. Reported in "Ripoffs—New American Way of Life," *U.S. News & World Report* (May 31, 1976), p. 30.

6. Howard S. Becker, *The Outsiders: Studies in the Sociology of Deviance* (New York: Free Press, 1963), pp. 8–9.

7. Kai T. Erikson, *Wayward Puritans: A Study in the Sociology of Deviance* (New York: John Wiley, 1966), p. 6.

8. Deena Weinstein and Michael Weinstein, *Living Sociology: A Critical Introduction* (New York: David McKay, 1974), p. 271.

9. Michael Mewshaw, "Irrational Behavior or Evangelical Zeal?" *The Chronicle of Higher Education*, October 18, 1976, p. 32.

10. Erikson, *Wayward Puritans*, pp. 5–6.

11. See Emile Durkheim, *The Rules of Sociological Method*, S. A. Solovay and J. H. Mueller, trans. (Glencoe, Ill.: Free Press, 1958); and Emile Durkheim, *The Division of Labor in Society*, George Simpson, trans. (Glencoe, Ill.: Free Press, 1960); and Robert A. Dentler and Kai T. Erikson, "The Functions of Deviance in Groups," *Social Problems* 7 (Fall, 1959), pp. 98–107.

12. Durkheim, *The Division of Labor in Society*, p. 102.

13. Earl Rubington and Martin S. Weinberg, *Deviance: the Interactionist Perspective*, 2nd ed. (New York: Macmillan, 1973), p. 1.

14. See Becker, *Outsiders*, p. 4; Weinstein and Weinstein, *Living Sociology*, p. 273; and Robert Ross and Graham L. Staines, "The Politics of Analyzing Social Problems," *Social Problems* 20 (Summer, 1972), pp. 18–40.

15. Edwin M. Schur, *The Politics of Deviance* (Englewood Cliffs, N.J.: Prentice-Hall, 1980), p. xi.

16. The section that follows is dependent on the organization and insights of Edwin M. Schur, *Radical Non-intervention: Rethinking the Delinquency Problem* (Englewood Cliffs, N.J.: Prentice-Hall (Spectrum Books), 1973).

17. For a summary of the biological and psycho-

logical theories on deviance, see Charles H. McCaghy, *Deviant Behavior: Crime, Conflict, and Interest Groups* (New York: Macmillan, 1976), pp. 5–40; Sue Titus Reid, *Crime and Criminology* (Hinsdale, Ill.: Dryden Press, 1976), pp. 130–171; and Albert K. Cohen, *Deviance and Control* (Englewood Cliffs, N.J.: Prentice-Hall, 1966), pp. 48–62. For a formal review of the sociological theories of deviance, see summaries provided by: Nanette J. Davis, *Sociological Construction of Deviance* (Dubuque, Iowa: Wm. C. Brown, 1975); McCaghy, *Deviant Behavior*; Earl Rubington and Martin S. Weinberg, *The Study of Social Problems; Five Perspectives* (New York: Oxford University Press, 1971); and Charles E. Frazier, *Theoretical Approaches to Deviance: An Evaluation* (Columbus, Ohio: Charles E. Merrill, 1976).

18. Chester D. Poremba, "Learning Disabilities, Youth and Delinquency: Programs for Intervention," in *Progress in Learning Disabilities*, Vol. III, Helmer R. Myklebust, ed. (New York: Grune & Stratton, 1975), pp. 123–149; Herb Stoenner, "Youth Crime, Learning Disability Found 90% Linked," *Denver Post*, April 9, 1974, p. D1; and Charles A. Murray, *The Link between Learning Disabilities and Juvenile Delinquency* (Washington, D.C.: U.S. Department of Justice, 1976).

19. Cohen, *Deviance and Control*, pp. 41–45.

20. Edwin Powers and Helen Witmer, *An Experiment in the Prevention of Delinquency* (New York: Columbia University Press, 1951).

21. David Matza, *Delinquency and Drift* (New York: John Wiley, 1964), p. 17.

22. Two representative sources for this approach are: Louis Wirth, "Urbanism as a Way of Life," *American Journal of Sociology* 44 (July, 1938), pp. 1–24; and Clifford R. Shaw and Henry D. McKay, *Juvenile Delinquency and Urban Areas* (Chicago: University of Chicago Press, 1942).

23. Milton L. Barron, "The Crimogenic Society: Social Values and Deviance," *Current Perspectives on Criminal Behavior*, Abraham S. Blumberg, ed. (New York: Alfred A. Knopf, 1974), p. 81.

24. Clayton A. Hartjen, *Crime and Criminalization* (New York: Praeger, 1974), p. 175. Excerpts from this work are reprinted by permission of Praeger Publishers, a division of Holt, Rinehart and Winston, © 1974 by Praeger Publishers.

25. Edwin H. Sutherland and Donald R. Cressy, *Principles of Criminology*, 7th ed. (Philadelphia: J. B. Lippincott, 1966), pp. 81–82.

26. Clayton A. Hartjen, *Crime and Criminalization*, p. 51.

27. Robert K. Merton, *Social Theory and Social Structure*, rev. ed. (Glencoe, Ill.: Free Press, 1957), pp. 131–160.

28. Reece McGee, *Points of Departure: Basic Concepts in Sociology* (Hinsdale, Ill.: Dryden Press, 1975), pp. 211–212.

29. Jack Doyle and Paul T. Schindler, "The Incoherent Society," paper presented at the meetings of the American Sociological Association, Montreal, August 25–29, 1974, p. 2.

30. See, especially, Walter B. Miller, "Lower Class Culture as a Generating Milieu of Gang Delinquency," *Journal of Social Issues* 14 (No. 3, 1958), pp. 5–19; and Edward C. Banfield, *The Unheavenly City Revisited* (Boston: Little, Brown, 1974), especially pp. 179–210.

31. For other criticisms of this approach, see Gwynn Nettler, *Explaining Crime* (New York: McGraw-Hill, 1974), pp. 150–153.

32. William Ryan, *Blaming the Victim* (New York: Random House (Vintage Books), 1972), p. 7.

33. Many of the insights that follow come from William Ryan, *Blaming the Victim* (New York: Pantheon Books, 1971); and two articles by Nathan Caplan and Stephen D. Nelson: "On Being Useful: The Nature and Consequences of Psychological Research on Social Problems," *American Psychologist* 28 (March, 1973), pp. 199–211; and "Who's to Blame?" *Psychology Today* 8 (November, 1974), pp. 99–104.

34. "Illiteracy: Invitation to Failure," editorial in *Kansas City Times*, January 26, 1974.

35. Quoted in *The New York Times*, March 11, 1973.

36. Edwin A. Roberts, Jr., ". . . It Is Dangerous for the Nation to Project a Tolerant Attitude Toward the Criminal," *The National Observer*, March 24, 1973.

37. Tom Wicker, "Nixon's Rhetoric on Crime Ignores the Real Problem," *Kansas City Times*, March 14, 1973.

38. Ryan, *Blaming the Victim*, pp. 10–18.

39. The following enumeration of the consequences of the person-blame model are taken primarily from Caplan and Nelson, "On Being Useful," and Caplan and Nelson, "Who's to Blame?"

40. Caplan and Nelson, "Who's the Blame?" p. 104.

41. Lee Stillwell, "Revenue Sharing Fails to Aid Poor, Study Says," *Rocky Mountain News*, December 11, 1974, p. 36.

42. Caplan and Nelson, "On Being Useful," p. 209.

43. For a critique of the traditional sociological assumptions of such pathology by deviants, see C. Wright Mills, "The Professional Ideology of Social Pathologists," *American Journal of Sociology* 49 (September, 1942), pp. 165–180.

44. James S. Wallerstein and Clement J. Wyle, "Our Law-Abiding Law Breakers," *Probation* 22 (April, 1947), pp. 107–112.

45. See F. Ivan Nye, James F. Short, Jr., and Virgil J. Olson, "Socioeconomic Status and Delinquent Behavior," *American Journal of Sociology* 63 (January, 1958), pp. 381–389; Ronald I. Akers, "Socioeconomic Status and Delinquent Behavior: A Retest," *Journal of Research and Delinquency* 10 (January, 1964), pp. 38–46; Harwin L. Voss, "Socioeconomic Status and Reported Delinquent Behavior," *Social Problems* 13 (Winter, 1966), pp. 314–324; and Maynard L. Erickson and LaMar T. Empey, "Class Position, Peers, and Delinquency," *Sociology and Social Research* 49 (April, 1965), pp. 268–282.

46. Travis Hirschi, *Causes of Delinquency* (Berkeley, Calif.: University of California Press, 1969), p. 66.

47. See August B. Hollingshead and Frederick C. Redlich, *Social Class and Mental Illness* (New York: John Wiley, 1958); and Jerome K. Myers and Lee L. Bean, *A Decade Later: A Follow-Up of Social Class and Mental Illness* (New York: John Wiley, 1968).

48. Becker, *Outsiders*, p. 14.

49. David Janzen, "Love 'em and Leave 'em Alone," *The Mennonite*, June 11, 1974, p. 390. See also William J. Chambliss, "The Saints and the Roughnecks," *Society* 11 (November/December, 1973), pp. 24–31.

50. For a complete discussion of the labeling approach to deviance, see Edwin M. Schur, *Labeling Deviant Behavior: Its Sociological Implications* (New York: Harper & Row, 1971).

51. William J. Chambliss, *Crime and the Legal Process* (New York: McGraw-Hill, 1969), p. 86.

52. Theodore G. Chiricos, Philip D. Jackson, and Gordon P. Waldo, "Inequality in the Imposition of the Criminal Label," *Social Problems* 19 (Spring, 1972), pp. 553–572. These data focus on the poor and the blacks. Similar results are found when examining the differential treatment of other minority groups in the criminal justice system. One study, for example, of native Americans and the system of justice substantiates the finding comparing whites and blacks; see Edwin L. Hall and Albert A. Simkus, "Inequality in the Types of Sentences Received by Native Americans and Whites," *Criminology* 13 (August, 1975), pp. 199–222.

53. Ramsey Clark, *Crime in America: Observations on Its Nature, Causes, Prevention and Control* (New York: Simon and Schuster, 1970), p. 335. See also Marvin E. Wolfgang and Marc Riedel, "Race, Judicial Discretion and the Death Penalty," *The Annals* 477 (May, 1973), pp. 119–133; and William J. Bowers, *Executions in America* (Lexington, Mass.: Lexington Books, 1974).

54. Marvin E. Wolfgang, Arlene Kelly, and Hans C. Nolde, "Comparisons of the Executed and the Commuted Among Admissions to Death Row," *Journal of Criminal Law, Criminology and Police Science* 53 (September, 1962), p. 311.

55. *The Challenge of Crime in a Free Society*, A Report by the President's Commission on Law Enforcement and Administration of Justice (New York: Avon Books, 1968), pp. 80–429.

56. David M. Petersen and Paul C. Friday, "Early Release from Incarceration: Race as a Factor in the Use of 'Shock Probation,' " *The Journal of Criminal Law and Criminology* 66 (March, 1975), pp. 79–87.

57. See Martin R. Haskell and Lewis Yablonsky, *Crime and Delinquency* 2nd ed. (Chicago: Rand McNally, 1974), pp. 629–630. See also Charles E. Reasons, "The Politicizing of Crime, the Criminal, and the Criminologist," *The Journal of Criminal Law and*

Criminology 64 (December, 1973), pp. 471–477.

58. See Campbell et al., *Law and Order Reconsidered*, pp. 628–637; Ronald L. Goldfarb, "American Prisons: Self-Defeating Concrete," *Psychology Today* 7 (January, 1974), pp. 20–24, 85–90; Haskell and Yablonsky, *Crime and Delinquency*, pp. 622–624; and Gresham Sykes, *The Society of Captives* (Princeton, N.J.: Princeton University Press, 1958), pp. 65–78.

59. "The Ex-Con's Unhappy Lot," *Newsweek*, February 25, 1974, pp. 84–85.

60. Edwin M. Lemert, *Social Pathology: A Systematic Approach to the Theory of Sociopathic Behavior* (New York: McGraw-Hill, 1951), pp. 75–78.

61. For an empirical verification of this assertion, see Richard D. Schwartz and Jerome H. Skolnick, "Two Studies of Legal Stigma," *Social Problems* 10 (Fall, 1962), pp. 133–138.

62. Nettler, *Explaining Crime*, p. 203.

63. See Thomas J. Scheff, *Mentally Ill* (Chicago: Aldine, 1966); and M. Balint, *The Doctor, His Patient, and the Illness* (New York: International Universities Press, 1957).

64. Ken Kesey, *One Flew Over the Cuckoo's Nest* (New York: Signet Books, 1962).

65. Stephen Cole, *The Sociological Orientation: An Introduction to Sociology* (Chicago: Rand McNally, 1975), pp. 141–142. See also Eli Glogow, "The 'Bad Patient' Gets Better Quicker," *Social Policy* 4 (November/December, 1973), pp. 72–76.

66. Edwin M. Lemert, *Human Deviance, Social Problems and Social Control* (Englewood Cliffs, N.J.: Prentice-Hall, 1967), pp. 42–43.

67. Hartjen, *Crime and Criminalization*, pp. 120–121.

68. Schur, *Radical Non-intervention*, pp. 117–173.

69. Ibid., pp. 154–155. Reprinted by permission of Prentice-Hall, Inc., Englewood Cliffs, N.J.; © 1973.

70. For critiques of labeling theory, see Carol A. B. Warren and John M. Johnson, "A Critique of Labeling Theory from the Phenomenological Perspective," in *Theoretical Perspectives on Deviance*, Jack D. Douglas and Robert Scott, eds. (New York: Basic Books, 1973); Jack P. Gibbs, "Conceptions of Deviant Behavior: the Old and the New," *Pacific Sociological Review* 9 (Spring, 1966), pp. 9–14; Davis, *Sociological Constructions of Deviance*, pp. 164–191; and, most important, Alexander Liazos, "The Poverty of the Sociology of Deviance: Nuts, Sluts, and Preverts," *Social Problems* 20 (Summer, 1972), pp. 103–120.

71. McCaghy, *Deviant Behavior*, p. 87.

72. McCaghy, *Deviant Behavior*, p. 88.

73. Liazos, "The Poverty of the Sociology of Deviance."

74. Ibid.

75. Ibid., p. 119.

76. Richard Quinney, *The Social Reality of Crime* (Boston: Little, Brown, 1970); Richard Quinney, *Critique of Legal Order: Crime Control in a Capitalist Society* (Boston: Little, Brown, 1974).

77. The following is taken largely from Richard Quinney, *The Social Reality of Crime*, pp. 29–97.

78. For a historical analysis of the role of powerful interest groups in the formation of laws concerning activities on Sunday, theft, antitrust, adulterated food, sex, drunkenness, drugs, and vagrancy, see Quinney, *The Social Reality of Crime*, pp. 65–97; and Hartjen, *Crime and Criminalization*, pp. 21–33.

79. Haywood Burns, "Black People and the Tyranny of American Law," *The Annals* 407 (May, 1973), p. 157.

80. The following examples are taken from Burns, "Black People and the Tyranny of American Law," pp. 156–166.

81. For discussions of the political nature of the system of justice, see George F. Cole, *Politics and the Administration of Justice* (Beverly Hills, Calif.: Sage Publications, 1973).

82. Hartjen, *Crime and Criminalization*, p. 11.

83. Gresham M. Sykes, "Criminology: The Rise of Critical Criminology," *The Journal of Criminal Law and Criminology* 65 (June, 1974), p. 210.

84. See Walt Anderson, "Breaking Out of the Establishment Vise," *Human Behavior* 2 (December, 1973), pp. 10–18; and Jerome Agel, *The Radical Therapist* (New York: Ballatine Books, 1971).

85. See Sykes, "Criminology," and Reid, *Crime and Criminology*, pp. 203–205.

86. Richard Quinney, *Criminal Justice in America* (Boston: Little, Brown, 1974), p. 25.

87. See Nanette J. Davis, *Sociological Constructions of Deviance: Perspectives and Issues in the Field* (Dubuque, Iowa: Wm. C. Brown, 1975), pp. 192–244; Gresham M. Sykes, "Criminology: The Rise of Critical Criminology," *The Journal of Criminal Law and Criminology* 65 (June, 1974), pp. 206–213; John Horton, "Order and Conflict Theories of Social Problems as Competing Ideologies," *American Journal of Sociology* 71 (May, 1966), pp. 701–713; Jerome H. Skolnick and Elliott Currie, "Approaches to Social Problems," in *Crisis in American Institutions*, Jerome H. Skolnick and Elliott Currie, eds. (Boston: Little, Brown, 1970), pp. 1–16; William J. Chambliss, *Functional and Conflict Theories of Crime*, Module 17 (New York: MSS Modular Publications, 1974), pp. 1–23; and William J. Chambliss, "Functional and Conflict Theories of Crime: The Heritage of Emile Durkheim and Karl Marx," in *Whose Law, What Order? A Conflict Approach to Criminology*, William J. Chambliss and Milton Mankoff, eds. (New York: John Wiley & Sons, 1976, pp. 1–28.

Part III

Social Inequality

10

The American System of Social Stratification

A sample of average annual salaries/ wages of workers in Denver, Colorado (1979), assuming a full year's work, included:[1]

David Thompson, professional basketball player	$800,000
President, Johns-Manville Corporation	235,000
President, Frontier Airlines	150,000
U.S. District Court Judge	61,500
Mayor	50,000
Geologist, oil and gas company	45,000
Full professor, University of Colorado	25,441
Electrician	24,960
Painter	23,251
Roofer	22,600
Airline ticket agent	19,560
Registered pharmacist	18,202
City bus driver	16,973
Supermarket checker	15,686
Denver Symphony Orchestra member	15,000
Garbage collector	13,065
Registered nurse	12,730
Meter reader, Public Service Company	11,040
Bank teller	9,900
Clerk-typist, state government	9,624
Laundry worker	7,296
Janitor	6,720
Medical office receptionist	6,600

These huge differences in the monetary rewards for labor shows dramatically the inequality present in American society. These differences in pay, along with education, family background, and race and ethnicity rank people in society. These ranks are social locations that have an enormous impact on our lives as individuals and as members of families. This chapter is devoted to an inquiry into two related questions: How are wealth and prestige distributed in society? and What are the consequences of an unequal distribution of wealth and prestige for individuals?

Inequality is a fact of social life. All known societies have some system of ranking individuals and groups along a superiority–inferiority scale. The thrust of this chapter is that the particular placement of individuals in the ranking system makes a significant difference—a difference in lifestyle, behavior, attitude, and self-images.

MAJOR CONCEPTS AND ASSUMPTIONS

People differ in age, physical attributes, and in what they do for a living. The process of categorizing persons by age, height, occupation, or whatever is called **social differentiation**. When people are ranked in a vertical arrangement (hierarchy) that differentiates them as superior or inferior, we have **social stratification**. The key difference between differentiation and stratification is that the process of ranking or evaluation occurs only in the latter. What is ranked and how it is ranked are dependent upon the values of the society.

Social stratification refers, in essence, to structured social inequality. The term "structured" refers to stratification being socially patterned.[2] This implies that inequalities are not caused by biological differences (for example, sex or race). Biological traits do not become relevant in patterns of social superiority or inferiority until they are socially recognized and given importance by being incorporated into the beliefs, attitudes, and values of the people in the society. Americans, for example, tend to believe that sexual and racial characteristics make a difference—therefore they do.

The social patterning of stratification is also found in the distribution of rewards in any community or society, since that distribution is governed by social norms. In American society few individuals seriously question the income differential between medical doctors and primary school teachers because the norms and values of society dictate that such inequalities are just.

Patterned behavior is also achieved through the socialization process. Each generation is taught the norms and values of the society and of its social class. The children of slaves and the children of the ruling family in a society are each taught the behavior "proper" for persons of their station in life.

Finally, the system of stratification is always connected with other aspects of the society. The existing stratification arrangements are affected by and have effects upon such matters as politics, marriage and the family, economics, education, and religion.

An individual's position (**social status**) in the social stratification system is determined by the degree to which he or she possesses those qualities highly valued by the society. The important criteria by which people are evaluated and ranked in the United States are (1) family background, which includes the status of the preceding generations of one's family, their ethnic and racial background, and religious affiliation; (2) the amount and type of an individual's wealth; (3) personal qualities, such as sex, age, beauty, and intelligence; (4) personal achievements, such as amount of education, type of job, and job performance; and (5) the amount of power and authority of the individual.

These criteria for evaluation can be viewed as either ascribed or achieved characteristics. **Ascribed characteristics** befall individuals regardless of their efforts. Individuals cannot control their age, sex, their race, or their family background—therefore, these characteristics are ascribed. **Achieved characteristics**, on the other hand, are those attained by individuals because of their own efforts, such as amount of education and type of job.* Ascribed characteristics determine an individual's **ascribed status**, while achieved characteristics determine his or her **achieved status**. An individual's **social rank** is determined by both types of status.

When a number of persons occupy the same relative economic rank in the stratification system, they form a **social class**. Persons of similar status form a **status group**. The members of a status group view one another as social equals. Interaction tends to occur most frequently among status equals. Although social classes and status groups often overlap, they may not—leading to the phenomenon of status inconsistency.

---

*This distinction between ascribed and achieved characteristics is a somewhat artificial one made for analytical purposes, since abscribed characteristics can and do have an effect upon educational attainment, type of job, and the other achieved characteristics.

The rigidity of the stratification system varies from society to society. The key indicator of rigidity is the extent to which ascribed characteristics "lock" the individual into a social class or status group. The more that achieved characteristics determine class or status position, the more open the system—the more movement is possible from one rank to another (**social mobility**).

Social Stratification from the Order and Conflict Perspectives

As we examine inequality in American society, let us keep in mind the alternative ways order and conflict theorists view this phenomenon. The position of the order theorists is basically supportive of inequality, since the unequal distribution of rewards is assumed to be not only inevitable but necessary. Conflict theorists, on the other hand, tend to denounce the distributive system as basically unjust, unnecessary, and the source of many social problems.

Adherents of the order model begin with the fact that social inequality is a ubiquitous and apparently unavoidable phenomenon. They reason that inequality must, therefore, serve a useful function for society. The argument, as presented in the classic statement by Davis and Moore, is as follows:[3] The smooth functioning of society requires that various tasks be accomplished through a division of labor. There is a universal problem, then, of allocation—of getting the most important tasks done by the most talented people. Some jobs are more important for social survival than others (typically persons involved in decision making, medicine, religion, teaching, and the military). The societal problem is how to get the most talented people motivated to go through the required long periods of training and to do these important tasks well. The universally found answer, according to Davis and Moore, is differential rewards. Society must provide suitable rewards (money, prestige, and power) to induce individuals to fill these positions. The rewards must, it is argued, be distributed unevenly to various positions because the positions are not equally pleasant or equally important. Thus, a differential reward system guarantees that the important societal functions are fulfilled, thereby ensuring the maintenance of society. In this way, differential ranks actually serve to unify society (functional integration through a division of labor and through the socialization of persons to accept their positions in the system). Although there probably is some truth to this argument, the analyst of American society must also ask: Is inequality primarily integrative or divisive? Is it necessary? Must the poor always be with us?[4]

Conflict theorists view stratification in a wholly different manner. Rather than accepting stratification as a source of societal integration, the conflict perspective assumes it to be a major source of discord and coercion. It is a source of discord because the "have-nots" will not be satisfied but rather resentful of their lowly position and lack of rewards. Coercion results from stratification as the powerful (who are coincidentally the wealthy) prey on the weak. The powerful make and enforce the laws, determine the distribution of rewards, and through control of the media and education make their value system paramount.

A major contention of the conflict theorists is that most oppressed peoples accept their deprivation because of **false consciousness**.[5] This concept refers to the acceptance of an untrue belief that works to one's disadvantage. The argument is that people adhere to beliefs damaging to their interests because of the power of the socialization process in society. The working classes and the poor in the United States, for example, tend to accept their lack of monetary rewards, power, and prestige because they believe that the system is truly meritocratic—and they lack the skills and brains to do the better-rewarded tasks in society. In short, they believe that they deserve their fate.[6] Consequently, they accept a differential reward system and the need for their supervision and decision making left to "experts."

While it is true that social stratification is an important source of societal friction, the conflict theorists have not answered the important question as to its necessity (neither have the order theorists for that matter, although they address themselves directly to that question). Both models have important insights that we must consider. The order theorists see stratification serving the useful function of societal maintenance by providing a mechanism (differential rewards) to ensure that all the slots in the division of labor are filled. Conflict theorists are equally valid in their contention that stratification is unjust, divisive, and a source of social instability or change.

SOCIAL CLASSES
IN THE UNITED STATES

There are several questions to be raised in this section: Is the United States a classless society? If not, how many classes are there and what are their characteristics? Are there real gaps between each of these classes? Are the classes national in scope or are they community-specific?

Economic and Status Differences
in the United States

There is a great deal of evidence that Americans differ greatly on a number of socioeconomic dimensions. Americans are also very status-conscious. Let us examine some of the documentation of the existence of economic and status differences in the United States.

In the first place, wealth is unquestionably maldistributed in the United States. There exists in the United States unbelievable wealth in the hands of a few and wretched poverty for some others. This is not to say that the bulk of Americans lack enough wealth to live comfortably, for most are reasonably comfortable. The median family income in 1977 was $16,009. The differences in family income by race were substantial for that year: white families, $16,740; black families, $9,560; and Hispanic families, $11,420. It is also important to note that in that year 9.3 percent of all families had incomes of less than $5,000.[7] Those at the low end of the wealth continuum experience malnutrition and inadequate health care while at the other end of the spectrum, a few other Americans have a superabundance of material blessings.*

Americans also vary considerably in educational attainment. The amount of formal education an individual receives is a major determinant of his or her occupation and income. Despite the standard belief by Americans in free mass education and the almost uniform requirement that persons complete at least eight years of formal schooling, very

---

*Chapters 11 and 16 will provide much greater detail about the unequal distribution of income in American society.

real differences in educational attainment exist. In 1978 some 34 percent of Americans aged twenty-five and over had less than a high school education and 15.6 percent had a college degree. At the low end of educational attainment, 32.1 percent of whites had not completed high school, while 52.4 percent of blacks and 59.2 percent of Hispanics were non-high-school graduates.[8]

There is an obvious correspondence between being inadequately educated and receiving little or no income. There is not only a generational correlation between these two variables but an intergenerational one as well. The children of the poor and uneducated tend not to do well in school and eventually drop out (regardless of ability), while the children of the educated well-to-do tend to continue in school (regardless of ability). Thus, the cycle of inequality is maintained.

Another demonstration that persons diverge in status is that occupations vary systematically in prestige. The degree of prestige and difference accorded to occupations is variable. A justice of the Supreme Court obviously enjoys more prestige than a bartender. But society makes much more subtle prestige distinctions. There is a rather uniform tendency to rate physicians slightly higher than college professors, who in turn are somewhat higher in rank than dentists. Further down the prestige scale, mail carriers outrank carpenters, who in turn have higher prestige than automobile repairmen.*

The culture provides a ready-made and well-understood ranking system. It provides a relatively uniform system based on several related factors. These are: (1) the importance of the task performed (that is, how vital the consequences of the task are for the society), (2) the degree of authority and responsibility inherent in the job, (3) the native intelligence required, (4) the knowledge and skills required, (5) the dignity of the job, and (6) the financial rewards of the occupation.

But society also presents us with warped images of occupations, which leads to the acceptance of stereotypes. The media, for example, through advertisements, television, and movie portrayals, evoke positive images for middle and upper class occupations and negative ones for lower-prestige occupations. Professional and business leaders are white, male, cultured, and physically attractive. They are decisive, intelligent, and authoritative. At the other end of the occupational spectrum very different characteristics are portrayed:

It is the incumbents of the lowest-prestige occupations who are portrayed in the least enhancing light. Blue-collar workers of all kinds are either the butt of comedy or the embodiment of ignorance or deviance. They are often ethnic, always lower class, sometimes immoral, generally unattractive, frequently bigoted, and not-too-bright. They are not superhuman; they are subhuman, often with personalities bent by a warp that evokes laughter or disgust.[12]

Occupation, then, is a very important variable that sorts people into hierarchically arranged categories. It is highly correlated with income and education level (see Table 10–1). There is a strong probability that highly educated persons will also have a high-

---

*C. C. North and Paul K. Hatt, the two sociologists who gathered these prestige rankings in 1947, found some degree of variation but a substantial agreement among a cross section of American adults ($N = 3000$).[9] This study was replicated in 1963 to ascertain if Americans had changed their ranking of occupations. The correlation between the two studies of 0.99 suggests that the rating of occupations by Americans has remained remarkably stable.[10] Incidentally, sociologists have found a high correlation in the ratings for occupations for a number of industrialized nations.[11]

ALL THE BUCKS STOP HERE

prestige job and have a good deal of wealth. Of these three variables, occupational level is the best single indicator of status postion in the United States.

Additional evidence for Americans being status-conscious is the importance attached to family background. An individual's social status is not immutably fixed by birth in American society, but family background remains an important determinant of status. Race and ethnicity are inherited from one's parents, and they have had and continue to have a profound effect upon socioeconomic status. Offspring almost invariably adopt the religion of their parents, and this, too, may have consequences for placement in the status hierarchy. Most important, the extent of family wealth determines in very large measure the lifestyle, amount and type of education, with whom one associates as equals, whom one marries, and the occupational niche one occupies. Family status is especially important at either extreme of the status hierarchy. In the middle range there is much greater fluidity, with family background being less important either as an obstacle (as with the lowest social category) or as a passport to prestige and wealth (as with the very highest category).

There is no doubt that most Americans are status seekers. They spend a great amount of effort seeking to rise in status. Many Americans "moonlight" (that is, work at two jobs),

TABLE 10-1   Summary Occupation Group for Employed Persons 25 to 64 Years Old, by Years of
School Completed, Sex, and Race: March 1979
(Numbers in thousands)

Class of worker, sex, and race	Total	Less than 4 years of high school	High school: 4 years	College		
				1 to 3 years	4 years	5 years or more
WHITE						
Male, total	38,110	8,044	13,654	6,770	5,117	4,523
Percent	100.0	100.0	100.0	100.0	100.0	100.0
White-collar workers	48.1	15.4	33.1	57.0	85.7	95.2
Blue-collar workers	42.4	69.7	55.7	34.1	9.3	3.1
Service workers	6.2	8.6	7.3	6.7	3.2	1.2
Farm workers	3.4	6.3	3.9	2.2	1.8	0.5
Female, total	25,235	4,416	11,778	4,370	2,761	1,910
Percent	100.0	100.0	100.0	100.0	100.0	100.0
White-collar workers	69.0	28.0	69.2	82.7	92.8	97.0
Blue-collar workers	14.3	39.4	13.4	4.7	2.5	0.8
Service workers	15.7	30.8	16.4	11.8	4.2	1.7
Farm workers	1.1	1.8	1.1	0.8	0.4	0.5
BLACK						
Male, total	3,429	1,342	1,218	490	220	160
Percent	100.0	100.0	100.0	100.0	100.0	100.0
White-collar workers	25.4	7.7	19.0	43.9	81.4	86.9
Blue-collar workers	57.2	68.2	64.9	44.5	13.2	5.0
Service workers	14.3	17.1	15.1	11.6	5.0	6.9
Farm workers	3.1	7.0	1.1	—	—	—
Female, total	3,330	1,110	1,233	557	227	173
Percent	100.0	100.0	100.0	100.0	100.0	100.0
White-collar workers	45.3	12.9	46.3	72.5	91.6	98.8
Blue-collar workers	19.1	26.6	22.6	9.3	1.8	0.6
Service workers	35.2	59.9	30.7	18.3	7.0	—
Farm workers	0.5	0.7	0.5	—	—	—

—Represents zero.
Source: Bureau of the Census, Current Population Reports, Series P-20, No. 356, Table F.

or both husband and wife work to get ahead financially. Others sacrifice to further their
education so that they might be better able to secure a more prestigious (and better-paying)
job.

There is also the propensity of Americans to purchase material goods that they feel will
impress others. Presumably this is done in order that persons might be accepted as social
equals by others higher in the stratificational "pecking order." The purchase of jewelry,
furs, large homes, art objects, luxury cars, the latest in clothing styles, and other ostentatious displays are examples of this phenomenon of **conspicuous consumption.**

A final piece of evidence leading to the conclusion that social inequality is a real
phenomenon in American society is the existence of patterns of deference. Persons of

CROSS-CULTURAL PANEL

Panel 10–1
Status Seeking Among the Kwakiutl

Competition for prestige so obsesses the Kwakiutl Indians of British Columbia that they act in what appears to outsiders in irrational ways. The Kwakiutl engage in activities where they destroy or give away their possessions to gain status. This practice of "conspicuous waste" (as opposed to "conspicuous consumption," the American practice of trying to outdo others in the accumulation and display of material possessions) occurs in a ceremony known as the potlatch.

Competition among the various village chiefs is heightened because each is insecure about his status and the status he will transmit to his heirs. The competition for status among the contenders occurs at the potlatch. Here a host chief and his followers give a rival chief and his followers great quantities of valuable gifts, there-

wealth are treated differently than poor persons in schools, churches, and community organizations. With few exceptions, their opinions are given greater weight, they are more likely to be elected or appointed to official posts, and they are automatically treated with greater respect.

American Social Classes: Statistical Categories or Social Groups?

The preceding section established that Americans are conscious of their position in the status hierarchy and that the range in status is quite large with respect to income, education, and occupation. This means, in effect, that there is social inequality in the United States and that it can be perceived as a continuum of status. This raises a question upon which social scientists are not in agreement: Are there breaks in this continuum that allow us to distinguish social classes and/or status groups? Put another way, are American social classes real, or are they artificial constructs?

The techniques employed by many sociologists ensure that the social strata they delineate are not real. Persons are assigned a social class position on the basis of their education, occupation, income level, place of residence, or other status characteristics. With such a techinque, placement is arbitrary, to say the least. The procedure is invalid if the goal is to delineate the exact boundaries of classes and their memberships. It is a valid technique, however, if the goal is to compare the behaviors and/or attitudes of persons at different status levels. The sociologists who use this technique tend either to accept the continuum approach to stratification, or to use it as a quick method to delineate approximately the members of real classes.

The "classes-are-real" adherents claim that there are distinct social strata whose members are conscious of their unity. They share common goals, interests, and values. Furthermore, they contend that there are boundaries separating each of the strata. The

by gaining in prestige. The recipients, though, belittle these gifts and vow to hold a return potlatch where they would give even more valuable gifts.

The gifts transferred are fish, fish oil, berries, animal skins, blankets, canoes, and others. The gifts are piled neatly before the guests while the host chief boasts of his incredible generosity and the relative poverty of his rivals. Accountants for each side carefully record the wealth being given away. Occasionally the ultimate in conspicuous waste—the destruction of valuable property—is accomplished in front of those the chief most wants to outdo. Blankets and even a house might be burned as a display of fabulous wealth. This will cause shame for the guests who then feel compelled to have an even bigger potlatch to shame their competitors.

The goal of the potlatch ceremony is to solidify a man's hereditary claims to chiefdom and the right to transmit them to his heirs. If he miscalculates, however, and is unable to give away or destroy more than his competitor, the prestige of the chief and his heirs will be in doubt and subject to serious challenge from within and outside the village. This fear of miscalculation causes the chief and his followers to work extra hard to produce the goods to be given away.

problem is that class consciousness, class unity, and the understanding of class boundaries are variables. They may be quite pronounced in some communities and not so in others. The valid point made by proponents of the "realist" perspective, however, is that persons in communities tend to think in terms of classes. They see themselves in a class and they can place others in the stratification system.

There is conflicting evidence for the "classes-are-real" thesis. A. B. Hollingshead found evidence in his study of Morris, Illinois, for the existence of five discrete classes. He found that respondents in that community believed in the existence of social classes, identified persons as members of specific classes, thought of themselves as members of classes, and associated behavior with class level. At one point in the research Hollingshead asked twelve knowledgeable persons to rank twenty representative families into classes. No instructions were given regarding the number of strata into which the families should be divided. Ten of the twelve raters divided the families into five strata. This Hollingshead interpreted as conclusive evidence for the existence of five discrete social class groups in that community.[13]

In contrast, Gerhard Lenski's study of Danielson, Connecticut, suggests the very opposite of Hollingshead's. Lenski selected 24 residents who were old enough (between 20 and 70) and who had lived in the community long enough (at least 7 years) to be considered "well-informed" members of that community of 6000. Each rater was given a pack of cards with the names and addresses of 173 families. They were asked to select from the pack only the names they knew and rank these families according to their relative "standing." They were not given any instructions regarding the number of classes or levels into which the families were to be divided. The raters, it was found, lacked a consensus on the number of strata and the placement of families within strata. For example, one rater identified three strata in the community, four raters discerned four strata, seven raters noted five strata, eight raters perceived six strata, and four raters believed the community to have seven strata. Lenski noted that the raters, in the course of the rating interview, constantly changed the number of strata they were using to classify the sample families. He concluded that, for this community at least, there was no system of discrete social classes. But Lenski delved further into the data. Perhaps some of the raters perceived the actual number of classes while others just were not keen observers of the community. If this were so, perhaps all the raters who agreed on the number of strata would agree as to the families belonging in each. There was virtually no agreement, however, among the raters who perceived the same number of strata. For example, the most common number of strata perceived was six, but some raters defined the top stratum in very narrow terms, including only two or three families in it. Others, by contrast, defined the top stratum so as to include twelve families in it. Lenski's findings, therefore, present the consistent conclusion that although status differences occur in the community, there are no real social classes.[14]

The studies by Hollingshead and Lenski suggest that the extent of class boundaries varies from community to community. The analyst of any particular community or the total society should look for two basic indicators of the existence of separate classes: the existence of **class consciousness** and **class segregation**.

The extent of class consciousness. Karl Marx believed that capitalist societies were composed of two broad classes—those persons who owned the instruments of production (bourgeoisie) and those who worked for the owners (proletariat). In other words, there would be a dichotomy based on the relationship to the means of production. Marx predicted (based upon his analysis of history and of how capitalism was working in mid-nineteenth-century England) that persons in these two classes would develop class consciousness—a necessary precondition for class conflict. The essential characteristics of class consciousness for Marx were, first, that persons in a similar economic position should realize they have common interests. In Marx's analysis, the proletariat will be profoundly dissatisfied with the distribution of economic rewards while the bourgeoisie will work to keep the status quo. The bourgeoisie will cooperate among themselves because they are outnumbered and fear the potential power of the lower class. These feelings of common interests lead naturally to the second characteristic of class consciousness—each class becomes hostile to the other. Marx designated these two classes as the oppressors and the oppressed. If these words describe the situation accurately, then hostility between them would be a natural outcome. Finally, class consciousness entails a collective commitment to a political ideology for the attainment of economic interests.

Implied in these three characteristics of class consciousness is the uniformity of belief by persons in a similar economic situation. Marx believed this would occur because of the unequal distribution of economic rewards. Because of similar economic interests, the bourgeoisie would unite to exert control over the proletariat, while the proletariat would band together for power. Finally, the relative ease of communication among the individuals in the same class position should lead to relatively uniform beliefs within each class.

Marx predicted that the natural development of class consciousness would lead ultimately to class conflict in capitalist societies. Does his prediction appear to hold for the United States? To answer this, we need to ask: Do Americans identify themselves with a class? Are blue-collar workers (or businesspersons) unified? Are they allied in a common cause? Do they vote for the same candidates and perceive issues in the same way? Are they organized? Is it clear who are members and who are not?

The empirical evidence for the existence of class consciousness suggests that this phenomenon is relatively low in the United States but not absent.

TABLE 10–2   Voting Preferences by Education in Presidential Elections (percentages)

Election	Educational attainment		
	College	High school	Grade school
1952			
Stevenson (D)	34	45	52
Eisenhower (R)	66	55	48
1956			
Stevenson (D)	31	42	50
Eisenhower (R)	69	58	50
1960			
Kennedy (D)	39	52	55
Nixon (R)	61	48	45
1964			
Johnson (D)	52	62	66
Goldwater (R)	48	38	34
1968			
Humphrey (D)	37	42	52
Nixon (R)	54	43	33
Wallace (I)	9	15	15
1972			
McGovern (D)	37	34	49
Nixon (R)	63	66	51
1976			
Carter (D)	42	54	58
Ford (R)	55	46	41
McCarthy (I)	2	a	1
1980			
Carter (D)	35	43	54
Reagan (R)	53	51	42
Anderson (I)	10	5	3

[a]Less than 1 percent.

Source: The Gallup Opinion Index, Report No. 183 (December, 1980), pp. 6–7.

Table 10–2 provides the data on political preferences from 1952 to 1980 in presidential elections. These data reveal that the voting patterns are relatively stable—the higher the education, the more likely to vote for the Republican candidate (although the data are not supplied here, the results are similar for occupation, with the holders of the higher-prestige jobs the greatest supporters of the Republican Party). Despite the apparent uniformity, the data also reveal that within each educational category, a minimum of one third of the persons differ in their political views from the others.

Other studies also document that people in various occupational, educational, and income levels differ significantly in their opinions on a number of social and political issues.[15]

Are Americans aware of class boundaries? Do they know what class they are in? Do they owe great allegiance to that class? These related questions lie at the core of class consciousness. Most of the evidence from studies of the United States suggests negative answers to these questions.

The study cited most often as a basis for the existence of class consciousness in the

United States was conducted by Richard Centers.[16] Centers gathered data from a representative cross section of American adult white males in 1945. Among other things, he asked if they belonged to the middle class, lower class, working class, or upper class. Here are the results:

Upper class	3%
Middle class	43%
Working class	51%
Lower class	1%
Don't know	2%

Centers felt that since only 2 percent of Americans did not know what class they belonged to, he had overwhelming evidence of a strong class consciousness in the United States.

Centers's study, however, raises more questions than it answers. Let us look at several of the criticisms, because they weaken what on the surface appears to be a very strong argument for class consciousness.[17] First, self-identification as to class in a questionnaire may not be reliable. Some individuals may claim a class position that represents only wish fulfillment or fantasy. For instance, 18 percent of the unskilled workers in Centers's study said they were middle class. Conversely, some individuals may be inclined to downgrade their actual class position because they are influenced by equalitarian ideology. In Centers's study 10 percent of the professionals identified themselves as working class instead of middle or upper.

A second criticism is the use of a forced-choice type of question. The situation was structured for the respondents, as they had four response categories. What if Centers had used five or six categories? Or better yet, what if the respondents were not given any prearranged choices? Neal Gross tested this in a study of 935 heads of households in Minneapolis. The respondents were asked to identify their social class with no hint as to what was meant by social class or how many the interviewer thought there might be. Over one third of the responses were in the "don't know" category (Centers only found 2 percent in this category).[18] Obviously, the open-ended method provides an opportunity for the respondent to express his lack of class identification as well as identification. We must conclude, therefore, that Centers did not measure class consciousness.

Oscar Glantz conducted a study better designed than Centers's to determine the extent of class consciousness. He gathered data from 400 white, adult males in Philadelphia. But rather than a cross section of citizens, he selected occupational groups that would most likely be class-conscious in the Marxian sense—big and small businessmen, on the one hand, and union and nonunion, on the other. To get at class consciousness, he asked: "To which of these groups do you feel you owe allegiance—business or labor?" He further asked them to respond to six questions, three of which were statements adopted by the National Association of Manufacturers and three from the Congress of Industrial Organizations. On the basis of group identification and the answers to the six questions, Glantz ascertained the degree of class consciousness. The methods, it would appear, were "stacked" in favor of finding class consciousness (as was the case for Centers), but the results revealed the opposite. He found that 40 percent of all big businessmen and 25 percent of small businessmen were class-conscious. Only 28 percent of all union members and 13 percent of nonunion workers were so designated. These findings, striking because the percentages are so much less than expected in the most class-conscious-prone groups, indicate that class consciousness certainly must be at a relatively low level in the United States.[19] Although this is the obvious conclusion, we should not ignore its existence for some individuals and groups. The very uppermost stratum in American society, the group that has had a great deal of money over several generations, whose children go to exclusive schools, and where intermarriage is the highest, constitute a social class with a high degree of class identification by the members. Toward the other end of the continuum there are persons who feel oppressed and who lack economic security. It has been demonstrated that these persons are especially likely to be conscious of their class and feel antipathy toward other classes.[20]

Marx's prediction of the class consciousness and the polarization of the classes has occurred but only minimally in the United States. Class conflict occurs only rarely, and more in the context of specific issues rather than a proletarian revolution. There are labor disputes and strikes, but they do not threaten the fabric of American society. The poor can, if organized, exert greater pressure for better living conditions. The Poor People's March on Washington, D.C., late in the 1960s is just such an example. Welfare mothers in various cities have also organized to bring about change.

Perhaps the two best examples of group consciousness leading to conflict in American society are not based on economics (as Marx envisioned) but rather on race and age. Among blacks, for instance, more and more leaders have recently emphasized racial pride, separateness, and violence. In-group solidarity (race consciousness) has been accomplished. Among different age groups there has also been building an "us" versus "them" feeling. There have been sporadic violent clashes between the young and the establishment, with the outcome generally being greater repression of the dissidents. The problem with "youth consciousness," of course, is that the young become the old; that is, the oppressed may become the oppressors, whether there is a revolution or not. On the opposite end of the age scale, another relatively neglected group, the "senior citizens," have begun organizing and protesting on their behalf.

Although racial and age groups approach the group consciousness that Marx envisioned, this consciousness has not really developed among social classes in the United States.* There are a number of possible explanations for the relatively low level of class consciousness in the United States. First, Americans, rich and poor alike, tend to share the belief that upward mobility is possible. Even workers who know they will never move to a better job often hold the hope that their children will be upwardly mobile. Because of this widespread belief in the opportunities for upward mobility, efforts to improve status are typically individual efforts rather than concerted collective effort.

A second reason for the low level of class consciousness is that the living standards of blue-collar workers have steadily improved. Skilled laborers (electricians, plumbers, masons) are paid more than many white-collar workers (clerks, teachers). Even assembly-line workers can make a more-than-adequate income.

Third, and related to the second reason, is that there has been a leveling of the differences in the lifestyles of manual and nonmanual workers. Many manual workers can afford cars, homes, boats, and clothes similar to those owned by higher-status persons and therefore do not feel separate from them.

---

*Marx's theory, however, has provided a fairly accurate model for considering the development process in the emerging nations of Latin America, Africa, and Asia.

The development of class consciousness is also inhibited by the existence of organizations whose memberships cut across class lines. Religious denominations, local churches, and organizations such as the American Legion have as members persons from a number of social strata.

Fifth, the blue-collar category, the most likely stratum to develop class consciousness according to Marx, is composed not only of whites but all manner of racial and ethnic group members as well. The animosities among these groups within the ranks of the blue collars is often so great that the possibility of unity, coordinated effort, and group pride necessary for class consciousness is precluded.

Class segregation. A second empirical technique that may be employed to ascertain whether there are distinct boundaries among the social classes is to determine the extent to which there is class segregation. There are two types of segregation to look for: social and spatial. Social segregation refers to barriers that restrict social interaction to the members of a certain category. This is often accomplished by economic factors. High rent, high cost of property, entrance fees, and dues have the function of restricting residents in some parts of town and membership in some clubs. "Undesirables" may also be kept out of certain areas or clubs by the vote of the members. This practice of "blackballing," as well as the economic factors, explains the separation of the wealthiest from the rest of the population.

There is also a voluntary segregation by status that occurs at all levels in the hierarchy. The status character of many organizations is well known and is accomplished often without restrictive entrance requirements. People just feel more comfortable interacting with others like themselves (in wealth, amount of education, type of occupation). Society matrons just have no desire to belong to the women's auxiliary of plumbers local 371, and the wives of plumbers would probably not be comfortable sipping tea with the ladies of the Junior League. Lower-class persons probably would feel uneasy in prestigious Episcopal, Presbyterian, or Unitarian churches, while the well-to-do probably would feel just as uncomfortable in a Pentecostal church.

To determine the extent of voluntary status separation, the analyst can: (1) compare the status characteristics of marriage partners, (2) determine the status characteristics of persons who spend their leisure time together, (3) ascertain the status characteristics of the members of voluntary associations (from the African Violet Society to the Veterans of Foreign Wars), and (4) compare the status characteristics of close friends.

Segregation also occurs in space. Residential segregation may be forced (as is often the case with minority racial groups) or voluntary. Some residential areas go to great lengths to remain exclusive. Devices such as "gentleman's agreements," restrictive covenants, and point systems have been used for such a purpose.

In summary, the evidence shows that class consciousness has not developed in the United States as Karl Marx predicted (that is, to the point of political unity). The degree of class consciousness varies with locality and status group. The best evidence for the existence of class consciousness seems to be the social and spatial boundaries separating the highest classes from the rest of the populace.

The Hierarchy of "Classes"

Although class consciousness is relatively low in the United States, Americans do have a conception of a stratification structure, and evaluate persons as social superiors, equals, or inferiors.

Since actual class boundaries are virtually nonexistent (or fuzzy beyond recognition), we will put some artificial closure around a number of strata and call them social classes. The reason for this exercise is to enumerate the characteristics that tend to cluster in the persons located at particular points along the status hierarchy. These characteristics aid in the understanding of behavioral and attitudinal differences found when comparing persons in different strata. They also aid in understanding and analyzing power differentials on the community and national levels. We should keep in mind, however, that the dividing line between strata is arbitrary and that we should conceive of the stratification system as a continuum with artificial lines designating social classes for analytical purposes only.

The assumption of this analysis is that at different points on this "class" continuum persons will have more or less distinctive characteristics. The units designated as social classes are aggregates of individuals and families who are in similar economic positions and therefore have similar opportunities. Moreover, there is a strong likelihood that they probably consider other persons in the aggregate as social equals.

The upper class (the old rich). Of the various social classes in the United States, the upper class of the old rich is the only class with real boundaries. There is strong in-group solidarity and it is clear to the members who is and who is not included. G. William Domhoff, after an extensive analysis, concluded that this category makes up 0.5 percent of the American population. His criteria for inclusion in the upper class are found in Panel 10–2.

Domhoff's criteria for inclusion suggest that the very uppermost stratum in American society is not only wealthy but exclusive. They belong to exclusive clubs and attended equally exclusive boarding schools. These clubs and schools are exclusive because they have very elaborate screening mechanisms to ensure that only certain people are allowed in—usually the persons whose parents were also wealthy. Great wealth by itself is not enough, for persons who acquired it only during their lifetime will never be fully accepted by the persons in the highest stratum.

One characteristic of the upper class is physical and social separation from the other strata. As mentioned above, members of the elite go to very private schools and they belong to private clubs where interaction is restricted to people like themselves. Living in restricted residential areas is another dimension of the exclusiveness prevalent in the upper strata. The lifestyle of the very wealthy also distinguishes it from the other strata. Expensive clothes, jewelry, furs, and cars, as well as distinctive speech and manners, serve to separate this group further from others.

The possession of great wealth and the benefits concomitant to having great wealth serve to make the elite very powerful, both in the local communities where each of the members resides, and nationally. Persons of wealth accumulate not only power, but also honor and deference. It is natural that such persons exude self-confidence, for their opinions are sought, their lifestyle is emulated, and they, by their presence, can legitimize an otherwise questionable activity.

Upper-class persons tend to be family oriented. There is a sense of extended family solidarity. This is a consequence of the emphasis on family heritage among the elite. Family solidarity is also maintained often by the joint holding of property. The main source of wealth for the elite is interest and dividends from investment of inherited wealth. Their typical jobs are those of high-ranking executives in established corporations or banks.

Panel 10-2
The Criteria for Upper-Class Membership

G. William Domhoff provides a number of criteria that distinguish the upper-most social stratum from all others:

1. A person will be considered a member of the upper class if he, his parents, his wife's parents, or any of his siblings are listed in any of the following registers and blue books: *The Social Register* (which has editions in twelve major cities), *Social Secretary* (Detroit), *Social Register* (Houston), *Blue Book* (Los Angeles), *Social Register* (New Orleans), and the *Blue Book* (Seattle).
2. A person will be considered a member of the upper class if he, his father, brother, or father-in-law attended any of the following schools: thirty-seven very private schools, including Choate (Wallingford, Connecticut), Deerfield (Deerfield, Massachusetts), Groton (Groton, Massachusetts), and St. Mark's (Southborough, Massachusetts).
3. A person will be considered a member of the upper class if he, his father, brother, or father-in-law belongs to any one of the following social clubs: forty exclusive clubs, including the Century and Knickerbocker Clubs (New York), Pacific Union (San Francisco), Idlewild (Dallas), Somerset (Boston), and the Racquet Club (St. Louis).

Persons in this category tend toward attitudes of political and economic conservatism. Because they benefit so much from existing political and economic arrangements, they work to maintain the status quo. The holding of similar interests (for example, maintaining the status quo) promotes class consciousness—a condition not found to any extent elsewhere in the stratification hierarchy.

Since the American system of social stratification is a continuum of social "classes," there are no rigid boundaries that mark this continuum into clearly defined classes except at the highest level. As Domhoff has asserted, "the social structure is made up of strata that shade off one into the other until we arrive at the highest level, where the continuum hardens into a social class with more or less definite boundaries and class consciousness."[21]

Domhoff argued that through in-group interaction and differential lifestyles, class consciousness is intensified among the elite. Evidence of in-group interaction is found in the large proportion of intermarriage that occurs among the very rich. The marriage between two elite young people provides further linkage between the two families. The linked families are often widely separated in space, but the marriage occurred because the children attended the same or neighboring private boarding schools or colleges.

The prestigious private schools that provide the milieu for mate selection have stringent requirements that usually admit only the uppermost stratum. The evidence is also that these schools provide havens for the interaction of rich children from all over the country. As an example of this, "Hotchkiss graduates are listed in the *Social Register* for the following cities: New York, 552; Chicago, 125; Philadelphia, 94; Cleveland 64; Pittsburgh, 64; Boston, 59; San Francisco, 40; Washington, 35; and St. Louis, 34."[22]

4. A person will be considered a member of the upper class if his sister, wife, mother, or mother-in-law attended one of the following schools: sixty-seven private schools, including Abbot Academy (Andover, Massachusetts), Baldwin (Bryn Mawr, Pennsylvania), Chatham Hall (Chatham, Virginia), Lenox (New York), and Westover (Middlebury, Connecticut).

5. A person will be considered a member of the upper class if his sister, wife, mother, or mother-in-law belongs to one of the following clubs: ten, including Acorn (Philadelphia), Chilton (Boston), Colony (New York), Fortnightly (Chicago), and Sulgrave (Washington, D.C.).

6. A person will be considered a member of the upper class if his or her father was a millionaire entrepreneur or a $100,000-a-year corporation executive or corporation lawyer, *and* (a) if he or she attended one of the 130 private schools listed in the back of Kavaler's *The Private World of High Society,* or (b) if he or she belongs to any of the exclusive clubs mentioned in Baltzell's *Philadelphia Gentleman: The Making of a National Upper Class* or in Kavaler. The list of private schools and exclusive clubs can be larger here than for the second, third, fourth, and fifth criteria because it is known that the person is a member of the second generation of a wealthy family.

Source: Summarized from G. William Domhoff, *The Higher Circles: The Governing Class in America* (New York: Random House, 1970), pp. 21–27. Copyright © by G. William Domhoff. Reprinted by permission of Random House, Inc.

The nationwide interaction of the rich is also found in club memberships. The exclusive clubs of the upper class have nationwide memberships.

Summer resorts are further evidence for the cohesiveness of the national upper class. Around the island of Mt. Desert in Maine, for example, are found the summer homes of *Social Register* listees from the following cities: Philadelphia, 92; New York, 80; Boston, 40; Washington, 12; Chicago, 7; Baltimore, 7; Cincinnati-Dayton, 6; and St. Louis, 5.[23] The same is true of such winter resorts as Palm Beach in Florida and Palm Springs in California.

In summary, the "old rich" are a distinct social class. They are separated from others in the stratification system by where they live, where they attend school, by lifestyle, and by the deference they receive from others. There is, therefore, a clear-cut boundary between the old rich and others.

The persons within the old rich category form a real social class because the members consider themselves as such—they know who belongs and who does not. Additionally, there are linkages between the members—through marriage, business, school, neighborhood, club, and mutual acquaintance. The members interact and hence form a social group.

The old rich social class, unlike any of the other strata, is national in scope. There is a considerable amount of intermarriage and social interaction linking wealthy families living in different cities. While it is clear that not everyone in the old rich category knows each other, it is highly probable (as Domhoff has asserted after a great deal of research on the subject) that everyone has friends and relatives who know someone from the uppermost stratum in every major American city. The upper-class person, therefore, has an entree into the highest social circles all over the country.[24]

The "new rich." We shall inaccurately refer to the "new rich" and the remaining status categories as "classes." They are not classes in the sense that the old rich are. Class consciousness is weak, within-stratum interaction is not as restrictive as in the elite, and the boundaries, which are fuzzy in the minds of many citizens, and therefore set arbitrarily according to objective criteria by social researchers. This arbitrariness of the boundaries, however, does not negate the existence of status differentials.

The new rich differ from the uppermost stratum in prestige, not wealth. Great wealth alone does not ensure acceptance by the elite as a social equal. A family tradition of wealth (of more than two generations) is a necessary condition for inclusion in the elite. The *nouveaux riches* of Houston, for example, could buy a membership in River Oaks Country Club with an initiation fee of many thousands of dollars, but membership in the Houston Country Club is closed except to members of old-guard families.[25] To have

---

Panel 10–3
Inflation and Inequality: The Making of the Superclass

The growing spread between income groups applies to corporations as well as to individuals. Companies have fueled much of their growth through loans and other debt financing. But the larger corporations, always better able to borrow, have evaded the country's attempts to control debt expansion by going overseas to borrow—raising billions from European banks, free of Federal Reserve restrictions. And, anticipating President Carter's announcement of new lending limits, they successfully lined up credit at major U.S. banks before controls were imposed, leaving them free of limits while small companies and individuals were left to face the cold winds of recession alone.

One frightening measure of this disparity between large and small corporations: according to *The New York Times*, oil companies alone represent almost one quarter of the value of all stocks trading today.

Looked at another way, inflation-fighting does not work because it is directed at a nonexistent entity called the American Economy, when in fact we live in the pluralism of mini-economies that operate semi-independently of one another. Briefly, they are:

The noneconomy: At least 16 million Americans survive off public welfare in one form or another. The median family income for the poor is less than $5,000 annually, and it is almost entirely consumed by food, energy and shelter. So far this year President Carter has fought inflation in the noneconomy by eliminating hot lunch and breakfast programs for poor children and cutting out 50,000 CETA jobs.

The subeconomy: Between the poor and the middle American lies the subeconomy, a world increasingly composed of single women and Third World workers. Eighty percent of women workers are concentrated in low-skill clerical and service jobs, the overwhelming majority unprotected by union contracts. Inflation here is taking a grievous toll: people in this group have little or no discre-

acquired wealth in one's lifetime means that one will not have had the time required to learn the ways of the wealthy (for example, language, manners, grace). This is accomplished only if one has been totally immersed from birth in the ways of the wealthy (private schools, extensive travel, interation limited to others of equivalent status and background).

The *nouveaux riches* often try to buy their way into elite circles by giving lavish parties, building very expensive homes, and by means of other forms of conspicuous consumption. Such overly ostentatious behavior is perceived typically by the elite as "too gauche" and therefore further evidence for exclusion from the most elite circles. One tenet of the old rich faith is that one should not have to prove oneself with ostentatious displays. This behavior, although it is often motivated by a desire to be accepted by the old rich, actually causes the opposite reaction.

The new rich stratum is thus composed of the self-made wealthy. These families have amassed fortunes typically through business ventures, or because of special talent in sports, music, or motion pictures. Additionally, some professionals (doctors, lawyers) may

tionary income, more often rent than own a home and in many instances have only partial protection against medical costs.

The very middle class: There is a portion of the economic landscape, covering incomes between $15,000 and $25,000, where survival is not a question, but where life is precarious. More than half this group relies on having two income earners per family; and in the blue-collar middle class, especially in the industrial Gray Belt, where the number of unemployed in the steel and auto industries alone is now over 500,000, keeping up with the cost of living is hard. Savings are quickly devoured if one earner is thrown out of work.

The superclass: Out of the '60s and '70s has come a new component in the inflationary landscape, the college-educated, two-income, non-child-rearing family. While a distinct minority of the population, these young couples have the rosiest of futures. According to *Fortune*, "The overwhelming majority of the added income that consumers will enjoy in the Eighties will go to households in the upper-income brackets." *Fortune* is not talking about the merely upper-middle-income earners; it is talking about the folks who will be earning $75,000 or more a year by 1990. It is estimating that eventually $1.2 trillion a year, or 60 percent of all income, will be in the hands of just 25 million people.

The clear and very ugly conclusion from this is that during the '80s we are headed for a kind of economic class war that will pit the superclass against the vast majority of Americans in their desire for a stable and reasonably prosperous life. Concentrating so much income in so few hands destroys the unified market. . .

Inflation is a cancer, one that has been endemic to capitalism for 150 years. And it is a disease none of us will recover from, unless we change the doctors and the diagnosis.

Source: Richard Parker, "The Making of the Superclass," *Mother Jones* 5 (July 1980), pp. 14, 18. Reprinted with permission from *Mother Jones* magazine, © 1980, the Foundation for National Progress.

become wealthy because of their practice and/or investments. Finally, a few persons because of their own talent may become very wealthy by working their way in corporations to top executive positions, where high salaries and stock options are common.

The new rich tend to be political conservatives. They are inclined toward the radical right groups that oppose the welfare state, the graduated income tax, and unions. They vigorously oppose communism and socialism because under these economic systems hard work and initiative are penalized while the ne'er-do-wells benefit. As the political sociologist S. M. Lipset has noted:

New wealth most often tends to have extremist ideologies, to believe in extreme conservative doctrines in economic matters. The man who makes money himself feels more insecure about keeping it than do people who possess inherited wealth. He feels more aggrieved about social reform measures which involve redistribution of the wealth, as compared with individuals, still wealthy, who have grown up in an old traditionalist background, which inculcates the values of tolerance traditionally associated with upper-class aristocratic conservatism. It is not without reason that the new millionaires, such as those in Texas, have given extensive financial support to radical right movements, politicians, and to such propaganda organizations as Facts Forum.[26]

The upper-middle class. The key distinguishing feature of this category is high-prestige jobs (but not the most remunerative in the society) that require a good deal of formal education and have a high degree of autonomy, responsibility, and security. This stratum is largely composed of professional people, executives, and business people. They do not make nearly as much money as the new rich but, as a category, they are usually better educated. Education is of particular importance to persons in this class because the members have found it important to their own careers. The children of this class are expected by the parents to receive a college education.

Much like the two upper classes, the upper-middle class is a bastion of conservatism in American society. They believe in the work–success ethic and capitalism. They are self-made persons, having accomplished prestige and a comfortable economic situation through hard work and sacrifice. They tend, therefore, to oppose many socialistic programs, especially welfare. Many of the more highly educated, however, tend toward liberalism on civil rights, civil liberties, and internationalism issues (but some notable exceptions may be doctors, dentists, and engineers).

The middle class. This category is composed of white-collar workers who may work primarily in minor jobs in bureaucracies. Also included are clerks, technicians, the owners of small businesses, and salespeople.

These workers are paid an adequate wage, but substantially lower than upper-middle-class persons. Their jobs require less skill, less responsibility, and do not involve as much decision making as the class above them in the stratification hierarchy.

These persons usually have some education beyond high school. Some college or training in specialized schools is typical. Most, however, have not graduated from college. This presents a severe limitation to career mobility unless they possess exceptional skills.

The heterogeneity of this stratum is clearly evident. There is a vast difference, for example, between white-collar workers in huge bureaucracies and the owners of small businesses. They differ in amount and type of education, income, degree of autonomy on the job, and job security. These differences affect attitudes, perceptions, motivation, and behaviors. Even child-rearing patterns are noticeably different between these two social categories. An interesting study by Miller and Swanson showed the diversity found within this stratum by comparing entrepreneurial parents (self-employed) with bureaucratic parents (employed in large-scale organizations). The researchers assumed that the different settings and demands of each category would be revealed in the way children were reared. They found that entrepreneurial families stressed self-control, self-reliance, and individual initiative because these traits were needed in the competitive business world. Bureaucratic parents, on the other hand, reared their children to adjust and accommodate to the wishes of others because these traits were especially appropriate for success in large organizations.[27]

The wide diversity found within the middle class demonstrates that this category is *not* a real social class. The persons designated as members by social scientists lack class consciousness and the boundaries are not well defined.

The lower-middle class. This category is composed of skilled craftsmen such as mechanics, electricians, plumbers, cabinetmakers, and masons, many of whom are self-employed. It also includes foremen in large industrial plants, who have authority over other workers.

This category receives relatively high wages, often higher than white-collar workers, allowing them to own homes and other possessions typical of middle-class Americans.

They differ from white-collar workers in that they are manual workers with less formal education. Although they rank relatively low in the hierarchy, they are "aristocrats" of the blue-collar workers.

Many persons in this stratum are likely to be status inconsistents (as are the "new rich"). This means that an individual's status attributes are unbalanced—that is, their income is higher than their educational background would appear to warrant. This condition often leads to strain and hostility in individuals, since they may not be accepted as equals by persons they feel are their equals (neighbors, colleagues, customers), who have similar incomes but more education and different lifestyles.

The upper-lower class. Semiskilled operatives who work in the mass production industries are the main component of this class. They are manual workers whose jobs allow little if any autonomy, are simple and repetitive, and require no creativity. Along with the boredom of these jobs is their relative insecurity because of strikes or because of unemployment brought about by economic recession.

These persons have not gone beyond high school and many have not even achieved that. Because of their lack of education and limited skills, they are severely blocked if they have aspirations to be upwardly mobile. There is really quite a large gap between semiskilled workers and white-collar workers. The gulf, for many, is too large to breach.

The lower-lower class. This class is composed of unskilled laborers whose formal education is often less than eight grades. The chronically unemployed are in this class. The bulk of those on welfare are in this class. Minority-group members—blacks, Puerto Ricans, Mexican Americans, Indians—are disproportionately found in this category.

These persons are those that are looked down upon by all others in the community. They live "on the other side of the tracks." They are considered by others to be undesirable as playmates, friends, organization members, or marriage partners. Lower-lowers are viewed as lazy, shiftless, dependent, and immoral—traits exactly opposite "good middle-class virtues."

SOCIAL MOBILITY

Societies vary in the degree to which individuals may move up in status. Probably the most rigid stratification system ever devised was the caste system of India. In brief, this system (1) determined status by heredity, (2) allowed marriage to occur only within one's status group (endogamy), (3) determined occupation by heredity, and (4) restricted interaction among the status groups. Even the Indian caste system, however, was not totally rigid, for some mobility has been allowed under certain circumstances.*

In contrast to the closed stratification system of India, the United States is a relatively open system. Social mobility is not only permitted, but it is part of the American values that upward mobility is good and should be the goal of all Americans.

The United States, however, is not a totally open system. All American children have the social rank of the parents while they are youths. As we shall see in the four chapters of this section, the status of parents has a tremendous influence on a child's attitudes and behaviors (particularly performance in school) and these determine in large measure whether the child can be mobile (upward or downward).

Concepts

Social mobility refers to an individual's movement within the class structure of society. **Vertical mobility** is movement upward or downward in social class. **Horizontal mobility** is the change from one position to another of about equal prestige. The shift in occupations from being an electrician to a plumber is an example of horizontal mobility.

Social mobility occurs in two ways. **Intergenerational mobility** refers to vertical movement comparing a daughter with her mother or a son with his father. **Intragenerational mobility** is the vertical movement of the individual through his or her adult life.

Societal factors affecting social mobility. There are societal factors that increase the likelihood of people's vertical mobility regardless of their individual efforts. The availability of cheap and fertile land with abundant resources gave many thousands of Americans in the nineteenth century opportunities for advancement no longer present. Similarly, the arrival of new immigrants to the United States from 1880 to 1920 provided a status boost for those already here. Economic booms and depressions obviously affect individuals' economic success. Technological changes too can provide increased chances for success as well as diminish the possibilities for those trained in occupations now obsolete. Finally, the size of one's age cohort can limit or expand opportunities for success (see Panel 10-4).

The extent of vertical mobility in the United States. The most comprehensive study of intergenerational mobility has been conducted by Peter Blau and Otis Dudley Duncan.[29]

---

*Some observers have charged that the stratification system of the United States is castelike with reference to race. Race, in many ways, presents a barrier that determines status, range of marriage partners, and discriminatory treatment of all kinds.[28]

Figure 10-1 summarizes their findings on the probability of mobility in American society for males. Some of their conclusions are that: (1) few sons of white-collar workers become blue-collar workers; (2) most mobility moves are short in distance; (3) occupational inheritance is highest for sons of professionals (physicians, lawyers, professors); and (4) the opportunities for the sons of non-professionals to become professionals are very small.

Another study, this one by the Carnegie Council on Children, found that only one male in five exceeds his father's social status through individual effort and achievement.[30] The advantages of the children of the rich over those of the poor are enormous, as seen in the following example from this study:

Jimmy is a second grader. He pays attention in school, and enjoys it. School records show he is reading slightly above grade level and has a slightly better than average I.Q. Bobby is a second grader in a school across town. He also . . . enjoys school and his

FIGURE 10-1 Percentage distribution of United States males' intergenerational mobility: Distance and direction by educational level

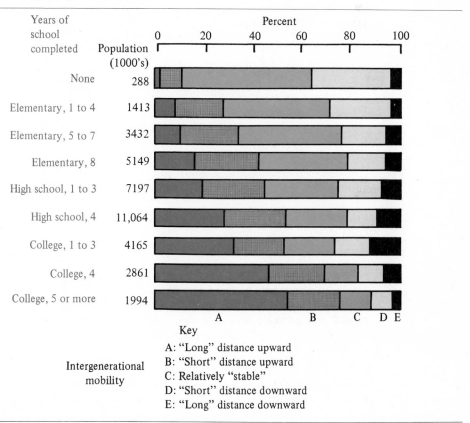

Key

Intergenerational mobility

A: "Long" distance upward
B: "Short" distance upward
C: Relatively "stable"
D: "Short" distance downward
E: "Long" distance downward

Source: Reprinted with permission of Macmillan Publishing Co., Inc. from *The American Occupational Structure* by Peter M. Blau and Otis Dudley Duncan, p. 159. Copyright © 1967 by Peter M. Blau and Otis Dudley Duncan.

METHODS PANEL

Panel 10–4
Baby Boomers and Social Mobility: A Cohort Analysis

An important tool of social scientists is the longitudinal study—research designed to permit observations over a long period. One type of longitudinal study is the *trend study*, in which changes in a population are noted over time. Figure 1

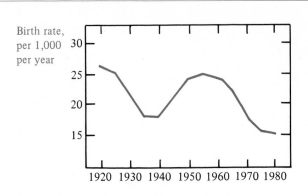

test scores are quite similar to Jimmy's. Bobby is a safe bet to enter college (more than four times as likely as Jimmy) and a good bet to complete it—at least twelve times as likely as Jimmy.

Bobby will probably have at least four years more schooling than Jimmy. He is twenty-seven times as likely as Jimmy to land a job which by his late forties will pay him an income in the top tenth of all incomes. Jimmy has one chance in eight of earning a median income.

These odds are the arithmetic of inequality in America. . . . Bobby is the son of a successful lawyer whose annual salary of $35,000 puts him well within the top 10 percent of the United States income distribution in 1976. Jimmy's father, who did not complete high school, works from time to time as a messenger and a custodial assistant. His earnings, some $4,800, put him in the bottom 10 percent.[31]

This example clearly demonstrates that the commonly accepted belief of Americans that ours is a meritocratic society is largely a myth. Equality of opportunity does not exist because (1) employers may discriminate on the basis of race, sex, or ethnicity of their employees or prospective employees; (2) educational and job training opportunities are

shows the results of a trend study noting the differences in birth rate (the ratio of births in a given year to the average population) for the United States since World War I.

This figure shows that following World War II (roughly from 1947 to 1960) there was a very high birth rate, preceded and followed by periods of relatively low birth rates.

Another type of longitudinal study—a *cohort study*—follows an age group (such as the people born in the depression, or those born in the 1950s) across time. As we saw in Chapter 4, the baby boom generation consists of an extra 10 million persons. Because of these extra numbers, those born in this cohort are having a more difficult time economically than those born during the "birth dearth" depression years. The baby boom generation is and will continue to find it tough sledding economically because of the pressure of numbers and the resulting keen competition for jobs and resources. Jobs are scarcer. The possibilities for advancement are rarer. Salaries are lower. Even "stagflation," a combination of high unemployment and accelerating inflation, is partly the consequence of this cohort. The result is that this accident of birth—being born in an overly populated cohort—will negatively affect the members of that cohort throughout their lives.

Source: Richard A. Easterlin, *Birth and Fortune: The Impact of Numbers on Personal Welfare* (New York: Basic Books, 1980), p. 8.

unequal; and (3) the family has great power to enhance or retard a child's aspirations, motivation, and cognitive skills.[32]

The schools play a major part in both perpetuating the meritocratic myth and legitimizing it by giving and denying educational credentials on the basis of "open and objective" mechanisms that sift and sort on merit.[33] The use of I.Q. tests and tracking, two common devices to segregate students by cognitive abilities, are highly suspect because they label children, resulting in a positive self-fulfilling prophecy for some children and a negative one for others. Moreover, the results of the tests and the placement of children in "tracks" because of the tests, are biased toward middle and upper class experiences.

Educational attainment, especially receiving the college degree, is the most important predictor of success in America. Bowles and Gintis have shown, for example, that those in the lowest tenth of the population in years of schooling have a 3.5 percent chance of being in the top fifth of the population in monetary income. At the other end, though, those in the highest tenth of the population in education have a 45.9 percent chance of being in the top 20 percent in income.[34] Moreover, among people with identical I.Q. test scores, those in the top tenth in schooling are eight times more likely to be in the top fifth in income than those in the lowest tenth in education.[35] Clearly, mental skills alone are not enough. They must be coupled with formal schooling to maximize the likelihood of economic success.

Just as important, Bowles and Gintis have also shown that family socioeconomic background determines how much education one receives: those in the lowest tenth in socioeconomic family background *with the same average I.Q. scores* as those in highest tenth in socioeconomic family background will receive an average of 4.9 *fewer years of education*.[36] In short, educational level determines socioeconomic position—and one's family's socioeconomic background determines one's educational opportunities. Thus, the ascribed status of family background has a profound impact on the probability of educational achievement and upward mobility.

Christopher Jencks and his associates have added to the work of Bowles and Gintis, providing the most current and methodologically sophisticated analysis of the determinants of upward mobility in their book *Who Gets Ahead?*[37] Their findings, summarized, show the following as the most important factors leading to success.

1. Family background is the most important factor. Children coming from families in the top 20 percent in income will, as adults, have incomes of 150 to 186 percent of the national average whereas those from the bottom 20 percent will earn 56 to 67 percent of the national average.

2. Educational attainment—especially graduating from college—is very important to later success. It is not so much what one learns in school but obtaining the credentials that counts. The probability of high educational attainment is closely tied to family background.

3. Scores from intelligence tests are by themselves poor predictors of economic success. Intelligence test scores are related to family background and educational attainment. The key remains the college degree. If high I.Q. people do not go to college they will tend *not* to succeed economically.

4. Personality traits of high school students, more than grades and I.Q., have an impact on economic success. No single trait emerges as the decisive determinant of economic success but rather the combined effects of many different traits are found to be important. These are self-concept, industriousness (as rated by teachers), and the social skills or motivations that lead students to see themselves as leaders and to hold positions of leadership in high school.

The picture drawn by Jencks and other experts on social mobility in America is of a relatively rigid society in which being born to the right family has a profound impact, especially on the probability of graduating from college. There are opportunities for advancement in society but they are clustered among the already advantaged. If the stratification system were open with equality of opportunity it would make sense that people, even the disadvantaged, would support it. The irony is that although the chances of the poor being successful are small indeed, the poor tend to support the inequality generated by capitalism—truly a case of false consciousness. This irony will become clearer as we see the consequences of inequality for individuals.

THE CONSEQUENCES OF SOCIOECONOMIC STATUS

We have conceived of social strata as aggregates of individuals and families with more or less similar economic positions, similar educational attainment, and holding occupations similar in prestige. These aggregates are ranked, and this creates a stratification hierarchy. Even though these "classes" do not possess real boundaries and class consciousness (except, as we have noted, at the very top), there are very real differences between an aggregate of people at one level of the status hierarchy and persons at another level. This section will illustrate these differences from research that has focused on the life chances of the various strata.

Life Chances

Perhaps Marx was right that the key to the class structure is economics. The extent of one's wealth is the determining factor in a number of crucial areas, including the chance to live and the chance to obtain those things (for example, possessions, education) that are highly valued in society. The term **life chances** refers to the chances throughout one's life cycle to live and to experience the good things in life. This is dependent almost exclusively on the economic circumstances of the family to which one is born. Gerth and Mills have contended that life chances refer to

everything from the chance to stay alive during the first year after birth to the chance to view fine art, the chance to remain healthy and grow tall, and if sick to get well again quickly, the chance to avoid becoming a juvenile delinquent—and very crucially, the chance to complete an intermediary or higher educational grade. . . .[38]

Life expectancy. Economic position has a great effect upon how long one will live or in a crisis who will be the last to die. For instance, the official casualty lists of the trans-Atlantic luxury liner, the *Titanic*, which rammed an iceberg in 1912, listed 3 percent of the first-class female passengers as lost; 16 percent of the second-class female passengers drowned, and among the third-class females 45 percent were drowned.[39] Apparently, even in a disaster, socioeconomic position makes a very real difference—the higher the economic status of the individual, the greater the probability of survival.

The greater advantage toward longer life by the well-to-do is not limited to disasters such as that of the *Titanic*. A consistent research finding is that health and death are influenced greatly by social status.*

Probably the most complete and valid (methodologically) study in this area was conducted by Kitagawa and Hauser, who matched 340,000 death certificates (for deaths occurring during the months May–August, 1960) to the 1960 Census records.[41] Using educational attainment level as an indicator of socioeconomic status, the researchers found the expected strong inverse correlation between mortality and educational attainment. Among white women between the ages of 25 and 64 years, for example, the mortality rate for those with less than eight years of school was 61 percent higher than among college educated women. Among white males in this age bracket, the mortality rate for those with less than eight years of school was 48 percent higher than for the college-educated men.

Principal cause of death. The data from Kitagawa and Hauser show very clearly the relationship between socioeconomic status (as measured by educational attainment) and the principal cause of death. The most striking finding was for white males between 25 and

*There is an excellent summary article (by Aaron Antonovsky) surveying over thirty studies done prior to 1950 in the United States and elsewhere which lead to the conclusion that socioeconomic status influences one's chance of staying alive.[40]

64; those with less than eight years of education had a mortality rate from tuberculosis of more than 800 percent higher than the college-educated. This relationship, although not as strong as found for tuberculosis, was also noted for death from influenza, pneumonia, accidents (motor vehicle and all others), and cancer of the stomach, lung, bronchus, and trachea.

Among the women of this sample, the same general pattern of the less educated having higher mortality rates from specific diseases was found with one exception. Cancer of the breast was found to be the cause of death more frequently in the more educated category.

Among men over 65 there were two interesting differences. The lower-educated persons were more likely to die of cardiovascular disease and cancer than the higher educated. But one form of cancer—cancer of the prostate—was much more likely to be the cause of death among the more highly educated men.

Physical health. The physical health of poor persons is more likely to be impaired than the health of the more well-to-do because of differences in diet, sanitation facilities, and adequate clothing and shelter. Poor people also cannot afford the best medical care. The following quotation from the United States Public Health Service summarizes the special health problems of the poor, in this case poor children:

Poor children are more likely to be in poor health or to have functional disabilities than children in families with adequate incomes. They are more likely to develop communicable diseases. They are no more likely to develop other conditions, such as myopia or asthma, but because they are less likely to receive adequate medical care, they are more likely to have some degree of functional disability as a result.

Physical illness, disability, and death are not independent of one another, nor are they independent of emotional illness and disability or the environment in which the child's life is spent. Emotional or behavioral problems can both cause and result from physical problems. The environment, both physical and social, affects physical and emotional health. Crowded and dilapidated housing, poor schools and teachers, poverty, and discrimination all increase the risk of physical and emotional illness and impairment. Adequate housing, good schools and teachers, enough money for food and clothing, and social acceptance all decrease the risk.

Strong relationships exist between family income and certain health indicators. The proportion of children in "fair" or "poor" health drops significantly as family income rises. About 9 percent of the children and youth in families with incomes of less than $5,000 per year, compared with 2 percent in families with incomes of $15,000 or more, are reported as being in "fair" or "poor" health. Children and youth in low income families are more likely to have days when their activity is restricted, when they are confined to bed, or when they are out of school. For example, school-age children in low income families lost an average 6.6 days from school per year during 1975–76 because of acute illnesses, while school-age children in high income families lost an average 4.7 days.[42]

Table 10–3 provides government data on the relationships between health and income. For example, children from families with incomes of less than $5,000 visit dentists less than once a year while those from families with incomes over $15,000 average 2.2 visits to the dentist annually. This does not mean that the teeth of the well-to-do are worse than those of the poor but rather that they can afford to do more to ensure that they will continue to have good teeth. The data also show that money translates into fewer days away from

TABLE 10-3   Selected Indicators of Health by Level of Income, 1976

Income Level	Number of bed disability days per person per year for ages 45–64	% self-assessed as in excellent health	Incidence of acute respiratory condition for ages 45–64 (per 100 persons per year)	Number of dental visits per year, under age 18 (per 1000 population)	% needing dental care for ages 1–5	% with private medical insurance or medicare
Less than $5,000	18.9	17.1	156.7	918.5	21.2	53.2*
$5,000–9,999	11.8	26.5	122.3	1030.9	19.2	69.3*
$10,000–14,999	7.6	32.3	126.1	1379.1	13.6	86.8
$15,000 or more	5.8	47.5	108.0	2225.3	8.4	92.3

*These percentages are approximations due to a slightly different breakdown by income for this category.
Source: Public Health Service, Health: United States, 1978, Department of Health, Education, and Welfare, Publication No. (PHS) 78-1232 (December, 1978), Tables 55, 59, 61, 64, 97, and 164.

work, a lower incidence of respiratory conditions, feeling healthy, and adequate medical insurance.

Mental health. The most consistent relationship reported in social psychiatric studies is the inverse relationship between socioeconomic status and psychological disorder. Probably the most often cited study is that conducted by Hollingshead and Redlich in New Haven, Connecticut.

Hollingshead and Redlich used objective variables to determine social class—level of occupation and education and quality of neighborhood. Despite the artificiality of the class boundaries, the findings are dramatic in that they show that the prevalence of all types of psychoses increases as the index of occupation, education, and neighborhood decreases. This classic study by Hollingshead and Redlich is representative of the findings of countless other studies.[43]

Family instability. Research relating socioeconomic status to family discord and marital disruption has found an inverse relationship—the lower the status, the greater the proportion of divorce or desertion. An explanation for this relationship is that lower-class families experience greater economic and job insecurity. Given the tremendous emphasis in the United States on success and achievement, lower-class persons (particularly men) will tend to define themselves and be perceived by others in the society as a failure. Such a belief will, doubtless, hinder rather than help a marriage relationship.

SOCIAL
DILEMMAS
AND CRITICAL
CHOICES

Panel 10-5
Political Ideologies and Inequality

Is inequality what has made the United States a powerful and affluent nation? If so, will it continue to do so? Are we responsible for those who are unsuccessful in society? Governmental decision makers may reduce or increase the extent of inequality in society by subsidies and tax reform. What would you encourage them to do?

There are essentially four political ideologies held by various groups and individuals in American society. You will certainly find political figures representing each position, whom you can work for or against. Let's briefly review the spectrum of political ideologies with respect to their positions on inequality in society.

Conservatism. This political philosophy favors inequality. Similar to the order model, this ideology believes that competition for unequal rewards is necessary to motivate people and ensure that the best people will do the most important tasks. The key is the need for unequal wages to persuade people to work harder and unequal profits to promote managerial efficiency. The government should, therefore, leave individuals alone and let the competitive market work unencumbered.

The draft. The draft system works to the disadvantage of the uneducated. In 1969 only 10 percent of the men drafted were college men—yet over 40 percent of college-age men go to college. The Supreme Court has further helped the educated by ruling that a person can be a conscientious objector either on a basis of religion or philosophy. Young intellectuals can use their knowledge of history, philosophy, and even sociology to argue that they should not serve. The uneducated will not have the necessary knowledge or sharpened intellect to make such a case.

For those educated young men who end up in the armed services, there is a greater likelihood of their serving in noncombat supply and administrative jobs than for the non-college-educated. Persons who can type, do bookkeeping, or know computer programming will generally be selected to do jobs where their skills can be used. Conversely, the nonskilled will generally end up in the most hazardous jobs. The chances for getting killed while in the service are greater, therefore, for the less educated than for the college educated.[44]

Justice. Chapter 9 provided strong evidence that the administration of justice is unequal in the United States. Low-status persons are more likely to be arrested, to be found guilty, and to serve longer sentences for a given violation than persons of middle and upper status. Let us review a small but representative portion of the evidence.

A study of California court decisions involving first-degree murder found blue-collar workers to stand a better chance of being sentenced to death than white-collar workers.

Liberalism. This political ideology prevails in contemporary American society. Governmental aid is advocated to provide minimum welfare payments, food stamps, and the like to reduce the misery of the poorest segments of society. Governmental intervention to limit inequality is minimal, however, so as not to displace the basic functioning of the competitive free market.

New populism. The goal of this philosophy is to change the American political and economic system from one that further enriches the rich and powerful to one that responds to the less-than-rich and the not-so-powerful. Leaders of this reform movement advocate the closing of tax loopholes, the increase of inheritance and estate taxes, the lowering of taxes that disproportionately hurt the poor (for example, the sales tax), free medical care for all, the expansion of Social Security, and the public ownership of all utilities.

Democratic socialism. Unlike the three previous political-economic ideologies, socialism rejects capitalism. Socialists would take over the ownership of private corporations, commit an enormous investment in welfare for all citizens (health, housing, food, minimum annual wage), and make the tax structure truly progressive (treat all income alike for tax purposes and increase the rate as income increases). The goal of these programs is to halt gross inequalities by guaranteeing adequate goods and services to all citizens.

These ideologies represent four possible responses to the societal problem of inequality. The dilemma is that at one extreme, conservatism condones people living in poverty, while at the opposite end, persons must give up some freedoms and sacrifice for the good of all. What is your position? Which direction should our government take?

This study, conducted by five Stanford University Law School students, examined 200 separate factors that might be related to getting the death penalty. Occupation was found to be the most important determinant.[45]

White-collar crime (for example, price fixing, using fraudulent advertising claims, embezzlement, and issuing fraudulent stock) often involves much more money than burglary or robbery, but the offenders of white-collar crimes seldom receive proportionate jail sentences or fines as Table 10-4 shows.

For example, a partner in a New York stock brokerage firm pleaded guilty to trading illegally $20 million in Swiss banks. He hired a prestigious lawyer, who got the judge to issue a fine of $30,000 and a suspended sentence. That same judge, when confronted a few days later with the case of an unemployed black shipping clerk who pleaded guilty to stealing a television set worth $100 from an interstate shipment, sentenced him to one year in jail.[46]

Why does justice let its blindfold slip? The rich can afford the services of the very best lawyers for their defense, detectives to gather supporting evidence, and expert witnesses such as psychiatrists. The rich can afford to appeal the decision to a series of appellate courts. The poor, on the other hand, must take court-appointed lawyers, who are usually among the least experienced lawyers in the community. All the evidence points to the regrettable truth that a defendant's wealth makes a significant difference in the administration of justice.

There is a class bias held by most citizens, including arresting officers and judges, that affects the administration of justice. There is a set of assumptions about persons according to their socioeconomic status. In a study of a small South Dakota community, police officials were found to deal severely with lower-class delinquents on the theory that they came from bad stock and therefore required strict punishment. Upper-class teenagers who violated the same laws were deemed by officials to be "accidental" cases to which their families were not accountable, and the cases were consequently dismissed after a warning.[47]

A Philadelphia attorney who specializes in representing juveniles has said:

A middle-class white juvenile delinquent—even if caught red-handed—almost never goes to jail, but for a poor kid, it's another story. I have represented many white

TABLE 10-4   Sentences for Different Classes of Crime

Crime Categories	Average Sentence (in months)	Average Time Until Parole (in months)
Crimes of the poor		
Robbery	133.3	51.2
Burglary	58.7	30.2
Larceny/theft	32.8	18.7
Crimes of the affluent		
Embezzlement	21.1	13.2
Fraud	27.2	14.3
Income tax evasion	12.8	9.7

Source: Federal Bureau of Prisons—Statistical Report, Fiscal Year 1973.

middle-class girls caught shoplifting, and almost none of them went to prison. This isn't due to my talents, but to the system. I'd say to the court: "Your honor, this girl wants to go to college, and her family is sending her to a psychiatrist." Then I'd put Momma on the stand, have her mention the psychiatrist's name—and that's all it would take.[48]

Education. In general, life chances are dependent upon wealth—they are purchased. The level of educational attainment (except for the children of the elite, where the best in life is a birthright) is the crucial determinant of one's chances of income.

Inequality of educational opportunity exists in all educational levels in many subtle and not so subtle ways. It occurs in the quality of education when schools are compared by district. The districts with a better tax base have superior facilities, better-motivated teachers (because the districts can pay more), and better techniques than the poorer districts. Within each school, regardless of the type of district, children are given standardized tests that have a middle-class bias. Armed with these data, children are placed in "tracks" according to "ability." These tracks thus become discriminatory, because the lowest track is composed disproportionately of the lower socioeconomic category. These tracks are especially harmful in that they structure the expectations of the teacher.

The classic study that demonstrates empirically the reinforcement of the stratification system by the educational system was done by A. B. Hollingshead.[49] He found that the lower the socioeconomic status of the high school student's family:

1. The higher the dropout rate.
2. The lower the vocational aspirations.
3. The lower the proportion planning on college.
4. The lower the course grades and the higher the percentage of failures.
5. The lower the IQ scores.
6. The greater the number of recorded discipline problems.

The net effect of these facts is that children tend to repeat the educational experience of their parents. Consequently, even bright youngsters from the lower classes have difficulty in school and probably will not attend college. These data are interpreted by social scientists as demonstrating that American schools systematically disadvantage the lower-class children in favor of upper- and middle-class children.

SUMMARY

Social stratification, the ranking of persons into superior and inferior statuses, is a universal phenomenon. Order theorists view this characteristic of society as having positive consequences. It provides for the smooth functioning of society by providing for a division of labor and ensuring that the most talented persons will be motivated to do the most sensitive and crucial tasks. Conflict theorists, however, see stratification not as a source of societal integration and survival, but as the major source of social problems and social discord. It leads to coercion by the powerful, who wish to retain their advantages, and to conflict between the "haves" and the "have-nots."

Both sides in this debate recognize the consistent relationship between socioeconomic status and achievement of the desirable things in life. The general pattern is that lower-status persons are disadvantaged—in school, in marriage, in the courts, in health, and so on. The research findings are consistent, regardless of whether socioeconomic status is measured by income, educational attainment, or occupational prestige, or a combination of these status characteristics.

CHAPTER REVIEW

1. The process of categorizing people on some dimension(s) is called social differentiation.

2. When people are ranked in a hierarchy that differentiates them as superior or inferior this is called social stratification.

3. An individual's position (social status) in the stratification system is determined by the degree to which he or she possesses those qualities highly valued by the society.

4. Those persons occupying the same relative economic rank form a social class.

5. Persons who consider themselves social equals constitute a status group.

6. Movement from one class or status position to another is called social mobility.

7. Order model theorists accept social inequality as universal and natural. They believe that inequality serves a basic function by motivating the most talented people to perform the most important tasks.

8. Conflict theorists tend to denounce social inequality as basically unjust, unnecessary, and the source of many social problems. The irony is that the oppressed often accept their deprivation. Conflict theorists view this as the result of false consciousness—the acceptance through the socialization process of an untrue belief that works to one's disadvantage.

9. Americans vary greatly on a number of socioeconomic dimensions. Wealth and income are maldistributed. Educational attainment varies. Occupations differ greatly in prestige and pay.

10. The extent of class boundaries varies from community to community. The two indicators of the existence of separate classes are class consciousness and class segregation.

11. Class consciousness is relatively low in the U.S. There are clusters of characteristics along the status hierarchy that individuals recognize and that make it possible to designate "social classes" more or less artificially.

12. Societies vary in the degree to which individuals may move up in status. The most rigid are called caste systems which are essentially closed to hereditary groups. Class systems are more open, permitting vertical mobility.

13. Although the U.S. is a relatively open class system, the extent of intergenerational mobility (a son or daughter surpassing his or her parents) is limited.

14. The prime determinants of upward mobility appear to be: (a) family background; (b) educational attainment; (c) graduation from college; and (d) personality traits.

15. The consequences of one's socioeconomic status are best expressed in the concept of "life chances," which refers to the chances to live and the chances to obtain those things highly valued in society. The data show that the higher one's economic position: the longer one's life; the healthier (physically and mentally) one will be; the more stable one's family; the less likely one will be drafted; the less likely one will be processed by the criminal justice system; and the higher one's educational attainment.

FOR FURTHER STUDY

Paul Blumberg, *Inequality in an Age of Decline* (New York: Oxford University Press, 1980).
Samuel Bowles and Herbert Gintis, *Schooling in*

Capitalist America (New York: Basic Books, 1976).
Ralf Dahrendorf, *Class and Class Conflict in In-*

dustrial Society (Palo Alto, Calif.: Stanford University Press, 1959).

Vincent Jeffries and H. Edward Ransford, *Social Stratification: A Multiple Hierarchy Approach* (Boston: Allyn and Bacon, 1980).

Christopher Jencks, and others, *Who Gets Ahead? The Determinants of Economic Success in America* (New York: Basic Books, 1979).

Louis Kriesberg, *Social Inequality* (Englewood Cliffs, N.J.: Prentice-Hall, 1979).

Gerhard Lenski, *Power and Privilege: A Theory of Social Stratification* (New York: McGraw-Hill, 1966).

Jeffrey H. Reiman, *The Rich Get Richer and the Poor Get Prison* (New York: Wiley, 1979).

Beth Ensminger Vanfossen, *The Structure of Social Inequality* (Boston: Little, Brown, 1979).

NOTES AND REFERENCES

1. These salaries are taken from Suzanne Weiss, "Have a Peek at How Much Your Neighbor Earns," *Rocky Mountain News* (October 29, 1979), p. 8.

2. The following discussion is indebted in part to the insights provided by Melvin M. Tumin, *Social Stratification: The Forms and Functions of Inequality* (Englewood Cliffs, N.J.: Prentice-Hall, 1967), pp. 12–18.

3. Kingsley Davis and Wilbert E. Moore, "Some Principles of Stratification," *American Sociological Review* 10 (April, 1945), pp. 242–249. For an elaboration of the order model's view of stratification, see Leonard Beeghley, *Social Stratification in America: A Critical Analysis of Theory and Research* (Santa Monica, Calif.: Goodyear, 1978), chapter 3.

4. There are some powerful criticisms of the Davis-Moore argument. See especially Melvin M. Tumin, "Some Principles of Stratification," *American Sociological Review* 18 (August, 1953), pp. 387–393; and George A. Huaco, "The Functionalist Theory of Stratification: Two Decades of Controversy," *Inquiry* 9 (Autumn, 1966), pp. 215–240.

5. L. Richard Della Fave, "Mass Support for Inequality," paper presented at the meeting of the Society for the Study of Social Problems, New York (August, 1975), pp. 5–7; Michael Parenti, *Power and the Powerless* (New York: St. Martin's Press, 1978), pp. 15–18; Albert J. Szymanski and Ted George Goertzel, *Sociology: Class, Consciousness, and Contradictions* (New York: D. Van Nostrand, 1979), pp. 137–138. For the original statement on "false consciousness" see Karl Marx and Friedrich Engels, "Manifesto of the Communist Party" in L. Feuer (ed.), *Marx and Engels: Basic Writings on Politics and Philosophy*

(New York: Doubleday, 1959), pp. 15–17. This was originally written in 1848.

6. See especially Richard Sennett and Jonathan Cobb, *The Hidden Injuries of Class* (New York: Random House (Vintage Books), 1973).

7. Bureau of the Census, "Population Profile of the United States," *Current Population Reports*, Series P-20, No. 336 (U.S. Government Printing Office, 1979), p. 51.

8. *Ibid.*, Table 15.

9. C. C. North and Paul K. Hatt, "Jobs and Occupations: A Popular Evaluation," *Public Opinion News* 9 (September, 1947), pp. 3–13.

10. Robert W. Hodge, Paul M. Siegel, and Peter H. Rossi, "Occupational Prestige in the United States, 1925–63," *American Journal of Sociology* 70 (November, 1964), pp. 286–302.

11. Robert W. Hodge, Donald J. Treiman, and Peter H. Rossi, "A Comparative Study of Occupational Prestige," in *Class, Status, and Power*, 2nd ed., Reinhard Bendix and S. M. Lipset, eds. (New York: Free Press, 1966), pp. 309–321.

12. Linda Burzotta Nilson and Murray Edelman, "The Symbolic Evocation of Occupational Prestige," *Society* 16 (March/April 1979), p. 60.

13. A. B. Hollingshead, *Elmtown's Youth: The Impact of Social Classes on Adolescents* (New York: John Wiley, 1949).

14. Gerhard Lenski, "American Social Classes: Statistical Strata on Social Groups," *American Journal of Sociology* 58 (September, 1952), pp. 139–144.

15. See, for example, William H. Form and Joan Huber (Rytina), "Ideological Beliefs on the Distribution of Power in the United States," *American Sociological Review* 34 (February,

1969); and any current poll by the Gallup or Roper organizations where the data are presented by income, education, and/or occupation levels.

16. Richard Centers, *The Psychology of Social Classes: A Study of Class Consciousness* (Princeton, N.J.: Princeton University Press, 1949).

17. For a summary of the criticisms of Centers's study, see especially Milton M. Gordon, *Social Class in American Sociology* (New York: McGraw-Hill, paperback edition, 1963), pp. 193–202.

18. Neal Gross, "Social Class Identification in the Urban Community," *American Sociological Review* 18 (August, 1953), pp. 398–404.

19. Oscar Glantz, "Class Consciousness and Political Solidarity," *American Sociological Review* 23 (August, 1958), pp. 375–382.

20. John C. Leggett, "Economic Insecurity and Working-Class Consciousness," *American Sociological Review* 29 (April, 1964), pp. 226–234. For other studies on class consciousness in the United States, see R. Vanneman and F. C. Pampel, "The American Perception of Class and Status," *American Sociological Review* 42 (June, 1977), pp. 422–437; and E. M. Schreiber and G. T. Nygreen, "Subjective Social Class in America: 1945–68," *Social Forces* 48 (March, 1970), pp. 348–356.

21. G. William Domhoff, *The Higher Circles: The Governing Class in America* (New York: Random House, 1970), p. 74.

22. *Ibid.*, p. 78.

23. *Ibid.*, p. 80.

24. *Ibid.*, p. 871; see E. Digby Baltzall, *Philadelphia Gentlemen: The Making of a National Upper Class* (New York: Free Press, 1958); and C. Wright Mills, *The Power Elite* (Fair Lawn, N.J.: Oxford University Press, 1959).

25. Lucy Kavaler, *The Private World of High Society* (New York: Pyramid Books, 1961), p. 184.

26. Seymour Martin Lipset, "The Sources of the 'Radical Right,'" in *The Radical Right*, Daniel Bell, ed. (Garden City, N.Y.: Doubleday (Anchor Books), 1963), p. 341.

27. Daniel R. Miller and Guy E. Swanson, *The Changing American Parent* (New York: John Wiley, 1958).

28. For an excellent discussion of the extent to which American society parallels Indian society, see Gerald D. Berreman, "Caste in India and the United States," *American Journal of Sociology* 66 (September, 1960), pp. 120–127.

29. Peter M. Blau and Otis Dudley Duncan, *The American Occupational Structure* (New York: Wiley, 1967).

30. Richard H. De Lone, *Small Futures: Children, Inequality, and the Limits of Liberal Reform* (Carnegie Council on Children), cited in Patricia McCormack, "Economic Gap Between Classes," *Rocky Mountain News* (August 22, 1979), p. 66.

31. De Lone, *Small Futures*, cited in Murray Kempton, "Arithmetic of Inequality," *The Progressive* 43 (November, 1979), pp. 8–9.

32. Christopher Jencks, et al., *Who Gets Ahead? The Determinants of Economic Success in America* (New York: Basic Books, 1979); and Herbert Gintis, "Who Gets Ahead?" *Saturday Review* (June 2, 1979), pp. 29–33.

33. Samuel Bowles and Herbert Gintis, *Schooling in Capitalist America* (New York: Basic Books, 1976), chapter 4.

34. *Ibid.*, pp. 110–112.

35. *Ibid.*, p. 113.

36. *Ibid.*, p. 31.

37. Jencks, *Who Gets Ahead?*

38. Hans Gerth and C. Wright Mills, *Character and Social Structure: The Psychology of Social Institutions* (New York: Harcourt, Brace, and World, 1953), p. 313.

39. Walter Lord, *A Night to Remember* (New York: Henry Holt, 1955), p. 107.

40. Aaron Antonovsky, "Social Class, Life Expectancy and Overall Mortality," *Millbank Memorial Fund Quarterly* 45 (April, 1967), pp. 31–73.

41. Evelyn M. Kitagawa and Philip M. Hauser, "Education Differentials in Mortality by Cause of Death: United States, 1960," *Demography* 5 (1968), pp. 318–353.

42. Public Health Service, *Health: United States 1978* (Department of Health, Education, and Welfare, Publication No. (PHS) 78-1232, December 1978), p. 55.

43. Robert Faris and H. Warren Dunham, *Mental Disorders in Urban Areas* (Chicago: University of Chicago Press, 1939); and Leo Srole, Thomas S. Langner, Stanley T. Mi-

chael, Marvin K. Oplea, and Thomas A. C. Rennie, *Mental Health in the Metropolis* (New York: McGraw-Hill, 1962).

44. Maurice Zeitlin, Kenneth G. Lutterman, and James W. Russell, "Death in Vietnam: Class, Poverty, and the Risks of War," in *American Society, Inc.*, 2nd ed., Maurice Zeitlin, ed. (Chicago: Rand McNally, 1977), pp. 143–155; and Laurence M. Baskir and William A. Strauss, *The Draft, The War, and the Vietnam Generation* (New York: Knopf, 1978).

45. "California Juries," *Parade*, November 2, 1969.

46. Glynn Mapes, "Unequal Justice: A Growing Disparity in Criminal Sentences Troubles Legal Experts," *The Wall Street Journal* (September 9, 1970), p. 21.

47. John Useem, Pierre Langent, and Ruth Useem, "Stratification in a Prairie Town," *American Sociological Review* 7 (June, 1942), p. 341.

48. Mapes, "Unequal Justice," p. 21.

49. A. B. Hollingshead, *Elmtown's Youth: The Impact of Social Classes on Adolescents* (New York: John Wiley, 1949).

11

Poverty in the United States

. . . but I do not mean to ignore the bodily ills of these children [of migrant workers]: the hunger and the chronic malnutrition that they learn to accept as unavoidable; the diseases that one by one crop up as the first ten years of life go by; diseases that go undiagnosed and untreated; diseases of the skin and the muscles and the bones and the vital organs; vitamin deficiency diseases and mineral deficiency diseases; and untreated congenital diseases and infectious diseases and parasitic diseases, and in the words of one migrant mother, "all the sicknesses that ever was." She goes on: "I believe our children get them, the sicknesses, and there isn't anything for us to do but pray, because I've never seen a doctor in my life, except once, when he delivered my oldest girl; the rest, they was just born, yes sir, and I was lucky to have my sister near me, and that's the way, you know." . . .

That is what the migrant child eventually learns about "life," and once learned finds hard to forget. He learns that each day brings toil for his parents, backbreaking toil: bending and stooping and reaching and carrying. He learns that each day means a trip: to the fields and back from the fields, to a new county or on to another state, another region of the country. He learns that each day means not aimlessness and not purposeless motion, but compelled, directed (some would even say *forced*) travel. He learns, quite literally, that the wages of work are more work, rather than what some of us call "the accumulation of capital." He learns that wherever he goes he is both wanted and unwanted, and that, in any case, soon there will be another place and another and another. I must to some extent repeat and repeat the essence of such migrancy (the wandering, the disapproval and ostracism, the extreme and unyielding poverty) because children learn that way, learn by repetition, learn by going through something ten times and a hundred times and a thousand times, until finally it is there, up in their minds in the form of what I and my kind call an "image," a "self-image," a *notion*, that is, of life's hurts and life's drawbacks, of life's calamities—which in this case are inescapable and relentless and unremitting.

Source: Excerpts from Robert Coles, *Uprooted Children: The Early Life of Migrant Farm Workers* (Pittsburgh: University of Pittsburgh Press, 1970), pp. 123–126. Reprinted by permission of the University of Pittsburgh Press. © 1970 by University of Pittsburgh Press.

The United States is envied by most peoples of the world. It is blessed with great natural resources, the most advanced technology known, and a very high standard of living. Despite these facts, a significant portion of American citizens live in a condition of poverty. Millions of Americans are ill-fed, ill-clothed, and ill-housed. These same millions are discriminated against in the schools, in the courts, in the job market, and in the market-place, all of which has the effect of trapping many of the poor in that condition. The "American Dream" is just that for millions of Americans—a dream that will not be realized.

The purpose of this chapter is both descriptive and practical. On the one hand, we shall examine the facts of poverty—who are the poor, how many are poor, where the poor are located, is the proportion increasing or decreasing, and what it means to be poor. On the practical level, we shall explore what needs to be done if extreme poverty is to be eliminated.

There are two underlying themes in this chapter. The first is important to consider as we examine the descriptive facts about the poor: The victims of poverty are not to be blamed for their condition, but rather the inequities present in American society are responsible. This is because the essence of poverty is inequality—in money and in opportunity. The second theme is most important when we take up the possible solutions to this social problem: The United States has the resources to eliminate poverty if it would give that problem a high-enough priority.

THE EXTENT OF POVERTY IN AMERICA

What separates the poor from the nonpoor? In a continuum there is no absolute standard for wealth. The line separating the poor from the nonpoor is necessarily arbitrary. The Social Security Administration (SSA) sets the official poverty line based on what it considers the minimal amount required for a subsistence level of life. To determine the poverty line the SSA computes the cost of a basic nutritionally adequate diet and multiplies that figure by three. This is based on a government research finding that poor people spend one-third of their income on food.* Using this standard, 11.6 percent of the population (24.7 million) was defined as living in poverty in 1977. In this chapter we shall consider the poor as those below this arbitrary line. In effect, though, "the poor" is anyone denied adequate health, diet, clothing, and shelter because of lack of resources.

Exact figures on the number of poor are difficult to determine. For one thing, the amount of money needed for subsistence varies drastically by locality. Compare, for example, the money needed for rent in New York City with that needed in rural Arkansas. Another difficulty is that those most likely to be missed by the U.S. Census are the poor. People most likely to be missed in the Census live in ghettos (where several families may be crowded into one apartment) or in rural areas where some homes are inaccessible and where some workers follow the harvest from place to place and therefore have no permanent home. Transients of any kind will probably be missed by the Census. The conclusion is inescapable that the proportion of the poor in the United States is underestimated because the poor tend to be invisible, even to the government.[2] This underestimate of the poor has important consequences, since U.S. Census data are the basis for political

---

*The government procedure is not only arbitrary, but it actually minimizes the extent of poverty in America. Some economists have argued that a more realistic figure would be 50 percent of the median income. In 1980, for example, the official poverty line was $8,450 for a nonfarm family of four, but if the 50 percent of median income standard were used, the line would have been over $10,000, adding many millions to the category.[1] Such a procedure might shock the government into more action to alleviate suffering in this country.

representation in Congress. These data are also used as the basis for instituting new governmental programs or abandoning old ones. Needless to say, an accurate count of the total population is necessary if the Census is so used.

Despite these difficulties and the understating of actual poverty by the government's poverty line, sociologists do know some facts about the poor.

1. Although most of the poor (in numbers) are white, racial minorities are disproportionately represented in this category. In 1978, 30.6 percent of all blacks and 21.6 percent of Hispanic persons were classified as poor, whereas the rate for whites was 8.7 percent. Black families in the United States lived on $57.10 for every $100 received by white families (and this was down from a high of $61 in 1969). Another way to demonstrate this disparity between black and white families is to compare median family incomes for 1978: $10,879 for blacks and $18,368 for whites.[3] The poverty rate among black families has risen from 3.75 times that of whites in 1969 to four times that of whites in 1978.

2. There were 3.6 million elderly persons (65 and over) below the poverty level in 1980 (an increase of 400,000 from 1979).[4]

3. Women who head families are disproportionately poor. The poverty rate for female-headed families, no husband present, was 31.7 percent, compared to 5.3 percent for husband-wife families, and 11.1 percent for male-headed families, no wife present.[5] A most significant change, comparing poverty in 1969 with 1979, was the rise in the number of poor families headed by females from 1.8 million to 3.2 million. This trend has been termed the "feminization of poverty" by the National Advisory Council on Economic Opportunity.[6]

4. The number of poor children is increasing. There were, for example, close to a quarter of a million more poor children under 18 in 1978 than in 1969.[7]

5. Although the poverty level moves up with inflation, this should not be interpreted as indicating an improvement in the living conditions of the poor. The proportionate total income of the bottom 20 percent of the nation's families did *not* improve from 1968 to 1977.[8] One could argue that the plight of the poor has actually become worse. The poverty line is established by the cost of food and rises with inflated food costs. Not included in the formula is the cost of energy, which has soared much faster than food. Present estimates are that the poor must pay at least 21 percent of their income for home heating and other utility bills (four times more than the 5.1-percent of income that middle-income families spend on household energy).[9]

WHO IS TO BLAME FOR POVERTY?

Basically there are two very different answers to this question. In the first instance, the poor themselves are believed to be at fault for their condition. Poverty is thus perceived as the result of persons being lazy, stupid, wasteful, and immoral. The second possibility places the blame on society. Some persons are poor because society has failed to provide equality in education, because of institutional discrimination against minorities, because of the failure of private industry to provide enough jobs, because automation has made some jobs obsolete, and so forth. In this view, society has worked in such a way as to trap certain persons and their offspring in a condition of poverty.

FIGURE 11–1 Percentage of People in Various Groups below the Poverty Level, 1978

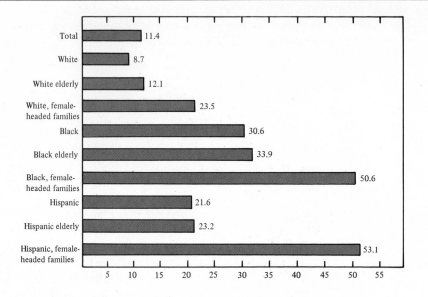

Source: U.S. Bureau of the Census, *Current Population Reports*, Series P-60, No. 123, "Characteristics of the Population Below the Poverty Level: 1978," (Washington, D.C.: U.S. Printing Office, 1980).

The weight of sociological evidence suggests strongly that the inequities of society are to blame for poverty, not the traits of individuals. The focus of this book is on the effects of social structure and this chapter will provide an illustration of how the structure itself can work to the detriment of certain categories of persons. But the citizenry tend to view social problems and poverty in particular from the opposite perspective—blaming individuals for their plight. A recent study of a national cross section of adults ($N = 1017$) examined beliefs about the cause of poverty. More than half (53 percent) gave the most weight to blaming the poor (because of their assumed loose morals, drunkenness, wastefulness, and lack of effort). Only 22 percent saw the workings of society as the fundamental reasons for poverty.[10] Americans, then, tend to blame victims for their condition. "We still blame the poor for being poor, which makes as much sense as blaming the sick for being diseased. Now that we have accepted no-fault auto insurance and even no-fault divorce, surely it is time to accept no-fault poverty as well."[11]

The prevalent view **(blaming the victim)** has extremely important ramifications for the way the war on poverty will be waged. Instead of looking for structural changes, this view focuses on changing the attitudes and behaviors of the individual poor. Thus it is imperative that we examine closely the rationale for blaming the poor because of its important implications.

Blaming the Poor

Although a number of causes are commonly given for why the poor themselves are at fault, they really boil down to two major reasons. One is that the poor have developed a deviant subculture that is antithetical to the American values of hard work, thriftiness, and mortality. The other basis for blaming the poor is the belief that the poor are poor because they are inferior. Let us examine these in turn.

One explanation of poverty is called the **"culture of poverty"** hypothesis. This view contends that the poor are qualitatively different in values and lifestyles from the rest of society *and that these cultural differences explain continued poverty*. In other words, the poor, in adapting to their deprived condition, are found to be more or less permissive in the raising of their children, less verbal, more fatalistic, less apt to defer gratification, and less likely to be interested in formal education than the more well-to-do. Most important to this position is the contention that this deviant cultural pattern is transmitted from generation to generation. Thus, there is a strong implication that poverty is perpetuated by defects in the lifeways of the poor. If poverty itself were to be eliminated, the former poor would probably continue to be unlikely to defer gratification, be immoral by middle-class standards, and so on. Panel 11–1 provides an illustration by an eminent political scientist who views the poor in this manner.

Banfield in Panel 11–1 presents a classic example of "blaming the victim." To him the poor have a subculture with values that differ radically from the other social classes. He does not see the present-time orientation of the poor as a function of the hopelessness of their situation. Yet it seems highly unlikely that the poor see little reason to complain about the slums: What about the filth, the rats, the overcrowded living conditions, the high infant mortality? What about the lack of jobs and opportunity for upward mobility? This feeling of being trapped seems the primary cause of a hedonistic present-time orientation. If the structure were changed so that the poor could see that hard work and deferred gratification really paid off, they could adopt a future-time orientation. Needless to say, there have been many severe critiques of Banfield's position.[12]

Alternatives to "Blaming the Poor"

The alternative view to the "culture-of-poverty" hypothesis is the thesis that the poor are an integral part of American society. They do not abandon the dominant values of the society, but rather retain them while simultaneously holding an alternative set of values. This alternative set is a result of adaptation to the conditions of poverty. Elliot Liebow in his classic study of lower-class black men has taken this view. For him, streetcorner men strive to live by American values but are continually frustrated by externally imposed failure.

From this perspective, the streetcorner man does not appear as a carrier of an independent cultural tradition. His behavior appears not so much as a way of realizing the distinctive goals and values of his own subculture, or of conforming to its models, but rather as his way of trying to achieve many of the goals and values of the larger society, of failing to do this, and of concealing his failure from others and from himself as best he can.[13]

But most Americans do not believe this. They believe rather that the poor are poor because they have a deviant system of values that encourages behaviors that lead to poverty. We shall review and attempt to refute each of these charges in the following section.

Panel 11-1
Blaming the Poor

A controversy that continues to rage is what to do about the urban poor. Edward Banfield, a distinguished professor of urban government at Harvard and chairperson of President Nixon's task force on model cities, has written a highly controversial book that presents the conservative assessment of the urban condition.

In Banfield's view, the urban poor have a culture of poverty that dooms them and their descendants to the lowest social class. The essence of the poor subcultures is a present-time orientation.

The lower-class individual lives from moment to moment. If he has any awareness of a future, it is of something fixed, fated, beyond his control: things happen to him, he does not make them happen. Impulse governs his behavior, either because he cannot discipline himself to sacrifice a present for a future satisfaction or because he has no sense of the future. He is therefore radically improvident: whatever he cannot consume immediately he considers valueless. His bodily needs (especially for sex) and his taste for "action" take precedence over everything else—and certainly over any work routine. He works only as he must to stay alive, and drifts from one unskilled job to another, taking no interest in his work (p. 61).

The poor are doomed by their hedonism. But, in the eyes of Banfield, the culture of poverty is such that it makes the slums actually desirable to the slum dwellers.

Although he has more "leisure" than almost anyone, the indifference ("apathy" if one prefers) of the lower-class person is such that he seldom makes even the simplest repairs to the place that he lives in. He is not troubled by dirt and dilapidation and he does not mind the inadequacy of public facilities such as schools, parks, hospitals, and libraries; indeed, where such things exist he may destroy them by carelessness or even by vandalism. Conditions that make the slum repellent to others are serviceable to him in several ways. First, the slum is a place of excitement—"where the action is." Nothing happens there by plan and anything may happen by accident—a game, a fight, a tense confrontation with the police; feel-

The most common belief is that the poor could escape poverty if they were not so lazy. This simply is not true. Table 11-1 shows that one-fifth of all heads of poor families *are fully employed*. These householders are working at low-paying jobs and may have relatively large families, making it impossible to raise their family income above the poverty level. Another 16 percent did not work at all or worked only part time because they were unable to find a job. These persons do not fit into the economy for a number of reasons, some of which are: the recession, government policies to keep unemployment at relatively high levels to keep inflation in check, automation, and new technology making some occupations obsolete.

Another factor reflected in Table 11-1 that makes work difficult for the poor to obtain is that 49 percent of all heads of poor households are female. Because of discrimination, the jobs they qualify for are typically very low paying. Also, most have children who require either their attention or child care during working hours. The low availability and

ing that something exciting is about to happen is highly congenial to people who live for the present and for whom the present is often empty. Second, it is a place of opportunity. Just as some districts of the city are specialized as a market for, say, jewelry or antiques, so the slum is specialized as one for vice and for illicit commodities generally. Dope peddlers, prostitutes, and receivers of stolen goods are all readily available there, within easy reach of each other and of their customers and victims. For "hustlers," the slum is the natural headquarters. Third, it is a place of concealment. A criminal is less visible to the police in the slum than elsewhere, and the lower-class individual, who in some parts of the city would attract attention, is one among many there. In the slum one can beat one's children, lie drunk in the gutter, or go to jail without attracting any special notice; these are things that most of the neighbors themselves have done and that they consider quite normal (p. 72).

As Banfield sees it, the poor are the cause of urban problems:

So long as the city contains a sizeable lower class, nothing basic can be done about its most serious problems. Good jobs may be offered to all, but some will remain chronically unemployed. Slums may be demolished, but if the housing that replaces them is occupied by the lower class it will shortly be turned into new slums. Welfare payments may be doubled or tripled and a negative income tax substituted, but some persons will continue to live in squalor and misery. New schools may be built, new curricula devised, and the teacher–pupil ratio cut in half, but if the children who attend these schools come from lower-class homes, they will be turned into blackboard jungles, and those who graduate or drop out from them will, in most cases, be functionally illiterate. The streets may be filled with armies of policemen, but violent crime and civil disorder will decrease very little. If, however, the lower classes were to disappear—if, say, its members were overnight to acquire the attitudes, motivations, and habits of the working class—the most serious and intractable problems of the city would all disappear with it. . . . The lower-class forms of all problems are at bottom a single problem: the existence of an outlook and style of life which is radically present-oriented and which therefore attaches no value to work, sacrifice, self-improvement, or service to family, friends, or community (pp. 234–235).

Source: Summarized from Edward C. Banfield, *The Unheavenly City Revisited* (Boston: Little, Brown, 1974). Copyright © 1968, 1970, 1974 by Edward C. Banfield. By permission of Little, Brown and Co.

high cost of child care make it difficult for many potential working mothers without husbands to work. Finally, fully one-fourth of poor families are headed by persons who are either retired, ill, or disabled.

The commonly held belief that the poor remain poor because they do not believe in hard work is refuted by several studies. Leonard Goodwin of the Brookings Institution compared 210 suburban Baltimore families with 307 welfare mothers to determine differences in attitudes. The results showed that welfare mothers believed in the work ethic just as strongly as the suburbanites did, and more strongly in some instances than the children of the affluent.[14] Leonard Reissman, in a study of 1500 heads of households in New Orleans, found that the poor, particularly the black poor, were very willing to learn new routines, or to leave the city, or to give up leisure time, in order to take a better job. Reissman concluded that the poor people in his sample believed in the same kind of achievement values that characterize the more prosperous classes.[15] Davidson and Gaitz

TABLE 11-1   Work Experience and Reasons for Not Working of Civilian Family Heads of Households Below the Poverty Level in 1977

Total Number of Poor Families	*5,300,000*	*100.00%*
Family head Worked	*2,568,000*	*48.5*
Worked all year	1,068,000	20.2
Worked part of the year	1,500,000	28.3
Unable to find work	599,000	11.3
Because of family needs	428,000	8.1
Ill or disabled	202,000	3.8
Other	271,000	5.1
Family head did not work	*2,722,000*	*51.4*
Keeping house	1,149,000	21.7
Ill or disabled	759,000	14.3
Retired	409,000	7.7
Unable to find work	207,000	3.9
Going to school	114,000	2.2
Other	84,000	1.6

Source: U.S. Census, *Current Population Reports*, Series P–60, No. 119, "Characteristics of the Population Below the Poverty Level: 1977," (Washington, D.C.: U.S. Government Printing Office, 1979), pp. 9–10.

studied a sample of Houston residents and found, contrary to the popular notion, that minority poor were as work-oriented as the Anglo-nonpoor.[16]

As a final piece of evidence concerning the willingness of the poor to work, consider what occurred in 1980 when the government advertised 25 jobs in Baltimore that paid $7,210 a year.[17] Over 26,000 persons, most of them black, unemployed, or on welfare, applied for these jobs within three days, waiting for hours in the heat just to pick up the application forms.

Michael Harrington, whose book *The Other America* was instrumental in sparking the "War on Poverty" by the federal government, has said, "The real explanation of why the poor are where they are is that they made the mistake of being born to the wrong parents, in the wrong section of the country, in the wrong industry, or in the wrong racial or ethnic group."[18] This is another way of saying that the society is to blame for poverty, not the poor. The customary ways of doing things, the prevailing attitudes and expectations, and the accepted structural arrangements work to the disadvantage of the poor. Let us look at several examples of the way in which the poor are trapped.

Most good jobs require a college degree, but the poor cannot afford to send their children to college. Scholarships go to the best-performing students. Children of the poor most often do not perform well in school, largely because of the low expectations of teachers and administrators for them. This is reflected in the system of "tracking" by ability as measured on class-biased examinations. Further evidence is found in the disproportionately low amounts of money given to schools in impoverished neighborhoods. All of these acts result in a "self-fulfilling prophecy"—the poor are not expected to do well in school and they do not. Since they are "failures" as measured by "objective" indicators

revolutionary or reform organizations, threats, complaints, destruction of property, or theft. In general, then, any repressed group (the poor in this case, but any minority group, as we will note in Chapter 12) has three basic responses. They can put up with the aversive situation, they can withdraw from it, or they can fight it.

But what of the consequences for the society if a significant proportion of the populace is poor? In economic terms, the cost is very high. In the first place, the poor constitute a relatively unproductive mass of people. In a sense these persons are wasted. Their work output is marginal. They pay little if any taxes (usually only sales tax, since they have little property and low incomes). The cost to other taxpayers, however, is quite large, because of welfare programs, urban renewal, and crime prevention. If the category of "poor" were eliminated through more better-paying jobs and more adequate monetary assistance to the permanently disabled or elderly, the entire society would prosper because of the purchasing power and the larger tax base from those who were formerly poor.

Economic considerations, while important, are not as crucial as humanitarian reasons. A nation that can afford it must, if it calls itself civilized, eliminate the human misery (physical and psychological) associated with poverty.

THE ELIMINATION OF POVERTY

There is an oft-quoted verse from the Bible that says, "and the poor shall always be with us."[34] While this has been true, must it always be? Can Americans, living in the midst of plenty, eliminate the paradox of poverty? The answer is yes, if we mean by poverty that condition of life that is intolerable because the necessities of adequate health facilities, diet, clothing, and shelter are denied certain persons. The methods to accomplish this goal, however, are elusive. The remainder of this chapter will enumerate some of the assumptions that appear basic to such a goal and some of the general programs that adoption of these assumptions demand.

Assumption 1: Poverty can be eliminated in the United States. Michael Harrington has argued forcefully that poverty must be eliminated because America has the resources. "In a nation with a technology that could provide every citizen with a decent life, it is an outrage and a scandal that there should be such social misery."[35] This paradox—poverty in the midst of plenty—can be eliminated if the people wish to make such a commitment. The nation's priorities would need to be reordered in order for economic human misery to be eliminated. Ronald Reagan's election as President is 1980, along with a number of conservative senators and representatives, indicates that this reordering will not take place during the first half of the 1980s (see Panel 11–2).

Assumption 2: Poverty is caused by a lack of resources, not a deviant value system. Basic to a program designed to eliminate poverty is the decision on what keeps some people in a condition of poverty. Is it lack of money and power, or is it the holding of deviant values and lifestyles? This question is fundamental because the answer determines the method for eliminating poverty. The "culture-of-poverty" proponents would tackle these undesirable, non-middle-class traits. The target would be the poor themselves— making them more socially acceptable. Elimination of those pernicious traits would bring an end to poverty. The focus here is on developing the social competence of the poor—not

Panel 11-2
THE REAGAN BUDGET
Who Wins, Who Loses?

THE BIG LOSERS

The Programs	Who Currently Benefits
Supplemental Food Programs	2.2 million needy pregnant women, new mothers, infants and children under 5 years
Food Stamps	Only families below poverty levels
Education	Every school district—economically and handicapped youth
Energy Assistance	Low income persons, the elderly
Medicaid	The poor, aged, blind and handicapped
Subsidized Housing	Low and moderate income families— 85,000 units
Community and Urban Development	61 major metropolitan areas, workers on community building and renovation projects
Aid to Dependent Children	The poorest families, 90% headed by women

changing the system. This approach places the blame on the victim rather than the source of the problem. Such attempts treat the symptom, not the disease. The disease can only be cured by attacking its sources within the society—the structural arrangements that maintain inequality. Thus, the attack must be directed at the structural changes that will enable lower-class persons to earn a living to support their families adequately.

Assumption 3: Poverty is not simply a matter of deficient income for the poor; it results from other inequities in the society as well. Poverty involves a reinforcing pattern of restricted opportunities; deficient community services; powerful predators who profit from the poor; prejudiced attitudes; unequal distribution of resources. These can be eliminated through structural changes. These include, first, the enforcement of the laws regarding equal opportunity for jobs, advancement, and schooling. Second, power on the local and national levels must be redistributed. The present system works in such a way as to keep the poor powerless. What is needed, rather, is the organization of the poor into viable groups with power to determine or at least shape policy in the local communities. The poor need to have some power over school policies. They need to have a voice in the decisions about the distribution of resources within the community (for example, money for parks and recreation, fire protection, street maintenance, refuse collection). The American system of representative democracy is one of "winner take all," and is therefore to blame for the powerlessness of all minorities. A system of proportional representation would guarantee a degree of power.

Minimum Social Security Benefits	3 million older and disabled persons
Unemployment Insurance	9.7 million unemployed workers per year
Public Service Employment	700,000 workers and the local government and private agencies that employ them
Legal Services	The poor, consumers, low income neighborhoods
Urban Mass Transit	Most urban Americans
Health Services	Low income communities, mentally ill, migrant workers
Social Services	Working mothers, abused children, the poor and poor communities

AND THE BIG WINNER!

Military Spending	1981—Up $ 6.8 billion—25% of budget
	1982—Up $25.8 billion—27% of budget
	1983—Up $37.2 billion—31% of budget
	1984—Up $29.4 billion—33% of budget
	1985—Up $48.3 billion—36% of budget
	1986—Up $38.8 billion—38% of budget

Source: *The Reagan Watch: The First 100 Days* (Washington, D.C.: Americans for Democratic Action, Spring 1981), p. 1.

A third structural change involves an increasing reliance upon central planning and action at the national level to alleviate the causes of poverty. This shift from a relative *laissez-faire* policy toward a relative socialism will be outlined in greater detail toward the end of the chapter.

Assumption 4: Poverty cannot be eliminated by the efforts of the poor themselves. The poor have neither the power nor the resources to bring about the structural changes necessary to eliminate poverty. A few of the individual poor by their own efforts may escape poverty, but poverty remains for the others unless the persons and groups with the power and the resources do change the system. This is not to say that the poor cannot have some effect. They can, but usually only indirectly through influential persons or groups who become concerned about the plight of the poor.

Assumption 5: Poverty cannot be eliminated by the efforts of the private sector of the economy. Assuming that private enterprises will not engage in unprofitable activities, we can assume also that private-enterprise efforts will never by themselves eliminate poverty. This is another way of saying that private profit will tend to subvert the human needs that are of public concern. This means that businesses will not provide jobs that they consider unnecessary or not immediately profitable. It also means that these businesses will not voluntarily stop activities that are profitable (for example, persistence in renting deteriorated housing because the unimproved land may increase in value; lobbying to keep certain occupational categories outside minimum-wage restrictions).

Conventional wisdom, however, suggests that private business is the answer, because it will generate new and better-paying jobs. This simply is not the case, because the "new poor," as Harrington has referred to them, differ dramatically from the "old poor."[36] The "old poor"—that is, the poor of other generations—had hopes of breaking out of poverty; if they did not break out themselves, then at least they believed their children would. This hope was based on the needs of a rapidly expanding economy. There were jobs for immigrants, farmers, and grade-school dropouts because of the needs of mass production. The poor of the present generation, the "new poor," however, are much more trapped in poverty. There is now a much greater probability of poverty being "hereditary"—hence a much greater pessimism by poor persons. The "new poor" could be called the "automation poor." They are workers (and their families) displaced by technological advancement. They left coal mining or the small farms, not because of the attraction of the cities, but because they were forced out. Whereas immigrants years ago without much skill were needed to supply muscle, these jobs are now done by machines.

The year 1956 marked a watershed, since it was the first time in history that there were more white-collar than blue-collar workers in the United States. The proportion of workers needed in blue-collar positions continues to decline. The less skillful white-collar jobs are also being replaced by computers and automated techniques. At the same time, however, the labor force grows at a rate of approximately 1.5 million a year. In other words, if the unemployment rate is to remain at the same level, 1.5 million new jobs must be generated annually. The private sector with its emphasis on profit (and therefore efficiency) will not generate the new jobs needed to meet this need, let alone reduce the unemployment rate.

Assumption 6: Poverty will not be eliminated by the efforts of state and local governments themselves. A basic tenet of political conservatism is decentralization of government. Relatively small and locally based governmental units are believed to be best suited for meeting the needs of the people. This belief, although logical, has not always worked in practice. In fact, it has increased the problems of some localities.

A good deal of money is gathered and dispensed at the city, county, and state levels for the purpose of alleviating the misery associated with poverty. Some federal programs function only through the local units of government. The basic problem is that these local units differ so dramatically in their willingness to attack poverty. For example, there are vast differences among states in their levels of welfare assistance. The average, 1980, maximum federal-state payment to a family of four was $339 per month. In Vermont such a family received $524; in New York $476; but in Texas it would receive a maximum of $140 and in Alabama $148.[37] These widely varying rates contribute to the migration of the poor from the South (where the lowest welfare payments tend to occur) to the heavily industrialized states and cities where jobs also pay workers more. Such interstate migration places an increasingly intolerable burden on some states and cities. This raises the question of whether these states and cities should give assistance to all who qualify and live within their boundaries. This is an unbearable situation, and the taxpayers have a legitimate reason to question the use of their money for aiding the poor who were forced to leave other localities where welfare payments and job opportunities were much less.

Assumption 7: Poverty is a national problem and must be attacked with massive, nationwide programs financed largely and organized by the federal government. Poverty can be eliminated through the massive infusion of money and compensatory programs, coupled with centralized planning. This is a form of socialism, and therefore is suspect by many. Governmental control and government subsidies are not new phenomena in the United States. It is the curious fact, however, that subsidies for the poor are generally decried, while the others go unnoticed or even praised. The federal government has subsidized, for example, defense industries (loans), the oil industry (oil depletion allowance), all corporations (tax write-offs), students (government scholarships and interest-free loans), professors (research grants), homeowners (the interest on mortgages is tax-deductible, usually saving homeowners hundreds of dollars a year), newspapers and magazines (through lower-cost postage), churches (no property tax or income tax), and farmers (farm subsidies).

What can the federal government do to achieve the goal of getting all persons permanently above the poverty line? Three quite different programs are needed, because there are three kinds of poverty: (1) the unemployed (or employed at jobs that pay below the minimum wage) because they lack the skills needed in an advanced technological society; (2) those who cannot work because they are too old, physically or mentally handicapped, or because they are mothers with dependent children; and (3) the children of the poor.

The poor who are able-bodied need three things: (1) adequate training; (2) guaranteed employment; and (3) guaranteed minimum income that provides the necessities of food, clothing, shelter, and medical care. An important need here is the creation of new jobs and even new occupational categories. Michael Harrington has suggested that these new jobs may involve working as "indigenous" neighborhood social workers, as teacher's aides, community organizers, or as research assistants. The new needs and opportunities would be in the service sector of the economy rather than in the goods-producing sector, which is where automation occurs.[38] Other jobs could be in such public-works areas as highway construction, mass transit, recycling waste materials, and park maintenance. An important component of such jobs is social usefulness. Jobs with high social productivity would also have some beneficial by-products (latent consequences) in less estrangement of the worker from his job and in overall improvements for the society itself.

All segments of society benefit under full employment. If the poor are paid adequately and therefore have more money to purchase products, the private sector of the economy will be stimulated, since more goods and services will be demanded. At the same time, full employment and decent pay will give power to the poor. The greater their resources, the greater their likelihood to organize for political and social power, to vote their interests, and to become respected by others.

The second type of poverty, involving the disabled and incapacitated who cannot or should not be employed, requires government subsidies to get these people above the poverty line. These subsidies may be in the form of money, food, housing, recreational facilities, or special care centers for the physically and mentally handicapped. An important need is adequate low-cost housing, since most of the poor currently live in deteriorated housing units. Whatever the cost, there must be a nationwide commitment to provide a decent standard of living for these persons. In the words of an editorial in the *Saturday Review*, "One hallmark of a civilized society is its willingness to care for its poor, ill, elderly, dependent young, and permanently handicapped."[39]

Panel 11–3
Who Benefits from Poverty?

Herbert Gans, a sociologist, has some interesting insights about the benefits of poverty that are important to consider if this phenomenon is to be eliminated. He begins with the assumption (from the order perspective) that if some social arrangement persists, it must be accomplishing something important (at least in the view of the powerful in society). What, then, does the existence of a relatively large number of persons in a condition of poverty accomplish that is beneficial to the powerful?

1. Poverty functions to provide a low-wage labor pool that is willing (or unable to be unwilling) to do society's necessary "dirty work." The middle and upper classes are really subsidized by the existence of economic activities that depend on the poor (low wages to many workers in restaurants, hospitals, and in truck farming).
2. The poor also subsidize a variety of economic activities for the affluent by supporting, for example, innovations in medicine (as patients in research hospitals or as guinea pigs in medical experiments) and providing servants, gardeners, and house cleaners who make life easier for the more well-to-do.[41]
3. The existence of poverty creates jobs for a number of occupations and professions that serve the poor or protect the rest of society from them (penologists, social workers, police, pawn shop owners, numbers racketeers, and liquor store owners). The presence of poor people also provides incomes for doctors, lawyers, teachers, and others who are too old, poorly trained, or incompetent to attract more affluent clients.
4. Poor people subsidize merchants by purchasing products that others do not want (seconds, dilapidated cars, deteriorated housing, day-old bread, fruit, and vegetables that otherwise would have little or no value).
5. The poor serve as a group to be punished in order to uphold the legitimacy of conventional values (hard work, thrift, honesty, and monogamy). *The poor provide living proof that moral deviance does not pay*, thus, an indirect rationale for blaming the victim.
6. Poverty guarantees the status of those who are not poor. The poor are at the

About one half of the poor are children. Present-day poverty tends to be passed on to succeeding generations, since the poor often drop out of school early because of the financial difficulties of the home or because they do not perform well in school. Changing this will require a crash program with massive investment of quality education in the ghetto as well as in rural pockets of poverty. Harrington has pointed to the need for compensatory programs:

The poor, so to speak, cannot be given the same voucher as everyone else. Having been systematically deprived for so long, they require the use of federal power to make the schooling market more favorable to them than to the children of affluent homes.[40]

Or, as Harrington argued in another article,

bottom of the status hierarchy, therefore providing a reliable and relatively permanent measuring rod for status comparison, particularly by those just above them (i.e., the working class, whose politics, for example, are often influenced by the need to maintain social distance between themselves and the poor).

7. The poor aid in the upward mobility of others. A number of persons have entered the middle class through the profits earned from providing goods and services in the slums (pawn shops, secondhand clothing and furniture stores, gambling, prostitution, and drugs).

8. The poor, being powerless, can be made to absorb the costs of change in our society. In the nineteenth century they did the back-breaking work that built the railroads and the cities. Today they are the ones pushed out of their homes by urban renewal, the building of expressways, parks, and stadia. Many economists assume that a degree of unemployment is necessary to fight inflation. Of course, the poor, since they are the ones who are "first to be fired and the last to be hired," are the ones who make the sacrifice for the economy.

In the words of Gans,

This analysis is not intended to suggest that because it is often functional, poverty *should* exist, or that it *must* exist. For one thing, poverty has many more dysfunctions than functions; for another, it is possible to suggest functional alternatives. For example, society's dirty work could be done without poverty, either by automation or by paying "dirty workers" decent wages. Nor is it necessary for the poor to subsidize the many activities they support through their low-wage jobs. This would, however, drive up the costs of these activities, which would result in higher prices to their customers and clients. . . .

In sum, then, many of the functions served by the poor could be replaced if poverty were eliminated, but almost always at higher costs to others, particularly more affluent others. Consequently a functional analysis [equivalent to the order model] must conclude that poverty persists not only because many of the functional alternatives to poverty would be quite dysfunctional for the affluent members of society. . . . Poverty can be eliminated only when they become dysfunctional for the affluent or powerful, or when the powerless can obtain enough power to change society (p. 24).

Source: Summarized from Herbert J. Gans, "The Uses of Power: The Poor Pay All," *Social Policy* 2 (July–August, 1971), pp. 20–24. Copyright Social Policy Corporation.

We should have a GI bill in the war against poverty and pay people to go to school, pay for their tuition, their books, and give them an additional living allowance if they have a family. The GI bill was one of the most successful social experiments this society ever had. Why does it require a shooting war for us to be so smart? Why can't we in the war on poverty say that the most productive thing a young person between ages 16 and 21 can do is go to school, and that this is an investment in the Great Society.?[42]

The positive consequences of this plan would be, first, that a significant segment of the potential workers would be kept out of the labor force for a period of time, thereby reducing the number of jobs needed. Second, individuals would learn the skills needed in an automated society. Third, the educated workers could command greater wages and therefore pay more in taxes to the government. The lifetime earnings for the veterans who took advantage of the GI bill was significantly greater than for those who chose to bypass the plan—so much so that they will pay back to the government in taxes approximately six times more than the government invested in their education. This could work for the poor, too.

The problem with this emphasis on education (and with alleviating poverty in general) is the creation of enough socially useful jobs with a decent American standard of pay. Leon Keyserling, former Chairman of the Council of Economic Advisors, has said that "education and training as a conduit to a job is itself a travesty unless the jobs are created first;

Panel 11-4
It's Time to Replace Welfare

A clear understanding of the dramatic changes in social-welfare policy in the 60's and 70's is a prerequisite to sound and wise policy-making in the 80's, for while much was accomplished, much remains to be done. After President Lyndon B. Johnson declared war on poverty in 1964, we substantially increased social-welfare expenditures. We threw money at problems; contrary to the popular myth, it worked.

Over half of the increased expenditures went to the aged. In consequence, the percentage of aged who were poor dropped from 35 to 14 percent. This could only have been achieved by giving the aged more income—by throwing dollars at the problems. Other programs, including many run by the now-defunct Office of Economic Opportunity, were equally successful. The Community Action Program, the heart of the O.E.O., provided entrée into government for thousands of blacks. In 1964, there were only 70 black elected officials at all levels of government in America; by 1979, the number had increased to 4,600. Over one-third came out of Community Action Program agencies. Even Head Start, after strong, early criticism, now appears to have long-term positive effects.

Yet, over half of the children in single-parent families headed by women and a quarter of all black families remain poor. (Poor means having less than 48 cents to spend per person per meal.) In our wealthy country, poverty is a national disgrace, and foolish: Since 40 percent of all our children will spend at least part of their time growing up in a single-parent family and over half of them will be poor, we are talking about a large proportion of the next generation.

Ironically, the very programs that help the poor make it difficult for them to escape poverty. The poor face tax rates from welfare and Social Security programs that are higher than any imposed by the institutions that tax us all. For each dollar earned by the average mother receiving Aid for Families with Dependent Children, she loses about 40 cents in A.F.D.C. benefits and about 25 cents in food stamps; in effect, she pays a tax on earnings of 65 percent. If she earns enough to leave welfare, she will lose Medicaid coverage—in effect, a tax rate in excess of 100 percent. The aged, disabled, working poor and unemployed also depend upon programs that, by reducing benefits, implicitly tax earnings at higher rates than everyone else pays. In short, the combined tax rates in our tax and social-welfare systems are regressive. The economic effect is that we reduce incentives for the poor to work; the moral effect is that we stack the deck against the

training for jobs can be meaningful only if the jobs are going to be available, and the training itself does not create jobs."[43] The creation of jobs, then, is the key to eliminating poverty. Since most of these jobs will no doubt be in the public sector of the economy, the government must divert its best minds to tackling this immense problem.

The general programs given above are indeed necessary if the United States is going to get everyone above the absolute minimum level of economic security. This goal is easily attainable because the productive capacity of the United States is great enough to make it possible without too great a strain. *These programs, however, will not solve the basic problem of inequality.* Thus, there is no insurance that these programs will eliminate urban

poor. They cannot improve their lot the way Americans are supposed to—through hard work. We thereby violate our commitment to equality of opportunity.

Tax rates on the poor must be reduced. It is possible to do so and simultaneously make the poor better off by replacing welfare with programs that benefit all, like Social Security and public education. A number of such reforms have been suggested: Substitute a $600 to $700 per-capita refundable income-tax credit for both the food-stamp program and personal exemptions in the Federal income tax; raise the per-capita credit for the aged and disabled high enough to replace the Supplementary Security Income program; replace Medicaid with a universal national health-insurance program; replace A.F.D.C. with a new child-support program.

A child-support program is worth special attention because it is a new idea and urgently needed. It would replace both A.F.D.C. and the judicial system of awarding and enforcing child support. Under it, all single adults caring for one or more children would be eligible for a benefit equal to either the amount of child support paid by the absent spouse or a minimum, whichever were larger. The minimum benefit would be set high enough to eliminate A.F.D.C. in most states.

Who would bear the cost of child support under such a plan? In large part, the absent spouses would pay, through a tax equal to some proportion of their income for each child not living with them. The Internal Revenue Service would administer this tax. If the tax paid by an absent spouse fell below the minimum benefit, the shortfall would be financed from general revenues.

The current child-support system fosters parental irresponsibility. Over three-quarters of absent parents pay nothing. A new child-support program is attractive because it fosters such conservative values as family responsibility and the reduction of welfare costs and caseloads, while simultaneously achieving liberal ends— by reducing the tax rates on welfare mothers and improving their economic status.

In the 60's and 70's, we extended a helping hand to the poorest among us. We can all be proud of this. But by relying so heavily on welfare programs, we created a system in which what we give with one hand we take away with the other. In the 80's, we must cease this unjust taxation of the poor by replacing welfare with programs that serve all citizens.

Source: Irwin Garfinkel, "It's Time to Replace Welfare," *New York Times* (January 3, 1980), p. A19. © 1980 by The New York Times Company. Reprinted by permission. Professor Garfinkel directs the Institute for Research on Poverty at the University of Wisconsin, Madison.

riots, demonstrations, or crime. They will not eliminate the anger and bitterness that persons feel as they experience relative deprivation. They can, however, eliminate the human suffering associated with extreme deprivation.

SUMMARY

Approximately one out of eight Americans is legally poor. Why are some people poor in a land of affluence? Order theorists see the fault in the individual poor. American society is an open society and people with the proper motivation and perseverance will eventually succeed. Clearly, if some do not succeed in such a system, they must lack the traits essential for success. The fatal flaws within the poor that keep them and their children poor are believed to be a deviant value system ("culture of poverty") and the inheritance of inferior genes.

Conflict theorists see the origins of poverty in the structure of society: (1) in the problems of the economy (inadequate wages for some types of work, unemployment, and automation); (2) in the schools where the poor receive an inferior education; (3) in the discrimination aimed at minority groups; and (4) in the political machinery of society that operates to keep the advantages of society among the already advantaged (for example, tax benefits and the exclusion of certain industries from minimum-wage laws). This last point is especially relevant, because American society has the resources to redistribute wealth and eliminate extreme poverty without undue hardship to the more favored segments of society. But the political apparatus continues to protect the nonpoor, passing legislation the effect of which has been to even increase the gap between the "haves" and the "have-nots".

CHAPTER REVIEW

1. According to the government's arbitrary dividing line, which minimizes the actual extent of poverty, 12 percent of the United States is officially poor. Disproportionately represented in the poor category are: blacks, Hispanics, the elderly, and women who head families.

2. The plight of the poor has not improved in recent decades.

3. One explanation for poverty is that the poor themselves are to blame. For example, the "culture of poverty" hypothesis contends that the poor are qualitatively different in values and life-styles from the nonpoor and that these differences explain their poverty and the poverty of their children.

4. Another position placing the blame on the poor for their condition is the "innate inferior-

ity" hypothesis. This position, a variant of Social Darwinism proposed by Arthur Jensen and Richard Herrnstein, argues that certain categories of people are disadvantaged because they are less endowed mentally.

5. Critics of both the "culture of poverty" and the "innate inferiority" hypotheses charge that they blame the victim. Both theories ignore how social conditions trap individuals and categories in poverty.

6. The consequences of being poor, aside from negative life chances, are: rejection, isolation, hopelessness, degradation, and anger. Three coping devices are: accommodation, avoidance, and aggression.

7. The elimination of poverty requires: (a) a commitment to accomplish that goal; (b) a pro-

gram based on the assumption that poverty results from a lack of resources rather than a deviant value system; (c) a program based on the assumption that poverty results from inequities in the society; (d) recognition that poverty cannot be eliminated by the efforts of the poor themselves; (e) recognition that poverty cannot be eliminated by the private sector; (f) recognition that poverty will not be eliminated by the efforts of state and local governments themselves; and (g) recognition that poverty is a national problem that must be attacked by mas-

sive, nationwide programs largely financed and organized by the federal government.

8. Three quite different programs are needed because there are three kinds of poverty. The unemployed or underpaid need adequate training, guaranteed employment, and a guaranteed minimal income that is adequate to provide the necessities. The disabled and incapacitated require government subsidies to meet their needs. Finally, the children of the poor need education and opportunities to break the cycle.

FOR FURTHER STUDY

Edward C. Banfield, *The Unheavenly City Revisited* (Boston: Little, Brown, 1974).

Herbert J. Gans, *More Equality* (New York: Pantheon, 1973).

Michael Harrington, *The Other America: Poverty in the United States* (Baltimore, Md.: Penguin, 1963).

Michael Harrington, *Decade of Decision*, (New York: Simon and Schuster, 1980).

Richard J. Herrnstein, *I.Q. in the Meritocracy* (Boston: Little, Brown, 1973).

Arthur R. Jensen, *Bias in Mental Testing* (New York: The Free Press, 1980).

Oscar Lewis, *Five Families: Mexican Case Studies in the Culture of Poverty* (New York: New American Library, 1971).

Elliot Liebow, *Tally's Corner* (Boston: Little, Brown, 1967).

Frances Fox Piven and Richard Cloward, *Regulating the Poor: The Functions of Public Welfare* (New York: Random House, 1971).

Harrell R. Rodgers, Jr., *Poverty Amid Plenty: A Political and Economic Analysis* (Reading, Mass.: Addison-Wesley, 1979).

Beth E. Vanfossen, *The Structure of Social Inequality* (Boston: Little, Brown, 1979).

NOTES AND REFERENCES

1. For problems with the various measures of poverty, see John B. Williamson and Kathryn M. Hyer, "The Measurement and Meaning of Poverty," *Social Problems* 22 (June, 1975), pp. 652–663. See also, Michael Harrington, *Decade of Decision* (New York: Simon and Schuster, 1980), pp. 225–231.

2. For a survey of problems with missing census data, see "The Census—What's Wrong with It, What Can Be Done," *Trans-action* 5 (May, 1968), pp. 49–56. For a complete analysis, see Jacob S. Siegal, "Completeness of Coverage of the Nonwhite Population in the 1960 Census and Current Estimates, and Some Implications," *Social Statistics and the City*, David M. Heer, ed. (Cambridge, Mass.: Harvard

University Press, 1968), pp. 13–54. See also, Beth Brophy, "The Billion-Dollar Count," *Forbes* (November 12, 1979), p. 185.

3. These data on poverty are taken from U.S. Bureau of the Census, *Current Population Reports*, Series P–60, No. 123, "Money Income of Families and Persons in the United States: 1978," (Washington, D.C.: U.S. Government Printing Office, 1980), p. 6.

4. *NBC Nightly News* (October 23, 1980).

5. Ann McFeatters, "Women Still on Poverty Rung of Economic Ladder," *Rocky Mountain News* (September 1, 1979), p. 76.

6. United Press International release (October 19, 1980).

7. Cited in *ibid*.

8. Woodrow Ginsburg, "The Poor Among Us,"

Rocky Mountain News (February 19, 1980), p. 40.

9. Associated Press release (July 22, 1980). See also Bob Swierczek and David Tyler, "Energy and the Poor," *Christianity and Crisis* 38 (October 16, 1978), pp. 242–244; and "The Real Disgrace of Welfare," editorial in *The New York Times* (February 21, 1980), p. A22.

10. Joe R. Feagin, "Poverty: We Still Believe That God Helps Those Who Help Themselves," *Psychology Today* 6 (November, 1972), pp. 101–110, 129.

11. Shana Alexander, "The Crime of Poverty," *Newsweek*, October 30, 1972, p. 53.

12. For an especially acerbic review of the first edition of Banfield's book, see William Ryan, "Is Banfield Serious?" *Social Policy* 1 (November/December, 1970), pp. 74–76. For a series of papers on the culture of poverty, see Eleanor Burke Leacock, ed., *The Culture of Poverty: A Critique* (New York: Simon and Schuster, 1971). For a summary of the culture of poverty theory, see Beth E. Vanfossen, *The Structure of Social Inequality* (Boston: Little, Brown, 1979), pp. 355–365.

13. Elliot Liebow, *Tally's Corner: A Study of Negro Streetcorner Men* (Boston: Little, Brown, 1967), p. 222. See also Hyman Rodman, "The Lower Class Value Stretch," *Social Forces* 42 (December, 1963), pp. 205–215; and Ulf Hannerz, "Roots of Black Manhood: Sex, Socialization and Culture in the Ghettos of American Cities," *Trans-action* 6 (October, 1969), p. 20.

14. Reported in "Viewing the Poor," *Transaction* 5 (May, 1971), p. 16.

15. Leonard Reissman, "Readiness to Succeed: Mobility Aspirations and Modernism among the Poor," *Urban Affairs Quarterly* 4 (March, 1969), pp. 379–395.

16. Chandler Davidson and Charles M. Gaitz, " 'Are the Poor Different?' A Comparison of Work Behavior and Attitudes among the Urban Poor and Nonpoor," *Social Problems* 22 (December, 1974), pp. 229–245.

17. David Treadwell, "Stampede for 75 Jobs Shows Human Cost of Troubled Economy," *Los Angeles Times* (September 25, 1980), Part I, p. 13.

18. Michael Harrington, *The Other America:*

19. Associated Press release, April 30, 1971.

20. Elie A. Schneour, *The Malnourished Mind* (Garden City, N.Y.: Doubleday (Anchor Books), 1974).

21. J. Skelly Wright, "The Courts Have Failed the Poor," *The New York Times Magazine*, March 9, 1969, p. 26.

22. William Ryan, *Blaming the Victim* (New York: Pantheon Books, 1971), p. 203.

23. Richard Hofstadter, *Social Darwinism in American Thought*, rev. ed. (Boston: Beacon Press, 1955).

24. See "An Epitaph for Sir Cyril?" *Newsweek*, December 20, 1976, p. 76; "Basic Study on IQ Pattern Challenged," *Christian Science Monitor*, November 30, 1976, p. 15; Oliver Gillie, "Did Sir Cyril Burt Fake His Research on Heritability of Intelligence?" *Phi Delta Kappan*, February, 1977, pp. 469–471; and the rejoinder by Arthur Jensen, *Phi Delta Kappan*, February, 1977, pp. 471, 492. See also, "The Father of Jensenism," *Psychology Today* 13 (December, 1979).

25. Arthur R. Jensen, "How Much Can We Boost IQ and Scholastic Achievement?" *Harvard Educational Review* 39 (Winter, 1969), pp. 1–123. The subsequent issues of the *Harvard Educational Review* include a large number of replies to Jensen's article. See especially the articles appearing in the Spring, 1969, and Summer, 1969, issues. Arthur R. Jensen, *Bias in Mental Testing* (New York: Free Press, 1980).

26. Richard J. Herrnstein, "I.Q.," *Atlantic* 228 (September, 1971), pp. 43–64; and Richard J. Herrnstein, *I.Q. in the Meritocracy* (Boston: Little, Brown, 1973). For critiques, see Noam Chomsky, "The Fallacy of Richard Herrnstein's IQ," *Social Policy* 3 (May/June, 1972), pp. 19–25; Karl W. Deutsch and Thomas Edsall, "The Meritocracy Scare," *Society* 9 (September/October, 1972), pp. 71–79; and Arthur S. Goldberger, "Mysteries of the Meritocracy," *Institute for Research on Poverty*, University of Wisconsin–Madison (October, 1974).

27. Herrnstein, "I.Q.," p. 63. For an essay on what might occur in a meritocracy, see Michael

Young, *The Rise of the Meritocracy 1870/2033: An Essay on Education and Equality* (Baltimore, Md.: Penguin Books, 1961).

28. William Ryan, "Postscript: A Call to Action," *Social Policy* 3 (May/June, 1972), p. 54. For an empirical study that verifies the importance of environment on IQ, see Sandra Scarr-Salapatek and Richard A. Weinberg, "When Black Children Grow Up in White Homes. . . .," *Psychology Today* 9 (December, 1975), pp. 80–82.

29. Joanna Ryan, "IQ—the Illusion of Objectivity," in *Race and Intelligence*, Ken Richardson and David Spears, eds. (Baltimore, Md.: Penguin Books, 1972), p. 54. For new attempts to solve the intelligence testing dilemmas, see Berkeley Rice, "Brave New World of Intelligence Testing," *Psychology Today* 13 (September, 1979), pp. 27–41; and Robert J. Sternberg, "Stalking the IQ Quark," *Psychology Today* 13 (September, 1979), pp. 42–54.

30. Ryan, "IQ—The Illusion of Objectivity," p. 44.

31. See Edmund W. Gordon, "Education, Ethnicity, Genetics and Intelligence; Jensenism: Another Excuse for Failure to Educate," *IRCD Bulletin* 5 (Fall, 1969), pp. 1–22. This justification of unequal schooling is patently false. See Maya Pines, "A Head Start in the Nursery," *Psychology Today* 13 (September, 1979), pp. 56–68.

32. From the official position of the Society for the Psychological Study of Social Issues, George W. Albee et al., "The SPSSI Statement," *Harvard Educational Review* 39 (Summer, 1969), pp. 625–627.

33. See Daniel Zwerdling, "Poverty and Pollution," *The Progressive* 37 (January, 1973), pp. 25–27.

34. *Matthew* 26:11.

35. Harrington, *The Other America*, p. 24.

36. The following is taken largely from two sources: Michael Harrington, "The Politics of Poverty," in *Poverty Views from the Left*, Jeremy Larner and Irving Howe, eds. (New York: William Morrow, 1965), pp. 13–38; and Michael Harrington, "Introduction," in *Poverty in America: A Book of Readings*, Louis A. Ferman, Joyce L. Kornbluh, and Alan Haber, eds. (Ann Arbor, Mich.: University of Michigan Press, 1965), pp. vii–xiv.

37. William Steif, "Recession Swells Welfare Rolls," *Rocky Mountain News* (June 23, 1980), p. 22.

38. Harrington, "The Politics of Poverty," p. 35.

39. "Welfare: Time for Reform," *Saturday Review*, May 23, 1970, p. 19.

40. Michael Harrington, "The Urgent Case for Social Investment," *Saturday Review*, November 23, 1968, p. 34.

41. Morton Mintz and Jerry S. Cohen, "Human Guinea Pigs," *The Progressive* (December, 1976), pp. 32–36.

42. Harrington, "Introduction," *Poverty in America*, pp. xii–xiii.

43. Leon H. Keyserling, "Programs: Present and Future," in *Dialogue on Poverty*, Paul Jacobs et al., eds. (Indianapolis, Ind.: Bobbs-Merrill, 1966), p. 93.

12

Racial and Ethnic Minorities

A heroic figure in American history died in Mississippi on March 14 [1977]. The relative lack of notice given to her passing reveals how little we honor our saints and prophets—reveals, in fact, how little we know and appreciate them when they are among us.

To the majority of Americans, the name of Fannie Lou Hamer was not a familiar one. For the first forty-five years of her life, she was completely unknown except to her black family and friends in the Mississippi delta, and to the few whites for whom they labored. During her last fifteen years, she inspired and influenced and challenged a much larger circle of people; still, too few ever knew who she was or what she had done to advance the cause of freedom and justice for us all.

She was born the last of twenty children in a family of sharecroppers, one generation removed from slavery and still confined under the oppressive grip of white supremacy. She was allowed six abbreviated years of education in a segregated school before she was compelled to work full-time on the land, even though she had been crippled by polio. She always remembered a lesson her mother taught her. "God made you black. Respect yourself." With that as her compass, and with the deep love and respect she felt for her parents, she arrived at middle age angry at injustice, determined to attack it, and yet miraculously free of bitterness and vengeance. "Hate is something destructive," she used to say. "If I hate you, then we're just two miserable people."

If anyone ever had justification to hate, Mrs. Hamer did. In 1962, she was thrown off the farm where she lived and worked because she had tried to register to vote, and her husband and their daughters were subsequently evicted too. They were harassed and threatened repeatedly. In 1963, in the town of Winona, she was arrested with five other persons and jailed for three days, during which she was viciously whipped and beaten.

She survived to tell that tale of horror at the Democratic Convention in Atlantic City the following year. Nonetheless, the Democrats could not bring themselves to unseat the white delegation from Mississippi which steadfastly resisted voter registration and political participation by blacks. The FBI and the Justice Department investigated the Winona assault, and the whites responsible were tried but acquitted.

Mrs. Hamer and others who formed with her the Mississippi Freedom Democratic Party tried again to stir the conscience of the nation's leaders, taking their challenge to the floor of the U.S. House of Representatives, but again they were rebuffed. "I don't want no *equal* rights anymore," Mrs. Hamer said. "I'm fightin' for *human* rights. I don't want to become equal to men like them that beat us." To a nation still unwilling to listen, she spoke the plain and terrible truth: "This ain't just Mississippi's problem," she said. "It's America's problem."

Slowly and reluctantly in the decade since then, Mississippi and the rest of America have moved to acknowledge that fact, and to begin to correct the injustice of it. Mrs. Hamer lived to see

307

some evidence of improvement in the lives of some black and poor Americans, and she was gratified by it. But she was not—and could not have been—satisfied by it. Too many lives remained untouched, and too much justice remained undelivered, for her to consider the job done. "I ain't givin' up," she said later in her life. "I'm stayin' right here in the South, in Mississippi. We got to treat each other right, 'cause we're in this thing together, and if the white people survive, we're gonna survive too."

She stayed, and with serene self-assurance she persisted in her nonviolent struggle for simple justice. She continued the fight until the day she died, at the age of sixty, of cancer, heart problems, and diabetes.

When Mrs. Hamer first dared to challenge the tyranny of white supremacy in the early 1960s, two of the people who gave assistance to her and were in turn inspired and strengthened by her courage were Andrew Young of the Southern Christian Leadership Conference and John Lewis of the Student Nonviolent Coordinating Committee. They, too, were later jailed and beaten, and like her, they held firmly to their faith in the ultimate power of nonviolence.

No doubt she was pleased by the accomplishments of Young and Lewis, and by the hundreds of other Americans, young and old, black and white, who have been emboldened by her example to commit themselves to the pursuit of human rights. But she would surely say now, to them and all of us, what she said many times over, and what her life spoke with such eloquence: Don't stop now. Discrimination is still alive. Racism and poverty still exist. People are sick, hungry, uneducated, out of work. We are still waiting for justice.

Not enough honor ever came to the life of Fannie Lou Hamer, but if that bothered her, she gave no indication of it. Honor and praise were not what she was about. What she was about was being right, and bringing justice like a mighty wave over the land and people she loved—over all of us. Honor came not so much *to* her life as *from* it, to the rest of the world. It was a gift outright. If she were awarded the Nobel Peace Prize posthumously—and she should be, for no one could be more deserving of it— our debt to her would still be enormous, and unpaid.

Source: John Egerton, "Fannie Lou Hamer," *The Progressive* (May 1977), p. 7. Reprinted by permission from *The Progressive*, 408 West Gorham Street, Madison, Wisconsin 53703. Copyright © 1977, The Progressive, Inc.

The United States is a mosaic of different social groups and categories. These are not equal in power, resources, prestige, or presumed worth. They are differentially ranked on each of these dimensions. But why is one group alleged to be superior to another? The basic reason is differential power—power derived from superior numbers, technology, weapons, property, or economic resources. Those holding superior power in a society establish a system of inequality by successfully imposing their will upon less-powerful groups, and this system of inequality is then maintained and perpetuated by power.[1] Inequality is maintained because the dominant group provides the standards (values and norms) by which individuals and groups are judged, and the reward–punishment system; thus the dominant group's institutions systematically disadvantage some groups while favoring others.[2]

THE CHARACTERISTICS OF MINORITY GROUPS

Because majority–minority relations is basically a power relationship, conflict or at least the potential for conflict is always present. Overt conflict is most likely when the subordinate group attempts to alter the distribution of power. Size is not crucial in determining whether or not a group is the most powerful. A numerical minority may, in fact, have more political representation than the majority, as is the case in the Union of South Africa and in most colonial situations. Thus, the most important characteristic of a subordinate "**minority**" group is that it is dominated by a more powerful group.

A second characteristic of a minority group is that it is composed of persons with similar characteristics that differ significantly from the dominant group. These characteristics are salient—they are visible and they make a difference.

The behavior and/or characteristics of minority-group members is stereotyped and systematically condemned by the dominant or majority group. Minority groups typically inspire stereotypes in the minds of the dominant group, presumably because these negative generalizations keep them "down." S. I. Hayakawa, in the following passage, has shown vividly how stereotyped ideas of minority groups are variable, irrational, and negative in their consequences.

Mr. Miller is a Jew. If Mr. Miller succeeds in business that proves that "Jews are smart"; if he fails in business, it is alleged that he still has "money salted away somewhere." If Mr. Miller has different customs than ours, that proves that "Jews don't assimilate." If he is indistinguishable from other Americans, he is "trying to pass himself off as one of us." If Mr. Miller fails to give to charity, that is because "Jews are tight"; if he gives generously, he is "trying to buy his way into society." If he lives in the Jewish section of town, that is because "Jews are so clannish"; if he moves to a locality where there are no other Jews, that is because "they try to horn in everywhere." In other words, because of our feelings towards Jews is general, Mr. Miller is automatically condemned, no matter who he is or what he does.[3]

A final characteristic that all minority groups have in common is that they are singled out for differential and unfair treatment. The discrimination may be subtle or blatant, but it is always detrimental to the minority group. A sizable portion of this chapter will focus on the various manifestations of discrimination toward minority groups in the United States.

Using these criteria—relative powerlessness, visible differentiation from the majority, negative stereotyping, and unfair discrimination—eight categories of people are commonly designated as "minority groups." **Race**, which refers to genetic and therefore immutable differences among individuals, is a typical basis for differential treatment in most societies. For some Americans, racial differences determine behavioral differences as well as skin color, shape of lips, and color of eyes. Although science belies this statement, the fact remains some segments within the society perceive behavioral differences as racial, thereby justifying differential treatment.

A second category, **ethnicity**, is also a traditional basis for inequality. An ethnic group has a culture distinctive from the dominant one. An Amish rural community or an Italian neighborhood in Boston are examples of ethnic groups. Of course, racial groups may also differ culturally from the dominant group—for example, the Chinese in San Francisco's Chinatown or any tribe of American Indians.

The third classification—**religion**—also places some categories in "inferior" positions. The Jews throughout most of their history have in one country after another been persecuted because of their religion (or assumed religious ties). Much of the unrest in Northern Ireland stems from religious differences. The Protestants in that country are dominant and the Catholics are the objects of discrimination.

Another category—the *impoverished*—comprise a minority group in all societies. As we found in Chapter 11, the American poor are powerless and victims of varied forms of discrimination.

A basis for differentiation that has only recently been recognized as a basis for minority status is *sex*. Women in American society are relatively powerless, presumed to have stereotyped qualities (for example, incapable of leadership because of being highly emotional), and are the victims of discrimination, as we will see in Chapter 13.

Certain *deviant* groups also have the characteristics of minority groups. Unmarried mothers (and their offspring), homosexuals, ex-criminals, and ex-mental patients are examples of deviant groups with minority status.

A seventh category, the *aged*, meet the criteria for a minority group in many societies. The elderly in the United States are clearly objects of discrimination, the possessors of negative stereotypes, and relatively powerless.[4]

The *physically different* also have minority-group status. The deformed, the handicapped,[5] the obese, the ugly,[6] and the short experience discrimination because they are different.

RACIAL AND ETHNIC GROUPS

Two types of minorities—racial and ethnic—are very significant in American society and these are the subjects of this chapter.

An ethnic group is socially defined on the basis of a common culture.[7] Ethnicity refers, then, to identification with a particular ethnic group. The culture that binds the members together is distinct from the culture of the majority. Some of the ethnic groups found in the United States are Vietnamese, Jews, Czechs, Mennonites, Chicanos, and Poles.

A racial group is socially defined on the basis of a presumed common genetic heritage resulting in distinguishing physical characteristics. Crucial to an understanding of race is an appreciation that the physical differences thought to cluster and form a race are socially defined. Scientists, however, do not agree on how many races there are or even if races exist. What happens is that "when people become convinced that two or more races exist, then those races do, in fact, exist in the everyday lives of the people who are labeled accordingly."[8]

Confusing the issue further, many racial groups have ethnic characteristcs as well. Whenever a racial group has a distinct culture or subculture, shares a common heritage, and has developed a common identity, then that group is also an ethnic group. In this chapter we will focus on two groups—blacks and Chicanos—that have both racial and ethnic characteristics. What is clear about both of these groups is that they are minority groups—subordinated by and discriminated against by the dominant majority.

Differences Among Ethnic Groups

Some ethnic groups have moved into the mainstream of society while others have remained in subordinate status. The Germans, Italians, and Irish, for example, experienced discrimination when they migrated here in the late nineteenth century but have since been accepted into the dominant majority. Native Americans, blacks, Chicanos and others, however, have not become assimilated and continue to be the objects of discrimination. Two factors combine to explain much of this apparent anomaly.

The first and most obvious reason is race. Those groups easily identified by physical characteristics find it difficult if not impossible to escape the devalued label. Second, the conditions under which the ethnic groups came into contact with the dominant majority appear to be crucial. A key to the way ethnic groups were ultimately treated is whether they migrated to the United States voluntarily or not.[9] Voluntary migrants came to the new world to enhance their inferior stature or to market their skills in a land of opportunity. They came with hope and sometimes with resources to provide a foundation for their hoped for upward mobility. Many had the option of returning if they found the conditions here unsatisfactory.

The voluntary migrants came to the United States in several waves. In colonial times the English, Scotch-Irish, and Germans were the most notable ethnic groups. The Catholic Irish came in great numbers just prior to the Civil War as a result of the great potato famine in Ireland. They were rural, unskilled, Catholic, and anti-English in sentiment. They settled in urban areas and experienced a good deal of discrimination. During this same period the Chinese and later the Japanese migrated to western states. They experienced great discrimination by whites apprehensive about job security.

From about 1870 to 1920 a great wave of voluntary migrants came to America mainly from the Catholic areas of Europe—Poland, Italy, and Eastern Europe—but also from the Jewish sections of Russia and Eastern Europe. These new immigrants were different from the dominant English/Protestant culture. As a result they were more discriminated against than many of the earlier immigrants. The anti-migrant feeling was exposed in a 1924 federal law, which restricted immigration from Southern and Eastern Europe and stopped it altogether for Asians.

The voluntary migrants came to America and experienced varying forms of labor exploitation and other forms of discrimination. In general, though, they fared better than those who came involuntarily. Those forced to enter a country are by definition powerless. From the beginning they are victimized. Also, unlike the voluntary migrants, they were unable to return home if dissatisfied with the move. To understand the special plight of the involuntary migrants, let's look at two such groups—blacks and Chicanos.

Blacks. The slave trade brought blacks to America from Africa from 1619 up until the Civil War, by which time they represented one-eighth of the population.[10] Slaves were defined as property and denied the rights given to other members of society. Families could be broken up for economic or punitive reasons. The slave owners used their power in several ways to maintain their dominance over their slaves. First, they demanded absolute obedience; to question the authority of the master meant physical punishment, often severe. Second, blacks were taught to defer to their masters and to accept their own inferiority. Third, the master used public displays of power to create in slaves a sense of awe. Fourth, slaves were taught to identify with their master's economic success. Finally, slaves were made to feel dependent on their master. This was accomplished primarily by restricting their education. Typically, it was against the law in the South to teach a slave to read or write.

Following emancipation the newly freed blacks, except for the brief period of Reconstruction, remained powerless. They did not have the skills and resources to break away from their dependence on whites.[11] Since whites owned the land, blacks were forced to enter into sharecropping agreements, whereby they would farm the land, take all the risks, and return a percentage of the crops harvested to the owner. Typically the sharecroppers would borrow on the next year's crop to purchase equipment as well as food and clothing. This often meant a cycle of indebtedness that bound the sharecroppers as if they were slaves.

During this same period many states passed the so-called "Jim Crow" laws demanding racial segregation in almost all areas of life (separate schools, transportation, neighborhoods, drinking fountains, public eating establishments). These laws, which legalized white domination, remained in effect until about 1965.

Beginning with World War I, a time of labor shortage and industrial expansion, blacks began to move from the rural South to the urban North. But following that war, blacks in the North experienced large scale discrimination as jobs became scarce. Similarly, World War II brought another great wave of migrants to the industrial cities of the North. And again, following the war, there was massive black unemployment and discrimination was aimed at them from many fronts.

Several conditions following World War II made the black experience different this time. Blacks were now concentrated in cities more than ever, increasing the likelihood of group actions to alter their oppression. Also more blacks were educated, providing the skills of leadership. Even more important, many blacks had served the country in the war and were now unwilling to accept continued inferiority. The result of these conditions, and others, was the civil rights movement of the 1960s. Although there were significant positive changes for blacks resulting from this movement—favorable legislation and court decisions—the lot of blacks in the 1980s remains one of inferiority and subordination (which will be documented fully later in this chapter).

Chicanos. Mexicans represent another ethnic group that experienced involuntary migration. Unlike the blacks who were transported to a hostile environment, Chicanos involuntarly became a part of the United States because of a shift in political boundaries.[12]

The southwestern part of the United States had been controlled by Spain (beginning around 1600) and later Mexico. In 1840, after the war with Mexico, these lands became part of the United States. At that time there were 60,000 Chicanos in New Mexico, 5,000 in Texas, 7,500 in California, 1,000 in Arizona, and a few settlements in Colorado.[13] Significantly, this minority came to the United States not by choice but as a result of conquest. In short, they were colonized.[14] Even in New Mexico where the Chicanos had a numerical majority they lost political control. The Anglo majority was clearly dominant economically and politically in the Southwest.

Since 1900 many Mexicans have migrated (legally and illegally) to the United States, mainly to the southwestern states. These persons have typically been unskilled and unable to speak English. When they have found work it has been in agriculture, on the railroads, and more recently as laborers in manufacturing. Inevitably many have been treated unfairly in the labor market. Even though these new migrants were technically voluntary, "their low status had already been established in the course of conquest, and their lives were very much at the mercy of the dominant Europeans who alternately used them and discarded them as the situation required."[15]

Chicanos in the Southwest remain an ethnic group. They are united by the Mexican culture, the Spanish language, the Catholic religion, and by being the objects of discrimi-

TABLE 12-1   Education and Income by Race, 1978

A. Years of School Completed by Persons 25 and Over and by Race, 1978 (percentages)

Race	Less than H.S.	High School	College 1-3	College 4 or more
White	32.1	37.0	14.4	16.4
Black	52.4	29.0	11.4	7.2
Hispanic	59.2	24.6	9.2	7.1

B. Median Income by Race, 1977

White families	$16,740
Black families	9,560
Hispanic families	11,420

C. Numbers Living Below the Poverty Line by Race, 1977

White	16.4 million (9 percent)
Black	7.7 million (31 percent)
Hispanic	2.7 million (22 percent)

Source: Bureau of the Census, *Current Population Reports*, Series P-20, No. 336, "Population Profile of the United States," (Washington, D.C.: U.S. Government Printing Office, 1979), Table 15, pp. 46-47, 51.

nation. The group is relatively large—8.8 million in 1980, with perhaps another 9 million uncounted because they are in the United States illegally.* East Los Angeles, for example, has more people of Mexican origin than any city in the world except Mexico City. Although large numerically, Chicanos are still relatively powerless. They are undereducated and underpaid. In short, they continue to be subordinate to the white majority. Table 12-1 shows this vividly.

Racial and Ethnic Minorities from the Order and Conflict Perspectives

Order and conflict theorists view the phenomenon of majority-minority quite differently.[17] The order model accepts America as the land of opportunity. The competitive marketplace provides ample opportunities for advancement on individual merit. There is recognition that racial and ethnic groups are disadvantaged but that their incorporation (**assimilation**) into the mainstream is inevitable. Thus the United States is a melting pot for voluntary *and* involuntary migrants, perhaps not now for the racial minorities but eventually. The immediate problem is racism, but this is seen as a psychological problem of individuals rather than a structural problem of the social system. From this perspective the

*Chicanos represent about 60 percent of the 15 million Hispanics in the U.S. (not including an estimated 9 million "illegals"). When the population of Puerto Rico (3.1 million) and the likely number of illegals was added, the Hispanic population of the United States exceeded 28 million in 1980 or 12 percent of the total.[16] Because about 1 million Hispanics enter the United States annually and their birth rate is twice that of whites (and 60 percent higher than blacks), it is likely that an ever increasing proportion of the United States population will be Hispanic.

fundamental fault lies in minority individuals. They resist the culture of the majority. They lack the skills and education required by the larger society for success. Their culture (language, attitudes, values) retards their progress toward equality. In short, if they gave up their distinctive ethnic characteristics and adopted those of the majority, they would achieve equality. The solution then is to expose the disadvantaged to middle-class values. With the right kind of education and social skills, they will become an integral part of society. As proof of this assertion, order theorists use the examples of those ethnic groups that entered society at the bottom but now are assimilated. Groups like the Irish overcame great obstacles to become accepted, therefore all racial and ethnic groups have the same opportunity.

From the conflict perspective, assimilation simply does not apply to blacks, Chicanos, Native Americans, and Asian Americans because they were colonized, and this determined their asymmetrical relationship with the dominant society and their continuing experience in America. According to Robert Blauner, internal colonialism is manifested in four ways: (1) colonization is involuntary with the colonized becoming part of a new society through force or coercion; (2) the colonizing power attempts to change or eliminate the culture of the colonized people; (3) the colonized people are legally controlled by the colonizers; and (4) the colonizers discriminate against the colonized.[18] These conditions make assimilation into the larger society a myth.

Racism is an integral part of American society, the conflict theorists assert, that serves the interests of the white majority. The existence of a continuously oppressed racial/ethnic group provides a labor pool to do society's dirty work at low wages. The political-economic system is *not* neutral. It is a system of power, privilege, and profit that dominates and disadvantages minorities. Parenti has criticized order theorists because they focus "on the poor and [ignore] the system of power, privilege and profit which makes them poor [which] is a little like blaming the corpse for the murder."[19]

A tenet of the conflict model is that only a major transformation in society's institutions will bring equity. One should not forget that majority-minority relations is a struggle for power and privilege in society.

The conflict perspective views group solidarity movements such as "black power" or La Raza (a Chicano organization) as rational attempts to unite members through a sense of common heritage and class interest. Although these groups are often divisive in society and may even lead to violence, they are logical responses to racism. It is the racism prevalent in society's institutions and the resistance of the powerful to change that are pathological, not the growth of these movements within oppressed minorities.

Finally, Marxian conflict theorists would envision that different minorities would eventually see their common oppression and unite to bring about the necessary structural transformation in society. For example, if blacks and Hispanics united today, they would be 50 million strong—a formidable group.[20]

DISCRIMINATION IN THE
UNITED STATES

Discrimination is a complex phenomenon. The forms discrimination may take can vary from a Polish joke to mass murder. The discriminators may be individuals, groups, or even society itself. Moreover, the motivations of the discriminators, as we have seen, may include or lack malice toward those discriminated against. The analysis that follows will examine the modes of discrimination and the characteristics of the types of discriminators. The cross-classification of these two phenomena will provide a paradigm of discrimination.[21]

Throughout human history, dominant groups have used coercion, segregation, defamation, and other techniques to keep the subjugated group "in its place"—that is, powerless and disadvantaged. Of the many types of discrimination, three distinctive modes—derogation, denial, and violence—incorporate most of the means employed and show the breadth of the discriminatory spectrum.

At the least violent end of the continuum is **derogation**. This type of discrimination is in the form of words that put the minority group "down." These words may be common sayings that emphasize the stereotypes held, such as "don't let them jew you down." Derogation is also found in jokes (Polish jokes, "Pat and Mike" stories, jokes about "Rastus") or stereotyped roles for minority-group members in movies and plays. Epithets referring to minorities, such as "nigger," "kike," or "greaser," are derogatory to these persons so labeled. Finally, derogation may occur in the form of the embittered oratory or writings by demagogues who focus on such things as the "mongrelization of the races" or the "international Jewish conspiracy."

A second type of discrimination, usually more direct than derogation, is **denial**. One form of denial—avoidance—is the practice of avoiding interaction with members of a minority group. Children are taught not to play with certain other children. Parents may take their children out of a newly integrated school to avoid the possibility of interaction with the minority group. Avoidance is also involved when whites move out of a neighborhood if a family of a minority group moves in.

Denial occurs when groups set up barriers limiting social interaction. Clubs, fraternities, and homeowners' associations have on numerous occasions set up policies that explicitly denied access to members of other groups. All manner of segregation policies have occurred in the United States. The "Jim Crow" laws of the South prior to the 1960s are a good example. Under these laws the whites and blacks could not use the same drinking fountains, restrooms, waiting rooms, or the same seating area in buses and trains.

The most extreme form of discrimination is **violence** or the threat of violence perpetrated upon minority-group members. The destruction of the property and lives of minority-group members has occurred throughout American history.

So much for the types of discriminatory acts. What about the sources of these acts? Robert Merton has developed a scheme by which he delineates four "types" of persons according to their consistency or inconsistency in prejudiced beliefs versus prejudiced actions.[22] Those whose actions and attitudes are consistent are the "active bigots" (whose beliefs *and* actions are bigoted) and the "all-weather liberals" (always tolerant). The other two types are interesting in that they show inconsistencies that are present in the large portion of the American populace. In each case persons go against their feelings, whether basically bigoted or basically tolerant, when faced with countervailing social pressures. They conform to the wishes of their friends, reference groups, or the law, even though they would rather not. "Fair-weather liberals," while perhaps basically unprejudiced, refuse to serve blacks in their places of business because they fear that they would lose customers. Similarly, unprejudiced real estate salespersons may nevertheless refuse to show certain homes to Mexican Americans because it may affect their jobs. This type of person presumably does not harbor feelings of malice toward minority groups, but the effects of their actions are no less discriminatory.

"Timid bigots" are also faced with social pressures, which in this case cause them to go against their true prejudiced feelings. They conform to the laws or customs which demand that they serve black customers, sell homes to any persons who can afford them, and hire minority-group members in their firms. *The social situation, then, is a powerful determinant of behavior regardless of personal feelings.*

Merton's scheme, while useful, focuses on the individual. Only indirectly (in the cases of the "fair-weather liberal" and the "timid bigot") is the source of discriminatory behavior found outside the individual. To focus only on the individual and his or her beliefs and acts is to ignore the direct and indirect ways that the institutions of society work to disadvantage minority-group members systematically. This phenomenon has been labeled "**institutional racism**." It refers to the established, customary, and respected ways things are done in the society that keep the minority in a subordinate position. For Carmichael and Hamilton there are two types of racism—individual and institutional. Individual racism consists of overt acts by individuals that harm other individuals or their property. This type of action is usually publicly decried and is probably on the decline in the United States. Institutional racism is more injurious to more minority-group members than individual racism, but it is not recognized by the dominant group members as racism. Carmichael and Hamilton illustrated the two types as follows:

When a black family moves into a home in a white neighborhood and is stoned, burned or routed out, they are victims of an overt act of individual racism which many people will condemn—at least in words. But it is institutional racism that keeps black people locked in dilapidated slum tenements, subject to the daily prey of exploitative slumlords, merchants, loan sharks, and discriminatory real estate agents. . . . Respectable individuals can absolve themselves from individual blame: *they* would never plant a bomb in a church; *they* would never stone a black family. But they continue to support political officials and institutions that would and do perpetuate institutionally racist policies. Thus *acts* of overt, individual racism may not typify the society, but institutionalism racism does. . . .[23]

For the sake of clarity, let us use the term **institutional discrimination** rather than institutional *racism*. The referent for racism is clearly race (and usually the black race). Institutional racism is present in American society, but this phenomenon is not limited to racial minority groups. The social system works to disadvantage *all* minority groups, thus suggesting the term "institutional discrimination."

Discrimination can be subtle or blatant, covert as well as overt. As we have seen, it takes many forms as it comes from several sources. In order to describe discrimination in a systematic fashion, the types of discriminators and the types of discriminatory acts will be combined. Table 12–2 provides the scheme that will be used. This paradigm is not exhaustive of all the possibilities, since there are other types of motives for discrimination and other types of discriminatory behavior. However, the major ones are included, and these are sufficient to illustrate the complex and ubiquitous character of discrimination in American society.

registered by blacks after 1960 and there is no evidence that the improvements among employed blacks have ceased during the present recession. Nevertheless these gains have not eliminated the very large gap between the occupations held by whites and those held by non-whites. *Despite three and one-half decades of improvements, the average prestige score for non-white workers in 1975 was inferior to that of white workers at the end of the Depression and the proportion of workers with white collar jobs was greater among whites in 1940 than among blacks in 1975.* (Italics added).[57]

Health

The differences between whites and blacks in income, education, and type of employment are revealed most vividly in the facts concerning health and life itself. Two statistics— infant mortality and life expectancy—show that blacks have become healthier in recent years but still lag behind whites. Comparing the number of deaths per 1,000 live births for 1940 and 1973, researchers found that the rate declined for whites from 43.2 to 15.8, and for blacks from 73.8 to 26.2.[58] While these data show a dramatic improvement for blacks, the difference between whites and blacks indicates a grim reality. For every 1,000 births by each race, black deaths exceed white deaths by ten, an improvement from 30 in 1940, but

FIGURE 12-4 Prevalence of significantly high blood pressure among adults, by age, sex, and race: 2-year average, 1971–1972

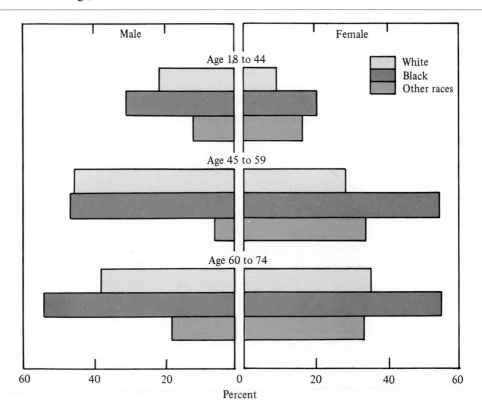

Panel 12-4
"I Have a Dream"
Martin Luther King, Jr.

I have a dream that my four little children will one day live in a nation where they will not be judged by the color of their skin but by the content of their character.

I have a dream today.

I have a dream that one day the state of Alabama, whose governor's lips are presently dripping with the words of interposition and nullification, will be transformed into a situation where little black boys and black girls will be able to join hands with little white boys and white girls and walk together as sisters and brothers.

I have a dream today.

I have a dream that one day every valley shall be exalted, every hill and mountain shall be made low, the rough places will be made plain, and the crooked places will be made straight, and the glory of the Lord shall be revealed, and all flesh shall see it together.

This is our hope. This is the faith with which I return to the South. With this faith we will be able to hew out of the mountain of despair a stone of hope. With this faith we will be able to transform the jangling discords of our nation into a beautiful symphony of brotherhood. With this faith we will be able to work to-

still a brutal gap. Worse by far, nonwhite mothers will die in childbirth at a rate four times greater than white mothers.[59]

This ultimate advantage for whites is also shown in the data on life expectancy (see Figure 12-3). The data show that for 1974, white males live six and one-half years longer than black males; white females exceed black females by five years. The reasons for these differences are obvious. Blacks, being poorer than whites, are less likely to have adequate diets and live in sanitary environments. Not only is medical care proportionately more expensive for the poor (that is, taking a larger segment of the family income) but it is practically nonexistent (as noted earlier in the section on institutional racism). With access to few doctors and resources, people who contract a disease have a much greater likelihood of dying. A study of 250,000 whites and blacks found, for example, that almost every form of cancer was more deadly for blacks than for whites, and higher percentages of blacks die within five years after cancer is diagnosed.[60] Finally, the degradation of minority status may affect their health (see Figure 12-4).

SUMMARY

This chapter has chronicled the differences between blacks and whites in American society. In 1963 some 250,000 civil rights marchers gathered at the Lincoln Memorial in Washington to hear Martin Luther King, Jr., deliver his most eloquent and famous speech (see Panel 12-4). King told his friends that he "had a dream" that one day racism would end in America. Fifteen years later data show that while blacks have made some absolute

gether, to pray together, to struggle together, to go to jail together, to stand up for freedom together, knowing that we will be free one day.

This will be the day when all of God's children will be able to sing with new meaning "My country 'tis of thee, sweet land of liberty, of thee I sing. Land where my fathers died, land of the pilgrim's pride, from every mountainside, let freedom ring."

And if America is to be a great nation this must become true. So let freedom ring from the prodigious hilltops of New Hampshire! Let freedom ring from the mighty mountains of New York! Let freedom ring from the heightening Alleghenies of Pennsylvania!

Let freedom ring from the snowcapped Rockies of Colorado!

Let freedom ring from the curvaceous peaks of California!

But not only that; let freedom ring from Stone Mountain of Georgia!

Let freedom ring from every hill and mole hill of Mississippi. From every mountainside, let freedom ring.

When we let freedom ring, when we let it ring from every village and every hamlet, from every state and every city, we will be able to speed up that day when all of God's children, black men and white men, Jews and Gentiles, Protestants and Catholics, will be able to join hands and sing in the words of that old Negro spiritual, "Free at last! Free at last! Thank God almighty, we are free at last!"

Source: "I have a dream," speech by Martin Luther King, Jr. Reprinted by permission of Joan Daves. Copyright © 1963 by Martin Luther King, Jr.

progress, they have not made progress relative to the majority. There remains a gap between the races in educational attainment. Unemployment is twice as high for blacks, the same as it was in 1963. Jobs for blacks are less prestigious and less rewarding financially than they are for whites. "The purchasing power of black families lags twenty years behind that of whites and 50 percent of the country's black children, compared to 14 percent of the white, live in poverty level families."[61] Finally, blacks receive less medical attention and die younger than whites. Although there is less conscious bigotry now, institutional racism persists, and King's dream evades fulfillment.

The differences between blacks and whites have remained despite the breakdown of legalized discrimination (voting rights, public accommodations, housing, and schooling). But the laws have often been circumvented to continue de facto segregation and discrimination. Building codes have been used to restrict homeowners in a neighborhood to a certain income bracket. Schools have remained segregated in the South by the creation of private academies for whites and in the North by faculty assignment, school site selection, and "optional attendance zones." A final example of continued discrimination despite the law is the "last hired, first fired" layoff provision of many union contracts. Thus, there remains systematic institutional barriers to first-class citizenship for blacks. There have been changes: forty years ago the discrimination was blatant; now it is subtle. The effects, however, are essentially the same.

There is the danger today that the minimal gains blacks and other minorities have won in recent years may be eroded with the reduction of government programs and the cancellation of progressive legislation and court decisions. The election of President Reagan and a decidedly more conservative Congress in 1980 enhances the likelihood of *increased* inequality. Although many of their plans may curb inflation and reduce unemployment, the overall impact suggests the distinct possibility that the gap between the "haves" and the "have nots" will increase. This prediction is based on:

1. The professed desire of the newly powerful to reduce social expenditures (Social Security, Medicare, food stamps, school lunch subsidies, youth employment programs, subsidized housing, and other forms of welfare), while expanding the military budget significantly.
2. The new Republican majority in the Senate has meant a major change in important committee chairs. The new chair of the Labor and Human Resources Committee, Orrin Hatch, has vowed to abolish affirmative action for women and minorities. The new chair of the Judiciary Committee, Strom Thurmond, has consistently opposed civil rights legislation since joining the Senate in 1954. Jesse Helms, the new chair of the Agriculture Committee, now has jurisdiction over food stamps and other nutritional programs for the needy, yet he has vowed to reduce such programs.
3. President Reagan's commitment to eliminating busing to achieve racial integration.
4. A number of measures to reduce civil rights, narrowly defeated in the past, which now seem more likely to pass: (a) the prohibition on using quotas or other numerical requirements in employment or admissions policies; (b) the prohibition on spending federal funds for bilingual education; (c) the repeal of Title IX, which insists on sexual equity in education programs receiving federal monies; and (d) the prohibition on spending federal funds for racial-integration busing.
5. The mood in government and among the majority of Americans to reduce or eliminate many social programs.

The implementation of these and other similar plans will directly impact minorities. Some will eliminate monetary, occupational, and educational gains of the recent decades. There may be increased hostility between the "haves" and the "have nots." The economic and social gulf between the two will widen. Violence, especially in urban ghettos, may escalate. In the short term, the "more guns and less butter" approach will bring increased misery to those already suffering. Vernon Jordan, executive director of the National Urban League, has called this governmental trend the "new minimalism." This philosophy, he has asserted, is a blueprint for continued inequality.

Less government means less protection for people without resources; less spending means fewer desperately needed social programs and stark hunger for those in poverty; fewer government employees means fewer public services, and less interference means abandonment of civil-rights enforcement. The "new minimalism," then, is a blueprint for rolling back progressive social policies and laying waste the hopes of those who look for a more just, more equal America. . . . the new minimalism proposes to institutionalize intolerable living conditions for the black and the poor, and to perpetuate continued decay of America's cities and rural poverty pockets.[62]

Finally, this "new minimalism" further reduces the credibility of the order theorists' belief in the assimilation model. The claim that racial minorities will assimilate into the mainstream of society seems further and further removed from the realities of race relations as found in the United States.

CHAPTER REVIEW

1. The characteristics of a minority group are that: it is dominated by a more powerful group; the members have some characteristics that make them different from the dominant group; the characteristics of the group are stereotyped and systematically condemned; and the members are the objects of discrimination.

2. Eight categories of people are commonly designated as minority groups: racial groups, ethnic groups, religious groups, the poor, deviants, the aged, and the physically different.

3. An ethnic group is a group socially defined on the basis of a common culture that is distinct from the culture of the majority.

4. A racial group is socially defined on the basis of a presumed common genetic heritage.

5. Whenever a racial group has a distinct culture, shares a common heritage, and has developed a common identity, that group is also an ethnic group.

6. Ethnic groups that have difficulty escaping the devalued status generally are easily identified by physical characteristics (race) and migrated to the United States involuntarily. Blacks and Chicanos in the United States are two groups fitting both of these criteria.

7. Order model theorists recognize that racial and ethnic minorities are disadvantaged. They feel that these groups will ultimately be assimilated into the mainstream because of the opportunities available to all members of American society. The main hindrance to assimilation, then, is created by individuals. They do not acquire the necessary skills and education; their culture retards their progress.

8. From the conflict perspective assimilation is impossible for racial groups because they were once colonized, and this experience continues to shape their existence. Moreover, it is not in the interest of the majority that the oppressed achieve equality. Conflict theorists further argue that the solution is a major transformation of society, brought about in part by the collective effort of the oppressed.

9. Discrimination occurs in three forms: derogation, denial, and violence. The sources of these acts are bigoted individuals and groups, those individuals and organizations that do not hate but conform to discriminatory norms, and the structure of society (institutional discrimination).

10. There are four basic themes of institutional discrimination: (a) it is related to the force of history in shaping present conditions; (b) it can occur without conscious bigotry; (c) it is more invisible than individual acts of discrimination; and (d) it is reinforced by the interrelationships among the institutions of society.

11. Although blacks have made some impressive gains in income, educational attainment, and employment, their relative position to whites has not improved.

FOR FURTHER STUDY

Robert Blauner, *Racial Oppression in America* (New York: Harper & Row, 1972).

Stokely Carmichael and Charles V. Hamilton, *Black Power: The Politics of Liberation in America* (New York: Random House, 1967).

Terry Eastland and William J. Bennett, *Counting by Race: Equality from the Founding Fathers to Bakke and Weber* (New York: Basic Books, 1979).

Franz Fanon, *The Wretched of the Earth* (New York: Grove Press, 1963).

Louis L. Knowles and Kenneth Prewitt (eds.), *Institutional Racism in America* (Englewood Cliffs, N.J.: Prentice-Hall, 1969).

Reid Luhman and Stuart Gilman, *Race and Ethnic Relations: The Social and Political Experience of Minority Groups* (Belmont, Calif.: Wadsworth, 1980).

Thomas F. Pettigrew (ed.), *The Sociology of Race Relations: Reflection and Reform* (New York: The Free Press, 1980).

Malcolm X, *The Autobiography of Malcolm X* (New York: Grove Press, 1966).

Norman R. Yetman and C. Hoy Steele (eds.), *Majority and Minority: The Dynamics of Race and Ethnicity in American Liffe*, 3rd ed. (Boston: Allyn and Bacon, 1982).

NOTES AND REFERENCES

1. Norman R. Yetman and C. Hoy Steele, "Introduction," in *Majority and Minority: The Dynamics of Race and Ethnicity in American Life*, 3rd ed., Norman R. Yetman and C. Hoy Steele, eds. (Boston: Allyn and Bacon, 1982); and Reid Luhman and Stuart Gilman, *Race and Ethnic Relations: The Social and Political Experience of Minority Groups* (Belmont, Calif.: Wadsworth, 1980), pp. 7–8.

2. Robert Bierstedt, "The Sociology of Majorities," *American Sociological Review* 13 (December, 1948), p. 709.

3. S. I. Hayakawa, *Language in Thought and Action* (New York: Harcourt, Brace, 1949), pp. 190–191.

4. See Simone de Beauvoir, *The Coming of Age* (New York: Warner Books, 1973); Vern L. Bengston, *The Social Psychology of Aging* (Indianapolis, Ind.: Bobbs-Merrill, 1973).

5. See John Gleidman and William Roth, "The Unexpected Minority," *The New Republic* 182 (February 2, 1980), pp. 26–30; Bruce P. Hillam, "You Gave Us Your Dimes . . . ," *Newsweek*, November 1, 1976, p. 13; and Terri Schultz, "The Handicapped, a Minority Demanding Its Rights," *The New York Times*, February 13, 1977, p. E9.

6. "Now, a Drive to End Discrimination against 'Ugly' People," *U.S. News & World Report*, August 23, 1976, p. 50.

7. For further conceptual clarification on race and ethnicity see George Ritzer, Kenneth C. W. Kammeyer, and Norman R. Yetman, *Sociology: Experiencing a Changing Society*, 2nd ed. (Boston: Allyn and Bacon, 1982), Chapter 12; and Luhman and Gilman, *Race and Ethnic Relations*, pp. 5–6.

8. Luhman and Gilman, *Race and Ethnic Relations*, p. 6.

9. The following is taken from ibid., pp. 8–27.

10. George Ritzer, Kenneth C. W. Kammeyer, and Norman R. Yetman, *Sociology: Experiencing a Changing Society*, (Boston: Allyn and Bacon, 1979), pp. 350–364.

11. Luhman and Gilman, *Race and Ethnic Relations*, pp. 21–23; and Pete Daniel, *The Shadows of Slavery: Peonage in the South 1901–1969* (New York: Oxford University Press, 1972).

12. Luhman and Gilman, *Race and Ethnic Relations*, pp. 23–25.

13. Joan W. Moore, *Mexican Americans* (Englewood Cliffs, N.J.: Prentice-Hall, 1976).

14. Joan W. Moore, "Colonialism: The Case of Mexican Americans," *Social Problems* 17 (1970), pp. 463–472.

15. Luhman and Gilman, *Race and Ethnic Relations*, p. 25.

16. These data on Chicanos and Hispanics are from two sources: Roberto Anson, "Hispanics in the United States: Yesterday, Today, and Tomorrow," *The Futurist* 14 (August, 1980), pp. 25–31; and Geoffrey Godsell, "Hispanics in the U.S.: Ethnic 'Sleeping Giant' Awakens," *The Christian Science Monitor* (April 28, 1980), p. 3, and "Hispanics on the Move," *U.S. News and World Report* (August 24, 1981), pp. 60–64.

17. This discussion comes from L. Paul Metzger, "American Sociology and Black Assimilation: Conflicting Perspectives," *American Journal of Sociology* 76 (January, 1971), pp. 627–647.

18. Robert Blauner, *Racial Oppression in America* (New York: Harper & Row, 1972).

19. Michael Parenti, *Power and the Powerless* (New York: St. Martin's Press, 1978), p. 24.

20. See Lilliam Calhoun and Ron Arias, "The Coming Black . . . Hispanic Coalition," *The Civil Rights Quarterly Perspectives* 12 (Spring, 1980), pp. 12–18; and Joel Dreyfuss, "Blacks and Hispanics: Coalition or Confrontation," *Black Enterprise* 9 (July, 1979), pp. 21–23.

21. The section that follows combines two different perspectives: (1) the modes of discrimination as presented by Peter I. Rose, *They and We: Racial and Ethnic Relations in the United States* (New York: Random House, 1964), Chap. 5; and (2) the types of discriminators as presented in several works, including: Norman R. Yetman and C. Hoy Steele, eds., *Majority and Minority: The Dynamics of Race and Ethnicity in American Life*, 3rd ed. (Boston: Allyn and Bacon, 1982), Part IV; Robert K. Merton, "Discrimination and the American Creed," *Discrimination and National Welfare*, R. M. MacIver, ed. (New York: Harper & Row, 1949), pp. 99–126; and Stokely Carmichael and Charles V. Hamilton, *Black Power: The Politics of Liberation in America* (New York: Random House (Vintage Books), 1967).

22. Merton, "Discrimination and the American Creed," p. 103.

23. Carmichael and Hamilton, *Black Power*, pp. 4–5.

24. For a classic summary of what is known about prejudice, see Gordon W. Allport, *The Nature of Prejudice* (Garden City, N.Y.: Doubleday (Anchor Books), 1956), especially Chap. 25, "The Prejudiced Personality."

25. Associated Press release (July 23, 1979).

26. Karl E. Taeuber, "Demographic Perspectives on Housing and School Segregation," *Wayne Law Review* 31 (March, 1975), pp. 840–841; and Karl E. Taeuber, "Racial Segregation: The Persisting Dilemma," *The Annals* 422 (November, 1975), pp. 91–92. See also, U.S. Commission on Civil Rights, *The State of Civil Rights: 1977* (Washington, D.C.: U.S. Government Printing Office, 1978), pp. 16–21.

27. Associated Press release (December 17, 1979). For an analysis of the lack of school integration in the North, see Robert Reinhold, "25 Years After Desegregation, North's Schools Lag," *The New York Times* (May 17, 1979), pp. A1, B11.

28. William Bruce Cameron, *Informal Sociology: A Casual Introduction to Sociological Thinking* (New York: Random Houe, 1963), p. 94.

29. Louis L. Knowles and Kenneth Prewitt, eds., *Institutional Racism in America* (Englewood Cliffs, N.J.: Prentice-Hall (Spectrum Books), 1969), p. 5.

30. Nijole Benokraitis and Joe R. Feagin, "Institutional Racism: A Review and Critical Assessment of the Literature," a paper presented at the meetings of the American Sociological Association, Montreal, Canada, (August, 1974).

31. Ibid., p. 6.

32. U.S. Commission on Civil Rights, *Window Dressing On the Set* (Washington, D.C.: U.S. Government Printing Office, 1979); and Christine Noschese, "The Ethnic Image in the Media," *Civil Rights Digest* 11 (Fall, 1978), pp. 28–34.

33. U.S. Commission on Civil Rights, *Characters in Textbooks: A Review of the Literature* (Washington, D.C.: U.S. Government Printing Office, 1980).

34. See John E. Williams and John R. Stabler, "If White Means Good, Then Black . . . ," *Psychology Today* 7 (July, 1973), pp. 51–54; and "Reversing the Bigotry of Language," *Psychology Today* 7 (March, 1974), p. 57.

35. David Steinberg, "Racism in America: Definition and Analysis," in *People Against Racism* (Detroit, n.d.), p. 3.

36. Skolnick, *The Politics of Protest*, p. 180.

37. Philip Goldberg, "Are Women Prejudiced against Women?" *Trans-action* 5 (April, 1968), pp. 28–30.

38. Durward Pruden, "A Sociological Study of a Texas Lynching," *Studies in Sociology* 1 (1936), pp. 1–9.

39. "Death Row: A New Kind of Suspense," *Newsweek*, January 11, 1971, p. 24.

40. Carmichael and Hamilton, *Black Power*, p. 4.

41. "In the National Interest," a pamphlet about black medical care distributed by Meharry Medical College, Nashville, Tenn.

42. Robert M. Press, "Why Suburbs May Take Decades to Open Housing to Minorities," *Christian Science Monitor* (April 26, 1976), p. 7.

43. *The World Almanac and Book of Facts* (New York: Newspaper Enterprise Association, 1981), p. 349.

44. The data for this section are taken essentially from two sources: one that argues that the gap is narrowing and one that purports the opposite. The former view is found in Ben J.

Wattenberg, *The Real America: A Surprising Examination of the State of the Union* (New York: G. P. Putnam/Capricorn Books, 1976), pp. 124–151; and the latter in Sidney M. Willhelm, "Black Obsolescence in a White America," *Social Problems in American Society*, 2nd ed., James M. Henslin and Larry T. Reynolds, eds. (Boston: Holbrook Press, 1976), pp. 102–119. For other excellent accounts of the gap between whites and blacks, see Joel Dreyfuss, " 'Black Progress': Myth and Ghetto Reality," *The Progressive* (November, 1977), pp. 21–25, and *The State of Civil Rights: 1977*, a Report of the United States Commission on Civil Rights (Washington, D.C.: Government Printing Office, 1978). See also, William A. Darity, "Illusions of Black Economic Progress," *The Review of Black Political Economy*, 10 (Winter 1980), pp. 153–168.

45. Willhelm, "Black Obsolescence," pp. 106–107.

46. Michael P. Johnson and Ralph R. Sell, "The Cost of Being Black: A 1970 Update," *American Journal of Sociology* 82 (July, 1976), pp. 189–190.

47. Reynolds Farley, "The Economic Status of Blacks: Have the Gains of the 1960s Disappeared in the 1970s?" (Ann Arbor, Mich.: Population Studies Center, 1975), pp. 31–32.

48. Bureau of the Census, *Current Population Reports*, Series P–20, No. 360, "School Enrollment—Social and Economic Characteristics of Students: October, 1979," (Washington, D.C.: U.S. Government Printing Office, 1980), p. 12. See also, Associated Press release (May 18, 1981).

49. Department of Health, Education and Welfare, *Equality of Educational Opportunity* (Washington, D.C.: U.S. Government Printing Office, 1966), p. 20.

50. G. Donald Jud and James L. Walker, "Discrimination by Race and Class and the Impact of School Quality," *Social Science Quarterly* 57 (March, 1977), pp. 731–749.

51. Bureau of the Census, *The Social and Economic Status of the Black Population, 1974*.

52. Cited in Wilhelm, "Black Obsolescence."

53. David E. Rosenbaum, "Life in America's Ghettos Mirrors Grim Statistics," *The New York Times* (May 25, 1980), p. B2.

54. David Anable, "Young and Black—and 40 percent Unemployed," *Christian Science Monitor*, July 26, 1976, p. 3. One estimate put the rate of black teenage unemployment at 53 percent in July, 1976, when the overall unemployment rate was 7.8 percent; CBS News, August 7, 1976.

55. Bureau of the Census, *Current Population Reports*, Series P–23, No. 80, "Economic Characteristics of the Black Population," (Washington, D.C.: U.S. Government Printing Office, 1979), p. 218.

56. Wattenberg, *The Real America*, p. 131.

57. Farley, "The Economic Status of Blacks," pp. 17–18.

58. Bureau of the Census, *The Social and Economic Status of the Black Population, 1974*, p. 126.

59. Bernard Gavzer, "Fuel for Riots in Ghetto Ashes," *Kansas City Times*, April 24, 1972, p. 35. See also *The New York Times*, August 26, 1973, p. 44L.

60. Don Kirkman, "Cancer Is Deadlier for Blacks Than Whites," *Rocky Mountain News*, April 21, 1975. For an overall analysis of the health delivery system for minorities, see June Jackson Christmas, "How Our Health System Fails Minorities," *Civil Rights Digest* 10 (Fall, 1977), pp. 3–11. For the special problems of American Indians receiving adequate health care, see Everett R. Rhoades, "Barriers to Health Care: The Unique Problems Facing American Indians," *Civil Rights Digest* 10 (Fall, 1977), pp. 25–31.

61. Farley, "The Economic Status of Blacks," p. 34.

62. Vernon E. Jordan, Jr., "The New Minimalism," *Newsweek* (February 23, 1976), p. 9.

13

Sexual Stratification

Sexism takes many forms. One involves the difference in the way promotions for men and women are interpreted in the corporate world. In one celebrated case, Mary Cunningham, age 29, was appointed vice president for strategic planning at Bendix Corporation just 15 months after she graduated from Harvard Business School. She began her work at Bendix as an executive assistant to Bendix chairman and chief executive officer, William A. Agee. She moved up quickly in the company, with each advance the result of Agee's recommendation. With each promotion the gossip about a sexual relationship between Agee and Cunningham accelerated. The couple worked together and traveled together. Agee's wife of 23 years obtained a divorce. It seemed obvious that Agee and Cunningham were having an affair and this explained her rapid rise up the Bendix ladder.

Both parties vehemently denied the rumors. Agee argued that Cunningham's promotions were justified by her extraordinary abilities and contributions to Bendix. The rumors persisted and Cunningham's effectiveness in the company was affected. As a result, she resigned.

Was Cunningham unfairly victimized by sexist suspicions that attractive women advance through the corporate ranks by sleeping with the right men rather than by utilizing their business skills? The clear message from this case is that young women who rise rapidly in positions of authority in a company will be suspect. Ironically men can rise rapidly in an organization, even as a result of being close friends with their boss, without risking such a stigma. In fact, one could argue that all promotions to the highest levels of a company are based in part on personal relationships. Bosses promote the people they like, know, and trust. Unfortunately, the rules differ according to the gender of the office seeker.

The decade of the 1970s was clearly a turning point in American society, dramatically altering the status of women in American society. Although equality has *not* been realized in such important areas as equal pay for equal work, Social Security benefits, and passage of the Equal Rights Amendment, some major advances were made in the 1970s:[1]

item: Women became more visible politically. By the end of that decade, women held about 11 percent of the political offices in the United States (double the rate for 1975) including the governorships of Connecticut and Washington and the mayorships of Chicago and San Francisco.

item: Title IX of the Educational Amendments Act of 1972 prohibited sex discrimination in education. This has had the dramatic effect of increasing the educational opportunities for females in higher education and especially in professional schools. Most notably, Title IX moved women toward equality in sports, resulting in a dramatic increase in female participation in athletics at all educational levels.

item: Affirmative Action and class action lawsuits were reasonably successful in correcting sex discrimination in hiring practices and criteria used for promotion.

item: Several Supreme Court decisions made important breakthroughs for women. For example, the Court ruled that unemployment benefits cannot be withheld from pregnant women before and after childbirth. Also, the Court legalized abortions in 1973.

item: Some other important legal landmarks occurred when, for example, girls won the right to play Little League Baseball, when the Service Academies were ordered to admit women, and when women became eligible for Rhodes scholarships.

These changes indicate a shift away from traditional sex roles. We are in an age of transition where many, perhaps the majority, continue to cling to tradition while others demand changes at an ever-accelerated pace. Even though there has been improvement recently in the status of women, men continue to have the advantages in power, decision making, money, and status. These extraordinary benefits for males are found in all major areas of social life: the family, economy, education, religion, sport, and politics. These consistent and patterned inequities between the sexes indicate a condition of sexual stratification. Men are dominant. Women are subordinate to men. Gender determines one's access to power, prestige, and privilege.

The two fundamental dimensions of sexual rank are rewards and power.[2] Inequality in material rewards is easily documented. Do men and women receive the same pay for equal work? Is one sex disproportionately found in the best paying positions in society, in an occupation or profession, or in a particular company? Which sex does the work for which there are no monetary rewards (e.g., homemaking)? Is differential reward by sex found throughout the social class structure?

The other significant aspect of sexual stratification is power. Is one sex dominant over the other? Is this dominance in all spheres of social life? Assuming that each sex has some autonomy (i.e., freedom from the control of the other sex), how do the areas of female control compare with the areas of male control—is one subsumed by the other, or do they exist in balance? As Schlegel has put it:

. . . the status of men and women within the dimension of power derives from their ability to control their own persons and activities and the persons and activities of others. Thus, if men control the persons and activities of women to a greater degree than women control the persons and activities of men, men are dominant. Where neither sex controls the other—a situation one is likely to find in societies where males and females either have equal control in all spheres, or where spheres of control are different but balanced—we can speak of sexually egalitarian societies.[3]

The discussion in this chapter will document the extent of sexual inequality in American society on the dimensions of reward and power. But first, let's look at how the proponents of the order and conflict models explain the subjugation of women in society.

SEXUAL STRATIFICATION FROM THE ORDER AND CONFLICT PERSPECTIVES

From the order perspective biology, history, and the needs of society combine to separate men and women into distinctive roles. Biologically, men are stronger and women bear and nurse children. These facts have meant that men have tended to be the providers while women have "naturally" dealt with childrearing and family nurturance. These interests in children and caring are manifested in the occupations in which women are disproportionately found—day care, elementary school teaching, social work, and nursing.

The necessity for women to nurse their infants and stay near home meant that for most of human history they have done the domestic chores while men were free to hunt and leave the village for extended periods. Thus, a whole set of customs and traditions supporting men as the providers and women as the nurterers set the expectations for future generations of men and women.

Although modern technology has freed women from the necessity of staying at home and has allowed them to work at jobs formerly requiring great strength, the order theorists believe that the traditional division of labor is beneficial for society as a whole. The clear-cut expectations for each sex fulfill many needs for individuals and provide order (see Panel 13-1). The traditional roles for men and women promote stable families and an efficient system of specialized roles with boys and girls trained throughout their youth to take their "natural" places. If gender does not serve as such a guide, people are left without direction. Society becomes less orderly and predictable. Moreover, with industrialization the role of homemaker has increased in importance. Talcott Parsons, a major order theorist, has argued that the husband in the competitive world outside the home needs a haven, a place of affection and acceptance apart from his achievements.[4]

The conflict theorists, in sharp contrast, describe the division of labor by sex with terms such as domination, exploitation, and oppression. From the beginning of human history men have used their greater physical strength to dominate and take advantage of women. They structured society to perpetuate their superiority by retaining leadership in all spheres of society such as the family, religion, politics, and in the world of work outside the home. Women have been and continue to be deprived of power and economic rewards, just as any minority group. They do the work that is devalued because it is unpaid (housework) or underpaid (maid, nurse, secretary, school teacher, stewardess). Their low or nonexistent pay leaves women with few resources. Women have but one road to success—to marry successful men.

Making a good marriage, which means finding a husband who can support her well, is a woman's road to success. To do this she should take care of her looks (but not look "cheap," meaning too overtly sexual), learn the skills of a good housewife, accept her destiny as devoted mother to her husband's heirs, and learn to be a good companion and provide essential emotional support to her husband. So girls are taught to be good listeners to their boyfriends, to be non-assertive and compliant to all but their sexual demands, to exhibit the appropriate inferiority and weakness by losing at games of skill and not outshining males in course work or grades.[5]

Panel 13–1
Sexual Suicide

There has emerged no institution that can replace the family in turning children into civilized human beings or in retrieving the wreckage of our current disorder.

Yet what is our new leading social movement? It's Women's Liberation, with a whole array of nostrums designed to emancipate us. From what? From the very institution that is most indispensable to overcoming our present social crisis: the family. They want to make marriage more open, flexible, revokable, at a time when it is already opening up all over the country and spewing forth swarms of delinquents and neurotics, or swarms of middle-aged men and women looking for a sexual utopia that is advertised everywhere, delivered nowhere, but paid for through the nose (and other improbable erogenous zones). At a time when modernity is placing ever greater strains on the institutions of male socialization—our families, sports, men's organizations—the women's movement wants to weaken them further, make them optional, bisexual, androgynous. Most of the books of the feminists speak of the need to "humanize" (emasculate?) men. . . .

The central position of the woman in the home parallels her central position in all civilized society. Both derive from her necessary role in procreation and from the most primary and inviolable of human ties, the one between mother and child. In those extraordinary circumstances when this tie is broken—as with some disintegrating tribes—broken as well is the human identity of the group. Most of the characteristics we define as humane and individual originate in the mother's love for her children.

Deriving from this love are the other civilizing concerns of maternity: the desire for male protection and support, the hope for a stable community life, and the aspiration for a better future. The success or failure of civilized society depends on how well the women can transmit these values to the men, to whom they come less naturally. The woman's sexual life and how she manages it is crucial to this process of male socialization. The males have no ties to women and children—or to long-term human community—so deep or tenacious as the mother's to her child. That is primary in society; all else is contingent and derivative.

Whereas the order model would accept this, the conflict model asserts that this is an example of false consciousness.

A woman's status is a result of her husband's accomplishments. In the view of conflict theorists this derivation of status through one's husband comes from the conception of the wife as the property of her husband, a common belief throughout history. The patriarchal family, according to Friedrich Engels the colleague of Karl Marx, emerged to guarantee male power.

Because of the . . . importance attached to property and inheritance, the paternity of children becomes a paramount concern of the males. The patriarchal family form arises in response to the new conditions. The wife becomes the property of the husband who can use whatever means necessary to guarantee her sexual fidelity and, thereby, the paternity of his children.[6]

This essential female role has become much more sophisticated and refined in the modern world. But its essence is the same. The woman assumes charge of what may be described as the domestic values of the community; its moral, aesthetic, religious, nurturant, social, and sexual concerns. In these values consist the ultimate goals of human life: all those matters that we consider of such supreme importance that we do not ascribe a financial worth to them. Paramount is the worth of the human individual, enshrined in the home, and in the connection between a woman and child. These values transcend the marketplace. In fact, to enter them in commercial traffic is considered a major evil in civilized society. Whether one proposes to sell a baby or a body or a religious blessing, one is conscious of a deep moral perversion.

The woman's place in this scheme is deeply individual. She is valued for her uniqueness. Only a specific woman can bear a specific child, and her tie to it is personal and infrangible. When she raises the child she imparts in privacy her own individual values. She can create children who transcend consensus and prefigure the future: children of private singularity rather than "child development policy."

Even the husband ultimately validates his individual worth through the woman. He chooses her for her special qualities and she chooses him to submit his marketplace reward to her—and to her individual values. A man in courtship offers not chiefly his work but his individuality to the woman. In his entire adult life, it may be only his wife who receives him as a whole human being.

One of the roles of the woman as arbiter, therefore, is to cultivate herself: to fulfill her moral, aesthetic, and expressive being as an individual. There is no standard beyond her. She is the vessel of the ultimate values of the society. The society is what she is and what she demands in men. She does her work because it is of primary rather than instrumental value. The woman in the home with her child is the last bastion against the technocratic marketplace.

Source: George F. Gilder, *Sexual Suicide* (New York: Quadrangle/The New York Times Book Company, 1973), pp. 6, 245-246. Copyright © 1976 by George Gilder. Reprinted by permission of *Times Books*, a division of Quadrangle/The New York Times Book Co., Inc.

In sum, the barriers to sexual equality are the institutions of society that were established in a time of unquestioned male dominance. Increasing numbers of women are realizing this and are organizing to break these barriers. Social action by the oppressed, in the view of conflict theorists, is the way toward a just society.[7]

SEX-LINKED DISCRIMINATION

The discrimination paradigm described in Chapter 12 is applicable to women as well as racial groups. Individuals, whether consciously sexist or not, discriminate against women, as do the impersonal institutions of society. The discussion in this section will be limited, however, to derogation, discrimination in employment (wages and type of job), and discriminatory laws.

Derogation

This type of discrimination uses language to put women "down." Derogation may occur in common sayings that emphasize negative stereotypes, such as "isn't that just like a woman," or in jokes about "women drivers" or "dumb blondes." It also occurs in stereotyped roles for women in movies, television, and advertising (sex object, dependent, irrational, and stupid).[8] School textbooks also tend to stereotype women and girls by typically featuring them as dependent and domestic.[9]

The English language is also derogatory to women by essentially ignoring them and thereby reflecting the dominance of men. In referring to humanity, we speak of "man" or "mankind." The pronoun "he" is used whenever the sex of the person is unspecified. These examples are demeaning to women.

Discrimination in Employment

Although women are the objects of discrimination in the economic sector in several ways, we shall focus on job-related discrimination. This requires that we analyze the work patterns of those women formally in the labor force and those who are homemakers.

Panel 13-2
The Essence of Sexism

Woman's condition, here and now, is the result of a slowly formed, deeply entrenched extraordinarily pervasive cultural (and therefore political) decision that—even in a generation when man has landed on the moon—woman shall remain a person defined not by the struggling development of her brain or her will or her spirit, but rather by her childbearing properties and her status as companion to men who make, and do, and rule the earth. Though she is a cherished object in her society, she shall remain as an object rather than becoming a subject; though she is exposed to education, wealth, and independence, apparently exactly as though she were an autonomous being and the equal of men, every genuine influence in her life is actually teaching her that she may educate herself only in order to be a more fit companion to her husband. She may use wealth but not make it; she may learn about independence only so that she can instill it in her male children, urge it forward in her husband, or admire its presence or despise its absence in her father. Her sense of these characteristics of adult life is sharply and distinctly *once removed*: it never really occurs to her that these necessities are there for her, as well as for those to whom she is attached. Everything in her existence, from early childhood on, is bent on convincing her that the reality of her being lies in bearing children and creating an atmosphere of support and nurturance for those who aggress upon the world with the intent of asserting the self, grasping power, taking responsibility—in other words, those who are living life as it has always been defined by human principle. Woman shall never be allowed to forget that her ego is passive and her will to independence lies fallow; that the urgent desire for self-assertion that spurs the development of intellect, genius, and complex capacities is, in her, a weak and flickering mechanism; that, in reality, woman is a

Discrimination in the latter case is immediately evident by the nature of the actual work done. In the role of wife and mother, women earn no money for their household chores of cleaning, ironing, cooking, sewing, and caring for the needs of the household members. Although this work is necessary, many would argue that the type of work is demeaning since much of it, if done in other contexts, is very low in prestige.

Five points are important here. First, housework is apportioned in this society by sex. Second, not only is the demeaning work done exclusively by women, but women are socialized to accept this role as their true calling. Komisar has forcefully made this observation:

In a country where the low status of maids probably cannot be matched, where the more than one and a half million household workers (98 percent female, nearly two-thirds black) have median year-round, full-time wages of $1,523—they are excluded from the federal minimum wage laws—it is an amazing feat of hocus pocus worthy of Tom Sawyer and Phineas T. Barnum to lovingly declare that domestic labor is the true vocation of women wearing wedding bands.[10]

Third, these tasks are unpaid. One argument is that this lack of payment for work leads to further debasement of housewives, since self-esteem and status are related to earnings.

---

differently made creature, one whose proportions are more *childlike*, if you will, less given to maturity than are the proportions of men.

This is the substance of sexism. This is the creation of thousands of years of thought and reinforced patterns of behavior so deeply imprinted, so utterly subscribed to by the great body of Western conviction, that they are taken for "natural" or "instinctive." Sexism has made of women a race of children, a class of human beings utterly deprived of self-hood, of autonomy, of confidence—worst of all, it has *made the false come true*. Women have so long shared acquiescently in society's patriarchal definition of them as beings composed of warmth, passivity, nurturance, inert egos, and developed intuition, that they have become the very thing itself and can no more see themselves in that mirror of life that declares independence, aggression, intellectual abstraction, and primary responsibility to be the silhouette of human development than can men. As a result, women have long suffered from an image of the self that paralyzes the will and short circuits the brain, that makes them deny the evidence of their senses and internalize self-doubt to a fearful degree. They have been raised to be the bearers of children by other bearers of children. They have been treated primarily as bearers of children by everyone they have ever known: parents, teachers, friends, lovers, busdrivers, landlords, employers, policemen, culture heroes. . . . Should they reveal strong wishes that their lives form themselves around an altogether other definition, they are branded unnatural.

Sexism, like any other cultural characteristic, lives through institutions—those that blindly perpetuate it and those that depend upon it for their very life.

Source: Excerpted from Vivian Gornick and Barbara K. Moran, *Woman in Sexist Society: Studies in Power and Powerlessness* (New York: Basic Books, 1971), pp. xix-xxi. Copyright © 1971 by Basic Books, Inc., Publishers, New York.

Panel 13–3
I Want a Wife

I belong to that classification of people known as wives. I am A Wife. And, not altogether incidentally, I am a mother.

Not too long ago a male friend of mine appeared on the scene fresh from a recent divorce. He had one child, who is, of course, with his ex-wife. He is obviously looking for another wife. As I thought about him while I was ironing one evening, it suddenly occurred to me that I, too, would like to have a wife. Why do I want a wife?

I would like to go back to school so that I can become economically independent, support myself, and, if need be, support those dependent upon me. I want a wife who will work and send me to school. And while I am going to school I want a wife to take care of the children. I want a wife to keep track of the children's doctor and dentist appointments. And to keep track of mine too. I want a wife to make sure my children eat properly and are kept clean. I want a wife who will wash the children's clothes and keep them mended. I want a wife who is a good nurturant attendant to my children, who arranges for their schooling, makes sure that they have an adequate social life with their peers, takes them to the park, the zoo, et cetera. I want a wife who takes care of the children when they are sick, a wife who arranges to be around when the children need special care, because, of course, I cannot miss classes at school. My wife must arrange to lose time at work and not lose the job. It may mean a small cut in my wife's income from time to time, but I guess I can tolerate that. Needless to say, my wife will arrange and pay for the care of the children while my wife is working.

I want a wife who will take care of *my* physical needs. I want a wife who will keep my house clean. A wife who will pick up after me. I want a wife who will keep my clothes clean, ironed, mended, replaced when need be, and who will see to it that my personal things are kept in their proper place so that I can find what I need the minute I need it. I want a wife who cooks the meals, a wife who is a *good* cook. I want a wife who will plan the menus, do the necessary grocery shopping, prepare the meals, serve them pleasantly, and then do the cleaning up while I do my studying. I want a wife who will care for me when I am sick and sympathize with my pain and loss of time from school. I want a wife to go along when

Given a capitalist society in which personal autonomy as well as status are gained through money, women do need to be wage earners in order to achieve the self-reliance and self-esteem which are the first steps toward equality.[11]

Moreover, the housewife is not insured, cannot claim sickness benefits, nor is she eligible for retirement benefits.

Fourth, the next generation is apparently much less willing than previous ones to see the homemaking role as their calling. A survey of 17-year-old girls in 1976 revealed that only 3 percent chose "housewife" as their first career choice.[12]

Finally, the apportionment of housework and child care tends to be a problem where both wife and husband work outside the home. Working wives average 4.8 hours of family

our family takes a vacation so that someone can continue to care for me and my children when I need a rest and change of scene.

I want a wife who will not bother me with rambling complaints about a wife's duties. But I want a wife who will listen to me when I feel the need to explain a rather difficult point I have come across in my course of studies. And I want a wife who will type my papers for me when I have written them.

I want a wife who will take care of the details of my social life. When my wife and I are invited out by my friends, I want a wife who will take care of the baby-sitting arrangements. When I meet people at school whom I like and want to entertain, I want a wife who will have the house clean, will prepare a special meal, serve it to me and my friends, and not interrupt when I talk about the things that interest me and my friends. I want a wife who will have arranged that the children are fed and ready for bed before my guests arrive so that the children do not bother us.

And I want a wife who knows that sometimes I need a night out by myself.

I want a wife who is sensitive to my sexual needs, a wife who makes love passionately and eagerly when I feel like it, a wife who makes sure that I am satisfied. And, of course, I want a wife who will not demand sexual attention when I am not in the mood for it. I want a wife who assumes the complete responsibility for birth control, because I do not want more children. I want a wife who will remain sexually faithful to me so that I do not have to clutter up my intellectual life with jealousies. And I want a wife who understands that *my* sexual needs may entail more than strict adherence to monogamy. I must, after all, be able to relate to people as fully as possible.

If, by chance, I find another person more suitable as a wife than the wife I already have, I want the liberty to replace my present wife with another one. Naturally, I will expect a fresh, new life; my wife will take the children and be solely responsible for them so that I am left free.

When I am through with school and have a job, I want my wife to quit working and remain at home so that my wife can more fully and completely take care of a wife's duties.

My God, who *wouldn't* want a wife?

Source: Judy Syfers, "I Want a Wife," *Ms.* (December 1979), p. 144. Copyright © 1970 by Judy Syfers.

work per day while working husbands in these homes average about 1.6 hours per day.[13] To survive they must be "superwomen" and many are rebelling because the time demands on them far exceed those on their husbands.[14]

Women in the labor force. For the 51 percent of adult women who are in the labor force (in 1980), discrimination is clearly found in the allocation of jobs by sex and in differential remuneration. Let's begin by examining the distribution of working women by type of job. The data show that women are concentrated in the lowest prestige jobs. Almost 7 out of 10 employed women held clerical, sales, and service jobs, whereas less than 22 percent of males were engaged in these occupations. For example, almost 99 percent of all stenog-

raphers, typists, and secretaries are women; 88 percent of all cashiers are women; and 71 percent of all elementary and high school teachers are women.

On the other hand, in the most prestigious professions the proportion of women is low: 3 percent of engineers, 13 percent of doctors, 10 percent of lawyers, and 32 percent of university professors.[15] The few women in medicine are over-represented in specialties that conform to the feminine role of caring (especially for children): pediatrics, child psychiatry, preventive medicine, and public health. They are vastly underrepresented in the most prestigious specialties: surgery, orthopedics, and cardiology. Women lawyers tend to be concentrated in two areas: trusts/estates and domestic relations, both of which are low prestige specialties with a large proportion of female clients.[16]

Although men continue to dominate the professions, positive changes for women have occurred recently. Table 13–1 shows that over a six-year period, the proportion of women receiving advanced degrees in medicine, law, dentistry, and veterinary medicine has at least doubled.

Discrimination against women is not limited to white collar jobs. In 1950 the proportion of women carpenters was 1.5 percent; yet by 1979 that percentage had slipped to 1.3 percent. In other well paid skill trades (e.g., plumbers, electricians, and house painters) the proportion of women is consistently less than 3 percent.[17]

TABLE 13-1 The Progress of Women in 4 Professional Fields

Medicine

	First-year enrollment		Total enrollment		Degrees awarded	
	No. of women	Per cent of total	No. of women	Per cent of total	No. of women	Per cent of total
1969–70	940	9.1%	3,385	9.0%	713	8.5%
1970–71	1,241	10.9%	3,873	9.6%	829	9.2%
1971–72	1,701	13.1%	4,730	10.8%	845	9.1%
1972–73	2,225	16.3%	5,836	12.7%	939	9.0%
1973–74	2,855	19.0%	7,701	15.6%	1,280	11.2%
1974–75	3,260	22.4%	9,659	18.1%	1,654	13.2%
1975–76	3,897	23.4%	11,386	20.5%	2,200	16.2%

Dentistry

	First-year enrollment		Total enrollment		Degrees awarded	
	No. of women	Per cent of total	No. of women	Per cent of total	No. of women	Per cent of total
1969–70	69	1.6%	227	1.4%	36	1.0%
1970–71	103	2.2%	274	1.7%	46	1.2%
1971–72	160	3.1%	355	2.0%	46	1.2%
1972–73	241	4.0%	556	3.1%	58	1.4%
1973–74	423	6.9%	892	4.6%	88	2.0%
1974–75	638	10.9%	1,403	7.0%	149	3.1%
1975–76	781	12.2%	1,987	9.7%	249	4.5%

Veterinary medicine

	First-year enrollment		Total enrollment		Degrees awarded	
	No. of women	Per cent of total	No. of women	Per cent of total	No. of women	Per cent of total
1969–70	159	11.5%	417	8.8%	90	7.5%
1970–71	158	11.0%	444	9.4%	98	7.8%
1971–72	228	15.1%	593	11.5%	117	9.4%
1972–73	327	18.6%	745	13.7%	133	10.2%
1973–74	350	23.0%	957	17.3%	155	11.2%
1974–75	453	25.3%	1,220	20.4%	225	15.9%
1975–76	462	28.0%	1,337	23.5%	277	18.1%

Law

	First-year enrollment		Total enrollment		Degrees awarded	
	No. of women	Per cent of total	No. of women	Per cent of total	No. of women	Per cent of total
1969–70	2,296	7.5%	4,719	7.0%	852	5.6%
1970–71	3,173	8.8%	6,469	8.0%	1,293	7.3%
1971–72	4,653	11.6%	9,075	9.6%	1,545	7.0%
1972–73	6,248	15.7%	12,571	12.5%	2,224	8.1%
1973–74	8,186	19.8%	16,730	16.1%	3,408	11.5%
1974–75	9,954	23.4%	21,504	20.0%	4,455	15.1%
1975–76	11,625	25.9%	26,403	23.3%	6,264	19.3%

Source: National Center for Education Statistics, reported in *The Chronicle of Higher Education* (January 16, 1978), p. 15.

Pay differentials. An important aspect of discrimination toward women in the work world is their disproportionately low wages. In 1955, for example, full time working women earned 64.3 cents for each dollar earned by men. Twenty-three years later, in 1978, the ratio was even lower—60 cents.[18] Put another and perhaps more dramatic way, Labor Department data show that a white man who dropped out of high school on the average makes more than a white woman with a college degree.

The following are some examples of the gulf between males and females in pay:[19]

item: A man's average retirement income after reaching age 65 is $5,500 compared to slightly under $3,000 for women.

item: Female administrative aides in the House of Representatives averaged $17,000 compared to $39,000 for their male counterparts.

item: 77 percent of the government employees in 1978 at the lowest grades (1–4, ranging in salary from $7,210 to $13,064) were women, but they constituted only 5 percent at the highest grades (16+, where the salary ranges from $47,889 to $65,750).

item: Women faculty at the college level earn more than $3,000 less per year than men faculty.

item: Regardless of race, men always average higher pay than women. In 1977, for example, there was a wage difference of $6,628 for whites; $3,510 for blacks; and $3,612 for Hispanics.

These disparities are the result of discrimination for two reasons. Foremost is the fact, previously documented, that women are found disproportionately in lower prestige and therefore lower-paying jobs. But—and this is the second point—within each job category women receive substantially lower income. Table 13–2 documents this trend.

A possible explanation for these income differences by sex might be that although women and men have the same job, their unequal pay is a reflection of men having greater educational attainment. Table 13–3 shows that this hypothesis must be rejected. In this table median income is presented for each educational level and, without exception, males outrank women by substantial margins. Amazingly, educational attainment is so inconse-

TABLE 13–2   Median Annual Earnings of Full-Time Workers, 1977

Type of Employment	Median Income		
	Male	*Female*	*Difference*
Professional and technical	$18,724	$12,211	$6,513
Managers and administrators	18,757	10,248	8,509
Clerical	13,771	8,797	5,974
Sales	16,415	7,396	9,019
Crafts	14,886	9,314	5,572
Operatives	12,895	7,588	5,307
Laborers	11,169	7,566	3,603
Service Workers	10,899	6,628	4,271

Source: Adapted from Bureau of Census, *Money Income in 1977 of Families and Persons in the United States, Current Population Reports*, Series P–60, No. 118 (Washington, D.C.: U.S. Government Printing Office, 1979), Table 51, pp. 212–215.

TABLE 13-3   Education and Median Income by Sex: Persons 18 Years Old and Over,
Year Round Fully Employed, 1977

Years of Schooling	Male	Female	Difference
Less than 8	$ 9,332	$ 6,022	$3,310
8	11,931	6,493	5,438
1–3 years high school	12,357	7,227	5,130
high school graduate	14,408	8,462	5,946
1–3 years college	15,548	9,471	6,077
college graduate	19,016	11,134	7,882
5 or more years of college	21,832	14,145	7,687

Source: Adapted from Bureau of the Census, *Money Income in 1977 of Families and Persons in the United States, Current Population Reports*, Series P–60, No. 118 (Washington, D.C.: U.S. Government Printing Office, 1979), Table 47, pp. 184–193.

quential that the median income of women with a college degree is even less than the median income of men with only eight years of formal education.

A second possible explanation for income differences between males and females is that the latter are more likely to work intermittently during their prime working years. As a result, women have less experience and less seniority, two prerequisites for mobility into higher-paying jobs. Suter and Miller conducted a study comparing men and women, ages thirty to forty-four, who worked steadily throughout their adult life.[20] By comparing women and men of equal education, occupational status, and work experiences, they were able to determine the differences in income that are probably the result of sexual discrimination. The data show that fully employed women, when compared to fully employed men, are consistently underpaid by thousands of dollars, even when equal in educational attainment or type of occupation. In a similar study, the Committee on the Status of Women of the American Economic Association surveyed a sample of Ph.D. economists, evenly divided by sex, by college, by year of degree, by continuity of experience, by research completed, and by specialization. Consistently, the women Ph.D. economists were 15 percent *below* that of their male peers in average income.[21] The conclusion, then, is inescapable: discrimination against women is a real and pervasive phenomenon.

Sexual Discrimination by Law

That the law has been discriminatory against women is beyond dispute. One need only to recall that women were specifically denied the right to vote prior to the 19th Amendment. Less well known, but very important, was the 1824 Mississippi Supreme Court decision upholding the right of husbands to beat their wives (the U.S. Supreme Court finally prohibited this practice in 1891). Another interesting case, which shows the bias of the legal system, was *Minor* v. *Happerset* (1874). Here the U.S. Supreme Court ruled that the "equal protection" clause of the 14th Amendment did not apply to women. Another ruling by the Supreme Court, at the time of the early feminist Susan B. Anthony, ruled that women are entitled to the right of counsel, but that it must be male counsel.

But legal discrimination against women is not limited to the distant past. Only in the past decade have major obstacles to equality been removed by new laws or court decisions. For example, sexist discrimination in the granting of credit has been ruled illegal; discrimination against pregnant women in the work force is now prohibited by law;[22] the structural bias against women has been removed by affirmative action; sexist discrimination in housing is prohibited; and the differential requirements by gender as traditionally practiced in the airline industry have been eliminated[23] (See Panel 13–4).

Legal discrimination remains, however, in a number of areas. There are still problems with Social Security and other pension programs. States vary considerably in their laws concerning property ownership by spouses, welfare benefits, and the legal status of homemakers. A major area of concern continues in the area of reproductive choice. In 1973 the Supreme Court ruled that a state could *not* prohibit any abortion during the first three months of pregnancy. During the second three months the state's only legal actions

---

Panel 13–4
Breakthroughs and Milestones Toward
Sexual Equity: 1970–1981

1970: Hawaii, Alaska, and New York become the first states to liberalize their abortion laws.
1970: The Department of Justice files first Title VII sex discrimination suit against Libby-Owens and the United Glass and Ceramic Workers.
1970: New York City is the first major city to pass a bill banning sex discrimination in public accommodations.
1970: First woman Lutheran pastor is ordained.
1971: U. S. Supreme Court rules that companies cannot refuse to hire mothers with small children unless the same policy applies to fathers.
1971: New York Board of Education votes to allow high school girls and boys to compete in noncontact sports.
1971: The University of Michigan becomes the first university to incorporate an affirmative action plan for hiring and promotion of women.
1971: The Boy Scouts of America admits girls into the Explorer Scout Division.
1972: Congress passes the ERA; Hawaii becomes the first state to ratify it.
1972: Title IX is passed prohibiting sex discrimination in federally assisted educational programs.
1973: The Supreme Court legalizes abortion.
1973: Women are admitted to the U. S. Coast Guard Officers-Candidate program.
1973: Men and women get equal prize money at the U. S. Open Tennis Tournament.
1973: The Supreme Court outlaws discrimination against women officers and their husbands in military benefits.
1973: The Federal Home Loan Bank Board bars sex bias by savings and loan associations.
1974: The Supreme Court outlaws mandatory maternity leaves for teachers.
1974: The Merchant Marine Academy admits women.
1974: National Little League Baseball, Inc. agrees to admit women.
1974: Housing and Community Development Act outlaws sex bias in housing.

regarding abortion may be related to regulations providing for safety in the abortion procedure. This controversial ruling was a major breakthrough for women, giving them the ultimate right to control their bodies. This principle has been reaffirmed by several later decisions by the Court (a major one occurred in 1979 when the court struck down a state law requring unwed women under the age of 18 to have the consent of their parents for an abortion). The Court ruled in 1980, however, that while a woman has the right to an abortion, she does not have a constitutional right to have the Federal government pay for it. This decision, which reaffirmed the 1976 Hyde Amendment passed by Congress, was a setback for abortion advocates because it made the option less likely for those women least able to afford children. The states have tended to pass similar laws restricting the use of state monies for abortion. These actions place a difficult burden on the poor who cannot afford the $150 to $300. In effect the denial of money to pay for the abortion is the

1974: McGraw-Hill publishes nonsexist guidelines for its nonfiction authors.

1974: Equal Credit Opportunity Act prohibits discrimination in credit on basis of sex or marital status.

1974: Lorene Rogers becomes the first woman president of a major university (University of Texas—Austin).

1975: The Supreme Court outlaws the automatic exclusion of women from jury duty.

1975: The Pentagon outlaws the automatic discharge of pregnant women from the armed services.

1975: Congress passes a bill requiring the service academies to admit women.

1976: The Supreme Court requires federal agencies to end discrimination in the industries they regulate.

1976: Barbara Walters signs $1 million contract with ABC.

1976: Janet Guthrie is the first woman driver to race in the Indianapolis 500.

1977: AT&T permits dual listings of married people in phone books.

1977: Women are assigned as permanent shipboard crew members by the Navy.

1978: Congress passes a bill prohibiting the introduction of the victim's reputation in cases of rape or attempted rape.

1978: Congress requires pregnancy disability benefits for pregnant workers.

1978: U. S. District Court rules that women sportswriters cannot be barred from major league baseball locker rooms.

1978: More women than men enter college for the first time in American history.

1979: The Supreme Court rules that welfare benefits must be paid to families left needy by the mother's loss of her job, just as to families with a father left unemployed.

1979: The Supreme Court rules in the Weber case that employers and unions can establish affirmative action programs including quotas.

1979: The Supreme Court rules that a minor has a constitutional right to an abortion.

1981: Sandra Day O'Connor becomes the first woman justice of the Supreme Court.

Source: Excerpts from Ellen Sweet, "A '70s Chronology," *Ms.* 8 (December 1979), pp. 60–94.

equivalent of denying the poor a legal abortion. Faced with this unsurmountable hurdle, the poor are forced to bear unwanted babies or try self-induced abortions. As one critic of these laws has argued:

> The practical consequence of the court's and Congress' actions is that thousands of poor women will again be forced to seek back-alley abortions or attempt self-induced ones, and that more thousands of children will be born annually to women who will need continuing public assistance to care for them. The situation is bound to lead to a rise in illegitimacy, child abuse, maternal and infant health problems and welfare cases. Justice Thurgood Marshall said as much in dissenting from the Supreme Court's majority opinion: The ruling will "brutally coerce poor women to bear children whom society will scorn," he said, "and will fall with great disparity on women of minority races" who obtain as many abortions as white women and depend more heavily on public medical care. Financially-secure women, of course, are unaffected by the Supreme Court ruling or congressional action They can afford to pay for abortions performed under decent conditions—just as they were able to travel to Europe or Scandinavia, if necessary, before abortion was legal in the United States.[24]

THE CONSEQUENCES OF SEXISM
FOR THE INDIVIDUAL

The society through cultural tyranny suppresses the choices of males and females. The socialization process forces males and females into those behavioral modes, personality characteristics, and occupational roles deemed appropriate by society. Most important, these constraints bring about a system that is biased in favor of males. Men possess power and status while women have inferior and supportive roles. Men have the opportunity to develop their talents fully while women may only within a severely limited range. In this section we shall enumerate the consequences of this pernicious system for individuals in American society.

Relative powerlessness of women. Women enjoy less political and economic power than their male counterparts. Politically, women are rarely found in elected positions.

In the world of work we have seen that women typically hold the less prestigious and authoritative jobs. They serve rather than lead. They are largely directed and supervised by men. Even in voluntary associations such as the church, women are generally excluded from leadership roles. They teach Sunday School classes while men preach and hold the positions of deacon, elder, and trustee.

Even within marriage, the spouses are unequal. Several studies note the strong tendency for husbands to dominate in the important areas (for example, job, moving, large purchases) while women make the lesser decisions on things such as food and choice of doctor.[25]

Limited range of occupations for women. Women in American society typically choose from a very narrow range of occupations. This limited choice for females is fostered, as we have seen in Chapter 7, by the attitudes of the family, children's books, and the school. The process is subtle but effective nevertheless. One study has shown, for instance, that by the fourth grade, girls essentially see four occupations for them—teacher, nurse, secretary, and mother. Boys of the same age, however, see the whole range of occupational opportunities open to them.[26]

Loss of academic potential for women. Because of the sex bias prevalent in American schools, many girls do not believe that they can compete with boys in college and graduate school. The evidence is that high school girls, although they achieve better grades than boys, are less likely to believe that they have the ability for college work. They are, therefore, less likely than boys to attend college and, if they do attend, to complete their degree. This is true even when comparing college males and females of equal intellectual ability.[27] This higher dropout rate continues in graduate school as well.[28] The reasons for the higher attrition rate for women are many: discrimination, marriage, parenthood, lack of commitment, felt necessity to work in order for their husband to complete his education (the reverse rarely happens), and low aspirations.[29] Most important, many women consider success and femininity to be incompatible.[30] All these factors imply the bias of the system that leads to many women dropping out of formal education prematurely, wasting their talents, and not qualifying for those careers highest in prestige, power, and financial rewards.

Lack of respect for women's abilities. A commonly held assumption is that women are not as talented as men in important areas such as creativity, decision making, mechanical aptitude, art, and intellectual activities. If personnel directors, administrators, publishers, and others who decide who is hired or not believe that women are inferior, then obviously men will receive preferential treatment. Several studies point to the existence of this bias against women.

In one study mythical biographies of young Ph.D.'s were sent to 228 colleges and universities. There were two forms, however. Half the candidates on Form A had female first names; the other half, male; on Form B the sexes were reversed. Administrators were asked at what rank they would hire these individuals. The results were that more jobs leading to tenure were suggested for the male versions of the mythical candidates, more "males" were thought to be eligible for the rank of full professor, and in 7 out of 8 cases more "men" than "women" were thought to be eligible for a post of associate professor.[31]

In another study men and women mental patients were asked if they would prefer a male or female psychotherapist. Interestingly, both sexes preferred a male psychotherapist. The reasons given by both men and women centered on such things as males having greater respect, competence, and authority. There was a specific fear and mistrust of women as authorities.[32] See Table 13–4 for the results of a nationwide Gallup Poll as to whether one would prefer to work for a man or woman boss for similar results.

The finding that men and women have more confidence in male psychotherapists supports the research of Goldberg, who found that even women have an antifemale prejudice. Goldberg asked college girls to read a number of articles and decide the extent to which the authors were good writers, experts, persuasive in their arguments, and so on. The students were given one of two forms. On each form half of the articles were written by a "male" and half by a "female," but the second form reversed the sexes of the authors. Invariably, the students ranked the "male" authors higher than the "female" authors even though, of course, the articles were identical.[33]

These studies show convincingly that men *and* women are biased against women and that this even affects perceptions. Clearly, the socialization process is powerful. Women

TABLE 13-4 *Question:* "If you were taking a new job and had your choice of a boss, would you prefer to work for a man or for a woman?"

	Among women (%)			Among men (%)		
	Man	Woman	No difference	Man	Woman	No difference
National	60	10	27	63	4	32
Race						
White	62	9	26	63	3	33
Nonwhite	38	20	37	63	11	25
Education						
College	50	10	39	60	3	36
High school	64	9	24	63	6	30
Grade school	59	13	23	69	1	29
Age						
Under 30	50	18	30	51	11	38
30–49 years	63	7	26	63	2	34
50 and older	63	8	26	72	1	25
Politics						
Republican	69	5	23	71	a	27
Democrat	58	13	26	66	3	30
Independent	55	10	32	59	6	35
Occupation						
Professional/Business	53	10	35	57	2	39
Clerical/sales	69	10	20	63	2	34
Manual workers	59	10	28	66	4	29

[a]Less than 1 percent.
Source: Gallup Opinion Index, Report No. 128 (March 1976), p. 45.

have been explicitly and implicitly taught to see themselves as inferior. This coupled with the predominance of males in positions of authority "proves" that women should not be taken seriously. Because women are rarely leaders, it is commonly assumed that they lack leadership qualities. As Kanter has put it:

The structure of power in organizations, rather than inherent sexual attitudes, can also explain why women sometimes appear to be less preferred as leaders. It is concluded that it is not the nature of women but hierarchical arrangements that must be changed if we are to promote equity in the workplace.[34]

Identity problem among women. Whereas leadership, intelligence, and aggressiveness are traits by which American males are judged competent or not, these are not relevant for the female. Her appearance is judged by many males to be more important in the business world than her intelligence or personality. Thus, she is considered a sexual object, not a person. Her achievements also make little difference for her social status depends on the achievements of her father, boyfriend, husband, and sons. As if in reinforcement of this, the prefix to the female's name indicates her married status, whereas the form of address for men is constant in American society. Moreover, women will most often be addressed as Mrs. Fred Smith, losing in marriage both first and last names. Society relates to the married woman not as an individual, but as a part of someone else. To combat this problem, the use of Ms. is increasing and many married women are retaining their maiden names.

Low self-esteem among women. An obvious consequence for the members of a social category that is thought to be intellectually inferior and who occupy the less-desirable and poorer-paying jobs is low self-esteem. Women face the same problems as other minority groups in this regard.

A study of adult men and women asked the respondents to select from a long list of adjectives those that most applied to themselves. The results were that adult females had acquired the expected self-image and that the personality traits comprising that image are the very ones that reduce one's chances of success in the occupational world.

The results showed that women strongly felt that they could accurately be described as uncertain, anxious, nervous, hasty, careless, fearful, dull, childish, helpless, sorry, timid, clumsy, stupid, silly and domestic. On the more positive side women felt they were understanding, tender, sympathetic, pure, generous, affectionate, loving, moral, kind, grateful and patient. This is not a very favorable self-image, but it does correspond fairly well to the myths about what women are like. The image has some "nice" qualities, but they are not the ones normally required for the kinds of achievement to which society gives its highest rewards.[35]

High self-esteem for women is typically associated with beauty. Women, consequently, tend to spend enormous amounts of time and resources to enhance their beauty (see Panel 13–5). Women are taught that

their looks are a commodity to be bartered in exchange for a man, not only for food, clothing, and shelter, but for love. Women learn early that if you are unlovely, you are unloved. The homely girl prepares to be an old maid, because beauty is what makes a man fall in love. . . . Don't we all think it strange when a man marries a girl who isn't pretty and not at all strange when he marries a dumb beauty? Is it therefore surprising that even the great beauty fears a man's love will not survive her looks, and the average woman is convinced that no man can really love her? How can he love her when she lacks what is needed to produce love? That is why she so desperately keeps up her looks and feels that although all the kids have measles, she ought to greet her husband with her beauty mask on.[36]

A major consequence of this obsession with beauty is that women will increasingly feel insecure and anxious as they age.[37]

Trials of the aging woman. Middle-aged and older women in American society face two problems from which men are relatively exempt. These are the loss of sexual attractiveness and the loss of their primary role—the bearing and raising of children. Let's examine these in turn.

Given the occupational patterns in American society, men generally gain in prestige and power as they age. They, therefore, tend to retain or even enhance their attractiveness to women. The reverse, however, is not the case. As one observer has said, "Women get wrinkles. Men's faces are 'lined with character.' "[38] The result is that widowed or divorced

CROSS-CULTURAL PANEL

Panel 13–5
The Cross-Cultural Search for Beauty by Women

She then begins woman's frantic pursuit of beauty, for she has read in innumerable ads that "every woman has the right to be beautiful. Makeup is magic! It can transform you, create the illusion of perfect feminine loveliness that every woman longs for." In every new jar of face cream, box of powder, tube of lipstick, mascara, eyeliner, she expects to find the magic formula that will transform her into a beauty. Every change of hairdo, every padded bra, every girdle, every pair of high heels or sandals, every mini skirt or midi skirt, every tight sweater or sack dress will somehow make her glamourous, captivating. She never gives up. Her blue hair waved, circles of rouge on her wrinkled cheeks, lipstick etching the lines around her mouth, still moisturizing her skin nightly, still corseted, she dies.

For centuries, in the pursuit of beauty, Chinese women used to bind their feet, trying to compress them to the ideal three inches. To achieve this ideal beauty, no suffering was too great. At about the age of four, a girl's feet were bandaged; the toes were pulled backward so tightly that blood and pus later oozed from the bandages, a toe or two might fall off, and death from gangrene was possible. If a girl survived, she would never be able to walk freely again without a cane or the support of attendants. But the excruciating pain and the loss of freedom were worth it, for the tinier her feet, the richer the husband she might get. She might also win first prize in one of the many tiny-foot beauty contests. All ladies had bound feet; it was fashionable; natural feet were ugly; only tiny feet were beautiful.

Not long ago when narrow-toed shoes were fashionable, many women had their little toes amputated so their feet would more comfortably fit the shoes. These women were like Cinderella's sisters, one of whom cut her big toe and the

men tend to remarry younger women. Widowed or divorced women either remain single or marry older men. Consequently, although the male–female ratio is approximately 1:1 in the 45 to 64 age bracket, there are three times as many single, divorced, and widowed women as there are single, divorced, and widowed men in that age category.

The second age-related problem for women occurs when their children leave home. This stage is critical for a woman who has been a totally committed "supermother." Her life has been one of self-sacrifice devoted to raising her children. Now, sometime between the ages of 40 and 59 her last child leaves home and she is faced with another 30 years or so of life void of a role that was all-consuming. Menopause thus becomes a special problem for American women, not only because of the hormone changes taking place, but because it represents symbolically their decline into "uselessness" or perhaps their realization of wasted potential. This empty-nest syndrome is a common source of depression among middle-aged women. This depression can result from several related factors.[39]

One source of depression is that women going through this transition period are presented no guidelines for dealing with their situation. There are no *rites de passage*. As Pauline Bart has put it, "There is no bar mitzvah for menopause."[40] Thus, women who

other the back of her heel in order to fit the glass slipper. These are extremes, perhaps, but few women alive today have not subjected themselves to the discomfort
of high heels, which produce such deformities as calluses, corns, bunions, clawed
toes, unduly high arches, and secondary shortening of the calf muscles, deformities
different only in degree from those of the bound foot.

In China it used to be said that a girl had to suffer twice—she had to have her
ears pierced and her feet bound. But today a girl in her first pair of high heels will
rarely admit that her feet hurt; almost every girl begs to have her ears pierced and
does not think of it as suffering or mutilation. Apparently, the pursuit of beauty is
a great anesthetic. Older women used to wince bravely as they plucked their eye-
brows, and who can doubt that if it became fashionable, many women would
pluck out every eyebrow hair, as Japanese women did not long ago. As it is,
women merely razor off the "unfeminine" hair on their legs and under their arms.
The women unlucky enough to have "masculine" facial hair endure the pain of
electrolysis; millions of women undergo surgery to have their freckles burnt off,
their skin peeled, their faces lifted, their noses reshaped, their breasts filled with sil-
icone. Millions of women wear tight girdles, live for weeks on celery and beef
broth, or sweat in gyms, or if rich, subject themselves to the luxurious rigors of a
beauty farm, just to keep thin. It is now fashionable to be thin, but if it were fashionable to be fat, women would force-feed themselves like geese, just as girls in
primitive societies used to stuff themselves because the fattest girl was the most
beautiful. If the eighteen-inch waist should ever become fashionable again, women
would suffer the tortures of tight lacing, convinced that though one dislocated
one's kidneys, crushed one's liver, and turned green, beauty was worth it all.

Source: Excerpted from Una Stannard, "The Mask of Beauty," in *Woman in Sexist Society*, Vivian Gornick and Barbara K. Moran, eds. (New York: Basic Books, 1971),
pp. 188–190. Copyright © 1971 by Basic Books Inc., Publishers, New York.

have spent their lives carrying out culturally defined tasks (e.g., raising and nurturing a
family) are now faced with a relative absence of societal expectations for them. Durkheim
called this condition of normlessness "anomie" and a prime source of suicide.[41]

Another source of depression, already alluded to, also stems from the loss of the
all-important role for women in American society of mother. There is a tendency for a
mother to expect her adult children to act as they did when they were children once
dependent on her. "To the extent that they no longer act this way, she is likely to feel
resentful; since . . . a woman is not 'allowed' to be hostile toward her children, she may turn
her resentment inward and become depressed."[42]

The third reason depression can result from the loss of the mother role is because of the
ensuing loss of self-esteem. Many in this condition feel a sense of worthlessness and
uselessness.

Pauline Bart made a serious study of menopause in a variety of societies and concluded
that: "Depressions in middle-aged women are due to their lack of important roles and
subsequent loss of self-esteem, rather than the hormonal changes in the menopause."[43]
The key, then, to psychic stress among middle-aged women is loss of the primary role of

mother with dependent children. Depression caused by role loss is found similarly in men but at retirement age. Since the primary role of the male in our society is occupational, retirement from that role leads to anomie, loss of self-esteem, and feelings of uselessness.

THE SOCIOECONOMIC–POLITICAL CONSEQUENCES OF SEXISM

If women are systematically kept from jobs requiring leadership, creativity, and productivity, the economy will obviously suffer. It will suffer because the pool of talent consisting of half of the population is underutilized and underproductive—in effect, constituting a massive "brain drain" for the society. This potential for creativity and leadership is lost because of the barriers that keep women "in their place." As one observer has summarized it:

Any society that ascribes low status to some of its members on such arbitrary grounds as race, caste, or sex is artifically restricting the economic contribution of part of the population. To be fully efficient, a modern industrial economy must allow social mobility on the grounds of merit, not restrict it on the grounds of an irrational, ascribed status.[44]

The economy is also negatively affected when the 50 percent of adult women who work outside the home are underpaid. This artificially reduces the gross national product, prosperity, and tax revenues.

An additional cost to society occurs as an oppressed minority becomes increasingly aware of its plight and faces the resistance of the majority. As the "consciousness is raised" for millions of women, the society and the economy are weakened because of the ensuing strikes, lawsuits, and other disruptive occurrences.

The Women's Movement

Sex-based inequality in the United States has led to a growing social movement dedicated to sexual equality. Feminists have organized in this country to overcome sexual discrimi-

SOCIAL DILEMMAS AND CRITICAL CHOICES

Panel 13–6
The Goals and Tactics of the Women's Movement

What is your position on improving the status of women? If you seek continued change, do you favor something close to an androgynous society where the sex-role differences between men and women would become blurred, or do you prefer leaving some sex-role differences undisturbed but pushing for a real equality between the sexes?

These preferences will somewhat influence the kind of movement for women's rights that you might support. Assuming that you might support some such

nation for over 150 years. Over the years the issues have been voting rights, dress, discriminatory laws, educational reform, working conditions, and job discrimination. Although there were notable successes—especially the passage of the 19th Amendment granting women the right to vote—progress was painfully slow until the 1960s.

The early activities by feminists, along with a number of other factors, set the stage for the dramatic changes of the past two decades.[45]

1. The traditional argument—that men must be dominant because work tasks require strength—was weakened by technological advances. In a mechanical and computerized age, strength obviously has given way to talents and skills unrelated to muscle.

2. Technology also released women from the confines of the home and child rearing. Contraceptive techniques made the controlling of family size and the spacing of children a reality. The result was smaller families. Also the role of wife, mother, and homemaker became less time consuming than in previous generations because of labor-saving devices. Women were thereby freed to become more involved in activities outside the home.

3. Since World War II more and more women were completing high school and college. The steady rise in the education of women coupled with a lack of improvement in economic rewards led to an increased number of persons with a type of status inconsistency (high investment—education—with relatively low rewards—occupational prestige and money) conducive to blaming outside forces for their plight rather than themselves.

4. Also since World War II increased numbers of women were employed in the labor force. These women discovered firsthand the reality of receiving disproportionately lower pay than men for similar work and the artificial ceilings placed on their advancement.

5. The civil rights movement of the 1960s spread the ideology of equality. This movement was instrumental in pointing to the previously unexamined and unrecognized inequities in society (at least by the middle and upper classes) and to the fact that the power structure was impervious to change unless the powerless organized.

---

movement, here are some choices you might have to make: Should the target be the change of people's attitudes or the change of the structure of society? The former requires efforts at "consciousness raising," propaganda, education, and other techniques designed to alter the attitudes of men and women, making them receptive to change. If, however, the choice is a change in laws and customs, the tactics demand political pressure, the election of sympathetic candidates, the passage of appropriate legislation, and court suits. And, if the normal legislative and judicial channels prove too slow or unyielding, one must decide whether the use of nonviolent resistance or even violence is justified.

So, in sum, which goal of the feminist movement do you favor? Just how committed are you to that goal? Can you suggest your own version of tactics that are appropriate to reach that goal?

6. The government's actions in the conduct of the Vietnam war caused many persons to question existing power relationships and established authority.
7. Writers and researchers also fed the resentment that many women felt by providing the data on such things as wage differentials between men and women and pointing out the sexist stereotypes that permeate the English language, and other manifestations of a sexist society.

All these forces converged to develop a **"class consciousness"** among millions of American women. These women perceived the same sources of injustice, they experienced similar feelings of hatred and resentment, and they felt a common urgency to change an unjust system. "Consciousness-raising" sessions occurred spontaneously among neighbors, colleagues, and in various organizations to air grievances, share experiences, and to plan strategies to cope with and to change the system. Formal organizations such as the National Organization of Women (NOW) emerged to lead the efforts to bring about societal-wide changes. Although these organizations often disagreed on tactics, they sought a common goal—equality.

During the 1960s and 1970s profound changes occurred to reduce but not fully eliminate sexual inequalities in the society. Many sexist laws were stricken from the law books. The government insisted on fair employment practices for hiring and compensation for all minorities (Affirmative Action). The government also demanded that schools provide equal facilities and experiences for boys and girls (Title IX). Predictably, these changes have been met by resistance from many men. The powerful rarely, if ever, give up their advantages without struggle. Curiously, many women have joined forces with men to resist the changes demanded by feminists (most notably fighting to defeat passage of the Equal Rights Amendment).[46] These "traditional women" favor the status quo. They provide testimony for the power of the socialization process. They are comfortable with and seek to retain sexual inequality, for this is viewed as "natural." Early in this book we used the following metaphor, borrowed from Peter Berger. Berger pointed out that society is like a prison, with the inmates, because of the power of the socialization process, busy keeping up its walls. These traditional women illustrate this principle very well. But the prison and the socialization process are not all powerful, as the existence and the persistence of the feminists attest.

SUMMARY

There are clear expectations for the behavior, feelings, personality, and occupational aspirations of persons based on gender. While this appears to be a universal process in human societies, the bases for the differences are social, not biological. The socialization process is a powerful force that influences most of us to conform to society's expectations. But these socially determined differences are detrimental to women. Men lead, women follow. Men are independent, women dependent. Success in the occupational world is reserved for men, and only indirectly devolves upon their wives. Women are paid less than men for equal work.

A sexist society has damaging consequences for women and the larger society. The personal penalties are low self-esteem, feelings of powerlessness, failure to attain full potential in school and work, and a relatively high probability of depression. Society is harmed by the underdevelopment of half of the population. This affects the economy as well as social relationships.

The many manifestations of inequality present in a sexist society have led many women to organize and use a variety of tactics, from violent confrontations to court cases to change society. Order theorists interpret these activities as harmful to society because they disrupt order and stability. Conflict theorists, on the other hand, applaud such behavior because it reflects the recognition that stable societal arrangements are themselves social problems. The social structure, in this view, is the problem, not aberrant women.

CHAPTER REVIEW

1. There is considerable evidence that American society is in a transitional stage regarding sex roles. Many gains for women have been achieved but men remain dominant. Gender continues to determine access to power, prestige, and privilege.

2. Order theorists view sexual stratification as natural and necessary. It is natural because men are physically stronger and only women can have children. Sexual stratification is necessary because society needs a division of labor. Traditional sex roles provide order for society and stable families. If gender did not serve as a guide to behavior, order theorists contend, people would be left without direction, causing mental anguish and anomie.

3. Conflict theorists view sexual stratification as a division of labor based on the domination of men and the exploitation and oppression of women. Society is structured through the various institutions to perpetuate male superiority. Women are deprived of power and economic rewards, just as any minority group. The work typically done by women is devalued and underpaid. Regardless of the work they do, women are generally accorded the status of their husbands, a practice that stems from the patriarchal family and the conception of the wife as the property of her husband.

4. Sex-linked discrimination takes several forms: derogation, low prestige and paying jobs outside

the home, demeaning housework inside the home, and a biased legal system.

5. Living in a sexist society has negative consequences for women: (a) they are relatively powerless; (b) their academic potential is lost; (c) their abilities are not respected; (d) they have an identity problem; and (e) they have low self-esteem.

6. The negative consequences of sexism for women heighten as women age. This is because they face two problems from which aging men are relatively exempt—the loss of sexual attractiveness, and the loss of their primary role of bearing and raising children.

7. The negative consequences of sexual stratification for the economy are significant. Most important the economy suffers as half of the population is underutilized, underproductive, and underpaid.

8. Although the feminist movement has been active in the United States for over 150 years, a number of social and historical factors have converged in the last two decades to give it momentum. These forces have led to a "class consciousness" among millions of women.

9. There are, however, millions of women who oppose equality for women. This demonstrates the power of the socialization process and false consciousness.

FOR FURTHER STUDY

Simone de Beauvoir, *The Second Sex* (New York: Knopf, 1953).

Jo Freeman, *The Politics of Women's Liberation: A Case Study of an Emerging Social Movement and Its Relation to the Policy Process* (New York: McKay, 1975).

Betty Friedan, *The Feminine Mystique* (New York: Norton, 1963).

Nona Glazer and Helen Y. Waehrer (eds.), *Woman in a Man-Made World* (Chicago: Rand McNally, 1977).

Germaine Greer, *The Female Eunuch* (New York: McGraw-Hill, 1971).

Charlotte G. O'Kelly, *Women and Men in Society* (New York: D. Van Nostrand, 1980).

Alice Schlegel (ed.), *Sexual Stratification: A Cross-Cultural View* (New York: Columbia University Press, 1977).

Jean Stockard and Miriam M. Johnson, *Sex Roles* (Englewood Cliffs, N.J.: Prentice-Hall, 1980).

NOTES AND REFERENCES

1. See "The Decade of Women," *Ms.* 8 (December, 1979), pp. 59–94.

2. The following discussion is taken from Alice Schlegel, "Toward a Theory of Sexual Stratification," in *Sexual Stratification: A Cross-Cultural View*, Alice Schlegel, ed. (New York: Columbia University Press, 1977), pp. 5–9.

3. Ibid., p. 8.

4. Talcott Parsons, Robert F. Bales, et al., *Family, Socialization and Interaction Process* (New York: Free Press, 1955), pp. 3–9.

5. Charlotte G. O'Kelly, *Women and Men in Society* (New York: D. Van Nostrand, 1980), p. 56.

6. Ibid., p. 46. This is a paraphrase of Friedrich Engels' theory of the family in Karl Marx and Friedrich Engels, "The Communist Manifesto," in *Marx and Engels, Selected Works in Two Volumes*, Vol. 1 (Moscow: Foreign Language Publishing House, 1958). For a contemporary major contribution to the conflict view of sex roles see Randall Collins, "A Conflict Theory of Sexual Stratification," *Social Problems* 19 (Summer 1971), pp. 3–21.

7. James William Coleman and Donald R. Cressy, *Social Problems* (New York: Harper & Row, 1980), p. 283.

8. See Christine Moschese, "The Ethnic Image in the Media: Ethnic Men and Particularly, Women Suffer from Typecasting, When Cast at All," *Civil Rights Digest* 11 (Fall 1978), pp. 28–34; and Civil Rights Commission, *Window Dressing on the Set: An Update* (Washington, D.C.: U.S. Government Printing Office, 1979).

9. Civil Rights Commission, *Characters in Textbooks: A Review of the Literature*, Clearinghouse Publication 62 (Washington, D.C.: U.S. Government Printing Office, 1980), pp. 10–12).

10. Lucy Komisar, "The Image of Women in Advertising," in *Woman in Sexist Society: Studies in Power and Powerlessness*, Vivian Gornick and Barbara K. Moran, eds. (New York: Basic Books, 1971), p. 307. Excerpts from this work are printed by permission of the publisher; © 1971 by Basic Books, Inc., Publishers, New York.

11. Carole Lopate, "Pay for Homework?" *Social Policy* 5 (September/October, 1974), p. 27.

12. Cited in Ellen Goodman, "What Our Daughters Have 'Chosen,'" *Rocky Mountain News* (November 23, 1976), p. 40.

13. Joseph H. Pleck, "The Work-Family Role System," *Social Problems* 24 (April, 1977), pp. 417–427. See also, Caryl Rivers, "Egalitarian Marriage: No More Ring Around the Collar," *Mother Jones* 2 (November, 1977), pp. 39–48.

14. "The Superwoman Squeeze," *Newsweek* (May 19, 1980), pp. 72–79; and Ellen Goodman, "Superwoman Myth Exploding," *Rocky Mountain News*, (December 22, 1979), p. 59.

15. Philippa Strum, "Pink Collar Blues: For

Women Who Work, It Still Doesn't Add Up," *The Civil Rights Quarterly Perspectives* 12 (Summer 1980), p. 34; and "Women Have Their Day in Court—as Lawyers," *U.S. News & World Report* (November 17, 1980), pp. 86–87.

16. Michelle Patterson, "Sex and Specialization in Academe and the Professions," in *Academic Women on the Move*, Alice S. Rossi and Ann Calderwood, eds. (New York: Russell Sage Foundation, 1973), pp. 313–331; and Pamela Avery, "Women Doctors Find Door to Surgery Closed," *Rocky Mountain News* (December 8, 1977), pp. 11–12c. See also Jill Quadagno, "Occupational Sex-Typing and Internal Labor Market Distributions: An Assessment of Medical Specialties," *Social Problems* 23 (April, 1976), pp. 442–453.

17. Strum, "Pink Collar Blues," p. 35.

18. Ibid., p. 33.

19. Ibid., pp. 33–37.

20. Larry E. Suter and Herman P. Miller, "Income Differentials Between Men and Career Women," *American Journal of Sociology* 78 (January, 1973), pp. 962–974. See also, William P. Bridges and Richard A. Berk, "Sex, Earnings, and the Nature of Work; A Job-level Analysis of Male-Female Income Differences," *Social Science Quarterly* 58 (March, 1978), pp. 553–565.

21. Reported in Strum, "Pink Collar Blues," p. 34.

22. See Peg Simpson, "A Victory for Women," *Civil Rights Digest* 11 (Spring 1979), pp. 13–21.

23. Alexsandra Lett and Harold Silverman, "Coffee, Tea and Dignity," *Civil Rights Quarterly Perspectives* 12 (Spring 1980), pp. 4–11.

24. Anthony C. Beilenson, "Equal Protection Is Threatened," *Los Angeles Times* (July 17, 1977), p. 1, Part VIII.

25. See Robert O. Blood, Jr., and Donald M. Wolfe, *Husbands and Wives: The Dynamics of Married Living* (New York: Free Press, 1960); and Dair L. Gillespie, "Who Has the Power? The Marital Struggle," *Journal of Marriage and the Family* 33 (August, 1971), pp. 445–458.

26. Robert O'Hara, "The Roots of Careers," *Elementary School Journal* 62 (February,

1962), pp. 277–280. For a study of sex differences among adolescents, see Judy Corder Tully, Cookie Stephan, and Barbara J. Chance, "The Status of Sex-Typed Dimensions of Occupational Aspirations in Young Adolescents," *Social Science Quarterly* 56 (March, 1976), pp. 638–649.

27. See Patricia Cross, "College Women: A Research Description," *Journal of Association of Women Deans and Counselors* 32 (Autumn, 1968), pp. 12–21; and Michelle Patterson and Lucy Sells, "Women Dropouts from Higher Education," *Academic Women on the Move*, pp. 79–91.

28. Patterson and Sells, "Women Dropouts," pp. 79–91; and Marilyn Mercer, "Sex Discrimination in Graduate Schools: How It Operates, and What You Can Do about It," *Glamour* (August, 1970), pp. 190–191, 246.

29. See Leonard L. Baird, Mary Jo Clark, and Rodney T. Harnett, *The Graduates* (Princeton, N.J.: Educational Testing Service, 1973).

30. Matina S. Horner, "Fail: Bright Women," *Psychology Today* 3 (November, 1969), pp. 36ff.

31. A study by Linda Fidell, cited in Mercer, "Sex Discrimination in Graduate Schools," pp. 190–191, 246.

32. Phyllis Chesler, "Patient and Patriarch: Women in the Psychotherapeutic Relationship," *Women in Sexist Society*, pp. 362–392.

33. Philip Goldberg, "Are Women Prejudiced against Women?" *Trans-action* 5 (April, 1968), pp. 28–30.

34. Rosabeth Moss Kanter, "The Impact of Hierarchical Structures on the Work Behavior of Women and Men," *Social Problems* 23 (April, 1976), p. 415.

35. Jo Freeman, "Growing Up Girlish," *Trans-action* 8 (November/December, 1970), p. 37.

36. Una Stannard, "The Mask of Beauty," *Woman in Sexist Society*, pp. 195–196.

37. For a novel that portrays this anxiety in the aging beauty, see Alix Kates Shulman, *Memoirs of an Ex-Prom Queen* (New York: Bantam Books, 1973).

38. Arthur J. Snider, "Trials of the Aging Woman," *Kansas City Times*, November 16, 1973.

39. The following is taken primarily from Pauline B. Bart, "Depression in Middle-Aged

Women," *Woman in Sexist Society*, pp. 163–186.

40. Bart, "Depression in Middle-Aged Women," p. 169.

41. Emile Durkheim, *Suicide*, John A. Spaulding and George Simpson, trans. (New York: Free Press, 1951), pp. 241–276. This book was first published in 1897.

42. Bart, "Depression in Middle-Aged Women," p. 170.

43. Ibid., p. 176.

44. Ian Robertson, *Sociology* (New York: Worth Publishers, 1977), p. 306.

45. William J. Goode, *Principles of Sociology* (New York: McGraw-Hill, 1977), pp. 356–361.

46. See Andrew Hacker, "E.R.A.—R.I.P." *Harper's* 261 (September, 1980), pp. 10–14.

Part IV
Social Institutions

14

The American Family

Everyone admired Joyce and Mike. They had a good marriage. They went skiing, golfing, and jogging together. And they had equal and interesting careers. She taught history in the local community college, and he owned the local sporting goods store.

Everything was fine until Joyce was promoted to dean at a salary that topped Mike's take from the store.

Neither of them thought it would make a difference, and at first it didn't. But as the work piled up, Joyce began to feel guilty about the cleaning she couldn't get done and the fancy meals she no longer had time to cook. Mike didn't bother to reassure her. On the contrary, he seemed to enjoy her guilt and even encourage it.

Eventually, he began to grumble about how nice things "used to be" when meals were on time, when the "poor dog" was taken to be groomed on a regular basis, in "the days before there was dust." And he began to find all sorts of little ways to show that he was still the boss.

Sometimes, for instance, he would demand sex when he knew she was tired. "What's the matter?" he would say if she refused. "Don't you love me any more?" It was as if he refused to recognize that anything had changed to give her a right to be tired.

When they went skiing, he spoiled the fun by becoming competitive with her, as if to prove that he was stronger and better. He would insist, for instance, on skiing the only one out of thirty-five slopes that was too hard for her. Not only did

that mean that they had to ski separate slopes, but he seemed more interested in proving something about himself than in sharing the pleasure with her.

The strain began to show in social situations. He started cracking jokes at Joyce's expense.

As it often does, the first verbal hostility was in humor. "What can I say?" he once cracked. "She makes more money than I."

"Yes, Madam Dear," he once said mockingly when she asked him to refill her drink while he was refilling his.

At home, Mike lost interest in Joyce's work as she had every reason to become more interested in it. He refused, for instance, even to read a newspaper article about one of her projects which had attracted a great deal of attention among their friends. When they brought it up, he just shrugged and said he hadn't had time yet to read it. The implication, of course, was that his own career was absorbing him totally.

Joyce pretended not to notice these digs. She hoped they would go away. Instead they got worse. Finally she could take it no longer. As she later put it, "Something inside of me snapped."

Source: Caroline Bird, *The Two-Paycheck Marriage: How Women at Work Are Changing Life in America* (New York: Pocket Books, 1979, pp. 74–76. Reprinted by permission from Rawson, Wade Publishers, Inc.

Social institutions are conservative. They serve to maintain society by clinging to proven patterns which ensure that certain important goals of the society are accomplished. The institution of the family (the stable arrangements of marriage, child rearing, and kinship relations) is foremost among the institutions in meeting the basic societal problems of stability and continuity. The family, for example, provides a regular input of new members to the society, who are physically and emotionally cared for in a stable environment. Most important, these new members will learn the society's culture primarily through the family. Family members act as a primary source of pressure on individuals to keep them within the behavioral limits prescribed by society, thus performing an important social control function.

Another function of the family, which serves to perpetuate the status quo, is that it is the primary agent of social location. Membership in a family, involuntary though it may be, automatically confers the family's social status to each offspring. Not only is status transmitted, but also wealth and property and the benefits that they can purchase ("life chances"; see Chapter 10). The family, then, is a primary source for the perpetuation of social inequality. From the standpoint of the society this is useful because it prevents chaos. People will automatically know their place, hence, stability will tend to prevail.

All known societies have rules (formal and informal) regarding the family to regulate and determine morality, responsibility for children, accessibility of marriage partners, type of marriages, line of descent, and other functions. The range of variation found around the world in each of these areas is staggering. For instance, some societies allow a plurality of wives, while others favor a plurality of husbands. Most commonly, the biological parents are responsible for the nurture of their children, but some societies demand that the biological mother and the maternal uncle will raise the child while the biological father cares for the children of his sister. Some societies forbid marriage partners from visiting or even seeing each other from a distance until the actual wedding ceremony. Although these customs may seem weird to Americans, they are normal to those practicing them. The important factor is not the variation, but rather that all societies have found it necessary to have rules regarding marriage and the raising of children. The primary task of this chapter will be to describe the typical American family patterns. This will be followed by a discussion of the American family of the future.

There is great risk in attempting to describe any American institution, since there is so much diversity. With respect to the family, there are regional, social-class, religious, and ethnic differences. Additionally, each family unit may have its own idiosyncratic role expectations, mode of socialization, and rules. Thus, the reader should remember that the description of the American family presented here is of the typical family. By necessity, such a description must be done with "broad brush strokes." Although subject to oversimplification, the description of the American family is important, because it will help us understand why Americans are the way they are and why they differ from persons in other societies.

American family customs, when compared with the family customs of other societies, are characterized by considerable freedom.[1] One instance of relative autonomy is that the American family is unusually equalitarian. Although there is a tendency for the male parent to be considered the head of the household, most families are relatively democratic. Certainly, there is wide variation by family unit in type of power arrangement.

An important source of freedom in American society is that Americans leave their families when they reach adulthood and set up their own nuclear family. Often there is a great distance from one's own home to that of one's parents. Thus, grown children are no longer under the direct influence of their parents, as is the case in many societies where there are extended families.

Characteristic of the American system is the free choice of mates. Unlike most societies where marriage is arranged by parents on practical grounds, Americans are free to "fall in love" with whomever they please. This freedom is, in part, illusory because there are social pressures that guide the selection process. Persons tend to marry individuals similar to themselves in social class, religion, race, and level of education (this tendency for like to marry like is called **homogamy**. This freedom is also illusory because what individuals perceive as desirable characteristics in the opposite sex are affected greatly by the values of one's parents, peers, and the influence of the media. Despite these constraints on mate selection, the individual is considered "free" to marry his or her choice, providing that party is also willing.

Finally, there is relative freedom of choice within each American family in the exact arrangements (rights, duties, obligations, spheres of authority, division of labor) between the husband and wife. The lack of the formalized and detailed blueprint for family roles found in some other societies is a source of strain in many marriages. With each change in family situation (e.g., moving to a new neighborhood, working a different shift, the arrival of children) there must be decisions about allocation of duties and expectations. While many of these decisions occur automatically, others create conflicts.

The relative freedom of choice that occurs in most American families is a mixed blessing. It can create ambiguities, strain, and conflict. Much of this freedom results from the relative isolation of each family unit from any larger kin group. This autonomy, while refreshing at times, means that many of society's most basic burdens (economic, emotional, and physical) must be borne by the nuclear family. The result is a relatively high rate of family instability (a topic to be covered later in the chapter), mental illness, and alienation.

THE AMERICAN FAMILY: PAST AND PRESENT

The nuclear family (parents and non-adult children living together) has prevailed in both pre-industrial times and under current conditions.[2] There are major differences, though, between families of 1800, 1900, and the 1980s. Families of the past were more likely than those of the present ot have a kinship group extending beyond the household living nearby. The presence of an extended family provided members with emotional and physical support, often lacking in today's mobile society. Today's family, however, has more freedom because of its isolation, which can be a blessing or a curse.

The family of the past was larger than today. The number of children was dramatically higher. In 1800 the average adult woman had seven children, in 1900 she had 4.7 children, while today the average number is less than two. This decline is the result of several factors: (1) In an urban setting children are a liability, rather than the asset they would represent in a rural setting. In 1980 the average cost of raising a child from infancy to age 18 for a mid-income family was $85,000—a serious constraint on large families.[3] (2) The almost universal employment of family planning techniques ensures that families can have just the number of children they want. The liberalization of abortion laws also limits family size.

Panel 14-1
The Baganda of Uganda

Polygyny is the dominant form of marriage among the Baganda of central Africa. Because wives are expensive, the wealthier the man, the more wives he will have (the king, for example, will have hundreds of wives, while commoners only two or three).

Polygyny is most logical in a society where females outnumber males, which is true for the Baganda among whom the ratio is about three females to one male. The reasons for this imbalance are the occasional practice of male infanticide, wanton executions of law violators, human sacrifice, and nearly continuous warfare with neighboring tribes.

The Baganda are farmers with a fairly high standard of living. Wives are considered a source of income and therefore a form of investment because wives do all of the cultivation work. Wives are purchased (usually at age 13 or 14) with a bride price. When a male chooses a mate, he visits the girl's brother and maternal

The family of the eighteenth and nineteenth centuries was composed of members considerably younger than is typical today. This was the result of a relatively low life expectancy. In 1900, for example, men lived for an average of 48 years and women 51 years compared to 69 and 77, respectively, today. This meant that the possibility of ties between several generations was lower in the past. The increased longevity of marriage partners today is one of the reasons for a higher divorce rate. In 1890 the average wife was a widow when her last child left home for marriage. By 1960 the average couple lived 15 years together in an "empty nest" after the last child left home. By 1970 they lived closer to 30 years together (increases in life expectancy and tendency for women to have all their children before age 30). This long time together with the concomitant shift in roles (especially for the female) places increased burdens on the marriage bond.

The family is less stable today in at least two respects. First, the family members are apart a good deal and are increasingly under the influence of constraints from other sectors (organizations, professions, peer groups). Second, and often related to the first, is the instability of marriage itself. Today the divorce rate is considerably higher (as will be documented later in this chapter) than in the past, when divorce was relatively rare. There is no evidence, however, that families were any happier then than they are now. The constraints of religion, community, and family made divorce an unacceptable option in the past even for incompatible couples.

Cultural beliefs concerning marriage and the family have shifted appreciably in the past 200 years. For most of American history the following beliefs were accepted virtually without question:[4]

1. Adults should be married.
2. Marriage was a lifelong commitment.
3. Sexual intercourse was limited to marital partners.

uncle. He offers a package of salt and if they accept this gift, then they have tentatively approved the match. Beer is served to the brother and uncle. The uncle asks the prospective bride if he should drink the beer. If she agrees, then this ratifies the marriage.

The uncle negotiates the bride price, which usually involves animals and money. The price is typically more than a young man can afford so there is a period, often lasting a year or so, when the groom is separated from his wife-to-be while he gathers the required amount. When the bride price is paid and divided among the bride's relatives, the wedding takes place. Divorce and the remarriage of widows is possible provided that the woman's relatives refund the bride price to the original husband or his family.

The wife's duties are to have children and to work. Her primary task is to cultivate her part of the family garden which means physical work from sunrise to dark. The male, in sharp constrast, works but a few hours a day at hunting, fishing, or clearing land, which is considered appropriate given his status relative to the female. The wife is expected to have many children, who, by the way, will be raised by their maternal uncles (and their uncles' wives). A well-to-do commoner may have as many as fifty children from his several wives. Large family size, promoted by polygyny, is not a problem because the land is fertile and plentiful.

4. Married couples should have children.
5. Parents should be responsible to their children at whatever cost and children should be obedient to their parents.
6. A wife's place was at home.
7. There was a sharp division of labor between men and women inside and outside the home.
8. The husband and father was the ultimate decision-maker.

These traditional beliefs, while still held by many, are under serious attack by many others today. Many adults opt not to marry. Some who marry choose to remain childless, a choice that would have brought social ostracism in the past. Divorce has become an acceptable option for troubled families. Sexual activity before marriage is now the norm. Marital infidelity is widespread. The majority of wives now work outside the home.

The relationship between the spouses is increasingly egalitarian in American society. In the past most families were **patriarchal**. Most homes today are relatively democratic. A good case can be made for a *de facto* **matriarchy** occurring in many homes because the father is absent so much of the time—in the well-to-do suburbs or the slums.

The increasing egalitarianism in the family is related to another trend—the changing role of women. Instead of always having subservient roles, women are now elected to political office and are making inroads in the professions. Women are organizing to fight male oppression. This liberation from the old ways will have a profound impact on the family of the future.

Another trend has been an enhanced tolerance for and recognition of a wide variety of lifestyles. This tolerance is not widespread, but it is increasing, especially among college students. The liberated female, the homosexual, the interracial couple, the couple living together without legal sanction, the individuals uniting in a commune—all probably face intolerance, even hostility from some segments of the American population, but the intensity and the numbers of the opponents have been diminishing in the past few years.

These significant shifts in cultural beliefs and behaviors place an increased burden on family relationships. For example, **dual career marriages** have, on the one hand, made wives more independent and relationships more egalitarian, yet they also have increased the conflicts between husbands and wives. Whereas the culture once provided a monolithic set of answers, couples now must resolve their problems without preordained rules. Conflicting solutions from peers, family, and the media often make the resolution to these problems difficult.

Another shift from the past—the loss of many family functions—has placed additional burdens on the modern family. The family of the past was a production unit (family farm or business). It was the primary socialization agent for the youngsters. The family provided the leisure-time activities for all members. Finally, the family provided for the affectional needs of its members. Actually, in the present family, all the functions but affectional have been lost or attenuated. Economically, the family is fragmented, as the family members tend to have various and often unrelated jobs. The family is now far less important as an instrument in the socialization of children. Pre-school children often go to nursery schools or are raised in the daytime hours by babysitters. The school itself has taken over many chores once the prerogative of the family (vocational training, citizenship training, sex education). Older children are away from home so much (school, leisure-time activities) that the peer group replaces the parents as the primary source for approval and belonging as well as attitudes and values.

This shift in family function from a productive unit to an emotional retreat cannot be overemphasized. Historical changes such as industrialization, migration, and urbanization have increased the division of labor among the institutions of society. The family is now much more specialized, focusing on the socialization of young children and the stabilization of adult personalities through identity and emotional gratification. The result is that the family has become *the* institution providing emotional stability for members working and living in an increasingly impersonal world outside the home. The intensity of feelings generated in modern families as a result is at once a bane and a blessing. Precisely because the family is the primary source for the satisfaction of personal needs, it is a powerful source of pain and conflict as well. Moreover, because we work, worship, and go to school in impersonal bureaucracies, "the family is one of the few *locations* where the expression of strong feelings is legitimate, thus increasing the likelihood that emotionally charged interactions—both positive and negative—will occur."[5]

THE MODERN FAMILY FROM THE ORDER AND CONFLICT PERSPECTIVES

From the order perspective, the family serves important survival functions for society (e.g., replacement of members, regulation of sexual behavior, socialization of new members, care and protection of members). In such ways the family is vital to maintaining order in society. Most important the family provides for the emotional needs of members in times of change. The trend toward greater depersonalization in society (living in densely populated cities and working in bureaucracies) is countered by families serving as havens.[6] Thus, the isolated nuclear family is an important adaptation making an achievement-oriented industrial society workable.

Although most order theorists would prefer the proven ways of custom, they would likely also see the new family forms (communes, cohabitation, and serial monogamy) as functional alternatives to the traditional nuclear family. In this view, although the forms differ the functions are the same. In short, societal order is still maintained.

The family, from the conflict perspective, is not necessarily the haven posited by the order theorists. First, conflict theorists argue that the isolated nuclear family has positive consequences for capitalism but is highly negative for individuals.[7] The economic system benefits when employers are able to move individuals from place to place without too much disruption. The economy is served when employers do not have to worry about satisfying the emotional needs of workers. Finally, the system benefits when the family is isolated and therefore cannot affect society.

This has negative consequences for individuals, conflict theorists maintain, because the family has sole responsibility for maintaining a private refuge from an impersonal society and for personal fulfillment, and is thus structured to fail. The demands are too great. The family, alone, cannot provide for all the emotional needs of its members although its members try to succeed through consumerism, "the joy of sex," and child-centered activities. Conflict theorists would argue that society should be restructured so that personal fulfillment, identity, and other individual needs are met not only in the family but also in the community, at work, and in the other institutions of society.

Second, the family is the primary socialization agent of youth and as such promotes the status quo by transmitting the culture of society. Children are taught to accept the inequalities of society as "natural." They are taught to accept the political and economic systems without question, yet these systems may need reform or even transformation to increase the likelihood of serving the needs of the masses. Thus, the family serves to promote false consciousness.

Third, the family is the primary mechanism which perpetuates the system of social stratification. As noted in Chapter 10, most children will have the same "life chances" as their parents. The "haves" will pass on their advantages to their children and likewise the "have-nots" will transmit their disadvantages to their offspring. While this transmission of social class position promotes stability in society, which the order theorists cherish, it also promotes inequality based on ascription rather than achievement.

Fourth, the shifts in the character of the contemporary family create conflicts within the family and for individuals. As families become more private and specialized, conflict is generated. As we will see in the remainder of this chapter, conflict in families is engendered by: (1) the strains resulting from sex role expectations, the demands of work, and economic hardships which often work against intimacy and companionship between spouses; (2) parent-child relationships which have become strained with the increased significance of peers; and (3) changing sex roles. Thus, the modern family is not a tranquil institution but one fraught with potential and actual conflict.

AGE AND SEX ROLES OF FAMILY MEMBERS

In the chapter on social groups (Chapter 2) we mentioned briefly the concept of **role**. This concept is borrowed directly from the theatre and is a metaphor intended to convey the idea that conduct adheres to positions (**statuses**) in a system. This is to say that because of one's position in an organization (for example, family, corporation, community) one has certain rights and privileges as well as duties and obligations to persons occupying other positions in that social structure. In occupying a specific position, a person experiences a number of normative expectations, and these expectations are the role. They specify what one should, ought, and must do, and usually how to do it. In this section we are especially concerned with the specific roles (that is, specific behavioral expectations) of American husbands, wives, and children. The sociological significance of this concept is that although millions of different persons occupy these family roles, the behaviors in each are so routinized that they are duplicated (varying somewhat by social class, region, and ethnicity, but within a given range of tolerance) throughout American society. Because roles provide guidelines for social actions and they are followed, they give regularity and predictability to our social interactions. Finally, with respect to family roles, they provide the social mechanism that ensures a continuous supply of adequately socialized new members.

The Roles of Women and Men

As we saw in Chapter 7, masculine and feminine roles are basically cultural, not physiological phenomena. The defining characteristics of masculinity in American society are assumed to be dominance, aggressiveness, competitiveness, and independence. To have these traits in American society is rewarding in the American system of values; that women lack these traits is a major explanation for their secondary status. If, on the other hand, a woman possesses these traits, she is "put down" for not being feminine. Consequently, it is a situation of being damned if you do and damned if you don't—typical of the dilemma all minority groups face. Thus, one basis for the current women's liberation movement is the drive for women to develop their own potential. They stress that the traditional masculine-feminine roles are archaic and of benefit only to the male.

To be "feminine" in American society is to have a role that is conforming, passive, and dependent. A crucial element, however, is self-sacrifice. The female in American society is taught to sacrifice her own wishes for those of her husband and children. The self-sacrifice of being a wife and mother may have benefits for some women as their husbands climb to the top occupationally or economically or as their children successfully reach maturity. Unfortunately, many self-sacrificing women have problems later in life because they find they have lost much of their sexual attractiveness and their children no longer need them. For them, their *raison d'être* has evaporated with the passage of time. As we have said before, menopause thus becomes a special problem for American women, not only because of the hormone changes taking place, but because it represents symbolically their decline into "uselessness" or perhaps their wasted life potential.

Although the women's liberation movement has made some headway, the adult female role in American society is now what it always has been. She has the fundamental responsibility for the home and the rearing of the children. It is now common for married women to work outside the home (31 percent in 1960, 37 percent in 1968, and 51 percent in 1980). It is not common, however, for men to stay home and care for the home and raise the children. For the male in American society, the key life role is his occupation.

Division of Labor in Marriage

Evidence for cultural prescriptions for the masculine and feminine roles is seen clearly in the way duties are divided in American families. Data from numerous studies indicate that men and women tend to do those tasks for which they have been culturally trained.[8] Males are expected to be more mechanical and muscular while females are trained to know more about cooking and cleaning. Clearly, there is a strong tendency for the division of labor to be along these lines, but there is variation. Each family unit must work out the particulars of its own division of labor.

Each family must also decide who will make decisions in the key areas. Whether the male or the female predominates in a particular decision-making area is culturally assigned, but as with division of labor, there is some variation.

Parental Roles

The vast majority in society consider parenthood very desirable for a variety of personal and social reasons. At the personal level, family continuity is one stimulus to parenting. Parenthood is seen as giving a fuller meaning to the marriage relationship. For many, raising children is a fundamental form of personal fulfillment as parents take pride in their children as extensions of themselves.

American society, like others, places a high value on becoming parents. Society expects married couples to have children. It is expected that normal people, especially women, will marry and have children. Young girls, for example, are socialized toward the parent role through a variety of play activities, by being given dolls, and by the literature they read.

Parenthood is one of the major roles that an individual may assume in adulthood, but it differs from other adult roles. Alice Rossi has noted four characteristics that are unique to parenthood:[9]

1. Women are exposed to greater cultural pressures to assume this role than men. Girls are socialized to be parents while boys are socialized toward competency for future occupational roles. Thus there is a societal bias for what is considered to be the primary focus of adult life for males and females.
2. The parental role is not always voluntarily assumed as are many adult roles. We can choose our jobs but unplanned pregnancies can occur despite advanced medical technology.
3. The parental role is irrevocable for most. Once the decision is made to continue a pregnancy and the birth occurs, one cannot back out of the commitment except by placing the child for adoption. So, except for unusual circumstances "We can have ex-spouses and ex-jobs but not ex-children."[10]
4. The preparation for parenting is generally worse than the preparation for other adult roles. Most people do not have specific educational experiences that will help them cope with the parent role (e.g., knowledge of diet, medicine, and developmental psychology).

This last point needs further elaboration. Society allows the crucial role of parent to fall on anyone capable of sexual intercourse. In some cases, religious beliefs and stringent government regulations on abortion leave a pregnant women no choice but to accept a parenting role. One critic feels that society should license parents to overcome this basic problem:

Almost all the professions that deal with a person's physical or mental health require extensive training. A license to practice as a lawyer, doctor, registered nurse, social worker, or teacher is given only after at least four years of college. Yet to become a parent—the person most responsible for a child's development—presently requires no training, license, or experience. Society demands that a person obtain a license before pursuing such relatively simple tasks as driving a car, operating a ham radio, wiring a house, or prescribing a pair of glasses. Yet to do the job of a parent—one much more complex and crucial to the lives of so many—requires no license at all.[11]

The transition to the parent role is an abrupt one. The infant is fragile and totally dependent and is, from the outset, a relentless 24-hour per day, seven days per week responsibility. The adjustment to this full time commitment is not easy. The first child becomes the center of the family's activities with all other things becoming secondary. Life is reorganized around the child's needs. No longer can the spouses travel or engage in forms of entertainment as they used to. Their social lives are disrupted. So, too, is their sex life. The child causes more domestic work and lost sleep. Moreover, children are expensive, causing a constant drain on family resources. In short, for many young couples the adjustment to parent roles is difficult and sometimes traumatic. The difficulties are minimized if the parents want the baby; if they are committed to the role of parent; and if the mother is in good health.[12] Of course, if soon-to-be parents were prepared for parenthood with training and experience, the adjustment problems would be minimal.

A primary responsibility of parents is to teach their children the attitudes, values, and behaviors considered appropriate by the parents (and society). This ensures that most children will be reared to take acceptable niches in the society when they reach adulthood. Parents, therefore, are the most important societal agents of socialization in the child's formative years. There is a wide latitude, however, in the mode of socialization.

There are two broad patterns of socialization that can be identified in American society. One stresses punishment for wrong behavior while the other emphasizes rewards for good behavior. One demands obedience of the child to adults. The other allows the child freedom to explore and find things out for himself. Thus, one is adult-centered while the other is child-centered. One is much more strict when it comes to thumb sucking, toilet training, cleanliness, and aggression control, while the other is more tolerant. The first mode of socialization for each of the comparisons above is called **repressive socialization**; the second has been named **participatory socialization**. Repressive socialization is based on the premise that children can and should be molded to conform, to be obedient. Participatory socialization, on the other hand, assumes that children should be given freedom to explore and develop their unique potentialities.

Although few parents are consistent in the manner in which they interact with their children, there appear to be discernible patterns by social class. The empirical evidence is that working-class parents tend toward repressive socialization while middle-class parents are more likely to practice participatory socialization.

Social class appears to make a difference in socialization modes because of the variance in life experience among the classes. The members of the middle class, for example, tend to have a good deal of autonomy in their occupations, while working-class persons are more likely to take orders under strict supervision. Parents, apparently, use the mode of socialization that they are comfortable with and the one that makes adjustment to life the easiest. The patterns continue over time because the social class behaviors are reinforced. Children live in relatively homogeneous neighborhoods by social class, thereby giving the impression that a particular mode is the most natural because almost everyone does it.

Persons also tend to marry within their social class. This, too, reinforces one type of socialization practice as the typical one for a particular social class.[13]

Participatory socialization has not always been the primary mode of the middle classes. Child-rearing practices, especially among the middle and upper classes, have vacillated according to the prevailing views of experts. The bulletin *Infant Care*, published by the United States Children's Bureau, has gone through a number of editions and has changed significantly since its inception in 1914. In that year the views of psychologist John B. Watson were enunciated. He believed that the development of the child was shaped entirely by the habits he acquired. Thus, mothers were instructed to never rock their baby, begin toilet training by the third month, and never let the child suck his thumb. In the 1930s the philosophy of Sigmund Freud prevailed. The concern then was with the emotional damage that could occur from unfavorable experiences during the first years of life. Parents were enjoined to make the child's environment supportive and loving.[14]

Participatory socialization, so prevalent in the contemporary American middle class, is in large measure due to the persuasive influences of Dr. Benajmin Spock, whose book *Baby and Child Care* had sold more than 21 million copies from 1947 to 1970.[15] Most parents (at least middle-class parents) were greatly influenced by the child-rearing philosophy of Spock. He argued that young children should be treated with kindness in a relaxed atmosphere. Babies should not be fed on a rigid time schedule, but when they want to eat. Children should be taught to love rather than fear their parents. In later editions (1957 and 1968) Spock was less permissive but the basic philosophy remained—that children should be raised in a relaxed, loving environment. Although accused by many of advocating wanton permissiveness, Spock, especially in his later editions, placed great emphasis on the child's need for parental control and the importance of not letting the child become a tyrant in the home.

There is another mode of socialization that characterizes s sizable minority of lower-class families (but is found in some families in the other social classes as well), and that is excessive freedom. This freedom is different from that found in participatory socialization, because in this case the freedom is not because of adherence to a particular philosophy of child raising, but because of either neglect by the parents or rebellion by the children. Either of these may prevail in the lower class as the result of several factors: (1) the chance of two parents being present in the home is reduced because of the conditions of lower-class life; (2) children living in an achievement-oriented society may not have respect for their parents and may therefore disobey their wishes; (3) for the minority-group families that are so predominant in this stratum, there is a huge "generation gap" because the youngsters consider their parents "uncle toms" for not fighting the system that keeps them in such a lowly state.

Adolescence

About 13 percent of the total population is between the ages of 13 and 19. This is a very significant category in American society for several reasons. First, they are a strong economic force. For example, they account for more than one fourth of the record sales and more than one third of the movie audiences. They spend collectively an enormous amount of money on clothes and toiletries. As they shift from fad to fad, fortunes are made and lost in the clothing and entertainment industries. Second, adolescents are a financial burden to society. Most adolescents are in school and not in the labor market. They are furnished with an education that they did not earn. Within each family, adolescents and the younger children are economic liabilities. They do not earn their way. The United States is probably the first nation to transform children from a family asset as labor to a family liability as student-consumer. A third basis for this category's importance is that many adolescents are disenchanted and alienated. This results in withdrawal, apathy, or rebellion.

For some of the young, their disenchantment is brought about by a moral gap—not a generation gap. They see older people as mainly interested in making money and oblivious to the social ills of the society. They want to put into practice what the Constitution says but the government does not enforce. Furthermore, they feel that young people are forced to fight in wars brought about by the older generation. Many young people become disenchanted because they are unsure of their identity. Unlike adults who find identity in their vocations or avocations, adolescents must find their identity elsewhere—in a cause, in religion, in sports, in sexual promiscuity, in being "tough." Adolescence is an age of "self" discovery. For many young persons, this is a difficult task.[16]

Why is the stage of adolescence in American society a period of stress and strain for so many? The most important reason is that it is an age of transition from one social status to another. There is no clear line of demarcation between adolescence and adulthood. Are people considered adult when they can get a full-time job, when they are physically capable of producing children, or when they can be drafted for military service? There is no clear distinction. Most primitive societies, by contrast, have "rites of passage" that seem cruel and barbaric but do serve the function of clearly identifying the individual as a child or an adult. Adulthood in American society is unclear. As Stephens has said, "The postponement of sociological adulthood produces a social status which is filled, somewhat uncertainly, by millions of our society's members. This is adolescence; the state of being physically mature but not working, sexually mature but not married, 'grown-up' but still dependent on parents."[17] Surely much of the acting out by adolescents in the United States can be explained partially at least by these status ambiguities.

These status ambiguities are probably unavoidable in a society where the state of technological development demands an extended period of education. Full-time schooling for a college degree or beyond tends to defer marriage well beyond the age of full biological maturity. This presents special problems for the adolescent. Young men and women are permitted and encouraged to date without chaperons. They are sexually mature and are members of a society that places a good deal of emphasis on sex (movies, novels, magazines, and advertising).

Children, too, are away from home a good deal at school activities, club meetings, on dates, and being with their friends. The time children spend with others tends to be more with peers than with adults (especially as the child becomes a teenager). The typical peer group of children tends to be homogeneous. This results from seeking friends who share the same interests. A less obvious reason is that young people are restricted in choice of friends by propinquity. The typical urban or suburban neighborhood is noted for its sameness—in architecture and age of homes, but more importantly in the characteristics of the inhabitants. The individuals tend to be of the same race, socioeconomic level, and even age. Thus, the relationships that children form tend to be limited to persons who are similar in important ways.

The typical American youngster at some point in time turns away from parents to peers for opinion, advice, or companionship. The impact of the peer group on the child is great.

A study by James Coleman of youngsters in ten high schools is especially instructive on this point. He found that although approximately three fourths of the boys' parents wanted their youngsters to be remembered as brilliant students, only 31 percent of the boys wanted to be so remembered (44 percent wanted to be remembered as athletic stars). Apparently, the attitudes of the students were not only anti-intellectual but antithetical to those of their parents.[18]

Adolescents have a tremendous need to be popular, to be acceptable, to belong. They are "other-directed," which means that their peer groups become so important that they are the sources of direction for the individual.[19] Thus, the sources for attitudes, clothing styles, hairstyle, slang, for most teenagers are their close friends.

The Aged

The age distribution of the population has shifted in recent years, with more and more Americans living past the arbitrary dividing line of 65 years of age. In 1940, for example, 9 million persons (6.8 percent) were 65 or older, whereas more than 25 million Americans (11.2 percent) were in that category in 1980. This change in the composition of the population has important effects upon family life and the society in general.

The elderly in American society are somewhat analogous to adolescents in the ambivalence they face, because they are in a transition stage (in this case between work and death). As a category they are neither self-sufficient nor productive. As a category, the elderly are accorded low status, unlike many societies where they are believed to be especially wise and therefore hold the power. In a sense they constitute a minority group, for they are subject to unfavorable treatment (forced retirement, difficulty in finding employment). They are believed by many to be inflexible, cantankerous, and unreliable—all false stereotypes.[20] These negative stereotypes are held by many Americans. They probably stem from the fear of old age that is prevalent in the youth-oriented American society.

Stereotypes of the aged are difficult to dispel, largely because research on aging is a recent development in both the biological and the social sciences and research findings reach the public at a snail's pace. Many widely held but inaccurate images, inadvertently repeated through the mass media, come from social workers who serve the poor, the lonely, and the isolated, and from physicians and psychiatrists who see the physically ill and the mentally ill. Thus, we base many of our current stereotypes on a picture of the needy rather than on a picture of the typical older person.

Studies of large and representative samples of older persons are now appearing, however, and they go far toward exploding some of our outmoded images. For example, old persons do not become isolated and neglected by their families, although both generations prefer separate households. Old persons are not dumped into mental hospitals by cruel or indifferent children. They are not necessarily lonely or desolate if they live alone. Few of them ever show overt signs of mental deterioration or senility, and only a small proportion ever become mentally ill. For those who do, psychological and psychiatric treatment is by no means futile.

Retirement and widowhood do not lead to mental illness, nor does social isolation. Retirement is not necessarily bad; some men and women want to keep on working, but more and more choose to retire earlier and earlier. Increasing proportions of the population evidently value leisure more than they value work. Nor do retired persons sicken physically from idleness and feelings of worthlessness. Three fourths of the persons

questioned in a recent national sample reported that they were satisfied or very satisfied with their lives since retirement. This is in line with earlier surveys. Most persons over 65 think of themselves as being in good health and they act accordingly, no matter what their physicians think.

But the most insidious stereotype of all, in many ways, puts the old (or, for that matter, the young or the middle-aged) into a distinct category or a distinct group. There is, in truth, no such thing as "the" young, or "the" old. People *do* differ; they also become increasingly different over time, as each person accumulates an idiosyncratic set of experiences and becomes committed to a unique set of people, things, interests, and activities. One has only to recall, for instance, the range of differences among the members of one's high school graduating class and then to see these persons at a class reunion 25 years later. They are much more varied as 40-year-olds than they were as 18-year-olds. In a society as complex as the United States, with increasing social permissiveness for people to follow their own bents, a good case can be made that—despite the counterpressures that create conformity—increased differentiation occurs over the life cycle.[21]

Despite the disclaimers just presented, the elderly in American society often are lonely. This is a consequence of the nuclear family system, which separates the aged from their children. Often the children of the elderly live a great distance from their parents. Added to this spatial separation is the social separation that occurs through social mobility. Many children surpass their parents in social status. Concomitant with a widening gap in social status but also a result of age differences are discrepancies in lifestyles, behaviors, and attitudes between parents and their adult children.

Another way in which the elderly tend to be isolated from kinship ties is through the death of one's mate—widowhood. There are about 11 million widowed persons with the present ratio of widows to widowers being more than 4 to 1. This dramatic difference results from a variance in life expectancy—a difference of almost eight years—and the tendency for males to marry someone younger than themselves (usually about a two-year differential). Thus, the average married female can expect ten years of widowhood—and, therefore, dependency upon Social Security, insurance, savings, or help from her family.[22]

Isolation of the elderly also occurs from a break in occupational ties. In the past when many persons farmed or owned small businesses, work was a lifetime process. In an industrial, bureaucratized society, however, retirement is usually abrupt. Many firms have established a policy that makes retirement compulsory at a given age (regardless of the individual's willingness to continue, expertise, and experience). Since one's work is the source of income, social status, and identity, to be cut off against one's will may be a traumatic experience from which it is difficult to recover.

A final source of isolation is the breakup of community ties. A relatively recent trend has been the creation of entire communities for the aged in Florida, California, and Arizona. Many old people are enticed to leave their home communities and live in these age-segregated communities. Another way in which the elderly may be separated from community life is by living in nursing homes or confined in mental hospitals.

Talcott Parsons, a highly esteemed sociologist, has wondered if two alleged behavioral consequences of old age are the result of the high probability of being isolated from kinship ties, occupational ties, and community ties. These factors may explain, at least partially, the increased political agitation among the elderly, on the one hand, and, on the other, the high incidence of psychosomatic illnesses and the well-known disabilities of older people.[23]

FAMILY STABILITY AND INSTABILITY

There is a tendency to think of marriage in idyllic terms. Two people marry for romantic reasons and they share a life of marital bliss ("and they lived happily ever after"). The marriage relationship, however, is fraught with tension. The spouses may differ in religious and political ideology. They may argue over sex role expectations. They may disagree on the number of children, their spacing, and how they should be raised. Habits may become irritating. The relationship in time may become so routinized as to be humdrum. While the majority of marriages adjust to these and other problems, for increasing numbers of people these disagreements and irritations may lead to ruptured relationships. In this section we will discuss two forms of family instability—violence and divorce.

Violence in the American Family

The family has two faces. Positively it is a haven from an uncaring, impersonal world, a place where love and security prevail. The family members love each other, care for each other, and are accepting of each other under all circumstances. But there is a dark side to the family too.[24] The family is a major location of violence in society. One fourth of all the murders in the United States involve the killing of spouses, parents, and children. The most common request for police help is for "domestic disturbances." More police personnel are killed (22 percent) trying to settle family fights than in any other line of duty. Millions of wives and children are regularly assaulted by husbands and parents. Even the elderly are sometimes physically abused by their adult children. Here we will consider only one form of family violence, husbands physically abusing their wives. Violence by wives directed at husbands, compared to the reverse type, is less likely to occur, is likely to cause less physical damage, and is often the result of self-defense toward an abusive husband. This is not intended to minimize the existence of physical violence by wives, because it does occur,[25] but because the frequency and severity are much less than husbands' attacks on wives, we will describe wife abuse in some detail.

The actual statistics on battered wives are impossible to obtain. The reasons for this are fairly obvious. Foremost, the events generally take place in private with no witnesses other than family members. Battered women are often attended by physicians who treat their wounds either without asking embarrassing questions or, if they know the cause, without reporting the abuse to the authorities. The victims, most commonly, lie about the causes of their injuries because of shame or fear. Last, many victims do not go to public agencies for help because they have often found them to be unresponsive. This is especially true of the police and the courts because they typically feel that most domestic violence is a private affair and none of their business. Also, the situation often comes down to the wife's word against her husband's, leaving prosecution difficult if not impossible.

Understanding the limitations of the data on spouse abuse, the following are some estimates of the extent of wife abuse:

—Extrapolating the data from a representative sample of the general population, it has been estimated that 1.8 million wives are beaten by their husbands. Since the data are surely underreporting the actual situation, the researchers suggested that the true incidence is probably closer to 50 or 60 percent of all couples.[26]

—A psychologist specializing in helping abuse victims has estimated that 50 percent of all women will be battering victims at some point in their lives.[27]

—Wife-beating is estimated by the FBI to be the most frequently occurring crime in the country.[28]

Although these are imprecise estimates, they reveal that wife abuse is a fairly common practice. We do know some facts about the conditions under which this phenomenon occurs. Foremost, "Battered women are found in all age groups, races, ethnic and religious groups, educational levels, and socioeconomic groups."[29] This counters the prevailing myth that wife abuse is most prevalent in the lowest classes. Pregnancy seems to be a time when wives are most vulnerable for attack. The National Institute of Mental Health has found that a quarter of battered women were victims while pregnant.[30]

Those couples given to verbal aggression are more prone to engage in physical violence than those couples who are not.[31] This is contrary to the catharsis hypothesis, while argues that verbal aggression allows couples to get rid of their pent-up hostilities, thereby reducing the potential for physical violence.

Research on husbands known to be abusers of their wives has tended to find that these men are underachievers, when compared to their wives. They may be less intelligent, less successful in their jobs or school, or lower in certain status characteristics compared to their wives. A common patterns is for the husband's occupational status to be lower than that of his father-in-law implying that a woman, in the eyes of her husband, retains the social status of her father.[32] The inability to be superior to one's wife in a male-oriented society apparently leads to the tendency to prove one's superiority over her in physical ways.

Wife-beating is also generated by a number of problems facing the husband in his marriage, his work, or other situation. These may include financial difficulties, sexual dysfunction, and jealousy.

The major contributing factor to being violent in a family situation is coming from a family that was itself violence prone. Husbands who batter their wives most often come from homes in which they were beaten by their parents or in which they had observed their own fathers beating their mothers. Much less likely, but significant nonetheless, is that women who are victims of wife abuse have tended also to come from homes where they were abused as children and/or their mothers were victims of physical abuse.

There are a number of psychological and interpersonal reasons for wife battering, and each case is in some ways idiosyncratic. For our purposes, though, let's focus on the societal supports for such violence, as argued by Murray Straus:

The causes of wife-beating are to be found in the very structure of American society and its family system. Demonstrating this, even in principle, is a vast undertaking. All that can be done here is to identify seven of the main factors and to give the general flavor of the argument. . . . They are:

—the family is a type of social group characterized by a high level of conflict;
—the United States is a nation which is fundamentally committed to the use of violence to maintain the status quo or to achieve desirable changes;
—the child rearing patterns typically employed by American parents train children to be violent.
This in turn:
—legitimizes violence within the family and
—builds violence into the most fundamental levels of personality and establishes the link between love and violence;
—the male dominant nature of the family system, with a corresponding tendency to use physical force to maintain that dominance when it is threatened;
—the sexual inequalities inherent in our family system, economic system, social services, and criminal justice system, effectively leave many women locked into a brutal marriage. They literally have no means of redress, or even of leaving such a marriage.

It is the combination of these factors which makes the family the most violent of all civilian institutions, and which accounts for that aspect of family violence which we call wife-beating.[33]

Divorce

Although some societies have a higher rate of family dissolution, the family in American society is especially vulnerable. A primary reason is that the most important bond in American marriages is romantic love, a feeling that may change as the partners age, or as they are upwardly or downwardly mobile.[34]

Panel 14–2
Wife-Beating: The Legacy of Patriarchy

The patriarchal family has prevailed throughout the history of western civilization. Much of the ideology and many of the institutional arrangements which supported patriarchy are still reflected in our culture and our social institutions. Let's look at this legacy of patriarchy.

In ancient Rome the law first proclaimed by Romulus in 753 B.C. stated that married women were to conform entirely to the wishes of their husbands and that husbands were to rule their wives as possessions. All property was owned by the husband. The husband was given legal right to punish his wife for any misbehavior such as adultery, drinking wine, attending public games without his permission or appearing unveiled in public. The husband was given full power to judge and punish her. Speaking about the appropriate response to marital fidelity Cato said in the fifth century B. C.: "If you catch your wife in adultery, you could put her to death with impunity, she, on her part, would not dare to touch you with her finger; and it is not right that she should."

Christianity embraced the hierarchical family structure and celebrated the subordination of wives to their husbands. Although the teachings did not advocate force, they did demand the obedience of the wife to her husband.

During the Middle Ages in Europe there were many laws of chastisement. The French code of chivalry specified that the husband of a scolding wife could knock her to the earth, strike her in the face with his fist and break her nose so that she would always be blemished and ashamed. Women in Spain, Italy, France and England could be flogged through the city streets, exiled for years or killed if they committed adultery or numerous "lesser" offenses.

Under English Common Law a married woman lost all of her civil rights, had no separate legal status and became the chattel of her husband. The right of the husband to chastise his wife was considered a natural part of his responsibilities. When the old common law was changed to the new civil law husbands were still

The data on divorce in American society indicate a strong trend toward an even higher rate. In an historical context, the number of divorces per 1000 couples was only 1.2 in 1860, 4.0 in 1900, 7.7 in 1920, and 21.1 in 1975. Table 14–1 and Figure 14–1 show this trend for the last 28 years in two ways.

The data in Table 14–1 show that the number of divorces is rising faster than the number of marriages in each year. They appear to indicate that for 1978 about one out of two marriages ended in divorce. This is a fallacy, however, because it compares those married in a given year (a relatively small number of persons are eligible) with all of those eligible for divorce (a relatively large nunber). A more accurate picture of divorce is obtained by determining the number of divorces per 1,000 married women (or men) in a given year. Thus, as noted above, the actual divorce rate nearly tripled from 1920 (7.7) to 1975 (21.1). Figure 14–1 shows this "divorce ratio" for different age levels. The rate has increased most rapidly at ages under 45. Above age 30, the divorce ratio for women has risen more rapidly than for men, as divorced men continue to have higher remarriage rates than divorced women.

allowed "for some misdemeanors to give his wife a severe beating with whips and clubs; for others, only to apply moderate correction."

All of the legal systems of Europe, England and early America supported a husband's rights to beat his wife and so did the community norms. Men were to rule their wives because "the man who is not master of his wife is not worthy of being a man. By this time, though, husbands were expected to show some restraint, at least in their public beatings of wives. The beatings were to conform to the rules of legitimate punishment (i.e., to not be too severe). Upon observing a man severely attacking his wife a neighbor exclaimed, "Oh, that's a bit much. We all know that wives need beating but you must be reasonable all the same."

In America various states legally gave husbands the right to chastise their wives physically. In 1824 the Supreme Court of Mississippi upheld this right. In 1865 a court in North Carolina ruled that the State could not interfere in cases of domestic chastisement unless permanent injury or excessive violence was involved. To not interfere, while seemingly a neutral statement, meant of course that husbands were to be allowed to continue to beat their wives.

Finally, in the late nineteenth century the laws in America and England allowing husband abuse were abolished. By 1878 in England women were allowed to use cruelty as a grounds for divorce. The rejection of the legal rights for husbands to physically assault their wives was complete in America in 1891 when the courts declared that "the moral sense of the community revolts at the idea that the husband may inflict personal chastisement upon his wife, even for the most outrageous conduct." Many groups objected to this change, and community norms often allowed it to continue in private. So little was done to bring about any meaningful change in the daily lives of women that by 1910 the Suffragettes made assaults on wives one of their platforms.

Source: Excerpted from R. Emerson Dobash and Russell P. Dobash, "Wives: the 'Appropriate' Victims of Marital Violence," *Victimology* 2, Numbers 3–4 (1977–78), pp. 426–432. Reprinted by permission of Visage Press.

TABLE 14–1   Incidence of Marriage, Divorce, and Children Involved for Selected Years

	# of Marriages	# of Divorces	# of Marriages to One Divorce	Average # of Children per Divorce
1955	1,667,000	385,000	4.3	.92
1960	1,523,000	393,000	3.9	1.18
1965	1,800,000	479,000	3.8	1.32
1970	2,159,000	708,000	3.1	1.22
1975	2,153,000	1,036,000	2.1	1.08
1978	2,243,000	1,122,000	2.0	1.00*

*1977 data

Source: Adapted from U.S. Bureau of the Census, *Statistical Abstract of the United States 1979*, 100th edition (Washington, D.C.: U.S. Government Printing Office, 1979), p. 81.

FIGURE 14-1   Divorced Persons Per 1,000 Married Persons With Spouse Present, by Sex and Age, for Selected Years: 1950–78

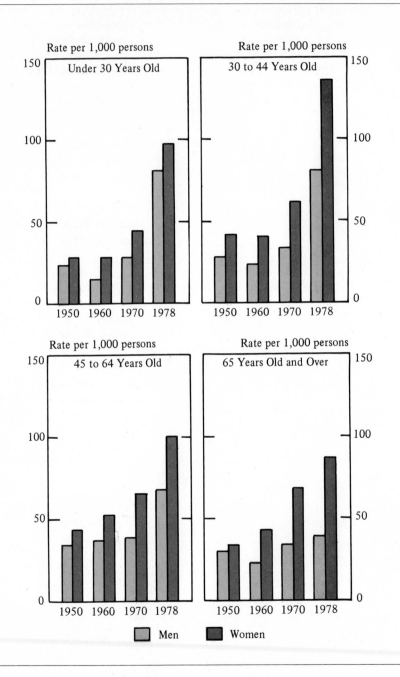

Source: U.S. Bureau of the Census, *Current Population Reports*, Series P-23, No. 104 (Washington, D.C.: Government Printing Office, 1980), Chart 6, p. 5.

There are many reasons for the increased divorce rate. Some of these are: increased independence (social and financial) of women; increased affluence, which has removed the barrier of divorce costs; greater tolerance of divorce by religious groups; and reform of divorce laws, especially the adoption of no-fault divorce (that is, it is no longer necessary in many states for one partner to prove that the other was at fault in order to obtain a divorce). Probably the most important reason, though, is the striking change in public attitudes toward divorce. While divorce is a difficult step and one that commands sympathy for the partners and children, "it is no longer considered a violation of public decency. Whether the individual is viewed as the sinner or as sinned against, divorce is generally accepted today as one possible solution for family difficulties."[35]

The following are some generalizations about divorce in the United States:[36]

1. Half of all divorces occur during the first seven years of marriage.
2. The divorce rate is related to economic conditions. The rate increases during prosperity. Apparently this is due to unwillingness to break up a marriage when wives and children will need greater economic support.
3. The younger the age at marriage of the partners, the greater the likelihood of divorce. "Women whose first marriage ended in divorce have been, on the average, about two years younger when they entered marriage than married women of the same age who have not been divorced."[37]
4. The higher the income, the less the likelihood of divorce.
5. The higher the education for males, the lower the incidence of divorce. In contrast to males, a more complicated pattern is found for women. The highest rate of divorce is found among the least educated women, followed by those with post-graduate degrees. The lowest rates were found for those women with high school and college eduations.[38]
6. About four out of every five of those persons who obtain a divorce will remarry, with men more likely than women to do so.[39]
7. Blacks have a higher incidence of divorce than whites or Hispanics. In 1978 the percentage of males over age 18 who were divorced was: blacks 6.9 percent, whites 4.5 percent, and Hispanics 3.5 percent. The rate for females by race was 9.3 percent, 6.3 percent, and 6.6 percent, respectively.[40]

THE FUTURE FAMILY

There are a number of marriage/family trends of the late 1970s and early 1980s that have interesting implications for the future of marriage. Some of the most important are:

1. The proportion of couples living together outside of marriage is increasing.
2. Individuals are marrying later.
3. Couples are having fewer children.
4. The number of childless couples is rising.
5. An ever greater proportion of wives are working outside the home.
6. The divorce rate continues to climb.
7. The proportion of nontraditional households is increasing rapidly. Only 7 percent of America's families in 1979, for example, consisted of a breadwinner father, homemaker mother, and children.[41]
8. The fastest growing family type is the household maintained by a woman with no husband present.

Do these trends indicate that the nuclear family is dying? We can safely predict that some form of the nuclear family will characterize American society for the foreseeable future. The turbulence of the future may even drive people deeper into their families rather than otherwise, since families may become *the* source of roots in a highly transient world.[42]

It could be argued that the family has gone through a great deal of turmoil because of being in the "shake-down" phase between agrarian life and the industrial world, between rural life and urban life, between frugality and affluence. Perhaps the family is now adapted to the modern world. This not to say that the family will no longer change. As Ira Reiss has said:

Change is inevitable, but the radical changes are behind us and not ahead of us. We now possess a family system congruent in many ways with our urban-industrial society . . . a number of indices point to the fact that the essentials of our current family system were formed in the early decades of this century and that they now come to be established in several relatively stable patterns. I expect mostly modest changes in the remaining three decades of this century. Nothing on the scale of the family system changes of the first three decades of this century should occur during the last three decades. . . .[43]

Alternative possibility I: pluralism.   Although the nuclear family will remain the choice of the majority, there will continue to be experimentation with alternative family forms. The future will be characterized by pluralism and freedom. Rainwater has predicted:

Life styles will increasingly be built out of a rapidly expanding multiplicity of choices— choices made possible by the interaction of affluence and cosmopolitanism. One of the most striking things about American society since World War II (or longer than that) has been the extent to which the lives of most Americans involve what they put together out of the choices available to them rather than what they are constrained to do

SOCIAL DILEMMAS AND CRITICAL CHOICES

Panel 14–3
The Effects of a Shrinking Job Market on Family Stability

How strong is the nuclear family? Could it withstand the economic pressures of a law forbidding more than one working adult per family unit? Let's examine just such a hypothetical case, keeping in mind what your personal decisions would be.

Three trends converge to exacerbate the unemployment crisis facing contemporary America: (1) a shrinking of jobs due to automation; (2) fewer jobs because of a decline in population growth, which lessens the demand for products; and (3) an ever-expanding proportion of women seeking to enter the labor force. The result is a societal-wide problem of job creation and job allocation.

The time may come, and perhaps sooner than we think, when the federal government may be forced to place a limit of one person active in the labor force per family to ensure a fair allocation of the scarce jobs. Such a ruling would have several possible negative ramifications for the family. First, it may lead to fewer mar-by their socioeconomic situation. Much of the conflict and turmoil in the society probably has as much to do with anxiety and uncertainty engendered by continuing massive increases in the range of choices available to people as with more frequently cited factors. Indeed the 'oppression' that many of these who 'protest' feel (aside from blacks and other minorities) is probably more the oppression of having many choices and not knowing how to choose among them than of being 'forced' to do things one does not wish to do.

Out of the current ferment about life styles is very likely to come the institutionalization of a set of pluralistic standards which legitimate a far wider range of ways of living in American society than has previously been the case. From the various liberation movements (black, brown, red, women, gay men, gay women, youth) will probably come a more widespread ethic of pluralism in life styles. (And this will be more than toleration in that it will involve recognition of the legitimacy of different kinds of identities and life styles).[44]

The acceptance of a wide diversity of lifestyles will enhance the probability of a greater proportion of interfaith and interracial marriages. Homosexuals will no longer hide their identities. More and more married couples will choose to remain childless.[45]

An alternative to the nuclear family for some is the commune. These are, generally speaking, conscious efforts on the part of several persons to recapture the warmth and intimacy of extended families. They result from the feelings of isolation and alienation that some persons feel in a depersonalized, segmented, bureaucratic, and mobile society. What is especially interesting about communes to the sociologist is that here the extended family is a chosen one (instead of one imposed by the accident of birth), by persons who share cultural, social, and/or political outlooks. They will be especially important phenomena of the future because they are havens for those persons who consciously choose an alternative lifestyle and/or to those who cannot cope with the pressures of rapidly changing society

riages, since many persons would not marry so that both partners could work. This would mean an increase in "cohabitation" arrangements which are less stable than formal marriages, and to "policing" efforts by the government to crack down on illicit living and working arrangements.

A second consequence of job limitation per family unit would be a drastic reduction in the incomes of married couples used to two incomes. This would cause a drastic change in lifestyles and perhaps increased family discord.

An additional pressure on married couples will be the decision and the acceptance of the decision as to who will be the breadwinner. Will it be the traditional male in the work force and the woman as homemaker? Will the partners each work one-half days or alternate by weeks, months, or by the year? Given the lower pay that women currently receive, the pressure will be for women to let men be in the labor force, but this will cause resentment and the loss of momentum for the women's movement. This possibility of one worker per family also poses serious questions for the male. Will he be willing to be a house-person part of the time while his spouse gets the recognition and the paycheck? Or will he insist on the traditional division of labor, bringing other stresses to the relationship?

A commune is by definition composed of people who want stability and security—two qualities missing in contemporary American society.

Another alternative to the present monogamous form of marriage has been mentioned by several observers.[46] They feel that the conditions of the future will augur against lifelong monogamy. Life expectancy rates are rising, which means people will be forced to live together for a longer time. As the rate of change in society accelerates and as the individual family moves geographically and socially, the interests and values of husband and wife will change, often away from the supports they had when the marriage was formed. These changes may not develop at comparable rates or perhaps not even in the same direction. Thus, the odds against the success of the lifelong marriage may become overwhelming. If this occurs, we can anticipate a somewhat more open public acceptance of serial monogamy (or temporary marriage).

Toffler predicts a three-step marriage career that departs radically from the present norms as the typical pattern of the future. At each stage the couple would sign a marriage contract. At the end of the contracted period they could decide whether to renew it or not. The first occurs in the late youth or early adult years. It is a probationary marriage ("trial marriage") with or without the benefit of the ceremony. This stage is a romantic one without children, where couples practice at cohabitational living. The second stage in the process is the time of child raising and career advancement. The couple at the end of stage one must decide if they want to terminate their arrangement and seek new partners or not for this very different part of the life cycle. The third stage occurs when the children leave home. It will probably last thirty years or so. The requirements of the partners are different than before. The persons are mature. They have only themselves and their career(s) to consider. By this time the interests, attitudes, and values are stable. The marriage partners at this stage can match their interests and psychological needs. The chances of this relationship enduring are quite good, although the time of retirement is a difficult stage for many and may necessitate one final change in marriage partners.

Alternative possibility II: societal constraints. The first set of future alternatives was essentially optimistic, since it envisioned a tolerance for different lifestyles. There is always the possibility, however, that individual choices will be curtailed by the government meeting some crisis. For example, the present low fertility rate may shift upward. The resulting population pressures may become so great that the government would have to impose a limit on family size (for pregnancies beyond the prescribed limit the government could demand abortion or an exorbitant fine).

If unemployment becomes a serious problem, the government may be forced to limit the number of "breadwinners" to one per family unit. High unemployment rates may also bring about lower mandatory retirement ages and government-imposed limits on the numbers of hours worked.

The limitation on individual freedoms may also occur because the values of Americans demand a change. Individuals and organizations may organize to pressure the legislatures and courts to curb communes, trial marriages, abortions, and easy divorces simply because they are convinced that these arrangements are wrong. Similarly, they may also attempt to pressure those in power to protect morals by a rigid censorship of movies, plays, magazines, and literature. Religious groups such as the Moral Majority, are the most likely to make such demands, but the pressure may become more widespread in reaction against the permissiveness that many believe pervades the family, school, church, and courts.

SUMMARY

The family is one of the most basic of all social institutions. Although the exact form of marriage and family varies by society, families universally provide society not only with a regular input of members but also serve as society's fundamental agent of socialization. Most significant, the family is the primary place where society's age and sex roles are learned and reinforced. Thus, like all institutions, the family is conservative, preserving the unity and stability of society.

The contemporary American family faces a number of potential crises. The divorce rate is the highest in history. Increasing numbers of couples are living together in temporary nonlegal arrangements. Illegitimacy is rising. Fewer couples want children. What do these trends mean for the future of the family? While there will be more variation and more experimentation in the family of the future, the nuclear family will remain. The family will be smaller, more egalitarian, and even more nuclear than at present. The family will continue because it will be the one source of stability, of primary relations, and of irrationality in a shifting, secondary, and overly rational social world.

CHAPTER REVIEW

1. The family, like all institutions, is conservative as it ensures that certain important goals of the society are accomplished. The family provides a regular input of new members. The family socializes these new members to fit in society. The family also provides them with a social location, thereby perpetuating social inequality and providing for societal stability.

2. The typical American family, when compared to the family in most other societies, is characterized by relative freedom. There is a relatively free choice of mates. Family units are generally established away from parents and kin. And, there are choices within the family regarding the division of labor, power arrangements, raising children, and the like.

3. The American family has always been nuclear (parents and their nonadult children living together). The family of the past was much more likely than the present family to have a kinship group living nearby, providing members with emotional and physical support. Families today have fewer children and the life expectancy is much higher. The divorce rate now is much higher. Many more wives are now working outside the home. A final difference between the family of the past and present is that the contemporary family has lost many functions

once part of the family. All of these differences have put stress on the members of modern families.

4. From the order perspective, the family provides important survival functions for society. Most important it provides for the emotional needs of members in a changing and impersonal world.

5. Although order theorists prefer the stability provided by the traditional family, they also see the new family forms of communes, cohabitation, and serial monogamy as functional alternatives. That is, societal order is still maintained although the forms of the family are different.

6. Conflict theorists argue that the burden on the family as the only institution providing for identity, personal fulfillment, and a refuge from an impersonal world, is too great. Society needs to be restructured so that these necessities are met in the community, at work, and in the other institutions.

7. Conflict theorists see the family as a major source of false consciousness through the socialization of children. The family is also the primary agent by which the system of social stratification is perpetuated.

8. The family is not a tranquil institution but one fraught with potential and actual conflict.

9. Changing sex roles have a direct impact on husband-wife relationships. This can be a major area of disagreement. Dual career marriages—the majority of families now have both spouses working outside the home—often cause major disagreement among spouses.

10. The parental role differs from other adult roles. Girls are socialized for this role but boys are not. This role may not be voluntary. The parental role is irrevocable. The preparation for parenting is worse than the preparation for other adult roles.

11. A primary responsibility of parents is to teach their children the culture—to fit into society. There are two basic modes of socialization used by parents. Repressive socialization demands conformity to rigid rules enforced by physical punishment. Participatory socialization allows children freedom to explore and develop their unique potentialities.

12. Adolescence is a difficult time for many young people and their parents in American society. The fundamental reason for this is that these people are in a transitional stage between childhood and adulthood with no clear distinction when adulthood is reached.

13. The aged also face ambivalence because they are in a transitional stage between work and death. Moreover, they are the objects of discrimination in a youth-oriented society.

14. The family is a major location of violence in American society. One fourth of all the murders in the United States involve the killing of spouses, parents, and children. Wife abuse is fairly common and occurs in all age groups, ethnic and racial groups, and educational levels.

15. The divorce rate continues to rise in American society. The reasons for this trend are: increased social and financial independence of women, increased affluence, greater tolerance by religious groups, passage of no-fault divorce laws, and a change in the public attitude toward divorce.

16. A number of trends indicate that the American family is changing such as the higher divorce rate, the rising number of childless marriages, and the fact that the fastest growing family type is the household with no man present. One possibility in the future is for increased pluralism and freedom with a wide diversity of acceptable lifestyles. An opposite scenario for the future is for ever greater societal constraints on the family. Society in this case may demand a narrow range of choices to meet some crises or because the majority demands conformity to their way.

FOR FURTHER STUDY

Mary Jo Bane, *Here to Stay: American Families in the Twentieth Century* (New York: Basic Books, 1976).

Caroline Bird, *The Two-Paycheck Marriage* (New York: Pocket Books, 1979).

Michael Gordon (ed.), *The American Family in Social-Historical Perspective*, 2nd ed. (New York: St. Martin's, 1978).

Kenneth Kenniston, *All Our Children: The American Family Under Pressure* (New York: Harcourt Brace Jovanovich, 1977).

George Masnick and Mary Jo Bane, *The Nation's Families: 1960–1990*, (Cambridge, Mass.: The Joint Center for Urban Studies of MIT and Harvard University, 1980).

Lillian Breslow Rubin, *Worlds of Pain: Life in the Working-Class Family* (New York: Basic Books, 1976).

Eli Zaretsky, *Capitalism, the Family, & Personal Life* (New York: Harper Colophon, 1976).

NOTES AND REFERENCES

1. This theme is elaborated in William N. Stephens, "Family and Kinships," in *Sociology: An Introduction*, Neil J. Smelser, ed. (New York: John Wiley, 1967), pp. 535–543.

2. This section on history is taken primarily from Barbara Laslett, "Family Membership, Past and Present," *Social Problems* 25 (June, 1978), pp. 476–490.

3. Population Reference Bureau, cited in Associated Press release (October 3, 1980).

4. John F. Cuber, Martha Tyler John, and Kenrick S. Thompson, "Should Traditional Sex Modes and Values Be Changed?" in Raymond H. Muessig, ed. *Controversial Issues in the Social Studies: A Contemporary Perspective* (Washington, D.C.: National Council for the Social Studies, 1975), pp. 87–121, cited in Thomas J. Sullivan, et al., *Social Problems: Divergent Perspectives* (New York: John Wiley & Sons, 1980), p. 221.

5. Laslett, "Family Membership, Past and Present," p. 487.

6. Talcott Parsons and Robert F. Bales, *Family Socialization and Interaction Process* (Glencoe, Ill.: The Free Press, 1955).

7. The following argument is from Eli Zaretsky, *Capitalism, The Family & Personal Life* (New York: Harper Colophon, 1976).

8. See Robert O. Blood, Jr., and Donald M. Wolfe, *Husbands and Wives* (New York: The Free Press, 1960).

9. Alice S. Rossi, "Transition to Parenthood," *Journal of Marriage and the Family* 30 (February, 1968), pp. 26–39.

10. Ibid., p. 32.

11. Jerry Bergman, "Licensing Parents: A New Age of Child-Rearing?" *The Futurist* 12 (December, 1978), p. 363.

12. Candyce Smith Russell, "Transition to Parenthood: Problems and Gratifications," *Journal of Marriage and the Family* 36 (May, 1974), pp. 294–301.

13. There are a number of sources that document the differences in mode of socialization by social class. Especially important is the article that summarizes twenty-five years of studies of parent-child relationships by Urie Bronfenbrenner, "Socialization and Social Class through Time and Space," in E. E. Maccoby, T. M. Newcomb, and E. L. Hartley, eds., *Readings in Social Psychology* (New York: Holt, Rinehart and Winston, 1958), pp. 400–425. See also Melvin L. Kohn, "Social Class and Parental Values," *American Journal of Sociology* 64 (January, 1959), pp. 337–351; and James D. Wright and Sonia R. Wright, "Social Class and Parental Values for Children: A Partial Replication and Extension of the Kohn Thesis," *American Sociological Review* 41 (June, 1976), pp. 527–537.

14. For an historical review of child-rearing patterns, see Robert R. Sears, Eleanor E. Maccoby, Harry Levin, et al., *Patterns of Child Rearing* (Evanston, Ill.: Row, Peterson, 1957).

15. Benjamin Spock, *Baby and Child Care* (New York: Simon and Schuster (Pocket Books), 1947).

16. David Matza, "Position and Behavior Patterns of Youth," *Handbook on Modern Sociology*, Robert E. L. Faris, ed. (Chicago: Rand McNally, 1964), pp. 200–216.

17. Stephens, "Family and Kinship," p. 542.

18. James S. Coleman, *The Adolescent Society* (New York: Free Press, 1961).

19. For a discussion of "other-directedness" in American society, see David Riesman, *The Lonely Crowd* (New Haven, Conn.: Yale University Press, 1950).

20. Milton L. Barron, *The Aging American* (New York: Thomas Y. Crowell, 1961), Chap. 4, "The Aged as a Quasi-Minority Group."

21. Bernice L. Neugarten, "Grow Old Along with Me! The Best Is Yet to Be," *Psychology Today*, 5 (December, 1971), pp. 46, 48.

22. Felix Berardo, "Widowhood Status in the United States: Perspective on a Neglected Aspect of the Family Life Cycle," *The Family Coordinator* 17 (July, 1968), pp. 191–203.

23. Talcott Parsons, "Age and Sex Structure of the United States," *Essays in Sociological Theory*, Talcott Parsons, ed. (New York: Free Press, 1949), pp. 102–103.

24. For some general statements about the violent side of the family, see Suzanne K. Steinmetz and Murray A. Straus, "The Family as Cradle

of Violence," *Society* 10 (September/October 1973), pp. 50–56; Richard Sennett, "The Brutality of Modern Families," *Trans-action* 7 (September, 1970), pp. 29–37; and Graeme Newman, *Understanding Violence* (Philadelphia: Lippincott, 1979), Chapter 6, "Recycling Violence: The Family," pp. 137–153.

25. For discussions of battered husbands, see Suzanne K. Steinmetz, "The Battered Husband Syndrome," *Victimology* 2, Numbers 3–4 (1977–78), pp. 449–509; Richard J. Gelles, "The Myth of Battered Husbands," *Ms.* 8 (October, 1979), pp. 65–66, 71–74; and "The Battered Husbands," *Time* (March 20, 1978), p. 69.

26. Murray A. Straus, "Wife Beating: How Common and Why?" *Victimology* 2, Numbers 3–4 (1977–78), pp. 449–451.

27. Lenore E. Walker, *The Battered Woman* (New York: Harper & Row, 1979), p. 1.

28. Reported in Laura Shapiro, "Violence: The Most Obscene Fantasy," *Mother Jones* 2 (December, 1977), p. 11.

29. Walker, *The Battered Woman*, p. 16.

30. Reported in William Steif, "U.S. Government Slowly Aiding Battered Wives," *Rocky Mountain News* (October 27, 1979), p. 76.

31. Richard J. Gelles, "No Place to Go: The Social Dynamics of Marital Violence," in *Battered Women*, pp. 57–58; see also, Murray A. Straus, "Sexual Inequality, Cultural Norms, and Wife Beating," *Journal of Marriage and the Family* 36 (February, 1974), pp. 13–30.

32. John E. O'Brien, "Violence in Divorce Prone Families," *Journal of Marriage and the Family* 33 (November, 1971), pp. 692–698.

33. Straus, "Wife Beating," pp. 449–451. See also Murray A. Straus, "A Sociological Perspective on the Prevention and Treatment of Wifebeating," in *Battered Women: A Psychosociological Study of Domestic Violence*, Maria Roy, ed. (New York: Van Nostrand, 1977), pp. 232–233.

34. See Bruno Bettelheim, "Untying the Family," *The Center Magazine* 9 (September/October, 1976), pp. 5–9.

35. William J. Goode, "Family Disorganization," in *Contemporary Social Problems*, 4th ed.,

Robert K. Merton and Robert Nisbet, eds. (New York: Harcourt Brace Jovanovich, 1976), p. 529.

36. Unless otherwise noted, the source used for the information below is Reiss, *The Family System in America*, Chap. 17.

37. Paul C. Glick, "Some Recent Changes in American Families," *Current Population Reports*, Series P-23, No. 52 (Washington, D.C.: U.S. Government Printing Office, 1975), p. 9.

38. Hugh Carter and Paul C. Glick, *Marriage and Divorce: A Social and Economic Study*, rev. ed. (Cambridge, Mass.: Harvard University Press, 1976), p. 403; and U.S. Bureau of the Census, *Current Population Reports*, Series P-20, No. 312 (Washington, D.C.: U.S. Government Printing Office, 1977), Tables 3 and F.

39. Glick, "Some Recent Changes in American Families," p. 2.

40. U.S. Bureau of the Census, *Statistical Abstract of the United States 1979*, 100th ed. (Washington, D.C.: U.S. Government Printing Office, 1979), pp. 41, 81.

41. American Broadcasting Company, "Good Morning America," (November 20, 1979). See also, George Masnick and Mary Jo Bane, *The Nation's Families: 1960–1990* (Cambridge, Mass.: Joint Center for Urban Studies of MIT and Harvard University, 1980).

42. Alvin Toffler, *Future Shock* (New York: Bantam Books, 1970), p. 239.

43. Reiss, *The Family System in America*, p. 414.

44. Rainwater, "Post-1984 America," p. 20.

45. See the entire issue of *The Family Coordinator* 24 (October, 1975), entitled "The Second Experience: Variant Family Forms and Life Styles."

46. Margaret Mead, "Future Family," *Trans-action* 8 (September, 1971), pp. 50–53; Toffler, *Future Shock*, Chap. 11; "Signing Up for Marriage," *The New York Times*, June 27, 1976, p. E7; and J. Gipson Wells, "A Critical Look at Personal Marriage Contracts," *The Family Coordinator* 25 (January, 1976), pp. 33–37.

15

Religion in America

"All human beings have an innate need to tell and hear stories and to have a story to live by. Religion, whatever else it has done, has provided one of the main ways of meeting this abiding need. Most religions begin as clusters of stories, embedded in song and saga, rite and rehearsal. Go back as far as the bloody Babylonian epic of Gilgamesh or to Homer's accounts of the gods and heroes of Hellas. Or read the tales told by Bantu priests, Cheyenne holy men or Eskimo shamans. They are all, in their own way, stories. The Hebrew Scriptures are largely stories; so is the New Testament. Rabbis, saints, Zen masters and gurus of every persuasion convey their holy teachings by jokes, kōans, parables, allegories, anecdotes and fables. There has never been a better raconteur than Jesus of Nazareth himself."

Source: Harvey Cox, *The Seduction of the Spirit: The Use and Misuse of People's Religion* (New York: A Touchstone Book, Simon and Schuster, 1973), p. 9.

Religion is a ubiquitous phenomenon that has a tremendous impact on any society and its members. It is part of a large social system, affected by and affecting the other institutions of the society—that is, patterns of the family, the economy, education, and the polity. Since religious trends may be responses to fundamental changes in society, and some religious ideas may constrain social behaviors in a narrowly prescribed manner, the understanding of any society is incomplete unless one comprehends the religion of that society.

But, what is religion? The variety of activities and belief systems that have fallen under this rubric is almost infinite. There are some elements essential to religion, however, that allow us to distinguish it from other phenomena.[1] A starting point is that religion is created by people (that is, it is a part of culture). It is an integrated set of ideas by which a group attempts to explain the meaning of life and death. Religion is also a normative system, defining immorality and sin as well as morality and righteousness. Let us amplify some of these statements further.

1. Religion deals with the ultimate of human concerns—the meaning of life and death. It provides answers as to the individual's place in society and in the universe.[2]
2. There is an emphasis on human conduct. There are prescriptions for what one ought to do as well as the consequences for one's misconduct.
3. There is a distinction between the sacred and the secular. Some objects and entities are believed to have supernatural powers and are therefore treated with respect, reverence, and awe. What is sacred and what is not is a matter of belief. The range of items believed to be sacred is limitless. They may be objects (idols, altars, or amulets), animals

CROSS-CULTURAL PANEL

Panel 15-1
The Cargo Cult of Melanesia

Some religions prophesy a radical change in the future (the end of the world, the 1,000 year reign of Christ, or a return to some golden age). One such "millenarian movement" is the cargo cult of Melanesia. The islands in Melanesia have been visited throughout history by foreigners in sailing ships, steamships, and airplanes. Each time the visitors brought riches unknown to the island people. The natives were greatly impressed by these goods, which they believed were being manufactured and sent to them by their ancestors.

or animal totems, parts of the natural world (mountains, volcanos, or rivers), transcendental beings (gods, angels, devils), or persons (living or dead, such as prophets, messiahs, or saints).

4. Because the sacred is held in awe, there are beliefs (theologies, cosmologies) and practices (rituals) to express and reinforce proper attitudes among believers about the sacred. The set of beliefs attempts to explain the meaning of life. Moreover, these beliefs present a set of guidelines for action toward the sacred, and toward one's fellows. Ritual, with its symbolism and action, evokes common feelings among the believers (awe, reverence, ecstasy, fear) which lead to group unity.

5. An essential ingredient of religion is the existence of a community of believers. There must be a social group that shares a set of beliefs and practices, moral values, and a sense of community (a unique identity).

One important consequence of a group of persons having the same religious heritage and beliefs is unity. All believers, whether of high or low status, young or old, are united through the sharing of religious beliefs. Thus, religion, through the holding of common values to be cherished, sins to be avoided, rules to be followed, and symbols to be revered, integrates. Group unity is also accomplished through the universal feeling that God or the gods look upon this particular group with special favor (the ethnocentric notion that "God is on our side"). An example of this is found in a verse of the national anthem of Great Britain:

O lord our God, arise
Scatter our enemies
And make them fall.
Confound their politics,
Frustrate their knavish tricks,
On thee our hopes we fix,
God save us all.

Another consequence of religion is that it constrains the behavior of the community of believers, thus providing a social control function. This is accomplished in two ways. First, there are explicit rules to obey which if violated will be punished. Second, in the process of

The natives were most impressed with the cargo brought to the islands by plane during World War II (canned food, clothing, tools, radios, watches, guns, and motorcycles). When the War ended, however, the supplies were used up and not replaced by new shipments. The island prophets proclaimed that if airstrips were built, these would entice back the planes with their fabulous cargo. As a result, the natives have built airstrips in the jungle, complete with hangars, radio shacks, beacon towers, and airplanes (all made out of bamboo sticks and leaves). The airports are manned 24 hours a day, with bonfires set at night to serve as beacons for the expected cargo planes.

Thus, 40 years or so after World War II the natives await the phantom cargo that will hail the beginning of a new age. When the planes finally arrive their lives will be filled with riches and plenty. They will be reunited with their deceased ancestors, heralding the beginning of heaven on earth.

socialization, children internalize the religious beliefs and rules. In other words, they each develop a conscience which keeps them in line through guilt and fear.

A final positive consequence of religion—positive in the sense that it aids in uniting persons—is the legitimation of social structures that have profane origins.[3] There is a strong tendency for religious beliefs to become intertwined with secular beliefs, thereby providing religious blessings to the values and institutions of society. In American society, for example, private property and free enterprise have become almost sacred. Democracy, too, is believed to be ordained by God.

The very same religious bases that promote group integration also divide. Religious groups tend to emphasize separateness and superiority, thereby defining others as inferior ("infidels," "heathens," "heretics," or "nonbelievers"). This occurs because each religious group tends to feel it has the way (and perhaps the only way) to achieve salvation or reach nirvana or whatever the goal.

Religious differences accentuate the differences among societies, denominations, and even within local churches. Since religious groups have feelings of superiority, there may be conflict brought about by discrimination, competition for converts, or feelings of hatred. Also because religious ideas tend to be strongly held, groups may split rather than compromise. Liberals and fundamentalists, even within the same religion, denomination, or local church, will, doubtless, disagree on numerous issues. A common result, of course, is division.

A major divisive characteristic of religion is its tendency, through established churches, to accept the acts of the state. American churches, for example, have condoned such things as slavery, segregation, white supremacy, and war.* Within the church, there have always been those who spoke out against the church's cohabitation with the secular. This ability of the church to rationalize the activities of the state no matter how onerous has split many churches and denominations. The slavery issue, for example, split Baptists into American Baptists and Southern Baptists.

---

* Actually, the church has sometimes actively pursued some of these policies. The Puritan Church of the early settlers condoned witch hunts. The defeat of the Indians was justified by most Christian groups on the grounds that they were heathens and in need of white man's religion. Finally, most religious denominations sought Biblical rationalizations for slavery.[4]

Conflict itself can occur between religious groups (with the sanction of each religion). Recent world history gives bloody evidence of this occurrence (for example, Moslems versus Hindus in India and Pakistan, Moslems versus Jews in the Middle East, Catholics versus Protestants in Northern Ireland). Religious conflict has also occurred within the United States at various times. Confrontations between Catholics and Protestants, between warring sects of Muslims (Black Muslims versus Sunni Muslims), as well as Protestants and Jews, have been fairly commonplace.[5] Clearly, religious values are reason enough for individuals and groups to clash.

RELIGION FROM THE ORDER PERSPECTIVE OF EMILE DURKHEIM

Durkheim, the French sociologist, wrote *The Elementary Forms of Religious Life* in 1912. This classic work explored the question of why religion is universal in human societies. He reasoned that religion must help to maintain society. Durkheim studied the religion of the Australian aborigines to understand the possible role of religion in societal survival.

Durkheim found that each aborigine clan had its own totem, an object it considered sacred. The totem—a kangaroo, lizard, tree, river, or rock formation—was sacred because the clan believed that it symbolized the unique qualities of the clan. Two of Durkheim's interpretations are important in this regard. First, people bestow the notion of the sacred onto something, rather than that object being intrinsically sacred. Second, what the group worships is really society itself. Thus, people "create" religion.* Because the members of a society share religious beliefs, they are a moral community and as such the solidarity of the society is enhanced.

The society is held together by religious rituals and festivals in which the group's values and beliefs are reaffirmed. Each new generation is socialized to accept these beliefs, ensuring consensus on what is right and wrong. Religion, then, whether it be among the pre-industrial Australian aborigines, the Muslims of the Middle East, the Buddhists of Asia, or the Christians of North America, serves the same functions of promoting order and unity.

RELIGION FROM THE CONFLICT PERSPECTIVE OF KARL MARX

Whereas Durkheim interpreted the unity achieved through religion as positive, Marx viewed it as negative. Religion inhibits societal change by making existing social arrangements seem right and inevitable. The dominant form of economics in society, the type of government, the law, and other social creations are given religious sanction. Thus, the system remains stable, which the order theorists see as good, when it perhaps should be transformed to meet the needs of all of the people.

---

*This raises an important question: Do we create God or is there is a supernatural somewhere that human beings grope to find? Durkheim is correct in stating that religion is a social product. This universal response, however, does not prove or disprove the existence of a God or Gods. Sociologists as individuals may have strong religious beliefs, but as sociologists they focus on the complex interrelationship between religion and society.[6]

Religion promotes the status quo in other ways. The powerless are taught to accept religious beliefs that are against their own interests. The Hindus, for example, believe that it is the person's duty to accept his or her caste. Failure to do so will result in being reincarnated to a lower caste or even as an animal. Christianity proclaims that the poor should accept their lot in this life for they will be rewarded in Heaven. In short, somehow oppression and poverty are reinterpreted by religion to be a special form of righteousness. Thus, religion is the ultimate tool to promote false consciousness.

SOME DISTINCTIVE FEATURES OF AMERICAN RELIGION

Civil Religion

One feature of American religion, traditionally, has been the separation of Church and State (established by the first amendment to the Constitution). This is both a consequence and the cause of the religious diversity found in the United States. There is a relationship between religion and the state in America, but it differs from the usual conception of one dominant church that is inseparable from the state. In many respects, God and Country are conceived by most Americans as one. This has been labeled the civil religion of the United States.[7]

America's **civil religion** is seemingly antithetical to the constitutional demand for separation of Church and State. The paradox is that on the one hand the government sanctions God (the Pledge of Allegiance has the phrase, "one nation, under God"; the phrase, "In God We Trust," is stamped on all money; every Presidential inaugural address except Washington's second has mentioned God; and present-day Presidents have regularly scheduled prayer breakfasts), while at the same time declaring it illegal to have prayer and/or religious instruction in the public schools. The basis for the paradox is that the civil religion is not a specific creed. It is a set of beliefs, symbols, and rituals that is broad enough for all citizens to accept. The God of the civil religion is all things to all people. One thing is certain—politicians, if they want to be successful, must show some semblance of piety by occasionally invoking the blessings of this nondenominational, nonsectarian God.

There are several central themes of the civil religion that are important for the understanding of American society. First, there is the belief that God has a special destiny for the United States. This implies that God is actively involved in history and, most important, that America has a holy mission to carry out God's will on earth. John F. Kennedy phrased this message well in the conclusion to his inauguration address: "With a good conscience our only sure reward, with history the final judge of our deeds, let us go forth to lead the land we love, asking His blessing and His help, but knowing that here on earth God's work must truly be our own."[8] This belief has been the source of self-righteousness in foreign relations. It has allowed Americans to subdue the "pagan" Indians, win the frontier, follow a policy of manifest destiny, and defeat fascism. Currently, the defeat of communism is seen as a holy crusade.

A second aspect of the civil religion is maintenance of the status quo. The God of civil religion is more closely allied to law and order than to changing the system. Thus, civil religion tends strongly toward uncritical endorsement of American values and the system of stratification. Order and unity are the traditional ways of God, not change and dissent. Thus, public policy tends to receive religious sanction.

At the same time, however, the civil religion enjoins Americans to stand up for certain principles—freedom, individualism, equal opportunity. Consequently, there are occasions when current governmental policy or the policy of some group is criticized because it does not measure up to certain ideals. The civil religion of America, then, accomplishes both the priestly (acceptance of what is) and the prophetic (challenging the existing system) roles of traditional religion, with emphasis, however, on the former.

The Variety of Religious Belief

Some societies are unified by religion. All persons in such societies believe the same religious ideas, worship the same deities, obey the same moral commandments, and identify strongly with each other. Superficially, through its civil religion, the United States appears to be homogeneous along religious lines. Moreover, 92 percent of Americans are Christians and 94 percent of all adults in 1978 expressed a belief in a Supreme Deity.[9] But the range of attitudes and beliefs among Christians in American society is fantastic. Among Catholics, for example, there are radical priests who disobey the instructions of bishops, cardinals, and even the Pope. At the same time, however, there are priests who rigidly adhere to all the rules set down by the church authorities. If anything, the range within Protestantism is even greater. In 1976, Gallup reported that 46 percent of Protestants believed that the Bible is to be taken literally, word for word;[10] for others, the Bible is purely allegorical. This difference has led to a schism in the Missouri Lutheran Synod.[11] Some religious groups have so much faith in the healing power of religion that their members refuse to see physicians under any circumstances. Within Protestantism are Amish, Quakers, high-church Episcopalians, Pentecostal Holiness groups, Congregationalists, and even snake handlers.

Further evidence for the diversity of religious expression in the United States is found in the variance of beliefs concerning basic tenets of Christianity. Glock and Stark have demonstrated in their study of a random sample of church members in four metropolitan counties in northern California the wide disagreement among the various denominations, Protestant and Catholic, on a number of presumably central tenets of Christianity. They found, moreover, that with few exceptions there is considerable within-denomination variation on each of these articles of faith.[12]

Religious Organization

Very broadly, American religious organizations can be divided according to their secular commitments into two categories—churches and sects.[13]

Religious groups have a choice—to reject and withdraw from the secular society, or to accommodate to it. The basis for a decision to reject the social environment is maintenance of spiritual and ethical purity. Such a choice, by definition, entails withdrawal from the world, thereby consciously avoiding any chance to change it. The opposite choice—accommodation—requires compromise and the loss of distinctive ideals but it also means that the group can influence the larger society. The accommodation or resistance to the secular world is the fundamental difference between a church and a sect.

The **church**, as an ideal type, has the following attributes:

1. The tendency to compromise with the larger society and its values and institutions.
2. Membership tends to occur by being born to parents who belong. Membership,

moreover, takes place through infant baptism, which implies that all members are "saved."

3. A hierarchy of authority, with those at the top being trained for their vocation.
4. Acceptance of a diversity of beliefs, since the membership is large, and for many the scriptures are interpreted metaphorically rather than literally.
5. There is a tolerance of the popular vices.

A **sect** in its perfect form is exactly opposite a church in every way.

1. There is a fundamental withdrawal from and rejection of the world. A sect is a moral community separate from and in many ways hostile toward the secular world.[14]
2. Membership is only through a "conversion" experience. Membership is therefore voluntary and limited to adults. Hence, adult baptism is the only accepted form of baptism.
3. Organization is informal and unstructured. Ministers are untrained. They became ministers by being "called" from the group.
4. The belief system is rigid. The Bible is the source and it is interpreted literally. The goal of the membership is spiritual purity as found in the early Christian Church.

5. There are rigid ethical requirements restraining the members from the popular vices of drinking, smoking, card playing, dancing, and cursing.

The church–sect dichotomy does not exhaust all the possibilities. Some religious groups would fit somewhere in between—as institutionalized sects. These groups (for example, Mormons, Disciples of Christ, and Southern Baptists) incorporate features of both a church (trained leadership, some accommodation to the larger society) with the sectlike attributes of adult baptism, and an unwillingness to compromise on some theological questions.

For our purposes, however, the church–sect dichotomy, while oversimplifying the situation, is useful in two ways: to depict a form of social change, and to show why certain categories of persons are attracted to one type and not the other.

The church–sect dichotomy illustrates an important sociological phenomenon—the very process of organization deflects away from the original goal of the group. A group may form to pursue a goal such as religious purity, but in so doing it creates a new organization, which means that some of the group's energies will be spent in organizational maintenance. Consequently, a sect may form with the explicit intention of eliminating a hierarchy and a codification of beliefs. Patterns of behavior emerge, however, as certain practices are found to be more effective. In particular, the selection of ministers tends to become routinized, and a system of religious instruction for children is developed so that they will learn the catechism in the proper sequence. Sects, then, tend to become churches. This is illustrated by the type of leader found in each. Often a sect is formed by a charismatic person and his followers. This person is followed because he is believed to possess extraordinary qualities of leadership, saintliness, gifts of prophecy, or ability to heal. What happens to such an organization when this leadership is gone? The organization is faced with a crisis of succession. Groups typically find ways to pass on the **charisma** ("routinization of charisma") by either: (1) selection of the successor by the original charismatic leader, (2) designation of a successor by the group closest to the original leader ("disciples"), (3) hereditary transmission, or (4) transmission of charisma by ritual ("laying on of hands").[15] In this last instance there is the recognition of a charisma of office—that is, whoever holds the position possesses charisma. When this occurs, the organizational machinery is advanced enough to move the group away from its sectlike qualities toward a church. The important sociological point here is that organizations seldom remain the same. The simple tends to become complex. But the process does not stop at complexity; as the original goal of the sect (religious purity with the necessity of separation from the world) is superseded when the organization gets larger and more bureaucratic, some persons will become dissatisfied enough to break away and form a new sect. Thus, the process tends to be cyclical.

Increased bureaucratization (and subsequent splintering) is characteristic of moderr urban society. This leads us to a final consideration relative to the church–sect dichotomy—the motivation to join sects. At the risk of oversimplification, we can identify two important features of sects that help explain why some categories of persons are especially prone to join sects rather than churches. The first is that a sect (more so than a church) may provide a total world of meaning and social identity, and a close circle of persons to whom members can turn when troubled. The sect provides precisely those things missing in the lives of many urban dwellers. They find meaning in a meaningless world. They find friends in a sea of strangers. They find stability in a setting that is rapidly undergoing change. Thus, the alienated are especially attracted to sects. So, too, are new migrants to the city. In the city, they are confronted with a variety of new and difficult problems—industrialized work, work insecurity, loss of kinship ties, and disruption of other primary group ties. The sects, unlike the established city churches, appeal to such persons by their form of worship, emphasis on individual attention, and lack of formal organization appeal.[16]

A second variable affecting attraction to a sect or church is social class. Generally, low-status persons tend to be attracted to sects rather than churches because religious status is substituted for social status (or as the Bible puts it, "and the last shall be first"). It makes sense for persons of low social or economic status to reject this world and the religious bodies that accommodate to it. Such persons would be especially attracted to a religious group that rejects this world and assures its followers that in the next world "true believers"—those who are religiously pure—will have the highest status. The sect represents to its followers a reaction against or escape from the dominant religious and economic systems in society. It is a protest against the failure of established churches to meet the needs of marginal groups.[17] The sect, moreover, rejects the social class as irrelevant and, in fact, a system of rewards that is in exact reverse order from God's will.*

Churches, on the other hand, attract the middle and upper classes. Since these persons are successful, they obviously would not turn to a religious organization that rejects their world. As Max Weber said over fifty years ago:

> Other things being equal, classes with high social and economic privilege will scarcely be prone to evolve the ideas of salvation. Rather, they assign to religion the primary function of legitimizing their own life pattern and situation in this world.[18]

Both the sect and the church, consequently, have well developed theodicies.[19] A **theodicy** is a religious legitimation for a situation that otherwise might cause guilt or anger (such as defeat in a war or the existence of poverty among affluence). Sects tend to have a theodicy of suffering—i.e., a religious explanation for their lack of power and privilege. Churches must explain the inequalities of society, too, but their emphasis is on legitimation of possessing power and privilege. This tendency to develop theodicies has the important social function of preserving the status quo. Churches convince their adherents that all is well, that one should accept one's fate as God-given. This makes people's situations less intolerable and the possibility of revolution remote—the suffering know they will be rewarded, while the guilt of the well-off is assuaged. Consequently, there is no reason to change the system.

The Relationship between Socioeconomic Status and Religion

The dominant religion in the United States, Christianity, stresses the equality of all men in the sight of God. All persons, regardless of socioeconomic status, are welcomed in Christianity. We might expect, therefore, that the distribution of members by socioeco-

---

* It is incorrect to say, however, that all lower-class persons who are alienated will join religious sects in order to attack the establishment. Their estrangement may lead them to join other kinds of social movements (e.g., labor or political) or toward social isolation.

nomic status within any denomination would be randomly distributed. We might also assume that the organization of any local congregation would ignore status distinctions. Although these two assumptions seem to have surface validity, the empirical situation refutes them.

We have seen that sects and churches tend to have a social class bias—the lower the socioeconomic status, the greater the probability of belonging to a sect. There also seems to be a ranking of denominations in terms of the socioeconomic status of their members. Although there is always a range of the social classes within any one denomination, there is a modal status that characterizes each. The reasons for this are varied: the proportion of members living in rural or urban areas, which immigrant groups brought the religion to the United States and during what historical period, the appeal of the religious experience (ritual, evangelism, close personal ties, salvation, legitimation of the social system, or attacks on the establishment). This last point is especially important because "life conditions affect men's religious propensities, and life conditions are significantly correlated with the facts of stratification in all societies."[20]

There is a relationship between socioeconomic status and denominational affiliation. Table 15–1 presents data from a national sample that orders the major Protestant denominations by decreasing status.

Even though Table 15–1 shows that the denominations can be ranked by socioeconomic status, it is clear that each denomination includes persons of high, middle, and lower status. As Demerath has stated, "Episcopalians may be *relatively* upper class, but more than 40 percent are from the lower class. Baptists may be *relatively* lower class, but they claim their Rockefellers as well."[21]

TABLE 15–1   Social Class Profiles of Major Protestant Denominations (percentages)

Dimension of social class	Total Protes- tants[a]	Episco- palians	Presby- terians	Meth- odists	Luther- ans	Baptists
Education						
College	24	54	41	27	24	16
High school	56	36	51	58	56	57
Grade school	20	10	8	15	20	27
Income						
$20,000 and over	14	28	25	16	19	10
$15,000–$19,999	13	19	18	15	19	12
$10,000–$14,999	22	20	28	27	25	25
$7000–$9999	11	8	10	13	14	12
$5000–$6999	11	12	8	12	10	14
$3000–$4999	10	8	8	10	9	15
Under $3000	19	5	3	7	4	12

[a] The category of "Total Protestants" includes sects as well as the major denominations and therefore provides an indirect measure of their distribution on the two measures of social class as well.

Source: "Religion in America," *Gallup Opinion Index*, Report No. 130 (no date, but the survey was conducted in 1975 and 1976), p. 40.

Local churches, even more so than denominations, tend to be homogeneous in socioeconomic status. This is partly the result of residential patterns—that is, neighborhoods are relatively homogeneous by socioeconomic status and the local churches are attended mostly by persons living nearby. Another reason, and perhaps just as important, is the tendency for persons to want to belong to organizations composed of persons like themselves. They do not want to feel out of place, so they are attracted to churches where the members have the same lifestyle (for example, speech patterns, clothing tastes, and educational background). The result, then, is that persons belonging to a particular denomination will often seek out the local congregation in the city where they feel most comfortable. To paraphrase Broom and Selznick, "although rich and poor, educated and uneducated are members of one denomination, they tend to worship under different roofs."[22]

There is some range, however, in every local church. Probably no one congregation is comprised totally of persons from exactly the same status niche. Although the status differentials may be minimal within a local congregation, they are evidently important to the parishioners. The rule is that the higher the socioeconomic status of the member, the greater his or her influence in the running of the local church. There is greater likelihood that such persons will be elected or appointed to office (elder, deacon, trustee, Sunday school superintendent) and that their opinions will carry greater weight than persons of lower social status. This may be partly a function of the disproportionately large financial contributions by the more well-to-do, but the important point here is that the secular world intrudes in the organization of each local congregation.

The common indicators of religious involvement—church membership, attendance at church services, and participation in the church's activities—all demonstrate a relationship to socioeconomic status. On each of these measures, persons of high status are more involved than those of low status.[23] Unfortunately, these are not very good measures of religiosity, although often assumed to be. The problem is that upper-class persons are much more likely to join and actively participate in all sorts of organizations. The joining of churches and attending services are but the manifestations of a more general phenomenon—the tendency for middle- and upper-class persons to be "joiners" while lower-class individuals tend to isolate themselves from all types of organizations. The spuriousness of the relationship between socioeconomic status and "religiosity" is more clearly seen when we analyze the importance of religion to persons of varying socioeconomic circumstances, as well as differences in religious beliefs and the degree to which church activities are secular by social class.

Goode, after comparing white-collar church members with working-class church members, found that while the former were more likely to belong and participate in formal activities of the church, the latter were in fact more religious.

They participate less in formal church activities, but their religious activity does not appear to be nearly so secularized. It is more specifically religious in character. This is indicated by the fact that on a number of other religious dimensions, dimensions not dependent on extraneous nonreligious variables, individuals of manual-status levels appear to display a considerably higher level of religious response. This is true particularly of psychological variables, such as religious "salience," the greater feeling that the church and religion are great forces in the lives of respondents. It is also true for "religiosity" as measured by a higher level of religious concern, and for religious "involvement," the extent to which the individual is psychologically dependent on some sort of specifically religious association in his life.[24]

Table 15–2 presents evidence for the "secularization of religion" by the upper classes and the difference by level of education on religious beliefs. Examination of Table 15–2 reveals that the higher the educational status of the respondent, the more likely to hold liberal religious beliefs. This means, in effect, that the middle- and upper-status categories have tended to abandon the bases of Christianity.

In summary, there is a rather complex relationship between socioeconomic status and religion. Although the relatively poor and uneducated are more likely to be indifferent to religion than the better educated and financially well-off, those who are religious tend to make religion a more integral part of their lives than better-off persons. They go to church more for religious than secular reasons. They believe much more strongly than the well-to-do in the fundamental beliefs as expressed in the Bible. Thus, we have the paradox that on many objective measures of religious involvement—church attendance and participation in formal church activities—the middle- and upper-status persons exceed those of lesser status, whereas if importance of religion in the lives of the individual is considered, the poor who go to church outstrip their more economically favored brethren.

RELIGIOUS TRENDS

Religion in American society is a paradox. On the one hand, religion seems to be losing its vitality. The data show that in the past 25 years or so there has been a downward trend and recently a leveling off in regular church attendance (see Table 15–3). Protestants during this period have stayed near the 40 percent attendance level while the percentage of Catholics attending church at least once a week has fallen from 72 percent in 1954 to 52 percent in 1979. The data also show that the percentage of young adults attending church regularly has fallen and that the largest denominations—Episcopal, Methodist, and Presbyterian—are falling in both attendance and membership.[25]

On the other hand, however, there are indications that Americans are just as religious as ever and in some areas there is even dramatic growth. On the first point, Americans have consistently and overwhelmingly believed in God. Gallup has reported that 94 percent of

TABLE 15–2   Religious Attitudes for a Sample of American Adults
By Level of Education, 1976

Level of Education	% feeling their religious beliefs very important	% saying they are "born again"	% believing in God	% believing in life after death	% believing the Bible is the actual word of God	% who have tried to "save" someone
College	49	27	91	66	17	37
High school	58	36	96	70	42	47
Grade school	70	42	96	75	60	65

Source: Gallup Poll, reported in George Gallup, Jr., "U.S. In Early Stages of Religious Revival," Journal of Current Social Issues 14 (Spring 1977), adapted from a number of tables, pp. 53–55.

TABLE 15-3   Percentage Attending Church During Average Week

1954	46	1968	43
1955	49	1969	42
1956	46	1970	42
1957	47	1971	40
1958	49	1972	40
1959	47	1973	40
1960	47	1974	40
1961	47	1975	40
1962	46	1976	41
1963	46	1977	41
1964	45	1978	41
1965	44	1979	40
1966	44	1980	40
1967	43		

Source: Gallup Polls, reported in "Religion in America," *Gallup Opinion Index*, Report No. 130 (no date), p. 26; *Public Opinion* 2 (March/May 1979), p. 34; *The New York Times* (December 30, 1979), p. 13; and The Gallup Poll news release (January 25, 1981).

adult Americans believe in God or a universal spirit, which is the highest rate found in the nations of North America and Europe. Similarly, more Americans (71 percent) believe in life after death than do these other nations. (Canada is the next highest at 54 percent and West Germany the lowest with only one-third of adults accepting this belief.)[26]

Contrary to the experience of the mainline churches, some religious groups are growing rapidly in members and interest. The fastest growing in percentage gain is the Mormon Church with a national growth of 83,000 new members annually. More significant because of their growing numbers nationwide and their political leverage, are the evangelican denominations and sects.

In this section we will highlight four major trends of American religion: (1) the decline of the mainline churches; (2) the rise of the evangelicals; (3) the new political activism of the evangelicals and the decline of religious pluralism; and (4) the consciousness movement. Since social conditions have led to these shifts, the focus will be on the societal conditions that have given impetus to these trends.

The decline of the mainline denominations.   The major churches have been experiencing declining membership, attendance, and revenues. The reasons for this are not altogether clear, but the following appear plausible. These denominations have lost their vitality as they have become more and more churchlike (and have moved away from the qualities characterizing sects). The beliefs within these churches have become so pluralistic that to many the faith seems "watered down." Many churchgoers want authority but they too often receive only more ambiguity.

Since other parts of society emphasize rationality, efficiency, and bureaucracy, many persons seek a religion that will emphasize feelings and fellowship. However, the mainline churches, for the most part, are just as impersonal and ossified as the other bureaucracies found in society.

The Catholic Church has been especially vulnerable to losses in attendance. In this case, the rigidity of the Catholic hierarchy is partly responsible. The Church has taken strong stances against contraception, abortion, and divorce. Many Catholics feel that the Church authorities are out of step with contemporary life. The Catholic and some other traditional churches have also lost credence with some for their refusal to accept women in leadership roles. This patriarchal emphasis by some churches, however, is a positive attraction for some individuals as we will see later.

The rise of the evangelicals.   The most obvious reason why the evangelicals are increasing in number is their great emphasis on saving souls. They stress this activity because Christ commanded "Go ye into all the world and preach the gospel to every creature."

The evangelicals provide for many the ingredients they find missing in the mainline churches. They offer friendship, emotional release, a personal relationship with Christ, and rigid guidelines for beliefs and behaviors. This last point is an important one. Modern life in American society is characterized by rapid change and a plurality of ideas and choices. Although many are comfortable with change, many others seek authority, a foundation to provide consistency and constancy in their lives. The evangelicals provide a rigid set of beliefs based on the infallibility of the Bible as the word of God. This desire for authority has increased in the populace through a number of societal factors roughly dating back to the assassination of President John Kennedy.

We lost our leaders. We lost a war, which tore us apart at home. We lost confidence in business and government. A president once admired by millions left office in disgrace. Inflation soars. Energy is scarce. International tensions mount one upon another. And for many who were over 30 during the '60s, the radical changes in young people's values and life styles underscored the loss of a taken-for-granted morality that was once as integral to American culture as baseball, popcorn and Chevrolet.[27]

The evangelicals have increased their popularity with a tremendous emphasis on the use of direct mail advertising, radio, and television. This type of ministry began with the advent of radio in the 1920s, and expanded greatly with the growth of television in the '50s and '60s and cable television in the late 1970s. The enormity of this impact is in the number of people affected and the amounts of money generated. The National Religious Broadcasters, an association of 900 programmers, estimated that in 1979 an average of 14 million Americans watched a religious television show and 115 million listened to a radio gospel program *each week*, which is more than go to church. The top five electronic preachers together received $205 million in contributions. The largest amount was the $51 million collected by Reverend Jim Bakker of the PTL (Praise the Lord) Club, which surpasses the national budgets of many entire denominations in the United States.[28]

The success of this electronic church has been enhanced by the use of sophisticated methods such as professional production of programs, computerized mailing lists, and personalized letters written by computers. The successful evangelical preachers have adapted the communication technologies used by business and politicians to reach and manipulate their audience with the greatest effectiveness.

The mailrooms of the more successful electronic church practitioners are paragons of modern communication technology. Mail is sorted first by the presence or absence of money. Then letters are sorted by topics, and appropriate paragraphs are retrieved by computer and woven into some appropriate prepared response that can thus be "personalized." On-line printers dash off these individualized answers. Several organizations reportedly have a mailroom capability for processing 20,000 or more letters a day.[29]

A final reason for the growth of the evangelical movement has to do with its base in the South and Southwest. The Bible Belt happens to correspond with the Sun Belt, the region of fastest population growth. As business enterprises and individuals leave the Northeast and Midwest for the warm South, they are entering a religious climate that is evangelical in tone and substance. In time, these migrants will be likely candidates for membership in the evangelical churches.

The political activism of the evangelicals and the decline of religious pluralism. The traditional emphasis of evangelicals on saving souls, while undiminished, has added a new dimension—saving the morals of society through political activism.[30] This concern has risen as the result of recent court decisions and legislative acts legalizing abortion, defining the rights of homosexuals, permitting pornography, liberalizing divorce through "no fault" laws, and prohibiting prayer in the schools. These acts, and others such as the possibility of an Equal Rights Amendment to the Constitution and Affirmative Action, are viewed as undercutting the traditional family and promoting immorality.[31] The foes, in this view, are liberal politicians who are allowing the nation's moral foundations to crumble. Deserving of support are those politicians who are conservative Christians, opposed to the ERA, gay rights, abortion, Communist expansion, and disarmament. In the 1980 election, for example, the evangelicals (led by Reverend Jerry Falwell's Moral Majority) worked for the election of Ronald Reagan as President and focused their attention on the defeat of key liberals in the Senate. The were successful on both counts.

One consequence of these political efforts by the Christian right wing is an upsurge in religious bigotry. The evangelicals assume that their position is the only correct one. They have the only answer for women's rights (against), capital punishment (for), and national defense (increased spending), and so on. As a result, there can be no compromise. Some Christians are good (Reagan) and others are bad (Carter). The conservative churches are right and the liberal ones wrong. The commonalities among Christians are forgotten as the issues divide.

Finally, the political activism of the evangelicals is spawned by and directed at moral concerns, narrowly defined. Their political efforts are not concerned with racial injustice, poverty, or other problems of inequity. In short, the moral outrage of the evangelicals is selective. This issue of political activism is a topic we will return to shortly.

The "Consciousness Revolution." A recent trend has been toward eastern religions such as Zen, Yoga, and Hare Krishna or toward quasi-religion (Transcendental Meditation),[32] personal awareness, and mysticism. Although there are obvious differences between these groups, there are some commonalities that may explain their appeal. The key words used in all of these diverse belief systems are "consciousness," "inner awareness," "peace," "authenticity," "natural," and "self." The assumptions that are shared by these philosophies are:[33]

1. We are at the beginning of a New Age. The past focused on conquering the external world, but the new frontiers are inner.
2. Changes in society will not occur until people are changed.

3. There are forces within us that are immensely powerful yet remain untapped (these forces are "supernatural," even "divine").
4. The goal, then, is to develop the "you that could be."

Tom Wolfe has termed this movement "The Age of Me." "The old alchemical dream was changing base metals into gold. The new alchemical dream is: Changing one's personality—remaking, remodeling, elevating, and polishing one's very self. . . ."[34]

There are some major differences between the eastern religions and the non-religious personality development movements. Harvey Cox, the esteemed theologian, has studied the converts to the eastern religions such as Zen Buddhism, Hare Krishna, and the Unification Church, and found that they have rejected western religions in search for:[35] (1) a supportive community; (2) experiential religion; and (3) strong authority.

These reasons are not too different from those given by converts to evangelical Christianity. They, too, are responding to society, and a malaise they feel keenly from impersonal bureaucracies. There is a major difference, however, in society's response to the converts to oriental religions. There have been legal attempts to close their temples, make their religions subject to taxes, and to disallow them from purchasing property. Parents have had their children kidnapped and "deprogrammed" because they are so appalled by their actions.[36] Ironically, their children are living a life of peace, sharing, and self discipline—traits that parents typically encourage in their children.[37] In this context, however, these traits are interpreted negatively because they reject Christianity, competition, materialistic consumption, and status striving—all so very much part of American society.

THE ROLE OF THE CHURCH: COMFORT OR CHALLENGE?

The contemporary Christian church is faced with a basic dilemma brought about by its two contradictory roles (analogous to order and conflict approaches to the social order)—to comfort the afflicted and to afflict the comforted (or to comfort and to challenge). It is the church's commitment to both of these functions that has generated much of the trouble in the contemporary church.[38] The comforting role is one of aiding individuals in surmounting trials and tribulations of sickness, the death of loved ones, financial woes, social interaction with family, neighbors, colleagues, or enemies. The church aids by such means as pastoral counseling and collecting and distributing food and clothing to the needy. Another way the church comforts the afflicted is through providing a rationale for suffering (theodicy), the consequence of which is sanctification of the status quo.

Three related criticisms of the comforting function are immediately apparent. First, some would say that the church (and the clergy) have allowed this function to supersede the other role of challenger. Second, if the church would do more challenging and less comforting, evils such as poverty would be reduced. By helping people to accept an imperfect society, the church preserves the status quo—that is, the injustice and inequality that caused the problems in the first place. In this way, religion *is* an opiate of the masses because it convinces them to accept an unjust situation rather than working to change it from below. Third, the comfortable will not feel guilty, thereby preventing them from working to change the system from above.

The other function of the church—to challenge—is the injunction to be an agent of social protest and social reform. The church, through its pronouncements and leadership, seeks to lead in the fight to right the inequities of the society. A fundamental problem is in winning the support of the members. Change is almost by definition controversial, since some persons benefit under the existing social arrangements. When the church takes a stand against racial segregation, abortion, war, the abuses of business or labor, some members will become alienated. They may withdraw their financial support or even leave the church. The church, of course, has a commitment to its members. Since it cannot afford to lose its membership, the church may compromise its principles. Such an action, however, may make others angry at the church because of its hypocrisy. Consequently, the church is in the unenviable position of trying to keep a very precarious balance between compromise and purity.

The evidence is that, in general, the contemporary Christian church has opted in favor of the comforting function (see Panel 15–3). The most popular preacher of the 1960s and 1970s was Billy Graham. His theology is an excellent example of the prevailing "comforting" view. He has said, for example: "We should work for peace but all we can really do is patch things up, because the real war is in man's *own* heart. Only when Christ comes again will the lion lie down with the lamb and the little white children of Alabama walk hand in hand with the little black children."[42] This philosophy is anti-interventionist. One does not attack society. One either waits until the Second Coming or one changes the hearts and minds of individuals. Social problems, by this philosophy, are a result of the sinful nature of human beings and are to be dealt with on that level rather than on the level of changing the law or the social structure. Religion in this light is essentially a private transaction between an individual and God, and not a force for overcoming social ills. But this refusal to become involved in social issues supports the status quo, which is a form of involvement. As the Reverend Malcolm Boyd has argued:

There is a brand of Christianity which tells the rest of the world that it awaits the Second Coming of Christ to solve pressing "social problems" such as hunger, starvation, war, racism, sexism, colonialism, grinding poverty, and the absence of equal opportunity. This brand of Christianity explains that it renders unto God what belongs to God, and renders unto Caesar what belongs to Caesar, and it remains uninvolved in the arena of social issues. It lies.

For it is, in fact, cohesively involved in social issues by its support of the status quo on which it is dependent. It is rewarded by privilege, tax exemptions, and deductible financial benefits, and that ineffable sort of prestige bestowed traditionally upon docile religion by seasoned manipulators of caesaropapism—which means to say, the state using religion for its own purposes.[43]

Of course, the clergy vary in their interpretation of the role of the church. They are truly people in conflict. There are conflicting expectations of the clergy from all sides (resulting in role conflict). The church hierarchy expects the clergy to behave in a particular way (consider the rules issued by the Catholic hierarchy, for example). Most parishioners will doubtless favor the comforting role. Most joined the church to be comforted (if poor, to know they will be rewarded later; if rich, to have their wealth and power legitimized). There will, however, be some parishioners who wish the clergy to take a stand on

SOCIAL DILEMMAS AND CRITICAL CHOICES

Panel 15-2
The Freedom of Youth to Differ from Their Parents

A commonly held assumption is that parents have the right to transmit their religious and moral views to their children. At what point are children free to shift away from their parents' views if they wish? Are we a free society? Do we adhere to the principle of religious freedom?

These questions have come to national attention as some parents have hired persons to "abduct" their adult children from religious cults such as Hare Krishna or Sun Myung Moon's Unification Church, and "deprogram" them from beliefs which they believe to be sinister (that is, different, very different from their religious views).[39]

Perhaps it is ironic that they seek to release their children from groups that control the behavior of children in a manner consonant with what most parents would want of their children. As Nicholas Von Hoffman has put it:

The real baffler is why the Moonies' parents object so vehemently to their children being members of the sect. The parents should be rejoicing. They ought to be sending the Moon Man contributions. He gets people to do what parents want their children to do. Moonies are always clean, neat and conservatively dressed; they abstain from sex, alcohol and other drugs of pleasure; they get up early and they work hard all the livelong day; they go to church frequently and pray incessantly; they espouse no radical causes, and they uphold

controversial issues and work for social change. A final source of the clergy's role conflict arises from their own definition of the role. These various expectations, and the resulting role conflict on the clergy, amount to one reason why they may drop out. Another is that if they take a stand (or do not), they may automatically alienate a segment of the parish and perhaps the church hierarchy. They may, consequently, be forced to resign.

Those who do not resign may solve their dilemma by being noncontroversial. This non-boat-rocking stance is all too familiar and results in another problem—irrelevancy. By not talking about social problems, one in fact legitimates the status quo. Hence, the inequities of the society continue, since the moral force of the churches is mainly quiet.

The evidence is that the majority of clergy are opting for the "comforting" function over the "challenging" function. A 1980 Gallup Poll of clergy found that:[44] (1) 65 percent thought their churches should concentrate more on personal renewal than social renewal (the percentage agreeing with this was significantly higher among clergy from evangelical, Southern Baptist, and Baptist churches); (2) only 6 percent of the clergy would like to see religious periodicals address themselves more effectively to "social dimensions of faith and ministry;" and (3) only 45 percent had tried to persuade church, religious, and government organizations to aid the poor.

Not all clergy are content with the emphasis on comfort. As noted in the previous section, increasing numbers of clergy have become politically active on the "moral" issues of abortion, homosexuality, pornography, and the like. Typically, though, this view of

established authority no matter how barbaric. The wonder is that parents aren't insisting their children join the sect. This Korean reverend is so successful at getting Americans to live up to what are popularly regarded as Christian norms the guy should rent himself out to school boards as a consultant.[40]

Back to our original question, however: At what point should these young people be free to defy their parents' views, and do they have an unconditional right to be defiant? Do the parents have any rights in this situation, and if so, on what grounds? If you were able to influence a city mayor or state senator on enforcing the law on this issue, which way would you argue?

In fact, however, many state and local authorities have already decided the issue without consulting you; they have sided with the parents on this issue. Many judges and other government officials have disregarded the First Amendment and attacked these religious groups that are so different (for example, taking away tax-exempt status, placing adults under the guardianship of their parents in order to be deprogrammed). The system, from the government to parents, not to our surprise, supports orthodoxy and persecutes nonconformity. Americans have a difficult time accepting groups with foreign ideas (groups that oppose values like individual competition, personal ambition, and materialism/consumerism upon which traditional American society rests). Some might say the actions of the authorities resemble the Inquisition prevalent in medieval Europe.[41]

What is your opinion? Do parents have the right to continue their control over the minds of their children beyond adolescence—and by force? When are the rights of the individual violated—for youth? For parents? What is the role of society in demanding ideological conformity?

morality ignores the social problems of inequalities and injustices. Other clergy are not content to let the church continue to perpetuate injustice by not speaking and acting out. They are committed to a socially relevant church, one that seeks social solutions to social problems. They speak out, they participate in marches, work for integrated housing, and demonstrate against excessive militarism. Such activities, however, are not acceptable to the bulk of American Christians. As a result, the socially active clergy often become the object of discrimination by their parishioners. Another consequence is that the laity trust their clergy less and less. As behavior in one area is questioned—e.g., social activism—church members are likely to withdraw confidence in others as well. Finally, churches have divided on this issue. Some want social action instead of just pious talk. Others want to preserve the status quo. The hypocrisy found in many churches forces splits, the formation of underground churches, or total rejection of Christianity as the source of social action. Others may leave because they feel that the church has wandered too far from the beliefs upon which the faith was founded. This dilemma accelerates the current dropout problem—by parishioners and clergy alike.[45] The problem (if the author may here interject his bias) seems to be that for the most part those who drop out are the social activists who leave the church with a residue of "comforters." If this is the case, the future of the church is bleak unless there is a reversal and prophets of social action ascend—an unlikely possibility given the propensity of most parishioners for the message of "comfort" over the message of "challenge."

Panel 15–3
The Church and the Establishment

The theme of this essay is that it is *normal* for the Church *not* to effectively protest or to actively seek solutions on behalf of those being victimized by the social order. I am not referring to the innocuous pap the Church routinely hands out in muted and safe tones on quiet Sunday mornings to yawning and bored parishioners. This it does with the regularity of ritual—and is regularly ineffectual. I am, rather, referring to the Church, with its millions of members and its potential power, not protesting the Established Order on behalf of the downtrodden of society, not taking a stand for those persons who are being systematically brutalized by a discriminatory social system.

Why, for example, is the Church largely silent when it exists in the midst of a white supremacist society which selected its most physically fit and able youth (primarily from the ranks of its lower income groups—those groups which didn't have the privileged protection of deferments—its blacks, Indians, and Appalachian whites) and sent them thousands of miles in a genocidal onslaught against a yellow peasant population? Where was the voice of the Church when our corporate warlords spouted their democratic ideology as the basis for napalming women and children, with never a word about the profits being raked off the war industries based on the production of wholesale death and destruction? Why didn't the Church protest when the military dehumanized our youth by teaching them to slaughter *groups* of yellow peasants as regular policy and ordered them by direct command to cold-bloodedly shoot *individual* peasants whose only "guilt" was that of being *suspected* of having collaborated with the Viet Cong? Where was the voice of the Church when those youth, who learned their lesson so well, applied it to a village such as My Lai? Why was the Church mostly silent when a dehumanized American public initially reacted with a "That's war" philosophy or a "We-don't-know-enough-about-it-to-make-a-judgment" attitude? Where is the Church when it is surrounded by a populace so brainwashed that it cannot see that the My Lai massacre was the logical extension of an inhuman, demoralizing policy being systematically and cruelly followed by the United States Government for the sake of profit and power?

Even when the social malaise came to the point where the poverty-stricken and our students began to riot and government troops, tanks, and helicopters were brought into play in order to hold down the masses, it was only a small part of the Church which responded in protest. When our corrupting and corrupted leaders dehumanize large numbers of our citizens by placing profits before human values,

SUMMARY

As usual, order and conflict theorists view this social phenomenon—religion—very differently. Also, as usual, the unity and diversity found within this institution suggest that both models of society are partially correct.

Adherents of the order model emphasize the solidarity functions of religion. Religion helps individuals through times of stress and it benefits society by binding people together

and when, through inadequate diets, the minds of our poor are blunted, their bodies debilitated, while at the same time others stuff themselves to the point that concern with too much fat on the figure becomes a major preoccupation, the Church is strangely silent.

One wonders where the Church is when more money is annually spent in the United States on alcohol . . . than the combined amount spent on public aid by federal, state, and local governments. . . . Or when more than *eight* times as much is spent on tobacco . . . than on funding the Job Corps. . . . Or when more money is spent annually on cat and dog food . . . than the total amount spent by all our federal, state, and local governments on meals for public school children. . . .

The reason the Church seldom joins social protest is because the Church itself typically sides with the Established Order of society. It does not view discriminatory and victimizing social arrangements as evil so much as it does the disturbances arising from these social arrangements. For example, the Church does not protest the conditions which lead to riots as much as it does rioting. It gives out insipid statements about deploring conditions which lead men to riot but then comes down firmly and with no hesitation solidly against those who riot, pointing to the evils of destroying that which is so sacred in American society—property. In this way the Church defends the propertied, those in control (and, not incidentally, its own larger contributors), and comes down hard with its predictable lines about "respect" for "law and order."

Can we really expect anything different from the Church? If we take the lessons of history seriously instead of paying attention to ecclesiastical ideology, we would find that it is normal for the Church *not* to speak out, *not* to take the side of the impoverished, the weak, and defenseless, or when it does speak out, to do so in such a muted and weak way that it affects no one. Historically, it is only rarely that the privileged classes of a society have effectively worked to change the conditions of the less fortunate of their society: This is because those very conditions serve to maintain the privileged in their exalted positions. Those who protest run the risk of bringing into play forces which lead to their own destruction. If members of the privileged classes were to protest, they would run the risk of losing their positions of privilege. And . . . the Church is part of the privileged sector of American society.

Source: Excerpted from James M. Henslin, "From Prophets to Profits: The Church and the Establishment," in *Social Problems in American Society*, 2nd ed., James M. Henslin and Larry T. Reynolds, eds. (Boston: Allyn and Bacon (Holbrook Press), 1976), pp. 270–272.

through a common set of beliefs, reaffirmed through regularly scheduled ceremonial rituals.

Conflict theorists acknowledge that religion may unify in small societies but in diverse societies religious differences divide. Religious conflict occurs commonly at all levels, however, from intersocietal religious warfare, to schisms in local congregations. From the conflict perspective, religious unity within a society, if it does occur, has negative consequences. Such unity is used to legitimate the interests of the powerful (for example, slavery, racial segregation, conquest of "pagans," and war). Similarly, the interests of the powerful are served if the poor believe that they will be rewarded in the next life. Such a "theodicy" prevents revolutions by the oppressed and serves, as Marx suggested, as "an opiate of the masses."

There are some contemporary trends in American religion that will be interesting to observe in the coming decade. Will the fundamentalist boomlet become the dominant mode of religious expression? Will religion become increasingly emotional? Will the "consciousness movement" gain momentum or be a passing fad? Will the rejection of social action by many religious persons encourage or discourage membership growth and with what other consequences for the mission of religion and the solutions to the pressing problems of society? What will be the effects of the politics of the evangelicals on American society?

CHAPTER REVIEW

1. Religion is socially created and has a tremendous impact on society. It is an integrated set of beliefs by which a group attempts to explain the meaning of life and death. Religion defines immorality and sin as well as morality and righteousness.

2. The consequences of religion are unity among the believers, conformity in behavior, and the legitimation of social structures. Religion also divides. It separates believers from non-believers, denominations, religions, and even the members of local religious groups.

3. Emile Durkheim, an order theorist, explored the question of why religion is universal. He reasoned that what any group worships is really society itself. The society is held together by religious rituals and festivals in which the group's values and beliefs are reaffirmed.

4. Karl Marx, a conflict theorist, saw religion as inhibiting social change by making existing social arrangements seem right and inevitable. Religion further promotes the status quo by teaching the faithful to accept their condition—thus religion is the ultimate tool to promote false consciousness.

5. Civil religion is the belief that God and Country are one. God is believed to have a special destiny for the United States. Order and unity are thus given religious sanction.

6. Although most Americans identify with Christianity, there is a wide variety of religious belief in American society.

7. American religious organizations can be divided according to their secular commitment into two categories. A *church* tends to compromise with the larger society, tolerates popular vices, and accepts a diversity of beliefs. A *sect*, in sharp contrast, rejects the world. It is a moral community with rigid ethical requirements and a narrow belief system.

8. A *theodicy* is a religious legitimation for a situation that otherwise might cause guilt or anger. Sects tend to have a theodicy of suffering, explaining their lack of power and privilege. Churches have theodicies that legitimate the possession of power and privilege.

9. There is a relationship between socioeconomic status (SES) and religion: (a) the lower the SES, the greater the probability of belonging to a sect; (b) there is a relationship between SES and denominational affiliation; (c) the higher the SES of the member, the greater his or her involvement and influence in the local church.

10. One trend is the decline in the mainline denominations. These churches are often bureaucratic and impersonal. Their beliefs are pluralistic. The Catholic Church is losing members

because its stands against contraception and divorce are out of tune with contemporary life.

11. Another trend is the rise of the evangelicals. These groups offer what many find missing in the mainline churches—friendship, emotional release, a personal relationship with Christ, and strong beliefs.

12. A third trend is the political activism of the evangelicals and the decline of religious pluralism. Evangelicals in 1980 became a major force in politics, exhibiting a narrow view and religious bigotry.

13. A final trend has been the upsurge toward eastern religions as a means to explore new levels of consciousness.

14. The contemporary Christian church is faced with a basic dilemma brought about by its two contradictory roles—to comfort the afflicted and to afflict the comforted. The comforting function is criticized because it focuses on helping the individual but ignores the problems of society. The challenging function—the injunction to be an agent of social protest and social reform—is criticized because it is divisive, alienating some members who disagree with the position taken. The evidence is clear that the majority of clergy are opting for the "comforting" function over the "challenging" function.

FOR FURTHER STUDY

Robert N. Bellah, *The Broken Covenant: American Civil Religion in Time of Trial* (New York: Seabury Press, 1975).

Peter L. Berger, *A Rumor of Angels: Modern Society and the Rediscovery of the Supernatural* (Garden City, N. Y.: Doubleday (Anchor Books), 1970).

Daniel Cohen, *The New Believers: Young Religion in America* (New York: Ballantine Books, 1975).

Harvey Cox, *The Seduction of the Spirit: The Use and Misuse of People's Religion* (New York: Simon and Schuster, 1973).

Alan Crawford, *Thunder on the Right: The "New Right" and the Politics of Resentment* (New York: Pantheon, 1980).

Emile Durkheim, *The Elementary Forms of Religious Life* (New York: The Free Press, 1965).

Donald B. Kraybill, *Our Star-Spangled Faith* (Scottdale, Pa.: Herald Press, 1976).

Max Weber, *The Protestant Ethic and the Spirit of Capitalism* (London: Allen and Unwin, 1930).

NOTES AND REFERENCES

1. These elements are taken primarily from Elizabeth K. Nottingham, *Religion and Society* (New York: Random House, 1954), pp. 1–11.

2. See especially Peter L. Berger, *The Sacred Canopy* (New York: Doubleday, 1967).

3. Peter L. Berger, "Religious Institutions," in *Sociology*, Neil J. Smelser, ed. (New York: John Wiley, 1967), pp. 343–344.

4. Pierre L. van den Berghe, *Race and Racism: A Comparative Perspective* (New York: John Wiley, 1967), p. 82.

5. Earl Raab, ed., *Religious Conflict in America* (Garden City, N.Y.: Doubleday (Anchor Books), 1964); see also Robert Lee and Martin E. Marty, *Religion and Social Conflict* (New York: Oxford University Press, 1964).

6. Emile Durkheim, *The Elementary Forms of Religious Life* (New York: The Free Press, 1965). Originally published in 1912.

7. The following is taken largely from Robert N. Bellah, "Civil Religion in America," *Daedalus* 96 (Winter, 1967), pp. 1–21; and Conrad Cherry, "American Sacred Ceremonies," in

American Mosaic: Social Patterns of Religion in the United States, Phillip E. Hammond and Benton Johnson, eds. (New York: Random House, 1970), pp. 303–316. For other scholarly treatises on the sources and measurement of civil religion, see William A. Cole and Philip E. Hammond, "Religious Pluralism, Legal Development, and Societal Complexity: Rudimentary Forms of Civil Religion," *Journal for the Scientific Study of Religion* 13 (June, 1974), pp. 177–189; Robert E. Stauffer, "Civil Religion, Technocracy and the Private Sphere: Further Comments on Cultural Integration in Advanced Societies," *Journal for the Scientific Study of Religion* 12 (December, 1973), pp. 415–425; and Ronald C. Wimberley, Donald A. Clelland, Thomas C. Hood, and C. M. Lipsey, "Measuring Civil Religion," paper read at the annual meeting of the American Sociological Association, Montreal, August, 1974. See also, Robert N. Bellah, *The Broken Covenant: American Civil Religion in Time of Trial* (New York: Seabury, 1975); and the entire issue of *Journal of Church and State* 22 (Winter, 1980).

8. Bellah, "Civil Religion in America," pp. 1–2. For other examples of civil religion in American society, see especially: "God-Language in the Inaugural," *The Christian Century* 94 (January 5–12, 1977), pp. 3–7; Leo Sandon, Jr., "James Reston: Prophet of American Civil Religion," *The Christian Century* 94 (January 5–12, 1977), pp. 15–18; and Donald B. Kraybill, *Our Star-Spangled Faith* (Scottdale, Pa.: Herald Press, 1976).

9. These data are from a Gallup Poll reported in *Public Opinion* 2 (March/May 1979), pp. 32–39.

10. Reported in "Born Again!" *Newsweek*, October 25, 1976, p. 68.

11. See Richard J. Cattani, "Missouri Lutheran Synod Makes Schism Official," *Christian Science Monitor*, December 8, 1976, p. 7.

12. Charles Y. Glock and Rodney Stark, *Religion and Society in Tension* (Chicago: Rand McNally, 1965).

13. Ernst Troeltsch, *The Social Teaching of the Christian Churches*, Olive Wyon, trans. (New York: Macmillan, 1931); and Liston Pope, *Millhands and Preachers* (New Haven, Conn.: Yale University Press, 1942), pp. 117–140.

14. For a contemporary analysis of the sect-church division, see John Scanzoni, "Resurgent Fundamentalism: Marching Backward into the '80s?" *The Christian Century* (September 10–17, 1980), pp. 847–849.

15. Max Weber, *The Theory of Social and Economic Organization*, A. M. Henderson and Talcott Parsons, trans. (Glencoe, Ill.: Free Press, 1947), pp. 358–366.

16. J. Milton Yinger, *Sociology Looks at Religion* (New York: Macmillan, 1961), pp. 21–25.

17. This is the conclusion of Liston Pope after his study of the rise of sects in a small town in North Carolina: Pope, *Millhands and Preachers*, p. 140.

18. Max Weber, *The Sociology of Religion*, Ephraim Fischoff, trans. (Boston: Beacon Press, 1963), p. 107.

19. Peter L. Berger, *The Sacred Canopy: Elements of a Sociological Theory of Religion* (Garden City, N.Y.: Doubleday, 1967), pp. 53–80.

20. Thomas O'Dea, *The Sociology of Religion* (Englewood Cliffs, N.J.: Prentice-Hall, 1966), p. 60. For an elaboration of this point, see the insightful discussion by Weber in *The Sociology of Religion*.

21. N. J. Demerath III, *Social Class in American Protestantism* (Chicago: Rand McNally, 1965), p. 3.

22. Leonard Broom and Philip Selznick, *Sociology*, 4th ed. (New York: Harper & Row, 1968), p. 321.

23. This relationship does not always hold, however, if other dimensions of religious involvement are examined. See especially Demerath, *Social Class in American Protestantism*, pp. 1–124.

24. Erich Goode, "Social Class and Church Participation," *American Journal of Sociology* 72 (July, 1966), p. 111.

25. *The New York Times* (December 30, 1979), p. 13.

26. Gallup Poll, cited in *Public Opinion* 2 (March/May 1979), p. 37.

27. Jeffrey K. Hadden, "Soul-Saving Via Video," *The Christian Century* (May 28, 1980), p. 611.

28. Cited in "Stars of the Cathode Church," *Time* (February 4, 1980), pp. 64–65.

29. Hadden, "Soul-Saving Via Video," p. 610.

30. See George F. Will, "Who Put Morality in

Politics?" *Newsweek* (September 15, 1980), p. 108; "A Tide of Born-Again," *Newsweek* (September 15, 1980), pp. 28–36; "Preachers in Politics," *U. S. News & World Report* (September 24, 1979), pp. 37–41; and Martin E. Marty, "Fundamentalism Reborn," *Saturday Review* (May 1980), pp. 37–42.

31. For a sample statement of the moral concerns of the evangelicals see C. Everett Kopp, "Corruption in Our Society: The Domino Effect," *New Wine* 12 (July/August, 1980), pp. 9–17.

32. A Gallup Poll found that approximately 10 million Americans are involved in eastern religions, reported in *Public Opinion* 2 (March/May, 1979), p. 27.

33. Melvin Maddocks, "America's Therapy Industry," *Christian Science Monitor* (January 10, 1977), pp. 16–17.

34. Tom Wolfe, "The Me Decade and the Third Great Awakening," *New West* (August 30, 1976), p. 36.

35. Harvey G. Cox, "Why Young Americans are Buying Oriental Religions," *Psychology Today* (July, 1977), pp. 36–42.

36. See Frederick Bunt, "Deprogramming and Religious Liberty," *The Humanist* (September/October, 1979), pp. 48–49.

37. Harvey G. Cox, "Four Big Ones," *Journal of Current Social Issues* 14 (Spring 1977), p. 28.

38. Much of the following discussion is taken from Charles Y. Glock, Benjamin B. Ringer, and Earl R. Babbie, *To Comfort and to Challenge: A Dilemma of the Contemporary Church* (Berkeley, Calif.: University of California Press, 1967), especially Chap. 9; and Jeffrey K. Hadden, *The Gathering Storm in the Churches* (Garden City, N.Y.: Doubleday, 1969).

39. For a defense of "deprogramming" by its leading practitioner, see Ted Patrick, *Let Our Children Go!* (New York: E. P. Dutton, 1976).

40. Nicholas Von Hoffman, "Moonies, Hare Krishnas Are Ideal American Kids, Right?" *Rocky Mountain News*, April 8, 1977, p. 51.

41. See Garry Wills, "The Secular Inquisition against Moonies," *Rocky Mountain News*, April 17, 1977; and "The Freedom to Be Strange," *Time*, March 28, 1977, p. 81.

42. "The Preaching and the Power," *Newsweek* (July 20, 1970), p. 52.

43. Malcolm Boyd, "Does God Have a Candidate?" *The Progressive* 41 (November, 1976), p. 27.

44. Cited in Robert T. Henderson, "Ministering to the Poor: Our Embarrassment of Riches," *Christianity Today* (August 8, 1980), p. 18.

45. Harold E. Quinley, "The Dilemma of an Activist Church: Protestant Religion in the Sixties and Seventies," *Journal for the Scientific Study of Religion* 13 (March, 1974), pp. 1–21.

16

The American Economy

Each new affirmation of unemployment renews the pain: the first trip to the employment agency, the first friend you tell, the first interview and, most dreaded of all, the first trip to the unemployment office.

Standing in line at the unemployment office makes you feel very much the same as you did the first time you ever flunked a class or a test—as if you had a big red "F" for "Failure" printed across your forehead. I fantasize myself standing at the end of the line in a crisp and efficient blue suit, chin up, neat and straight as a corporate executive. As I move down the line I start to come unglued and a half hour later, when I finally reach the desk clerk, I am slouching and sallow in torn jeans, tennis shoes and a jacket from the Salvation Army, carrying my worldly belongings in a shopping bag and unable to speak.

You do eventually become accustomed to being unemployed, in the way you might accept a bad limp. And you gradually quit beating yourself for not having been somehow indispensable—or for not having become an accountant. You tire of straining your memory for possible infractions. You recover some of the confidence that always told you how good you were at your job and accept what the supervisor said: "This doesn't reflect on your job performance; sales are down 30 percent this month."

But each time you recover that hallowed self-esteem, you renew a fight to maintain it. Each time you go to a job interview and give them your best and they hire someone else, you go another round with yourself and your self-esteem. Your unemployment seems to drag on beyond all justification. You start to glimpse a stranger in your rearview mirror. The stranger suddenly looks like a bum. You look at her with clinical curiosity. Hmmm. Obviously into the chronic stages. Definitely not employable.

We unemployed share a social stigma similar to that of the rape victim. Whether consciously or subconsciously, much of the work-ethic-driven public feels that you've somehow "asked for it," secretly wanted to lose your job and "flirted" with unemployment through your attitude—probably dressed in a way to invite it (left the vest unbuttoned on your three-piece suit).

But the worst of it isn't society's work-ethic morality; it's your own, which you never knew you had. You find out how much self-satisfaction was gained from even the most simple work-related task: a well-worded letter, a well-handled phone call—even a clean file. Being useful to yourself isn't enough.

But then almost everyone has heard about the need to be a useful member of society. What you didn't know about was the loneliness. You've spent your life almost constantly surrounded by people, in classes, in dorms and at work. To suddenly find yourself with only your cat to talk to all day distorts your sense of reality. You begin to worry that flights of fancy might become one way.

But you always were, and still are, stronger than that. You maintain balance and perspective, mainly through resorting frequently to sarcasm and irreverence. Although something going wrong in any aspect of your life now seems to push you into temporary despair much

431

more easily than before, you have some very important things to hang on to—people who care, your sense of humor, your talents, your cat and your hopes.

And beyond that, you've gained something—a little more knowledge and a lot more compassion. You've learned the value of the routine you scorned and

the importance of the job you took for granted. But most of all, you've learned what a "7.6 percent unemployment rate" really means.

Source: Jan Halvorsen, "How It Feels to Be Out of Work," *Newsweek* (September 22, 1980), p. 17.

Economic activity involves the production and distribution of goods and services. An urban and industrialized society such as the United States requires a complex network to transform raw materials into finished products, to transport these products, to merchandise these products. Services, too, are varied. People need things repaired, they want advice, they desire credit, they seek investments. The list is endless but the point is clear—American society is composed of persons doing highly specialized tasks which, because of the interdependence of the parts, result in the production and distribution of the materials goods and the services that people want.

The task of this chapter is to describe the American economy. Four areas will be emphasized: the domination of huge corporations, the domestic and international impact of multinational corporations, the maldistribution of wealth, and the unequal distribution of governmental largesse. We begin, though, with a brief description of the two fundamental ways societies can organize their economic activities.

CAPITALISM AND SOCIALISM

All the ways that industrialized societies organize their economic activities can be divided into one of two fundamental forms: capitalism and socialism. I will examine each of these types in its pure form (that is, how it might exist in ideal circumstances). Although no society has a purely capitalist or socialist economy, examining these ideal types provides examples of extremes so that we can assess the American economy more accurately.

Capitalism

Several crucial conditions must be present for pure capitalism to exist. The first is private ownership of property. Individuals are encouraged to own, not only private possessions, but most important, the capital necessary to produce and distribute goods and services. In a purely capitalist society there would be no public ownership of any potentially profitable activity.

The pursuit of personal profit is the second essential ingredient of capitalism. This goal implies that individuals are free to maximize their personal circumstances. Most important, the proponents of capitalism argue that this profit-seeking by individuals has positive consequences for the society. Thus, the act of seeking individual gain through personal profit is considered morally acceptable and socially desirable.

Competition is the mechanism that keeps individual profit-seeking in check. Potential abuses such as fraud, faulty products, and exorbitant prices are negated by the existence of competitors who will soon take business away from those who violate good business judgment. So, too, economic inefficiency is minimized as market forces cause the inept to fail and the efficient to succeed.

These three elements—private property, personal profit, and competition—require a fourth condition if true capitalism is to work. This is a government policy of laissez-faire (literally, to leave alone). The government must allow the marketplace to operate unhindered. This requires a minimum of government interference in economic life. Any government intervention in the marketplace will, argue capitalists, distort the economy by negatively affecting incentives and freedom of individual choice. If left unhindered by government, the profit motive, private ownership, and competition will achieve the greatest good for the greatest number. This "greatest good" is translated into individual self-fulfillment and the general material progress of society.

Socialism

The three goals of socialism are democratism, egalitarianism, and efficiency. True socialism must be democratic. Representatives of a socialist state must be answerable and responsive to the wishes of the public they serve. Nations that claim to be socialistic but are totalitarian counter this fundamental aspect of socialism. The key to differentiating between authentic and spurious socialism is to determine who is making the decisions and whose interests are being served. Thus it is a fallacy to equate true socialism with the politicoeconomic systems found in Russia, China, or Cuba. These societies are socialistic in some respects; that is, their material benefits are more evenly distributed when compared to those in the United States. But the economies and governments of these countries are controlled by a single political party in an inflexible and authoritarian manner. Although they appear to have democratic elections, these countries are far from democratic. The people have no electoral choices but to "rubber stamp" the choices of the ruling party. The people in these repressive societies are denied civil liberties and freedoms that should be the hallmark of a socialist society. In a pure socialist society democratic relations must be found throughout the social structure: in government, at work, at school, and in the community.

The second principle of socialism is egalitarianism. This goal is equality: equality of opportunity for the self-fulfillment of all; equality rather than hierarchy in making decisions; and equality in sharing the benefits of society. Thus, there is a fundamental commitment in socialism to achieving a rough parity by leveling out gross inequities in income, property, and opportunities. The key is a leveling of the advantages so that all citizens receive the necessities (food, clothing, medical care, living wages, sick pay, retirement benefits, and shelter).

The third feature of socialism is efficiency. This refers to the organization of the society to provide, at the least possible individual and collective cost, the best conditions to meet the material needs of its citizens. This means that production of the necessary goods must be assured, as well as the distribution of the goods produced, and services offered must be planned and managed. The key method to accomplishing this economic efficiency for socialism is the substitution of public for private ownership of the means of production. The people own the basic industries, financing institutions, utilities, transportation, and communication companies. The goal is serving the public, not making profit (as is the case in capitalism). Thus the government would plan to achieve societal goals such as protecting the environment, combatting pollution, saving natural resources, and developing new technologies. Socialism, it is argued, is efficient because public policy is decided by rationally assessing the needs of society and how the economy might be organized to best achieve them. This requires, of course, that the economy be regulated by the government, which acts as the agent of the people. Prices and wages are set by the government. Important industries might be run at a loss if necessary. Dislocations such as surpluses or shortages or unemployment are minimized by central planning. The goal is to run the economy for the good of the society.

THE CORPORATION-DOMINATED ECONOMY

The American economy has always been based on the principles of capitalism; however, the present economy is far removed from a free enterprise system. There are two important discrepancies between the ideal system and the real one we operate in. The American economy is no longer based on competition among more or less equal private capitalists. It is now dominated by huge corporations that, contrary to classical economic theory, control demand rather than being responsive to the demands of the market. However well the economic system might once have worked, the increasing size and power of corporations disrupt it. This calls into question just what is the appropriate economic form for a modern industrialized society. We will examine the consequences of concentrated economic power domestically and internationally, for they create many important social problems. The second contradiction of American economic life is the existence of what has been called corporate socialism: the dependence of corporations on governmental largesse, contracts, and regulation of the market for profit. We will examine these developments in turn.

Monopolistic Capitalism

Karl Marx, over 100 years ago when bigness was the exception, predicted that capitalism was doomed by several inherent contradictions that will produce a class of people bent on destroying it. The most significant of these contradictions for our purposes is the inevitability of monopolies.* Marx hypothesized that free enterprise will result in some firms becoming bigger and bigger as they eliminate their opposition or absorb smaller competing firms. The ultimate result of this process is the existence of a monopoly in each of the

---

* Marx prophesied that capitalism carried the seeds of its own destruction. In addition to resulting in monopolies, capitalism: (1) encourages crises—inflation, slumps, depressions—because the lack of centralized planning will mean overproduction of some goods and underproduction of others; (2) encourages mass production for expansion and profits but in so doing a social class, the proletariat, is created that has the goal of equalizing the distribution of profits; (3) demands the introduction of labor-saving machinery, which forces unemployment and a more hostile proletariat; and (4) will control the state, the effect of which is that the state will pass laws favoring the wealthy, thereby incurring the further wrath of the proletariat. All these factors increase the probability of the proletariat building class consciousness, which is the condition necessary before class conflict and the ushering in of a new economic system.[1]

various sectors of the economy. Monopolies, of course, are antithetical to the free-enterprise system because they, not supply and demand, determine the price and the quality of the product.

For the most part, the evidence in American society upholds Marx's prediction. Although there are a few corporations that are virtual monopolies (Xerox, American Telephone and Telegraph, and IBM), most sectors of the American economy are dominated by **shared monopolies**. Instead of a single corporation controlling an industry, the situation is one in which a small number of large firms dominate an industry.

When four or fewer firms supply 50% or more of a particular market, a shared monopoly results, one which performs much as a monopoly or cartel would. Most economists agree that above this level of concentration—a four-firm ratio of 50%—the economic costs of shared monopoly are most manifest. Familiar examples of such oligopolistic industries are automobiles (GM, Ford, and Chrysler), aluminum (Alcoa, Kaiser, and Reynolds), rubber tires (Goodyear, Firestone, U.S. Rubber, and Goodrich), soaps and detergents (Procter & Gamble, Colgate, and Lever Brothers), cigarettes (Reynolds, American, Philip Morris, L & M), and electric bulbs (GE, Westinghouse, Sylvania).[2]

Shared monopolies exists also in subparts of a larger industry. In the food industry, for example, four or fewer corporations control many of the various sectors. This is true of the breakfast cereals (where four firms control 90 percent of sales), bread and prepared flour (75 percent of sales by the shared monopoly), baking (65 percent), fluid milk (60 percent), dairy products (70 percent), processed meats (56 percent), sugar (65 percent), canned goods (80 percent), and soups (90 percent by just one company, Campbell's).[3]

Shared monopolies raise the cost to consumers considerably and thus are a major source of inflation. Two examples make this point:

—In 1980 the Federal Trade Commission, after an eight year study, released data showing that consumers had paid more than $1.2 billion in higher prices for ready-to-eat cereals over a 15-year period. These overcharges of 15 percent, it was alleged, were the direct result of the monopoly in the cereal industry by Kellogg, General Mills, and General Foods. In one year alone, consumers paid $100 million more than they would have for cereals if there had been a more competitive market.[4]

—In April 1979 the sales of American cars declined by 42 percent. Under the principle of supply and demand, auto prices should have fallen under these conditions, yet they were raised an average of $500 per car.[5]

The existence of shared monopolies is an indicator of the extent of concentration of American business. Clearly the assets of America's business are highly concentrated in the hands of a few giants. At the end of World War II the 200 largest corporations had 45 percent of all assets of American industry. In 1978, they owned 60 percent. Examined another way:

Of the almost two million corporations in America, one-tenth of 1 percent controls 55 percent of the total assets; 1.1 percent controls 82 percent. At the other end of the spectrum, 94 percent of the corporations own only 9 percent of the total assets.[6]

Defenders of a free and competitive enterprise system should attack the existence of monopolies and shared monopolies as un-American. There should be strong support of governmental efforts to break up the largest and most powerful corporations.[7]

Huey Long once prophesied that fascism would come to the United States first in the form of antifascism. So too with socialism—*corporate* socialism. Under the banner of free enterprise, up to two-thirds of American manufacturing has been metamorphosed into a "closed enterprise system." Although businessmen spoke the language of competitive capitalism, each sought refuge for themselves: price-fixing, parallel pricing, mergers, excessive advertising, quotas, subsidies, and tax favoritism. While defenders of the American dream guarded against socialism from the left, it arrived unannounced from the right.[8]

So instead of a free enterprise system, the American economy is controlled by huge corporations, which have political power to guarantee their privileged positions. This means that these companies need not be concerned with sound business principles and quality products because there is no real threat of competition. In other words, the concentration of industrial wealth means that the rules of free enterprise cannot work.[9]

Ironically, many large corporations devote considerable efforts to convincing the public that the American economy *is* competitive when the evidence is to the contrary. Why do they seek to delude the public? What do they gain from such hypocrisy? We see advertisements that depict the economy as an Adam Smith style of free market with competition among innumerable small competitors. This, however, is a dream world. There *is* competition among the Mom-and-Pop stores, but these stores control only a minute portion of the nation's assets. The largest assets are located among the very large corporations, and competition there is virtually nonexistent.[10]

Multinational Corporations

The thesis of the previous section was that there is a trend for corporations to increase in size resulting, eventually, in huge enterprises that join with other large companies to form effective monopolies. This process of economic concentration provides the largest companies with enormous economic and political power. Another trend—the globalization of America's largest corporations—makes their power all the greater.[11] This fact of international economic life has very important implications for social problems, both domestically and abroad.

There has been a tendency of late for American corporations to increase their foreign investments sharply. The U.S. petroleum industry, for instance, invests about $40 billion annually, approximately half of which goes outside of the United States. Mobil Oil, the U.S. corporation most heavily dependent on foreign operations, had foreign earnings of $654 million in 1974 compared with $258 million domestically. Why are American corporations shifting more and more of their total assets outside of the U.S.? The obvious answer is that the rate of profit tends to be higher abroad. Resources necessary for manufacture and production tend to be cheaper in many other nations, but labor costs are substantially lower. Wages in general are much lower than in the U.S., and unions are nonexistent.

The consequences of this shift in production from the U.S. to outside are significant. Most important is the decline in domestic jobs. As Barnet and Muller have put it:

The production of the industrial goods that have been the mainstay of the American economy is being transferred from New England factories that paid workers three dollars and forty cents an hour to factories in the "export platforms" of Hong Kong and Taiwan, where workers makes as little as thirty cents an hour. . . . The effect is to eliminate traditional jobs on the assembly line and to replace them with other jobs, probably fewer in number—jobs requiring special skills. For a growing number of Americans, unemployment and reduced income are the result.[12]

Thus, the transfer of American plants overseas has the consequence of drying up many semi- and unskilled jobs. The effects of the increased unemployment are twofold: increased welfare costs and increased discontent among those in the working class.

Another significant result of the corporate shift overseas is a crippling of the power of unions to get management to meet their demands. Barnet and Muller have argued that:

Capital, technology, and marketplace ideology—the bases of corporate power—are mobile; workers and their national unions, are not. The ability of corporations to open and close plants at will and to shift their investment from one country to another erodes the basis of organized labor's bargaining leverage—the strike. The power of corporations to neutralize the strike weapon is not merely theoretical; it is used.[13]

The problems of domestic unemployment exacerbated by overseas investment are the problems of lost revenues through taxes and a negative balance of payments. Tax revenues are lost because corporations can escape domestic taxes by having goods produced overseas and by undervaluing exports and overvaluing imports. Indirectly, taxes are also lost by increased unemployment. The balance-of-payments problem is aggravated by the flow of investment money overseas and the purchase of goods produced in foreign countries.

Another result of the twin processes of concentration and internationalization of corporations is the enormous power wielded by the gigantic multinational corporation. In essence, the largest corporations control the world economy. Their decisions to build or not to build, to relocate a plant, to start a new product, or to scrap an old one have a tremendous impact on the lives of ordinary citizens in the countries they operate from and invest in.

In their desire to tap low-wage workers the multinational corporations have tended to locate in poor countries. On the surface this would appear to have positive consequences for these nations (e.g., by providing a higher standard of living and access to modern technology). Unfortunately, this has not been the case. One reason is that the profits generated in these countries tend to be expatriated back to the United States in the form of dividends. Second, global companies do not have a great impact in easing the unemployment of the poor nations because they use advanced technology whenever feasible, and this reduces the demand for jobs. Third, the multinational companies tend to exploit the natural resources of the poor countries. An important consequence of this abuse is that exploited countries are beginning to unite in order to curb the abuses of the corporations. The Organization of Petroleum Exporting Countries (OPEC) was formed to demand higher prices in order to compensate for many years of exploitation and to achieve independence from the multinationals. The immediate result was an increase in the price of oil by approximately 500 percent. Organizations are being formed also among the countries exporting copper, tin, bauxite, coffee, and tea. Unfortunately, these efforts, although directed at the multinational companies, are paid for by the American consumer since the U.S. companies merely raise their retail prices accordingly.

Barnet and Muller have summarized the negative impact of global corporations on underdeveloped countries in the following statement:

It is an unhappy fact that the development policies pursued by international corporations . . . contributed more to the exacerbation of world poverty, world unemployment, and world inequality than to their solution. . . . The unfortunate role of the multinational business in maintaining and increasing world-wide poverty results primarily from the dismal reality that global corporations and poor countries have different— indeed, conflicting—interests, priorities, and needs. The primary interest of the corporation is profit maximization, and this means that it is often advantageous for the balance sheet if income is diverted from poor countries. Eager as they are to be good corporate citizens, the managers owe their primary allegiance to company shareholders. Their businesses, they like to say, are neither charities nor welfare organizations, although some do devote modest resources to good works. The claims of the global corporations rest instead on a theory of the marketplace which says, in effect, that by enriching themselves they enrich the whole world. This, unfortunately, has not been the reality.[14]

Finally, multinational corporations tend to meddle in the internal affairs of other nations in order to protect their investments and maximize profits. The following representative cases show how corporations put this policy into practice:[15]

item: ITT worked in Chile to remove the Allende government from power.

item: Exxon spent some $46 million between 1963 and 1971 to receive tax favors in Italy.

item: United Brands paid a $1.25 million bribe to a Honduras official in an effort to reduce that country's export tax on bananas.

item: From 1970 to 1975, Lockheed paid $202 million to foreign government officials, political parties, and sales agents. $106 million of this went to promote sales in one country: Saudi Arabia.

item: G. D. Searle & Company paid $1.3 million to foreign governmental employees from 1973 to 1975.

item: From 1970 to 1975, Tenneco paid $12 million in bribes to persons in twenty-four countries.

CORPORATE SOCIALISM

Economic and political issues combine to form a particular characteristic of the contemporary American economy: corporate socialism. We have seen in this chapter that the free enterprise system that many Americans favor has been subverted by the rise of huge corporations that dominate single industries. Competition, the hallmark of true capitalism, is missing for the most part because of these monopolies or near monopolies. Competition is further diminished by government practices that artifically stimulate corporations and industries regardless of their degree of efficiency or productivity. These governmental policies include favorable tax laws, governmental loans, artificially high rates for transportation, fair trade laws, and the large proportion of economic activity generated by governmental contracts.

The justification for these practices by many political leaders is that increased business profits create a more prosperous economy, and expanding job opportunities will result. Whether this rationale is true or not, the net effect is a subsidy to corporations. Let's examine the governmental subsidies by type of industry.

Corporate Socialism via Military Spending

The next chapter will describe the direct and obvious ties between the Pentagon and industry. There is evidence that producing goods for the military is more profitable, less competitive, and more susceptible to control through lobbying in Washington than commercial work. In short, there are tremendous profits to be made in defense contracting, and many if not most of the risks are borne by the Government. The irony is that this is in opposition to the free enterprise system. Apparently, American capitalism is in fact a form of corporate socialism where very large corporations receive government aid while smaller business ventures must operate on the principle of "survival of the fittest."

Because military spending is so high (it reached $180 billion in fiscal 1982), the American economy and millions of American workers and manufacturers have become dependent on the government. Some examples of those directly dependent on military expenditures are:

1. About 10 percent of the American work force is employed in military related activities: in the Pentagon bureaucracy, in the armed services, or in defense industries.
2. Numerous communities with military bases or defense contractors are dependent on the military for jobs, increased sales, and continued prosperity. The impact of defense spending on a local community's economy is seen when either: a large industry does or does not receive a major governmental contract; or the Pentagon decides to build or deactivate a major defense installation. Virtually all segments of the community (businesspeople, teachers, homeowners, blue-collar workers, and professionals) favor increased defense work or at least continuance of what they already have at the local level.
3. About 50 percent of all research financed by the government is defense related. Universities and professors have become particularly dependent upon government-sponsored research. Grant-winning professors are thrice blessed: they have money for research which, in turn, means more prestige, as well as higher salaries. Universities benefit because they often receive special equipment and about one-half of all monies for overhead. For more research-active universities, the overhead amounts to millions of dollars annually.

These examples show the impact of the military on American economic life. Thus, a ready-made pressure group, working with the corporations, fights to keep military spending high. The result is that the United States has continued to increase its stockpile of weapons.

It is estimated that the United States now possesses something on the order of 40,000 megatons of nuclear force, or about 100 times more destructive power than is required to devastate any potential enemy. The human mind is incapable of comprehending either this kind of power or its implications. One way of visualizing the size of the nuclear stockpile is to think of 43 million tons of TNT being manufactured every day for 6,000 years—or the time span of recorded history. The sum total of all that explosive force now resides in our arsenals and is getting bigger every day.[16]

Panel 16-1
The Globalization of Capitalism

. . . we should not expect the globalization of capitalism to occur smoothly. At issue is a world-shaking bid for power between the nation-state and the multinational corporation. Ironically, the rise of the multinational corporation has coincided with the development of scores of new nation-states. As increasing nationalist pressures have led to decolonization and to greater national political independence (at least in form), the multinational corporations have grown apace. And these newest repositories of power are mounting an ever greater challenge to the sovereignty, stability, and even the *raison d'etre* of the nation-state.

The multinationals have been able to amass enormous power through their control of four aspects of economic life:

1. Through their control of modern technology, they exert powerful influence over the nature of the process of production and the types of goods and services produced.
2. Their command over long-term finance capital enables them to control somewhere between 300 and 350 billion dollars of liquid assets—one and one-half to two times all the reserves held by governments.
3. Multinational corporations are—at least allegedly—capable of thwarting the countervailing power of national labor unions by threatening to move production to other countries rather than yield to labor's demands.
4. The multinational corporations purportedly wield increasing control over their product markets by psychologically bombarding their clients with the ideology of consumerism—the notion that the good life comes from the consumption of the things they produce. They spend billions on advertising to convince people around the globe that the good life is derived primarily from consumption of goods and services.

The multinationals have in the last few years helped to create domestic and international instability among the developed capitalist countries. For instance, just before the devaluation of the dollar in August 1971, the MNCs helped bring about an enormous flight from the dollar into deutschemarks, gold, and other assets thought to be more devaluation-proof than the dollar. The global giants were instrumental in triggering a balance of payments crisis for the United States that rocked the international monetary system to its foundation.

What are the potential options for dealing with the problems presented by the globalization of capitalism under the driving force of the multinational corporation? The present system seems so unstable that it may provoke investment wars. How can capitalism avoid the seemingly inevitable chaos? Among the options that have been proposed are:

1. Give the MNCs sovereignty. They would join the nation-states as equal partners. The President of Dow Chemical went far along this line of reasoning when he argued that his company should buy and locate its corporate headquarters on an unclaimed island—so that it would not be responsible to any nation-state.

2. Regulate the MNCs through world government. Some proponents of this approach are encouraged by the recent U.N. conference on control of the sea and its resources as a step in this direction. Some MNCs have themselves expressed the need for some form of world government regulation. They realize that the present international capitalist system requires some type of agreed-upon rules and regulations and governmental intervention from an international body. Some corporate leaders would point to the experience of the 1930s when capitalism broke down in the U.S. and Western Europe and was only revived and sustained by massive governmental intervention. They see the same need on an international scale today.

3. Regulate the MNCs through regional or special interest groups or blocs of nations. One could think of the Organization of Petroleum Exporting Countries (OPEC) as one such attempt, although it is not yet clear that the OPEC countries are regulating the oil companies so much as they are joining them in plundering the consumers of oil around the world. Another example of this approach is the Andean Pact nations of South America which have been trying to come up with a common position in their relationships vis-a-vis the MNCs.

4. Regulate the MNCs through an international condominium, i.e., joint sovereignty by two or more nations. Perhaps the nations of Western Europe and Japan will get together with the United States to establish policies which the MNCs must follow. The OECD Committee on Investment and Multinational Enterprise is striving for this sort of solution.

5. Develop countervailing power through the growth of multinational unions. These unions would represent all the workers employed by the MNC worldwide and would be able to block efforts to shift production from one country to another to minimize wage costs, break strikes, etc. In Denmark and Sweden, there seems to be a movement toward worker self-management. There are discussions of using the assets of the pension funds in Sweden to buy out the Swedish capitalists, to pay them off with interest-bearing bonds and to turn over management of Swedish industry to the workers in those industries. The workers would then elect workers' councils which would elect management. Since 1973, the membership of boards of all Swedish corporations must, by law, include two representatives elected by the workers. It is hard to know how this will affect the Swedish economy and the Swedish MNCs. But since Sweden has so often been the pace-setter for other capitalist countries, this is a development to be studied very carefully.

6. Attempt to re-establish U.S. hegemony and control of the mechanism of the international economy. Discussions are being held on the possibility of breaking the oil cartel, of re-establishing fixed exchange rates and of re-establishing U.S. competitive advantage vis-a-vis the West European and Japanese MNCs. However, it is unclear as to what might be done in terms of concrete measures to strengthen the U.S. position.

Source: Excerpts from James H. Weaver and Jon D. Wisman, "Smith, Marx, and Malthus—Ghosts Who Haunt Our Future," *The Futurist* 12 (April 1978), pp. 93–104.

Is this amount enough? Do we need to continue to accumulate even more? Apparently enough of the public benefits economically from this military machine that the military-industrial complex can't be challenged successfully. Conservative politicians also argue that the massive build-up in armaments by the Soviet Union requires a like response from us. Consequently, President Reagan has vowed to spend $1 trillion on defense over a five-year period.

In addition to the threat of annihilation of human life on this planet, the military behemoth is the source of another important economic and social problem. Former Senator McGovern has stated it well: "The arms industry is parasitic. It consumes our resources, but returns nothing that can be bought or sold or used to add to the national wealth."[17] In essence this statement is correct, but there is one area in which the arms industry does add to the national wealth: the sale of military goods abroad. That this is a growth industry is evidenced by the $13.7 billion in sales for fiscal 1978 compared to $8.3 billion in fiscal 1974. Proponents claim a number of benefits from these sales: (1) reducing the balance-of-payments deficit; (2) providing jobs in defense industries; and (3) increasing profits to corporations. The fundamental disadvantage of supplying arms to other nations is that it may increase the probability of war. In the Middle East, for example, the U.S. sells arms to both the Arab countries and their enemy, Israel. Ironically, part of the 1979 peace pact between Israel and Egypt was the agreement that each side would purchase weapons from the U.S.

Subsidies to Petroleum Companies

Congress has provided special tax laws for the oil industry that reduce its tax burden significantly below that of other industries and allow the companies to make enormous profits.[18] In 1977, for example, the fifteen largest oil companies earned $10.7 billion after taxes, for a 14 percent average return on invested capital.

Until 1975 the tax benefits to oil companies resulted from three provisions in the tax code. The most visible subsidy was the oil depletion allowance, which exempted the first 22 percent of oil and gas income from taxation. This tax provision alone cost the U.S. Treasury approximately $1.3 billion a year. In other words, it amounted to a gift of that much money to individuals and companies in the petroleum industry. This part of the tax code was repealed in 1975 for the larger oil corporations but retained for the smaller producers to stimulate continued efforts to drill for more oil.

A more costly subsidy ($1.6 billion) than the oil depletion allowance and one retained for the industry are deductions allowed for "intangible drilling expenses." This allows all drilling expenses to be considered as capital costs. Unlike the situation for other industries where such costs must be deducted gradually over the useful life of the property, three-fourths of this expense for oil drilling is immediately deductible. On a $100,000 operation, then, the oil driller gets a first-year deduction of $75,000 rather than $5,000 or $10,000, which would be the case in other industries.

A third tax provision that unusually benefits petroleum companies pertains to their foreign investments. American oil companies make payments to foreign governments for their oil. These costs are considered by the U.S. to be a tax and therefore a totally deductible expense. If the land were privately owned, however, the oil extracting companies would have to pay a "royalty." That the payment is considered a tax rather than a royalty has meant yet another subsidy to the oil companies. Stern has explained it this way:

> The difference is this: suppose Aramco makes a $100 million payment to the government of Saudi Arabia. If that is considered a royalty payment, it is merely treated as a deduction from Aramco's *income* in computing its U.S. taxes. At the current 48 percent corporate tax rate, Aramco is out of pocket $52 million, the remaining $48 million in effect being diverted from the U.S. Treasury to the government of Saudi Arabia. If, on the other hand, the $100 million is labeled a *tax* payment, the *law allows Aramco to reduce its U.S. tax payments by the full $100 million.* . . . Uncle Sam ends up bearing the entire load.[19]

This tax subsidy actually encourages foreign investment. Coupled with other advantages, this tax break makes foreign investment more profitable. The consequence is that American companies actually are spending more overseas than domestically. So, in sum, investments by American companies damage the American economy in at least three ways: loss of tax revenues, a negative balance of payments, and increased unemployment. Ironically, these problems are the result of the tax laws.

Subsidies to Banking

Federal and state governments commonly subsidize banks by allowing government monies to be deposited at little or no interest in private banks. These banks loan the monies out for their financial benefit. Typically, the choice of the banks where the money will be deposited is made on political grounds (i.e., how supportive have the bank officers and board directors been to the current administration).

The amount of money involved at the federal level is substantial. In 1975 Senator William Proxmire, chairman of the Senate Banking Committee, proposed that banks pay interest on federal deposits—averaging $4 billion daily—which they held interest-free. The cost to the banks would be a daily fee of $1 million in interest payments if Proxmire's plan were put into effect. Since no interest has been paid in the past, the government has been giving some banks a total of $1 million daily.

Subsidies to Transportation

The U.S. government has a long tradition of actively supporting transportation with subsidies. The railroads were built originally because the government gave companies huge parcels of land for their efforts. Currently, the government subsidizes ship building to cover the extra cost of building ships in the U.S. rather than abroad. Airlines are also subsidized by government monies that build airports, provide weather information, and pay air controllers. Federal agencies regulating transportation (e.g., Interstate Commerce Commission, Civil Aeronautics Board) have traditionally kept passenger and freight rates artificially high for railroads, trucking firms, and until recently the airlines. Financially troubled transportation companies often receive loans and outright gifts from the government to keep them operating. From 1970 to 1975 Penn Central received approximately $180 million in federal aid. In 1975 Congress passed a measure authorizing an additional $222 million in grants and loans to Penn Central and $125 to other bankrupt railroads.

In fiscal 1972 federal spending on transportation amounted to $1.8 billion for aviation, $1.6 billion for merchant marine and other water transportation, $1 billion for mass transit, and about $5 billion for highway construction. These monies help individual Americans (especially middle- and upper-class consumers, as well as people employed on various projects), but especially they subsidize and increase the profits of the manufacturers of planes, ships, trucks, and cars, contractors, suppliers, shippers, and, of course, the corporations involved in transportation.[20]

Subsidies to the Housing Industry

The federal government has aided the home construction industry in a variety of ways.[21] It has made mortgage money available to middle-income buyers through FHA and Veterans Administration insured mortgages. For years laws have allowed individuals to deduct interest and taxes paid on homes from their federal income taxes (a loss to the Treasury of over $9.6 billion).[22] Although aimed at individuals, the intent of the provision was to encourage the home-building industry. The home-building industry could be served just as well if the Federal government allocated subsidies to build housing for people who currently live in slums, but clearly the system is biased toward the middle and upper classes (a point we will return to later in this chapter).

In summary: The executive and legislative branches are supportive of subsidies to business because of: (1) the lobbying activities of the corporate rich; (2) the high cost of political campaigns requires that candidates either be rich or accept political contributions from the rich; and (3) people appointed to high government positions tend to come from the business sector. These facts should not be construed to mean that there is a conspiracy between big business and government to "line the pockets" of both. To the contrary, government decisions that favor corporate interests are usually justified by the commonly held rationale that "What's good for General Motors is good for the country." Such a belief implies that prosperous corporations result in plentiful jobs and high wages, which, in turn, further stimulate the economy by stimulating the purchasing of the products of industry. Another reason for subsidizing the profits of industry is to discourage the dependence on foreign companies for resources and products.

But regardless of the rationale for encouraging corporations, the consequence is that some businesses and some industries receive special favors (subsidies) at the expense of the taxpayer. These subsidies should be recognized as a form of corporate welfare.

INDIVIDUAL INEQUALITY IN RESOURCES AND GOVERNMENT BENEFITS

In theory, societies may distribute their goods in ways that range from a totally unequal distribution of wealth (income and propety) to total equality. The former is common in varying degrees in a number of societies, but the latter, while a goal for some, has never been fully attained. Since the American economy is a mixture of capitalism and socialism, it fits somewhere in between the two extremes of inequality and equality.

Whatever its ideological position with respect to other societies, in America income and wealth are vastly unequal, and the gap between the poor and the affluent is widening. The facts are these: the richest 10 percent of American families receive 26 percent of the income, while the poorest 10 percent receive only 1.7 percent. In terms of wealth, the top 20 percent owns 80 percent of all that is privately owned while the bottom 25 percent owns nothing.[23] Study after study provide data to support the conclusion that the distribution of income and wealth is not only unequal in the United States, but it continues to worsen. This section shows how the political-economic system actually works to increase income and wealth differentials rather than minimizing them.

Inequality and Government Policy

The government can make the distribution of wealth more equitable in two ways: (a) by taxing the more well to do, and (b) giving these monies to the poor through specially designed programs. A favorite device through the years has been the progressive income tax: the higher the taxpayer's income, the higher the tax rate he or she is assessed. The inheritance tax is another useful technique that could, if set at 100 percent, eliminate inherited wealth. A third type of tax that aids in redistributing the wealth is the property tax, a device where property is taxed according to its value.

Another possibility would be for the government to subsidize depressed industries. Or the government could create public service jobs, similar to the WPA program instituted by President Roosevelt during the Depression years of the 1930s. That program not only provided millions of jobs to the needy, it ". . . constructed nearly 600 airports, built or rebuilt 110,000 public buildings, half a million miles of roads and city streets and more than 100,000 bridges."[24] Although costly, this program had the dual effects of redistributing income in a more equitable way and, through its accomplishments, provided services for the entire society.

But while the government could do these things, it has not, for the most part. Either by action or inaction, it has tended to indulge corporations and punish individuals, especially the poor and the wage earner.

The progressive income tax and welfare programs should, theoretically, increase equality in the United States. The facts, however, lead to the opposite conclusion. *This is because the tax structure is not progressive, and welfare goes primarily to the well-to-do.* Let's examine the evidence to support this statement.

1. *Taxation and inequality.* Taxes are designed both to raise money and to effect the distribution of wealth. To accomplish the latter they can be designed to increase inequality by taking a larger proportion of a poor person's income than a rich person's. This type of tax, called "regressive," is based on a more or less fixed amount of tax for everyone, regardless of income levels, which means, in effect, that the poor pay a larger percentage of their incomes. Social security taxes and sales taxes are two examples of regressive taxes. The latter is especially important because more than one-half of all state revenues come from this regressive source.

Progressive taxes, on the other hand, take a larger proportion of a rich person's income than a poor person's. In theory, progressive taxes should result in a leveling of economic differences. The federal income tax rates, for example, range from 20 percent to 70 percent (the wealthier paying the larger percentage). In practice, however, loopholes in the tax structure allow the wealthy to avoid paying high taxes. These loopholes occur because not all income is treated alike. Income from municipal bonds is totally exempt from taxes. Sixty percent of long-term capital gains income goes untaxed. Twenty percent of income received from oil also is not affected by taxes. These tax privileges benefit only those who have capital to make investments: the wealthy. As former Senator George McGovern has put it,

Two taxpayers with the same annual income pay quite different taxes. A factory worker or a schoolteacher whose taxes are withheld from his wages cannot take advantage of loopholes. He may expect to pay almost $1,000 in taxes on earnings of $10,000. A wealthy person who receives $10,000 income from state and local bonds will pay no federal taxes at all. Clearly this system is unfair.[25]

Such inequities exist because of provisions in the tax law that permit the wealthy to exempt some types of income, but also because of such schemes as deferred compensation (the postponement of part of one's income until after retirement) and stock options (allowing part of salary to be taxed at capital gains rate since it is in the form of stock rather than a wage). As Gabriel Kolko has stated,

The conclusion is inescapable: Taxation has not mitigated the fundamentally unequal distribution of income. If anything it has perpetuated inequality by heavily taxing the low- and middle-income groups—those least able to bear its burden.[26]

The conclusion from the data provided in this section is clearly that the tax system, although commonly believed to be a mechanism to reduce inequality, actually reinforces inequality.

2. *Government subsidies and inequality.* The tax loopholes just considered are in fact a form of subsidy—gifts to the wealthy—since the money not taxed is of course not given to the government but kept for private (or corporate) use. The well-to-do are also subsidized by government programs that aid transportation, provide low-cost tuition and scholarships for college and graduate training, and many others. These direct and indirect subsidies to the nonpoor in American society have worked to reinforce inequality rather than minimizing it. The result has been the creation of a dual welfare system: one system favors the nonpoor through tax breaks and subsidies; the second systematically disadvantages and condemns the poor through subsidy programs.

This dual welfare system has important implications for American society. Foremost is the tremendous cost of subsidizing the nonpoor. If these tax "welfare" payments to the well-to-do were closed, governmental revenues would have increased by $114 billion in 1977.[27] If this were accomplished, not only could taxes be reduced, but many social programs could be added that would alleviate human misery.

A second characteristic of the dual welfare system is that it is hypocritical. A double standard operates when one type of welfare is condemned while another is accepted. One type is degrading while the other is uplifting. The effect is that many eligible poor refuse welfare.

A most important consequence of this dual system is that welfare programs are not redistributing wealth in American society. Wealth continues to be maldistributed. The bitter irony is that the welfare system benefits the nonpoor more than the poor. Thus, the gap between the two widens. An extreme example shows that the tax system provides average benefits of $148 for people making between $3,000 and $5,000, while those making over $1,000,000 receive an average yearly tax welfare of $720,490.[28]

A reasonable expectation for a welfare program is that it will increase the probability that its participants will acquire traits that pay off in society. Programs for the nonpoor accomplish this goal while those for the poor actually encourage those traits considered negative in American society. The poor are encouraged to be dependent rather than independent, unemployed rather than employed, separated rather than married, and ashamed rather than proud.

Finally, because the welfare to the affluent is concealed, the hostility of the lower income nonpoor is directed almost exclusively toward the poor, whom they see as parasites living off their taxes. The result is hostility between the two categories of have-nots rather than a recognition of their common interests.

AMERICAN CAPITALISM IN CRISIS

In this section we shall deal with a number of problems endemic to the American economy. We have already considered the problems of monopoly, multinationals, disproportionate largess to the wealthy, and the dependence of the economy on huge outlays for defense. Now we will consider briefly some additional serious economic problems.

Economic Cycles

Like other industrial nations, the United States is subject to periodic inflation and deflation. This disequilibrium occurs for two fundamental reasons. First, the American economy is strongly affected by international events.[29] We are part of an interdependent network where decisions in other countries concerning war or peace, monetary policies, price of products, boycotts, strikes, and price increases or decreases can profoundly affect our economy. The availability and price of goods, employment patterns, and expansion or contraction of output in this country are also affected by wars, famine, drought, floods, and other disasters that occur around the world.

The second fundamental cause of economic cycles in the United States is the general governmental policy of noninterference in private business affairs. Of course, the government exerts some control through taxation, control of interest rates, and regulation of utilities and transportation, but for the most part the companies act independently. They decide what to produce, how much to produce, where to locate their plants, what to charge, how many people to employ, and how much to spend on research and development. The traditional assumption by government is that a market governed by the law of supply and demand will work for the greatest good to the greatest number. This leads to a situation where some products are overproduced while others are underproduced, creating problems of distribution, employment, and pricing. Such a system increases the probability of times when too many dollars chase too few goods, a period called inflation.[30] But rather than focus on why these stages occur, let's look at the consequences of each.

1. *The Consequences of Inflation.* Inflation is a time of rapidly rising prices. For example, comparing prices in 1967 to those in 1977, the cost of a new car increased from

TABLE 16-1   Who Gains from Tax Breaks

Benefits from Personal Deductions and Credits	Estimated Tax Loss in 1980 (millions)
State, local taxes on income, sales, personal property	$12,450
Mortgage interest in owner-occupied homes	$ 9,290
Charitable contributions	$ 7,955
Property tax on owner-occupied homes	$ 6,615
Medical expenses	$ 3,120
Interest on consumer credit	$ 2,945
Earned-income credit	$ 2,070
Exemption for people age 65 and over	$ 1,855
Parents' exemption for students 19 and over	$ 1,020
Child and dependent-care credits	$ 705
Casualty losses	$ 475
Residential energy credits	$ 435
Tax credit for elderly	$ 160
Political contributions	$ 100
Exemption for the blind	$ 35
Total	**$49,230**

Benefits for Investors, Business Owners and Farmers	Estimated Tax Loss in 1980 (millions)
Special treatment for capital gains	$10,720
No tax on full capital gains at death	$10,005
Investment tax credit	$ 3,090
Exemption of interest on state, local debt	$ 3,050
Deferral of capital gains on home sales	$ 1,010
Extra depreciation write-offs	$ 690
Deferral of interest on U.S. savings bonds	$ 625
Deduction for energy exploration, development	$ 505
Excess energy-depletion allowance	$ 485
Dividend exclusion	$ 450
Deduction of certain capital outlays in agriculture	$ 430
Employment tax credits	$ 175
Deduction of construction-period interest, taxes	$ 145
Incentives for preservation of historic structures	$ 65
Others	$ 75
Total	**$31,520**

TABLE 16-1   (Cont.)

Benefits from Income Not Taxed	Estimated Tax Loss in 1980 (millions)
Pension plans—company contributions plus annual earnings of plan investments	$12,925
Company-paid insurance, other nonwage benefits	$10,970
Social Security benefits	$ 8,105
Interest on life-insurance savings	$ 2,720
Pension contributions, earnings of self-employed	$ 2,205
Unemployment insurance	$ 1,935
Maximum tax on personal-service income	$ 1,625
Military benefits, allowances	$ 1,600
Workers' compensation	$ 1,285
Veterans' benefits	$ 1,230
Income earned abroad by U.S. citizens	$ 555
Capital gains on home sales of persons age 55 and over	$ 535
Public assistance	$ 395
Scholarship, fellowship income	$ 365
Railroad-retirement-system benefits	$ 305
Disability pay	$ 150
Others	$ 80
Total	**$46,985**

Corporations	Estimated Tax Loss in 1980 (millions)
Investment tax credit	$15,490
Reduced rates on first $100,000 of income	$ 6,940
Exemption of interest on state, local debt	$ 4,695
Extra depreciation deductions	$ 3,130
Research, development deductions	$ 1,745
Special treatment for corporations in world trade	$ 1,710
Excess energy-depletion allowance	$ 1,265
Deduction of energy-exploration, development costs	$ 1,160
Charitable contributions	$ 1,015
Capital gains	$ 1,010
Excess bad-debt reserves of financial institutions	$ 855
Credits for companies doing business in U.S. possessions	$ 730
Employment tax credits	$ 680
Deduction of construction-period interest, taxes	$ 555
Noncash patronage dividends of farm cooperatives	$ 540
Investment credit for employee-stock-ownership plans	$ 450
Credits for energy conservation, new technology	$ 390
Others	$ 450
Total	**$42,800**

Source: Reprinted from *"U.S. News & World Report,* June 18, 1979, p. 64. Copyright 1979 U.S. News & World Report, Inc.

$3,200 to $6,120; groceries for a family of four went from $35 to $67 per week; the cost of the average gas bill increased from $122 to $274; and the (average) cost of monthly home mortgage payments soared from $152 to $430.[31] Clearly those on fixed incomes lose purchasing power in times of inflation. The elderly who must survive on fixed pensions are especially hard hit. The poor are also disproportionately affected since they must spend larger shares of their incomes on food and housing, two items which usually experience rapid increases.[32]

Efforts by the federal government to fight inflation usually have negative effects on social programs. Since a primary source of inflation is government spending, an obvious

TABLE 16-2   Compounding Inflation: 1962–1999

	What things may cost				
			Compounded rate of increase	Cost assuming same rate of increase	
Items	*1962*	*1979*		*1989*	*1999*
35-foot cabin cruiser	$22,500	$59,700	6.3%	$109,978	$202,599
One-family house	19,300*	68,300	8.8	158,748	368,975
Chevrolet Impala 4-door	2,529	5,828	5.4	9,861	16,685
Annual college costs†	980	2,230	5.3	3,738	6,264
Two-week London vacation for 2	893	1,508‡	3.3	2,086‡	2,887‡
Refrigerator-freezer	470	530	0.7	568	609
Medical bills	468**	1,070	7.1	2,125	4,219
Annual Social Security deduction	150	1,403	15.0	3,561††	6,770††
Man's wool suit	130	238	3.9	349	512
Auto insurance premium	87	250	6.8	483	932
Monthly electric bill	8	30	8.6	68	156
Prime-rib dinner	4.65	10.95	5.5	18.70	31.94
Haircut	1.00	3.50	8.2	7.70	16.93
Paperback novel	.95	2.60	6.5	4.88	9.16
Movie ticket	.81	2.46	7.2	4.93	9.88
Gasoline per gallon	.31	.79	6.0	1.41	2.53
Hamburger (McDonald's double)	.28*	.80	7.2	1.60	3.21
Pizza (slice)	.15	.70	10.1	1.83	4.80
Hershey bar	.05	.25	10.6	.68	1.88
Daily newspaper—*N.Y. Times*	.05	.20	9.1	.48	1.14
First-class postage stamp	.04	.15	8.6	.34	.78

*1963 data   † For state resident   ‡ Assumes Laker Airways fare   **1966 data   †† Amounts set by legislation in effect.

Sources: Bureau of the Census, Bureau of Labor Statistics; Chris-Craft; Edison Electric Institute; General Motors; Hart, Shaffner & Marx; Hershey Foods; Indiana University; McDonald's; Motion Picture Assn. of America; Publisher's Weekly; State Farm Insurance; Whirlpool Corp.

TABLE 16–2   Compounding Inflation: 1962–1999

| | What you may earn | | | | |
| | | | Compounded rate of increase | Cost assuming same rate of increase | |
Earnings	1962	1979		1989	1999
In-house attorney					
Gross earnings	$16,440	$42,318	6.1%	$76,502	$138,302
Aftertax earnings	12,872	30,113	5.5	41,860	56,878
Aftertax adjusted for inflation	29,577	30,113		23,155	17,404
Aftertax earnings as % of gross	78%	71%		55%	41%
Production worker					
Gross earnings	$5,021	$13,850	6.5%	$25,998	$48,802
Aftertax earnings	4,420	11,795	6.3	19,698	30,615
Aftertax adjusted for inflation	10,156	11,795		10,494	8,688
Aftertax earnings as % of gross	88%	85%		76%	63%

Assumptions: Married taxpayer; joint return; two dependent children; standard deduction; no change in 1979 tax structure for subsequent years; gross earnings less net tax liability, state and local income taxes (assuming the same proportion of state and local taxes to federal taxes); Social Security tax for 1989 and 1999 from legislation in effect.

Source: Reprinted by permission of *Forbes* Magazine from the June 11, 1979 issue, p. 108.

solution to the problem is to curtail or eliminate certain forms of government spending. The question then is one of priorities: where will the cuts be made? Should defense spending be reduced, or will programs to alleviate human suffering be cut? As a rule, defense spending has rarely been reduced, and social programs are the victims. This is true in Democratic as well as Republic administrations.

Another casualty of inflation is home ownership. Inflation drives up the cost of mortgage interest rates, taxes, insurance, and especially the cost of homes to the point where the American dream of owning a home is beyond the financial capabilities of the majority of Americans. According to a survey by the Commerce Department, the median cost of new homes in July 1978 was $61,500, up from the average of $35,100 in 1973. This meant that a family would have to earn at least $24,000 to qualify for a mortgage loan. Consequently, three-fourths of Americans would not qualify in 1978.[33] One coping strategy for couples is for both spouses to work outside the home. This is a necessity for many couples who wish to own their own home.[34]

Other victims of inflation are organizations dependent on tax revenues. State agencies, school districts, universities, communities, and states all suffer from the burden of increased expenses (fuel, goods, services, salaries) in inflationary times. New York City provides an extreme example of the problem: New York went $120 million in debt in fiscal 1975 and another $900 million further in debt in fiscal 1976.[35] Quality education is also a victim of inflation. Inflation forces school districts to allot greater portions of their budgets to noneducational expenditures: fuel, construction, power, and interest costs. Unless these districts raise taxes to cover the increased inflation, the amount spent for actual education (teachers, equipment, special programs) declines. Typically, however, the answer is to reduce special education classes, increase class size, and spend less on teaching materials.

2. *The consequences of recession and deflation.* The most obvious effect of an economic downturn is increased unemployment. As consumers lower their rates of consumption, companies let employees go. The automobile industry provides a good illustration of this cycle. Because the auto industry uses 65 percent of all the rubber in the United States, 30 percent of the zinc, 24 percent of the steel, 17 percent of the aluminum, and 13 percent of the copper, workers in all of these allied industries are laid off when car sales fall. This affects some 50,000 companies supplying materials, parts, and services to automobile manufacturers. One estimate by the Nobel laureate economist Wassily Leontif is that for every $1 billion in reduced auto sales, 22,900 auto workers are laid off, and an additional 34,100 unemployed in allied industries.[36]

Recessions are hardest on those already disadvantaged. Unemployment rates are always highest for minorities.[37] But unemployment is only one of their special problems. One expert, Harvey Brenner, a medical statistician from Johns Hopkins University, has studied death statistics in the United States from 1914 to 1970 and concluded that every recession caused increased deaths of unborn and infants, particularly among ethnic minorities and poor whites. He has estimated that a recent two-year recession cost the lives of 10,000 to 15,000. Brenner listed three reasons for additional deaths during a recession:

the inability of lower income women to pay for prenatal care, substandard nutrition, and mental depression. The problem is compounded as poverty and inadequate diets make the subjects more susceptible to infectious diseases and other illnesses.[38]

An obvious consequence of deflationary times is a rise in bankruptcies. In 1980, for example, a time of recession, about 355,000 bankruptcies were filed—120,000 more than the previous record set in 1975, another year of economic woes.[39] Companies owned by blacks are hit especially hard by an economic recession.[40] There are two reasons for this stronger effect: (1) the vast majority of black businesses are small and marginal; and (2) they tend to operate in low-income neighborhoods where unemployment is especially high. These two factors combine to make banks and other financial enterprises wary of loaning money to black businesses to keep them afloat in hard times.

The economic deprivation caused by hard times provides the impetus for many social changes and problems. Family life is directly affected in at least two ways. First, the fertility rate goes down. Marriages and children are postponed, and there is increased use of abortion and contraceptive methods. Second, marriages seem to reflect the tensions caused by economic worries, resulting in raised rates of divorce, separation, and desertion.[41]

There appears to be a direct relationship between bad economic times and mental problems.[42] The stress of losing a job or the fear of losing one can cause anxiety, hypertension, depression, and low self-esteem. One study found that admissions to mental hospitals increased between 1926 and 1968 whenever the economy turned downward, then leveled off as it stabilized.[43] After the 1980 recession in Iowa, for example, researchers found increases over the same six month period in the previous year ranging from 10 to 30 percent in new patients/clients in state mental hospitals, mental health clinics, and alcohol abuse programs.[44] We also know that 1,000 additional suicides can be expected nationally for every increase of one percentage point in the unemployment rate.[45]

Increased crime also appears to be an inevitable consequence of economic hard times. A study done by the Federal Bureau of Prisons documents this trend. Researchers found that the federal prison population tended to increase noticeably roughly fifteen months (accounting for processing of criminals) after periods of high unemployment.[46]

These personal and social problems associated with recession raise some serious doubts about governmental policies that actually encourage economic downturns. The Federal Reserve Board, for example, typically fights inflation by raising interest rates. This credit tightening affects the housing industry, slows down new business investment, and dampens consumer spending. Ignored, however, are the human costs of such a policy. Also disregarded are the other sources of inflation such as price fixing through shared monopolies, the increased cost of importing oil, enormous military expenditures, unbalanced government budgets, and corporate socialism.[47]

The National Debt

In response to the demands of various pressure groups, the assumed need to grow, and the problems of the business cycle, in the last forty years government has tended to spend more tax dollars than it has taken in. We have seen how the economy has become dependent on the huge defense industry. These enormous expenditures (in excess of $180 billion annually) are considered sacrosanct by most, and they are increased yearly. These and other subsidies drain the government coffers. Recession, too, is especially costly to the government. This is because government spending grows to create jobs and increase the flow of money in circulation. Recessions also cause the national debt to mount because tax revenues are smaller (because of declining profits by businesses and high unemployment), and welfare costs increase. The result is a staggering budget and a huge national debt. The debt reached the half-trillion point in 1975 and $993 billion by the end of fiscal 1981.[48] This presents the federal government with financial problems of unprecedented magnitude. If the national debt is $993 billion and the government must pay 9 percent interest, the interest alone amounts to $80 billion a year, or $219 million a day.

Dependence on Foreign Oil

In 1953 the United States imported 648,000 barrels of oil a day at $1.82 a barrel—a daily cost of $1,179,360. In 1980 we imported an average of 6,043,000 barrels of oil a day at approximately $26 a barrel—a daily cost of $157,118,000. This represents a tremendous drain on the United States, a negative balance of payments of many billions of dollars annually.[49] The result is a terrific strain on the American economy that will not lessen until the U.S. becomes self-sufficient in energy resources. This is unlikely in the near term because: (1) the huge demand for energy in this country continues; and (2) the government has not committed sufficient resources to the development of alternative sources of energy (wind, tides, sun, geothermal, methane from waste, coal, and oil shale). Federal research monies have been committed mainly to nuclear energy.

United States dependence on foreign oil means that if the supply were to be cut off or reduced significantly, there would be tremendous dislocations in the economy of the country and the lifestyle of Americans. The probability of a disruption in the flow of international oil is relatively high, because most of the world's oil exports come from politically sensitive areas where war, acts of terrorism, and international blackmail are always possible.[50]

Lack of Economic Planning

The inability of governments to plan adequately for energy shortages indicates a weakness of free enterprise economies. The philosophy dating back to Adam Smith is that the government should stay out of economic affairs. According to this view, the marketplace will force businesses to make the decisions that will best benefit them, and indirectly, the citizenry. Yet when the government does receive valuable information with which it could make decisions to avert future crises, the strong tendency in the United States is to remain aloof. For example, in 1951 President Harry Truman named a commission to plan what the country should do about the likelihood of scarce resources in 1975. That commission, although underestimating the problems, foresaw the trends accurately. The report called for immediate efforts to conserve energy, for ways to safeguard outside oil sources, and for massive increases in energy output. The report was not implemented.

Ironically, the government is involved in central planning in the areas of space exploration and defense. As one commentator has said:

The U.S. launched Mariner 10 on Nov. 3, 1973, and it flew to Venus and then to Mercury, which it circled for a total of a billion miles. It performed magnificently and sent back photographs. That took years of planning. But planning for a thing like that is one thing. Social planning and foreseeing energy shortages before they happen, that is different, and to some, slightly sinister.[51]

The issue of central planning revolves around whether the society is able *and* willing to respond to present and future social problems. Is a capitalist society capable of meeting the problems of poverty, unemployment, social neglect, population growth, energy shortages, environmental damage, and monopoly? Robert Heilbroner, a distinguished economist, has argued that we will not prepare for the problems of the future: ". . . the outlook is for what we may call 'convulsive change'—change forced upon us by external events rather than by conscious choice, by catastrophe rather than by calculation."[52]

The lack of central planning points to the undemocratic nature of American society. It is commonly believed that the people, through their economic choices, actually govern business decisions. While this is partially true, it ignores the manipulation of the public by business interests through advertising and other "hypes."[53] Neither the public nor its elected representatives are involved in the economic decisions of the giant corporations—and these decisions often have dire consequences domestically and internationally. As the historian Andrew Hacker has argued:

The power to make investment decisions is concentrated in a few hands, and it is this power which will decide what kind of a nation America will be. Instead of government planning there is boardroom planning that is accountable to no outside agency: and these plans set the order of priorities on national growth, technological innovation, and ultimately, the values and behavior of human beings. Investment decisions are sweeping in their ramifications—no one is unaffected by their consequences. Yet this is an area where neither the public nor its government is able to participate.[54]

The lack of central planning is also a result of the resistance of powerful interest groups in society. Short-term goals such as employment for labor groups or profit for corporations lead special interests to block government efforts to meet future needs. The oil industry, for example, has systematically fought any plans that would threaten its profits. Thus, the power of the economic dominants has the effect of superseding the interests of the nation.

Coping with Zero Economic Growth

The strong tendency of capitalism is continual expansion.[55] A kind of boosterism has prevailed and continues to dominate which "equates growth with progress, and finds in the concept of expansion the first principle of the American Dream."[56] Individuals, corporations, communities, and the society itself seemingly demand growth in technology, profits, size, and level of affluence. The history of the United States bears vivid testimony to this proclivity. But the present situation and the foreseeable future strongly suggest that the U.S. (and all advanced technological societies) will soon be approaching a steadying state. This situation will result from the depletion of resources and the drastic ecological dangers of industrial expansion, especially from pollution and increased heat.

Will capitalism be able to meet the demands of an economic system in which growth has ceased or been very greatly reduced? The most profound problem will arise from the maldistribution of income. The efforts of the lower and middle classes to improve their positions can only be met by diminishing the absolute incomes of the upper classes. This will present a classic confrontation between the "haves" and the "have nots" that was not probable in an expanding economy where all could improve. This problem will pose extreme political and economic difficulties for capitalism. According to Heilbroner, this situation will likely lead to a more authoritarian system:

The struggle for relative position would not only pit one class against another, but also each against all, as lower and middle groups engaged in a free-for-all for higher incomes. This would bring enormous inflationary pressures of the kind that capitalism is already beginning to experience, and would require the imposition of much stronger control measures than any that capitalism has yet succeeded in introducing—indeed, than any that capitalist governments have yet imagined.

In bluntest terms, the question is whether the Hobbesian struggle that is likely to arise in such a straight-jacketed economic society would not impose intolerable strains on the representative democratic political apparatus that has been historically associated with capitalist societies. . . .

It is possible that some capitalist nations, gifted with unusual political leadership and a responsive public, may make the necessary structural changes without surrendering their democratic achievements. At best, our inquiry establishes the approach of certain kinds of challenges, but cannot pretend to judge how individual nations may meet these challenges. For the majority of capitalist nations, however, I do not see how one can avoid the conclusion that the required transformation will be likely to exceed the capabilities of representative democracy.[57]

Unemployment

Most jobs in a capitalist society are in the private sector. This creates two problems leading to increased unemployment. First, since businesses are interested in profits, it is often in the interest of owners to replace workers with robots, computers, or other labor-saving devices. Second, plants may be closed or moved for business reasons, thus displacing workers. As noted earlier, multinationals often move their operations overseas where labor is less costly and unions nonexistent.[58] Also, a recent trend has been for businesses to move to the sunbelt states. Studies have shown that plants shifting locations typically hire locals at lower pay than at the old location. Thus, while jobs are created in the sunbelt states, serious dislocations are experienced by individuals and local economies in the previous locales.[59]

The problem of unemployment provides a fundamental dilemma for the government in an unplanned economy. It would seem reasonable to assume that society should provide enough jobs so that all able-bodied people would be able to secure employment at a reasonable wage. This is a critical problem in the United States. The question is whether the government should subsidize jobs to reduce or eliminate unemployment. Except for the WPA programs of the Great Depression the federal government has not attempted to guarantee employment to all who are able to work. The Nixon and Ford Administrations especially resisted legislation that would have created millions of jobs because they felt it was too expensive. A stronger argument, however, is that unemployment is the more expensive of the two options.

The involuntary idleness of 8 to 10 million unemployed Americans is costing the tax-payers about $40 billion a year in unemployment compensation, welfare payments, food stamps, subsidized housing and other benefits, which is more than it would cost to put almost everybody to work through government-guaranteed full employment. . . . [Moreover] the economy loses about $16 billion a year for every million out of work, to say nothing of the billions in tax revenues that are also lost through reduced payrolls.[60]

Of special interest are college graduates who will be forced either to be unemployed or to take jobs previously held by non-college graduates. The Bureau of Labor Statistics has estimated that between 1975 and 1985 the number of college graduates will exceed the number of jobs requiring their skills by 800,000.[61] The result will be a large number of individuals with inconsistent statuses. Research has shown that this type of status inconsistency (i.e., high on education and relatively lower on occupation or income) propels people toward radical political solutions, even violence.[62] The lack of jobs ought also to increase the political volatility among the less educated. With increased technology, semiskilled and unskilled jobs will become virtually nonexistent.

Clearly, then, the creation of jobs is critical. But left to operate guided only by the whims of the market, the private sector will decrease jobs rather than increase them.

The Trend toward Reducing the Scope (and Cost) of Government

The current political mood in the United States is toward limiting the role of government at all levels. Inflation and the high cost of government programs have brought about a taxpayers' revolt. The passage of the Jarvis-Gann bill (Proposition 13) in California by a 2 to 1 margin in 1978 showed clearly that the voters wanted to lower their taxes, even at the cost of restricting governmental activities (indeed, for some the goal was the reduction of government because they believed that the larger the role of the government, the fewer the freedoms of the individuals). The Jarvis-Gann plan, although not successful in all states, appears to have set a precedent as legislators in other states and at the federal level have introduced similar legislation with widespread legislative, corporate, and citizen support. The election of Ronald Reagan and a number of conservatives to Congress in 1980 also indicates this trend.

This trend has several important implications. First, it will curtail the ability of the government to reduce unemployment. The rate of employment will be a function of the economy. Conservatives argue that lower taxes will encourage businesses to expand, thereby increasing the demand for workers. Others are concerned, however, that employers will take the increased profits resulting from lower taxes and increase their dividends to stockholders, which will not have the effect of easing the employment problem. Or, if plant expansion is desirable, money will be spent on automated equipment, which actually would reduce the demand for workers.

A second probable consequence of this trend will be reduced government power to plan effectively for the future. Central planning, subsidies for developing new forms of energy or methods to curb pollution, and the like will be ineffectual.

Another result, if the Jarvis-Gann fever spreads appreciably, would be the curtailment of all but essential government services. What is essential depends on "whose ox is being gored," but we can safely predict that social services such as food stamps, rent supplements, aid for dependent children, day care centers, bilingual education programs, and others will be drastically reduced or eliminated. Moreover, legislation to spread benefits to all segments of the population (such as a national health insurance program) will be soundly defeated. If these programs are curtailed, then the gap between the haves and have-nots will continue to widen, increasing the possibility of conflict.

SUMMARY

The economy, like the polity, is an institution. By this, sociologists mean that the economy is a patterned, organized way that has evolved in society to accomplish a key survival need—in this case the way society is organized to insure that the goods and services required for societal and individual survival are produced, distributed, and consumed. But there is a paradox to all institutions that is illustrated by the economy. While the economy is absolutely necessary, it is a source of social problems.

The particular way the American economy is organized—its norms, values, and the distribution of people in economic roles—causes some very important problems. Some of these are economic cycles, unemployment, broad differentials in remuneration by type of work, discrimination in the labor market, a consumption ethic in a time of energy and resource shortages, subsidization of the already advantaged, taking advantage of the powerless in the United States and abroad, the profit motive superseding humanitarian values, and the concentration of economic power among a relatively few huge corporations that minimizes or even destroys competition.

American society must not only cope with these problems but deal with the new ones of the present era: pollution, shortages, worldwide interdependence, stagflation, the extraordinary power of multinational companies, and increased tensions (domestically and internationally). Four fundamental changes appear necessary to this observer if the U.S. is to be even moderately successful in meeting these problems: (1) central planning to meet societal goals and anticipated problems; (2) a shift away from an economy dependent on defense to one that has productive consequences (mass transit, energy creation, renewal of resources, and other public works); (3) a redistribution of wealth to alleviate material suffering among the impoverished by guaranteeing decent work at an adequate minimum annual wage, and adequate health care; and (4) extension of public ownership to utilities, transportation, and all natural resources.

CHAPTER REVIEW

1. Economic activity involves the production and distribution of goods and services.

2. There are two fundamental ways society can organize its economic activities—capitalism and socialism.

3. Capitalism in its pure form involves: (a) the private ownership of property; (b) the pursuit of personal profit; (c) competition; and (d) a government policy of allowing the marketplace to function unhindered.

4. Socialism in its pure form involves: (a) democracy throughout the social structure; (b) equality—equality of opportunity, equality rather than hierarchy in making decisions, and equality in sharing the benefits of society; and (c) efficiency in providing the best conditions to meet the material needs of the citizens.

5. Marx's prediction that capitalism will result in an economy dominated by monopolies has been fulfilled in the United States. But rather than a single corporation dominating a sector of the economy, the United States is characterized by the existence of *shared monopolies*—where four or fewer corporations supply 50 percent or more of a particular market.

6. The power of America's largest corporations is increased by their international activities. Multinational corporations have important consequences: (a) decline in domestic jobs; (b) crippling of the power of unions; (c) hurting the government through lost revenues in taxes and a negative balance of payments; (d) increased power of corporations over the world economy and world events; and (e) exploitation of workers and natural resources in Third World countries.

7. The United States is not capitalistic but has a form of corporate socialism whereby the government ensures the profitability of the largest corporations through subsidies, tax breaks, contracts, and market regulation. Corporate social-

ism is found in military spending, subsidies to petroleum companies, subsidies to banking, transportation, and the housing industry, to name a few.

8. The United States political-economic system works to increase income and wealth differentials among citizens. This occurs especially through regressive taxes and tax loopholes, through which benefits accrue to the affluent rather than the poor.

9. A major economic problem facing society is economic cycles. In inflationary times people on fixed incomes are especially hurt, home ownership declines, and organizations dependent on tax revenues suffer. During economic downturns, unemployment and bankruptcies increase, minorities and the poor are especially hard hit, and crime and mental illness increase.

10. Other economic problems facing the United States are: (a) an enormous national debt; (b) dependence on foreign oil; (c) a lack of economic planning; (d) coping with zero economic growth; and (e) unemployment.

FOR FURTHER STUDY

George W. Ball, ed., *Global Companies: The Political Economy of World Business* (Englewood Cliffs, N.J.: Prentice-Hall, 1975).

Richard Barnet and Ronald Muller, *Global Reach: The Power of the Multinational Corporations* (New York: Simon and Schuster, 1974).

John M. Blair, *The Control of Oil* (New York: Random House, 1976).

Robert M. Brandon, Jonathan Rowe, and Thomas H. Stanton, *Tax Politics* (New York: Pantheon, 1976).

Harry Braverman, *Labor and Monopoly Capital* (New York: Monthly Review, 1974).

Richard C. Edwards, Michael Reich, and Thomas E. Weisskopf, eds. *The Capitalist System: A Radical Analysis of American Society*, 2nd ed. (Englewood Cliffs, N.J.: Prentice-Hall, 1978).

Stuart Ewen, *Captains of Consciousness: Advertising and the Social Roots of Consumer Culture* (New York: McGraw-Hill, 1976).

David Hapgood, *The Screwing of the Average Man: How the Rich Get Richer and You Get Poorer* (New York: Bantam, 1975).

Michael Harrington, *Decade of Decision* (New York: Simon and Schuster, 1980).

Seymour Melman, *The Permanent War Economy: American Capitalism in Decline* (New York: Simon and Schuster, 1974).

Ralph Nader and Mark J. Green, eds., *Corporate Power in America* (New York: Grossman, 1973).

James O'Conner, *The Fiscal Crisis of the State* (New York: St. Martin's Press, 1973).

Michael Parenti, *Power and the Powerless* (New York: St. Martin's Press, 1978).

Sumner M. Rosen, *Economic Power Failure: The Current American Crisis* (New York: McGraw-Hill, 1975).

Anthony Sampson, *The Arms Bazaar: From Lebanon to Lockheed* (New York: Viking, 1977).

Leonard Silk with David Vogel, *Ethics and Profits: The Crisis of Confidence in American Business* (New York: Simon and Schuster, 1976).

Philip Stern, *The Rape of the Taxpayer* (New York: Random House (Vintage Books), 1973).

Albert Szymanski, *The Capitalist State and the Politics of Class* (Cambridge, Mass.: Winthrop, 1978).

Maurice Zeitlin, ed., *American Society, Inc.: Studies of Social Structure and Political Economy of the United States*, 2nd ed. (Chicago: Rand McNally, 1977).

NOTES AND REFERENCES

1. See Robert J. Werlin, "Marxist Political Analysis," *Sociological Inquiry* 42 (No. 3-4, 1972), pp. 157-181; *Karl Marx: Selected Writings in Sociology and Social Philosophy*, T. B. Bottomore, trans. (New York: McGraw-Hill, 1956), pp. 127-212. See also Michael Harrington, *The Twilight of Capitalism* (New York: Simon and Schuster, 1976).

2. Mark J. Green, Beverly C. Moore, Jr., and Bruce Wasserstein, *The Closed Enterprise System* (New York: Bantam Books, 1972), p. 7.

3. Daniel Zwerdling, "The Food Monopolies," *The Progressive* 39 (January, 1975), p. 15. See also Louis M. Kohlmeier, "Snap, Crackle and Divestiture," *The New York Times*, April 25, 1976, Sec. 3, pp. 1, 9.

4. Associated Press release (October 3, 1980).

5. Sidney Lens, "Blaming the Victims," *The Progressive* 44 (August, 1980), p. 27.

6. Herbert J. Gans, "The New Egalitarianism," *Saturday Review* (May 6, 1972), p. 43.

7. For a discussion of the efforts by the U.S. Senate to break up the largest corporations see Jaime Friedman, "Break 'Em All Up! A Senator's Plan for Dismantling Big Business," *The National Observer* (February 1, 1975), pp. 1, 15.

8. Mark J. Green, "The High Cost of Monopoly," *The Progressive* 36 (March, 1972, p. 4.

9. George S. McGovern, "The State of the Union," *Rolling Stone* (March, 13, 1975), p. 25.

10. TRB, "Why Mobil Isn't Loved," *The New Republic* (October 14, 1978), p. 3.

11. The following section depends largely on the insights of Richard Barnet and Ronald Muller, "Global Reach-1," *The New Yorker*, December 2, 1974, pp. 53-128, and December 9, 1974, pp. 100-159; and Gurney Breckenfeld, "Multinationals at Bay," *Saturday Review* (January 24, 1976), pp. 12-22.

12. Barnet and Muller (December 9, 1974), p. 102.

13. Ibid., p. 132.

14. Barnet and Muller (December 2, 1974), p. 80.

15. See Brickenfeld, "Multinationals at Bay"; "How Clean is Business?" *Newsweek* (September 1, 1975), pp. 50-54; "Payoffs: The Growing Scandal," *Newsweek* (February 23, 1976), pp. 26-33; and "The Big Payoff," *Time* (February 23, 1976), pp. 28-36.

16. Norman Cousins, "Target for Taxpayers," *Saturday Review* (August, 1978), p. 59.

17. McGovern, "The State of the Union," p. 25.

18. This section is taken largely from Philip M. Stern, *Rape of the Taxpayer* (New York: Vintage, 1974), pp. 228-251. See also John M. Blair, *The Control of Oil* (New York: Random House, 1976).

19. Stern, *Rape of the Taxpayer*, p. 239. For a history of this tax break, see Frederick Andrews, "Behind Foreign Oil Tax Credits," *The New York Times* (May 15, 1979), p. D2.

20. James O'Conner, *The Fiscal Crisis of the State* (New York: St. Martins, 1973), pp. 105-110 and 169.

21. Ibid., pp. 126-128.

22. Stern, *Rape of the Taxpayer*, pp. 355-359.

23. Lester C. Thurow, "The Myth of the American Economy," *Newsweek* (February 14, 1977), p. 11.

24. *Newsweek* (May 8, 1972), p. 99.

25. George McGovern, "On Taxing and Redistributing Income," *The New York Review of Books* 8 (May 4, 1972), p. 7. For additional evidence see also: Ferdinand Lundberg, *The Rich and the Super-Rich* (New York: Bantam Books, 1968), pp. 388-464; Howard P. Tuchman, *The Economics of the Rich* (New York: Random House, 1973), pp. 108-123; and Stern, *Rape of the Taxpayer*.

26. Gabriel Kolko, *Wealth and Power in Amer-*

ica: An Analysis of Social Class and Income Distribution (New York: Praeger, 1962), pp. 44–45.

27. Associated Press release (April 9, 1977). See also Gary Hart, "The Economy Is Decaying, the Free Lunch Is Over," *The New York Times* (April 21, 1975).

28. Stern, *Rape of the Taxpayer*, p. 6.

29. See, for example, Steven Rattner, "World Slump's Impact on U.S.," *The New York Times* (May 7, 1980), p. D2.

30. For analyses on the causes of inflation, see Robert L. Heilbroner, "The Inflation In Your Future," *The New York Review of Books* (May 1, 1980), pp. 6–10; Robert M. Solow, "All Simple Stories About Inflation Are Wrong," *The Washington Post* (May 18, 1980), pp. G1, G4; and Robert D. Hershey, Jr., "Inflation at 13.3%: What Is This Rapacious Thing?" *The New York Times* (February 3, 1980), Section 3, p. 1, 8.

31. "Inflation: Who Is Hurt Worse?" *Time* (January 15, 1979), pp. 58–60; "Next Round Against Inflation," *Time* (April 24, 1978), p. 66; see also "The Inflation Surge," *Newsweek* (May 29, 1978), pp. 68–82.

32. Sidney Margolius, "Inflation: Another Blow to the Poor," *Kansas City Times* (July 12, 1974), p. 15. See also "Inflation: Where Do We Go from Here?" *U.S. News & World Report* (October 2, 1978), pp. 20–51.

33. See "For Housing Costs, the Sky's the Limit," *U.S. News & World Report* (August 28, 1978), pp. 48–49, and John F. Lawrence, "U.S. Housing Buyers Keep Up with Pace," *Los Angeles Times* (September 3, 1978).

34. "Two Incomes: No Sure Hedge Against Inflation," *U.S. News & World Report* (July 9, 1979), pp. 45–46.

35. "The Big Apple on the Brink," *Time* (April 7, 1975), pp. 50–51. See also Robert Dietsch, "U.S. Cities Pounded Into 'Concussion' by Economic Ills," *Rocky Mountain News* (May 22, 1975), p. 12.

36. Cited in Edwin McDowell, "Stalled Autos: As Detroit Goes, So Goes Toledo," *The New York Times* (June 22, 1980), Section 3, p. 4.

37. "Where It Hits Hardest," *Newsweek* (May 5, 1975), p. 63; and "All about Unemployment," *Newsweek* (March 17, 1975), pp. 77–79.

38. Don Kirkman, "Two-Year Recession Toll of 10,000 Babies Forecast," *Rocky Mountain News* (October 24, 1974), p. 28.

39. "A Rush to Personal Bankruptcy," *Newsweek* (August 11, 1980), pp. 59–60.

40. The following is taken from Joann S. Lublin, "Black Firms' Blues: Recession Hits Hard at Many Companies Owned by Minorities," *Wall Street Journal* (April 1, 1975), pp. 1, 12.

41. Nancy Keebler, "Recession Leaves Its Mark on Family Structure," *The National Observer* (March 29, 1975), p. 4.

42. For a classic examination of this relationship see Emile Durkheim, *Suicide*, John A. Spaulding and George Simpson, translators (Glencoe, Ill.: The Free Press, 1951). This book was first published in 1897.

43. M. Harvey Brenner, *Mental Illness and the Economy* (Cambridge: Harvard University Press, 1973).

44. Roger Moore, "Suicide Rises as Economy Dips in Iowa," *Des Moines Register and Tribune* (September 28, 1980), pp. 1A, 3B.

45. Cited in *ibid.*, p. 1A.

46. Cited in Keebler, "Recession Leaves Its Mark," p. 4.

47. See "Three Cheers for Recession," *The Progressive* 43 (December, 1979), pp. 9–10.

48. "The U.S. Economy in Crisis," *Newsweek* (January 19, 1981), p. 40.

49. See, Ehud Levy-Pascal, "Will the Rising Price of Energy Push Us Over the Cliff?" *The Futurist* (December, 1979), pp. 477–480.

50. See Michael Rounds, "Hormuz Could Put U.S. In Sticky Straits," *Rocky Mountain News* (October 19, 1980), pp. 82, 89.

51. TRB, "The Case for More Planning, *Rocky Mountain News Trend* (March 30, 1975), p. 2.

52. Robert L. Heilbroner, *An Inquiry into the Human Prospect* (New York: W. W. Norton, 1974), p. 132.

53. See Stuart Ewen, *Captains of Consciousness: Advertising and the Social Roots of the Consumer Culture* (New York: McGraw-Hill, 1976).

54. Andrew Hacker, *The End of the American Era* (New York: Atheneum, 1970), p. 52.

55. This section is taken primarily from Heilbroner, *The Human Prospect*, pp. 82–95.

56. Wallace Stegner and Page Stegner, "Rocky Mountain Country," *The Atlantic Monthly* 241 (April, 1978), p. 86.

57. Heilbroner, *The Human Prospect*, pp. 88–90.

58. See Bob Tamarkin and Lisa Gross, "Starting Over in Chicago," *Forbes* (April 28, 1980), pp. 74–86.

59. Associated Press release (April 13, 1980).

60. Clayton Fritchey, "Should Texas Subsidize Work or Idleness," *Rocky Mountain News* (January 15, 1976), p. 63.

61. "Too Many College Graduates," *Parade* (May 4, 1975), p. 20.

62. See Linda Baer, D. Stanley Eitzen, Charles Duprey, Norman J. Thompson, and Curtis Cole, "The Consequences of Objective and Subjective Status Inconsistency," *The Sociological Quarterly* 17 (Summer, 1976), pp. 389–400; and Report to the National Advisory Commission on Civil Disorders (New York: Bantam, 1968), pp. 128–135.

17

The Structure of Power in American Society

In Washington, D.C. there are about 15,000 lawyers, association executives, public relations experts, and technical workers who are lobbyists. These lobbyists work on behalf of interest groups to influence legislators and regulatory agencies. Lobbyists' tactics include supplying information, doing favors, providing entertainment, giving campaign contributions, flooding Congress with telegrams, and furnishing transportation.

The phenomenon of lobbying can be interpreted in two opposite ways—*each of which illustrates a fundamental view of the distribution of power for the whole society*. The first view is that lobbying is the essence of democracy, as competing pressure groups each present their best case to the decision-makers. These officials, faced with these countervailing forces, tend to compromise and make decisions most beneficial to the public.

In contrast, others view lobbying as another instance of the privileged few consistently getting their way. Interest groups are not equal in power. Some have enormous power and are not challenged by effective opposition. For example, the American Petroleum Institute speaks for 350 corporations and has an annual lobbying budget of $30 million. Also, the United States Chamber of Commerce has a $20 million budget and represents 89,500 corporations and 2,500 local communities. These and other business-oriented lobbies are extremely well organized and financed. Their opposition is negligible. Clearly, from this perspective, power in Washington is centralized and represents the powerful few.

The compelling question of this chapter is: Who are the real power wielders in American society? Is it an elite, or are the people sovereign? The location and exercise of power is difficult to determine, especially in a large and complex society such as the United States. Decisions are necessarily made by a few people, but in a democracy these few are to be representatives of the masses and therefore subject to their influence. But what of nonrepresentatives who aid in shaping policy? What about the pressure on the decision-makers by powerful groups? What about those pressures on the decision-maker which are so diffuse that the leaders may not even know who is applying the pressure?

MODELS OF THE NATIONAL POWER STRUCTURE

There are two basic views of the power structure—**elitist** and **pluralist**. The elitist view of power is that there is a pyramid of power. Those persons at the apex control the rest of the pyramid. The pluralists, on the other hand, see power as dispersed rather than concentrated. Power is broadly distributed among a number of organizations, special interests, and the voters. This chapter is devoted to the examination of different elitist and pluralist conceptions of power in the United States. As we survey each, the fundamental question we should ask ourselves is: How does this model mesh with the facts of contemporary America? Does the model portray things as they are or as they should be?

Pluralist Models

Pluralism I: representative democracy. Many Americans accept the notion promoted in high school civics books that the United States is a "government of the people, by the people, for the people." Democracy is the form of government in which the people have the ultimate power. In a complex society of over 230 million persons, the people cannot make all decisions; they must elect representatives to make most decisions. So, decision making is concentrated at the top, but it is to be controlled by the people who elect the decision-makers. This model is shown in Figure 17-1.

The most important component of a democratic model is that the representatives, because they are elected by the people, are responsive to the wishes of the people.

This model, however, does *not* conform to reality. The United States is undemocratic in many important ways. The people, although they do vote for their representatives every few years, are really quite powerless. For example, who makes the really important decisions about war and peace, economic policies, and foreign policy? The people certainly do not. And in the light of the Pentagon Papers, which concerned the conduct of American leaders in the Indochina War, it is clear that the American people have been deliberately misinformed by the leadership. The record shows that many times the American people have been deceived when the object was to conceal clandestine illegal operations, mistakes, undemocratic practices and the like. The following events are instances of official U.S. deceit during our involvement in Southeast Asia:[1]

item: In 1963, the U.S. supported—but officially denied its involvement in—the coup against South Vietnam's President Ngo Dinh Diem.

item: In 1964 President Johnson used an incident in which American ships were allegedly shot at in the Tonkin Gulf to give him a free hand to escalate the war in Vietnam. Congress was deliberately misled by the official representation of the facts.

item: President Johnson praised our Asian allies for sending "volunteers" to fight in Vietnam when in fact our government had paid Thailand and the Philippines $200 million each if they would make this gesture.

item: President Nixon and his advisors told the American public that the neutrality of Cambodia had not been violated when U.S. pilots had already conducted 3,600

FIGURE 17-1   Representative Democracy

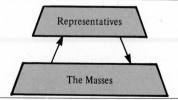

bombing missions in a five-year period in that country. To carry out this deception, the death certificates of Americans who died in Cambodia were falsified by our government.

These examples could be multiplied many times over with cover-ups of the CIA involvement in the takeover of the Allende government in Chile; the U.S.-sponsored invasion of Cuba in 1961; the attempted whitewashing of sheep deaths in Utah because of an unintended release of chemicals used in biological warfare; the denial by Attorney General Mitchell that ITT had offered $400,000 to underwrite the 1972 Republican National Convention, and so on.

Not only have the American people been misinformed, but the basic democratic tenet that the public be informed has been defied. On the one hand, Congress has shown its contempt for the electorate by the use of secret meetings. The executive branch, too, has acted in secret. Recent presidents have gone months without a press conference, have used "executive privilege" to keep presidential advisors from testifying before congressional committees, and have refused to debate opponents in election campaigns.

Many persons who are appointed rather than elected wield tremendous power. Technical experts, for example, evaluate extremely complicated issues; they can virtually dictate to the president and Congress what is needed for defense, shoring up the economy, or winning friends abroad, because they are the experts. The coterie of advisors may convince the president to act in particular ways. The members appointed to the regulatory agencies have tremendous power to shape various aspects of the economy.

Perhaps one of the most undemocratic features (at least in its consequences) of the American political system is a result of the manner in which campaigns are financed. Political campaigns are expensive, with statewide campaigns sometimes costing hundreds of thousands of dollars while a national campaign runs into the millions (excluding primaries, President Nixon spent more than $36 million and McGovern spent in excess of $18 million in the 1972 election campaign). This money is raised from contributions. Nixon, for example, received over $14 million from 100 persons for his 1972 campaign. Such contributions are given for a number of reasons, including the hope of future favors or payoffs for past benefits. Thus, the passage of favorable laws, beneficial governmental rulings, maintenance of tax loopholes, or appointment to prestigious government posts such as ambassador may be the reward for financing candidates. Some individuals and interest groups even donate to the candidate of both parties to ensure that their interests are served regardless of the election outcome. The result is that the wealthy have power while the less well-to-do and certainly the poor have no hold on office holders.[2]

To counter the potential and real abuses of large contributions, the Presidential campaigns of 1976 and 1980 were financed from public funds. Congressional candidates, however, were allowed to accept contributions from individuals and special interest groups. Most of the money has come from special interest groups through Political Action Committees (PACs). In 1974 PACs gave $12.4 million to Congressional candidates. In 1976 they gave $22.6 million, which increased to $35 million in 1978. PACs contributed another $50 million to Congressional races in 1980, leading some cynics to comment that we have "the best Congress money can buy."[3] These PACs are formed to represent interests such as labor unions, doctors, realtors, auto dealers, teachers, and corporations. Each PAC may give up to $5,000 to any candidate in a primary and another $5,000 in a general election. As *U.S. News & World Report* editorialized, "PACs of every ilk have a way of contributing their allowed $5,000 chunks to candidates who either have voted 'right' or had better do so shortly."[4] Although no one can prove conclusively that receiving a PAC contribution buys a vote, there is evidence leading to such a conclusion. In 1979, for example, the National Association of Realtors supported legislation that weakened government enforcement power in real estate fraud cases. The amendment passed the House of Representatives. "Of the 51 freshmen Representatives who supported the realtors' position 43 had received contributions, averaging $4,272 apiece, from the realtors' political action committee. Of the 29 freshmen who opposed the realtors, 13 had received no money from that committee at all."[5]

Money presents a fundamental obstacle to democracy because only the interests of the wealthy tend to be served. Elections are very expensive. In 1980, for example, five Senators spent over $2 million each to wage their campaigns. One governor—Jay Rockefeller of West Virginia—spent $11.6 million ($28.92 per vote received) to win.[6] Moreover, the data show consistently that the winners outspend the losers. In the 1978 Senate races candidates who outspent their opponents won 28 of the 33 contested races. Thus, it takes money and lots of it to be a successful politician. The candidate must either be rich or be willing to accept contributions from others. In either case, the political leaders will be part of or beholden to the wealthy.

There are a number of other undemocratic features that belie the validity of this model. The "seniority system" in Congress gives extraordinary power to those individuals with longevity of service. The electoral college system is undemocratic. So is the party nomination system; the people choose from among the nominees for President, but they have little voice in their selection as nominees. The establishment of voting district boundaries is often "gerrymandered" by the party in power to keep themselves in power. Minority groups of all kinds may have little if any representation because of the many "winner-take-all" electoral systems.

Another objection, and a most telling one, is that the majority of citizens are relatively uninformed and apathetic about politics—thereby giving power to those already in office by default. Surveys

show that 65 percent of the eligible voters do not regularly vote, half cannot name their congressperson, 68 percent cannot identify anything their representative has ever done, 96 percent cannot identify any policy the representative stands for—all rather minimal tests of political activity, and the figures are worse for state and municipal levels.[8]

A final objection to this model is that it neglects the vast power of the various interest groups on specific issues. Organized labor, the American Medical Association, environmentalists, farmers, and other interest groups often mobilize and get beneficial legislation involving tariffs, taxes, contracts, subsidies, or whatever.

Pluralism II: veto groups. Although some groups have more power than others and some individuals have more power than others, the power structure in the United States is viewed according to the "veto groups" model as a plurality of interest groups.[10] Each interest group (for example, the military, labor, business, farmers, education, medicine, law, veterans, the aged, blacks, and consumers) is primarily concerned with protecting its own interests. The group that primarily exercises power varies with the issue at stake. There is a balance of power, since each "veto group" mobilizes to prevent the others from actions threatening its interests. Thus, these groups tend to neutralize each other.

FIGURE 17-2   Veto-Groups Model

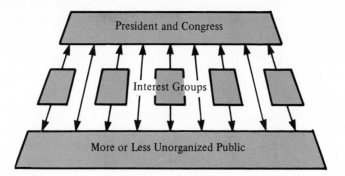

The masses are sought as an ally (rather than dominated, as is the case in the various elitist models) by the interest groups in their attempts to exert power over issues in their jurisdiction. Figure 17–2 shows the relationship between the various levels in this model.

This pluralist model assumes that there are a number of sectors of power. The most powerful persons in each are usually wealthy—probably upper class. But, the pluralist view is that the upper class is not a unified group—there is considerable disagreement within the upper-class category because of differing interests. Power is not concentrated, but is viewed as a shifting coalition depending upon the issue. The basic difference between pluralists and elitists is on the question of whether there is a basic unity or disagreement among the powerful from different sectors (basically, those who are wealthy enough to be upper class).

There are several criticisms of this pluralistic model. They stem from the knowledge that it, like the other pluralistic model (for representative democracy), is an idealized conception of the distribution of power—as such, it does not conform with reality and is subject to question on several grounds. First, is the power structure so amorphous that power shifts constantly from one power source to another? Second, are the interest groups so equal in power that they neutralize each other? The special bias of this view is that it does not give attention to the power differentials among the various interest groups. It is absurd to claim that the power of big business is neutralized by the countervailing power of farmers. A more probable occurrence is that there is a hierarchy of power among these "veto groups."

A final criticism is that the leaders in each sector come disproportionately from the upper economic strata. If this assertion is correct, the possibility of a power elite that transcends narrow interest groups is present, since they may know each other, tend to intermarry, and have similar economic interests (as we will see later).

The pluralist models are not altogether faulty. There are a number of possible power centers that often compete for advantage. Shifting coalitions are possible. There are instances when selected officials are responsive to public opinion. However, it seems to this observer that most of the evidence supports an elitist view, although each of the three types described below also has its faults.

The elitist views of societal power are usually structured quite similarly to those of Karl Marx. For Marx economics was the basis for the stratification system (that is, unequal distribution of rewards including power). The economic elite, because of similar interests (that is, keeping the status quo) and limited social interaction patterns, is a unified group. The economic elite controls the state and its inhabitants.

Implicit in the Marxian conception of the powerful is the notion of conspiracy. The elite manipulate the masses through religion, nationalism, control of the media, and control of the visible governmental leaders.[10]

Elitist Models

Power elite I: communist conspiracy. The "communist conspiracy" view is not taken seriously by social scientists, and most citizens would see little reality in its assumptions. However, G. William Domhoff has estimated that it is shared by 5 to 15 million adult Americans.[11] In this ultraconservative view of the power structure, the United States is led by a small, cohesive group of ideologues. This group is thought to be a "conspiracy" which shares an ideology that is collectivist (anti-capitalism and pro-welfare) and internationalist (one-world government), ridiculing the traditional virtues of rugged individualism and blind patriotism. As evidence of this "conspiracy," there is the existence of a bipartisan group called the Trilateral Commission. This is a group of 275 prominent businessmen, scholars, and politicians from North America, Western Europe, and Japan. It was formed in 1973 under the initial leadership of David Rockefeller, head of Chase Manhattan Bank. Its proponents argue that this organization strengthens the ties among the United States and its allies. Its conservative opponents see the Trilateral Commission as an international elite, whose interests transcend national loyalties. They see it as the forerunner of world government. They also fear its influence on domestic politics. President Carter, a former member, had on his administration team other Trilateralists—Zbigniew Brzezinski, Walter Mondale, Cyrus Vance, and Harold Brown. The Reagan Administration is also represented by Trilateral members in high places—George Bush and Caspar Weinberger.

An important component of this view is that the leaders act together, and secretly, to manipulate the masses so that certain agreed-upon goals are accomplished. They are motivated by an ideology that is antithetical to all that America has stood for in the past.

Within the ultra-right-wing literature, some variations are found as to who comprises the conspiracy. For some, it is composed of Jews. For others, it is the "Eastern Establishment" of bankers and industrialists who control the Republican Party. Another variation is that the leaders are either card-carrying communists or the dupes of the communists. The founder of the John Birch Society, Robert Welch, has written, for example, that President Dwight D. Eisenhower was a Communist. He said, "My firm belief that Dwight Eisenhower is a dedicated, conscious agent of the Communist conspiracy is based on an accumulation of detailed evidence so extensive and so palpable that it seems to me to put this conviction beyond any reasonable doubt."[12]

Although there is a tendency by academics not to take this model seriously, there are at least two aspects of this view that make sense. First, the ultra-right-wingers are convinced that the big money interests (heads of major banks, industrial giants, and insurance companies) actually run the country. This can make a good deal of sense, as we will see later, although the degree to which they are unified in trying to run the country is debatable. Second, both political parties are dominated largely by the same kinds of people—the wealthy. From that viewpoint it really does not make very much difference which party is in power or who is appointed to the highest government posts—the interests of the wealthy tend to be served.

There are some notable points of this model that do not fit the facts. The government is not dominated by Jews or Communists who work for the overthrow of the government. As Domhoff has asked: Is David Rockefeller a communist? Is he against capitalism?—not likely. There is no "conspiracy." The leaders tend to have similar economic interests, and they work for what they consider best for the country and its economy; this means a strong defense, protected industry, prosperity, and economic growth. They are not a tightly knit organization that works secretly for the goal of America's downfall. This is a paranoid view of the world that is just plain false.

Power elite II: the thesis of C. Wright Mills. C. Wright Mills' view of the American structure of power posits that the key persons in three sectors—the corporate rich, the executive branch of the government, and the military—all combine to form a **power elite** that makes all important decisions.[13]

The elite is a small group of persons who routinely interact together. They also, as Mills assumed, have similar interests and goals. The elite is the power elite because the members have key institutional positions—that is, they command great authority and resources in a specific and important sector, and each sector is dependent upon the other sectors.

There are three levels in Mills' pyramid of power. The uppermost is the power elite—composed of the leaders of three sectors. Mills implied that of the three, the corporate rich are perhaps the most powerful (first among "equals"). The middle level of power is comprised of local opinion leaders, the legislative branch of government, and the plurality of interest groups. These bodies, according to Mills, do the bidding of the power elite. The third level is the powerless mass of unorganized people who are controlled from above. They are exploited economically and politically. The three levels of power are depicted in Figure 17–3.

Mills believed that the power elite was a relatively new phenomenon resulting from a number of historical and social forces that have enlarged and centralized the facilities of power, making the decisions of small groups much more consequential than in any other age.[14]

FIGURE 17-3   Mills's Pyramid of Power

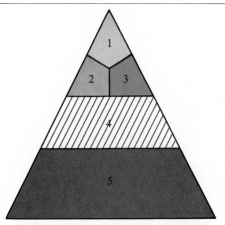

Legend: 1, corporate rich: 2, executive branch; 3, military leaders; 4, leaders of interest groups, legislative branch, local opinion leaders; 5, unorganized masses.

The two important and related factors giving rise to the recent emergence of the power elite are: (1) the means of power and violence are now infinitely greater than they were in the past, and (2) they are also increasingly centralized. The decisions of a few become ultimately crucial when they have the power to activate a system that has the capabilities of destroying hundreds of cities within minutes. Transportation, communication, the economy, the instruments of warfare are examples of several areas that have become centralized—making a power elite possible. The federal government taxes, regulates, and passes laws so that the lives of almost all Americans are affected. This same bureaucratic process is evident in the military, where decisions are more and more centralized. The Pentagon, which oversees the largest and most expensive feature of the government, is a relatively new phenomenon. The economy in the United States was once composed of many, many small productive units that were more or less autonomous. But over time the number of semiautonomous economic units has dwindled through mergers, interlocking directorates, and chainstores, putting the financial squeeze on the small businessperson. The result is that the economy has become dominated by less than 200 giant corporations.

The tremendous advances in transportation and communication have made it much more likely that the persons holding key positions in the political, economic, and military hierarchies can be in contact with each other if they wish to do so. If, as Mills assumed, they have similar interests, then they must be in contact so that their activities can be coordinated to the best mutual advantage.

The key decision makers also have instruments to influence the masses, such as television, public relations firms, and techniques of propaganda that are unsurpassed in the history of mankind. Hence, if there is a power elite and they want to manipulate the masses to accept their decisions, they have the instruments of mass persuasion at their disposal.

Mills also contended that the importance of institutions has shifted. Whereas the family and religion were once the most important American institutions, they (along with education) have become subordinate to the three power institutions of the economy, polity, and military—thus making the leaders of these three domains the power elite. Mills said, "Families and churches and schools adapt to modern life; governments and armies and corporations shape it; and, as they do so, they turn these lesser institutions into means for their ends."[15] For example, religious institutions supply chaplains to the armed forces, where they increase the effectiveness of the combat units by raising morale. Schools train persons for their places in the giant corporations. Fathers and sons are sometimes taken from their homes to fight and die for their country. And, Mills said, the symbols of these lesser institutions are used to legitimate the decisions of the power elite who dominate the powerful institutions.

A most important impetus for the formation of the power elite was World War II. American participation in a war worldwide in scope and where the possibility of defeat was very real meant, among other things, that a reorganization of various sectors had to be accomplished. The national government, particularly the executive department, had to be granted dictatorial powers so that the war could be conducted. Decisions had to be made quickly and in secret, two qualities not compatible with a democracy. The nation's corporations had to be mobilized for war. They made huge profits. Finally, the military became very prominent in decision making. Their expertise was essential to the making of wartime strategy.

Following World War II, the United States was faced with another threat, the spread of communism. This meant, in effect, that the executive department, the corporations, and the military did not shift back to their peacetime ways. The military remained in the decision-making process, the corporations remained dependent upon lucrative defense contracts, and the executive branch continued to exercise its autonomous or at least semiautonomous powers.

All these factors, according to Mills, ensured that the domains of the polity, economy, and military were enlarged and centralized. Decisions made in each of these domains became increasingly crucial to all citizens, but particularly to the leaders of the other key domains. The result had to be a linkage between the key persons in each domain. It was in their interests to cooperate. Since each sector affected the others, the persons at the top of each hierarchy had to interact with the leaders from the other sectors, so that the actions and decisions would benefit all. Thus, they have come to form a triangle of power, an interlocking directorate of persons in the three key domains making coordinated decisions—a power elite.

An important ingredient in Mills' view is that the elite is a self-conscious cohesive unit. This unity is based on three factors: psychological similarity, social interaction, and coinciding interests.

1. *Psychological similarity.* The institutional positions men occupy throughout their lifetimes determine the values they will hold. For example, career military men hold certain values by virtue of being socialized into the military subculture. The famous quote that "What's good for General Motors is good for the country" by Secretary of Defense (under President Eisenhower) Charles Wilson is also indicative of this probability. Thus, for Mills, the psychology of these leaders is largely shaped by the values they develop in their institutional roles. Additionally, the psychological similarity among the members of the elite is derived from their similar social origins and style of life.

2. *Social interaction.* Mills stated that the ruling elite are involved in a set of overlapping groups and intricately connected cliques.

The people of the higher circles may also be conceived as members of a top social stratum, as a set of groups whose members know one another, see one another socially and at business, and so, in making decisions, take one another into account. The elite, according to this conception, feel themselves to be, and are felt by others to be, the inner circle of "the upper social classes." They form a more or less compact social and psychological entity; they have become self-conscious members of a social class. People are either accepted into this class or they are not, and there is a qualitative split, rather than merely a numerical scale, separating them from those who are not elite. They are more or less aware of themselves as a social class and they behave toward one another differently from the way they do toward members of other classes. They accept one another, understand one another, marry one another, tend to work and to think if not together at least alike.[16]

3. *Coinciding interests.* A third unifying condition hypothesized by Mills is the existence of similar interests among the elite. The interest of the elite is, among other things, maintenance of the capitalist system with themselves at the top. Additionally, the government needs adequate defense systems, to which the military agree and which the corporations gladly sell for a profit. The huge corporations have large holdings in foreign

countries. They therefore expect the government to make policy decisions that will be beneficial (profitable) for American interests. These similar interests result in a unity and a need for planning and coordination of their efforts. Since each sector affects the other, the persons at the top of each hierarchy must interact with leaders of the other sectors so that their actions will benefit all. Top decisions, Mills argued, thus become coordinated decisions.

Empirical evidence for the existence of a military-industrial power elite. Mills postulated that there was an interlocking directorate uniting key persons in the business, military, and economic sectors. The relationships among the three are therefore:

There is much evidence supporting the linkages for each of the three relationships pictured above.

On the surface the federal government appears to have great power over business— through taxation, the power of the regulatory agencies (for example, Federal Trade Commission, Interstate Commerce Commission, and Securities and Exchange Commission), the power to determine interest rates and the flow of money, and so on. But who are the people who wield power in the executive branch of the government? The evidence is that they tend to be wealthy businesspeople.[17] The leaders either are rich or they are dependent upon contributions from the wealthy. The important appointees of the President (cabinet members, members of regulatory agencies, Supreme Court justices, ambassadors) most often are executives in the large corporations, corporation lawyers, or bankers. The implication is clear, if Mills was correct, that the linkage between the executive branch and business is very strong and that the leaders in both areas are alike in attitudes and actions because of similar interests.

The Defense Department is dependent upon Congress for money, including the appropriations for new programs. The Defense Department, according to the Constitution, must be headed by a civilian appointed by the president and approved by the Senate. The president is also Commander-in-Chief of the Armed Forces, and the final authority for important policy decisions.

The alliance between the government and the military is not a one-way relationship, however, since Congress and the executive department are influenced in many ways by the military. Frequently, they must rely upon the testimony of military experts, and the assessment of America's spy network determines to a significant degree what course of action the government will take. Furthermore, the Pentagon has thousands of public relations personnel around the world. One of their jobs is to convince the public and the government of the importance of its programs and of the need for new weaponry.

Government officials also receive great pressure from state and local governments to keep and/or to increase military expenditures in their local areas. In fiscal 1979, California had $12.3 billion in contracts, followed by Texas, $4.8 billion; New York, $4.6 billion; Connecticut, $3.8 billion; Missouri, $3.4 billion; Virginia; $3.3 billion; and Massachusetts, $3.1 billion.[18] Even Colorado, a state that receives defense spending in the middle range, was the recipient of $1.6 billion, with 10 percent of its citizenry directly dependent on military-related activities.[19] The military payrolls and other revenues generated locally by military expenditures affect all segments of local communities: businessmen, teachers, homeowners, blue-collar workers, and professionals. For this reason a critic of the military-industrial complex, Senator William Proxmire from Wisconsin, has suggested that the system should rather be called the "military-industrial-bureaucratic-labor-intel-lectual-technical-academic complex."[20] Proxmire's label indicates the interconnectedness and extent of military dominance in American life.

But while all of these groups exert pressure on governmental officials to continue huge outlays for defense, the greatest coercion comes from business (hence, the term "military-industrial complex"). In many respects the military cannot be separated from business. The military needs weapons, ammunition, vehicles, clothing, and other materials. Indus-tries gladly supply them for a profit.* The needs of both are apparently rarely satiated. The military continually seeks more sophisticated weaponry and delivery systems, while industry seeks more contracts and profits.

In the United States, the pressure applied to governmental decision makers by the military has reaped great monetary benefits for large military contractors. Business prospers handsomely because, as we have seen, all the risks of military contract business are underwritten by the taxpayers. Profits are higher than in the competitive consumer market. Because weapon systems rapidly become technologically obsolete, there is a constant demand for new generations of such systems, resulting in endless demand and profit. Finally, each new weapon system is more sophisticated than its predecessor, making weapons production profits escalate.[22]

It appears that fear of Communism, need for an adequate defense, *and* pressures from the military, local government officials, businessmen, and corporations have helped to keep military budgets very high since World War II.[23] This raises questions about what constitutes an adequate budget for defense. The current Pentagon budget is bigger than those of the Soviet Union and China combined. Moreover, the American stockpile of weapons is capable of killing all of the earth's beings many times over.

The United States possesses 9,000 nuclear warheads. . . . These are hydrogen bombs, each having from four to 450 [times] the explosive power of the weapon that devas-tated Hiroshima. In a war, only about 400 warheads would be needed to wipe out half the Soviet Union's urban population and two-thirds of its industrial capacity.[24]

But instead of reducing the budget or at least maintaining it at its present level, Congress increases the budget yearly. This growth is due in part to inflation and the costs of an all volunteer army, but it also results from the Pentagon and its corporate friends seeking larger expenditures for more sophisticated weaponry and delivery systems. For example, the military budget following the U.S. withdrawal from Vietnam *increased*. When Presi-dent Reagan was faced with the twin problems of rampant inflation and a severely unbalanced budget, his solution was to reduce the budget while *increasing* the military budget. Moreover, his commitment was to a tremendous increase in military spending—

---

*In fiscal 1979 the four largest defense contractors were: General Dynamics ($3.5 billion), McDonnell Douglas ($3.2 billion), United Technologies ($2.6 billion), and General Electric ($2.0 billion).[21]

to spend $1 trillion from 1981 to 1985.[25] This program requires that government programs in other areas, most notably social programs for the disadvantaged, be curtailed severely.*

The greatest impetus for huge outlays for defense comes from business. The military continually seeks more sophisticated weaponry and delivery systems, while industry seeks more contracts and profit.† But why is industry so interested in obtaining governmental contracts? Kaufman has pointed out that producing goods for the military is more profitable, less competitive, and more susceptible to control through lobbying in Washington than commercial work.[29]

Kaufman stressed first that there is much less competition for defense contracts. The general rule for government procurement is that purchases shall be made through written competitive bids obtained by advertising for the items needed. In World War II this rule was suspended. After the war the rule was put back into force, but with seventeen exceptions. According to Kaufman, about 90 percent of the Pentagon's contracts are negotiated under these seventeen exceptions. The meaning is clear that in all but 10 percent of the cases, contracts are made on a basis other than competitive bids.

What does it take to get a contract, if it is not being the lowest bidder? The answer is not easy, for there are many possibilities, including superior design, more efficient programs, performance on schedule, and better quality control. Perhaps more important is convincing a few key men in the Pentagon. A good deal of time and money is spent in trying to influence these men. Not the least of these methods is the practice in industry of hiring former military officers. As Jack Anderson has put it:

The giant contractors, such as Northrop Corporation and Rockwell International, court Pentagon officials assiduously. The way to many a defense contract has been greased by a mixture of booze, blondes and barbeques. The brass hats and the industrialists shoot together in duck blinds. They ski together on the Colorado slopes. They drink together and play poker together. And invariably, the tab is picked up by some smiling corporate executive. The relationship is so cozy that many Petagon officials, upon retirement, go to work for the companies that had come to them for contracts. The last time we counted them, we found 715 former Pentagon bigwigs scattered over the payrolls of the top defense contractors. It's a rare contractor that doesn't employ a few retired generals and admirals who are on a first-name basis with the Pentagon's big brass. Northrop Corporation, for example, has 64 ex-Pentagon officials on the payroll. This may help to explain how Northrop has managed to wangle a whopping $620.3

*This tremendous emphasis on defense is not limited to the United States. The world's outlay for defense in 1977 was $434 billion, easily topping the $186 billion spent for health and the $374 billion for education. Thus, defense is the world's biggest business. It buys more industrial products than any other customer. It employs more people, including 25 percent of the world's scientific talent.[26]

†One proposed project is the MX missile system, which will deploy 200 nuclear-armed missiles on mobile platforms to a variety of launch sites in Arizona, Nevada, New Mexico, and Utah. The estimated cost is conservatively put at $33 billion (Martin Marietta is to receive $3.5 billion, Rockwell $3 billion, and Northrop $1 billion). The biggest benefactor, however, is the cement industry because the system will require some 5,000 concrete launching shelters and more than 7,000 miles of roads or underground trenches.[27] Some other weapons systems to be purchased are: 1,377 F/A-18 jet fighters at a cost of $17.5 million each; 7,958 XM-1 battle tanks at a total cost of $12.1 billion; the Trident submarine fleet at a cost of $28.7 billion; the purchase of 18 Aegis cruisers by the Navy for $16.6 billion; one nuclear aircraft carrier for $2.1 billion; the purchase of 200 CX cargo planes for $12 billion; and a number of army helicopters for $11.2 billion.[28]

million in military contracts. Boeing Corporation, which is doing a $1.56 billion business with the Pentagon, has 48 former Pentagon bigwigs on the staff. And Rockwell International, with $732.3 million in defense contracts, has 36 ex-officials in key jobs.[30]

In addition to reduced competition, defense contractors receive other benefits from the government. The Pentagon generously provides capital (land, buildings, and equipment) to its contractors. Since 1976 all money spent to buy or lease plant and equipment has been charged to the government. Moreover, all development expenses are now paid for by the Pentagon. Congress may even "bail out" a contractor facing bankruptcy, but only, it would seem, if the corporation is very large and a prime supplier of defense material. The Lockheed Corporation in 1971, for example, received a government loan of $250 million. Moreover, if a defense contractor has been inefficient or careless in its cost estimates, resulting in cost overruns, the government may absorb some of the additional cost. This is done under a 1958 law authorizing modification of defense contracts whenever such action is necessary to "facilitate the national defense" in times of declared national emergency. Thus, when Lockheed had cost overruns of approximately $1.1 billion on its C-5A jet transport and other procurement disasters, the government ruled that Lockheed's liability would be for only $200 million.

The gist of these assertions is that there are tremendous profits to be made in defense contracting, and many, if not most, of the risks are borne by the government. The irony is that this is in opposition to the free-enterprise system. Apparently, American capitalism is, in fact, a form of corporate socialism where very large corporations receive government aid while smaller business ventures must operate on the principle of "survival of the fittest."

Critique of Mills' thesis. Much of Mills' argument seems to fit with the realities of American politics. Certainly the men at the top of the key sectors wield enormous power. The last several decades have seen shifts in this power with the decline of the role of Congress and the rise in military clout.

There are some elements in Mills' thesis, however, that are not consistent with the facts. First, Mills believed that the three subelites that comprise the power elite are more or less equal, with the corporate rich probably having the most power. The equality of these groups is not proved. Certainly, the military seems second-rate compared to the executive branch, Congress, and the large corporations. Military leaders are influential only in their advisory capacities and their ability to convince the executive branch and Congress. What looks like military power is often actually the power of the corporations and/or the executive branch carried out in military terms. In the view of many observers (especially Domhoff, as we will see in the next section), the business leaders comprise the real power elite. While this is debatable, the fact is that they far surpass the military in power, and since the executive branch is composed of ex-businesspeople, the logical conclusion is that business interests prevail in that sector as well.

Conflict occurs among the three sectors. There is often bitter disagreement between corporations and the government, between the military and the executive branch, and between the military and some elements in the business community. How is this conflict to be explained if, as Mills contended, the power elite is a group that acts in concert, with joint efforts planned and coordinated to accomplish the agreed-upon goals? There is a good deal of empirical evidence that the heads of the three major sectors do *not* comprise a group.

Mills relegates a number of powerful (or potentially powerful) forces to the middle ranges of power. What about the power of pressure groups that represent interests other than business or the military? Certainly organized labor, farmers, professional organizations such as the American Medical Association, and consumers exert power over particular issues. Sometimes business interests even lose. How is this to be explained?

Finally, is Congress only in the "middle level" of the power structure? In Mills' view, Congress is a rubber stamp for the interests of business, the executive branch, and the military. Congress is apparently not composed of "puppets" for these interests, although the laws most often seem to favor these interests. But Congress does have its mavericks, and some of these persons, by virtue of seniority, exert tremendous power (for either the blockage or passage of legislation). Should not the key congressional leaders be included in the power elite? The problem is that they often have interests that do not coincide with those of the presumed "elite."

Power elite III: Domhoff's "governing class" theory. While in the Mills view, power is concentrated in a relatively small, cohesive elite, G. William Domhoff's model of power is more broadly based in a "governing class."[31] Domhoff defined this "governing class" as the uppermost social group (approximately 0.5 percent of the population), which owns a disproportionate amount of the country's wealth and contributes a disproportionate number of its members to the controlling institutions and key decision-making groups of the country. This status group is composed mainly of rich businessmen and their families, many of whom are, according to Domhoff's convincing evidence, closely knit through stock ownership, trust funds, intermarriages, private schools, exclusive social clubs, exclusive summer resorts, and corporation boards (see Chapter 10).

The "governing class" in Domhoff's analysis controls the executive branch of the federal government, the major corporations, the mass media, foundations, universities, and the important councils for domestic and foreign affairs (for example, the Council on Foreign Relations, Committee for Economic Development, National Security Council, National Industrial Conference Board, the Twentieth Century Fund). If they can control the executive branch, this governing class can probably also control the very important regulatory agencies, the federal judiciary, the military, the Central Intelligence Agency, and the Federal Bureau of Investigation.

The "governing class" has greater influence (but not control) than any other group upon Congress and state and local governments. These parts of the formal power structure are not directly controlled by the "governing class" in Domhoff's analysis, but since he claims that such a class controls the executive and judicial branches, the Congress is effectively blocked by two of the three divisions of government. Thus, American foreign and domestic policies are initiated, planned, and carried out by members and organizations of a power elite that serves the interests of an upper class of rich businesspeople.[32] Decisions are made that are considered appropriate for the interests of the United States—a strong economy, an adequate defense, and social stability. While perhaps beneficial to all Americans, policies designed to accomplish these goals especially favor the rich. Consequently, American corporations overseas are protected, foreign trade agreements are made that benefit American corporations, and the tax structure benefits corporations or the very wealthy (by means of allowances for oil depletion, for capital gains and capital losses, for depreciation of equipment, and for other business expenses).

Domhoff has demonstrated in detail the manner in which the governing class interacts (which we have already examined in Chapter 10). Once he established the interlocking ties brought about by common interests and through interaction, he cited circumstances that show the impact of individuals and subgroups within the elite upon the decision-making structure of the United States. To mention a few:

1. Control of presidential nominations through the financing of political campaigns: The evidence is clear that unless candidates have large financial reserves or the backing of wealthy persons, they cannot hope to develop a national following or compete in party primaries.
2. Control of both major political parties: Even though the Democratic Party is usually considered the party of the common man, Domhoff shows that it, like the Republican Party, is controlled by aristocrats.
3. Almost total staffing of important appointive governmental positions (cabinet members, members of regulatory agencies, judges, diplomats, and presidential advisors): These appointees are either members of the upper class or persons who have held positions in the major corporations, and are thereby persons who accord with the wishes of the upper class.

As a result of the circumstances above (and others), all the important foreign and domestic decisions are seen as made by the governing class. Domhoff's view of the power structure is reconstructed graphically in Figure 17–4.

In many ways, Domhoff's model of the American power structure was a refinement of the one posited earlier by Mills. Domhoff's assessment of the power structure was similar to Mills' in that they both: (1) view the power structure as a single pyramid; (2) see the corporate rich as the most powerful interest group; (3) relegate Congress to a relatively minor role and place the executive branch in an important role in the decision-making process; and (4) view the masses as being dominated by powerful forces rather than having much grass-roots power.

The major difference between the views of Mills and Domhoff is that Domhoff has asserted the complete ascendancy of the upper class to the apex of power. The executive branch is controlled by upper-class businesspeople, industrialists, and financiers rather than the two groups being more or less equal partners in the power elite, as Mills saw it. Moreover, the placement of the military in the pyramid of power is quite different. Mills saw the military as part of the alliance of the "troika," while Domhoff saw the military as having much less power and being dominated by the corporate rich through the executive branch.

Critique of Domhoff's thesis.   Domhoff's book is quite persuasive, but there are several criticisms that should be mentioned. First, much of Domhoff's proof is in the form of listing the upper-class pedigrees of presidential advisors, cabinet members, ambassadors, regulatory agency members, and so on. While persons in these positions are disproportionately from upper-class backgrounds (as evidenced by their attendance at prestige schools, their membership in exclusive social clubs, and their placement in the various social registries), we are given no proof that these persons actually promote the interests of the corporate rich. This is an assumption by Domhoff that appears reasonable, but it is an oversimplification. There is always the possibility of wealthy persons making decisions on

FIGURE 17-4   Domhoff's View of the Structure of Power

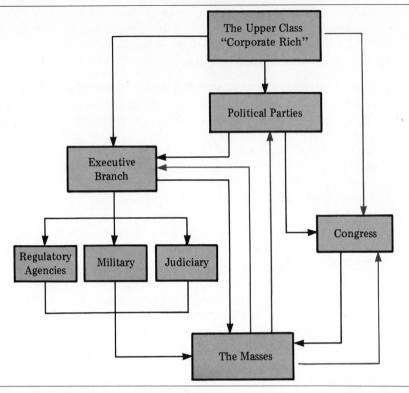

Legend: Black line, control; color line, influence. This model is based on my interpretation of Domhoff and is therefore subject to minor errors in emphasis.

bases other than economics, such as religious or moral altruism or civil rights or human rights. Thus, Domhoff's assumption is one of Marxian economic determinism, and as such is subject to the criticism of oversimplification of a complex process. While an economic motive of some kind may explain a great deal of social behavior, its operation with other prestige factors may be very complex, and it will not explain all of human behavior.

Although Domhoff has denied his belief in an upper-class conspiracy, his books strongly suggest that he does hold this view, at least implicitly. The upper class is shown to get its way either by force or fraud. His chapter on social legislation showed, for example, that workmen's compensation, social security, and collective bargaining were accomplished not by pressure from working people, but because the upper class felt it was in their long-range economic interest to pass such seemingly socialistic legislation. Domhoff, therefore, viewed the efforts of the upper class (assuming that they indeed form an elite) as only self-seeking, never altruistic. Moreover, the power of labor and other pressure groups in the forming of social legislation was virtually ignored.[33]

Power elite IV: Parenti's "bias of the system" theory.[34] Commonly we think of the machinery of government as a beneficial force promoting the common good. While the government can be organized for the benefit of the majority, it is never neutral.[35] The state regulates; its stifles opposition; it makes and enforces the law; it funnels information; it makes war on "enemies" (foreign and domestic); and its policies determine how resources are apportioned. And in all of these areas, the government is generally biased toward policies that benefit the wealthy, especially the business community.

Power in America is concentrated among those who control the government and the largest corporations.[36] This assertion is based on the assumption that power is not an attribute of individuals but rather of social organizations.[37] The elite in American society is composed of those persons who occupy the power roles in society. The great political decisions are made by the President, the President's advisors, cabinet members, the members of regulatory agencies, the Federal Reserve Board, key members of Congress, and the Supreme Court. The individuals in these government command posts have the authority to make war, raise or lower interest rates, levy taxes, dam rivers, and institute or withhold national health insurance.

Once economic activity was the result of many decisions made by individual entrepreneurs and the heads of small businesses. Now a handful of companies have virtual control over the market place. The decisions by the boards of directors and the management personnel of these huge corporations determine employment and production, consumption patterns, wages and prices, the extent of foreign trade, the rate at which natural resources are depleted, and the like.

The few thousand persons who comprise this power elite tend to come from backgrounds of privilege and wealth. It would be a mistake, however, to equate personal wealth with power. Great power is only manifested through decision making in the very large corporations or in government. We have seen that this elite exercises great power. Decisions are made by the powerful and these decisions tend to benefit the wealthy disproportionately. But the power elite is not organized and conspiratorial.

The interests of the powerful (and the wealthy) are served, nevertheless, because of the way society is organized. This bias occurs in three ways—by their influence over elected and appointed governmental officials at all levels; through systemic imperatives; and through the ideological control of the masses.

As we saw in an earlier section, the wealthy are able to receive favorable treatment by actually occupying positions of power or by having direct influence over those who do. The laws, court decisions, and administrative decisions tend to give the advantage.

More subtly, the power elite can get its way without actually being mobilized at all. The choices of decision makers are often limited by various **systemic imperatives**. Whoever is in power is constrained in their decision making by tradition and by economic imperatives. There are pressures on the government to do certain things and not to do others. Inevitably, this bias favors the status quo, allowing those with power to continue. For example, no change is always easier than change. The current political and economic systems have worked and generally are not subject to question, let alone change. In this way the laws, customs, and institutions of society resist change. Thus the propertied and the wealthy benefit while the propertyless and the poor continue to be disadvantaged.

In addition to the inertia of institutions, there are other systemic imperatives that benefit the power elite and the wealthy. One such imperative is for the government to strive to provide an adequate defense against our enemies, which stifles any external threat to the status quo. Moreover, this means that Congress, the President, and the masses tend to support large appropriations for defense, which provides extraordinary profit to many corporations. In addition, the government will protect our multinational companies in their overseas operations, which, of course, promotes a healthy and profitable business climate for them. Domestically, government policy is also shaped by the systemic imperative for stability. The government promotes domestic tranquility by squelching dissidence.

Power is the ability to get what one wants from someone else. This can be achieved by force or by getting that someone to think and believe in accordance with your interests. "The ability to control the definition of interests is the ability to define the agenda of issues, a capacity tantamount to wininng battles without having to fight them."[38] This is accomplished by the schools, churches, and families in society. The schools, for instance, consciously teach youth that capitalism is the only correct economic system. This is indoctrination with conservative values that achieves a consensus among the citizenry concerning the status quo. In other words, the people tend to accept the system, even though it may work against their interests (false consciousness). Through the very powerful socialization process each of us comes to accept the system, obey the law, favor military solutions, and accept the present arrangements in society because they seem the only options that make sense. Thus, there is a general consensus on what is right—and wrong. In sum, the dominance of the wealthy is legitimized. "The interests of an economically dominant class never stand naked. They are enshrouded in the flag, fortified by the law, protected by the police, nurtured by the media, taught by the schools, and blessed by the church."[39]

Finally, the belief in democracy works to the advantage of the power elite, as Parenti has noted in the following passage:

As now constituted, elections serve as a great asset in consolidating the existing social order by propagating the appearances of popular rule. History demonstrates that the people might be moved to overthrow a tyrant who shows himself provocatively indifferent to their woes, but they are far less inclined to make war upon a state, even one dominated by the propertied class, if it preserves what Madison called "the spirit and form of popular government." Elections legitimate the rule of the propertied class by investing it with the moral authority of popular consent. By the magic of the ballot, class dominance becomes "democratic" governance. According to the classical theory of democracy, the purpose of suffrage is to make the rulers more responsive to the will of the people. But history suggests the contrary: more often the effect and even the intent of suffrage has been to make the enfranchised group more responsive to the rulers, or at least committed to the ongoing system of rule. In the classical theory, the vote is an exercise of sovereign power, a popular command over the rulers, but it might just as easily be thought of as an act of support extended by the electorate to those above them. Hence, an election is more a *surrender* than an *assertion* of popular power, a gathering up of empowering responses by the elites who have the resources for such periodic harvestings, an institutionalized mechanism providing for the regulated flow of power from the many to the few in order to legitimate the rule of the few in the name of the many.[40]

The Consequences

The way power is concentrated in American society raises the question—who benefits? At times most everyone does, but for the most part, the decisions made tend to benefit the wealthy. Whenever the interests of the wealthy clash with those of other groups or even the majority, the interests of the wealthy are served. As examples, examine carefully how the President and Congress deal with the problems of energy shortages, inflation, or deflation. Who is asked to make the sacrifices? Where is the budget cut—are expenditures for the military reduced or are funds for food stamps slashed? When the Congress considers tax reform, after the roar of rhetoric recedes, which groups benefit by the new legislation or by the laws that are left alone? When a corporation is found guilty of fraud, violation of antitrust laws, bribery, or whatever, what are the penalties? How do they compare with the penalties for crimes committed by poor individuals such as "welfare chiselers," and thieves? When there is an oil spill or other ecological disaster caused by huge enterprise, what are the penalties? Who pays for the cleanup and the restoration of nature? The answers to these questions are obvious—the wealthy benefit at the expense of the less well-to-do. In short, the government is an institution made up of people—the rich and powerful or their agents—who seek to maintain their advantageous positions in society.

Before we examine the bias of the system in the contemporary scene, let's briefly describe its continuation throughout American history.[41] The government's policy has primarily, although not exclusively, favored the needs of the corporate system.

The Founding Fathers were wealthy members of the upper class. The Constitution they wrote gave the power to people like themselves—property owners. This bias continued throughout the nineteenth century as bankers, railroad entrepreneurs, and manufacturers joined the landed gentry to make the power elite. The shift from local business to large-scale manufacturing during the last half of the nineteenth century saw a concomitant increase in governmental activity in the economy. Business was protected from competition by protective tariffs, public subsidies, price regulation, patents, and trademarks. Throughout that century when there was unrest by troubled miners, farmers, and laborers, the government inevitably took the side of the strong against the weak. The militia and federal troops were used to crush the railroad strikes. Antitrust laws, which were not used to stop the monopolistic practices of business, were invoked against labor unions. President Cleveland's Attorney General, Richard Olney, a millionaire owner of railroad stocks

used antitrust laws, court injunctions, mass arrests, labor spies, deputy marshals and federal troops against workers and their unions. From the local sheriff and magistrate to the President and the Supreme Court, the forces of "law and order" were utilized to suppress the "conspiracy" of labor unions and serve "the defensive needs of large capitalist enterprises."[42]

During this time approximately 1 billion acres of land in the public domain (almost 1/2 of the present size of the United States) were given to private individuals and corporations. The railroads in particular were given huge tracts of land as a subsidy. These lands were and continue to be very rich in timber and natural resources.

This active intervention of the government in the nation's economy during the nineteenth century was almost solely on the behalf of business. "The federal government did exercise a kind of laissez-faire in certain other areas: little attention was given to unemployment, poverty, education, the spread of urban slums, and the spoilation of natural resources."[43]

The early 20th century was a time of great governmental activity in the economy, which gave the appearance of restraining big business. However, the actual result of federal regulation of business was to increase the power of the largest corporations. The Interstate Commerce Commission, for instance, helped the railroads by establishing common rates to replace ruinous competition.[44] The federal regulations in meat packing, drugs, banking, and mining weeded out the weaker cost-cutting competitors, leaving a few to control the markets at higher prices and higher profits.[45] Even the actions of that great "trust-buster," Teddy Roosevelt, were largely ceremonial.[46]

Toward business he manifested bluster but virtually no bite. His major legislative proposals reflected the desires of corporation interests. Like other Presidents before and since, he enjoyed close relations with big businessmen and invited them into his administration.[47]

World War I intensified the governmental bias toward business. Industry was converted to war production. Corporate interests became more actively involved in the councils of government. Governmental actions clearly favored business in labor disputes. The police and military were used against rebellious workers because strikes were treated as efforts to weaken the war effort and therefore treasonous.

The New Deal is typically assumed to be a time when the needs of those impoverished by the Great Depression were paramount in government policies. But "the central dedication of the Franklin Roosevelt administration was to *business recovery* rather than *social reform*."[48] Business was subsidized by credits, price supports, bank guarantees, stimulation of the housing industry, and the like. Welfare programs were instituted to prevent widespread starvation, but even these humanitarian programs also worked to the benefit of the big business community. The government provided jobs, minimum wages, unemployment compensation, and retirement benefits, which obviously aided those in dire economic straits. But these programs were actually promoted by the business community because of benefits to them. The government and business favored social programs at this time not because millions were in misery but because of the threat of violent political and social unrest. Two social scientists, Piven and Cloward, after an historical assessment of government welfare programs, have determined that the government institutes massive aid to the poor *only* when the poor constitute a threat.[49] When large numbers of people are suddenly barred from their traditional occupations, the legitimacy of the system itself may be questioned. Crime, riots, looting, and social movements bent on changing the existing social, political, and economic arrangements become more widespread. Under this threat, relief programs are initiated or expanded by the government to diffuse the social unrest. During the Great Depression, Piven and Cloward contend, the government remained aloof from the needs of the unemployed until there was a surge of political disorder. Added proof for Piven and Cloward's thesis is the contraction or even abolishment of public assistance programs when stability is restored.

The historical trend for government to favor business over less powerful interests continues in current public policy. Let's look at some examples.

Subsidies to big business. There is a general principle that applies to the government's relationship to big business—business can conduct its affairs either undisturbed by or encouraged by government, whichever is of greater benefit to the business community. The following are some illustrative cases in which governmental decisions benefitted business:

item: The government has consistently bailed out huge corporations on the verge of bankruptcy. Recently the government has come to the aid of Penn Central,

Lockheed, and Chrysler. The irony, of course, is that the big companies receive emergency help while the government refused to aid the thousands of small businesses that go bankrupt annually.

item: Quotas are placed on imports of beef, wheat, oil and other products to protect the profits of American industry.

item: Although the House had passed a bill to create a Federal Consumer Protective Agency by 293 to 94, it was defeated in the Senate by a filibuster. The bill was opposed by the National Association of Manufacturers, the National Association of Food Chains, and some 300 other companies and trade associations.[50]

item: The government has rarely imposed rigorous penalties on businesses that pollute the air or water.

item: The automobile industry got the Justice Department to sign a consent decree which blocked any attempt by public or private means to sue them for damages occurring from air pollution.

item: A number of major United States corporations such as DuPont, General Motors, Ford, Exxon, and ITT owned factories in enemy countries during World War II. These factories produced products *for* the Axis war effort. "After the war, rather than being prosecuted for trading with the enemy, ITT collected $27 million from the United States government for war damages inflicted on its German plants by Allied bombings. GM and Ford subsidiaries built the bulk of Nazi Germany's heavy trucks which served as 'the backbone of the German Army transportation system.' GM collected more than $33 million in compensation for damages to its war plants in enemy territories. Ford and other multinational corporations collected lesser sums."[51]

item: The federal government directly subsidizes the shipping industry, the railroads, the airlines, and exporters of iron, steel, textiles, paper, and other products.

item: Government regulated industries such as trucking and railroads result in excess prices and profits. The federal government "maintains prices at noncompetitive, monopolistic levels in 'regulated' areas of the economy at an estimated annual cost of $80 billion to American consumers."[52]

item: "As in the olden days, government continues to give away, lease or sell at bargain rates the national forests, grasslands, wildlife preserves and other public lands containing priceless timber, minerals, oil and water and recreational resources— with little consideration for environmental values or for desires other than those of the favored corporations. From 1965 to 1967, for instance, several major petroleum companies leased acreage in Alaska for oil exploration, paying a sum of $12 million for leases worth upwards of $2 billion. In a subsequent oil lease auction, the companies paid the government $900 million for lands that are expected to be worth some $50 billion within a decade."[53] In 1979, during the midst of an oil shortage crisis, the government leased 33,749 acres of land surrounding an area of active wells *without competitive bids* for $1 dollar per acre. The value of the leases has been estimated at $10 million.[54]

item: The government develops new technologies at public expense and then turns them over to private corporations for their profit. Using the case of nuclear energy, Ralph Nader has said: "Nuclear power would never have existed if it weren't for the government. The government funded the basic research, funded the technology, gave the designs to the utilities gratis, enriched the uranium, protected the utilities from liability under the Price-Anderson Act, and has now decided to pay the costs for nuclear wastes. From start to finish, it's a classic case of an industry that has been sponsored, shielded, and protected by the government."[55]

Perhaps the best illustration of how business benefits under current governmental policies is the legal loopholes allowed them on Federal income taxes. Although the maximum statutory tax rate on corporate profits is 48 percent, corporations including the most profitable can escape with a very much lower rate. Some corporations may even escape Federal taxes altogether. Congressman Charles Vanik found that 17 American companies with combined worldwide net incomes of over $92 billion paid no United States income tax in 1977.[56] Twenty-nine other of the largest companies paid less than 10 percent of their total income in federal income taxes. In contrast, the average family of four earning $20,000 paid 16.7 percent. In 1975, the eight largest banks in the United States all showed a profit but none paid taxes. Ford Motor Company, by using foreign tax credits and investment tax credits, not only avoided paying any federal income taxes for 1974 and 1975, but received a $189 million refund for those years at the taxpayers' expense.[57]

Foreign policy for corporate benefit. The operant principle here is that "foreign policy seems to be carried on in the light of the needs of the munitions makers, the Pentagon, the CIA, and the multinational corporations."[58] Several examples make this point. First, military goods are sold overseas for the profit of the arms merchants. Sometimes arms are sold to both sides in a potential conflict, the argument being that if we did not sell them the arms, then the Russians would, so we might as well make the profits.[59]

The government has supported foreign governments that are supportive of American multinational companies regardless of how tyrannical these governments might be. The Shah's government in Iran or Chiang's regime in China or Chung Hee Park's dictatorship in South Korea are but three examples of this tendency.

Our government has directly intervened in the domestic affairs of foreign governments to protect American corporate interests. The most blatant example occurred when ITT encouraged the government (through the CIA) to depose the Allende government in Chile because Allende favored policies that threatened ITT's presence in Chile.[60]

The powerless pay the burden. Robert Hutchens, in his critique of American governmental policy, characterized the basic principle guiding internal affairs as: "Domestic policy is conducted according to one infallible rule: the costs and burdens of whatever is done must be borne by those least able to bear them."[61] Let's review several examples of this.

When threatened by war the government institutes a military draft. A careful analysis of the draft reveals that it is really a "tax on the poor."[62] During the height of the Vietnam War, for instance, only 10 percent of men in college were drafted, although 40 percent of draft-age men were in college. Even for those educated young men who ended up in the armed services, there was a greater likelihood of their serving in noncombat jobs than for the non-college-educated. Thus, the chances for getting killed while in the service were about three times greater for the less educated than for the college educated.[63] Even more blatant was the practice that occurred legally during the Civil War. The law at that time allowed the affluent who were drafted to hire someone to take their place in the service.

The poor, being powerless, can be made to absorb the costs of societal changes. In the nineteenth century the poor did the back-breaking work that built the railroads and the cities. Today they are the ones pushed out of their homes by urban renewal, the building of expressways, parks, and stadia.[64]

The government's attempts to solve economic problems generally obey the principle that the poor must bear the burden. A common "solution" for runaway inflation, for example, is to increase the amount of unemployment. Of course the poor, especially minorities (whose rate of unemployment is consistently twice the rate for whites), are the ones who make the sacrifice for the economy. This "solution," aside from being socially cruel, is economically ineffective because it ignores the real sources of inflation—excessive military spending, excessive profits by energy companies (foreign and domestic), and administered prices set by shared monopolies, which, contrary to classical economic theory, do not decline during economic downturns.[65]

More fundamentally a certain level of unemployment is maintained continuously, not just during economic downturns. Genuine full employment for all job seekers is a myth. But why, since all political candidates extol the work ethic and it is declared national policy to have full employment? Economist Robert Lekachman has argued that it is no accident that we tolerate millions of unemployed persons. The reason is that a "moderate" unemployment rate is beneficial to the affluent. Among these benefits are.[66] (1) people are willing to work at humble tasks for low wages; (2) the children of the middle and upper classes avoid the draft as the unemployed join the volunteer army; (3) the unions are less demanding; (4) workers are less likely to demand costly safety equipment; (5) corporations do not have to pay their share of taxes because local and state governments give them concessions to lure them to their area; and (6) the existing wide differentials between white males and the various powerless categories such as females, teenagers, Hispanics, and blacks are retained.

"Trickle down" solutions. Periodically the government is faced with the problem of finding a way to stimulate the economy during an economic downturn. One way to accomplish this goal is to spend federal monies through unemployment insurance, government jobs, and housing subsidies. In this way the funds go directly to those most hurt by shortages, unemployment, inadequate housing, and the like. Opponents of such plans advocate that the subsidies should go directly to business, which would help the economy by encouraging companies to hire more workers, add to their inventories, and build new plants. Thus, by subsidizing business in this way, the advocates argue, everyone benefits. To provide subsidies to businesses rather than directly to needy individuals is based on the assumption that private profit maximizes the public good.

There are two possible reasons why government officials tend to opt for these "trickle down" solutions. First, because they tend to come from the business class, government officials believe in the conservative ideology that says what is good for business is good for America. The second reason for the pro-business choice is that government officials are more likely to hear arguments from the powerful. Since the weak, by definition, are not organized their voice is not heard or, if heard, not taken seriously in decision-making circles.

Although the government most often opts for "trickle down" solutions, such plans are not very effective in fulfilling the promise that benefits will trickle down to the poor. The higher corporate profits generated by tax credits and other tax incentives do not necessarily mean that companies will increase wages or hire more workers. What is more likely is that corporations will increase dividends to the stockholders, which further exacerbates the existing problem of the maldistribution of resources. Job creation is also not guaranteed because companies may use their newly acquired wealth to purchase labor-saving devices. If so, then the government programs will actually have widened the gulf between the "haves" and the "have nots."

In summary, this view of power argues that the power of wealthy individuals and the largest corporations is translated into public policy that disproportionately benefits the power elite. Throughout American history there has been a bias that pervades government and its policies. This bias is perhaps best seen in the aphorism once enunciated by President Calvin Coolidge and repeated in 1981 by President Reagan: "The business of America is business."

SUMMARY

Power is unequally distributed in all social organizations. In our examination of the structure of power at the societal level, two basic views were presented—the pluralist and the elitist. The former is consistent with the world view of order theorists, while the latter is congruent with the way conflict theorists perceive reality (see Table 17–1).

TABLE 17-1   Assumptions of the Order and Conflict Models about Politics

Order model	Conflict model
1. People in positions of power occupy bureaucratic roles necessary for the rational accomplishment of society's objectives.	1. People in positions of power are motivated largely by their own selfish interests.
2. State works for benefit of all. Laws reflect the customs of society and ensure order, stability, and justice—in short, the common good.	2. State exists for the benefit of the ruling class (law, police, and courts protect the interests of the wealthy).
3. Pluralism: (1) competing interest groups; (2) majority rule; (3) power is diffused.	3. Power is concentrated (power elite).

One glaring weakness of many pluralists and elitists is that they are not objective. Their writings tend often to be polemics because so much effort is spent attempting to prove what they believe is the nature of the power structure. The evidence is presented so as to ensure the absolute negation of the opposite stance. This points to a fundamental research problem. Are the data reliable? Are our observations distorted by bias? Sociologists or political scientists are forced in the study of power to rely on either the perceptions of others (who are presumed to be knowledgeable) or their own observations, which are distorted by not being present during all aspects of the decision-making process. Unfortunately, one's perceptions are also affected by one's model (conflict or order; Marxian or democratic). Ideological concerns often cause either faulty perceptions or a rigidity of thought that automatically rejects conflicting evidence.

The task for sociologists is to determine the real distribution of power without ideological distortion. Given these problems with objectivity, we must ask ourselves: (1) What is the power structure really like? (2) What facts are consonant with the pluralist model and what facts fit the elitist model? With these questions in mind, let us enumerate some conditions of societies that affect the distribution of power.

All societies are composed of different segments. The bases for segmentation may be sex, age, race, religion, physical prowess, social class, occupational specialty, or special interest. The extent of segmentation and the degree of competition among such groups are variables. It is safe to assume that most segmented parts of a society would hope for and work toward greater power (and therefore advantage) in that society (although some may not if they have been socialized to accept their role and to accept that attempts to change it would bring serious religious or other sanctions).

The second basic condition of societies is that they all require some coordination among the various segments. The more complex the society, the greater the problem of coordination. Complex societies also require rapid decision making. Both of these requirements—rapid decision making and coordination—mean that decision making *must* be concentrated in a few persons. It is an empirical question as to whether power is concentrated in one or several elites or whether the "people" retain power while not actually making most decisions.

Finally, the degree of power centralization is a variable. The logical range is from absolute equality of all individuals and groups on the one hand to total power in one person or group on the other. All societies are found somewhere between these two extremes. Various factors affect change in the degree of power centralization. As Mills noted, World War II and the Cold War were important factors giving increased power to the executive branch and the military sector of American society. Force and fraud may also be used by certain individuals and groups to increase their power.

These conditions are accepted by elitists and pluralists. Where both of these theorists go wrong is in their distorted interpretations of the real world. Let us examine the *real* situation which, hopefully, will aid in the formulation of a more realistic view of the power structure. First, what is there about the elitist position that fits reality?

1. A contemporary trend has been for federal government to assume more and more power, thereby lessening the power of the state and local governments.
2. The executive branch has a tremendous amount of power, particularly in foreign affairs. Congress has tried to reassert its historic role, but the executive branch continues to have great power in this area. Some examples are sending the military forces to various places, fighting undeclared wars, diplomatic decisions, and CIA activities.
3. There is no question but that the wealthy in America have great influence in Congress and in the executive branch. This influence is accomplished through campaign contributions, control of the political parties, occasional bribes, and through being either elected or appointed to high offices. It is also fair to say that American foreign and domestic policy is, for the most part, based on the assumption that if business interests benefit, all Americans benefit.
4. Even if there are a number of different sectors of power present (the pluralist position), the leaders of each are almost universally wealthy, members of the establishment who more or less favor the status quo. This is true, for example, in industry, in banking, for labor, and for the farm bloc. Because of great wealth they probably have some interests in common (the economic status quo, an adequate defense system, protecting American interests abroad, and an expanding economy).

What is there about the pluralist position that fits reality?

1. There are many separate power structures. Each operates generally within its own sphere of influence—the AFL-CIO in labor, the AMA in medicine, the NEA in public education, the NAM for large business concerns, and so forth. Each tries to influence Congress and the executive branch on issues affecting it. Within each of these domains there is a hierarchy of power. A powerful elite then makes decisions and in other ways influences its public (and this influence is often reciprocal).
2. The various power structures are unequal in power. The economic elite is the most powerful. But there are shifting coalitions that may at times effectively counterbalance the unequal power of the corporate rich. Or one group may band with the corporate rich against some other coalition.
3. Pressure groups exert a tremendous influence on decision making. They may be organized or diffuse, but they can and do bring change. Blacks, migrant workers, young people, the aged, consumers, have by individual and collective efforts caused a shift in policy on occasion.

A realistic view of the power structure must incorporate the valid points mentioned above from both pluralistic and elitist views. The resulting model of power hinges on the empirical answer to the basic question: how democratic is the political process in American society?

CHAPTER REVIEW

1. In answering the question: Who are the real power wielders in American society? there are two contrasting answers from pluralists and elitists.

2. The "representative democracy" version of pluralism emphasizes that the people have the ultimate power. The people elect representatives who are responsive to the people's wishes. This version ignores the many instances in which the people have been deliberately misled by their leaders, secrecy, and the undemocratic manner in which election campaigns are funded.

3. The "veto groups" version of pluralism recognizes the existence of a number of organizations and special interest groups that vie for power. There is a balance of power, however, with no one sector getting its way. The groups tend to neutralize each other resulting in compromise. Critics of this view of power argue that it is an idealized version that ignores reality. The interest groups are not equal in power. Power does not shift from issue to issue. Also, at the apex of each of the competing groups are members of the upper class, suggesting the possibility of a power elite.

4. One version of the elitist view of power is the belief in a communist conspiracy. The power structure in the United States is led by a conspiratorial elite that share an anti-capitalist and internationalist ideology. The placement of members of the Trilateral Commission in high government places regardless of whether there is a Democrat or Republican president is evidence of such a conspiracy. This view of power is not taken seriously by social scientists but it is held by millions of Americans.

5. C. Wright Mills' view of power is that there is a power elite composed of the top people in the executive branch of the federal government, the military, and the corporate sector. Although these persons represent different interests they tend to perceive the world alike because of their similar social class backgrounds and similar role expectations; because they interact socially; because their children go to the same schools and intermarry; and because they share similar interests. There is considerable evidence for the linkages among these three sectors. There are some problems with this view, however. The equality of these three groups is not a fact. There is conflict among the three sectors. There are other sectors of power that are ignored.

6. G. William Domhoff's view of power is that there is a governing class—the uppermost social class. The very rich control the nation's assets, control the corporations, are overrepresented in the key decision-making groups in society, and through contributions and activities they control both major political parties. The major criticism of this view is that while the people in key positions tend to have upper-class pedigrees, there is no evidence that these people actually promote the interests of the corporate rich.

7. Michael Parenti's "bias of the system" view is another elitist theory. The powerful in society (those who control the government and the largest corporations) tend to come from backgrounds of privilege and wealth. Their decisions tend to benefit the wealthy disproportionately but the power elite is not organized and conspiratorial. The interests of the wealthy are served, nevertheless, by the way society is organized. This bias occurs by their influence over elected and appointed officials, systemic imperatives, and through the ideological control of the masses.

FOR FURTHER STUDY

Paul A. Baran and Paul M. Sweezy, *Monopoly Capital* (New York: Monthly Review Press, 1968).

G. William Domhoff, *The Powers That Be: Processes of Ruling Class Domination in America* (New York: Random House (Vintage Books), 1979).

Thomas R. Dye, *Who's Running America*, 2nd

ed. (Englewood Cliffs, N.J.: Prentice-Hall, 1979).

Martin N. Marger, *Elites and Masses: An Introduction to Political Sociology* (New York: Van Nostrand, 1981).

C. Wright Mills, *The Power Elite* (New York: Oxford University Press, 1956).

Marvin E. Olsen (ed.), *Power in Societies* (New York: Macmillan, 1970).

Michael Parenti, *Power and the Powerless* (New York: St. Martin's, 1978).

David Reisman, *The Lonely Crowd* (New Haven, Conn.: Yale University Press, 1951).

Leonard Silk and Mark Silk, *The American Establishment* (New York: Basic Books, 1980).

NOTES AND REFERENCES

1. The following examples are summarized from David Wise, *The Politics of Lying: Government Deception, Secrecy, and Power* (New York: Random House (Vintage Books), 1973).
2. See Warren Weaver, Jr., "What Is a Campaign Contributor Buying?," *The New York Times* (March 13, 1977), p. E2.
3. Barbara Haddad Ryan, "Common Cause: Special Interests Won on Nov. 4," *Rocky Mountain News* (November 16, 1980), p. 4. See also, Jack Bass, "For Regulating Corporate Political Action Committees," *The New York Times* (May 30, 1979), p. A23.
4. Marvin Stone, "Political Spending: Running Wild," *U.S. News & World Report* (October 23, 1978), p. 112.
5. David E. Rosenbaum, "Politics: Business Antes Up," *The New York Times* (January 13, 1980), Section 3, p. 5.
6. "Election Tab: A Billion Dollars, and Rising," *U.S. News & World Report* (December 15, 1980), pp. 32–33.
7. See Marlys Harris, "The Candidates' Family Finances," *Money* 9 (March 1980), pp. 82–90.
8. John Walton, "Economic Order," *Society Today Resource Letters* (Del Mar, Calif.: CRM Books, 1971), p. 2.
9. The fullest description of this pluralistic model is found in the classic by David Riesman with Nathan Glazer and Reuel Denney, *The Lonely Crowd* (New Haven, Conn.: Yale University Press, 1951), pp. 213–217.
10. Karl Marx and Friedrich Engels, *The German Ideology* (New York: International Publishers, 1947), p. 39. For a review of other classical elitist theorists, see Marvin E. Olsen, "Elitist Theory as a Response to Marx," in *Power in Societies*, Marvin E. Olsen, ed. (New York: Macmillan, 1970), p. 106–113.
11. This model of the American power structure is described in G. William Domhoff, *The Higher Circles: The Governing Class in America* (New York: Random House (Vintage Books), 1971), Chap. 8. Three ultraconservative books provide the bases for Domhoff's description: Dan Smoot, *The Invisible Government* (Dallas: Dan Smoot Report, 1962); Phyllis Schlafly, *A Choice Not an Echo* (Alton, Ill.: Pere Marquette Press, 1964); and William S. McBirnie, *Who Really Rules America: A Study of the Power Elite* (Glendale, Calif.: Center for American Research and Education, 1968).
12. Associated Press story in the *Christian Science Monitor*, April 1, 1961.
13. The model described here was first put forth in the classic book by C. Wright Mills, *The Power Elite* (New York: Oxford University Press, 1956). It contains the first assertion of the existence and threat of a military-industrial complex in the United States.
14. The following is taken from C. Wright Mills, "The Power Elite," in *Reader in Political Sociology*, Frank Lindenfeld, ed. (New York: Funk & Wagnalls, 1968), pp. 263–276.
15. Ibid., p. 267.
16. Mills, *The Power Elite*, p. 11. See also G. William Domhoff, "How Fat Cats Keep in Touch," *Psychology Today* 9 (August, 1975), pp. 44–48.
17. Mills, *The Power Elite*, Chap. 10, gives the evidence up to 1954. More recent evidence is found in G. William Domhoff, *Who Rules America?* (Englewood Cliffs, N.J.: Prentice-Hall, 1967), Chap. 4.

18. "Where Federal Dollars Give Business a Lift," *U.S. News & World Report* (July 28, 1980), pp. 62–63.

19. Robert Schware, "Colorado's Becoming a Military Junkie," *Rocky Mountain News* (August 19, 1979), p. 84.

20. William Proxmire, *America's Military-Industrial Complex* (New York: Praeger, 1970).

21. "Where Federal Dollars Give Business a Lift," p. 62.

22. Michael Parenti, *Power and the Powerless* (New York: St. Martin's, 1978), p. 86.

23. Michael Parenti, *Democracy for the Few*, 2nd ed. (New York: St. Martin's Press, 1977), pp. 83–90.

24. Morton Kondracke, "Carter's Nuclear Confidence Gap," *The New Republic* (April 15, 1978), p. 15.

25. Although this policy for ever increased military budgets is very popular, some observers have raised serious questions. See Emma Rothschild, "Boom and Bust," *New York Review of Books* (April 3, 1980), pp. 31–33; *The Progressive* 44 (July, 1980), entire issue.

26. United Press International release (October 4, 1979).

27. "The MX Missile: A Moving Target," *Forbes* (August 6, 1979), p. 31.

28. "The Pentagon's Multibillion Shopping List," *U.S. News & World Report* (June 23, 1980), pp. 40–42.

29. The following account is taken largely from Richard F. Kaufman, "The Military-Industrial Complex," in *Crisis in American Institutions*, Jerome H. Skolnick and Elliott Currie, eds. (Boston: Little, Brown, 1970), pp. 178–192. See also Paul Lewis, "All Systems Are Go for the Arms Makers," *The New York Times* (May 23, 1976), Sec. 3, pp. 1, 4; "The New Face of the Defense Industry," *Business Week* (January 10, 1977), pp. 52–58; and "A 'Cheerful' Military-Industrial Complex," *The Washington Spectator* (July 15, 1976), pp. 1–3.

30. Jack Anderson, "Weapons Makers and Pentagon Brass Are Happy Family," *Rocky Mountain News* (February 1, 1976), p. 51.

31. The discussion below is taken from Domhoff's books: *Who Rules America?* and *The Higher Circles: The Governing Class in America*.

32. See Chapter 5 of Domhoff's *The Higher Circles* for "how the power elite makes foreign policy," and Chapter 6 for "how the power elite shapes social legislation." Both of these chapters are persuasive in showing empirically the power of the upper class in the making of key decisions.

33. Domhoff, *The Higher Circles*, Chap. 6.

34. See Parenti, *Power and the Powerless*; and Parenti, *Democracy for the Few*, 3rd ed. (New York: St. Martin's, 1980).

35. See John C. Leggett, "The Political Institution," in Larry T. Reynolds and James M. Henslin, *American Society: A Critical Analysis* (New York: David McKay, 1973), pp. 66–108; and Parenti, *Power and the Powerless*.

36. This position is supported by the arguments and the empirical evidence found in: Thomas R. Dye, *Who's Running America? Institutional Leadership in the United States* (Englewood Cliffs, New Jersey: Prentice-Hall, 1976); Adolph A. Berle, Jr. and Gardiner C. Means, *The Modern Corporation and Private Property*, Rev. ed. (New York: Harcourt, Brace and World, 1968); Paul A. Baran and Paul M. Sweezy, *Monopoly Capital: An Essay on the American Economic and Social Order* (New York: Monthly Review Press, 1968); and C. Wright Mills, *The Power Elite* (New York: Oxford University Press, 1959).

37. Dye, *Who's Running America?*, pp. 5–8.

38. Parenti, *Power and the Powerless*, p. 41.

39. *Ibid.*, p. 84.

40. *Ibid.*, p. 201.

41. The following is taken largely from Parenti, *Democracy for the Few*, pp. 63–74. See also, Alan Wolfe, *The Seamy Side of Democracy*, 2nd ed. (New York: Longman, 1978), pp. 21–50.

42. *Ibid.*, p. 65. See also, Matthew Josephson, *The Politicos, 1865–1896* (New York: Harcourt, Brace, 1938).

43. Parenti, *Democracy for the Few*, p. 66.

44. See Samuel P. Huntington, "The Marasmus of the ICC," *Bureaucratic Power in National Politics*, Francis Rourke, ed. (Boston: Little, Brown, 1965), pp. 73–86.

45. *Ibid.*, p. 67.

46. See Patrick Renshaw, *The Wobblies* (Garden City, New York: Doubleday, 1968), p. 24.

47. Parenti, *Democracy for the Few*, p. 67.
48. *Ibid.*, p. 69.
49. Frances Fox Piven and Richard A. Cloward, *Regulating the Poor* (New York: Pantheon, 1971).
50. Morton C. Paulson, "What Is Business Afraid of?," *The National Observer* (October 5, 1974), p. 14.
51. Parenti, *Democracy for the Few*, p. 77. See also Bradford Snell, "GM and the Nazis," *Ramparts* (June, 1974), pp. 14–16; Thomas Di Baggio, "The Unholy Alliance," *Penthouse* (May, 1976), pp. 74–91; and Joseph Borkin, *The Crime and Punishment of I. G. Farben* (New York: The Free Press, 1978).
52. Parenti, *Democracy for the Few*, p. 78.
53. *Ibid.*, pp. 79–80. See also, James Ridgeway, *The Politics of Ecology* (New York: E. P. Dutton, 1970); and Barry Weisberg, "Ecology of Oil: Raping Alaska," *Eco-Catastrophe* (San Francisco: Canfield, 1970), pp. 107–109.
54. Associated Press release (September 13, 1979).
55. Quoted in "Alternatives for American Growth," *Public Opinion* 2 (August/September 1979), pp. 12–13.
56. Reported by Pat Ordovensky for Gannett News Service (June 24, 1979).
57. *Facts on File* (November 13, 1976).
58. Hutchins, "Is Democracy Possible?," p. 4.
59. United Press International release (October 3, 1978). See especially, Anthony Sampson, *The Arms Bazaar: From Lebanon to Lockheed* (New York: Viking, 1977).
60. See Anthony Sampson, *the Sovereign State of ITT* (Greenwich, Conn.: Fawcett, 1974).
61. Hutchens, "Is Democracy Possible?," p. 4.
62. See Peter Ognibene, "The Politics of the Draft," *Saturday Review* (June 23, 1979), p. 12.
63. See Maurice Zeitlin, Kenneth G. Lutterman, and James W. Russell, "Death in Vietnam: Class, Poverty, and the Risks of War," *American Society, Inc.*, 2nd ed., Maurice Zeitlin, ed. (Chicago: Rand McNally, 1977), pp. 143–155; and Lawrence M. Baskier and William A. Strauss, *The Draft, The War, and the Vietnam Generation* (New York: Knopf, 1978).
64. See Herbert J. Gans, "The Uses of Power: The Poor Pay All," *Social Policy* 2 (July–August, 1971), pp. 20–24.
65. Michael Harrington, "Social Retreat and Economic Stagnation," *Dissent* 26 (Spring, 1979), pp. 131–134.
66. Robert Lekachman, "The Specter of Full Employment," in Jerome H. Skolnick and Elliot Currie, eds. *Crisis in American Institutions*, 4th ed. (Boston: Little, Brown, 1979), pp. 50–58.

Epilogue

Any analyst of American society has the option of emphasizing either the social system as a smoothly functioning unit or the disunity and lack of harmony within it. American society for the most part does work rather smoothly. If we examine the whole of history, we must conclude that the system has improved in many respects. But this society has severe problems—the persistence of poverty, racial discrimination, injustice, violence, and the intransigence of the institutions to change, to name but a few. We must recognize that American society has many paradoxical dichotomies—unity and disunity, affluence and poverty, freedom and oppression, stability and change.

The topics selected for this book, the order in which they were presented, and the emphases have tended to focus on the problems, faults, and weaknesses of American society. This strategy was employed because these aspects of society are often minimized, but more important, because the society needs reform. Since institutions are made by people, they can be changed by people. As long as there are problems we cannot be content with the status quo. A full understanding of the complex nature of society must, however, precede the implementation of social change. That has been one goal of this book.

The primary purpose of any sociology book is to make the reader more perceptive and more analytical regarding social life. It is the author's hope that readers have gained new perspectives and new insights about our society from the reading and thinking required for analyzing American society. Hopefully, readers will build upon this knowledge in a lifelong quest to understand better this complex system called American society and to work for its improvement.

Glossary

Accommodation. Acceptance of one's position in a situation without struggle.

Achieved status. A position in a social organization attained through personal effort.

Ageism. Discrimination against the elderly.

Aggregate. A collection of individuals who happen to be at the same place at the same time.

Alienation. An individual's feeling of separation from the surrounding society.

Altruistic suicide. The sacrificing of one's life for the good of the group.

Androgyny. Having the characteristics of both males and females.

Anomie. Durkheim's term that indicates a social condition characterized by the absence of norms or conflicting norms. At the individual level, the person is not sure what the norms are, which leads to a relatively high probability of suicide.

Anticipatory socialization. Learning and acting out the beliefs, norms, and values of a group before joining it.

Argot. The specialized or secret language peculiar to a group.

Ascribed status. Social position based on such factors as age, race, and family over which the individual has no control.

Assimilation. The process by which individuals or groups voluntarily or involuntarily adopt the culture of another group, losing their original identity.

Baby Boom. A term referring to a 15-year-period in American history following World War II when an extraordinary number of babies were born.

Blaming the victim. The reason why some individuals are poor, criminals, or school dropouts is that they have a flaw within them.

Bourgeoisie. Marx's term for the class of persons that own the means of production in a capitalist society.

Bureaucracy. A system of administration that is characterized by specialized roles, explicit rules, and a hierarchy of authority.

Bureaucratization. The trend toward greater use of the bureaucratic mode of organization administration within society.

Capitalism. The economic system based on private ownership of property, guided by the seeking of maximum profits.

Case study. The research strategy that involves the detailed and thorough analysis of a single event, community, or organization.

Caste system. The closed system of social stratification. Membership is fixed at birth and is permanent.

Caveat emptor. The Latin phrase that means "let the buyer beware."

Charisma. The extraordinary attributes of an individual that enable the possessor to lead and inspire without the legal authority to do so.

Church. The highly organized, bureaucratic form of religious organization that accommodates itself to the larger society.

Civil religion. The set of religious beliefs, rituals, and symbols outside the church that legitimates the status quo.

Class consciousness. Karl Marx's term that refers to the recognition by persons in a similar economic situation of a common interest.

Class segregation. Barriers that restrict social interaction to the members of a particular social class.

Cloning. The artificial production of genetically identical offspring.

Cohabitation. The practice of living together as a couple without being married.

Commune. A small, voluntary community characterized by cooperation and a common ideology.

Conflict perspective. A view of society that posits conflict as a normal feature of social life, influencing the distribution of power and the direction and magnitude of social change.

Consensus. Widely held agreement on the norms and values of society.

Conspicuous consumption. The purchase and obvious display of material goods to impress others with one's wealth and assumed status.

Constraint. The state of being controlled by some force.

Contraculture. A culturally homogeneous group that has developed values and norms that differ from the larger society because the group opposes the larger society.

Control group. A group of subjects in an experiment who are not exposed to the independent variable but are similar in all other respects to the group exposed to the independent variable.

Correlation. The degree of relationship between two variables.

Counterculture. A subculture that fundamentally opposes the dominant culture.

Crime. An act that is prohibited by the law.

Cultural relativity. Customs of another society must be viewed and evaluated by their standards, not by an outsider's.

Cultural tyranny. The socialization process forces narrow behavioral and attitudinal traits on persons.

Culture. The knowledge that the members of a social organization share.

Culture of poverty. The view that the poor are qualitatively different in values and life styles from the rest of society and that these cultural differences explain continued poverty.

Deferred gratification. The willingness to sacrifice in the present for expected future rewards.

Deflation. The part of the economic cycle when the amount of money in circulation is down, resulting in low prices and unemployment.

Democracy. The form of government where the citizens participate in government, characterized by competition for office, public officials being responsive to public opinion, and the citizenry having access to reliable information upon which to make their electoral choices.

Demography. The scientific study of the size, composition, and changes in human populations.

Dependent variable. A variable that is influenced by the effect of another variable (the independent variable).

Deprogramming. The process where persons believed to be "brainwashed" by cults are abducted and retrained against their will.

Derogation. Discrimination in the form of words that put a minority "down."

Deviance. Behavior that violates the expectations of society.

Differential association. The theory that a person becomes deviant because of an excess of definitions favorable to the violation of societal expectations over definitions supporting the norms and values.

Direct social control. Direct intervention by the agents of society to control the behavior of individuals and groups.

Discrimination. To act toward a person or group with partiality, typically because they belong to a minority.

Division of labor. The specialization of economic roles resulting in an interdependent and efficient system.

Dual career marriage. A marriage in which a husband and wife both are employed outside the home.

Dysfunction. A consequence that is disruptive for the stability and cohesion of the social organization.

Economy. The institution that ensures the maintenance of society by producing and distributing the necessary goods and services.

Ego. According to Freud, the conscious, rational part of the self.

Egoistic suicide. Persons lacking ties to social groups are, Durkheim found, more susceptible to suicide than those with strong group attachments.

Elitist view of power. The assumption that power

is concentrated in a few rather than dispersed (the pluralist view).

Epistemology. The philosophical position that all reality is socially constructed.

Ethnic group. A social group with a common culture distinct from the culture of the majority because of race, religion, or national origin.

Ethnocentrism. The universal tendency to deprecate the ways of persons from other societies as wrong, old-fashioned, or immoral and to think of the ways of one's own group as superior (as the only right way).

Ethnomethodology. The subdiscipline in sociology that studies the everyday living practices of people to discover the underlying bases for social behavior.

Eugenics. The attempt to improve the human race through the control of hereditary factors.

Experimental group. A group of subjects in an experiment who are exposed to the independent variable, in contrast to the control group, which is not.

False consciousness. In Marxian theory, the idea that the oppressed may hold beliefs damaging to their interests.

Family. A particular societal arrangement whereby persons related by ancestry, marriage, or adoption live together, form an economic unit, and raise children.

Feral children. Children reputedly raised by animals, who have the characteristics of their peers (animals) rather than human beings.

Fertility. The frequency of actual births in a population.

Folkways. Relatively unimportant rules that if violated are not severely punished.

Function. Any consequence of a social arrangement that contributes to the overall stability of the system.

Functional integration. Unity among divergent elements of society resulting from a specialized division of labor.

Functionalism (the order perspective). The theoretical perspective that emphasizes the order, harmony, and stability of social systems.

Gender. Refers to the biological facts of maleness and femaleness.

Generalized other. Mead's concept that refers to the internalization of the expectations of the society.

Genetic engineering. The scientific effort to manipulate DNA molecules in plants and animals.

Glossolalia. The emotional religious experience involving the incoherent "speaking in tongues."

Group. A collection of people (two or more) who, because of sustained interaction, have evolved a common culture.

Hedonism. The pursuit of pleasure and self-indulgence.

Hidden curriculum. That part of the school experience that has nothing to do with formal subjects but refers to the behaviors that schools expect of children (obedience to authority, remaining quiet and orderly, etc.).

Hierarchy. The arrangement of people or objects in order of importance.

Horizontal mobility. Change in occupations or other situations without moving from one social class to another.

Id. Freud's term for the collection of urges and drives persons have for pleasure and aggression.

Ideal type. An abstraction constructed to show how some phenomenon would be characterized in its pure form.

Ideological social control. The efforts by social organizations to control members by controlling their minds. Societies accomplish this, typically, through the socialization process.

Ideology. The shared beliefs about the physical, social, or metaphysical world.

Independent variable. A variable that affects another variable (the dependent variable).

Inflation. The situation when too much money purchases too few goods, resulting in rising prices.

Institution. Social arrangements that channel behavior in presented ways in the important areas of societal life.

Institutional derogation. This occurs when the normal arrangements of society act to reinforce the negative stereotypes of minority groups.

Institutional discrimination. When the social arrangements and accepted ways of doing things in society disadvantage minority groups.

Institutional racism. When the social arrangements and accepted ways of doing things in society disadvantage a racial group.

Institutional sexism. When the social arrangements and accepted ways of doing things in society disadvantage females.

Institutional violence. When the normal workings of the society do harm to a social category.

Interest group. A group of like-minded persons who organize to influence public policy.

Intergenerational mobility. The difference in social class position between a son and his father.

Internalization. In the process of socialization society's demands become part of the individual, acting to control his or her behavior.

Intragenerational mobility. The movement by an individual from one social class to another.

Labeling theory (societal reactions). The explanation of deviant behavior that stresses the importance of the society in defining what is illegal and in assigning a deviant status to particular individuals, which in turn dominates their identities and behaviors.

Latent function. An unintended consequence of a social arrangement or social action.

Life chances. Weber's term that refers to the chances throughout one's life cycle to live and experience the good things in life.

Looking-glass self. Cooley's concept that refers to the importance of how others influence the way we see ourselves.

Machismo (macho). An exaggerated masculinity, evidenced by male dominance, posturing, physical daring, and an exploitative attitude toward women.

Macro level. The large-scale structures and processes of society, including the institutions and the system of stratification.

Majority group. The social cetegory in society holding superordinate power and who successfully impose their will on less-powerful groups (minority groups).

Male chauvinism. Exaggerated beliefs about the superiority of the male and the resulting discrimination.

Manifest function. An intended consequence of a social arrangement or social action.

Marginality. The condition resulting from taking part in two distinct ways of life without belonging fully to either.

Matriarchal family. A family structure in which the mother is dominant.

Meritocracy. A system of stratification in which rank is based purely on achievement.

Micro level. The social organization and processes of small-scale social groups.

Military-industrial complex. The term that refers to the direct and indirect relationships between the military establishment (the Pentagon) and corporations.

Minority. A social category composed of persons that differ from the majority, are relatively powerless, and are the objects of discrimination.

Modal personality type. A distinct type of personality considered to be characteristic of the members of a particular society.

Model. The mental image a scientist has of the structure of society. This influences what the scientists look for, what they see, and how phenomena are explained.

Monogamy. The form of marriage in which an individual may not be married to more than one person at a time.

Monopolistic capitalism. The form of capitalism prevalent in the contemporary United States, where a few large corporations control the key industries, destroying competition and the market mechanisms that would ordinarily keep prices low and help consumers.

Monopoly. When a single firm dominates an industry.

Mores. Important norms, the violation of which results in severe punishment.

Mortality rate. The frequency of actual deaths in a population.

Multinational corporation. A corporation that operates in more than one country.

Myth of peaceful progress. The incorrect belief that throughout American history disadvantaged groups have gained their share of power, prosperity, and respectability without violence.

Nominalist. A philosophical position that a group is nothing more than the sum of its parts.

Nomos. Literally, meaningful order. The opposite of anomie.

Norm. This part of culture refers to rules that specify appropriate and inappropriate behavior (in other words, the shared expectations for behavior).

Nuclear family. A kinship unit composed of husband, wife, and children.

Nuptiality. The proportion of married persons.

Ontology. The philosophical position that accepts the reality of things because their nature cannot be denied.

Order model. The conception of society as a social system characterized by cohesion, consensus, cooperation, reciprocity, stability, and persistence.

Paradigm. The basic assumptions a scientist has of the structure of society (see **Model**).

Participatory socialization. The mode of socialization in which parents encourage their children to explore, experiment, and question.

Patriarchal family. A family structure in which the father is dominant.

Peer group. Friends usually of the same age and socioeconomic status.

Peter Principle. The view that most people in an organization will be promoted until they eventually reach their level of incompetence.

Pluralism. A situation in which different groups live in mutual respect but retain their racial, religious, or ethnic identities.

Pluralist view of power. The diffuse distribution of power among various groups and interests.

Polity. The societal institution especially concerned with maintaining order.

Population implosion. The trend for people to live in ever-denser localities (the movement of people from rural areas to the urban regions).

Poverty. A standard of living below the minimum needed for the maintenance of adequate diet, health, and shelter.

Power. The ability of A to get B to do its wishes whether B agrees to or not.

Power elite. Mills' term for the coalition of the top echelon of military, executive branch of the federal government, and business.

Prestige. The respect of an individual or social category as a result of their social status.

Primary deviance. The original illegal act preceding the successful application of the "deviant" label.

Primary group. A small group characterized by intimate, face-to-face interaction.

Progressive tax. A tax rate that escalates with the amount of income.

Proletariat. Marx's term for the industrial workers in a capitalistic society.

Protestant ethic (Puritan work ethic). The religious beliefs, traced back to Martin Luther and John Calvin, which emphasize hard work and continual striving in order to prove that one is "saved" by material success.

Psychosurgery. A form of brain surgery used to change the behavior of the patient.

Pygmalion effect. Students placed in a track are treated by teachers in a way which ensures that the prophecy is fulfilled.

Racism. The domination and discrimination of one racial group by the majority.

Radical nonintervention. Schur's term referring to the strategy of leaving juvenile delinquents alone as much as possible rather than processing (and labeling) them through the criminal justice system.

Random sample. The selection of a subset from a population so that every person has an equal chance of being selected.

Realist. The philosophical position that a group is more than the sum of its parts (referring to the emergence of culture and mechanisms of social control that affect the behavior of members regardless of their personalities).

Recidivism. Reinvolvement in crime.

Reference group. A group to which one would like to belong and toward which one therefore orients his or her behavior.

Reform movement. A social movement that seeks to alter a specific part of society.

Regressive tax. A tax rate that remains the same for all persons, rich or poor. The result is that poor persons pay a larger proportion of their wealth than affluent persons.

Reliability. The degree to which a study yields the same results when repeated.

Religion. The social institution that encompasses beliefs and practices regarding the sacred.

Repressive socialization. The mode of socialization in which parents demand rigid conformity in their children, enforced by physical punishment.

Resistance movement. The organized attempt to reinforce the traditional system by preventing change.

Revolutionary movement. The collective attempt to bring about a radical transformation of society.

Rites of passage. The ritual whereby the society recognizes the adult status of a young member.

Role. The behavioral expectations and requirements attached to a position in a social organization.

Role performance (role behavior). The actual behavior of persons occupying particular positions in a social organization.

Routinization of charisma. The process by which an organization attempts to transmit the special attributes of the former leader to a new one. This is done by various means, for example, "laying on of hands" and the old leader choosing a successor.

Sacred. That which inspires awe because of its supernatural qualities.

Secondary deviance. Deviant behavior that is a consequence of the successful application of the deviant label.

Secondary group. A large, impersonal, and formally organized group.

Sect. A religious organization, in contrast to a church, that tends to be dogmatic, fundamentalistic, and in opposition to "the world."

Secular. Of or pertaining to the world; the opposite of sacred.

Segregation. The separation of one group from another.

Self-esteem. The opinion of oneself.

Self-fulfilling prophecy. An event that occurs because it was predicted. The prophecy is confirmed because people alter their behavior to conform with the prediction.

Sexism. The individual actions and institutional arrangements that discriminate against women.

Sex role. The learned patterns of behavior expected of males and females by society.

Sexual stratification. A hierarchal arrangement based on gender.

Shared monopoly. When four or fewer companies control 50 percent or more of an industry.

Sibling. A brother or sister.

Significant others. Mead's term referring to those persons most important in the determining of a child's behavior.

Social class. A number of persons who occupy the same relative economic rank in the stratification system.

Social control. The regulation of human behavior in any social group.

Social Darwinism. The belief that the principle of the "survival of the fittest" applies to human societies, especially the system of stratification.

Social differentiation. The process of categorizing persons by some personal attribute.

Social inequality. The ranking of persons by wealth, family background, race, ethnicity, or sex.

Social interaction. When individuals act toward or respond to each other.

Socialism. The economic system where the means of production are owned by the people for their benefit.

Socialization. The process of learning the culture.

Socialization agents. Those individuals, groups, and institutions responsible for transmitting the culture of society to newcomers.

Social location. One's position in society based on family background, race, socioeconomic status, religion, and other relevant social characteristics.

Social mobility. The movement by an individual from one social class or status group to another.

Social movement. A collective attempt to promote or resist change.

Social organization. The order of a social group as evidenced by the positions, roles, norms, and other constraints that control behavior and ensure predictability.

Social problem. There are two types of social problems: (1) societally induced conditions that cause psychic and material suffering for any segment of the population; and (2) those acts and conditions that violate the norms and values of society.

Social relationship. When two or more persons engage in enduring social interaction.

Social stratification. When people are ranked in a hierarchy that differentiates them as superior or inferior.

Social structure. The patterned and recurrent relationships among people and parts in a social organization.

Social system. A differentiated group whose parts are interrelated in an orderly arrangement, bounded in geographical space or membership.

Society. The largest social organization to which individuals owe their allegiance. The entity is located geographically, has a common culture, and is relatively self-sufficient.

Socioeconomic status (SES). The measure of social status that takes into account several prestige factors, such as income, education, and occupation.

Sociology. The scholarly discipline concerned with the systematic study of social organizations.

Stagflation. The contemporary economic phenomenon that combines the problems of inflation and deflation—high prices, high unemployment, wage-price spiral, and a profits squeeze.

Status. A socially defined position in a social organization.

Status group. Persons of similar status. They view each other as social equals.

Status inconsistency. The situation in which a person ranks high on one status dimension and low on another.

Stereotype. An exaggerated generalization about some social category.

Stigma. A label of social disgrace.

Structured social inequality. This refers to the patterns of superiority and inferiority, the distribution of rewards, and the belief systems that reinforce the inequities of society.

Subculture. A relatively cohesive cultural system that varies in form and substance from the dominant culture.

Subsidy. Financial aid in the form of tax breaks or gifts granted by the government to an individual or commercial enterprise.

Suburb. A community adjacent to a city.

Superego. Freud's term that refers to the internalization of society's morals within the self.

Survey research. The research technique that selects a sample from a larger population in order to learn how they think, feel, or act.

Symbol. A thing that represents something else, such as a word, gesture, or physical object (cross, flag).

Synthesis. The blending of the parts into a new form.

Systemic imperatives. The economic and social constraints on the decision makers in an organization, which promote the status quo.

Technology. The application of science to meet the needs of society.

Theodicy. The religious legitimation for a situation that might otherwise cause guilt or anger (such as defeat in a war or the existence of poverty among affluence).

Tracking. A practice of schools of grouping children according to their scores on IQ and other tests.

Transcience. Toffler's term that refers to the rapid turnover in things, places, and people characteristic of a technological society.

Underemployment. Being employed at a job below one's level of training and expertise.

Undocumented immigrant. Immigrants who have entered the United States illegally.

Urbanism. The ways in which city life characteristically affects how people feel, think, and interact with one another.

Urbanization. The trend referring to the movement of people from rural to urban areas.

Urban region (AKA megalopolis, conurbation, strip city). The extensive urban area that results when two or more large cities grow together until they are contiguous.

Validity. The degree to which a scientific study measures what it attempts to measure.

Value neutrality. The attempt by scientists to be absolutely free of bias in their research.

Values. The shared criteria used in evaluating objects, ideas, acts, feelings, or events as to their relative desirability, merit, or correctness.

Variable. An attitude, behavior, or condition that can vary in magnitude from case to case (the opposite of a constant).

Voluntary association. Organizations that people join because they approve of their goals.

White flight. Whites leaving the central cities for the suburbs to avoid interaction with blacks, especially the busing of children.

Index